THE TWO VIET-NAMS

A POLITICAL AND MILITARY ANALYSIS

THE TWO VIET-NAMS

The
TWO
VIET-NAMS

A Political and Military Analysis

REVISED EDITION

BERNARD B. FALL

Revised edition, 1966

To

THE VALIANT AND LONG-SUFFERING
VIETNAMESE—NORTH AND SOUTH

Preface

THIS is a book in praise of no one. I have written it not to plead a cause or to propound a pet theory, but simply to attempt to bring some understanding to the plight of a valiant people that happens to find itself, no doubt much against its will, at one of the focal points of a world-wide struggle.

It may well be that many readers will draw from this book the impression that numerous young television viewers draw from seeing either a "Western" or a Shakespearean tragedy: "Everybody gets killed in the end." Or, in the case of divided Viet-Nam, that life is not exactly pleasant in either zone of Viet-Nam; that each zone has its own set of economic and political troubles; and that both sides are engaged in military efforts which, having grown beyond their own control, may well overwhelm them in the end.

This seems to be, alas, the case at this writing, and it is unlikely to improve in the immediately foreseeable future. And again in the manner of most human tragedies, there are in both zones heroes with some fairly villainous character traits and some villains with a few likable human characteristics, but above all, there are the Vietnamese people, with their admirable qualities of frugality, incredible endurance, patience in the face of unavoidable adversity, and deep love for their war-torn homeland.

An important part of this book—and I hope this will be its particular contribution to the body of knowledge about Viet-Nam—is devoted to a comparison of the governmental and economic institutions of both zones *not* as they have been designed on paper to impress their friends and fool their foes, but as they *really operate* in everyday practice. This may not please the most ardent advocates of either regime, but the time for semantic niceties—if there ever was such a time in Viet-Nam—is long past. The weaknesses and strengths of each zone of Viet-Nam deserve our most careful attention; for, at a time when American and other Western troops may be committed in one form or another to holding South Viet-Nam, what we *don't* know may most definitely hurt us.

Although much of this book had been written before the Buddhist crisis erupted and the Diem regime was overthrown in South Viet-Nam, the reader will, I trust, find that the handling of that crisis by the then ruling government was entirely in accordance with its behavior during similar challenges earlier, and thus does not warrant any substantial revision of the present text. Similarly, no analysis can yet be made of the Saigon military *coups d'état* of November 1, 1963, and January 30, 1964, for they are only the beginning of a long-overdue reform process—not an end in themselves.

This book is the result of a ten-year-long research and decantation process. Some of its elements go back to my earliest stay in North Viet-Nam, in 1953; others to my recent stay in Indochina. Thus, it would be difficult to acknowledge any particular thanks to a few persons without being unfair to many others—Vietnamese, American, French—who have, in one way or another, made an invaluable contribution to my knowledge of the subject. I wish, however, to express my particular thanks to Phyllis Freeman, of Frederick A. Praeger, for patiently coping with more than a year of transoceanic correspondence and for giving final form to wads of manuscript.

Part of the final field research for this book was carried out under an International Relations research grant of the Rockefeller Foundation, for which I wish to acknowledge my gratitude. The Foundation, of course, is in no way responsible for the opinions expressed in my work; these are strictly my own.

B. B. F.

Phnom-Penh, Cambodia
July, 1962

Washington, D.C.
April, 1964

Contents

ix

Part Three: INSURGENCY IN THE SOUTH

APPENDIXES

MAPS AND CHARTS

TABLES

ONE

THE COMMON GROUND

1

The Physical Setting

"Like two rice baskets at the opposite ends of their carrying pole" —that is the way Vietnamese often describe their country, which uncoils in the form of an elongated S for more than 1,200 miles, from the 9th parallel north to the 26th, covering 127,300 square miles (about 330,000 square kilometers).

As one approaches it from the air—whether from Hong Kong to Hanoi, the northern capital; or from Bangkok or Manila to Saigon, the southern capital—one sees vast expanses of lush vegetation or endless rice fields stretching the metallic mirror of their flooded surfaces to the horizon during the rainy season, or presenting the velvety green of growing rice at other times. About 80 per cent of the country is covered with trees or brush, and 49 per cent of that is high-stand tree cover or outright jungle. The remainder consists of the open plains of the rice-bearing deltas.

It is those deltas—that of the Mekong in the south and of the Red River (Song-Coi) in the north—which indeed are the "rice baskets" of the country. Their vast alluvial plains (the Mekong Basin

3

covers three-fifths of neighboring Cambodia as well) produce in good times 9 *million tons* of rice: 5 million and more in the south, and 4 million in the north. In addition, a whole series of smaller deltas, often built around rivers less than 100 miles long, dot the shore line of Central Viet-Nam: Thanh-Hoa, Ha-Tinh, Quang-Ngai, Binh-Dinh, Khanh-Hoa, etc.

The "carrying pole" of those rice baskets is a series of mountain chains whose watershed roughly constitutes Viet-Nam's western border with Laos and Cambodia and is known as the Annamite Cordillera. Its mountains vary in height from more than 10,000 feet close to the Chinese border to about 4,000 feet as they drop in a sheer cliff into the sea near Cape Varella, to the north of the Khanh-Hoa plain.

Thus, Viet-Nam can be divided into eight natural regions—three low-lying plains, three mountain areas, and two that fall between the two other categories in altitude and configuration: (1) the Red River and Mekong deltas and the smaller Central Vietnamese deltas; (2) the Annamite Cordillera, the Thai Hill area of northwestern Tongking, and the northeastern Tongking mountain area; and (3) the North Vietnamese Midlands (Moyenne Région), which forms a wedge of terraced hills and soft-shouldered mountains to the north of the Red River Delta; and, finally, the vast Southern Mountain Plateau (still referred to by its French initials PMS, for Plateaux Montagnards du Sud), which covers two-thirds of all Viet-Nam south of the 17th parallel.

As can readily be seen, this is a country with no geographic unity whatever, and since the bulk of its population exists by cultivating rice on lands irrigated by gravity or by a system of often still primitive pumps and sluices, they live to an overwhelming extent in the tiny lowland pockets, leaving the vast uplands to ethnically alien mountain tribes. The results, in terms of human geography, are startling.

Whereas in the United States an average of 60 persons lives on a square mile of land, the average, in the Red River Delta, is 1,256—reaching in Nam-Dinh Province the fantastic figure of 3,800 inhabitants to the square mile. While in the PMS, often fewer than 5 inhabitants can be found per square mile, the neighboring Central Vietnamese delta of Binh-Dinh has an average of 1,380 to the square mile. In the open plains of the fertile Mekong Delta, the population figure is far less heavy; few areas reach a figure of 500 to the square mile, and many provinces have about 260 inhabitants to the square mile.

Thus, of Viet-Nam's 30.5 million inhabitants in 1962 (16.5 million in the zone north of the 17th parallel and 14 million south of the parallel), close to 29 million live on about *20 per cent* of the national territory, while the remaining 1.5 million roam—and the term can be applied literally, since many of them are at least seminomads—over more than 100,000 square miles of plateau and mountain areas. In American terms, this would mean that 175 million Americans were settled between the Eastern seaboard and the Appalachians, while another 8 million would have the rest of the country, all the way to the Pacific Ocean, to themselves.

It is obvious that such a situation would have far-reaching social and economic consequences. In Viet-Nam, the chaotic geography has conditioned the whole political and historical outlook of the country to this very day. For 1,000 years, the history of the Vietnamese people was one tenacious "Long March" to the south, from one small rice-bearing delta to the next, until the wide-open plain of the Mekong was reached and put to the plow.

In spite of their highly diversified racial origins, the Vietnamese today are largely an ethnically and culturally homogeneous people. The whole Indochinese peninsula appears to have been inhabited at first by an Austro-Indonesian population not unlike that which inhabits New Guinea today. Those aboriginal inhabitants were pushed farther and farther into the mountain areas of their country by Thai and Mongolian invaders from the north and by seafaring Indians from the west. The Thai migration began probably around 2000 B.C. and has not yet come to a complete halt.* The Indian influx culminated in the creation of the Khmer empire, which still survives in the present-day kingdom of Cambodia, and in the creation of the kingdom of Champa, which was subsequently destroyed by the Vietnamese.

The present-day Vietnamese language, with its blending of monotonic Indonesian and variotonic Mongolian elements, bears further evidence of the racial heritage of the Vietnamese. A flourishing indigenous Bronze Age culture—the Dong-Son civilization—existed in Viet-Nam about 200 B.C. According to Joseph Buttinger,[1] "in the Red River valley the New Stone Age was only beginning to give way to the Age of Bronze when Chinese imperial expansion suddenly thrust the Vietnamese onto a higher level of civilization." Very recent

---

* For example, in 1961–62, several Black Thai tribal groups, fleeing Pathet-Lao Communist elements, descended into the Mekong Valley and crossed over into Sayaboury Province in an exact repetition of the age-old process of migration of those tribes.

archaeological findings suggest that Bronze Age culture may be even older by a few centuries than hitherto believed.[2]

The various Chinese occupations that followed over the next 1,000 years also left a profound physical imprint upon the Vietnamese, while in the deep south of the country, intermarriage with the Cambodian inhabitants produced yet a different ethnic strain. The mountaineers who were pushed back into the hills have held onto their original culture to this day. In the north, the Thai, Muong, and Meo dominate the whole back country and their high cultural level—in many cases equal to that of the lowland Vietnamese—makes them a political factor that cannot be ignored. In the south, the more primitive tribes of the PMS, inaccurately called "*Moi*" ("savages"), have also maintained their elaborate tribal and social structure against heavy odds. Although their exact numbers are not known, spot censuses have shown that there may be as many as 1 million southern mountaineers living in the PMS area. For the northern mountain areas, the 1960 census gives a figure of 2,600,000 mountaineers.

Two other important ethnic minorities exist in Viet-Nam, and both live south of the 17th parallel: the Khmer (Cambodians) and the Chinese. The Chinese as rulers or residents have lived with the Vietnamese for 2,000 years. Although recent nationality laws enacted in South Viet-Nam have given Vietnamese citizenship to these Chinese, the ethnic and economic reality of the presence of 1 million Chinese—merchants, butchers, bankers, and rice millers—cannot be disregarded. The half-million Cambodians (or Khmer Krom, "Southern Khmer," as they are called in Cambodia), whose presence in South Viet-Nam is a living reminder of how recently Viet-Nam colonized the area, are concentrated in and west of the Mekong Delta. It is likely that they will disappear as a separate ethnic entity within a few generations. Realistically, the present Cambodian leadership—though defending the minority rights of the Khmer Krom—seems to have abandoned all thought of liberating the area by force.[3]

Thus, it can be reliably estimated that in 1962, 15 per cent of Viet-Nam's population consisted of ethnic minorities, about equally divided between both zones.

A third physical reality that is as important as the unequal distribution of Viet-Nam's population is the unequal distribution of its mineral and agricultural wealth. Accidents of climate and geology make the two zones of Viet-Nam not economic rivals, but, in normal times, perfect complements to each other. The northern zone pos-

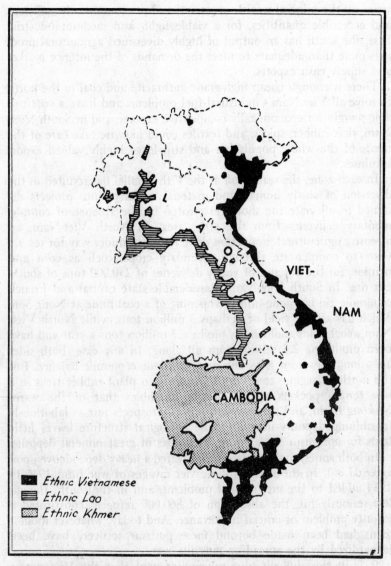

MINORITY AND MAJORITY POPULATIONS IN INDOCHINA

sesses all the mineral wealth necessary, and in economically sufficient and accessible quantities, for a viable light- and medium-industrial base; the south has an output of highly diversified agricultural products more than adequate to meet the demands of the interior market and supply cash exports.

There is enough cheap high-grade anthracite and coal in the north to solve all Viet-Nam's industrial fuel problems and leave a comfortable margin for economically competitive exports; and in South Viet-Nam, rice, rubber, spices, and textiles could likewise take care of the needs of the whole population and still leave highly valued export surpluses.

In each zone, the sealing-off at the 17th parallel has resulted in the diversion of costly human and material resources into projects designed to alleviate the shortages created by the absence of complementary deliveries from the other area. In North Viet-Nam, an intensive agricultural-production drive has been under way for several years to compensate through secondary crops, such as corn and manioc, for the absence of yearly deliveries of 250,000 tons of southern rice. In South Viet-Nam, considerable state capital and French economic aid has gone into the opening of a coal mine at Nong-Son, which has a *total* yield of perhaps 3 million tons, while North Viet-Nam's coal fields could easily produce 3 million tons a year and have been producing 2.5 million tons all along. In any case, both sides are a long way from self-sufficiency, let alone economic balance. But the northern regime continues laboriously to plant rubber trees in a few terrain pockets whose climate resembles that of the warm Mekong Basin, and the southern regime prospects just as laboriously for mining deposits in soils whose geological structure leaves little basis for optimism as to future discoveries of great mineral deposits.

In both zones, this imbalance has created a heavy dependence upon external aid. In the north, the heavier ravages of war from 1946 to 1954 added to the area's usual problems; and in the south, though less seriously hit, the absorption of 860,000 refugees constituted a priority problem of crucial importance. And today, whatever modest gains had been made beyond mere postwar recovery have been jeopardized by the spreading guerrilla war.

It is in this difficult physical environment that the Vietnamese people, fighting against overwhelming odds for more than 2,000 years, carved for itself a niche along the eastern rim of the Indochinese peninsula.

2

A Glimpse of the Past

Much of Viet-Nam's history before 200 B.C. is shrouded in legend —but so is much of Europe's past beyond the Mediterranean basin. A kingdom known as Van Lang and, briefly, Au Lac, seems to have existed between 500 and 207 B.C.,[1] apparently covering most of what is today China's Kwang-tung Province and North Viet-Nam. The latter, as will be seen, has been a border zone more than once in Viet-Nam's long and stormy history.

Conquered by Chinese generals who had broken with the Ch'in emperors and had adopted the mores of the "barbarians," Au Lac became known as "Nam-Viet" ("South[ern country of the] Viet").* As often later on in Vietnamese history, the small state could main-

* The word "Viet" has always designated the people of Viet-Nam, with the additional word "Nam" ("south") indicating that they were located to the south of their Chinese-dominated kinsmen. Therefore, the term is properly divided into two words, with a separation between place (or ethnic) name and location, just as in North Dakota, West Germany, East Berlin, and Southern Rhodesia. The hyphen between the words is dictated by Vietnamese grammar and pronunciation.

tain its integrity only when its huge neighbor fell on hard times, which happened more often than is usually believed. With the rise of the stronger Han in China, Nam-Viet was slowly pushed out from Kwang-tung into its North Vietnamese redoubt. In 111 B.C., the victorious Han crushed the young Vietnamese state, and save for a few brief but glorious rebellions, it remained a Chinese colony for more than 1,000 years.

Viet-Nam became a Chinese protectorate ruled by a governor and subdivided into military districts. By the beginning of the first century A.D., the country had absorbed, along with many Chinese settlers— a great many of them refugees from the Han dynasty—much of what was worthwhile in the culture of the occupying power: the difficult árt of rice planting in artificially irrigated areas, Chinese writing skills, Chinese philosophy, and even Chinese social customs and beliefs. But—and in this the Vietnamese are almost unique—they succeeded in maintaining their national identity in spite of the fact that everything else about them had become "Chinese." Opposition to Chinese rule built up as the Chinese presence became more ubiquitous and brutal. Finally, what could be called a routine "occupation incident," the execution of a minor feudal lord, brought about a conflagration. In 39 A.D., Trung Trac, the wife of the slain lord, and her sister Trung Nhi raised an army that, in a series of swift sieges, overwhelmed the Chinese garrisons, which had grown careless over the years. In 40 A.D., the Vietnamese, much to their own surprise, found themselves free from foreign domination for the first time in 150 years and the Trung sisters were proclaimed queens of the country.

Naturally in so huge an empire, Chinese reaction was slow, but when it came, it was effective. Old General Ma Yuan began his counterattack in 43 A.D., and the Vietnamese troops of the two queens made a fatal error: They chose to make a stand in the open field against the experienced Chinese regulars, with their backs against the limestone cliffs at the edge of the River Day—not far from the place where Communist General Vo Nguyên Giap was to pit his green regulars against French Marshal de Lattre's elite troops 1,908 years later. The result was the same in both cases: The more experienced regulars destroyed the raw Vietnamese levies. The two queens, rather than surrender to the enemy, chose suicide by drowning in the nearby river. "Sinization" now began in earnest, with Chinese administrators taking the place of the traditional Vietnamese leaders. Two more rebellions took place. One, in 248 A.D., also led

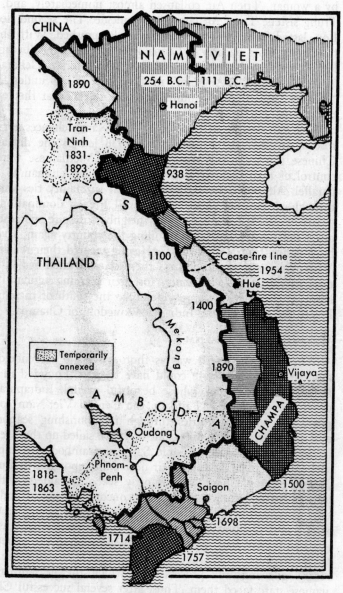

VIET-NAM'S IMPERIAL MARCH
111 B.C.-1863 A.D.

by a woman, Trieu Au, collapsed almost immediately, and, like the Trung sisters, Trieu Au committed suicide. The second, led by Ly Bon, lasted from 544 to 547 and was also crushed. With the rise of the strong Tang dynasty in China after 618, resistance became hopeless: Viet-Nam became the Chinese Protectorate General of the "Pacified South" ("An-Nam" in Chinese). It was under the name "Annam," a symbol of humiliation and defeat, that the region was to become best known to the outside world.

With the decline of the Tangs, Viet-Nam's chances for freedom rose again. A rash of rebellions in 938 led to the defeat of the Chinese the following year. By 940, the Vietnamese were in full control of their country from the foothills of Yünnan to the 17th parallel. Although they retained formal suzerainty ties with China throughout most of their history until French domination became complete in 1883, their northern neighbor, despite sporadic threats, never quite succeeded in controlling the country again, save for the brief period from 1407 to 1427. Having secured their rear areas, the Vietnamese now could address themselves to their major historical mission—securing *Lebensraum* for their teeming agricultural population in the relatively empty deltas to the south of their boundary. But to the south lay the Indianized kingdom of Champa.

VIETNAMESE COLONIALISM

What happened next was as thorough a job of genocide as any modern totalitarian state could have devised. Founded in 192 A.D., the Champa kingdom, whose beautiful capital, Indrapura, was located near present-day Faifo on the Central Viet-Nam coast, prospered for several centuries through its flourishing seaborne trade and its powerful battle fleets, one of which sailed up the Mekong and across the Great Lake (Tonlé Sap) of Cambodia to capture and sack Angkor in 1177. Like their near contemporaries in Europe, the Norsemen, the Chams were mostly seaborne raiders, with all the advantages and drawbacks of the concomitant social and political organization. They were the scourge of the area as long as they were strong and capable of carrying the war to their neighbors in their swift ships, but having neglected agriculture and the penetration of their own hinterland, they were incapable of resisting the slow but steady gnawing-away process with which the peasant-based Vietnamese state faced them. Thus, after several successful Cham raids into the Red River Delta, the Vietnamese finally beat them off, and the Chams were pushed onto the defensive.

Slowly, Vietnamese rice farmers peacefully occupied the untilled northern plains of the Champa kingdom, very often with the consent of the Chams, who felt that this process would serve their own enrichment. But as the settlements of the Vietnamese grew, so grew the willingness and ability of the neighboring Vietnamese state to protect its own citizens. Slice by slice, delta by delta, the process was repeated. There were a few temporary setbacks in the process, but by the end of the eleventh century, all the coastal provinces north of Hué had been conquered. The next important slice, including Hué, later Viet-Nam's imperial capital, became Vietnamese in the course of the mid-fifteenth century, thanks to a marriage between the sister of the Vietnamese king and the king of Champa. But in 1471, after renewed bitter warfare, in the course of which the Vietnamese conquered the Chams' second capital, Vijaya—Indrapura having been lost earlier—the once-flourishing Champa kingdom was near collapse. It lost more than 300 miles of shore line and, in fact, became little more than a beachhead stretching precariously over the small deltas of Khanh-Hoa, Phan-Rang, and Phan-Thiet.

One and a half centuries later, the Champa kingdom had simply disappeared. Today, all that is left of it is a series of watchtower ruins at the landward edge of the Central Vietnamese coastal plains and a small group of perhaps 30,000 handsome Indian-featured people eking out livings as fishermen and artisans around the Vietnamese cities of Phan-Rang and Phan-Ri.

In the course of this successful venture into colonialism (for it was nothing else), the Vietnamese state decided to institutionalize the process, and in 1481, the *don-diên*[2] were created. Like the Roman *coloniae* 1,500 years earlier or the Israeli *nakhal* settlements 500 years later (or the Austro-German *Wehrbauern* in the 1700's), the *don-diên* were agricultural settlements given to farmers who were, for the most part, army veterans and who, in return for free land, defended the new frontier. The members of the *don-diên* were a tough, hardy lot, not only willing to defend what they already had, but usually not loath to push the border farther west—this time at the expense of the decaying Khmer (Cambodian) state. It was obvious that such a situation was fertile in border incidents, which were further exploited to round out the Vietnamese domain. In 1658, all of South Viet-Nam north of Saigon (then the fishing village of Prey Kor) was in Vietnamese hands; Saigon itself fell in 1672.

The next step in colonial conquest was also typical. A Chinese merchant, Mac-Cuu, had established himself in southwestern Cambodia and, like the well-known European trading companies of the time, had taken physical possession of several provinces stretching from Kampot to Camau. When the Cambodians and their Siamese allies threatened Mac-Cuu's "state within a state," he appealed for help to the neighboring Vietnamese, who were only too happy to oblige. By 1757, Viet-Nam had occupied the rest of the Mekong Delta and the swamp-infested Camau Peninsula. Vietnamese settlers began to pour into the empty provinces, which became a vast "Far West" for the Vietnamese state. To this day, the areas on the western side of the Mekong are known to the Vietnamese as "Mien-Tay" ("the New West"). By the end of the eighteenth century, Viet-Nam had expanded to the full extent of its present shore line.

Vietnamese intervention in Cambodian affairs had begun in 1623, when Chey Chettha II, a king of Cambodia who had married a Vietnamese princess, attempted to shake Siam's overlordship with the help of the Nguyên. In exchange for that help, the Hué government requested Cambodia's authorization to send settlers to Prey Kor, and a Vietnamese general was sent with a security detachment to protect the new settlers. In 1658, a Vietnamese expeditionary force again had to intervene in the endless internecine struggles of the various pretenders to the Cambodian throne, and in 1660, Cambodia began to pay a regular tribute to the Vietnamese court.

But the Vietnamese yoke on Cambodia was to take a shape far more direct than the highly theoretical suzerainty China still exercised over Viet-Nam. The declining Khmer state was split into three Vietnamese "residences" under the control of a Vietnamese Chief Resident at the Cambodian court at Oudong. The Vietnamese began an acculturation process that, as in the neighboring provinces and in the case of the Chams, amounted to veritable genocide: destruction of the Buddhist temples and shrines, compulsory wearing of Vietnamese clothing and hairdress, Vietnamization of city and provincial names, and, finally, abolition of the royal title of the Cambodian sovereigns. By the early nineteenth century, the queen, Ang Mey (1834–41), held a virtual prisoner in her palace, was officially referred to as merely "chief of the territory of My-Lam."[3]

From 1841, Cambodia was purely and simply incorporated into Viet-Nam, but after a Cambodian rebellion encouraged by Siam and a brief war in which Siam and Viet-Nam fought each other to a stand-off, both countries agreed in 1845 to a condominium that ended only when France's protectorate was established, in June, 1863. A similar condominium policy in northern Laos also had brought the important Tran-Ninh Plateau—now better known as the Plaine des Jarres—under intermittent Vietnamese control beginning in the sixteenth century.

It is interesting to compare the Vietnamese colonization process with the corresponding process of state-building going on in Europe at that time; for too many well-intentioned writers (particularly those in the United States who feel that Europe must continually make amends for her colonial performance) tend to gloss over the *non-European* colonial processes that were going on simultaneously. In Europe, the sixteenth and seventeenth centuries witnessed what could be called a national "regroupment" process: Spain left the Low Countries; non-German states lost their influence in Germany; and the Turks, after a high tide that had brought them to the gates of Vienna in 1529 and 1683, returned to the lower reaches of the Balkans. In Europe outside Russia, only Austria-Hungary was to survive as a major multinational state until 1918, and no new state rose to power by ethnic assimilation of alien areas. Viet-Nam was obviously doing exactly the opposite: It carved out its territory through military conquest over states whose level of indigenous culture was at least equal, if not superior, to its own. In other words, it did not invoke the moralistic rationale of "Manifest Destiny," "*la Mission Civilisatrice*," or "the White Man's Burden"; its action, like the German *Drang nach Osten*, was simply a manifestation of the vitality of its people. It was simply and purely a process of colonial conquest for material gains, no more, no less. The fact that it took place on contiguous territory does not make it any more respectable than, say, the Russian conquest of Hungary.

But what makes the Vietnamese colonial process unique in Asia is that it took place in competition with that of several European powers—and the Vietnamese beat them to the punch on several occasions! By 1750, nearly all the later European colonial powers had appeared on the scene: the Dutch and Spaniards in the Spice Islands, the French and British in India, and the Portuguese throughout Southeast Asia, even as far inland as Laos. All of them, at one time or another or simultaneously, had trading stations in Viet-Nam. Whether through superciliousness or plain ignorance, none of the "traditional" colonial powers consciously reacted to the Vietnamese colonial process. But it was not without reason that the French consolidated their position in South Viet-Nam first when they set out to conquer the country one century later; after all, it had been Vietnamese for so short a time that its conquest proved easiest, for its inhabitants were the least secure in their social structure and institutions. This assertion appears to be borne out by the fact that the South appeared more "pro-French" (or simply more "French") than Central and North Viet-Nam and that French colonial penetration became more difficult as it advanced farther north.

Thus, much of what today is the Republic of Viet-Nam south of the 17th parallel has been "Vietnamese" for a shorter span of time than the Eastern seaboard of the United States has been "American." This is a reality that cannot be simply talked away, for it affects the very fabric of the nation in times of stress and crisis, as in the 1960's.

Having consolidated their hold on the lowlands, the Vietnamese committed virtually the same error as their Cham predecessors: They failed to give their country sufficient depth. Literally teeming in their narrow deltas, few Vietnamese had any particular desire to face the inhospitable forests and primitive tribes of the highlands, and save for a few government-sponsored settlements in the mountain areas of both zones, 95 per cent of all those who are Vietnamese ethnically, rather than by political fiat, live at an altitude of less than 900 feet (300 meters).

In the highlands, the fierce Thai, Muong, and Thô tribes tolerated Vietnamese overlordship with about as much good grace as the latter tolerated their own submission to the Chinese. Tribute in ivory, precious woods, and spices was exacted by Vietnamese mandarins who otherwise left the tribes to their traditional leaders, and Vietnamese annals are full of mountaineer uprisings. In fact, the tribal Thai were left almost entirely to themselves from the middle of the eighteenth century until the arrival of the French in 1893. The primitive southern tribesmen presented a problem of their own. The Vietnamese kings sagely recognized that they constituted a buffer zone against the still dangerous Khmer empire, and simply left them to their own devices, after the tribal chieftains had made their formal submission and paid a symbolical tribute. That direct relationship between the Vietnamese crown and the mountain tribes continued until 1955.

Nevertheless, the failure to integrate the mountain minorities into the Vietnamese national community has remained a serious problem to this day and is unlikely to be resolved satisfactorily in the near future.

The Vietnamese themselves, for all their cultural and social homogeneity, suffered politically from their own overrapid growth and their separation from the Tonkinese homeland. With the means of communication then in existence, the government in the Red River plain was simply incapable of exercising effective control over 1,400 miles of deltas. Divisions occurred, with local feudal lords taking matters into their own hands. In the north, the exhausted Lê dynasty had been overthrown by the Governor of Hanoi, Mac Dang Dung, who had, in Buttinger's words, "built himself a staircase of lordly and royal corpses right up to the throne," which he reached in 1527. In the south, another feudal lord, Nguyên Kim, had set up a Vietnamese government-in-exile in Laos, built around a descendant of the Lê. When Nguyên Kim died in 1545, murdered by supporters of the Mac clan, the struggle degenerated into a long civil war that, save for some brief spells of unity, lasted almost two centuries—with both sides claiming to represent the interests of the hapless legitimate Vietnamese kings while, in fact, merely watching over their own privileges. In the apt words of one French historian, the Vietnamese kings "were reduced to reigning over all Viet-Nam while being incapable of ruling over even the smallest district."[4]

In this indecisive struggle, the south remained largely on the defensive. In the 1630's, the Nguyên rulers built two huge walls across the Vietnamese plain of Quang-Tri near its narrow waist at Dong-Hoi—barely a few miles to the north of the present dividing line at the 17th parallel—and for 150 years the country remained divided on that line, just as it now has been since 1954. A *de facto* truce existed between the north and the south from 1673 to 1774, although the feudal Trinh lords (who, in the north, had succeeded the Mac as "protectors" of the Lê kings) still demanded the surrender of the southern "rebels," and the Nguyên in the south refused to agree to reunification as long as the Lê kings were helpless puppets of the Trinh. It is apparent that the Vietnamese people have had abundant experience in the kind of bitter internal division that was to rend it again 180 years later, after a brief period of independence and unity. There has been much debate over why the Trinh, with four-fifths of Viet-Nam's population in their area, never succeeded in breaking the hold of the Nguyên over the south, especially since the Nguyên not only had to hold the line against their northern foes, but also had to fight several bitter wars on their own southern frontiers with Cambodia, where Vietnamese settlers were advancing into the Mekong Delta. Economic and social reasons have been invoked by some historians who accept the Marxist interpretation of history as the only valid one, but that interpretation does not quite hold here.

for the economic and social organization of the Nguyên area was a carbon copy of that of the north. Militarily, also, both sides operated along similar lines, and both sides received "foreign aid" (a situation not unknown today). The Dutch backed the northern regime, while the Portuguese backed the Nguyên by providing modern artillery and military advisers. Since neither side was willing to consider a flanking maneuver through the inhospitable jungles to the west of the Wall of Dong-Hoi, a military stand-off resulted, which left the way open to a politico-ideological struggle. It was in the ideological sphere that the Nguyên side had the overwhelming advantage, for in the eyes of their own population, the Trinh lords had lost the "mandate of heaven." In an explanation of that important aspect of the attitude of the Vietnamese toward his government, a Vietnamese nationalist wrote in 1948:

> If the sovereign oppressed the people, he no longer deserved to be treated as the sovereign. His person was no longer sacred, and to kill him was no longer a crime. Revolt against such tyranny not only was reasonable but was a meritorious act and conferred upon its author the right to take over the powers of the sovereign.[5]

In the name of this right to revolution, the Nguyên were eventually victorious over the decadent Lê and Trinh; Ho Chi Minh defeated the French; Ngo Dinh Diem overthrew the discredited Nguyên ruler, Bao-Dai; and the Communist-led "Southern Front of Liberation" now seeks to gather a popular following against the stagnant Ngo Dinh Diem regime.

But an unforeseen event was to change for a brief moment the course of Vietnamese history. This was the rebellion of the three brothers from Tay-Son, a small village not far from Ankhé, on the northeastern edge of the PMS. The uprising began in 1772; by 1777, the Nguyên had been defeated and the last surviving prince of the family, Nguyên Anh, had been driven into the inhospitable swamps of the Mekong Delta. The Trinh, who had thought the moment ripe to settle their accounts with the southern regime, became the next victims of the victorious Tay-Son. By 1786, most of North Viet-Nam had fallen into the hands of the Tay-Son, who officially abolished the moribund Lê dynasty in 1787, although the youngest of the Tay-Son brothers, Hué, took care to marry the daughter of the last Lê king. Between 1789 and 1792, Viet-Nam was once more united under a single ruler, but the reunification brought in its wake a bitter civil war waged by the Nguyên, the Tay-Son, and the Trinh, which left

Viet-Nam more devastated than had 150 years of division. Present-day Marxist sources like to describe the Tay-Son as "progressive" rulers who lost their "mandate of Heaven" because they failed to solve the "social contradictions" then prevailing in Viet-Nam. The actuality seems to be less poetic: They were simply the first Vietnamese rulers to try to attempt to establish a military dictatorship in a country where the military were regarded with somewhat less than high admiration.

Thus, when Nguyên Anh began his campaigns of reconquest with the help of a French force of Katanga-type adventurers, the populace, mindful of the relatively efficient administration built up through competitive examinations under the Nguyên, began to flock again to the latter's banners. The fact that, thanks to his experienced French cadre and its better artillery, he outclassed the Tay-Son militarily, also had a great deal to do with the renewed enthusiasm for the Nguyên. But the final victory of Nguyên Anh over the Tay-Son was also the beginning of a new era: that of European political and military intervention in Vietnamese affairs.

THE EUROPEANS

The earliest recorded contacts between Viet-Nam and the West go as far back as 166 A.D., when the annals of the Giao-chi (the Chinese-administered area around the Red River Delta) relate that a Roman, sent by Emperor "An-Tun" (Marcus Aurelius Antoninus, who reigned from 161 to 180 A.D.), visited the country. A Roman gold medal, dating to 152 A.D., was found at Oc-Eo, in South Viet-Nam. It was in fact the word "Giao-chi," mispronounced by Marco Polo, that eventually gave rise to the word "Cochin," to which the term "China" was added for clarification, and "Cochinchina" was for several centuries the name under which Viet-Nam was best known in the West.

But the first lasting contact between Viet-Nam and Europe began with the landing of one of the Duke of Albuquerque's Portuguese captains, Antonio da Faria, at Faifo in 1535, and the subsequent establishment of rival Portuguese and Dutch trading posts. Catholic missionaries may have come to Viet-Nam even earlier than da Faria, but not until 1615 was a permanent Catholic mission established in Viet-Nam.

However, it was left to a French priest (said to have been of Jewish descent), Monsignor Alexandre de Rhodes, to establish Catholicism in Viet-Nam as not only a religious but also a cultural factor. Arriving in Viet-Nam in 1626 at the age of thirty-five, he set about unifying the various transcriptions of Vietnamese made by his predecessors into a coherent Latin alphabet supplemented with diacritical marks. This Latinized alphabet, called *quoc-ngu*, permits the writing of Vietnamese with almost as much facility as a Western language and represented a great step forward in opening Viet-Nam to Western culture. When Monsignor de Rhodes died, in 1660 in Persia, Catholicism had become a flourishing religion among the Vietnamese, who were matched in number of converts and fervor only by the Filipinos. For 100 years, however, the very competitiveness of the Portuguese, Spanish, and French clergy—and the openly commercial undertone of some of their enterprises—hobbled their success until, in 1767, another young and determined priest was appointed to Viet-Nam: Monsignor Pigneau de Behaine, later Bishop of Adran. His career in Viet-Nam began with a term in iron stocks, and his attempt to set up a Catholic seminary in Ha-Tien Province, at the extreme western end of Viet-Nam, ended in dismal failure. Then the Tay-Son rebellion added further woes to those the young bishop already faced, and provided him with yet another lost cause to espouse, that of the fleeing sixteen-year-old Nguyên prince, Nguyên Anh.

With the help of Bishop Pigneau, Nguyên Anh reassembled a small army, and while the Tay-Son concentrated on North Viet-Nam, he conquered and held several South Vietnamese provinces for four years. But his troops were no match for the full wrath of the Tay-Son, and Nguyên Anh was driven into exile to Siam. Pigneau did not despair; he went to France in 1787—a France whose financial and moral bankruptcy was to bring about the French Revolution two years later—in the forlorn hope of raising an army for his beloved "second fatherland." Meeting with no success in France, he returned to the Far East and, by sheer dint of personal persuasiveness, extracted from the French merchants in India, though skeptical of the whole scheme, sufficient funds to raise an army of about 300 men equipped with a few field pieces and two ships. Nguyên Anh, who, in the meantime, had returned to Saigon, had very little to offer the recruits except some land grants in the Mekong area—and he was shrewd enough to offer areas that then were largely still on Cambodian soil. The expedition set out for Viet-Nam on June 19, 1789. On July 14, the people of Paris stormed the Bastille.

Thanks to the modern methods of warfare of this French "military advisory group," the Nguyên forces now held victory in their grasp.

Bishop Pigneau, though his health was badly undermined by the long years of hardship he had endured, participated in the military campaigns at the side of his royal pupil. He died on October 9, 1799 under the walls of the Central Vietnamese fortress of Qui-Nhon and was buried a few miles north of Saigon with all the honors due a duke of the Vietnamese realm. Nguyên Anh himself defeated the last of the Tay-Son in 1801, brutally murdering the survivors, and then proclaimed himself emperor under the name of Gia-Long. The Chinese emperor confirmed Gia-Long in his title by sending him a new tributary seal in 1802, and Gia-Long gave the country he ruled its present name of "Viet-Nam."

With the end of the war, the role of Gia-Long's French advisers diminished markedly, as had their numbers, for they had not been supplemented by replacements during the French revolutionary and Napoleonic wars. Many of the Frenchmen had died in action or from the insalubrious climate; others had simply gone home. Very few had settled on the land grants offered by Gia-Long. In fact, by the time Gia-Long died, only two of Bishop Pigneau's original companions were still left at Hué, the new, centrally located capital. But rarely had so small a group of men in so short a time had so much influence in reshaping a country both physically and psychologically as did those 300 Frenchmen.

Their engineers had provided Viet-Nam with a series of star-shaped forts like those Vauban had designed in Europe and which had been imitated by all Western military powers everywhere from Fort Pitt to Malacca (even Viet-Nam's imperial castle is actually built inside a Vauban fort of vast proportions). Their armorers had taught skilled Vietnamese metalworkers to cast better and larger cannon, and some of the more peacefully minded Frenchmen had improved canals and sluices. Little wonder that Gia-Long showed great esteem for his little band of French advisers. Some sources assert that he had his own tomb built in the form of a French fortress out of esteem for what the French volunteers had done for Viet-Nam.[6] This esteem, however, did not extend to the religion of the Frenchmen; under Gia-Long's reign, the number of Vietnamese Christians is said to have diminished by 60 per cent.

In an interesting revision of history, the Vietnamese Communists have recently declared Gia-Long a "traitor king," very much as the Soviet leaders have posthumously purged Stalin. Gia-Long's "treachery" consisted in having brought in foreign advisers, which permits convenient, if inaccurate, comparisons with the Ngo Dinh Diem

Administration of South Viet-Nam. The fact that Gia-Long's foreign advisers all left the country and that North Viet-Nam has its own share of foreign advisers is, of course, conveniently forgotten.

END OF FREEDOM

The successors of Gia-Long—Minh Mang, Thieu Tri, and Tu Duc —lacked his imagination, as well as his appreciation of Western strengths and weaknesses. Further, Gia-Long dealt with the West at a time when it was embroiled in a Europe-wide "civil war"—the Napoleonic wars—but his successors had to deal with Western states whose power was directed once again toward overseas expansion. Practicing physical as well as spiritual isolationism (Catholics were now persecuted, missionaries expelled, and even the few remaining European traders forced to leave), the Vietnamese emperors soon cut themselves off completely from news of events outside. Their armed forces remained at the stage to which Bishop Pigneau's advisers had brought them forty years earlier—just as they had stagnated twice before, after the Portuguese and the Dutch had provided them with modern weapons. They had no knowledge of the newer and more accurate weapons developed by the West and, of course, had not sought to acquire them. Thus, when the inevitable collision with the West came, in the mid-1800's, Viet-Nam was not, like Japan and, to a lesser extent, Thailand, prepared to compromise some of its principles in order to survive as an independent state. It fought heroically but uselessly until its inevitable defeat.

French intervention in Viet-Nam was part of the over-all European design of opening China to Western trade. Britain had obtained Hong Kong from China in 1842, as well as the opening of five other ports to trade. In 1845, a French naval squadron obtained the same advantages for France, plus a promise to allow the practice of the Christian faith in the empire. While the French squadron was still in Chinese waters, news came of the imprisonment and death sentence of a French missionary, Monsignor Dominique Lefèbvre, by the Vietnamese. After an earlier rescue attempt by the U.S. Navy frigate *Constitution* had failed, a French warship obtained his release. But Lefèbvre was rearrested in 1846 and again sentenced to death, and again French ships sped to Tourane to obtain his release. Unbeknown to them, however, Bishop Lefèbvre already had been deported by the Vietnamese. After waiting in vain for two weeks in the port for an answer the Vietnamese Government failed to provide—probably through an oversight understandable to anyone familiar with governmental operations in the Far East even today—the nervous French were suddenly faced, on April 15, 1847, by four Vietnamese warships seemingly engaged in maneuvers that might have cut off the French vessels from the open sea. The French opened fire, and the outcome of the fight was hardly in doubt.

Buttinger later tallied the costs: "In seventy minutes French guns had taken a hundred times more lives than all the Vietnamese governments in two centuries of religious persecution."[7] While the image may be colorful, it is, on the basis of factual evidence, wholly inaccurate. In Tongking alone, Thieu-Tri and Tu-Duc had put to death 10 European priests, 100 Vietnamese priests, and 20,000 faithful in less than 15 years. In Cochinchina, 15 European missionaries, 200 Vietnamese missionaries, and 10,000 Vietnamese faithful had been put to death during that same period.[8] It is somewhat difficult to believe that four Vietnamese sailing ships of the 1840's were manned by 30,325 men—let alone by "a hundred times more."

A present-day Vietnamese historian, Lê Thanh Khoi, provides a simple explanation for what was to happen next—an explanation that has distinct resemblances to the contemporary situation:

. . . the mandarins hid from the ruler, isolated from his people by the high walls of the Forbidden City [i.e., the palace in Hué], national realities as well as the gravity of the crisis in foreign relations. It is their blind pride as well as their narrowness of views which bears a large measure of responsibility for the fall of Viet-Nam.[9]

On August 31, 1858, a Franco-Spanish squadron under Admiral Rigault de Genouilly anchored in front of Tourane. On the following day, landing parties stormed the forts and met perfunctory resistance. But Tourane proved to be no prize, and on February 18, 1859, Saigon was taken. Though only a fishing village at the time, Saigon showed excellent promise as a deep-water port. Two years later, much of the Mekong Delta had become a French bridgehead, but Emperor Tu-Duc still refused to capitulate, and well-organized guerrilla forces made life miserable for the French. What finally forced Tu-Duc to agree to French demands for freedom of religious practice, freedom of commerce, and possession of Saigon was a rebellion that had broken out in North Viet-Nam under the leadership of a remote descendant of the Lê dynasty. But in France, "the party of aggressive imperialism" (to use Buttinger's phrase)[10] outweighed the arguments of an anticolonial legislature, which reminded Emperor

Napoleon III that his little Mexican adventure had already cost France 260 million gold francs, while the Cochinchinese swamps had swallowed another 60 million without the justification of a corresponding increase in trade. At the same time, the Mekong—which had been hailed as yet another easy avenue to the riches of China—was found to be of no value whatever as a navigable river since it was cut by waterfalls at the Lao-Cambodian border. The Franco-Prussian War of 1870–71 put a temporary halt to French expansion in the Far East.

In fact, far from being the "grand design" elaborated by a group of greedy militarists at the beck and call of French financiers—a simple, picture-book view of colonialism that many Americans share with their Soviet Russian contemporaries—the occupation of Viet-Nam was a jigsaw puzzle of isolated and contradictory moves. Thus, in 1873, a French Navy lieutenant, Francis Garnier, with a landing force of 110 Marines, was sent to Hanoi to deport an unscrupulous French trader, Jean Dupuis, who had made himself thoroughly obnoxious to the Vietnamese. With an independence of mind that seems to be the hallmark of the French military (and the bane of the civilian governments who have to work with them)', Garnier decided to "liberate" all Tongking instead. For a while, the firepower and discipline of his small band prevailed. Soon, however, he was killed in an ambush, but only after having shattered the authority of the Vietnamese emperor in the north.

The case of Jules Ferry further indicates how limited France's involvement in Indochina was—both militarily and emotionally. Ferry, who had earned himself the nickname "*le Tonkinois*" because he was as dedicated to the acquisition of Tongking as Secretary Seward was to that of Alaska by the United States, was toppled from the Premiership on March 30, 1885, after a small force he had sent to the Tonkinese border had lost twelve men in a skirmish. Ferry was called a "traitor" in the Chamber of Deputies for having diverted precious resources to a faraway enterprise when all of France's strength was to be devoted to a "second round" with Germany.

In Viet-Nam, every French move was answered by renewed attacks from patriotic Vietnamese, aided by Chinese volunteers whom the French labeled "pirates" but who nonetheless fought extremely well. It was not until June 6, 1884; that Viet-Nam officially accepted the French protectorate. China, in a belated move to reassert her sovereignty over Viet-Nam, protested against the treaty, and Chinese forces in the Tonkinese border area attacked French forces. A French naval force landed in Formosa, bombarded Fu-chow, and occupied the Pescadores. In June, 1885, the Chinese, in turn, saw the futility of further resistance and signed a treaty with France at Tien-tsin, recognizing French suzerainty over Viet-Nam.

This settled the theoretical aspect of the problem, but not that of the effective occupation of the country by the French. A young emperor, Ham Nghi, came to the throne in July, 1884, and with his court, largely made up of Vietnamese scholars, he held the field against the French until his capture in 1888. He was to die in exile in an area the French then considered absolutely "safe"—Algeria. One last Vietnamese leader, Dê Tham, held out in the Yên-The area north of the Red River Delta until he was betrayed in 1913. The North Vietnamese Communists have made him a national hero.

Now 50 years of French administration were about to begin—a short span in comparison to the 1,000 years of Chinese occupation Viet-Nam had known earlier. But in their impact upon Viet-Nam's future, those 50 years proved as fateful as the full 1,000.

3

Colonial Interlude

PROBABLY few colonial enterprises have aroused as much bitter controversy in the United States—with fewer hard facts to rely on—than the fifty-year-long French rule in Indochina. This was due chiefly to the circumstances that, as a French-speaking area, it was less accessible to Americans than the various British colonies. Although Indochina was physically very close to the American-administered Philippines, there was little commerce or travel between the two areas. Little wonder that, prior to America's direct involvement in the area late in World War II, the popular view of Indochina in general and Viet-Nam in particular was the black-and-white stereotype of the all-bad "white exploiter" lording it over the all-good "natives."[1]

Thus, no less knowledgeable a person than President Franklin D. Roosevelt, on January 24, 1944, told Lord Halifax, then the British Ambassador to Washington:

France has had [Indochina]—thirty million inhabitants—for nearly one hundred years, and the people are worse off than they were at the beginning. . . . France has milked it for one hundred years. The people of Indochina are entitled to something better than that.

Yet, a severe Indian critic of the West, and former Indian Ambassador to Egypt and Red China, later appraised French performance in far less absolute terms:

In fact, during the first three decades of the twentieth century, French administration of Indochina was as well run and as efficiently organized as the best colonial governments and created a vast system of roads, railways, and other communication facilities . . . and economic measures meant to benefit large numbers. It also showed an interest in the history and culture of Indochina, preserving with care the monuments of the past. . . .[2]

In fact, French imperialism in the Far East remained a haphazard enterprise based more on local initiatives than on government policies, and more on prestige factors than on economic considerations. Buttinger asserts that "to enter Vietnam was at no time a desire of the French people and only very rarely the project of a government of France."[3] And in his superb study on *The Roots of French Imperialism in Eastern Asia*, John T. Cady shows conclusively that prestige—that "conspicuous consumption" of governments—was the major motivating factor behind France's colonial drive.[4]

For that matter, even a cursory analysis of French colonial budgets —not only in Indochina but throughout the world—indicates how expensive those overseas establishments were and how often their very survival depended upon an eleventh-hour appeal of the French Government to the legislature, not in the name of economic logic, but in the name of prestige. In a hardheaded analysis of the subject, the French historian Henri Brunschwig wrote recently:

The colonies were not supposed to be sources of revenue.. Their role consisted in disputing the mastery of the seas with Britain and affirming to the face of the world the *présence*, the *grandeur*, and the *rayonnement* of France. It was normal that all this was to be paid for, like all expenditures of sovereignty.[5]

In other words, in the 1870's to have colonies was, at least as far as France was concerned, largely a matter of "keeping up with the Joneses"—even if this analysis does not fit in with the Marxist theories on the purposes and aims of imperialism.

There remains a last-ditch argument for the traditional anti-colonialists—to wit, that the colonies were at least a magnificent

exclusive market for the colonial power's private citizens, whose
scandalous profits, re-exported from the colony to the homeland,
fattened the national treasury. That may have been true in a very
few specialized cases, but as an over-all view of Western or French
colonial economic policies, it is sheer nonsense. In most cases, France
set up effective protectionist barriers only after World War I, with
the result that from 1901 through 1910, as Brunschwig proves,[6]
foreign imports to French colonies *exceeded* French imports throughout the whole decade except the year 1901, and exports from those
colonies to countries other than France *exceeded* colonial exports to
France throughout the whole decade!

Similarly, the Chamber of Deputies' budget committee presented
in 1896 a report on the 1894 budget that contained the following
devastating facts: The total trade of France's colonies had been 476
million francs. Of that sum, trade with foreign countries represented
259 million, trade with France 217 million. Purchases by the colonies
had amounted to 126 million abroad and 95 million in France.
French purchases in the colonies had amounted to 118 million. However, of the 95 million exported by France to the colonies, 80 million
represented purchases made by the French Army and civil administration in those territories—from appropriations paid for by the French
home budget. And the budget committee concluded: "A market of
95 million costs us 80 million a year, and the foreign traders get a
market of 126 million without spending a cent." This, naturally, led
to many acrimonious debates in the Chamber of Deputies, since the
legislators were constantly asked to provide funds for colonial ven-
tures whose economic potential was perpetually described to them
as being on the verge of realization.

That this phenomenon was not limited to France, but was characteristic of other Western empires as well, is shown by John
Strachey's study of British trade relations with her empire and also
in the studies of the Swedish economist Gunnar Myrdal.[7]

Thus, the myth of the economic advantages of colonies can be
quietly laid to rest, no matter how temptingly simple it makes the
explanation of a rather complex problem. One last general figure
will show how unimportant the whole matter of colonial trade was
to France during the crucial period of colonial expansion: Trade
between France and her colonies in the years 1882–1913 rose from
6.7 per cent to 10.9 per cent of her total external trade—and her total
external trade, in turn, represented about 3 *per cent* of her gross national product. Whether Viet-Nam did or did not buy 100 million

francs' worth of French products in the 1900's may have been important to a few French special interests; it certainly had no bearing whatever òn a French trade volume of 20 billion francs.[8]

There remains yet another myth: that Viet-Nam was made an exclusive economic preserve of France. That line, assiduously fostered by Marxist economists, has found a ready audience among American professional anticolonialists whose ignorance of the real facts it suits well. Here, a recent economic study by Ton That Thien, an anti-French Vietnamese who until recently was President Ngo Dinh Diem's press chief, sheds an interesting light on the situation:

In 1939, the last year of normal trade under the colonial regime, Ton That Thien notes, Vietnamese exports to the French franc area amounted to 32.2 per cent of the country's total exports, and imports from France to 55.7 per cent of all imports. In comparison, exports to the United States amounted to 12 per cent and imports from the U.S. to 4.2 per cent. In 1957, when all of North Viet-Nam had been lost for three years and South Viet-Nam had eradicated the last traces of French imperialism, her exports to France amounted to *50.8 per cent* (a jump of 18.6 per cent over 1939), while her exports to the United States, her new exclusive backer, had increased by barely 1.7 per cent, accounting for 13.7 per cent of all her exports. At the same time, imports from France to Viet-Nam had been cut by 26.4 per cent, amounting to 29.3 per cent of the total, while imports from the United States (paid for by U.S. aid) had increased by 18.3 per cent, amounting to 22.7 per cent of the total. As will be seen later, Viet-Nam was *more dependent* than ever upon France's willingness to buy her overpriced (averaging 15 per cent above world-market prices) goods.[9]

In other words, very little has changed from 1896, when the French legislators complained that France was spending 80 million francs in order to earn 95 million—except that the United States is operating on a much more expensive scale than the French did—and American taxpayers' funds are now financing American exports for correspondingly low returns.

There remains, finally, the old saw about "capitalistic monocultures," i.e., the colonial power compelling a particular territory to devote all its energies to a single economic endeavor, or perhaps to two products (cocoa in Ghana, cotton in Egypt, coffee in Brazil, tobacco and sugar in Cuba, etc.). In that case, also, Viet-Nam was singularly fortunate, for, under the colonial regime, her ancient and almost exclusive rice culture was supplemented by the production of spices, tea, coffee, corn (650,000 tons in 1938; almost none now), and such raw materials as rubber, coal, tin, and wolfram. Thus, in 1938, rubber and rice represented only 56.2 per cent of all Vietnamese exports—an indication of a certain amount of healthy diversification. In 1958, those same products represented 89.5 per cent of all Vietnamese exports, and with the growing insecurity of the years 1961–63 and the resultant reduction of rice exports, rubber became a quasi-monopolistic product representing almost 90 per cent of the total value of all exports. This is certainly not a healthy situation, but one can scarcely blame French colonialism for it.

Brunschwig gives the following explanation of the French colonial process and its economic rationales, and for all its irony, his explanation appears to be as correct as any thus far in print:

> It was characteristic of that colonial policy always to bet its chips on the future: Military credits were voted because conquest would allow for development; [basic] investments were made because the railroads and other technical installations would permit the rational exploitation of resources; hospitals and schools were built because they would bring about a useful labor force. One constantly bet on the future, and in the last analysis, it was this speculation that led the colonizers to equip the colonized population instead of purely and simply exploiting it.[10]

Thus, it can be said that the "scandalous profits" the unsophisticated mind usually associates with a colonial economy were made in Viet-Nam at two specific periods: when the colonial system was established, and when it collapsed. When it was established, large-scale land grants (like those on which some early American fortunes were based) became a source of unlawful profiteering until strict legislation plugged the loophole; and when Indochina was about to be lost, the huge expenditures of the French Army and the inflated value of the Indochinese piaster in relation to the French franc gave rise to a system of graft and corruption that rotted everything it touched—and it touched nearly everything and everybody.

Between those two periods were forty years of steady and unspectacular development. In 1938, the last full peacetime year (France entered the war in September, 1939), the *total* value of stock dividends, interest, and shares distributed by all the French capital invested in Indochina amounted to a conservative return of 2.3 per cent.[11]

Where the French remained perfectly orthodox in colonial economics was in persisting almost to the end in considering Viet-Nam as little else but a source of raw materials. To be sure, textiles were produced on an industrial scale in Nam-Dinh, in North Viet-Nam; rice mills were established; the Haiphong cement plant began to export cement in 1935—but French vested interests fought against any kind of medium or light industry, which the country could have well afforded and needed. It was only in the face of the rising Japanese threat, and the belated French realization that Indochina might be cut off from France, that the French military decided to build an ammunition factory and even an aircraft-assembly plant at Tông, north of Hanoi. That ambitious program was far short of completion by the time France was overrun by the Nazis and Indochina occupied by the Japanese. But all in all, France's sins in the economic field were not her major ones; her major errors were all political.

GOVERNORS AND GOVERNED

It may be considered an axiom of colonial administration that no colonial government can export a better administrative system than it possesses at home. Thus, it would be rather surprising to find flourishing representative government and a free press in Spanish and Portuguese colonies, when the two mother countries concerned are full-fledged military dictatorships; or to have seen the Philippines develop Cabinet government with a Prime Minister and a weak President, when the American example pointed toward a strong Presidency. In the case of Indochina in general, and Viet-Nam in particular, the French system took hold with a vengeance.

In Paris, French governments fell with incredible speed, and colonial governors in Indochina followed the political fortunes of their backers at home, when they were not removed at the behest of influential Frenchmen in Indochina. During the forty-three years of French civil administration in Indochina, from October, 1902, to March, 1945, no less than twenty-three governors or acting governors had ruled the area! Several times, there was no chief executive at all in Indochina for more than a year, and some governors general lasted less than eight months before being recalled. It was obvious that under such conditions the pursuit of a consistent colonial policy was almost impossible—the more so as there *was no* French colonial policy. Incredible as it seems, the only constitutional text that served as a base for colonial policy-making from May, 1854, until the constitution of the Fourth French Republic was ratified in October,

1946, was this brief pronouncement by Emperor Napoleon III: "Colonies will be ruled by decree of the emperor until a decision has been taken by the *senatus-consulte*." And since Napoleon and his rubber-stamp *senatus-consulte* disappeared in the chaos of the Franco-Prussian War of 1870 before a decision had been taken, and the Third Republic completely forgot the matter, French colonial affairs became an almost private preoccupation of the Minister of Colonies and of the colonial governors. Ironically, the colonies—contrary to American practice—could at least send an increasing number of vóting representatives to the French legislature. But in the French protectorates, such as Annam, Tongking, Tunisia, and Morocco, all power lay in the hands of their respective residents general. With such lack of direction at the top, policy in Indochina was left very much to the governor general and depended upon his enthusiasm or concern for his charges. Under the governors general, Viet-Nam in 1902 was divided into three major territories: the two protectorates, Tongking and Annam, each administered by a *résident supérieur*, and the colony of Cochinchina, administered by a governor. In addition, the cities of Tourane, Haiphong, and Hanoi, ceded by Viet-Nam to France in 1884, also were administered as French colonies.

Each Vietnamese province was directed by an official of the French Indochinese Civil Service, called a *chef de province* in the colonies and a *résident* in the protectorates. In the protectorates, the *résidents* were theoretically "advisers" to Vietnamese mandarins; in reality, they held full powers, including those of the police and, often, the judiciary.

To be sure, the Vietnamese emperors continued to exist, surrounded by the antiquated court ceremonial of Hué, and seconded by Cabinet ministers whose resounding titles belied their total impotence (the Minister of War, for example, had authority over the palace guard). But every one of their acts, except those dealing with such minor religious matters as setting the exact dates of movable holidays, required the signature of the *résident supérieur*. In Tongking, whatever difference existed between the "protectorate" and direct colonial administration was strictly a matter of terminology.

At the lower echelons, Vietnamese retained their posts and gained access to many careers, such as forestry or surveying, that hitherto had not existed. However, at all echelons, even the most humble, they were confronted by Frenchmen holding exactly the same or lower jobs but being paid two or three times more. Thus, the French janitor at the University of Hanoi received a base pay that was slightly higher than that of a Vietnamese professor with a Ph.D. from the University of Paris.[12] In 1927, at last, under the enlightened rule of Governor General Varenne (November, 1924–April, 1928), Vietnamese and Frenchmen with comparable academic records were given equality of access to executive positions, and soon—a shift in a way from one extreme to the other—one could find Vietnamese holding important positions in the French colonial administration in neighboring Cambodia and Laos. The citizens of the latter countries thus felt *twice* colonized: first by the French, and second by the Vietnamese, whose own colonial activities in the two small states in the eighteenth and early nineteenth centuries had left anything but fond remembrances.

Those moves toward liberalization were fought tooth and nail by the European colonial population, and much of what was done in education and social welfare—and in the fields of work conditions, child labor, and tuberculosis prevention particularly, it was a great deal more than any other colonial power had done—was done in the face of the fiercest opposition and counterpressure from the Europeans. Thus, the decision of the French Government to allow Vietnamese to become officers in the French regular army even prior to 1914 brought forth the following prophetic outburst from a rich *colon:*

> Either they will be worthy of becoming French officers, in which case their highest ideal will be to liberate the soil of their fatherland and their most noble endeavor should be to throw us into the sea. Or those people will content themselves with getting their pay and wearing a beautiful uniform while preserving a servant's soul—and in that case, I don't want them as officers in the French Army.

And the Vietnamese officers who served with the French Army fell into exactly those categories thirty-five years later. In the meantime—and this is suppressed with all diligence in Saigon while, for example, the Indians, Pakistanis, and Moroccans are rightfully proud of their military achievements under the colonial banner—the Vietnamese in the French Army fought well. One of them became an air ace in World War I; another, Captain Do Huu Vi, died while leading the charge of a French unit at a vital sector of Verdun; and in December, 1945, a French major by the name of Vinh-San died in an air crash. He had been the holder of the highest French decorations for bravery and, as one of General de Gaulle's early followers, had earned the coveted title of Companion of the French

Liberation. Major Vinh-San was Viet-Nam's former emperor, Duy-Tan, forcibly removed from his throne by the French colonial administration in 1917 for his anti-French activities. Like Field Marshal Ayub Khan of Pakistan and General El-Kittani of Morocco (who, as a French colonel, lost a leg at Cassino), Duy-Tan had borne arms for the colonial power without ever forgetting the "most noble endeavor."

But what probably rankled most in the administrative relations between colonizers and colonized was the absence of any truly representative assemblies in which the Vietnamese could make their viewpoints known effectively. Only Cochinchina, being a colony, was able to send a deputy to the French legislature; and since that deputy was elected by the French citizens of the colony, he actually represented only the Europeans and the few thousand Vietnamese (out of a population of 5 million) who had gone through the French naturalization process. Needless to say, no Asian ever was elected to that post. (In French Africa, where the same system operated but where the base of local citizenship was far larger, the preponderance of those elected to the French legislature were African and soon rose to key posts. A French Negro from Martinique, Gaston Monnerville, has been President of the French Senate—i.e., No. Two man of the French Republic, after President de Gaulle—since 1947.)

However, each of the three territories was provided with an assembly having limited advisory powers and in which the Vietnamese were represented. In Cochinchina, this was the Colonial Council, in which fourteen seats out of twenty-four were held by Frenchmen; and in the two protectorates, there were Chambers of the People's Representatives. The Chamber in Annam was wholly elective and dominated by Vietnamese; in Tongking, it was also Vietnamese-dominated but one-fourth of its members were local citizens considered "safe" by the French authorities and appointed to the Chamber without election. Although their legislative powers were limited to expressing their "opinions" on economic and social legislation, these assemblies nevertheless provided a sounding board for heated debates in which the Vietnamese members faced their French colleagues with many an unpleasant truth about local conditions.[13] This may not have been representative government, but it was a good preparation for it—and, unfortunately, the rubber-stamp legislatures that have represented both zones of Viet-Nam since independence are hardly an improvement in terms of freedom of expression over their colonial predecessors.

An Indochina-wide legislature came into being in November, 1928. Called the Grand Council of Financial and Economic Interests, it was designed to represent the views of the inhabitants of Indochina to the governor general. Of its fifty-one members, twenty-three were native (eighteen Vietnamese and five Lao and Cambodian). The Grand Council represented a step forward in the sense that the governor general was compelled to consult it before the colonial budget could be approved, but in practice its native members wielded less influence than those in the territorial assemblies and were totally dominated by the economic "giants"—the Bank of Indochina, the rubber plantations, and some of the larger firms, such as Denis Frères and Descours et Cabaud, whose representatives figured importantly in the Grand Council.

In the field of jurisprudence, Cochinchina and the three French cities were provided with French courts, and cases could regularly be appealed to the highest courts in France. Such was not the case in the protectorates, whose traditional courts were provided with French advisers and dispensed justice through their own codes (the Lê code of the fifteenth century and the Gia-Long code of the early nineteenth century), adapted to European standards of punishment. Excessive imprisonment for minor violations and mutilation as a punishment for certain crimes were abolished. But in the protectorates, the French authorities remained a law unto themselves. In one test case, in 1936, the French Conseil d'Etat (Administrative Supreme Court) decided that the French protectorate authorities were in reality working under the jurisdiction of a "foreign" state (i.e., Annam) and thus not liable to suit before French courts—and it was unlikely that any Vietnamese would have had much success suing a French official before a Vietnamese court.[14]

All this spelled a great deal of frustration for the increasing numbers of young Vietnamese intellectuals who returned from France after having completed their university studies, or who completed them at the University of Hanoi, and then found their professional horizons blocked or encumbered by Frenchmen. As Isoart points out in a single eloquent figure, "the Viceroy of India governed in 1925 a total of 325 million Indians with 4,898 European civil servants, while the [French] Governor General administered 30 million Indochinese with 5,000 French civil servants."[15] And the situation worsened rather than improved between 1925 and 1954. This writer recalls seeing one last French white policeman directing traffic in the streets of Hanoi as late as September, 1953—a menial job no-

British colonial governor would have permitted a white man to do even a hundred years ago.

This brought into Indochina a marginal group of *petits blancs*—the French equivalent of "poor white trash"—whose living standards (and, above all, living habits) were barely a cut above those of the poorer urban Vietnamese and who bitterly competed with them for precisely those jobs that would have enabled the Vietnamese to create an urbanized middle class. If familiarity ever bred contempt, Indochina was probably the one area in the Far East in which the local population had become thoroughly familiar with its colonial overlords. It would, however, be too easy to dismiss out of hand the whole French colonial period as one vast cipher in everything but economics. Lest it be forgotten, the French have done a creditable job—better than the British in India or the Dutch in the East Indies —in eradicating illiteracy; the public-health services of the French colonial administration were among the best in Asia, with the unique network of Pasteur Institutes that from 1924 on were able to export vaccines to other Asian countries. It is perhaps worthy of note that to this day a French lycée exists in North Viet-Nam and that even the Communists do not object to the fact that it bears the name "Albert Sarraut," after a governor general who ruled Viet-Nam and all Indochina between 1911 and 1919 and whose long struggle (continuing until his death in 1962) for the peoples of Indochina is gratefully remembered.

Legislation on work conditions is another field in which the French colonial administration did pioneering work. Like most other underdeveloped countries, Viet-Nam had a *corvée* system of compulsory labor, in which villagers who did not pay monetary taxes were compelled to participate in public works. In the more advanced Western countries, the *corvée* system has been replaced by the more convenient system of working one day a week at one's *own* job for the government; this is called the income tax, and it is likewise compulsory. Since 1960, most newly independent African states have reinstated the *corvée* to an extent never known before, but now it is called "valorization of human capital." In Viet-Nam, the *corvée* system went out of existence in the 1920's, but a more abusive labor practice persisted: the recruitment of labor for plantation work. Carried on by native recruiters (*cai*) whose methods were brutal and who gouged the workers of much of their salary, the system rightfully was attacked as degrading. Here, the rise of left-wing governments in France came to the rescue of the hapless local laborers; when the

Popular Front of Léon Blum took power in 1936, one of its most important actions in the field of labor legislation was to decree the strict application of all domestic laws in the overseas territories: The eight-hour day was introduced as of January 1, 1937, supplemented by paid leaves, weekly rest periods, interdiction of night labor for women, pensions in case of work accidents, etc. And most important of all, the enterprise recruiting labor via a *cai* was now held fully liable for his acts. Enforced by teams of young labor inspectors who had no fear of vested interests, the legislation was obeyed and soon most firms began to recruit their own labor rather than be responsible for a *cai*.

When the International Labor Organization (then an organ of the League of Nations, and now an agency of the U.N.) surveyed labor conditions in the Far East in 1937, it found that conditions in French Indochina were far better than those everywhere else in the region. For example, indépendent Japan had no work-time limit for men, and women and youths were "limited" (*sic*) to eleven hours of work a day, with no compulsory weekly rest periods. In India, the workday for both sexes was twelve hours, and in China and Thailand, there were no restrictions at all. Let it be noted that even the Popular Front forbade unionizing activities in Viet-Nam, although since 1928 there had been an illegal Communist labor union whose increasing effectiveness began to be apparent in several well-conducted strikes for limited economic objectives. While still professing not to recognize the unions, French employers soon found it expedient to discuss matters with "workers' representatives," who were in fact presidents of union locals.[16]

When the world-wide economic crisis brought a collapse of rubber and rice prices and concomitant labor unrest, the French colonial administration was again in an interregnum. The well-liked Governor General Pasquier had been killed in an airplane accident in January, 1934, and had been replaced by a local colonial official, Robin, who saw his task mainly as a matter of "repressing agitation." The ensuing tension helped rather than hindered the Vietnamese nationalists, for the weakness of the French colonial administration persuaded them of the value of burying their internecine struggles for the sake of presenting a united front.

In one such operation, the Trotskyite Party of Cochinchina, under Ta Thu Thau, made an alliance with the orthodox Communists of the Indochinese Communist Party (ICP), which had been founded in 1930, and both parties presented a joint slate of candidates in the

January, 1933, elections for the Colonial Council. It is, in a way, evidence of the fairness of the colonial election process that candidates of *both* parties were elected (much to the shock of their French colleagues). Debates in the Colonial Council took a much livelier turn henceforth. It should be noted that in the 1953 municipal elections—held in the midst of the Indochina war—the Saigon Taxi Drivers' Union also put up a Trotskyite candidate, who won handily. (Both Vietnamese independent regimes have since done away with such paraphernalia as fair elections. Ta Thu Thau himself was murdered in 1946 by his former ICP allies, and South Viet-Nam has yet to hold a local election. It is furthermore doubtful that a Trotskyite candidate could present himself at the polls in either zone.)

The Popular Front government brought with it a change in colonial governors. The new appointee, Brévié (1936–39), came from Africa and thus had not been under the influence of the Indochinese vested interests. In rapid succession, he rammed through an amnesty that reduced the number of political prisoners from 10,000 to 3,000— today there are probably more than 100,000 political prisoners in *each* of Viet-Nam's two zones—including most of Viet-Nam's present Communist leadership; he modified the tax base so as to reduce the excessive load on the poorer sections of the population; he greatly simplified acquisition of French citizenship by Vietnamese; and in Cochinchina he authorized political parties and their newspapers to operate openly. In Tongking, although the Communist Party was banned, an "Indochinese Democratic Front," under Pham Van Dong and Vo Nguyên Giap, put out its own newspaper *Tin-Tuc* (*The News*), soon followed by no less than eight openly pro-Communist newspapers.[17]

In other words, in French-ruled Viet-Nam there had been notable strides between 1936 and 1939 in the field of political activities. Unfortunately, the absence of a concerted colonial policy in Paris— such as the viewpoint that allowed Britain or the United States to offer their Indian and Filipino colonial charges definite promises of reform and eventual independence—made any far-reaching arrangement between French interests and Vietnamese nationalism almost impossible. Not that the most enlightened of the French governors general had not warned both their countrymen in Viet-Nam and their governments at home that changes were long overdue—Albert Sarraut had advocated self-government as early as 1919, and Varenne in 1928 and Brévié in 1939 had warned of the political pressure that was building up without a safety valve—but there never seemed to be any particular urgency about the situation. Viet-Nam had no Gandhi to inflame the whole country to peaceful resistance, nor did it yet have the kind of armed rebellious movement[18] that could force the colonial rulers to yield.

In fact, Viet-Nam in the late 1930's, slowly recovering from the Great Depression, was very far from being ruled by the iron hand of military oppression and the fear of the police—a stereotype writers with a Communist bent like to perpetuate in the public mind.[19] On January 1, 1938, there were exactly 10,779 French soldiers and 292 police officers in all of Cambodia, Laos, and Viet-Nam with their 30 million inhabitants. (In 1960, the 8 million people of the city of New York were protected by a police force of 24,000 men.)

The outbreak of World War II found the French as unprepared in the Far East as they were in mainland France: Local reserves were called up, a total of fifteen modern combat aircraft could be spared for Indochina, and one lone light cruiser, *Lamotte-Picquet*, was dispatched to protect the open coast. Again, as in World War I, thousands of Vietnamese troops were levied to go to France.

Inside Viet-Nam, the brief Communist honeymoon with the colonial administration was over. The Communists, faithful to their Russian masters, who had just carved up Poland in a joint aggression with Nazi Germany, switched to an antiwar policy and went underground when France, in September, 1939, outlawed the Communist Party both at home and in the overseas area. In a policy statement on November 13, 1939, the ICP sought to reconcile the irreconcilable by attacking France's war against Nazi Germany as "imperialist" while asking its adherents to struggle against Japan (which at that time threatened Soviet positions in the Far East):

> Our Party finds it to be a matter of life and death . . . to struggle against the imperialist war and policy of thievery and massacre of French imperialism . . . while at the same time struggling against the aggressive aims of Japanese fascism. . . .

The lights were going out for the white man in Asia, but the Frenchmen in Indochina were not aware of it. In any case, not yet.

4

White Man's End

No period of Vietnamese history is less well known in the United States than that between 1940 and 1945, and for several good reasons: During those years, there were virtually no American observers in Viet-Nam—probably fewer than were inside either Nazi Germany or Japan—and the French themselves were reluctant to go into the details of what was happening in Viet-Nam, since much of it did not precisely redound to their glory. Today, however, sufficient historical sources are available on both sides of the Atlantic to enable us to retrace a good part of the tortuous path of both French and Allied policies in the area.

One point must be made at the outset: Contrary to popular belief —and to the accounts presented by most American writers and historians—the United States was deeply involved in shaping the postwar fate of Viet-Nam, an involvement that began well before the war was over. In large measure, American policy weakened France's postwar position in the Far East (as it was intended to), and French politicians and military men involved in the situation then or later developed a lively grudge against the United States that makes itself felt to this day.* As long as this is not fully understood in the United States, French reaction to certain American policy moves will remain a mystery to American policy-makers.

INDOCHINA IN ISOLATION

When the French mainland was overrun by the Germans, in the spring of 1940, and France signed an armistice with the Third Reich, on June 25, 1940, Indochina could no longer count on any help from France. Although a loose coordination of defense measures in the Far East had been agreed upon by the British and French during talks in June, 1939, and similar talks had taken place with the Dutch, the loss of both France and Holland and the dire straits of Britain after Dunkirk ruled out the possibility of an effective defense of Southeast Asia against Japanese aggression.

There always remained the possibility of an alliance with the only other major democratic power in the Pacific—the United States. But in the summer of 1940, the United States still clung to its policy of noninvolvement. On June 30, 1940, Under Secretary of State Sumner Welles told the French Ambassador in Washington:

. . . considering the general situation, the Government of the United States did not believe that it could enter into conflict with Japan and that, *should the latter attack Indochina, the United States would not oppose such an action.*[1]

This policy was apparently based on a State Department estimate of the situation, according to which it was doubtful that the Japanese, involved as they were in mainland China, were ready to take on additional military commitments; in other words, Washington believed that Tokyo was bluffing. This explains the statement a few days later by Sumner Welles's chief, Secretary of State Cordell Hull, that America's policy in Southeast Asia should be limited to encouraging "countries like Indochina . . . to delay and parlay [sic] and hold out to the last minute against Japanese demands [since] Japan would not dare make a military attack at this time."[2]

* For example, Pierre Messmer, President de Gaulle's Minister of the Armed Forces since 1960, was one of the senior officials parachuted into Viet-Nam shortly before V-J Day and imprisoned by the Viet-Minh. An American OSS (Office of Strategic Services) detachment operating with the Viet-Minh refused to intervene in his behalf with his captors. This, understandably, did not sit too well with Messmer and his associates. For the reasons the OSS did not intervene, see the following pages.

General Douglas MacArthur, who then commanded the American and Filipino forces in the Philippines and had a keener appreciation of the ultimate dangers to his own position if the French and Dutch were forced to yield to Japanese pressure, had intervened in their behalf with his own superiors in Washington, but he had been turned down. On September 15, 1940, a last request was made by General Martin, the French commander in Tongking, to the Commander of U.S. Naval Forces in the Philippines for a naval demonstration in the Gulf of Tongking when Japanese pressure became intolerable. This, too, was not acted upon.[3]

With the Vichy government of Marshal Pétain under the thumb of Japan's German ally, and Indochina totally isolated from outside help, the outcome of the next round was never in doubt.

On June 19, 1940, as France's government lay dying—it had just fled Paris and was incommunicado for several days until it could be installed in Bordeaux, only to flee that city a few days later as Nazi tanks approached—Japan addressed an ultimatum to the French governor general, General Catroux, demanding joint control of the Tonkinese border. (Tongking, with its Yünnan railroad, was Nationalist China's "iron lung," pumping in supplies from the outside world.[4]) When, in the absence of orders from Paris, Catroux acceded to the Japanese demand, the moribund Third Republic relieved him of his command—on June 25, the very day France signed an armistice with Germany—and replaced him with tough and able Admiral Jean Decoux, who, when faced with similar Japanese demands, told his home government that he would rather fight and die than see Indochina "reduced to becoming another Manchukuo."[5]

Historians have failed to record, however, that Catroux's hands were tied not only by France, but also by the United States and Britain. Prior to his assent to the Japanese conditions, Catroux had sent a purchasing mission to the United States with orders to acquire 120 modern fighter aircraft and modern antiaircraft artillery to be supplied out of the sizable orders France already had placed, and paid for, with American manufacturers—only to be informed that *delivery of that equipment to Indochina had been forbidden by the U.S. Government.*[6] And Donald Lancaster, a British diplomat turned historian, pointed out: "When he had completed this bleak assessment of his resources and had made every effort to get American or British help, Catroux had no alternative but to accept the Japanese demands."[7]

Catroux's own feelings are perhaps best indicated by the fact that he left Indochina to join the Free French and fought with them gallantly in North Africa and the Middle East. His successor still had to face the insatiable Japanese military. In the best tradition of Cordell Hull's formula of "delaying and parlaying," Decoux told the Japanese to take up the problem with the government in Vichy. Before Vichy agreed to make some concessions to the Japanese, its ambassador in Washington once more beseeched the United States to strengthen France's hand. On August 22, 1940, Sumner Welles let Vichy know that the United States was unable to come to the aid of Indochina but that it "appreciated the difficulties with which the French Government was faced and did not consider that it would be justified in reproaching France if certain military facilities were accorded Japan."[8]

On August 30, 1940, Vichy signed an accord with Japan that recognized Japan's "pre-eminent position" in the Far East and granted the Japanese in principle certain transit facilities in Tongking, subject to agreement between the military authorities on the spot. This qualification gave Decoux one more opening for further "delays and parlays." The Franco-Japanese negotiations, conducted by Generals Martin and Nishihara, began on September 5 at Hanoi and dragged on for weeks. Martin still expected American naval support and thus delayed the talks in the hope that an American naval demonstration might induce the Japanese to scale down their demands. That outside support failed to materialize, and the Japanese, growing impatient with the progress of the negotiations, decided to give the French a graphic demonstration of their own power: Without warning, on September 22, Japanese troops stationed in neighboring Kwang-tung and Kwang-si suddenly attacked the French border forts at Lang-Son and Dong-Dang, while Japanese aircraft bombed Haiphong and, on the evening of the twenty-fourth, began to land troops. Outnumbered and outgunned, the border forts fought to the last cartridge, losing 800 men in two days of fighting. Further fighting broke out in Haiphong when Japanese troops attempted to occupy several airfields.

By now, the Japanese had made their point. General Nishihara termed the whole matter a "dreadful mistake"; Vichy wired Decoux to accept the Japanese demands without further delay, and Decoux told Martin to stop the useless heroics and get on with the negotiations. Even so, the determination of the French field commanders had bought time for Nationalist China and also had reduced Japanese demands substantially. In the end, only three airfields in Tongking were occupied; the permanent Japanese occupation force was limited to 6,000 men; and no more than 25,000 Japanese were authorized to transit through Indochina.

To Decoux and the French in Indochina, however, their abandonment by everybody (including their own home government) had been a rude awakening. They knew that henceforth no course was left to them but to "play ball" with the Japanese. They had had their own miniature Pearl Harbor a full fifteen months before the United States, and the only outside attention the event attracted was a tongue-in-cheek editorial in an American newspaper entitled: "Who Wants to Die for Dear Old Dong-Dang?" The answer, apparently, was obvious.

THE WAR WITH THAILAND

In addition to his tribulations at the hands of Japan, Decoux also faced a trial with Japan's little ally, Thailand. Like Italy's *il Duce*, Thailand's Marshal Phibul felt he could settle minor scores in the shadow of the major conflict. Having signed a nonaggression pact with France on June 12, 1940—in true Axis fashion, a sure sign of aggressive designs—Thailand sent its troops, equipped and trained by the Japanese, into Cambodia on January 9, 1941. After some confused fighting on land and some fighting in the air, in which the fifteen French Moranes gave a good account of themselves, the "war" was brought to a climax in a naval battle near the Thai island of Koh-Chang. There, on January 17, 1941, a small force headed by the light cruiser *Lamotte-Picquet* intercepted the Thai battle fleet on its way to bombard Saigon: two battleships with 8.5-inch guns, one British-built and nine Italian-built torpedo boats—the latter noted for high speed and maneuverability—and several service ships. The battle began at 1814 hours. At 1845 hours, two of the torpedo boats were afire and sinking, and five minutes later, the battleship *Dhomburi*, shot to pieces, ran itself aground in order to forestall sinking in deep water. The second battleship, the *Ahidea*, also badly damaged, capsized near Chantabum.[9]

The Japanese concluded that the Thai were in need of some further training and imposed their "good offices." The cease-fire of January 28 was followed by an agreement signed in Tokyo on March 11, 1941, by which the French were forced to yield to Thailand three Cambodian and two Laotian provinces (which the Thai were forced to return after World War II). To this day, a huge victory monu-

ment, greeting the traveler going from Bangkok's airport into the
city, commemorates Thailand's military achievements in the nine-
teen-day war.

From the moment that agreement was signed in Tokyo, it was
obvious that French sovereignty over Indochina had become a farce.
The Japanese now "negotiated" over Decoux's head, directly with the
Vichy regime (that is, they told the Germans what they wanted, and
the Germans saw to it that Vichy fell into line). In a further agreement on July 29, 1941, Japan acquired *de facto* control of all vital
airports and port facilities. On the night of the strike against Pearl
Harbor, Japanese troops surrounded all the French garrisons, and
Decoux was faced with yet another ultimatum: to stay put and
cooperate with the Greater East Asia Co-Prosperity Sphere, or face
the immediate destruction of his garrisons as well as the loss of even
nominal French sovereignty. Decoux yielded, thus saving 40,000 of
his countrymen from the immediate ordeal of Japanese concentration
camps and saving for France at least the appearance of being in command of the local population.

Perhaps one of the most important but least-known facets of
the struggle to keep Indochina from falling into Japanese hands is
the last-minute intervention of the United States. It would not be
an exaggeration, in fact, to say that, in July, 1941, Indochina became
the watershed that separated peace from war in the Pacific. Until
the Japanese occupation of French airports in South Viet-Nam,
Washington had clung to its noncommittal attitude, but on July
26, 1941, when it became obvious that Vichy would no longer resist
Japanese demands, the President ordered the freezing of all Japanese
assets in the United States and an embargo on petroleum exports to
Japan. Japanese views of those events are now available,[10] and they
shed much light on subsequent events. In his memoirs, the then
Foreign Minister of Japan, Togo Shigenori, tells of a meeting on
July 24 between Admiral Kichisaburo Nomura, then Japan's Ambassador to Washington, and President Roosevelt, in which F. D. R.
proposed the complete neutralization of Indochina in exchange for a
guarantee of Japan's "right of acquisition . . . of supplies and raw
materials therefrom on a basis of equality."[11] But that solved neither
of Japan's two desperate problems: her need for oil (obtainable only
in Indonesia) and the necessity to cut off the Haiphong-Yünnan
life line through which American equipment sustained the Chinese
Nationalists. The issuance of the Executive Order on July 26, before
Japan's reply was received, hardened the Japanese Navy's insistence

upon an attack on Southeast Asia before its petrol supplies were totally exhausted.

Indochina's role in Japanese-American relations during the crucial days before Pearl Harbor became even more evident in the last round of negotiations, in November, 1941. On November 26, Secretary of State Hull handed Japan a note that, in effect, was a draft for a mutual declaration of policy. In Paragraph 2 of Section II, the "Hull Note" proposed negotiations between the British, Chinese, Japanese, the Dutch government in exile, and Thailand, in order to guarantee Indochina's neutrality and to provide "for each of the signatories equality of treatment in trade and commerce with French Indochina." The remarkable aspect of that part of the Hull Note was that it simply sidestepped the fact that there still existed a French administration in Indochina itself and the Vichy governn.ent in France, with which the United States had diplomatic relations at the ambassadorial level.

It is not without a touch of irony that Japan brought up this point in its notification of a state of war, delivered to the Department of State on December 7, 1941, a few hours after Japanese bombers had attacked the U.S. naval base at Pearl Harbor. Tokyo asserted that the Hull Note's provisions with regard to French Indochina would be tantamount to establishing a six-power protectorate over the country and, further, that "apart from the fact that such a proposal totally ignores the position of France, . . . [it was] unacceptable to the Japanese Government," which considered it merely as an extension to Indochina of the open-door policy. In those historic hours when what had been a European conflict turned into World War II, President Roosevelt addressed one last message to the Japanese Emperor, offering Japan a nonaggression guarantee in exchange for the evacuation of Indochina. That, in Togo Shigenori's words, was "the only concrete subject touched upon in the President's message."[12]

As will be seen in the following pages, President Roosevelt's preoccupation with Indochina and the attitude of the French there did not abate to his dying day. And, considering the negligible role that Viet-Nam, Laos, and Cambodia played throughout World War II, they probably absorbed more of the President's attention than they deserved. Indochina thus became the object of several high-level decisions of fateful importance to its postwar development—decisions that might perhaps have been better adapted to local realities had they been made at a lower level. Admiral Decoux, however (and in all likelihood, his superiors in Vichy), was hardly aware of what those decisions were, and operated in a frame of reference that was as much divorced from reality as that in which the decisions regarding Indochina were ultimately made.

Later, Decoux was to say with a measure of pride that, thanks to his action, France's was the only Allied flag not to have been struck in the whole Far East.[18] That, in retrospect, is nonsense. While Decoux's acts were wholly defensible (and even commendable) up to July, 1941—just as Pétain's rule was defensible until the Nazis overran the so-called Free Zone of southern France, in November, 1942—the maintenance of French rule beyond that point merely gave rise to personal and political ambiguities that weakened France's position with her allies and certainly did not enhance it with the natives of Cambodia, Laos, and Viet-Nam.

But the key question in appraising the situation must be whether or not the situation in Indochina hampered the Allied war effort. In terms of active military cooperation with Japan, no French units fought against Allied troops, as Vichy troops did in Syria or Morocco. In terms of passive cooperation, Indochinese raw materials went to Japan, just as those from Manchuria, the Philippines, and Malaya did, as long as Japanese shipping was available (i.e., until June, 1944). The assertion that French resistance to the end and direct Japanese administration of the area would have required the immobilization of large bodies of Japanese troops does not hold water. Postwar research has shown that the Japanese held their occupied territories quite thinly, and the continued presence until March, 1945, of 50,000 armed French troops compelled the Japanese to maintain a far larger force "in being" in Indochina than would have been required had those forces been destroyed once and for all in September, 1940, when all the other Allies were sitting on their hands. Those are the objective facts of the situation; they do not make the French attitude look particularly heroic or moral—but in eminently practical terms (and those were the terms under which the situation should have been considered at all times, instead of the high-level emotionalism that did prevail), it served the Allied cause in the Far East a great deal better than has been admitted.

INSIDE VIET-NAM

Ironically, the waning years of French rule in Viet-Nam were accompanied by some of France's most solid achievements, in terms of social and political development of the native population. The frankly fascist character of the Decoux Administration, coupled with the isolation from the outside and the absence of an increasing number of imported goods, provided it with all the impetus for the Rostowian "economic take-off": Under Navy Captain Ducoroy, a "Youth and Sports" movement was created, which gave hundreds of thousands of Young Vietnamese a chance to develop discipline and a sense of leadership (more Viet-Minh company commanders were to graduate from that Pétainist youth corps than from all the Viet-Minh Communist cadre schools); more children went to more schools under more Vietnamese teachers than ever before;[14] the University of Hanoi added a science department to its liberal arts curriculum and a *cité universitaire* (an American-style "campus"); and yearly literary prizes and painting *salons* markedly stimulated Vietnamese artistic development.

In the field of administration, Decoux upgraded the quality of the mandarinal cadres in the protectorates by salary reforms as well as stiffer professional requirements, and in 1942, he abolished salary differentials between European and Vietnamese civil servants, since Viet-Nam had become "homeland" for both. As French replacements were no longer arriving, Vietnamese nationals rose to increasingly senior posts in the administration.

Since Haiphong-produced cement was freely available, public works were undertaken on a grand scale: More kilometers of roads and bridges and more impressive public buildings were constructed during those four war years than during the preceding fifteen years of peace. But Decoux's most "revolutionary" move—a move no parliamentary government in France would have permitted, for the influential French *colons* would have immediately aroused their friends in Paris —was the transformation of the Grand Council into a Federal Council in 1941, and the appointment to it, as of May 31, 1943, of a *majority* of Indochinese members (thirty, as against twenty-three French).

It can, of course, be argued that such changes were entirely meaningless since Decoux ruled with fully dictatorial powers anyway, but this fails to take cognizance of the psychological factor that, for the first time, a French administration was conceding even *theoretically* that the Vietnamese should have a preponderant voice in their own affairs—a point that the whites in the Rhodesias or in Mississippi do not readily concede today to their respective nonwhite fellow-citizens.

In the economic field, the need for local replacements of unavailable imported goods created a variety of auxiliary industries Viet-Nam had never before possessed (and in some cases does not again today). The absent gasoline was replaced by rice-alcohol compounds and petroleum lubricants by palm-oil products; the Pasteur Institutes turned out a wide variety of hitherto-imported drugs; the cotton mills of Nam-Dinh switched to local fibers; a Vietnamese industrialist built Viet-Nam's first blast furnace in 1943 and succeeded in filling the country's most urgent requirements in pig iron and even simple steels. A wet-cell-battery plant began operations in 1942 and, finally, automobile tires were manufactured, with local production rocketing from 365 in 1943 to 13,000 the following year. The return of peace brought a resumption of the import of cheaper Western goods and the consequent demise of all those nascent industries.

Despite the relative merits of the Decoux regime, it was in most respects a carbon copy of its Vichy masters: It was anti-Semitic, anti-Masonic, anti-Gaullist, and pro-Axis. But there was also a dim realization, as the war turned against the Japanese, that it was they who were going to be the real engineers of France's downfall in the Far East, and not the "predatory Anglo-Saxons." A curious footnote to history: Pierre Boulle, later the author of *The Bridge over the River Kwai*, served as a subaltern on Decoux's staff. It seems beyond doubt that the novel's British Colonel Nicholson, who sought to preserve British "superiority" by serving the Japanese, was a faithful rendition of Admiral Decoux's complex character and ultimate failure.

As Japan's control over Viet-Nam increased, so did Decoux's touchy assertion of French "authority." Two native uprisings—one around Lang-Son after its destruction by the Japanese, and another, started on November 22, 1940, in Cochinchina—were ruthlessly crushed by the French. Even according to Communist sources, these were the only armed rebellions of any size[15] against French rule during World War II until Vo Nguyên Giap's guerrillas crossed from China into Viet-Nam in December, 1944. The Japanese protected some Vietnamese nationalist leaders (including Ngo Dinh Diem) from harm at the hands of the Decoux regime, but in fact, they interfered far less internally than is generally supposed

THE AMERICAN VIEW

Of all this, very little was known on the Allied side, but this did not prevent the rapid formulation of an American policy on Indochina and its postwar fate. Even after the refusal of the United States to help Indochina to defend itself, American concern for the area was expressed repeatedly to the Vichy authorities. Thus, on July 19, 1941, when Vichy was readying itself to sign the treaty of July 29 with Japan, the American Ambassador to Vichy, Admiral William D. Leahy, transmitted an oral message from President Roosevelt stating "bluntly that if Japan was the winner, the Japanese would take over French Indo-China; and if the Allies won, *we* would."[16] The statement was delivered to Pétain and his No. Two man, Admiral Darlan, at a time when the United States was still six months away from war with Japan.

Once the United States became involved in the war with Japan, a subtle process of "double-think" took place, which was superbly described by one of America's greatest contemporary diplomats, George F. Kennan, in his remarkable *Russia and the West under Lenin and Stalin:*

> There is, let me assure you, nothing more egocentrical than an embattled democracy. It soon becomes the victim of its own war propaganda. It then tends to attach to its own cause an absolute value which distorts its own vision on everything else. *Its* enemy becomes the embodiment of all evil. *Its* own side, on the other hand, is the center of all virtue.[17]

Far from admitting that American impotence in the Western Pacific, and America's repeated refusals (in 1931, 1934, and 1937) to join Britain and France in an anti-Japanese alliance to protect the area, were in good part responsible for the disaster that engulfed Southeast Asia, American policy-makers—often contradicting their own statements of the year before—now began to heap scorn on the French in general and their rule in Indochina in particular. The Indochinese situation, especially in the eyes of President Roosevelt, became the scapegoat for all of America's woes in the Pacific. As Hull noted in 1943:

> The President . . . himself entertained strong views on independence for French Indochina. [It] stuck in his mind as having been the springboard for the Japanese attack on the Philippines, Malaya, and the Dutch East Indies. He could not but remember the devious conduct [of the French], the right to station [Japanese] troops there, without any consultation with us. . . .[18]

The fact that this view was patently wrong on almost every count— i.e., neither the Philippine invasion nor the East Indies invasion was launched from Indochina (the Malayan invasion was backed by aircraft based in Saigon), and Washington *had* been repeatedly consulted with regard to Japan's encroachments in Indochina—did not prevent F. D. R. from sticking to it throughout the war and formulating American policies accordingly. Evidently, Roosevelt did not feel himself bound by Welles's promise in August, 1940, not to "reproach France if certain military facilities were accorded Japan." F. D. R.'s profound aversion to French actions in Indochina came to the fore repeatedly, in front of both his own entourage and foreign heads of state. Thus, while en route to the Casablanca Conference, F. D. R. told his son Elliott:

> The native Indochinese have been so flagrantly downtrodden that they thought to themselves: Anything must be better than to live under French colonial rule! . . . Don't think for a moment . . . that Americans would be dying tonight, if it had not been for the shortsighted greed of the French, the British and the Dutch.[19]

This is indeed an amazing interpretation of why World War II broke out in the Pacific, an interpretation that well-nigh absolved the Japanese of any wrongdoing. Needless to say, modern historians and the Japanese Government files that became available after the end of World War II do not bear out such an oversimplified view of world affairs. Nevertheless, that view prevailed at the various summit conferences that determined the fate of postwar Southeast Asia—just as similarly simplistic views about Europe determined the fate of Poland, Hungary, and Germany. There is only one difference: In the case of Eastern Europe, the fallacy of those premises has now been openly admitted. In the case of Indochina, the evidence has remained buried in the scattered files of various government departments or in the memoirs of the participants—and the American public has remained largely unaware and uninterested in this important area of the world in which their country has been actively fighting for more than twenty years.

Once it had been decided that France had "misruled" Indochina, the next logical step was to prevent France from reasserting her sovereignty over the area and to substitute another administration. The idea of substitution was first officially broached at the inter-Allied level during a White House conference on March 27, 1943, in which the President suggested to British Foreign Secretary Anthony Eden that a trusteeship be established for Indochina. The President also instructed Hull to present the trusteeship idea to the Russians at the

October, 1943, Moscow Conference, and he himself spoke of it to Turkish and Egyptian representatives and to Chiang Kai-shek during his brief stay in Cairo in November, 1943. According to General Joseph W. Stilwell, the U.S. commander in the China Theater, F. D. R. had in mind a trusteeship under three commissioners—an American, a Chinese, and a Briton.[20]

As the recently published secret documents on the Cairo and Tehran conferences show, F. D. R. did his best to convert Stalin (who was present at Tehran) to his own views on Indochina in order to outvote the very reluctant Churchill. According to the record (kept on the American side by Charles Bohlen, now U.S. Ambassador to France), F. D. R. stated that the first necessity "for the French, not only the government but the people as well, was to become honest citizens"; to this, Stalin replied that he was in full agreement and "went on to say that he did not propose to have the Allies shed blood to restore Indochina, for example, to old French colonial rule . . . and that the French must pay for their criminal collaboration with Germany."

President Roosevelt "said he was one hundred per cent in agreement with Marshal Stalin and remarked that after one hundred years of French rule the inhabitants were worse off than they had been before. . . ." The State Department record shows in a footnote that Churchill objected to these assertions, but that F. D. R. cut him off with a curt: "Now look, Winston, you are outvoted three to one." (The "three" included Chiang Kai-shek, present at Cairo but absent from the Tehran Conference.)

As the sorry record of the Tehran Conference unfolds, one is struck by the unrealistic world views held by both Stalin and F. D. R. The latter, among other plans for postwar France, proposed to "eliminate from the future government of France anybody over forty years old" whereupon Stalin remarked that Charles de Gaulle was "of little importance as a real factor in political or other matters." And all this was said while Free French soldiers were fighting and dying side by side with their Allies from the North Atlantic to Cassino, and while inside France 400,000 French men and women (including an impressive number of people "over forty") were marched off to Nazi death camps, torture chambers, and execution posts. Only Winston Churchill preserved his full sanity during this interchange. Having heard the postwar plans of his fellow-summiteers, he stated simply that "he could not conceive of a civilized world without a flourishing and lively France. . . ."[21]

Churchill came away from this conference gravely perturbed, and on January 3, 1944, the British Ambassador to Washington, Lord Halifax, asked Cordell Hull for further clarification of America's Indochina policy. President Roosevelt took up the matter personally with Halifax around January 20, 1944, and informed Hull on January 24 of their conversation:

> I saw Halifax last week and told him quite frankly that it was perfectly true that I had, for over a year, expressed the opinion that Indochina should not go back to France but that it should be administered by an international trusteeship.

And F. D. R. then repeated what by now had become his *leitmotiv* on the subject: that the French had been in control for a hundred years and the natives were worse off than ever before, that the French had milked Indochina dry, and that the people "are entitled to something better than that."

The trusteeship idea went through several other evolutions. For a time, when Chiang Kai-shek's fortunes were at a low ebb and there was some risk of China's dropping out of the war altogether, F. D. R. had offered China *all* of Indochina (including the "Hinduized" states of Cambodia and Laos!) as an outright grant.[22] It is to Chiang Kai-shek's honor (or an indication of his political realism) that he turned down the gift. Mindful of China's previous experience with the Vietnamese—of which the President and his advisers seemed unaware—Chiang explained his refusal by pointing out that the Indochinese were "not Chinese. They would not assimilate into the Chinese people."[23]

The trusteeship question was again brought up at Yalta in February, 1945. By that time, Roosevelt was willing to include one or two "Indochinese" and even a Frenchman in the Indochinese Trusteeship Council but insisted they be counterbalanced by a Filipino, a Chinese, and—a Russian ("because they are on the [Pacific] coast"). But this time, apparently, Churchill vetoed the whole scheme. F. D. R. decided to leave things as they were, since he wanted Churchill's support on more important matters. But on his return to the United States aboard the cruiser *Quincy*, F. D. R. vented to the journalists present his disappointment at having been foiled: "Stalin liked the idea. China liked the idea. The British don't like it. It might bust up their empire...."

It is a further indication of how little Roosevelt understood either the French or de Gaulle that during a personal meeting with de

Gaulle, the President offered him Filipino experts and advisers to help France establish "a more progressive policy in Indochina." De Gaulle, the record says, received the offer in "pensive silence."[24] (It is likely that the word "icy" would have been more appropriate.) Almost to his dying day, F. D. R. found time to turn his thoughts to the Indochina problem. In the words of his son Elliott, F. D. R. held that Indochina, "liberated in main part by American arms and American troops, should never simply be handed back to the French, to be milked by their imperialists."

The disaster that was to overtake the French in Indochina was thus as foreordained as a Greek tragedy—and when it came, the French were, as at Lang-Son and Dong-Dang in 1940, left to face it alone.

THE FREE FRENCH IN INDOCHINA

While Decoux ruled Indochina for Pétain and the Japanese, other Frenchmen began in Indochina, as elsewhere in Axis-held territory, to work for liberation. Three French generals, Mordant, Alessandri, and Sabattier, set about to prepare plans for an uprising in conjunction with an Allied landing or Allied pushes out of neighboring Yünnan or Burma—or at least the continuance of a maquis-type protracted defense, with Allied airborne help, in case the Japanese attempted to seize the remaining French garrisons.[25] After France had been liberated, in the summer of 1944, it was obvious that Decoux no longer could rule Indochina in the name of the defunct Pétain regime, but he was kept on as a front for Mordant, who had officially been placed on the retired list, but was in fact de Gaulle's *délégué-général* in Indochina. Several intelligence networks were operated by Frenchmen working with the American OSS, while Britain's elite commando and intelligence unit, "Force 136," parachuted equipment and men (both British and French) into the country.

Militarily, from the Allied side, Indochina was not a major objective. With Japan's transport fleet being hacked to pieces by American air and submarine action and Britain's 14th Army driving the Japanese to the wall in Burma, it was obvious that the days of Japanese rule in Southeast Asia were numbered. One major danger remained, however, even in late 1944, and that was that Chiang's China, as corrupt and inefficient as ever, might collapse—in spite of massive American aid—and give Japan a lease on iire. Thus, "Operation

Carbonaro" was planned, to open a South Chinese port close to North Viet-Nam, which would provide a short, large-scale supply line to Chungking. Cooperation with the French in Indochina would have been desirable, and in any case, intelligence as to Japanese movements and capabilities certainly was; but the whole matter became embroiled in a major jurisdictional fight between Britain's South-East Asia Command (SEAC) and Lord Mountbatten, its chief, in Ceylon, and General Wedemeyer, the American commander in chief in the China Theater (nominally operating under Chiang's authority). Although "Carbonaro" itself was called off for other reasons, Indochina became the center of a hot dispute when the China Theater command accused SEAC of "empire-building" in trying to extend its operations to Indochina. The matter was finally settled by an informal agreement along typically Chinese lines: Mountbatten's SEAC recognized Chiang's (and Wedemeyer's) jurisdiction over Indochina but was allowed to continue operations up to the 16th parallel.

This, however, still left the bothersome question of what to do with the French resistance in Indochina. Here, Washington followed the logical implications of its decision to evict the French from the country. On October 13, 1944, the President addressed a memorandum to Secretary of State Hull, stating that it was his "judgment on this date that we should do nothing in regard to resistance groups or in any other way in relation to Indochina." And on November 3, 1944, this instruction was implemented with another to American field commanders in Asia, enjoining them from giving "American approval . . . to any French military mission being accredited to the South-East Asia Command." Translated into actual military terms, those instructions meant an automatic death sentence for any French attempt at organized resistance in case of Japanese attack, and that is exactly the way it turned out.

On March 9, 1945, at 2130, the Japanese struck without warning. One by one, the French garrisons had been surrounded by Japanese troops, and French senior commanders, almost without exception, were captured in their own homes or in those of Japanese officers with whom they were dining. The French underground movement bungled its operations miserably; having operated more and more in the open, its members were for the most part well-known to the Kempetai, the Japanese secret police, and were as easily arrested as the army. Only in Tongking did Generals Sabattier and Alessandri get wind of what was afoot through their own intelligence and place their troops on alert status. They broke through to the Thai mountain areas, established themselves around the airfields of Dien Bien Phu and Son-La, and began calling for Allied supplies and air support.

In South Viet-Nam, some smaller groups withdrew into the roadless swamps of Camau and began guerrilla warfare. In Laos, French resistance probably was the most effective. Some French troops, with the help of Lao (including Prince Boun Oum, Premier of Laos in 1960–62), harassed Japanese communications along the Mekong until V-J Day, receiving airdrops and reinforcements from British Force 136 teams throughout.

But in much of the rest of Indochina, particularly in the vital Tongking area, Japanese action was brutal and effective. In Ha-Giang, they used the French women and children of the garrison as shields when they stormed the French fort. At Fort Brière de l'Isle, the whole garrison was machine-gunned to death, singing the *Marseillaise*. And ill-fated Lang-Son was again the center of a tragedy. The fort had secretly been rebuilt after its capture by the Japanese in 1940, and its defenders gave a good account of themselves. When the Japanese brought the captured military governor, General Lemonnier, and the civilian resident, Auphelle, under the walls of the fort and told them to ask the garrison to surrender, both men refused and both were beheaded by their enraged captors.

In the meantime, the nearest American field commander, General Claire L. Chennault, the famous father of the "Flying Tigers" and commander of the 14th U.S. Air Force in neighboring Yünnan, had moved into action. Following his own generous instincts, he had immediately sent liaison officers with small aircraft to make contact with Sabattier's forces. They had made a rapid survey of the most urgent needs of the French and arranged for airdrops and coordination of air support—and then had again vanished into Yünnan. No major airdrops materialized and many urgent radio messages simply went unanswered. Doomed Lang-Son also was calling for air support. The last message from the garrison that Sabattier's headquarters received said: "Still holding three-fourths of citadel— No water— Request air support and supply drops— Where are the Americans?" The garrison was massacred by the Japanese; only one man survived, after having been left for dead among the heaps of bodies thrown pell-mell into an open ditch.

What had happened to the 14th Air Force and General Chennault? After the war, Chennault provided the answer:

. . . orders arrived from theater headquarters stating that no arms and ammunition would be provided to French troops under any circumstances. I was allowed to proceed with "normal" action against the Japanese in Indochina provided it did not involve supplying French troops. . . . General Wedemeyer's orders not to aid the French came directly from the War Department. Apparently it was American policy then that French Indochina would not be returned to the French. The American government was interested in seeing the French forcibly ejected from Indochina so the problem of postwar separation from their colony would be easier. . . . While American transports in China avoided Indochina, the British flew aerial supply missions for the French all the way from Calcutta, dropping tommy guns, grenades and mortars.

I carried out my orders to the letter but I did not relish the idea of leaving Frenchmen to be slaughtered in the jungle while I was forced officially to ignore their plight.[26]

A few days later, Wedemeyer actually complained to the British SEAC commander that the latter's transport planes were overstepping operational boundaries by parachuting equipment to the dying French! Yet those British transport aircraft, operating at maximum range without fighter escort 1,500 miles inside enemy territory, stood by their French allies while U.S. aircraft, a bare 150 air miles from Sabattier's forces, were "forced officially to ignore their plight."

After the war, Wedemeyer, too, explained the reasons for his rigid refusal to aid, or to countenance aid to, the French:

[March, 1945, visit to F.D.R.] I had not seen the President for several months and was shocked at his physical appearance. His color was ashen, his face drawn, and his jaw drooping. I had difficulty conveying information to him because he seemed in a daze. Several times I repeated the same idea because his mind did not seem to retain or register. He evinced considerable interest in French Indo-China and stated that he was going to do everything possible to give the people in that area their independence. . . . He admonished me not to give any supplies to the French forces operating in the area.

[At a lunch with Secretary of War Stimson.] Mr. Stimson asked me about my conference with the President and I recounted the instructions I had received concerning the French. He expressed surprise and suggested that I mention this to General Marshall, which I did at the earliest opportunity.[27]

In view of the foregoing, it seems clear that F.D.R., in his personal instructions to Wedemeyer, apparently went beyond what had been the agreed policy in his desire to eliminate the French from Indochina at all costs. This explains Stimson's surprise and his urging Wedemeyer to take up the matter with General Marshall. What the latter's instructions were on the subject has never been made clear, but it seems probable that he somewhat softened the President's admonition. Wedemeyer's testimony adds considerable weight to my view that, to the last, President Roosevelt accorded Indochina—and, in particular, French activities there—an importance far out of proportion to its actual position within the scheme of things; his preoccupation amounted almost to a fixation.

Meanwhile, the battle was continuing in Washington, where the Free French Military Mission pleaded daily with the American military to release Chennault's supply-loaded aircraft to support of Sabattier's forces. The telegrams the French Government sent to its diplomats in the United States at that time tell again and again of the bewilderment and shock that assailed the French officials concerned with the problems. They could not bring themselves to believe that such American inaction was deliberate (since they were unaware of F. D. R.'s decisions on the subject) and continued to believe that the absence of American support was due simply to an incredible ignorance of the desperate plight of the French troops in Indochina. In the meantime, the last surviving French troops in Viet-Nam could watch, thousands of feet above their heads, the condensation trails of hundreds of American bombers flying imperturbably on "normal" operations against the Japanese in Borneo, Bangkok, and Saigon—but not against Lang-Son or Japanese columns near Son-La.

It was only at the end of March—after the last organized French units in Viet-Nam had been destroyed and Sabattier's troops were reduced to haggard bands of disease-ridden stragglers—that Admiral Leahy succeeded in obtaining the President's permission to release Chennault's aircraft for support missions in Indochina.[28] But by that time, the Japanese had settled the whole problem in their own way.

Of the approximately 13,000 French troops who were not immediately overwhelmed by the Japanese attack, 200 officers and 4,000 soldiers were, according to de Gaulle's *Mémoires,* killed or massacred in the course of the fighting retreat to China.[29] A total of 320 officers, both French and Vietnamese, and 2,150 European and 3,300 Vietnamese soldiers[30] survived the 800-mile trek to Yünnan. In his inimitable style, de Gaulle took the long view of the whole affair:

As painful as that development was locally, I must say that from the point of view of national interest, I willingly envisaged that hostilities would commence in Indochina . . . in view of our position in the Far East, I thought it essential that the conflict should not end without us having become, there also, [involved as] belligerents . . . French blood shed on Indochinese soil would give us an important voice [in later settlements]. Since I did not harbor the least doubt as to Japan's ultimate aggression, I desired that our troops should fight, no matter how desperate their situation.[31]

Inside Viet-Nam, the Japanese administration had taken things in hand: All male Frenchmen were herded into concentration camps, some of which, such as Hoa-Binh, gained a reputation as sinister as Dachau's. Other less lucky Frenchmen, and Vietnamese known for their pro-French sentiments, were locked up in the infamous "monkey cages" of the Kempetai.

On March 10, 1945, the Japanese Ambassador to Saigon came to Hué and announced to Vietnamese Emperor Bao-Dai that his country was now "independent." On the following day, after deliberation with his Cabinet ministers, Bao-Dai repudiated the protectorate treaty of 1885 and expressed the "confidence of the Government of Viet-Nam in Japan's loyalty and its own determination to collaborate with [Japan] within the framework of the Greater East Asia Co-Prosperity Sphere."[32]

France's rule over Viet-Nam had lasted a few months less than 60 years. Considering Viet-Nam's 2,200 years of recorded history, it had been a very brief interlude.

5

"Doc-Lap!"

IN FACT, that new-found, Japanese-granted independence was a
farce, with Japanese "advisers" taking the place of the French
governors, but in form, Vietnamese were again in positions of authority: Vietnamese mandarins took over the provincial administration,
a Vietnamese Council of Ministers and a Prime Minister, the well-
known professor and writer Tran Trong Kim, were appointed on
April 17; on May 2, Bao-Dai appointed a *Kham-sai* (Viceroy) for
Tongking; in July, the French towns of Hanoi, Haiphong, and
Tourane were ceded back to Viet-Nam; and on August 8, Cochinchina returned to the fatherland. For the first time since 1858,
Viet-Nam was reunified.

But all was not rosy in the reborn country. The war cry of "*Doc-
lap!*" ("Independence!") could not hide the fact that the 1945 rice
crop in North Viet-Nam was disastrously low. In peacetime, this
was a minor problem since from its traditional surpluses, South Viet-
Nam could be counted upon to ship north via boat and train the
quarter-million tons of rice necessary to tide the North Vietnamese

over until the next crop. But in 1945, strategic bombing had hacked the Transindochinese Railroad to pieces, and all the French and Japanese ships in Vietnamese ports had been sunk by the Allies. Rather than shouldering their new burden, Donald Lancaster has observed, many of the young nation's leaders preferred instead to "indulge unchecked their political pretensions and childish vanity in an orgy of demonstrations, processions, and public meetings, which contributed towards the paralysis of the administrative machine."[1] In the resulting famine, close to *1 million* people were to die of hunger and disease while the Vietnamese national administration floundered in chaos and despair and the Japanese, preoccupied with their own forthcoming doom, did little but plunder valuables and seek to escape from prospective Allied war-crimes trials.

Ho Chi Minh's Communist guerrillas seized control of Hanoi, on August 19, 1945, and on August 25 sent a mission to Hué to demand Bao-Dai's abdication and the surrender of the imperial seal. By then, Viet-Nam's first national government had already evaporated. Tran Trong Kim had resigned on August 7, and many of free Viet-Nam's Cabinet ministers had not even awaited his resignation before fleeing what was obviously a sinking ship. A similar situation was aptly described by Dean Acheson in 1949: "It was not overthrown, because there simply was nothing to overthrow."

Although Acheson was speaking of the Chiang Kai-shek government's loss of mainland China, that was precisely the case in Viet-Nam in 1945. Control of Viet-Nam could be taken by anyone bold enough to claim it, and Old Bolshevik Ho Chi Minh and his Viet-Minh were the men who staked out their claim with sufficient organizational ability, ruthlessness, and armament to make it prevail over all latecoming rivals.

The Birth of the Viet-Minh

In the wake of the outbreak of World War II, the ICP command had left Viet-Nam in November, 1939, for the safety of the neighboring Chinese provinces. Though the ICP had been badly mauled by the large-scale arrests that followed its outlawing in 1939 and the abortive Cochinchina rebellion of 1940, its essential organs and, above all, its central leaders had escaped destruction.

As the war continued in Asia, the ICP went along with the new "United Front" line, though in its own good time. Ironically, it was the South Chinese generals Lu-Han, Lung-Yün, and Chiang Fa-k'uei who sheltered the ICP leaders and who, for their own shortsighted purposes, pushed the wartime alliance between Vietnamese Communists and nationalists to its ultimate conclusion. All three generals had designs upon prosperous, mineral-rich Tongking, and they realized that the non-Communist Vietnamese parties, small, divided, and led by men in their seventies who had not set foot in Viet-Nam for several decades, would be incapable of "delivering" the area. But, they also realized, Ho Chi Minh and his well-disciplined Communists could.

Where the Chinese generals made their fatal mistake was in believing that they, in conjunction with their Vietnamese puppets, could control the ICP and maneuver it into docility. Ho Chi Minh and his followers, cut off from the outside world, at first did not know what line to follow; only after almost eighteen months of being dragged in stocks from Chinese prisons in Kweilin to other prisons in Liuchow did Ho Chi Minh agree to a collaboration with the warlords and their Vietnamese followers. The decision (though ideologically "correct" when he finally consented, in 1944) must have been prompted largely by the knowledge that his chances of surviving in jail much longer were becoming increasingly slim.

But even before he was jailed, Ho had taken certain measures to broaden the base of the Party's struggle. In May, 1941, during the eighth session of the Central Committee of the ICP, it had been resolved to create "an enlarged National Front to include not only workers and peasants . . . but also patriotic landowners"; and with the true opportunism that the circumstances demanded, "the Central Committee decided to adopt momentarily a somewhat milder slogan in the agrarian field: 'Confiscation of the land owned by traitors for distribution to the poor farmers.' "[2] That very much milder slogan was to remain the basis of Vietnamese Communist agrarian policy until ultimate victory was assured in 1953 and the cooperation of the landowning bourgeoisie was no longer deemed necessary.

Having decided on a "National Front" policy, the ICP made approaches to various non-Communist groupings which, on May 19, 1941, agreed to form the Viet-Nam Doc-Lap Dong Minh Hoi (Revolutionary League for the Independence of Viet-Nam), better known by its short name of Viet-Minh.

It was the Viet-Minh that in 1943 agreed to cooperate with the Chinese warlords. Too well-known in Chungking and elsewhere as a Communist leader, the man who hitherto had been Nguyên Ai-Quoc now adopted the name of Ho Chi Minh (He Who Enlightens), under which he was to become famous; and on March 28, 1944, a "Provisional Republican Government of Viet-Nam" was proclaimed in Liuchow under the aegis of the Chinese. The Viet-Minh represented a reassuring minority in that government—surely no danger to the non-Communist majority and its Chinese backers. No one objected when the Viet-Minh elements volunteered to return to the dangers of Japanese-occupied Indochina while the pro-Kuomintang Vietnamese awaited V-J Day in China.

Thus, it was the Viet-Minh that created the first anti-Japanese guerrilla forces in Viet-Nam, that rescued American fliers shot down in Indochina, that provided intelligence to the Allies, that spread its propaganda among the civilian population, and that received all the credit for anti-Japanese activities during the war.

But the ICP's master stroke came with V-J Day. On August 13, 1945, it held a "national conference" at the village of Tan Trao, in the hill province of Tuyên-Quang, in the course of which the ICP decided to make a strike for power before the Allies had a chance to land, and present them with the *fait accompli* of Communist control. In a small book published a year later, Truong Chinh, then secretary general of the ICP, described what went on:

> During the historic Congress, the Indochinese Communist Party advocated an extremely clear policy: to lead the masses in insurrection in order to disarm the Japanese *before the arrival of the Allied forces in Indo-China;* to wrest power from the Japanese and their puppet stooges and finally, *as the people's power,* to welcome the Allied forces coming to disarm the Japanese troops stationed in Indo-China [italics added].[3]

The passage is self-explanatory. It fits perfectly into the Communist pattern then being applied from Lublin to Athens to Singapore—and thanks to Allied blundering, it worked with signal success. At Tehran and Potsdam, it had been decided that Indochina would be occupied by Chinese Nationalist forces down to the 16th parallel, while Commonwealth forces would occupy the southern half of the peninsula. Both occupations worked in favor of what the Viet-Minh and ICP now set out to do. British occupation (mainly 1,400 men of the 20th Indian Division of Major General D. D. Gracey) was prompt but was spread far too thin to have any effect on the ICP apparatus establishing its control throughout the country. As for the Chinese occupation forces under Lu-Han, who later defected to the Chinese Communists, they were, on the contrary, enormous. They were composed of the 60th, 62nd, and 93rd armies, reinforced by the 23rd,

39th, and 93rd divisions, comprising more than 152,000 men; and it took them almost six weeks to cover the 100 miles from the border to Hanoi as, like a swarm of locusts, they slowly pilfered their way through the countryside. In the process, they not only gave the Viet-Minh sufficient time to gain control over much of Viet-Nam, but they also revived the century-old Vietnamese hatreds for all things Chinese and thus thoroughly discredited the Vietnamese nationalists who had hoped to be able to use Chinese support in their forthcoming struggle against Ho Chi Minh.

The "Provisional Government" created in 1944 in China was quietly forgotten as the Viet-Minh, on August 16, 1945, proclaimed, on the basis of the Tan Trao "national conference" held three days earlier, the creation of a National Liberation Committee of Viet-Nam. In striking fashion, the "Lublin process" was about to repeat itself in Southeast Asia—but without even the presence of an overwhelmingly strong Communist force. In the face of the disintegrating Bao-Dai Administration, the imprisoned French, the defeated Japanese, and the careless Chinese and Americans, the job of taking over the country as the "People's power" was an easy one for the Viet-Minh: Communist agitators inside Hanoi staged a brief uprising on August 17–18, 1945, and on the following day Ho's forces entered the capital city without firing a shot.

On August 25—the day when Bao-Dai, deserted by all his advisers, handed over the Grand Seal to the new regime—the Viet-Minh's "Committee of Liberation of the Nam-Bô" (Cochinchina) under Tran Van Giau, took control of Saigon and much of the South Vietnamese countryside. The doors of the prison on the island of Poulo Condore were thrown open, and hundreds of the old ICP leaders now swelled the ranks of the victorious movement. A "Provisional Government of the Democratic Republic of Viet-Nam" was formed on August 29 in Hanoi by Ho, in which the ICP or the Viet-Minh held all key posts. And on September 2, 1945, the independence of the "Democratic Republic of Viet-Nam" (D.R.V.N.) was solemnly proclaimed from the balcony of the Hanoi opera house to the cheers of a crowd 500,000 strong, the majority of which had not even known its new leaders a week earlier. Asia's second-oldest Communist state (Outer Mongolia was the first) was born.

So far, the ICP had completely outmaneuvered its adversaries. It was to suffer a few setbacks in the south, where General Gracey dealt with the Nam-Bô Committee of Tran Van Giau on a "no-nonsense" basis. ("They came to see me and said 'welcome' and all that sort of thing. It was an unpleasant situation and I promptly kicked them out," he told the Royal Central Asian Society in 1953.) He released the French troops who were still held in Japanese PW camps south of the 16th parallel and thus started a flurry of fighting, of which the take-over of Viet-Nam had until then been largely free.

But in Hanoi, the Chinese Nationalists, through their greed and shortsightedness, saw to it that the Communist take-over would be as painless and thorough as possible. When the Viet-Minh held a "gold week," during which residents of North Viet-Nam were compelled to give their gold for the "purchase" of weapons from the Chinese, it was thoroughly successful and provided the nascent "Viet-Nam People's Army" (VPA) with 3,000 rifles, 50 automatic rifles, 600 submachine guns, and 100 mortars of American manufacture— plus the substantial French and Japanese stocks (31,000 rifles, 700 automatic weapons, 36 artillery pieces, and 18 tanks) that the Chinese were supposed to have secured but did not.[4]

In the political field, the Viet-Minh fared equally well. Fully aware of its temporary dependence upon non-Communist good will, it took the unusual step of "dissolving" the ICP, on November 11, 1945, thus becoming, no doubt, the only "people's democracy" to operate without an official Communist Party. Then, again following the Polish experience, it promised the Kuomintang generals that it would give the Vietnamese non-Communist parties 70 seats in the first legislature, elected in January, 1946—provided that the non-Communist parties would not compete in the electoral contest.[5] Knowing that in a fair fight they would not be able to gain even 70 seats (out of a total of about 400), the nationalists agreed with alacrity, and thereby sealed their doom—for the Vietnamese electorate, which until then had known only the Viet-Minh, was deprived of a chance to see their competitors, much less vote for them.[6]

The government that resulted from the January, 1946, elections was, predictably, *not* openly Communist-dominated, in order to forestall adverse reactions from the Kuomintang generals and to gain, if possible, a measure of recognition in the West. With cold realism, the ICP leadership, acknowledging that the "Socialist motherland" was far away and unlikely to get embroiled in Viet-Nam, made a determined drive to win American recognition and a seat in the United Nations. Both efforts failed.

Behind the façade of respectability, a relentless struggle for the consolidation of Viet-Minh power went on. Provincial mandarins (among them, Ngo Dinh Khoi, brother of Ngo Dinh Diem) were murdered, a massive drive against the well-entrenched Trotskyites in South Viet-Nam began,[7] and a clumsy attempt was made at dismantling the religious sects by killing some of their leaders (such as Huynh Phu So, the young "prophet" of the Hoa-Hao).

Thus, through the sheer energy and organizational ability of its Communist leadership, Viet-Nam had become a "people's democracy," in fact as well as in name—even while its territory was still occupied by Chinese Nationalist, British, and French military forces and American observers, and while the nearest Soviet Russian and Chinese Communist troops were still thousands of miles away. This was surely a unique feat among present-day Communist regimes, and yet another indication of how thoroughly bamboozled the West was about events in Southeast Asia.

THE WEST IN DISARRAY

The sudden collapse of Japan after atom bombs had leveled Hiroshima and Nagasaki caught everyone unprepared to deal with the political consequences. There were far from enough Allied troops available to supervise and disarm enemy forces spread over a water and land area of close to 4 million square miles—let alone to take in hand the civil administration of those vast and largely devastated territories. Also, the death of Roosevelt on April 12, 1945, had created a hiatus in American postwar planning that the new American leadership, capable though it was, could not immediately fill. In France, likewise, postwar planning for Indochina had reckoned on a possible reoccupation in late 1946, or perhaps even in 1947, and there were many more urgent problems at hand than the constitutional structure of an enemy-occupied land halfway arour 1 the globe.

A declaration on Indochina had been issued by the Ministry of Colonies on March 24, 1945, that more or less accepted the Federal Council ideas of Decoux and also promised the Indochinese Federation "all democratic freedoms," economic autonomy, and the right to industrialize. That program, which might have been considered a step forward in 1925 or 1935, no longer had any correspondence with the situation inside Indochina; it was merely one of those theoretical exercises at which French politicians excel and which, in the absence of any real grasp of the facts, they like to substitute for a practical approach. In a resolution of April 8, 1945, a delegation of the 25,000 Vietnamese soldiers and workers stationed in France informed the French Government that it considered the March 24 declaration insufficient.[8] There is no evidence that the warning was heeded, much less acted upon.

In the Far East itself, the Free French build-up had been equally slow. With a rear base in Calcutta under the command of General Blaizot, the French had a Corps Léger d'Intervention (CLI) of about 800 men; about 200 additional officers and men operated with the British Force 136 in Burma, Malaya, and Laos; and the French battleship *Richelieu* and its escort vessels operated with the U.S. Navy in the Pacific. French intelligence maintained "Mission 5" (M-5), a French intelligence group, at Kunming, in Yünnan; and General Sabattier's surviving forces, totaling 2,140 Europeans and 3,223 Vietnamese, also were stationed in Yünnan—but disarmed and interned by their Chinese "allies." The presence of a Vietnamese majority among the French troops is noteworthy, for they, of all people, could just as easily have deserted and melted away among their own population instead of following the French in their ordeal. But as an OSS operator, with some surprise, reported at the time, "contrary to what was expected, the native troops remained faithful to the French."[9] In fact, because of the paucity of supplies, Sabattier and his officers had begged hundreds of their Vietnamese troops to disperse, but most of them stubbornly hung on. There was also a handful of French officers who had been attached to Chinese Nationalist forces and were now slowly being transferred to the French Army. In all, this did not amount to an awe-inspiring army, the more so as it depended entirely on the good will of its British and American allies for its supplies.

The Japanese forces inside Indochina comprised the 38th Area Army (2d and 55th Infantry Divisions and 34th Independent Mixed Brigade), plus the headquarters and communications troops of Marshal Count Terauchi's Southern Army Group, stationed at Saigon—a total of about 50,000 men.

American forces in Viet-Nam (there were no Americans in neighboring Cambodia and Laos, which were left to Force 136) comprised five OSS teams operating with the Viet-Minh; some AGAS (Air-Ground-Air Service) teams in charge of rescuing downed American fliers; and JANIS (Joint Army-Navy Intelligence Service), which collected long-range intelligence for the armed forces.

Added to this were the Chinese hordes of Generals Lu-Han, Lung-Yün, and Chiang Fa-k'uei and Ho Chi Minh's guerrillas, plus assorted sect zealots and outright bandits who roamed the countryside. Predictably, utter chaos now befell the hapless country, and countless intrigues sprang up among the various forces so as to neutralize each other's influence. In the end, no one but the Viet-Minh came out a winner.

French official reaction to V-J Day came in a telegram addressed by Calcutta to M-5 in Kunming: "Caught unprepared by Japanese capitulation, [Government] counts upon us to take care of most urgent matters." Implicitly, Calcutta "passed the buck" to M-5 and its energetic leader, Jean Sainteny, a Resistance hero from France whom de Gaulle had recently appointed to head the Kunming mission. In Sainteny's view, his mission was obvious: to reassert French sovereignty at the earliest possible moment and liberate all French citizens imprisoned by the Japanese and the Viet-Minh. The American theater commander, General Wedemeyer, saw his own mission as defined by the Roosevelt instruction of November 3, 1944, and as in the case of the 14th Air Force's aborted supply missions to Sabattier, he adhered strictly to it.[10] Thus, various obstacles were laid in Sainteny's path when he attempted to have his group embarked on U.S. aircraft leaving with OSS personnel for Viet-Nam. When the French finally received their own aircraft, Wedemeyer bluntly forbade "the departure from Kunming of any airplane, whatever its nationality, for Hanoi."

This difference in instructions, which had never been ironed out or even discussed at the highest level, since F. D. R. had never communicated to the French his ulterior plans for Indochina—and it is unlikely that Churchill had done so, either—was bound to bring about a crisis in Franco-American relations that, to a certain extent, has *never* been thrashed out and dogs relations between French and American missions in Cambodia, Laos, and Viet-Nam to this very day. Finally, after French threats to infiltrate their men into Viet-Nam by other means (and after the British had on their own parachuted French teams into Viet-Nam), Wedemeyer relented and allowed Sainteny to leave for Hanoi in the company of the OSS team of Major Archimedes L. Patti. Relations between Sainteny and Patti were never very cordial, especially after Patti informed Sainteny that the Potsdam agreements had made no mention of French sovereignty over Viet-Nam and that the French, therefore, no longer had any "rights to intervene in affairs which were no longer of any concern" to them.[11]

Thoroughly disillusioned, Sainteny radioed his superiors in Calcutta that he was "face to face with a deliberate Allied maneuver to evict the French from Indochina" and that "at the present time the Allied attitude is more harmful than that of the Viet-Minh." In fact, the arrival of the Chinese units made the situation even worse. Accompanied by the U.S. Combat Section, South China Command, under Major General Philip E. Gallagher, the Chinese and their American advisers acted as if the French did not exist. Although their attitude toward Sainteny's M-5 could be explained on the basis of orders from Washington, their personal attitude of callousness toward the Frenchmen who, two months after V-J Day, were still being detained in prison camps by mixed guard units of Japanese and Viet-Minh exacerbated matters needlessly.

The Frenchman Paul Mus, a severe critic of his own country's policies in the Far East, tells in his remarkable *Viet-Nam—Sociologie d'une guerre* of the visit of an American officer to one of the grimmer prison camps. When a young French officer cried out to the American to liberate them from their imprisonment, he retorted: "Those fellows must have had a reason for putting you in there. So why don't you just stay where you are?" The name of that young French officer was Jean Ramadier; two years later, his father was to become Premier of France. Humiliation was piled upon humiliation: On September 10, 1945, the Chinese bodily evicted Sainteny and his group from the French governor's building they occupied, and when the official surrender of the Japanese forces in Tongking took place, on September 27, no French flag was flown (although Soviet and Viet-Minh flags were prodigally displayed), and gallant General Alessandri, who in the meantime had returned from Yünnan, was offered seat No. 115 at the ceremony, behind the Viet-Minh leaders (then unrecognized) and a bevy of Chinese junior officers. No Frenchman accepted an invitation to attend the ceremony.

On October 17, 1945, a "Viet-Nam–American Friendship Association" (VAFA) was created in Hanoi. In the course of its inaugural meeting, attended by high Viet-Minh officials, General Gallagher even consented to sing over the Viet-Minh–controlled broadcasting station.

The consequences of all this for Franco-American relations are not difficult to assess, the more so as many of the French officials who were involved in Indochina then are still in high posts in the French Government today, or were in such posts in recent years: de Gaulle himself and his Minister of Defense, Messmer, already have been mentioned; General Massu, who now commands French troops in eastern France, commanded the first regimental combat team that landed in Viet-Nam in October, 1945; Sainteny, after having served again in North Viet-Nam in 1954–57, is now Minister of Veterans' Affairs; Hoppenot, French Delegate to the U.N. in the 1950's, was the man who pleaded in vain for U.S. air support in Washington in March, 1945; and hundreds of present-day French majors and colonels were lieutenants interned in Japanese concentration camps, and to this day, they term American actions of that period a rank "betrayal" of a loyal ally.

Yet, until the publication of these lines, available evidence, although on the nonsecret list, was hidden from the American public probably because it simply did not fit in with the "honest-broker" stereotype in which American diplomacy delights to see itself.[12] Thus, it is not surprising that an officially sponsored American study on Viet-Nam published late in 1961 describes the same events in the following terms:

> The French, although determined to reoccupy Viet-Nam, were for the moment stymied by their lack of troops and transportation. *The Allies, however, came to their aid.* In mid-September, British troops occupied the southern half of Indochina, and Chinese Nationalists the northern portion [italics added].[13]

The reason that such transportation was not available was that orders had *made* it unavailable; and the "aid" provided the French by the Chinese was of the kind the former would rather have dispensed with. The same American writer, George K. Tanham, admits, however, for the first time in public what the French had known since 1945:

> Early in the [Indochina] war, a considerable amount of equipment was shipped from Thailand to the Viet-Minh. . . . Nationalist China sent aid by land and sea . . . and some matériel came from the Philippines.[14]

What he refrains from stating explicitly is that all this equipment from Thailand, China, and the Philippines was *American* equipment, brought in on American aircraft, by American pilots. French reconnaissance pilots brought back aerial photographs of those aircraft parked on Communist-held airstrips at Vinh and Thanh-Hoa, in northern Central Viet-Nam, unmarked except for their serial numbers—and some of those pilots, now discharged and flying in Indochina for civilian airlines, maintain that a small number of the American "privately chartered" aircraft flying at present in behalf of the Lao Government bear the same serial numbers as those identified earlier on the Viet-Minh airfields.

Only very recently did the then French commander in chief for southern Indochina openly admit how the French finally dealt with the problem of private American contraband for Ho Chi Minh: The French Deuxième Bureau set up in the Philippines a "well-working network of intelligence and liaison agents" who would report the departure of ships or airplanes for the Viet-Minh strongholds before the craft even left Philippine territorial waters. And, as General Pierre Boyer de Latour added with quaint understatement, "we took some liberties with the Maritime Code";[15] i.e., contraband craft were sunk without further ado even on the high seas and unidentified planes shot down on the spot if they were found in forbidden areas. Such drastic actions on the French side eventually cut down on that contraband after 1947.

All this needs to be said and brought to public attention, because it strikes at the root cause of why there is not (and cannot be) any Western "united front" in Southeast Asia today, and why de Gaulle proves difficult today. France has no reason whatever to trust American actions on the basis of past performance; and Britain, having been an interested bystander of those American policies since their beginning, can be expected to cooperate only to the extent that American actions do not interfere to an alarming degree in areas Britain considers essential to her own position in the Far East. Although American contacts with Ho Chi Minh cooled off considerably as the Viet-Minh's Communist character became more evident, this shift came far too late to allay French suspicions, and events from Dien Bien Phu onward only further poisoned what already was a delicate situation at best and was never frankly discussed on either side.

PREPARATIONS FOR WAR

With the arrival of French reinforcements, through British help, early in October, 1945, and the release of French troops in Japanese hands south of the 16th parallel, the situation changed somewhat, although neither the British nor the French could prevent the murder of 450 French and Eurasian women and children at the Cité Heyraud housing development near Saigon on September 25 by mobs incited by the South Vietnamese Communist leader Tran Van Giau. It was Giau who, in the face of the strengthening French position, ordered a scorched-earth policy for South Viet-Nam and engaged in terror tactics that the Hanoi regime found, for the time being, at least, premature and embarrassing. Giau was quickly seconded by Nguyên

Binh on the military side. Binh was even more ruthless and soon alienated the important politico-religious sects to which almost two-thirds of the Cochinchinese population belonged. (When his terror tactics failed, he was recalled to North Viet-Nam in 1952, and was killed by a French patrol while traveling in disguise through Cambodia. There is some evidence that the French might have been deliberately tipped off about his trip.)

At the same time, the Ho Chi Minh government had slowly come to its senses. Faced with another famine, totally penniless thanks to its own demagogic abolition of taxes and a confiscatory exchange rate imposed by the Chinese warlords between the valuable piaster and the worthless Chinese dollar, the government was to be dealt yet another blow: The State Department, which, in the words of British diplomat Donald Lancaster, "had now asserted some measure of control over the policy-framing proclivities of OSS,"[16] informed the Viet-Minh that it could not hope for American political support. This placed the Vietnamese once more in the frightening position of being left alone to face *both* their colonial masters—the Chinese and the French. And even the Vietnamese Communists were "Vietnamese" enough to realize where the greater danger lay. Sweet reasonableness toward the Sainteny mission broke like a ray of sun through the dark clouds of Franco-Vietnamese relations.

But while in Hanoi a better mood prevailed, in Saigon, France committed its major postwar blunder in Southeast Asia: It appointed Admiral Thierry d'Argenlieu as the first High Commissioner (the title of governor general had been dropped) to Indochina. D'Argenlieu had spent most of his life between the two World Wars—he had served in both of them—as a Carmelite monk. Fiercely loyal to de Gaulle, he shared the latter's love for French grandeur but without his breadth of view. D'Argenlieu's was a world strictly of "good" and "evil," and "evil" was to be eradicated, not compromised with. As one wag on his staff used to say (paraphrasing a Franz Werfel play), d'Argenlieu had "the most brilliant mind of the twelfth century." The trouble was that he was about to be faced with one of the most delicate problems of the twentieth—decolonization—and he had neither the patience nor the tact for negotiating with "natives."

France, the Viet-Minh, and Nationalist China began a three-cornered round of negotiations aimed first at eliminating at least the Chinese from the tangle. The Chinese finally agreed to withdraw, but not until they had taken their full revenge for a century of humiliation: On February 28, 1946, at Chungking, France signed away all her special rights in China and, in return, granted China rights on the Yünnan railway and the port of Haiphong that were almost tantamount to what were known in the nineteenth century as "capitulations." But in true Chinese fashion, the warlords in Tongking were not entirely satisfied, and as the first French naval elements entered the port of Haiphong at dawn on March 6, the local Chinese commander opened fire on them on the grounds that he had not been informed in a "sufficiently official" manner of the terms of the agreement. When a French direct hit exploded 600 tons of Chinese ammunition stored on the rocks, the Chinese commander felt that he had been sufficiently informed and ceased fire.

On the same day, at Hanoi, Ho Chi Minh and Sainteny signed an accord that just *might* have become historic. In its brief three articles, France recognized "the Republic of Viet-Nam as a Free State having its own government, parliament, army, and treasury, and belonging to the Indochinese Federation and the French Union."[17] Before India, Burma, or the Philippines, Viet-Nam had come to terms with its colonial master. The military clauses of the treaty were equally generous on both sides: A total of 15,000 French troops were to be stationed north of the 16th parallel, to be relieved progressively by Vietnamese troops within five years, and France was to train and equip the Viet-Minh forces. General staff accords were signed on April 3, 1946, establishing the size and location of French and Vietnamese garrisons. They were signed by Vo Nguyên Giap for Viet-Nam; General Raoul Salan, later of Algerian Secret Army fame, signed for France. On March 16, French troops, impressive with their freshly arrived American armor and transport, were greeted with delirious enthusiasm by the French civilian population. Among the Vietnamese, the mood was pensive.

In the meantime, d'Argenlieu had not remained inactive in South Viet-Nam. There, the conservative elements of the reconstituted Colonial Council, frightened at developments in neighboring Annam and Tongking, decided to preserve its area from "outside encroachments." D'Argenlieu was only too happy to help the Colonial Council in its endeavor. The propitious moment came when Ho Chi Minh and several of the Viet-Minh and nationalist coalition leaders were called to Paris to negotiate final agreements with France. They left by French warship on May 31, 1946. On May 30, d'Argenlieu, *without authorization from Paris,* recognized the Republic of Cochinchina as a "free state" with its own army, finances, etc., in exactly the same terms as the Republic of Viet-Nam had been recognized on March 6!

On June 2, Cochinchina proclaimed itself a "republic" and, on the following day, signed a convention with Cédile, the French Commissioner for Cochinchina.

To the Viet-Minh, this appeared a rank betrayal of their confidence. What made matters worse was that, upon their arrival in France, they found the country both without a government and without a constitution. The first projected constitution of the Fourth French Republic had been rejected by the voters on May 5; general elections had been held on June 2, and a new French government could not be formed until two weeks later. The talks finally began at Fontainebleau, near Paris, on July 6. But both sides continued to make serious mistakes: Hô Chi Minh, overconfident of the strength of his Communist friends in Paris, took an inflexible position. In Indochina, d'Argenlieu arranged a "federal conference" in Dalat for August 1 and invited the governments of Cambodia, Cochinchina, and Laos—but not the Viet-Minh. From that point, the conference was headed for inevitable failure, for inside Viet-Nam, the Chinese-backed nationalists seized upon the Cochinchina issue as a pretext to undermine the authority of the Ho Chi Minh government, asserting that it was "subservient to French colonialism." This strategy among Vietnamese non-Communist nationalists of forcing the other side to outbid it in verbal intransigence continues to this very day, with Saigon propaganda media speaking of "Communo-colonialists" and accusing Hanoi of having "divided" the country at Geneva in 1954.

A last-minute *modus vivendi* signed by Ho Chi Minh and French Overseas Minister Marius Moutet on September 14, 1946, at least confirmed the successes achieved by the March 6 accords and held out the promise of further negotiations in January, 1947, but in Viet-Nam itself events marched inexorably on toward open conflict. On August 3, a French convoy on an authorized mission was ambushed and nearly destroyed at Bac-Ninh, in North Viet-Nam; several French soldiers were murdered;[18] and, vice versa, in Cochinchina, French troops continued with mop-up operations in spite of the existing accords that provided for a cease-fire throughout the country. On both sides, also, institutional developments further worsened the situation: In October, 1946, the French people finally agreed upon a new constitution (which was to rule France until 1958) which, contrary to all hopes, did not provide for fully independent member states within the French Union; and on November 9, 1946, Ho Chi Minh's D.R.V.N. approved its own constitution, which did not even mention the Republic's membership in the Indochinese Federation or the French Union and also claimed Cochinchina as an integral part of its territory. On the following day, Nguyên Van Tinh, the President of the French-sponsored Republic of Cochinchina, committed suicide in Saigon, exposing to the whole world the fragility of the political house of cards built in Viet-Nam by Admiral d'Argenlieu.

Militarily, the situation also reached a critical point for both sides. Thanks to the equipment the Viet-Minh had received from its foreign backers, its armed forces (numbering about 50,000 in November, 1946), trained by Japanese deserters, felt that they could still defeat the French in a short war, i.e., before the latter could complete their build-up. The French military, on the other hand, confident of their armor and mechanized equipment, which had just helped defeat the Wehrmacht in Europe, also felt that a military solution could still provide a cure-all for the hopelessly tangled political situation. As this writer has stated elsewhere:

> The French forces sent to Indochina [in 1946] were too strong for France to resist the temptation of using them; yet not strong enough to keep the Viet-Minh from trying to solve the whole political problem by throwing the French into the sea.
> The outbreak of the Indochina war can be traced back to that single, tragic erroneous estimate....[19]

The final spark that turned the whole situation into a general conflagration was the much talked-about "Haiphong incident." On November 20, 1946, a French Navy patrol boat had stopped a Chinese junk loaded with contraband and brought it into Haiphong harbor. As both ships anchored, a local post of Viet-Minh militia opened fire on the French ship. When the shots were heard in the nervous town, the Viet-Minh closed the barricades already established in the streets, thus cutting off French detachments from each other, and killed and wounded several unarmed French soldiers who were at the Vietnamese central market purchasing vegetables for their units. Twenty-three French soldiers were killed that day without any French counteraction. Through the intervention of mixed Franco-Vietnamese liaison teams, the whole incident seemed settled on the following day. But on November 22, a French burial detail collecting the bodies of the Lang-Son garrison, which had been murdered by the Japanese in March, 1945, was attacked by Viet-Minh units and lost six dead. The French commander in chief, General Valluy, afraid that his forces would be simply whittled away in a series of similar incidents, instructed Colonel Debès, commander of French forces in Haiphong, to give the Viet-Minh a "hard lesson." On November 23, Debès delivered a two-hour ultimatum demanding that the Viet-Minh forces evacuate the Chinese quarter of town. When the Viet-Minh refused, French ground troops moved into the Chinese quarter. Thus far, however, fighting had been desultory, but at the sound of the shooting, thousands of Vietnamese—as it turned out, unarmed civilians for the most part—streamed out of town in direction of the open country and the important French air base of Cat-Bi. At the sight of the mob, and unaware that it was unarmed, the French heavy cruiser *Suffren*, anchored offshore, opened fire with its turret guns. In the ensuing panic, 6,000 Vietnamese civilians were killed by gunfire or trampled to death.[20]

That appalling carnage could only strengthen the hand of extremists on both sides. Fighting once more ceased at Haiphong on November 28, and Sainteny returned hurriedly from leave in France to see whether, in view of his good personal relations with Ho, he could save the day, but on both sides, the military were now in the "driver's seat." Valluy's deputy in the north, General Morlière, demanded full control of the Hanoi-Haiphong road, and when the Viet-Minh withdrew its regulars from Hanoi and replaced them by an increasing number of trigger-happy Tu-Vê (militia), he demanded that security duties in the city be taken over by joint military-police detachments. To that, the opposing commander, Vo Nguyên Giap, answered by erecting barricades in Hanoi and by ordering the population to pierce house walls so as to permit direct communications from block to block without having to cross streets.

On the morning of December 19, 1946, Ho Chi Minh wrote a friendly letter to Sainteny, expressing the hope that an amicable resolution of the tension could be reached, and Giap suggested to his counterpart, Morlière, that a cancellation of the order restricting French troops to their quarters would also have a relaxing effect on the atmosphere. Morlière agreed and leave passes were issued to French soldiers as of noon. But at 1800, a Eurasian intelligence agent brought the news that a general uprising was planned for that very evening. With desperate hurry, Morlière sent out messengers to retrieve his soldiers on leave, while Sainteny himself set out in an armored car, in the hope of persuading Ho Chi Minh to call off the attack. At precisely 2000, the electric-power plant of Hanoi blew up, plunging the city into total darkness, and screaming waves of Tu-Vê threw themselves upon French installations and the houses of the defenseless French civilian population. Sainteny himself was severely wounded when his car was blown up by an electrically triggered mine detonated from the house of the mayor of Hanoi.

Within a few hours, all the French garrisons throughout Viet-Nam were likewise under attack, and what is generally known as the "Indochina War" had begun. The question remains whether it was the Vietnamese or the French who actually started it. To this, it can be replied that now even the Communist historians in Hanoi admit that it was their side that started the fighting on December 19, although in response to "bloody French provocations."[21] Evidence captured later, which this writer has seen, clearly shows that the coup had been meticulously planned and well executed. Had this not been the case, many of Ho Chi Minh's government would have been taken prisoner by the French.

On the other hand, it cannot be said that the French were planning a military strike against the D.R.V.N. just then—or they would have seen to it that thousands of their own civilians in small towns such as Hué, Tourane, Nam-Dinh, and Vinh would not have been exposed to capture or massacre by the enemy. They would also have seen to it that their small outlying garrisons were prepared either to fight their way out or to retreat into the jungle. Instead, both the civilians and some of the small garrisons fought desperate battles for nearly three months, cut off from the outside world save for a few hastily improvised airlifts. Hue was not relieved until February, 1947, while Nam-Dinh, defended by a paratroop battalion grimly fighting for its life in the shambles of the textile factories, was not liberated until March. Vinh's garrison was overwhelmed. In Hanoi itself, only 43 French civilians were killed but more than 500 French civilians, including women and children, were abducted there and in other towns. Some of them were released quickly; others spent eight years in Communist prison camps.

Viet-Nam, as a unified independent state, had again disappeared—if it can be said to have had time to bloom in the few chaotic months of the Tran Trong Kim regime under Japanese protection, and of the Ho Chi Minh regime under Chinese aegis. As in the sixteenth century, so again Viet-Nam was divided into two distinct states, but from 1946 until 1954, this was to be a new, strange, urban-rural division rather than a north-south division, with the Viet-Minh holding much of the countryside, including the hill-tribe areas; while the

French and, later, the non-Communist Vietnamese administration were to hold the lowlands and, especially, the cities. In 1954, the "normal" north-south division of Viet-Nam was to appear again, only a few miles to the south of the ancient Wall of Dong-Hoi.

And, once more, the two Viet-Nams began to build their own separate institutions.

TWO

REVOLUTION IN THE NORTH

6

The Rise of Ho Chi Minh

IT is indicative of the depth of the gap in Western knowledge of Vietnamese affairs that such a major personality of the Communist world as Ho Chi Minh has not thus far been subjected to any solid biographical research.[1] Unlike many other Communist leaders today, Ho still seems to delight in cultivating an air of mystery about himself even on such prosaic details as his exact birth date. A perusal of a dozen Communist sources on his background will produce at least ten different birth names and as many as six or seven birth dates, and even less is known about his immediate family and those other little details about a man's life that are meaningless per se but so important in fleshing out the personage. In the case of his South Vietnamese rival, Ngo Dinh Diem's large family of brothers and other relatives has become a major factor of the political equation. But Ho Chi Minh is presented by his propagandists more or less as if his life had begun in 1920, when he officially became a Communist, and as if he had never had any personal life since. And his non-Communist biographers until now simply lacked the minimal amount of firsthand information to be able to draw some valid conclusions.

Both northern and southern apologists for their respective leaders note, however, one essential trait their chiefs share: They are both *personally lonely*. Both are bachelors and both are thus presented as "fathers" of their country, but since the "father" image in Viet-Nam is too much wrapped up in the old mandarinal tradition—which Ngo accepts but Ho rejects—the latter is presented to his public as "uncle" instead, i.e., as a man who still commands respect but not with the forbidding sternness of a father. This difference in "image" is clearly reflected in their propaganda photographs: Ngo appears either in full traditional mandarin's dress or in the snow-white Western business suit of the French colonial tradition; Ho is shown either in the "Mao Tse-tung suit" of his party or in the dark peasant *cu-nao* and open-toed rubber sandals of the Vietnamese farmer or guerrilla fighter. There can be no doubt that these conflicting propaganda images of the two men are an important element in the struggle that divides Viet-Nam in the 1960's.

Opinions about Ho vary sharply not only among Communists and non-Communists, but also among observers within the two camps or from neutral nations. Thus, Nehru found Ho "extraordinarily likable and friendly"; while the Indian ex-Communist M. N. Roy, who attended with Ho the University of the Toilers of the East in Moscow in 1924, remembers him as an "unimpressive personality and not even a very good student." An American OSS officer who had worked closely with Ho for several months prior to V-J Day describes him as an "awfully sweet guy" whose outstanding quality was his "gentleness." Paul Mus, the French Orientalist who in 1946 and 1947 carried out some very delicate negotiations with Ho, speaks of him as an "intransigent and incorruptible revolutionary, *à la* Saint-Just"; while French Socialists who worked with Ho in Paris in the 1920's remember him as "not fanatical at all, and very witty." French Navy Commander Gerbaud, as captain of the French aviso *Dumont d'Urville*, had Ho as guest on his ship for twenty-one days on his return from France in September, 1946. Thus, Gerbaud had an opportunity, almost unique among Westerners, to observe Ho at close quarters. At the conclusion of the trip, Gerbaud reported to his superiors that Ho was an "intelligent and charming man who is also a passionate idealist entirely devoted to the cause he has espoused." Gerbaud also noted Ho's "naïve faith in the politico-social slogans of our times and, generally, in everything that is printed."[2]

That faith in "everything that is printed" may be the typical reaction of the self-taught man Ho largely is, or it may be a deliberate "know-nothing" pose assumed by him—Ho is known to be a talented comedian—as part of the man-of-the-people image he seeks to project even in the presence of foreigners. The same pose may underlie the stress Communist sources place on the apocryphal story that, within the compound of the former French governor general's palace that is now the residence of the President of the D.R.V.N., Ho has a small peasant hut in which he "really" lives and works. For the record; I can say that I was unable to see such a peasant hut when I walked around in the Presidential gardens in July, 1962.

It is obvious that such a mosaic of divergent impressions cannot replace an adequate biography. Yet, as will be seen, the verifiable facts are often pitifully few and contradictory, with gaps that extend over almost whole decades. Even Ho's exact year of birth is uncertain. Communist sources cite 1890, 1891, and 1892, with the consensus in favor of the earliest date. The exact day and month, being now a day of rejoicing in the D.R.V.N., is well established: May 19. He was born (there is full accord on that subject) in the village of Kim-Lien, district of Nam-Dan, in the province of Nghé-An, in Central Viet-Nam, not far from the Tonkinese border. His exact birth name, however, is part of the man's myth. Many Western Communist sources give his name at birth as Nguyên Ai-Quôc, which translates roughly as "Nguyên the Patriot." French Communist sources, wishing to stress the folksiness of Ho, equate the very common Vietnamese name "Nguyên" with the French "Jean" and thus translate Nguyên Ai-Quôc as "Jean-le-Patriote." The late German ex-Communist Ruth Fischer, who knew him in Moscow during the early Comintern days, stated that Ho's father's name was Nguyên Sinh Huy and Ho's own name was Nguyên That Thanh (Nguyên Who Will Be Victorious).[3] The Australian Communist writer Wilfred Burchett, who lived in Hanoi for several years after 1954 and got to know Ho well, affirms that Ho's name was Nguyên Van Thanh, which, considering the construction of Vietnamese male names, sounds extremely likely. In addition, Ho has used at least a dozen aliases during his long career as a Communist agent.

Ho was probably the youngest of a family of three children. His sister, Thanh,* was born in 1884 and his brother, Khiêm, in 1888.

---

* Although both Ho's name and his sister's appear identical in the Roman transliteration provided by the D.R.V.N. Government, diacritical marks in the Vietnamese probably indicate a differentiation in pronunciation between the masculine and feminine forms.

Both seem to have avoided politics and to have stayed in their native village throughout the period of resistance against the French, tilling the family rice fields. Khiêm died in 1950, and his sister (sources refer to her as "Miss," indicating that she may never have married) died in 1953. Ho's father was of the "village aristocracy." That is, he was barely richer than most of the rice peasants around him—the photos I saw of the family home in Kim-Lien bear this out—but, by dint of grueling work and learning acquired by rote, he passed the mandarinal examinations entitling him to a job in the imperial administration at the precise moment when the latter was buckling under the pressure of French military might. According to Admiral Decoux,[4] hardly a friend of Ho's, his father had been one of the imperial officials best versed in the difficult art of Chinese ideography, and had remained so thorough an anti-French nationalist that he was among the small group of mandarins who refused to learn the language of the conquerors.

That refusal may have been a contributory reason for his eventual dismissal from government service, although Communist sources cite his participation in anti-French secret societies as the cause, while French sources cite allegations of petty corruption. Either set of reasons would have been plausible in the Viet-Nam of the 1890's. A recent East German source[5] went so far as to say that Ho's father had been imprisoned at the notorious Poulo Condore island prison off the South Vietnamese coast. No other source, French or Communist, confirms this.[6] There is no doubt, however, that Ho's father was an ardent nationalist and that the young boy soon learned from his elders about the humiliation Viet-Nam had to endure at the hands of the foreign occupiers. At the age of nine, little Nguyên That Thanh had already begun carrying messages for his father's network of anti-French conspirators. But Ho's father had to earn a living for his family and entered the practice of "Oriental medicine," i.e., healing based on Chinese or Vietnamese traditional precepts.

Apparently, he was quite successful and moved to South Viet-Nam to practice his new profession. Tran Huy Lieu, an old revolutionary associate of Ho's and one who knew his family personally, told me in 1962 that Ho's father could be seen in the early 1930's— that is, at an advanced age—walking spryly through the Cochinchinese countryside, prescribing Oriental potions (and perhaps also some of the old nationalist ideas or even some of the new ideas of his youngest son). He died in the mid-1930's.

"I remember quite well when he died," said Tran Huy Lieu.

was in a French prison when I heard about it." According to Pham Van Dong, Ho's sister and brother also were imprisoned for a time because of Ho's activities. Ho's mother, allegedly of humble peasant origins (although this may be part of the "man-of-the-people" myth), probably died at the family home. Ho never speaks of her.

There is only hearsay evidence for the reports about Ho's marrying and having a family. It is possible that, while posing as a Chinese merchant after his escape from Hong Kong in 1931, Ho temporarily acquired a "family" to make the disguise more plausible. Ho and his associates deny the existence of such family ties. Several times during the Indochina War, Frenchmen in enemy prisons saw a young German Foreign Legionnaire who allegedly had been adopted by Ho and therefore bore the name Ho Chi Long. It is not unusual for an eminent man in the Far East to "adopt" a young adult (as will be seen, this was the case with Ngo Dinh Diem), and Ho may well have adopted this German. Ho Chi Long, however, has not been seen since the cease-fire and may never have been more than a clever device to break down prisoner morale.

At least it is certain that Ho's revolutionary career started early. He first acquired a basic Sino-Vietnamese education in the village school and from his father, who had attained the *pho-bang* (a minor doctoral degree). Many early sources state that Ho then attended the French *lycée* at the provincial capital of Vinh. However, there is corroborative evidence that Ho later attended what was then Viet-Nam's best high school, the Lycée Quôc-Hoc at Hué.[7] Probably much in Ho's life was shaped by the fact that he attended Quôc-Hoc: That school had been created at the initiative of Ngo Dinh Kha, a high official of the Hué imperial court and father of South Viet-Nam's Ngo Dinh Diem, for the express purpose of perpetuating in Viet-Nam a type of education that, though providing the young Vietnamese elite with Western knowledge, would be untainted by French views. The name of the school, which means "national" but with the connotation of "nationalist," gives in itself a key to its importance; and a list of the students who graduated from it or were dismissed from it over the past forty years reads like a "Who's Who in Vietnamese Revolution" on both sides of the 17th parallel; to name a few: Ho Chi Minh, Vo Nguyên Giap, Pham Van Dong—and Ngo Dinh Diem.

According to Pham Van Dong, Ho left Quôc-Hoc in 1910, without receiving a diploma, because of his anti-French activities. That would account for Ho's activities between the ages of twelve and twenty, left a complete blank in earlier sources, which spoke of his dismissal from the junior *lycée* of Vinh at the age of twelve or fourteen. He now had to earn a living; he drifted south and became an adjunct teacher at the Lycée Dac-Thanh, a private school in the small South Annam fishing town of Phan-Thiet that was run by anti-French Vietnamese along the Quôc-Hoc school's lines of modernism without colonialism. Almost twenty years later, another Vietnamese was to come to Phan-Thiet and there establish his reputation, not as a scholar but as an administrator for the province. His name: Ngo Dinh Diem. But Ho probably felt stifled in the sleepy fishing town; in spite of all the propaganda to the contrary, this intellectual-looking man was never a true man of letters in the old Vietnamese tradition, but rather a "doer," a political operator.

Small wonder, then, that the sum total of his writings amounts to little more than collections of speeches, a slim volume of verse he wrote while in a Chinese prison, and one play, *Le dragon de bambou* (*The Bamboo Dragon*), which was a flop in Paris in 1923 and has not been heard from since. His only work of some importance, *Le procès de la colonisation française*, published in Paris in 1926, was a slapdash, naïve pamphlet indicting French colonialism. One can safely predict that none of his writings will ever influence Marxism-Leninism in a lasting way. Ho has made his mark on history in a different manner.

It was at Phan-Thiet that Ho decided to go to France and see the world. Here he acted fully in the Vietnamese tradition, since his older brother had stayed home to take care of their mother and sister, while Ho, with his training, stood a better chance of earning a living elsewhere. Leaving Phan-Thiet in the summer of 1911, he entered a trade school in Saigon for a three-month course in October of that year. There is no record of what he studied at this school, but as he was hired soon after as a kitchen boy and later worked as a pastry cook's apprentice, he may have taken a "quickie" course in that field, then considered very desirable since it opened the doors to lucrative employment with the Europeans. To this day, Ho has a reputation as a gourmet and occasional cook.

The date of Ho's departure for Europe finds even the Communist sources divided. Some of them, perplexed by that hitherto unbridged gap between the ages of twelve and twenty, say that he left as early as 1907; others mention 1910 or 1911. The recent East German source cited above gives the summer of 1912 as the time of his departure. This date, in view of the foregoing, is probably accurate. And thus

Ho was signed on aboard the *Latouche-Tréville* as a kitchen boy. Not wishing to dishonor his good family name by so humble an employment, he took his first pseudonym: Ba. As Ba, he visited Marseilles, with its big-port squalor and its prostitutes, and on other vessels of the giant Messageries Maritimes line, he visited the west coast of Africa and North America.

His contacts with the white colonizers on their home grounds shattered any of his illusions as to their "superiority," and his association with sailors from Brittany, Cornwall, and the Frisian Islands— as illiterate and superstitious as the most backward Vietnamese rice farmer—did the rest. Ho still likes to tell the story of the arrival of his ship at an African port where, he claims, natives were compelled to jump into the shark-infested waters to secure the moorings of the vessel and were killed by the sharks under the indifferent eyes of passengers and crew. But his contacts with Europe also brought him the revelation of his own personal worth and dignity; when he went ashore in Europe in a Western suit, whites, for the first time in his life, addressed him as "monsieur," instead of using the deprecating "*tu*," reserved in France for children but used in Indochina by Frenchmen when addressing natives, no matter how educated.

With the beginning of World War I, Ho decided to live in London, working by day as a snow cleaner in a London school and by night as a cook's helper at the Carlton Hotel, then the domain of the great Escoffier, acknowledged as the master chef of his generation. The agile and quiet Vietnamese, who also spoke good French, found favor with Escoffier; he was promoted to a choice spot—in the pastry division. But Ho also had made friends with other Asians residing in London and joined the Lao-Dong Hai-Ngoa, the Overseas Workers' Association, which was largely under Chinese leadership. The organization, like other similar groups then in Britain, supported Ireland's struggle for independence, and thus Ho received his first lesson in anticolonial agitation. But as the war continued, the need for pastry cooks diminished and Ho went to sea again. According to North Vietnamese sources, Ho then visited the United States and for a time lived in Harlem. "There," according to Pham Van Dong, "he found the barbarities and ugliness of American capitalism, the Ku Klux Klan mobs, the lynchings of Negroes. He also witnessed the American workers' strikes against war and for higher wages."[8] He was sufficiently impressed by what he saw (or said he saw) to write, during his stay in Moscow in 1924, a pamphlet entitled *La*

Race Noire (*The Black Race*), which was bitterly critical of American and European racial practices.

He returned to France late in 1917 or early in 1918. His knowledge of Chinese ideograms had disciplined his hand to the use of delicate brushes, and he turned to photo retouching to earn a living. The Socialist newspaper *La vie ouvrière* carried in many of its issues of 1918 a tiny classified advertisement with the following text:

> You who wish a living remembrance of your parents, have your photos retouched at Nguyên Ai-Quôc's. Handsome portraits and handsome frames for 45 francs. 9, Impasse Compoint, Paris XVIIth District.

The collapse of Germany and the Versailles Conference brought Ho for the first time into the vortex of world politics. Excited by the hope of seeing President Wilson's Fourteen Points become the charter of independence for all colonial peoples, Ho rented a black suit and a bowler hat and began to haunt the gilded corridors of the royal castle along with other self-styled representatives of such nationalities or pseudo nations as the Croats, Transylvanians, Caucasians, and Turkomans. And the twenty-eight-year-old young man with the intense eyes shared the fate of those other representatives of stillborn nations: None of the great leaders, Clemenceau, Lloyd George, or Wilson, was willing to receive him. In fact, it is doubtful whether his request for an audience ever went further than the hands of some minor clerk, and the name of Viet-Nam or Annam is nowhere to be found among the records of the Versailles Peace Conference. Yet, Ho's very modest eight-point program did not demand even independence; it sought only equality between rulers and ruled, basic freedoms, more schools, replacement of rule by decree with rule by law, and appointment of a Vietnamese delegation to advise the French Government on local affairs. The failure of the Versailles Conference to settle the colonial question brought consequences that in the long run were perhaps as fateful as those produced by its unsatisfactory settlement of the German question.

It was after Versailles that Ho met face to face a man with whom he was later to tangle, at a distance, for more than twenty years: Louis Arnoux, the chief of the Vietnamese section of the French police's political intelligence branch, and who later headed all French security services in Indochina. Almost forty years after Versailles, Arnoux still warmly remembered his political discussions with the young Vietnamese firebrand at a little café near the Opéra. With the instinct of the policeman, Arnoux felt that Ho would "amount to something" and attempted to persuade Albert Sarraut, bv then risen from governor general of Indochina to Minister of Colonies, to meet with Ho. Sarraut refused (he finally met Ho in Paris in 1946) but allowed his Chief of Cabinet to meet Ho in his stead. Nothing conclusive came from the meeting (except that the French police succeeded in getting their first photograph of Ho as he left the Ministry), but Arnoux, who had to fight Ho and his associates for the remainder of his active career, prided himself that Ho never returned to his native soil while Arnoux headed the police there.[9] It is that series of strange encounters between the revolutionary and the policeman which later gave rise to the accusation by some Vietnamese nationalists that Ho had actually worked as an *agent-provocateur* for the French Sûreté. Although the possibility exists— Stalin is said at one time to have rendered some small services to the Czar's Okhrana—there is no evidence whatsoever at present to prove that assertion.

In post-Versailles France, the left wing was engaged in a great debate between the traditionalists in the Socialist Party, who sought to achieve their aims within the existing system of government, and the extremists in their ranks, who saw salvation in the kind of revolution that was then taking place in Russia. Ho, a party member, joined eagerly in the debate. Far too unsophisticated for the major philosophical issues, he considered the touchstone of the debate to be the attitude of the two wings on the colonial question. The traditional Socialists, while recognizing the validity of colonial claims to eventual independence, could not bring themselves to break with French national policies on the question. The Communist wing of the party had no such compunctions and advocated the immediate independence of all colonial areas in line with Lenin's theories on the subject (which, of course, were promptly changed when it came to applying them to Russia's own possessions). The equivocations of the French Socialist Party on the colonial question continued to dog it to the very end of the Algerian war in 1962: Both there and in Indochina, Socialist ministers became the advocates of military solutions for the sake of maintaining Cabinet solidarity.

The French Socialist Party national congress at which the issue was to be decided opened on Christmas Day, 1920, in the quiet provincial city of Tours. Ho Chi Minh was an accredited delegate from the colonial areas. A contemporary photograph shows us a sallow young Asian among the well-fed, mustachioed faces of the

French delegates. Ho's contribution to the debate clearly summed up his own simple criteria:

> I don't understand a thing about strategy, tactics, and all the other big words you use, but I understand very well one single thing: The Third International concerns itself a great deal with the colonial question. Its delegates promise to help the oppressed colonial peoples to regain their liberty and independence. The adherents of the Second International have not said a word about the fate of the colonial areas.

And he voted with the Communist wing against the Socialists, thus becoming on December 30, 1920, a *founding member* of the French Communist Party, ten years before he was to found, in turn, a Communist Party in his homeland. From then on, his careers as an international agent of Communism (he was to work successively for the French Communists; Russia; China; the Comintern in Europe, China, and Southeast Asia; and, finally, his own country's Communist apparatus) and as a Vietnamese "nationalist" were to be so completely intertwined as to fool all but the most penetrating observers. In much of Asia and among many American specialists on Southeast Asia, Ho was considered a nationalist first and a Communist second—almost until the battle of Dien Bien Phu. In actual fact, he has always been a dedicated Communist with Vietnamese reactions, just as Gomulka is a Polish Communist or Khrushchev a Russian Communist. This means that Ho is probably equipped with an instinctive Vietnamese fear of Chinese domination (no matter what its color) just as most observers agree that to Khrushchev *any* Germany might be slightly suspect. Thus, all his life, Ho has used the nationalist catch phrases, the references to traditional heroes and values—just as Khrushchev invokes God in almost every one of his public utterances—but without ever losing sight of his Party's goals. The fact that this was not understood by naïve outsiders was certainly not his fault; his career as a Communist has been on record since 1920.

From this point, Ho's future path was clear. Taken in hand by the senior French Communist leaders themselves—Marcel Cachin and Paul Vaillant-Couturier—Ho became the Party's expert on colonial affairs. As such, he created the Intercolonial Union in 1921, and became the editor of its more-or-less weekly journal, *Le Paria*, whose other collaborators were Algerian, Senegalese, and West Indian Communists. *Le Paria*'s masthead reflected the gradual evolution of its editor. When it first appeared, its subtitle was: "Tribune of the

Colonial People." By January, 1924, it read: "Tribune of the Colonial Proletariat." Ho also traveled extensively throughout France in 1919–21, addressing large crowds of Vietnamese war workers and soldiers awaiting repatriation to the Far East. Thus, tens of thousands of Vietnamese who had come into contact with the white man's world and seen its failings from close up, were for the first time given an interpretation of what they were seeing and how it could affect their future. That interpretation was both nationalist and Communist, and its seeds matured slowly over the next two decades. How well and how early those Communist ideas had begun to take hold among the Vietnamese is perhaps best illustrated by the case of Ton Duc Thang, since 1960 Vice-President of the D.R.V.N.: While serving as a sailor aboard the French heavy cruiser *Waldeck-Rousseau*, operating in 1919 in the Black Sea in support of anti-Communist Russian elements, Ton helped another French sailor, André Marty,[10] organize a mutiny in order to turn the warship over to the Bolsheviks. The mutiny was crushed at the last moment, and Ton served seventeen years in French jails for his deed.

The timetable of Ho's next travels is somewhat in doubt. According to Ruth Fischer, who was Chairman of the German Communist Party's Political Bureau until 1926 and therefore attended all the early Comintern conferences in Moscow, Ho attended the Fourth Comintern Congress in Moscow in November–December, 1922, which was the last public meeting Lenin attended.[11] This would support his later remark that he had personally met Lenin.[12] At the Fourth Congress, Ho allegedly became a member of the newly constituted Southeast Asia Bureau of the Comintern, in whose service he became very active later on. After this first trip to Russia, Ho may perhaps also have visited several other European countries on his way back to France. Assertions that he may have gone to Boston as a member of a Soviet economic mission[13] during that period or shortly thereafter have not been verified. In their conversations with me, his close associates denied that he had been a member of such a mission.

However, Ho had made his mark in the Comintern as one of the most vocal and energetic of the "colonial" leaders. Little wonder, then, that the French Communist Party sent Ho again to Moscow a few months later, to organize the Peasant International (Krestintern). Ho remained in Moscow from June to early November, 1923, making the acquaintance of the greats and near greats of the international Communist movement: Radek, Zinoviev, Bukharin,

Dimitrov, and Trotsky. On October 16, 1923, Ho was elected as the Colonial Representative to the ten-man Executive Committee of the Krestintern, and shortly thereafter he once more returned to France, filled with the excitement of the new world he thought was in the making in Moscow. When a Japanese writer Ho knew in France, Kyo Komatsu, refused Ho's invitation to come with him to Moscow, Ho exclaimed: "What kind of art can you practice in this rotten society? We'll make the revolution and then you can write for free men in a classless society!"

And Ho left France at the end of 1923, not to return until 1946 as President of the fledgling D.R.V.N. Wearing a borrowed fur coat, he reached Leningrad aboard an ice-covered Soviet vessel on January 23, 1924, and immediately proceeded to Moscow, a city stunned by the death of Lenin two days earlier. Now a period of intensive study and writing began for Ho. He attended the University of the Toilers of the East and acquired a thorough grounding in theoretical Marxism. At the same time, he wrote three pamphlets, including his famous *Le Procès de la Colonisation Française*, and contributed articles to French Communist newspapers. With the help of his long-time friend Nguyên Thé Truyên, he organized an "underground railroad" to send other promising Vietnamese recruits from France to Moscow.[14]

From June 17 to July 8, 1924, Ho participated in the Fifth Congress of the Comintern "as a member of the French Communist Party and delegate from the colonies."[15] For a man who four years earlier had not known the difference between the Second and Third Internationals, Ho had certainly climbed fast up the ladder of the Communist hierarchy. Ho also had made all the right political decisions: He did not get embroiled in the Stalin-Trotsky struggle but began to carve a niche for himself as an "expert" on colonial peasantry problems. The fact that Ho's role was strictly technical probably saved him from being purged a decade later when Stalin sent most of Ho's erstwhile Comintern associates to the firing squads or the execution chambers of the Lubianka prison.

It was during this second stay in Moscow that Ho's writing began to exhibit a doctrinaire hatred of France that was too strong even for the French Communist Party. According to Ruth Fischer, Jacques Doriot, its overseas-affairs specialist, told Ho to curb his tongue when he began to sign his articles "Nguyên-O-Phàp" ("Nguyên Who Hates the French").

In the meantime, international Communism, stalled in Europe

after Communist-inspired revolutions had collapsed in Germany, Hungary, and Poland, had turned to a "second front," China. In Canton, Chiang Kai-shek had established himself as one of Sun Yat-sen's leading heirs and, with Soviet help, was in the process of consolidating his regime against the northern warlords. A Soviet political and military mission, under Michael Borodin on the civilian side and General Vassily Bluecher (then known as "General Ga-lin") on the military, had become very active. But Canton for two decades had also been a major center of agitation for Vietnamese nationalist exiles. To the *agitprop* specialists at the University of the Toilers of the East, Ho was an obvious choice to take those elements in hand and spread the spirit of the revolution into Southeast Asia. In December, 1924, Ho began his trip to Canton (soon to be followed there by the Indian M. N. Roy), thus launching nearly twenty years of revolution in Asia. Ho's "European period" was almost over.

Officially, Ho was assigned to Canton as Borodin's interpreter but he soon developed an intense training and recruiting operation among his compatriots. He took over an existing refugee group, the Tam Tam Xa (Heart-to-Heart Association), set up in Canton in 1923 by Lê Hong Phong,[16] and rechristened it, in June, 1925, the Viet-Nam Cach Menh Thanh-Nien Dong Chi Hoi (Viet-Nam Revolutionary Youth Association). At the same time, he organized a League of Oppressed Peoples of Asia, patterned on the Paris-based Intercolonial Union. The League, which included members from Korea, Indonesia, Malaya, India, China, and Viet-Nam, was the Comintern front organization for the whole Far East and soon became the Nan-yang (South Seas) Communist Party. That Party supervised Communist activities in the Southeast Asia area until the time was ripe to set up national Communist parties.

Ho quickly had an efficient Party organization. The best-qualified young Vietnamese were sent to Chiang Kai-shek's own military academy at Whampoa, to be trained by General Bluecher's officers; some key elements were sent for advanced political training to Moscow; and Ho himself ran an accelerated training course that graduated 20 to 30 Vietnamese political agitators every three months. Between January, 1925, and July, 1927 (when Chiang broke with the Communists), Ho formed 200 *can-bo* (cadres), which were infiltrated back to Indochina. For those who proved unreliable or who, upon graduating from Whampoa, refused to follow Communist orders, Ho had a simple but effective cure: Their names were leaked by the Communists to French intelligence and the Sûreté in Viet-

Nam was only too glad to pick them up on arrival. One of the most brilliant Communist Vietnamese graduates from Whampoa was a young, high-ranking mandarin whose father had been Chief of Cabinet to Emperor Duy-Tan and had been involved in the Emperor's anti-French rebellion in 1917. The young mandarin henceforth became one of Ho's most reliable and devoted associates. His name is Pham Van Dong, and in 1955, he became Prime Minister of the D.R.V.N.

The Sino-Russian rupture sent Ho fleeing to the U.S.S.R., via the arduous route across the Gobi Desert, while Lê Hong Phong carried out the reorganization of the Thanh-Nien on a completely underground basis from Hong Kong. What Ho did next is again shrouded in mystery. In conversations with East German journalists, he mentioned that he had been sent to Berlin and fondly recalled the working-class district of Neukölln, where he had lived.[17] To this day, Ho speaks fluent French, Russian, English, Mandarin and two other Chinese dialects, and some German. What Ho Chi Minh did for the Comintern in pre-Nazi Germany has never been disclosed, but early in 1928, he attended the Communist Congress Against Imperialism in Brussels and also visited Switzerland and even fascist Italy, and may have made a short trip to France. It is not known on what kind of passport Ho undertook his many trips; several sources allege that, like many other Communist leaders of his stature, Ho had taken out Soviet citizenship.[18]

But the Far East remained Ho's major field of activity. Hunted in China, too well known to the Sûreté in Indochina, Ho made the Vietnamese settlements in eastern Thailand his temporary headquarters. Disguised as a Buddhist monk, wearing a saffron robe and with his head shaved, Ho walked from one village to another, setting up "Mutual-Help Associations" and starting two newspapers, which were smuggled back to Viet-Nam.

These were hard times for the Communists in the Far East. Their flourishing Chinese organization had been crushed through what was probably Stalin's first major foreign blunder, and the Nan-yang Communist Party, which had led a precarious existence for two years, had to be dissolved in April, 1930, after the British and Dutch had struck decisive blows against Malay and Indonesian Communist organizations. And in French Indochina, a bitter intra-Party struggle raged among the Indochinese Communist Party, the Annamese Communist Party, and the League of Indochinese Communists. And some of the rival Communist factions did not object to settling their differences by selling out their opponents to the colonial police. The Comintern, concerned at the situation, ordered Ho to settle it as expeditiously as possible. From the slim evidence available—one good American source, Gene Hanrahan,[19] and Lacouture—it appears that for once, Ho found himself overtaken by the changing Party line. Hanrahan makes the point that Ho adopted the attitude that the Chinese Communist Party no longer should play the role of "elder brother" to the Southeast Asian Communist movements. At the same time, Lacouture mentions that Ho and his faithful were attacked by the Communist elements inside Viet-Nam as "jokers" and "petits-bourgeois" for not pushing hard enough in the direction of an autonomous, centralized Indochinese Communist Party.[20] The Executive Committee of the Third International finally settled the problem through a message whose terseness clearly implied disapproval:

> The hesitations of certain groups concerning the immediate creation of a Communist Party are an error. The division within the Communist groups and elements under the present circumstances constitutes an even graver error and a great danger. . . . The most important and most urgent task for all Indochinese Communists consists in founding a revolutionary party of the proletariat, i.e., a mass Communist Party. It should be a unified party and the only Indochinese Communist Party.[21]

According to most sources and interviews with Ho's associates, he called the reunification meeting into session in Hong Kong on January 6, 1930. It took place in the bleachers of a stadium while a soccer game was in progress and probably went on at different other places for three weeks.[22] This explains why the Vietnamese Communist Party, and its successor, the Vietnamese Workers' Party (Dang Lao-Dong), alternately date their creation as of January 6 or February 3, 1930.[23]

The year 1930 in the Far East, like 1848 in Europe, was one of abortive revolutions and uprisings, made more acute by the shattering impact of the world-wide Depression on the colonial economies. In Indochina, Vietnamese nationalists of the Viet-Nam Quôc Dan Dang (VNQDD, or Vietnamese Nationalist Party) subverted a Tonkinese rifle battalion which mutinied on February 9, 1930, at Yen-Bay; but the Communists, realizing the hopelessness of the enterprise (and perhaps not unwilling to see the French do away with the non-Communist competition, although this theory is energetically denied by D.R.V.N. historians), remained aloof. But in July, 1930, a peasant rebellion broke out in Ho's native province of Nghé-An; the farmers, driven to desperation by low prices and a poor harvest, began to kill landlords and set up local *xo-viet* (soviets) as they went along. The Vietnamese Communists knew that the Nghé-An rebellion also was foredoomed, but they decided to take charge of the movement in order to provide the young Party with revolutionary experience— and martyrs.[24] It soon was to have both. The French police cracked down on the insurgents, and such Party stalwarts as Pham Van Dong, Vo Nguyên Giap, Truong Chinh, and the first secretary general, Tran Phu, received prison terms. Ho himself, under the alias of Tong Van So, had watched the operation from the safe haven of Hong Kong, where the Vietnamese Communist Party was being enlarged to embrace Cambodian and Laotian Communists as well and was renamed the Indochinese Communist Party (Dong Duong Cong-San Dang) in October, 1930.

In the meantime, however, Western intelligence agents had made a rare catch: On April 27, 1930, a French Comintern agent, Joseph Ducroux (alias "Serge Lefranc"), had secretly arrived in Singapore with extensive documents covering much of the Comintern's operations in the Far East. He was arrested on June 1 by the British and, contrary to expectations, made a clean breast of all he knew. British, French, Dutch, and Nationalist Chinese agents began to close in on Communist hideouts from Java to Shanghai. Ho, who then was either in charge, or at least a senior official, of the Southern Section of the Far Eastern Bureau of the Comintern, in Hong Kong, was arrested on June 5, 1931, by the British authorities and given a six-month prison sentence for subversive activities. Moreover, *in absentia*, Ho had been sentenced to death by the French tribunal in Vinh (the capital of Nghé-An Province) for his anti-French activities; and the French now requested his extradition from Hong Kong, since, technically, Ho was a French national.

A young British lawyer, Frank Loseby, took on Ho's case, and British respect for law prevailed. The case was appealed all the way to the Privy Council in London (where it was eloquently pleaded by the late Sir Stafford Cripps), and Ho was found to be a political refugee and thus not subject to extradition. He was released from prison in Hong Kong early in 1932 and hidden by Loseby from the waiting French agents until, disguised as a Chinese merchant, he could flee to Amoy in isolated Fukien Province. For the second time in Ho's life, assertions were made that he had bought his freedom by agreeing to serve a Western police force—this time that of the British, rather than the French. It is, of course, unknown whether Ho ever "delivered" on that promise, but the possibility is not as remote as it may seem. After all, ten years later, as will be seen, Ho made such offers to the American Office of Strategic Services—and they were accepted.

With the strengthening of Chinese Nationalist control in South China, Amoy apparently became too dangerous for Ho. It is also likely that the Comintern had assigned him new tasks. By November, 1933, Ho was in the International Settlement of Shanghai, ostensibly teaching school. There he met his one-time Communist chief from France, Vaillant-Couturier, who put him in touch with the apparatus of the Chinese Communist Party, and the latter filtered Ho back to the U.S.S.R. early in 1934.

It is possible that Ho was now in temporary disgrace, for his enterprises since 1930 had been somewhat less than successful. The new "national" Communist Parties set up in Malaya, Indonesia, Siam, and Indochina were in serious difficulty, if they survived at all; the ICP's leadership was in jail, and Ho himself and his all-important Party files in Hong Kong had fallen into British hands. According to most recent information on the subject, he spent the years 1934 and 1935 attending Party schools in Moscow; first the Institute for National and Colonial Questions, and then the famous Lenin School, where senior Communist leaders do their "graduate" work. During that period, Ho must have witnessed the purge trials of his Comintern friends of the past, including foreign Communist leaders like himself. That he himself was spared by the ever-suspicious Stalin is significant; perhaps, as a practitioner rather than a theoretician of revolution, Ho was not considered dangerous by Stalin—or perhaps he was considered absolutely loyal.

His days of study over, Ho returned to the Communist bases in northwestern China late in 1937 or early in 1938, during the Kuomintang-Communist "honeymoon"—a union produced by the Japanese aggression. He at first occupied low-level jobs as communications operator with the signal section of the Communist 8th Route Army and as secretary of the Chinese Communist Party cell of his unit. His assignment to this humble post may have been the result of a temporary disgrace, or part of the attempt to build the image of "Ho, the man of the people," or simply to provide additional training for his next job. For in 1940, Ho reappeared in the Tongking border area as part of the special Chinese Communist mission sent there to train Chinese Nationalist guerrillas. The mission was headed by Mao's most capable guerrilla expert, General (later Field Marshal) Yeh Chien-ying, and Ho was the "Party Secretary" (i.e., political commissar) assigned to the mission. Ho and Yeh apparently remained on good terms—a fact that was to have some importance twenty-two years later.

But Viet-Nam was still Ho's main preoccupation. There, as has been shown earlier, the French Popular Front had brought about a liberalization of the colonial regime and had released from prison many of the ICP's best leaders. The Seventh Comintern Congress in August, 1935, had advocated collaboration with the Western democracies against the rising forces of fascism, and, obediently, the ICP dropped the slogan "Down with French Imperialism" from its program during the meeting of its Central Committee in July, 1936. It also decided to drop its campaign against Viet-Nam's feudal leadership and even its demands for national independence and an effective legislature. But faithful to the Moscow line in its most minute aberrations, Ho reported to the Comintern in July, 1939, that the ICP had refused all offers of cooperation with the strong Vietnamese Trotskyite group: "As regards the Trotskyites—no alliances and no concessions. They must be unmasked as the stooges of the fascists, which they are."

Neither information nor speculation is recorded in any source concerning Ho's activities and whereabouts after he left Yeh Chienying's mission at the time the Chinese Red guerrillas were withdrawn from Chiang Fa-k'uei's Fourth War Area. However, a small nucleus of Vietnamese ICP and nationalist revolutionaries already had assembled at Liuchow, in Kwang-si Province, and it is likely that Ho joined them. Apparently, his first visit on Vietnamese soil in *thirty* years took place soon after, in December, 1940, at Pac-Bo, in the border province of Cao-Bang, after the Japanese had crushed the French garrisons in the area in September and a small rebellion of tribesmen had kept the French from reoccupying the area for a time. It was at Pac-Bo that the Central Committee of the ICP—severely depleted by French arrests[25]—held its eighth meeting, between May 10 and 19, 1941. The Museum of the Revolution in Hanoi now carefully preserves mementoes of Ho's stay in the Pac-Bo grottoes: his small rattan suitcase, his inkwell, and papers bearing some of his instructions to the ICP. And it was in such humble beginnings that the ICP gave birth to its front organization, the Viet-Minh, on May 19—Ho's fifty-first birthday.

Since the most likely recruits for a Vietnamese liberation movement still were in China and the only likely outside support for such a movement would have to be Chinese, Ho returned once more to China. Chiang Fa-k'uei set up a Vietnamese Special Training Group at the village of Ta Ch'iao, near Liuchow. According to statements the old general made to the previously cited young Chinese scholar, King Chen, during a visit to the United States in 1961, the Chinese spent NC$100,000 a month on the Vietnamese Training Group. Lecturers to the Group included Communists, such as Chou En-lai, and Catholic prelates, such as Archbishop Paul Yu. But while the Vietnamese nationalists of the group, many of whom had been in China for forty or more years—such as Nguyên Hai Than, an associate of the grand old man of Vietnamese nationalism, Phan Boi Chau—were quite content to leave the future of their country in the hands of the South Chinese warlords, Ho apparently soon fell out with his erstwhile Chinese protectors and was arrested by Chiang Fa-k'uei on August 28, 1942, on the conflicting charges that he was (a) a Communist and (b) a French spy.

What really happened is still a matter of controversy. Authoritative sources, such as Philippe Devillers and Harold R. Isaacs, support the above two theories. General Chiang himself denies that the whole affair took place and alleges that Ho was "sent to Kunming for training at the request of American military men there."[26] While, as will be seen below, contact between Ho Chi Minh and Americans (notably those of the Office of Strategic Services, the OSS) at that time was quite possible, there is solid evidence in the form of photographs and Ho's published *Prison Diary*[27] that he was imprisoned by the Chinese. The date for his release from Chinese imprisonment is given as September 16, 1943, and here again, a new allegation of American intervention in his behalf has come to light. According to a West German source published in 1960, "American representatives with [Generalissimo] Chiang [Kai-shek]" pleaded for Ho's release. Chungking gave way to the American request and thus, the German author asserts, "the Americans handed the Soviets, as often elsewhere during the war years, another trump card."[28]

That stay in Chinese jails convinced the Vietnamese revolutionary of the overwhelming, even if temporary, might of the warlords and the remoteness of his own Communist friends. When Ho was released from prison, he agreed to cooperate with Chiang Fa-k'uei in the formation of a unified Vietnamese revolutionary organization, from which the ICP was to be barred, but in which its stooge, the

Viet-Minh, was to be a full-fledged member. That unification conference, held in Liuchow on October 4–16, 1943, produced few tangible results, for the nationalists continued squabbling and Ho and his men remained aloof in order to prove to the Chinese that they, and they alone, were capable of welding the Vietnamese exiles into an effective force. During the next reunification congress, held at Liuchow on March 25–28, 1944, General Chiang allowed Ho to accept a portfolio in what was pompously christened the "Provisional Republican Government of Viet-Nam." Ho and his men were in the saddle, never to leave it again.

However, with the good measure of cold realism that, along with his kindly manners, has been his hallmark all his life, Ho realized that neither the Chinese Communists nor the U.S.S.R. could be relied on as a counterpoise to the growing influence of the Chinese warlords in Viet-Nam, or to that of the French, who would probably return to Indochina after V-J Day. The Americans in South China seemed Ho's only and best bet, and he set out to woo them with a will. He made several contacts in the winter of 1944–45 with Colonel Paul Helliwell, then head of OSS intelligence operations in South China, with headquarters in Kunming. Although according to Colonel Helliwell, "the only arms or ammunition which were ever given by OSS/China to Ho were six .38 caliber revolvers,"[29] the fact remains that Ho and his guerrillas soon were reinforced by several OSS teams that also provided the Viet-Minh guerrillas with American arms and ammunition.[30] For the time being, Ho discarded all Communist trappings; and the name Ho Chi Minh (He Who Enlightens) itself—which did not figure on any roster of known Communist agents, since Ho was generally known until 1944 as Nguyên Ai-Quôc, and in China as Tong Van So—was a good enough cover to fool most people. Emphasis was laid on "nationalism" alone, and the fact that the Chinese Nationalist warlords worked with Ho seemed to constitute satisfactory credentials for OSS. Soon, the OSS missions operating in North Viet-Nam and even China had acquired a number of Vietnamese aides, many of whom turned out to be good Vietnamese Communists. When Ho's forces took over Hanoi, the presence of American senior officers at Viet-Minh functions and the flying of the American flag over their residence made it easy to convince the unsophisticated population (and even the surviving French who began to emerge slowly from their various internment camps) that the United States had established "official relations" with the Viet-Minh regime and was giving the revolutionaries its fullest backing. Later, it was learned that the belief in Ho's American backing led Bao-Dai and his nationalist supporters to abandon the reins of government to the Viet-Minh without a struggle.[31]

When it became obvious that effective American support was not forthcoming, Ho once more made a 180-degree policy switch and began to advocate cooperation with France. It was during this period, from 1945 to 1946, that he acted as a "Vietnamese" first and a "Communist" second, in his grim determination to see the Vietnamese state survive at almost any price. But the pro-Western honeymoon was of short duration—if, internally, it had ever actually existed; for while Ho was negotiating with French Government officials in Fontainebleau, his ablest deputies—Vo Nguyên Giap, Tran Van Giau, Nguyên Binh, and Pham Van Bach—were liquidating the "internal enemies of the regime": leaders of religious sects, mandarins (such as Ngo Dinh Khoi, brother of South Viet-Nam's President Ngo Dinh Diem), intellectuals (such as Pham-Quynh), Trotskyites, and anti-Communist nationalists. In Cochinchina, both the sects and the Viet-Minh dealt with each other's sympathizers in the following manner: They tied them together in bundles like logs and threw them into the Mekong to float down to the sea while slowly drowning. This was called "crab fishing." But the myth of "good old Uncle Ho" was so well entrenched that it has survived unimpaired to this day.

The outbreak of the Indochina War greatly simplified Ho's political problems. No longer did the opposition have to be treated with kid gloves: It simply became *viet-gian* (traitors to Viet-Nam). The non-Communist elements within the Viet-Minh were either completely taken over, or reduced to the role of insubstantial puppets, which they still play today—for North Viet-Nam, like East Germany, is *not* a "single-party" state. There exist tiny Socialist and Democratic parties without the slightest shred of power but with carefully selected candidates who stand for re-election and are voted their seats in the rubber-stamp parliament at comfortable majorities of 83–93 per cent of the votes (Communist Party candidates, of course, are elected with 99.8 per cent of the votes).[32]

Much that has been said about the frail man with the iron grip is little more than wishful thinking. French intelligence pronounced him dead on the average of twice a year since 1930, and elaborate theories were concocted to "prove" that today's Ho and the Ho of the 1930's are in reality two different people. But there is an almost unbroken line of photographs available, from the 1920 Tours congress to his stay in a Chinese prison in 1942 and beyond, to show beyond a doubt that we are dealing with one and the same man— an intelligent, resourceful, well-trained senior Communist leader with a breadth of experience outside his own narrow national Party environment that far outstrips that of *any* other Communist leader now in power save perhaps Chou En-lai. He presides over a Party structure that has not suffered a major purge since its creation and that has thus far succeeded in staying out of all the major Party fights that in recent years have embittered relations between the Soviet Union and Red China—perhaps by seeking refuge behind his own immediate problems of industrialization and reunification; saying, in effect, again, what he said at Tours in 1920: "I don't understand a thing about strategy, tactics, and all the other big words you use . . ." and thus carefully preserving Khrushchev's friendship without losing Chou En-lai's aid and protection.

No event provides a better example of Ho's attitude than the Twenty-second Party Congress, held in Moscow in October–November, 1961, in the course of which the Red Chinese delegation stomped out of the proceedings in a huff. Ho was truly caught in a quandary: He had witnessed the yearly October parade from atop the Lenin mausoleum as an honored guest, standing immediately to the right of Khrushchev, but he could not possibly defy Red China by remaining seated in the Congress hall. Thus, he left the meeting, but instead of returning home as the Chinese did, he went on a tour of European Russia, shaking hands and kissing babies as if he were running for re-election in Minsk or Kovno. And before leaving Moscow, he wrote a brief article for the Russian press in which he specifically thanked the U.S.S.R. and her European satellites for their "generous and fraternal disinterested economic aid," and specifically omitted Red China from the list of donors, in spite of the fact that Red China is, by a wide margin, the biggest contributor of foreign aid to North Viet-Nam! But as always, Ho steers clear of direct involvement in Party disputes: Neither Albania nor Khrushchev is even mentioned by name in the article, which confines its wrath to routine and hackneyed attacks on the United States, SEATO, and Formosa, no doubt considered "safe topics" whatever change the Party line may undergo.[33]

Yet, upon his return to Hanoi, Ho dutifully praised Albania through a special exhibit celebrating the seventeenth anniversary of the tiny republic (but, of course, without criticizing the U.S.S.R.)—

thus no doubt clearing his slate with Peking. Throughout 1962, the delicate balance between pro-Moscow and pro-Peking gestures was skillfully maintained in Hanoi: The first part of the year witnessed the West's defeat in Laos in the face of Pathet-Lao and neutralist forces backed by the Soviet Union and North Viet-Nam, but not Red China. A Chinese Communist friendship mission to Hanoi in January, 1962, led by Ho's old friend Yeh Chien-ying, was more than balanced by the visits later in the year of two high-level Soviet missions, one civilian and one military. And for three months during the summer of 1962, contrary to usual practice, Red China had no ambassador in Hanoi.

The ever-acrimonious Sino-Soviet debate over Party policies again found the D.R.V.N. caught in the crossfire of competing ideological pulls and the brutal facts of geopolitical life: to wit, that Red China was next door but that the Soviet Union was 5,000 miles away. As in Moscow in 1961, the North Vietnamese delegation attending the Berlin Communist Congress of January, 1963, fell silently into line with Peking after pleading for "understanding." But Ho Chi Minh himself, after he received touring Czechoslovak President Antonin Novotny on January 28, 1963, signed a joint communiqué with him that explicitly endorsed the Soviet stand and lauded the U.S.S.R. as "the center of the Socialist camp . . . making great strides forward in building Communism."[34] As if to rebuke Ho, Kim Il Sung of North Korea resoundingly endorsed the Chinese stand on the following day.

Thus Ho, the gentle-looking "Uncle" with the iron fist, still pursues what essentially is a pragmatic policy—playing for time in the hopes of staying ahead of the young Party bureaucrats in his entourage who might be swayed by Peking's siren song and be willing to trade what is essentially still a *Vietnamese* policy (though fully Communist) for promises of Chinese support in the war against South Viet-Nam. No one has yet tried to defy Ho openly—for Ho *is* North Viet-Nam in the same sense as de Gaulle (who is Ho's age) is France's Fifth Republic. And for forty years Ho has led Vietnamese Communism from success to success.

The Road to Dien Bien Phu

PRESENT-DAY developments in Viet-Nam, Cambodia, and Laos are a direct product of the impact the Indochina War had on later developments. A simple comparison suffices: The cease-fire negotiated in March, 1962, for Algeria provides extremely wide-reaching political, military, and economic guarantees to the French for the simple reason that the Algerian Armée de Libération Nationale never defeated the French Army in battle and had, in fact, been whittled down to ineffectual squads. In Indochina, on the other hand, within two years after the 1954 cease-fire, France had disappeared from the scene as a military and political factor—for one simple reason: Dien Bien Phu and its aftermath. Ironically, South Viet-Nam's total liberation from French tutelage and replacement of the latter by an American protective shield in 1961 was brought about at bayonet point, not by the Vietnamese nationalists, but by their Viet-Minh opponents. Every political concession wrested by the nationalists from the French was first bought by a Vietnamese Communist victory on the battlefields of Tongking, Laos, or the Southern Highlands. There can be no doubt that this historical fact—no matter how well it may be camouflaged behind high-sounding slogans— accounts for the ambivalence of the southern leadership about its role in achieving its now embattled independence.

Perhaps the best illustration of this is a passage from a speech made in the United States by a high South Vietnamese official whose anti-Communism cannot be placed in doubt. Addressing a large gathering in New York, attended by many State Department and Pentagon officials, the Vietnamese spoke of "powerful modern French armies [defeated] by poorly armed Vietnamese fighters who . . . never were helped by Russian or Chinese troops."[1] The interesting omission of the Communist character of those fighters, in the hope that the Americans, knowing nothing to the contrary, would attribute the victory to the nationalist side; the equivocal assertion that no Russian or Chinese *troops* had ever helped the Viet-Minh (while conveniently omitting the fact that large quantities of Russian and Chinese matériel, the latter serviced in part by Chinese specialists, were at least instrumental in turning the tide for the Viet-Minh in the later stages of the war)—these provide a clear-cut example of the conflicting motivations. Within the South Vietnamese Army the morale problem also prevails: One cannot brand anyone who worked with the French as a "colonialist puppet" and, at the same time, run the South Vietnamese Army with senior commanders who all received their initial officer's stripes in the French colonial forces and look back upon their careers with a certain amount of professional pride. One cannot admire the "poorly armed Vietnamese [Communist] fighters" who defeated the French at Dien Bien Phu and, at the same time, draw pride and strength from the heroic stand made by the Vietnamese paratroop battalions and regimental combat teams who fought side by side with the French Union Forces to the bitter end.

How high morale was among the Vietnamese troops who fought on the French side has never been described, because the truth clashes with official dogma and widespread prejudice. The foredoomed battle of Dien Bien Phu again must be mentioned as a shining example of what the Vietnamese soldier could do—but on *both* sides. As the garrison began to run short of specialists, the French High Command issued a call for volunteers to be parachuted into the flaming hell that was that valley in the last days of the battle. Of the 1,800 volunteers who stepped forward, *close to 800 were Vietnamese.* The last group of reinforcements, 94 men, was dropped in at 0530 on May 6, 1954—eighteen hours before the fortress fell—and that group contained a good many Vietnamese. As one French officer said admiringly: "It would be easy to call those men 'mercenaries'—but there isn't enough money around to pay anyone for where they're going."

The Vietnamese Communist forces, on the other hand, have seen to it that all their military exploits became part of their own military tradition, which thus stretches back to the first Communist guerrilla groups in Tongking in 1944; and as will be seen, they connected their own military operations to Viet-Nam's earlier military past by giving their offensives the names of heroes of Vietnamese history. Through their own choice, the South Vietnamese forces, on the other hand, trace their exploits only to 1955, the year of the creation of the Republic of Viet-Nam—unlike the armed forces of, say, India, Pakistan, Israel, Morocco, and Senegal, all of which view with legitimate pride their military achievements while under colonial rule. Indians need not be ashamed of their troops who died at Ypres, nor need the Israelis apologize for the Jewish Brigade's conquest of Münster or the "Battle of Britain" ribbons of its air-force commanders; and the battle streamers from Italy, France, Germany, and Indochina that adorn the flags of Moroccan and Senegalese regiments today are eloquent witnesses of their people's continuing military traditions. It is this rightful part of its history that the Saigon regime has voluntarily forfeited. Yet it is an important, and perhaps a vital, part of its troops' psychological armament, and one no amount of modern armor or aircraft can replace. That is why a brief sketch of the military operations that brought about the present political situation is well-nigh indispensable if one wishes to penetrate the whole complex of events in the two Viet-Nams today.

WAR AIMS

French objectives in the Indochina War, at first, obviously envisioned little more than a campaign of colonial reconquest along classic lines, like Marshal Lyautey's campaign against Abd el Krim's Riff Kabyles in Morocco in the 1920's. That method, known as the "*tache d'huile*" (the "oil slick"), involves securing some solidly held key centers from which the "pacification" forces spread an ever-tightening net around the rebellious natives. In the wide, open spaces of Africa, the oil-slick tactics had always worked satisfactorily as the thinly spread population was easily watched or concentrated near forts. In the more arid stretches, the conquest of a few oases and watering holes could bring about the rapid surrender of whole tribes.

Even more classic methods of warfare succeeded when the natives tried to match the European power in open battle, as in the Sepoy Rebellion against the British in India and Viet-Nam's wars against France, in the nineteenth century. In such cases, overwhelming European firepower did its work, and the discovery of new weapons such as aircraft and armor further worked to the advantage of the powers who had them, as was evident in the Italo-Ethiopian war of 1935–37.

In the Indochina War of 1946–54—which, in fact, was first and foremost a war fought in and for Viet-Nam—the French clung to the oil-slick tactics until almost the bitter end, and in good part because, politically and militarily, no other course seemed open to them.

When Marshal Leclerc's armored forces landed in South Viet-Nam in October, 1945, they were used exactly as cavalry had been used 100 years earlier: Columns of tanks and personnel carriers were sent scurrying through the countryside, securing one town after another— but never meeting an enemy force head-on. Within a few months, much of what was still called Cochinchina was in French hands—to the extent of 100 yards on either side of all major roads. It is possible that, had Leclerc had 150,000 troops available for an intensive mop-up within the areas cleared by his armor, he might have had a chance of securing at least the bulk of the Vietnamese lowlands. The trouble was that he only had about 40,000 men, and budgetary pressures at home would not let him count on even that many for the following year! These circumstances were well-nigh fatal to the use of the oil-slick method, whose key element is the subsequent *quadrillage*, the splitting-up into small squares, or "gridding," of the countryside, with each grid being carefully "raked over" (the "*ratissage*") by troops thoroughly familiar with the area, or guided by experts who know the area well. When carried out with sufficient care and adequate numbers of troops, the *ratissage* would result in the cornering of the rebel elements and their eventual destruction.

Until late in 1947 or early 1948, the French tried oil-slick pacification in combination with stabs designed to destroy the enemy's battle force or to capture his politico-military leadership. As yet unacquainted with the principles of revolutionary war, the French were thus unaware that capture of the enemy's leadership might be only a temporary blow, not necessarily knocking the enemy out of the fight. The Dutch, for example, captured Sukarno and his staff without altering the fate of their war with the Indonesians; and the capture of several senior Algerian leaders (notably Ben Bella) by the French in 1956 in no way altered the outcome of the Algerian War. Yet, "Operation Léa," to which the French committed a good portion of their scarce troops and supplies during five months in 1947, was devoted almost exclusively to the capture of Ho Chi Minh and his associates and the destruction of their main battle troops. "Léa" failed in both objectives, while leaving much of Viet-Nam's countryside open to Communist infiltration.

The leveling-off at a minimal level of French effectives in 1948–49 gave the French High Command very little choice of strategy. It cleaned up much of Cochinchina, with the help of the religious sects, whom the Viet-Minh had alienated, and also consolidated its hold on the Tonkinese delta by occupying the hitherto-"neutral" Catholic bishoprics of Bui-Chu and Phat-Diem ("Operation Anthracite"). But despite French control, the Sino-Tonkinese border had become virtually a sieve through which equipment for the Communist forces filtered at an ever-increasing pace. When Red China occupied all the provinces bordering on Tongking, late in 1949, and thus provided the Viet-Minh with a "sanctuary" where its troops could be trained and its supplies stored and replenished, the war had, for all practical purposes, become hopeless for the French. The French Government, alarmed at these developments, sent a high-level study mission under the personal leadership of France's army chief of staff, General Revers, to Viet-Nam in May, 1949. He recommended the immediate withdrawal of all French forces from the outlying border areas and their concentration upon the low-lying fertile rice deltas that constituted the *"Viet-Nam utile"* (the "useful Viet-Nam") without which the enemy could not hope to feed itself or win the war. The top-secret Revers Report was "leaked" to the Communists, and verbatim passages of it were broadcast over Viet-Minh transmitters by April, 1950![2] Even so, it was inevitable that the French Army would carry out those withdrawals, regardless of the fact that the enemy was aware of their preparation.

In actual fact, however, the French had lost the initiative late in 1949. A Viet-Minh offensive of fifteen battalions against the small French outpost line in the Black River Valley—an operation dubbed "Lê-Loi" after a Vietnamese king who had defeated Chinese invaders —sealed off part of the Red River Delta from the Thai Highlands[3] in January, 1950. This was followed from February to April by an even larger-scale offensive—called "Lê Hong Phong I" in memory of the first secretary general of the ICP, who had died in a French prison in 1942—against the Red River Valley. Five Viet-Minh regiments stabbed deep into the French defensive belt, briefly conquered Tan-Uyên, laid siege to Nghia-Lô, and took the key frontier town of Lao-Kay. By the end of "Lê Hong Phong I," the whole vast northeastern corner of Tongking had become a Viet-Minh stronghold—except for an attenuated string of border posts stretching more than 160 miles south from Cao-Bang via Dong-Khé, That-Khé, and ill-fated Lang-Son to the Gulf of Tongking, along a single-lane highway known as Colonial Road 4 (RC 4). By May 25, four of the Viet-Minh battalions newly trained on nearby Red Chinese firing ranges at Ching-hsi, and supported by impressive amounts of American howitzers obtained from captured Chinese Nationalist stocks, had overwhelmed the three infantry companies defending Dong-Khé, but the French had retaken the post in a costly airborne counterattack on May 27. Throughout the summer of 1950, the Lang-Son–Cao-Bang supply run became a constant battle whose rising toll of casualties could no longer be hidden. A French parliamentary move further encouraged Viet-Minh designs: On August 14, the French Government decided to *reduce* the French forces in Indochina by 9,000 men despite urgent pleas for reinforcements, while the French National Assembly made its further support of combat operations and the Government's policy dependent upon assurances that no draftees would be used in this "police action." The French Government acquiesced in the bargain—and thus sealed the doom of the frontier forces.

But one further mistake was committed, and it is entirely imputable to the military command in Indochina itself: Even after three years of unsuccessful campaigns, the army still underestimated the enemy and grossly overestimated its own valor. As a French regular officer stated in a study of his own army's defeat: "the High Command had substituted for the hard facts of the real situation—i.e., for the results of the detailed intelligence at its disposal—the preconceived ideas it had about the enemy."[4]

Under such conditions, Giap's "Operation Lê Hong Phong II" could hardly fail. The attacking forces of "Lê Hong Phong I" veered toward Cao-Bang via the Red Chinese sanctuary and, at Long-Chow, joined ten newly formed Viet-Minh battalions, reinforced by a complete artillery regiment. On September 16, 1950, the offensive opened once more with an attack on Dong-Khé, which fell forty-eight hours later, cutting off Cao-Bang and the northern garrisons from the southern forts of RC 4. This time, the French High Command reacted more swiftly, albeit still belatedly: It ordered the commanding officer at Cao-Bang to blow up all his heavy equipment and all his motor transport and to march out of Cao-Bang; meanwhile a Moroccan task force of 3,500 men under the command of Colonel Le Page was directed to fight its way north from That-Khé to Dong-Khé, and to retake the latter, and hold it long enough for the Cao-Bang force of 2,600 men and 500 civilians to join up with Le Page's group. On October 3, the Cao-Bang force began its eighty-five-mile trek southward, *but with its artillery and trucks*. Its commander, not recognizing the extent of the threat hanging over his head, had decided—against orders—to save his equipment along with his men. He was to lose both in short order, and engulf the whole border line in his own catastrophe.

RC 4 winds for long stretches between high jungle-covered limestone cliffs and over flimsy bridges. Had the Cao-Bang force operated according to orders, it could have chosen footpaths, rather than using the main road, which was well covered by enemy troops, and in any case, it could have bypassed most bridges. But with its trucks and cannon, it was road-bound and ran almost immediately into a succession of ambushes and blown-up bridges. After one day of arduous work, the force had covered *nine* miles! Moving entirely on foot, it could beyond a doubt have covered at least twice as much ground, and in the meantime, the Le Page task force, outnumbered three to one, was bitterly holding onto its stretch of road, waiting for the Cao-Bang column. By the time the commander of the Cao-Bang force decided that his High Command had been right after all, and that the trucks and artillery were a useless and dangerous impediment, it was too late for both him and Le Page. The remnants of the two forces met in the hills around Dong-Khé just long enough to die together on October 7, in spite of last-minute go-for-broke parachute drops of three battalions, whose commitment increased the long list of French casualties without in any way changing the outcome of the battle.

From overconfidence, the French mood now veered to near panic. On October 17, Lang-Son, which had not even been under attack and whose open fields of fire and good airfield could have permitted a prolonged defense, was abandoned with most of its 1,300 tons of supplies intact (later French aerial bombings did not fully succeed in destroying them). By the end of the month of October, 1950, almost the whole northern half of North Viet-Nam had become a

Viet-Minh redoubt, into which the French were—with the brief exception of a paratroop raid on Lang-Son in July, 1953—never to penetrate again. As I have observed elsewhere:

> When the smoke cleared, the French had suffered their greatest colonial defeat since Montcalm had died at Quebec. They had lost 6,000 troops, 13 artillery pieces and 125 mortars, 450 trucks and three armored platoons, 940 machineguns, 1200 submachineguns and more than 8,000 rifles. Their abandoned stocks alone sufficed for the equipment of a whole additional Viet-Minh division.[5]

For the French, the Indochina War was lost then and there. That it was allowed to drag on inconclusively for another four years is a testimony to the shortsightedness of the civilian authorities who were charged with drawing the political conclusions from the hopeless military situation. American military aid—the first trickle of which had made its appearance in the form of seven transport planes in June, 1950, after the Korean War had broken out—was to make no difference whatever in the eventual outcome of the war.[6]

On the Communist side, war aims were politically simpler and militarily more complex than those of the French. Politically, the Viet-Minh program consisted of the one magic word *"doc-lap"* ("independence"). Militarily, the Viet-Nam People's Army (VPA) command applied a slightly altered version of Mao Tse-tung's teachings on the subject of guerrilla war, protracted war, and, above all, revolutionary war. The Viet-Minh commander in chief and some of the senior Viet-Minh commanders, such as the late General Nguyên-Son, had actually undergone training at Yenan; other officers had graduated from Whampoa, and most of the rising regimental commanders had attended at least a brief training course at Nanning, Ching-hsi, or Long-Chow when the new 'regular regiments and divisions were formed in Red China. Thus, unity of doctrine was relatively easy to obtain, even if there were often difficulties in its application.

Mao, in his basic *Strategic Problems of China's Revolutionary War*,[7] defined China's situation before 1948 as being that of (1) a semicolonial country of great size faced (2) with a powerful enemy opposed (3) by a weak Red Army endowed (4) with Communist leadership based on an agrarian revolution. It is obvious that this is not exactly comparable to Viet-Nam's situation for (1) although Viet-Nam was colonial, it was certainly not overwhelmingly large; (2) although the French forces until 1950 exceeded the Viet-Minh's in firepower, they never reached the ten-to-one minimal ratio neces

sary to win in a guerrilla war (and the ratio was to get worse rather
than better as the war went on); and (3) although Communist
leadership on the Viet-Minh side was a plus factor because it provided
an excellent channel to Communist bloc military aid, its Marxist
slogans were of very little importance in comparison to its appeals to
the national pride and traditional xenophobia of the Vietnamese.

Had land reform, for example, been a major item in the Viet-
Minh's psychological arsenal, then the Viet-Minh's popularity
should have been strongest in Cochinchina (where 2 per cent of
the landowners at one time owned 30 per cent of the land), while
in Tongking, with its 1 million Catholics and independent farmers
(98 per cent of whom cultivated their *own* plot of land), it should
have been weakest. But the situation was precisely the reverse; the
Viet-Minh was strongest in the north and weakest in the south.
There were other anomalies in the Viet-Minh's operations that did
not fit Mao's theories or even the pet theories developed by latter-day
Western theorists on the subject; for example, the fact that although
Ho Chi Minh and nearly all his major subordinates were Vietnamese
from the lowlands, all major Viet-Minh strongholds were in areas
inhabited by mountain minorities that traditionally *hate* the Vietnamese! It must be considered one of the Viet-Minh's signal achievements that it succeeded in at least partly winning over the mountain
tribes of Viet-Nam; without the successful wooing of those tribes,
Ho and his staff would sooner or later have been betrayed to the
French. A Thô tribal chieftain, Chu Van Tan, quickly rose to the
rank of major-general in the VPA; and one of the elite divisions,
the 316th, was largely recruited from mountain tribesmen, which
explains its efficiency in highland operations. Two other People's
Army divisions, the 325th and the 335th, included large groups of
minorities. At no time did Mao Tse-tung—with the exception, perhaps, of a brief period during the "Long March"—have to rely on
the good will of the non-Han tribes of China as Ho had to rely
on the non-Vietnamese tribes of Viet-Nam for almost eight years.
This demanded a *political* rethinking of the situation, which the
Viet-Minh never left in the hands of its military commanders, but
placed where it properly belonged—with its Party thinkers.

Thus, contrary to what has recently been asserted, it was not
General Vo Nguyên Giap who wrote what "to this day remains the
fullest expression of Viet-Minh [military] doctrine,"[8] but the then
secretary general of the Indochinese Communist Party, Truong
Chinh (Long March). It was Truong Chinh who, in a small book

written in 1947 and entitled *The Resistance Will Win,* first formulated a Vietnamese adaptation of Mao's *On Protracted War,* with its three-stage principles of strategic defensive, a period of equilibrium, and a final stage of the victorious general counteroffensive (*Tong tan-cong*). Giap's own *La guerre de libération et l'armée populaire* (1952) is only a restatement of Mao's principles in a simplified form and a résumé of VPA operations from 1945 until 1950. Giap's brochure *L'armée populaire de libération du Viet-Nam dans la lutte pour l'indépendance nationale, la démocratie et la paix* (November, 1951) merely emphasized the importance of the "war of movement" during the second phase and also claimed that the VPA was learning from "the Korean People's Army how a weak nation can vanquish modern American[-type] troops."

Giap's own best contribution to the art of revolutionary war was probably his estimate of the *political-psychological shortcomings* of a democratic system when faced with an inconclusive military operation. In a remarkable presentation before the political commissars of the 316th Division, Giap stated:

> The enemy will pass slowly from the offensive to the defensive. The blitzkrieg will transform itself into a war of long duration. Thus, the enemy will be caught in a dilemma: He has to drag out the war in order to win it and does not possess, on the other hand, the psychological and political means to fight a long-drawn-out war. . . .

In all likelihood, Giap concludes, public opinion in the democracy will demand an end to the "useless bloodshed," or its legislature will insist on knowing for how long it will have to vote astronomical credits without a clear-cut victory in sight. This is what eternally compels the military leaders of democratic armies to promise a quick end to the war—to "bring the boys home by Christmas"—or forces the democratic politicians to agree to almost any kind of humiliating compromise rather than to accept the idea of a semi-permanent antiguerrilla operation. There is little indication in the 1960's that logical conclusions have been drawn from earlier lessons.[9]

For the final stage of the war, Giap foresaw three major conditions: (1) superiority (numerical and, in the case of some key weapons, material) of VPA forces over French forces; (2) a favorable international situation (Communist-bloc military assistance and political support at the conference table); and (3) a favorable situation (i.e., favorable to the Viet-Minh) within Viet-Nam in general and the enemy camp in particular: political dissension in France, demoralization among pro-French Vietnamese politicians and troops, etc. This long-drawn-out timetable was one that the Viet-Minh apparently did not accept with a light heart, for it imposed tremendous sacrifices upon their army and even greater deprivation upon the sorely tried population. As will be seen, Giap himself made the fatal mistake of thinking that the French were ready for Phase Three as early as the spring of 1951; he lost a major part of three new divisions before he saw the error of his ways. In his postwar book on the subject, *People's War, People's Army,* Giap made a mild attempt at self-criticism:

> The application of this strategy of long-term resistance required a whole system of education, a whole ideological struggle among the people and Party members. . . . Sometimes erroneous tendencies appeared, trying either to by-pass the stages to end the war earlier, or to throw important forces into military adventures. The Party rectified them by a stubborn struggle and persevered in the line it had fixed.[10]

There is no doubt that, within the Vietnamese Communist high command, a struggle of a similar nature must be going on with regard to the guerrilla war that began in South Viet-Nam late in 1957 (and *not* in 1960, as some people claim). There must be considerable pressure by certain military leaders to match the American build-up by the open commitment of Viet-Minh regulars, and, perhaps, again the Party is at work, rectifying the erroneous views "by a stubborn struggle." In any case, there is no reason whatever to believe that Giap's doctrine and views of revolutionary war have changed since the 1950's, and they need not have—for they were eminently successful then.

The Battle in Balance

Almost duplicating the game of musical chairs played with governors general before the war, now in Indochina *la valse des généraux* began—a rapid succession of commanders in chief often replaced after only a few months: Leclerc, Valluy, Blaizot, Carpentier, de Lattre, Salan, Navarre, Ely—and all, with the exception of de Lattre, who left to die of cancer, departed under the shadow of frustration or of defeat. The fate of Viet-Nam looked particularly grim at the conclusion of the battle for RC 4: Demoralized troops were flowing back into the Red River Delta only to meet the demoralized French civilians whose recent acquaintance with Viet-Minh rule and camps was still a vivid nightmare and who viewed the approach of Giap's divisions with hysteria. Ho Chi Minh himself, relying on Giap's erroneous interpretation of the Mao Tse-tung timetable, promised the Vietnamese he would return to the capital for the Têt, the lunar New Year, in February, 1951, and the French Government at home sent the largest passenger liner available, the *Pasteur*, to evacuate all French civilians from North Viet-Nam. As a final gesture of French determination, General (he was to become a field marshal posthumously) Jean de Lattre de Tassigny was appointed on December 17, 1950, commander in chief and civilian high commissioner in Indochina—presumably to preside over its demise.

But de Lattre was not the kind of man to accept retreats lightly. Known as *"le roi Jean"* in the French Army because he always insisted upon regal elegance among his staff officers and a military ceremonial recalling the more civilized days of the eighteenth century, he was, at the same time, a shrewd and demanding commander.[11] In brief, what changed with de Lattre's arrival in Indochina was the "tone"— and at that juncture, that was a vital element. In his first address, he promised little: no improvements, no reinforcements, no easy victories. But he made one promise he kept to his dying day: "No matter what, you will be *commanded.*" And to troops who had sorely lacked the knowledge of a clearly explained mission, this was all-important. De Lattre fired the area commander of Hanoi five minutes after landing there because the honor guard was not turned out the way he felt it should be; he also insisted that French WAC detachments turn out for parades just as male units did; and it was de Lattre who invented the impressive paratroop parades in full battle gear: camouflage uniform with rolled-up jacket sleeves and all portable weapons, including mortars and recoilless cannon. It was de Lattre who sent the *Pasteur* back to France empty except for wounded soldiers (to the outcries of parliament); who drafted French civilians in Indochina for guard duties; who requisitioned all civilian aircraft as they landed, unaware, in Saigon, and used them to airlift reinforcements; and who, once the battle was joined, flew into the small outpost of Vinh-Yen in a two-seater aircraft, and answered the frantic radio pleas of his chief of staff that Vinh-Yen was in grave danger of being overrun with the laconic sentence: "Well, break through and get me out." Finally, it was also de Lattre who had the guts to meet head-on the problem of how to get the non-Communist Vietnamese to fight for their own country. He began to create wholly Vietnamese units commanded by Vietnamese officers and bluntly told a class of fastidious Vietnamese high-school graduates (of the type that were always willing to tell American reporters how they hated the French—provided they could spend the next four years at the University of Paris) to act "like men. If you are Communists, then go and join the Viet-Minh. There are people there who fight well for a bad cause."

It is unlikely that the Indochina War could have been won by the French, even had de Lattre lived. But there is no doubt that de Lattre would have been able to put a stop to the war on the day he saw that it had become hopeless—as de Gaulle was the man who had the prestige to stop the Algerian War.

In the meantime, General Giap committed the mistake of throwing his green divisions into a flatland battle against de Lattre's regulars. By January 13, Divisions 308 and 312 were assembled at the northern tip of the Red River Delta for the final thirty-mile dash on Hanoi, ready to pounce on two French regimental combat teams hurriedly thrown into and around Vinh-Yen. On January 16, at 1700, long waves of Communist infantry began to emerge from the forest-covered mountains of the Tam-Dao Massif—and "Operation Hoang Hoa Tham I" (named after Dê Tham, the Vietnamese guerrilla leader who had held off the French from 1887 to 1913 in precisely that area) was under way. After initial Communist successes, French firepower won the day. When Giap's troops left the battlefield on January 17, they left 6,000 dead and 500 prisoners behind. But Giap was still convinced that the time was ripe for the "general counteroffensive." In his next stab, "Operation Hoang Hoa Tham II," he tried to cut the French off from the sea by occupying their only major port, Haiphong, a bare twenty-five miles from the northern flank of the battle line. The freshly organized 316th Division, reinforced by the retrained elements of the 308th and 312th, fell upon a lone French and Vietnamese battalion protecting the pit head of a coal mine at Mao-Khé, in the Dong-Trieu coal belt. The pit head itself, defended by a company of Thô mountaineers and commanded by a Vietnamese lieutenant and three French NCO's, held out for a whole day against a Viet-Minh division, thus buying time for the arrival of a paratroop battalion. When the Viet-Minh broke off "Operation Hoang Hoa Tham II," on March 26, 1951, it had suffered yet another bloody defeat. A third, more limited offensive, again with the sorely tried 308th Division, but also involving the new 320th and the experienced 304th, returned to Viet-Minh control the southern corner of the Red River Delta, with its three-crop rice fields and prosperous Catholic bishoprics. On the Viet-Minh side, the sole innovation (and it was an important one) was the prebattle infiltration by an entire Communist regiment, the 64th Infantry, *inside* the French battle line. As a result, when the Viet-Minh offensive broke loose on May 29—it was called "Ha Nam Ninh" for the provinces of Ha-Nam and Ninh-Binh, which were its objective—the French were violently attacked from both the front and the rear. In spite of some initial gains, Giap failed to anticipate the difficulties of feeding three divisions operating on the left bank of the wide Day River, controlled by French aircraft and armored launches. On June 18, the third battle for the delta ended in a Communist defeat, and Giap retreated to the mountains to lick his wounds and ponder his mistakes.

This series of French victories at a time when the Korean War was at a stalemate not only was balm for French pride, but also considerably helped de Lattre in his plea for more American aid—a plea he made personally on a much-publicized visit to the United States. But prior to his departure from Viet-Nam, personal tragedy struck him: His cherished only child, Lieutenant Bernard de Lattre, was killed during the first day of "Operation Ha Nam Ninh," defending an important rock crag jutting out over the city of Ninh-Binh. But the sacrifice of young de Lattre and his platoon had blunted the attack of Division 308 and saved the day for the French.

On the Communist side, it probably took all Ho's prestige to keep Giap in the saddle; or, more probably, Giap was retained because the erroneous decision to launch the offensive had been made collectively by the whole senior Party hierarchy. The VPA retreated in full to Phase Two of Mao's precepts: refusing to accept battle except on its own terms, and pursuing peripheral military objectives remote from French centers of power, while undermining the non-Communist Vietnamese authorities and waiting for the break in French home-front morale that French Communist sources were freely predicting, and doing their best to produce.

Probing stabs in the Thai Highlands in September, 1951, had shown the Viet-Minh the weakness of French positions there, strewn in dribbles over roadless expanses at the end of precarious supply lines and far away from French airfields: *It was those highlands that now became the Viet-Minh's major military target, rather than the thickly populated ethnically Vietnamese lowlands.* This single strategic decision was a stroke of genius that ultimately resulted in the destruction of sizable French battle groups in mountainous areas where the traditional French superiority in mobile firepower (airplanes, tanks, and ship-borne and land-borne artillery) was more than matched by the cross-country mobility of the enemy foot-soldier and cannoneer. In carrying out this decision, the Viet-Minh concentrated its attacks on such outlying areas as the Thai High-lands, Central Laos, and the PMS. Thus, the Red River Delta and the Mekong Delta became, not the "two major theaters of opera-tions,"[12] but the *major prizes*.

It was de Lattre himself who was to provoke the first important battle outside the delta area. Relying on increasing arrivals of Amer-ican equipment and apparently impressed by the "meat-grinder" battles into which the North Koreans and Chinese Reds (apparently less sophisticated in this than Giap) had let themselves be drawn by U.S. forces in Korea, the French C in C decided to launch a major offensive against the major north-south Viet-Minh road con-necting the Tonkinese redoubt with Interzone IV—a block of four North Annam provinces solidly held by the VPA since 1945. The key point in the battle was the city of Hoa-Binh on the Black River, connected with the Red River flatlands by Colonial Road 6 (RC 6), winding for twenty-five miles through jungle thickets and dominated on both sides by cliffs and crags that are difficult to control.

As often before and after in Indochina, the initial occupation phase by a parachute drop of three battalions was the easiest part of the play, which was completed in less than twenty-four hours, on November 14, 1951. On the following day, de Lattre's informa-tion services—his hardest-working unit, as some of his critics used to observe—provided the world press with the understatement that "the conquest of Hoa-Binh represented a pistol pointed directly at the heart of the enemy." It may have been pointed, but it cer-tainly was not fired; Hoa-Binh did become a meat-grinder battle—but for both sides. By the time Hoa-Binh was evacuated by the French on February 24, 1952 (de Lattre, who had remained in Indochina until December 19, when he could no longer stand on his feet, had died in Paris on January 11), the battle, like the cancer that ate at the vitals of the French commander, had ground up all the French reserves available throughout the theater: paratroop battalions, armor, aircraft, naval river squadrons. Every other front in Viet-Nam, Cambodia, and Laos had been stripped below the danger level for the sake of feeding Hoa-Binh. Finally, twelve infan-try battalions and three artillery groups had to be used to cover a life line leading to four battalions precariously perched in a small valley where they were guarding absolutely nothing, for the Viet-

Minh had (in its usual fashion) built a bypass road around Hoa-Binh within thirty days after the French had occupied the town.

By the end of the battle of Hoa-Binh, the Red River Delta was Communist-infiltrated as never before, with major elements of the 316th and the 320th Divisions operating inside the French battle line and laying siege to such provincial seats as Thai-Binh and Nam-Dinh. And now *all* Communist divisions—though they had paid a collective price of perhaps 12,000 casualties for the experience—had had a close-quarters object lesson in French methods of fighting. They could see for themselves the limitations of French rocket- and napalm-firing aircraft, the comparative abilities of Moroccans and Foreign Legionnaires in jungle warfare or in defending a fortified position; they could shake down their own flaws in fire control and communications—and all this without ever vitally endangering their own positions. After all, the whole battle took place in the section of Tongking farthest from Ho Chi Minh's underground "capital," and any Viet-Minh unit that was badly mauled or whose commander lost his nerve had only to retreat two miles back into the jungle to be completely safe, for the French had their hands full holding onto Road 6 without sending scarce battalions on wild-goose chases.

Armed with newly gained knowledge of French abilities and limitations, Giap now prepared for his next play: the conquest of the Thai Highlands. Three VPA divisions—the elite 308th, the 312th, and the mountaineer 316th—crossed the Red River on October 11, 1952, in a three-pronged move. By October 17, great numbers of the small posts in the highlands had been swept from the map; one crack paratroop battalion, the 6th Colonial, under Major Bigeard, was offered up for sacrifice at Tu-Lê Pass to buy time for the other units falling back to the Black River, but to little avail. Two French airheads were hastily organized: one at Lai-Chau, the capital of the Thai tribes, and the other at Na-San, on the bare plateau near the Black River. They were both bypassed (although Giap did try to overrun Na-San and suffered bloody casualties) as the Red juggernaut ground on into the empty spaces of Viet-Nam's northwest frontier. On November 30, 1952, the first Viet-Minh advance units appeared on the Lao border. The Communist divisions, in the face of French mastery of the air, had covered 180 miles in six weeks of fighting, without using a single road or a single motor vehicle.

The French had not remained inactive during this time. It was, of course, impossible to build a defense line through the roadless jungle of the Thai Highlands, but de Lattre's successor, Raoul Salan, attempted to cure the illness at its source by attacking the VPA supply bases at Phu-Doan, in the hope that this threat would force Giap to return in haste in order to protect his own rear. The French offensive, "Operation Lorraine," involved four motorized or armored regimental combat teams, three airborne battalions, five commandos, two tank-destroyer squadrons, two naval assault divisions, and assorted support units—a total of more than 30,000 men and by far the largest force ever assembled in a single attack in Viet-Nam. But again Giap refused to fight the war by the traditional rulebook. Knowing that the French could not divert such an important body of troops for a long time, he decided to sacrifice Infantry Regiments 36 and 176 in a delaying mission. Begun on October 29, 1952, "Lorraine" stabbed almost 100 miles into Communist territory. Some important Viet-Minh depots at Phu-Doan were found (including, for the first time, Soviet-built trucks), but the vital major depots at Yen-Bay were never reached, and on November 14, "Lorraine" was called off. The inevitable retreat, which Giap had foreseen, proved delicate in the face of a fully alert enemy; heavy losses were incurred when Viet-Minh Regiment 36 ambushed French Mobile Groups 1 and 4 in the gorges of Chan-Muong. By December 1, the French were back behind the fortified but penetrable belt of the "de Lattre Line." And Giap was still poised on the Lao border.

In the plateau area of the PMS, the war also developed favorably to the Viet-Minh. Anchored on the three provinces of Quang-Ngai, Binh-Dinh, and Phu-Yen, which, as Interzone V, had been a Communist bastion since 1945, Viet-Minh control had slowly spread to the large Bahnar, Jarai, and Rhadé mountain tribes and smaller groups. Thus, they literally "hollowed out" Franco-Vietnamese areas in Central Viet-Nam to the point where they merely covered a few narrow beachheads around Hué, Tourane (today known as Danang), and Nha-Trang. The only areas where the Viet-Minh was visibly losing ground were South Viet-Nam proper (i.e., Cochinchina), and neighboring Cambodia. In Cochinchina, the religious sects that controlled two-thirds of the population had resolutely turned against the Communists; the Buddhist Cambodians detested the Communists not only on religious grounds but because they represented Vietnamese invaders—and Vietnamese invaders of any kind are unwelcome in Cambodia. Laos, thus far, had remained untouched by the fighting. Four VPA battalions (Numbers 80–83) were stationed in Laos, and one of them went as far as Muong-Lene in the Burmese southern Shan States, but until early 1953, they avoided contact and concentrated on training the pro-Communist Pathet-Lao, whose leader, Prince Souphanouvong, had set up his own phantom government on August 13, 1950, at one of Ho Chi Minh's North Vietnamese hideouts, Tuyên-Quang, and had signed an agreement with Ho on March 11, 1951 (along with the Cambodian Communist Sieu-Heng). According to the Australian Communist Burchett, "the creation of the Viet-Khmer-Lao alliance . . . paved the way for Vietnamese volunteers to help in the struggle. The latter were greatly reinforced by local Vietnamese."[13]

In the early spring of 1953, Giap was ready for his first foreign invasion. Laos, with an army of only 10,000 troops, backed up by 3,000 Frenchmen, was an inviting target, and Giap's initial three-division force, now backed up by a secondary prong composed of Division 304 and supported from within by 4,000 Pathet-Lao, was fully up to its task. For comparative purposes, it may be helpful to remember that in 1942 the Japanese ousted the British Army—reinforced by General Joseph Stilwell's Sino-American troops—from Burma with *four* divisions. Hence, the small Lao-French force never had even a remote chance of stemming the Red tide. Rather than sacrifice its small posts—as it had done the year before in the Thai Highlands—the French High Command withdrew most of them inland, leaving only a Lao battalion under a French captain, which was ordered to make a stand at Muong-Khoua to buy time for the other garrisons. Told on April 12, 1953, to hold out fourteen days against the bulk of the 316th Division, it fought on for thirty-six days; there were four known survivors. The retreating garrison from Samneua was overtaken in the course of its 110-mile dash westward and lost all but 180 of its 2,400 men.

Once more, the French were compelled to disperse their forces. A new airhead was hurriedly established at the Plaine des Jarres, a vast open plain midway between the border and Vientiane, and a round-the-clock airlift began to ferry in troops, barbed wire, and even tanks. Supplying those 10 battalions 500 air miles from Hanoi, and almost twice as far from Saigon, mortgaged all the air transport available in Indochina (not to speak of the 10,000 men still bottled up at Na-San, who also depended upon an airlift) and further depleted French reserves. On April 21, at 2200, the forward elements of two Communist divisions, hoping to be able to overrun the Plaine des Jarres before it was fully organized, began their assault against the hastily thrown-up French positions, and were soundly beaten back. A subsequent smaller stab against the royal capital of Luang-Prabang also failed, and the onset of the rainy season in May forced Giap to fall back upon his major supply depots. Laos was saved for another summer, but at the price of a steady deterioration of the over-all French position in the Red River Delta and Central Viet-Nam.

"GENERAL COUNTEROFFENSIVE"

The arrival of a new French commander in chief, General Henri Navarre, in July, 1953, coupled with promises of extensive American aid, gave rise to a new wave of euphoria both in France and in the United States. Much space was devoted in the press of both countries to the so-called Navarre Plan, which John Foster Dulles, then Secretary of State, explained to a Senate committee as being designed to "break the organized body of Communist aggression by the end of the 1955 fighting season." That, of course, like much that has come out of Washington about Viet-Nam since, was wildly wishful thinking. Navarre himself, once he had taken stock of the situation in his widely dispersed command, was a great deal less sanguine. In a secret report addressed to his government in 1953 and published in 1956 in his memoirs,[14] Navarre stated that the war simply could not be won in the military sense (just as the Korean War could not, without drawing Red China into it) and that all that could be hoped for was a *coup nul*—a draw.

And even that draw required an immediate reinforcement of the French Expeditionary Corps in such key fields as artillery and mobile infantry, merely to keep pace with the rapid build-up of Communist forces, thanks to the inflow of Chinese instructors and American equipment obtained in Korea, which had been at peace since July, 1953. Little has thus far been disclosed publicly about the agreements reached in 1952–53 between the United States and France regarding coordination of military strategy in the Far East. It is nevertheless known that the two allies realized that the Korean and Indochinese theaters of operations were interdependent battlefields, since in both, the enemy forces drew upon Red China for their major support. Although it has not been admitted publicly that the two allies exchanged formal agreements guaranteeing that neither would conclude a peace without the other, it has nevertheless been admitted by highly reliable French sources (and, at least once, mentioned before an American Congressional committee) that the United States

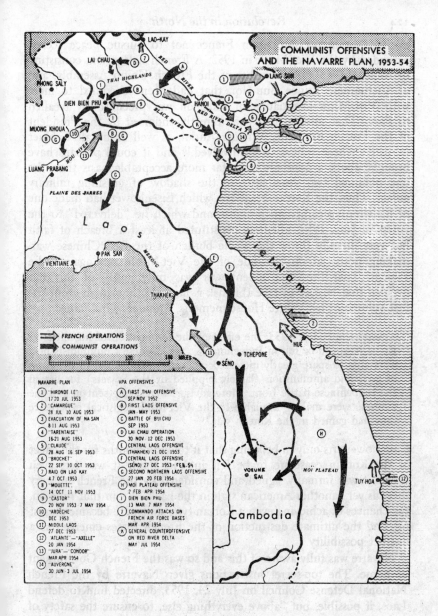

COMMUNIST OFFENSIVES
AND THE NAVARRE PLAN, 1953-54

FRENCH OPERATIONS
COMMUNIST OPERATIONS

0   50   100   150 MILES

NAVARRE PLAN

1 "HIRONDE LE"
   17-20 JUL 1953
2 "CAMARGUE"
   28 JUL-10 AUG 1953
3 EVACUATION OF NA SAN
   8-11 AUG 1953
4 "TARENTAISE"
   16-21 AUG 1953
5 "CLAUDE"
   28 AUG-16 SEP 1953
6 "BROCHET"
   22 SEP-10 OCT 1953
7 RAID ON LAO KAY
   4-7 OCT 1953
8 "MOUETTE"
   14 OCT-11 NOV 1953
9 "CASTOR"
   20 NOV 1953-7 MAY 1954
10 "ARDÈCHE"
   DEC 1953
11 MIDDLE LAOS
   27 DEC 1953
12 "ATLANTE — "AXELLE"
   20 JAN 1954
13 "JURA — CONDOR"
   MAR-APR 1954
14 "AUVERGNE"
   30 JUN-3 JUL 1954

VPA OFFENSIVES

A FIRST THAI OFFENSIVE
   SEP-NOV 1952
B FIRST LAOS OFFENSIVE
   JAN-MAY 1953
C BATTLE OF BUI CHU
   SEP 1953
D LAI CHAU OPERATION
   30 NOV-12 DEC 1953
E CENTRAL LAOS OFFENSIVE
   (THAKHEK) 21 DEC 1953
F CENTRAL LAOS OFFENSIVE
   (SÉNO) 27 DEC 1953 - FEB. 54
G SECOND NORTHERN LAOS OFFENSIVE
   27 JAN-20 FEB 1954
H MOI PLATEAU OFFENSIVE
   2 FEB-14 FEB 1954
I DIEN BIEN PHU
   13 MAR-7 MAY 1954
J COMMANDO ATTACKS ON
   FRENCH AIR FORCE BASES
   MAR-APR 1954
K GENERAL COUNTEROFFENSIVE
   ON RED RIVER DELTA
   MAY-JUL 1954

exerted strong pressure upon France not to pursue peace feelers extended by the Viet-Minh in 1952. A French delegation, consisting of Raphaël-Leygues, a member of the French Union Assembly, and of Vietnamese Prince Buu-Hoi, that had been scheduled to meet with Viet-Minh negotiators in Rangoon was precipitously recalled to Paris. That mission had been directly endorsed by the President of the French Republic, Vincent Auriol, as well as by all Cabinet ministers whose spheres were involved;[15] and it could perhaps have brought about a cease-fire on a far more acceptable basis than the one obtained two years later in the shadow of crushing military defeat. Thus, the Korean cease-fire, which Eisenhower had made one of his winning campaign promises and which he "delivered" to the voters in July, 1953, not only constituted at least a breach of faith but very literally threw the whole burden of the Red Chinese war-making potential on the side of the Viet-Minh and against the French. That President Eisenhower was fully aware of this but decided that he had to take this risk is now clearly evident from the first volume of his White House memoirs, *Mandate for Change:*

> Toward the end of 1953, the effect of the termination of hostilities in Korea began to be felt in Indochina . . . the Chinese Communists now were able to spare greatly increased quantities of matériel in the form of guns and ammunition (largely supplied by the Soviets) for use in the Indochinese battle front. More advisers were being sent in and the Chinese were making available to the Viet-Minh logistical experience they had gained in the Korean war.[16]

Eisenhower errs only in believing that it took six months for the effect of the Korean cease-fire to be felt in Viet-Nam. It was felt even before it was formally signed and considered by the French military there as yet "another American stab in the back." From that time on, the chances of achieving even a Korean-type stalemate became almost nil, and the ultimate destruction of the French forces emerged as a distinct possibility.

Navarre was fully aware of this and so was the French Government at home. The top-secret instructions given Navarre by the French National Defense Council on July 24, 1953, directed him to defend Laos, if possible, but "above everything else, to ensure the safety of our Expeditionary Corps." This Navarre set out to do by attempting to scrape together an operational reserve within the theater through the elimination of unnecessary static posts. At the same time, he sought to forestall the impending enemy build-up around the key Viet-Minh prize, the Red River Delta, by a series of rapid stabs designed to throw him off balance. The first part of the maneuver was successful: The airhead of Na-Sam was airlifted out on August 13 in such secrecy that the last French truck had been put down at the Hanoi airfield before the surprised Viet-Minh even attempted to occupy the deserted and useless position. The Thai tribal capital, Lai-Chau, was evacuated in similar fashion in December, 1953. At the same time, the Vietnamese National Army began to emerge from the limbo in which French checkreins and delays in American arms deliveries had left it. Gradually, whole sectors were transferred to Vietnamese military jurisdiction (notably the whole Trans-Bassac area of Cochinchina; Hung-Yen and Bui-Chu provinces, in North Viet-Nam; and Phan-Rang and Khanh-Hoa, in Central Viet-Nam, and a separate Vietnamese General Staff emerged under energetic General Nguyên Van Hinh, who had served as a colonel in the French Air Force.[17]

But all this came too little and too late. General Giap, too, had read the signs and knew he had to defeat the French before the impact of increased American aid could make itself felt and permit, as in Korea, the arming of a large indigenous force closely directed by Western units. Undeterred by Navarre's stabs,[18] Giap set about concentrating a battle force of four infantry divisions reinforced by the ill-famed 351st "Heavy Division" (a unit made up of two artillery regiments and one combat-engineer regiment) that was supposed to conquer all of Laos and perhaps overrun Cambodia, and then to join up with the Viet-Minh's southern bastion of Interzone V and carry the fight to the doors of Saigon. In the meantime, the 60,000 guerrillas and five regular regiments operating *inside* the "de Lattre Line" would wreak havoc in the Red River Delta and there paralyze French supply activities—essential to the support of Laos.

The plan, bold as it was, was executed like clockwork and succeeded in full. In a first stab by parts of the 304th and 325th Divisions, stealthily executed in December, 1953–January, 1954, all of central and south Laos was invaded. Indochina was cut in two at Thakhek on Christmas Day, 1953, with the help of Vietnamese "refugees" who crossed over from nearby complacent Thailand. Central Viet-Nam was cut off from Laos through the destruction of French posts along Roads 12 and 9, and the important Séno air base in south Laos had to be reinforced hurriedly by paratroops when

VPA Regiment 66 appeared seemingly out of nowhere in front of its gates. Two weeks later, the southernmost feelers of the VPA task force were encircling Voeune Sai in northeastern Cambodia, which proclaimed a state of mobilization. In the meantime, the main Viet-Minh task force readied itself for its major stab at northern Laos.

The stab had been foreseen by Navarre—but the only answer he could find to the problem was to create an airhead even larger than those he had evacuated the year before because they were a drain on supplies and manpower! Although admitting that it was a mediocre solution at best, Navarre felt that, while "it would not prevent light enemy detachments from roaming the countryside," it would leave "essential points" in French hands and thus prevent an outright invasion.[19] As it turned out, the "light enemy detachments" that roamed the Lao countryside in February, 1954, amounted to the bulk of Giap's battle force, while Navarre was frantically scraping together troops for an increasing number of airheads, including the new base at Dien Bien Phu, on the Lao-Vietnamese border, whose garrison increased from 9,000 to 15,094 men as the battle mounted in intensity. But as General Catroux (who had been governor general of Indochina in 1940) said after he had filed his report of inquiry on the battle of Dien Bien Phu: "There are no blocking positions in a country lacking European-type roads. . . . Dien Bien Phu [could] neither protect northern Laos nor exercise a mission of external aggressiveness."

Thus, Giap had succeeded in getting Navarre to fritter away his reserves into a dozen airheads around Indochina, from Muong-Sai, 100 miles north of Luang-Prabang, to Ankhé, on the Southern Mountain Plateau. Now Giap suddenly called off his northern attack and threw his four divisions on Dien Bien Phu. What happened there is history and need not be repeated here at length. It would be at least slim consolation if one could record that the battle of Dien Bien Phu saved any of the other vital objectives in Viet-Nam, but this was not the case. As early as February, 1954, the Viet-Minh 320th Division, which had recovered from its mauling of the previous September, began to infiltrate the southern corner of the Red River Delta, and by March, its full three regiments were inside the French main line of resistance. In an incredibly daring raid, Viet-Minh infiltrators, penetrating through the sewage system, entered the completely fortified airport of Haiphong–Cat-Bi and destroyed thirty-eight aircraft that were absolutely essential for the daily supply runs to the encircled fortresses. Late in March, the vital road and railroad between Hanoi and Haiphong were under daily attack along almost their whole length and their disruption threatened the resupply of Hanoi and the various large units depending upon it.

In the PMS, two regular VPA regiments, 108 and 803, operated in broad daylight, playing cat-and-mouse with the last remaining mobile combat team in the hill area, Mobile Group 100, made up of French volunteers who had recently returned from U.N. duty in Korea and who were totally bewildered by the incredible conditions of jungle war. The whole combat team was destroyed in one large ambush on June 24, 1954, and when hostilities ended, the Franco-Vietnamese hold on the PMS was reduced to a narrow pocket around Ban Mé Thuot and Dalat. Yet, in the midst of this chaos, with the French supply services stretched to the breaking point, Navarre decided to launch a counterthrust. "Operation Atlante" involved a seaborne landing at Tuy-Hoa, in the southern part of the Interzone V bastion. According to Navarre's own book, he decided upon this operation, launched in January, 1954, in order to draw enemy troops away from the main northern theaters—which demonstrates how Europe-oriented Navarre's thinking was. Even a cursory examination of all his predecessors' operations should have taught him that the Viet-Minh would never stand battle in an area so far away from its centers of strength but would simply wait for the moment when the French offensive ran out of steam (as it soon did). And in any case, Giap's troops from northern Laos could not have come to the succor of their comrades at Tuy-Hoa even if Giap had had the suicidal idea of trying it—as a passing glance at a terrain map of Viet-Nam would have readily shown. Thus "Atlante" merely ate into the last French reserves and the third-line French and Vietnamese troops used in the operation covered themselves with shame, while the young Vietnamese administrators made themselves hated for their arrogant attitude toward a population that had spent almost a decade under Communism.

At 0153 local time, on May 8, 1954, the last guns fell silent at Dien Bien Phu after a desperate bayonet charge of the Algerian and Foreign Legion garrison of strongpoint "Isabelle" had been smothered by the sheer numbers of the victorious Viet-Minh, and the war that had lasted eight years was almost over. A French survey mission, made up of Generals Ely and Salan, went to Viet-Nam and recommended—in a top-secret report that was "leaked" to both right-wing and Communist French elements within days—that France immediately evacuate all of North Viet-Nam and concentrate on the

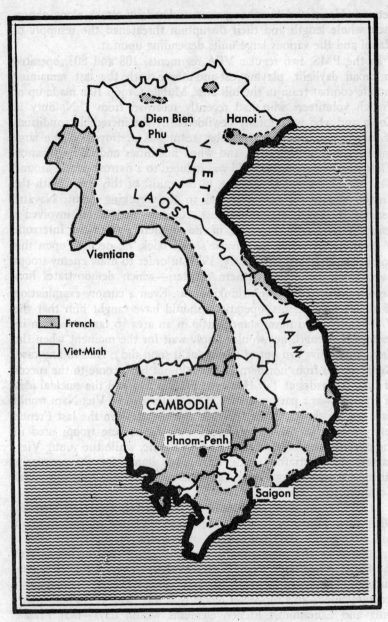

INDOCHINA, JULY, 1954

Dien Bien Phu

Hanoi

VIET-

LAOS

Vientiane

NAM

French

Viet-Minh

CAMBODIA

Phnom-Penh

Saigon

areas south of the 16th parallel. The last major battle of the war, "Operation Auvergne," began on June 11, as the French and Vietnamese troops in the southern part of the Red River Delta began to fight their way toward the Hanoi-Haiphong life line, abandoning to the tender mercies of the VPA close to 1.5 million Vietnamese Catholics.

The Indochina War ended on July 21, 1954, at 0343 Geneva time. It had cost the French Union Forces a total of 172,000 casualties and forever broke France's hold on Viet-Nam. The Viet-Minh's casualties probably ran three times as high, and perhaps another 250,000 Vietnamese civilians were killed during the fighting.

And as during the bitter 200-year-long feud between the Trinh and the Nguyên, the rival Viet-Nams began to go their separate ways. In the South, a shattered nationalist regime had to make its start almost from scratch, for the remaining shreds of the imperial structure had disintegrated in the nonchalant hands of the last Nguyên emperor, and 860,000 northern refugees began pouring into Saigon. In the North, grim-faced Viet-Minh commissars exchanged correct military salutes with grim-faced French officers as tricolors were hauled down in town after town and fort after fort in the shrinking French perimeter.

In the areas south of the 17th parallel, similar scenes were going on, but in reverse: There, Viet-Minh fighters, who for eight years had bitterly held onto stretches of swamp in the Camau Peninsula or hills and jungles in Interzone V, now came gingerly into the daylight to walk to the Polish and French ships that were to bring them and their families northward. A smaller group of elite guerrillas never came out into the open; it quietly buried its well-greased weapons, hid its portable radio transmitters, and simply returned for the time being to the humdrum tasks of sowing and harvesting rice.

On May 15, 1955, the first Indochina War ended as the last French ship left the outer harbor of Haiphong in North Viet-Nam. By accident or design, its name was *Espérance—Hope.*

8

Garrison State

E VEN before the outbreak of hostilities, the D.R.V.N. had prepared the terrain politically so that it would have a monopoly on all elements likely to emerge as leading members in an independent Vietnamese government—or in a "resistance government," in the event of war with the French.

In a series of lightning-like raids in the summer of 1946, Vo Nguyên Giap, Minister of the Interior (i.e., the security police), neutralized the armed nationalist groups one by one, forcing such leaders as Vu Hong Khanh, who had fought against the French in the abortive 1930 rebellion, to flee once more to China, never to return. On July 11, 1946, following a pattern that was to be repeated from North Korea to Czechoslovakia, Giap "purged" the last nationalist leaders still free in Hanoi and closed down Viet-Nam, their only remaining news organ. When it resumed on July 18, it was the same paper with the same masthead—and even the same editorial staff. Only its "line" had changed: Its front page was devoted to a groveling "constructive self-critique," and the rest of the paper contained only encomiums for the Viet-Minh regime it had lambasted a week earlier.

.There still remained the *Gleichschaltung* of the National Assembly. Among the 444 members elected in January, there were, theoretically, still 70 opposition members. When the Assembly convened for its second session—its first meeting; in March, had been concerned only with approving Ho Chi Minh and his ministers—on October 28, 1946, there were only 291 members present and of those, according to neutral press correspondents, only 37 were of the opposition. When one of the opposition candidates, with touching naïveté, asked about the fate of his colleagues, Cu Huy Can, the Viet-Minh Minister of Agriculture, answered from the Government bench that "they had been arrested with the approval of the Permanent Committee for common-law crimes."[1] That foolhardy legislator mysteriously disappeared with all but two of his colleagues while the session was in progress, and while their parliamentary immunity was supposedly in force. When the National Assembly finally voted on the D.R.V.N.'s first constitution, on November 8, 1946, more than a dozen of the Viet-Minh's own legislators had disappeared, and the final vote was 240 to 2..On the following day, Ho promulgated the constitution, which remained in force (in theory if not in fact) until January 1, 1960. Its text, like many earlier Communist constitutions (including that of the Soviet Union of 1936), contains several basic democratic principles. In this, Ho again showed his profound realism: The American observers were right in Hanoi, General Leclerc's armor was in Haiphong, Chiang Kai-shek's troops were just across the border, and Mao Tse-tung and his Red Chinese troops were still bottled up in Yenan and, for all Ho knew, would stay there for another decade. Thus, many of the constitution's passages had a ring that was closer to Jefferson than to Stalin. Here is a sentence from the Preamble:

Permeated by the spirit of unity symbolized in the struggle of the entire nation and manifested in an enlarged and democratic regime, Viet-Nam now goes forward confidently in consonance with the progressive movements of the world and the peaceful aspirations of mankind.

This is a far cry from the hate-filled, doctrinaire indictment of the West that serves as a Preamble to the 1960 constitution, drafted when one might assume that the regime, now solidly in the saddle, could have afforded to show some leniency in linguistics, if in nothing else:

> But French imperialism, supported by American imperialism, again lighted up the flames of invasion war in the hope of enslaving our country a second time. Under the direction of the Party of the Working Class and of the D.R.V.N. Government, our entire people rose unanimously to participate in the war of salvation. . . .

The remainder of the 1946 constitution provides the traditional liberties of speech, religion, and free movement of all citizens; the equality of all citizens and the protection of racial minorities; a limited habeas corpus; and free and compulsory education. The voting age for both sexes was eighteen; the age for eligibility to office was twenty-one; and amendments to the constitution were subject to popular approval by referendum. The People's Parliament, a unicameral body elected for three years at a ratio of 1 deputy per 50,000 inhabitants, had, in addition to the usual law-making powers, copied provisions from the French model regarding the election of the chief executive. Both the President and the Vice-President of the D.R.V.N. were to be elected by a two-thirds majority from among the membership of the Parliament; the President, in turn, was to choose the Premier from among the deputies and submit his choice for their approval, in the manner of the Third and Fourth French republics. The Premier, also along French lines, would then pick his whole Cabinet—save the under secretaries—from the members of the People's Parliament. As under the French system of that time, power was held by the Premier and his Cabinet.

In one important point, however, the D.R.V.N. constitution of 1946 differed from the French model and openly borrowed from that of the Soviet Union. That was in the inclusion of a Permanent Committee in the National Assembly and People's Parliament. Articles 36–39 of the constitution provided extensive legislative powers for the Permanent Committee in the absence of the regular legislature —and that legislature was to sit for a total of less than 100 session days in the first sixteen years of its existence! In fact, after its November, 1946, meeting, the legislature failed to meet again until December, 1953, when it was convened for a single day somewhere in the jungle to vote unanimously for a sweeping land-reform law. In fact, it never transformed itself into a People's Parliament, for the original constitutional assembly acted as a temporary legislature until the first regular legislative elections, held on May 8, 1960, the sixth anniversary of the victory over the French at Dien Bien Phu.

Similarly, none of the guarantees and freedoms contained in the 1946 constitution was ever put into effect, and even the basic structural features were not respected. Ho Chi Minh simultaneously held the posts of President and Premier until September 20, 1955, when he relinquished the Premiership to his faithful companion Pham Van Dong, without, however, relinquishing any real power. That, again contrary to the constitution, remained in Ho's hands. The Permanent Committee was presided over by Ton Duc Thang. The Viet-Nam People's Army had remained in the hands of Vo Nguyên Giap since its inception on December 22, 1944, as the "Armed Propaganda Brigade for Liberation."

To be sure, the Ho Chi Minh regime contained (and still does) some non-Communists: the Socialist Hoang Ming Giam, who was Foreign Minister as long as the D.R.V.N. had no foreign relations but was shunted to the Ministry of Culture in 1954, as soon as some serious negotiating began; the Catholic Nguyên Manh Ha, a son-in-law of the French Communist deputy Marrane, who held the Ministry of Economics in 1946 but has preferred since then to profess his Viet-Minh sympathies from the more congenial climes of Paris and Geneva, where he acts as a go-between for various Vietnamese exile groups. But from the very beginning of the North Vietnamese revolution, the *real* levers of power have been in the hands of old-line ICP members. Outside observers who failed to see this were either blinded by their own partisan views or simply ill-informed.[2] The D.R.V.N.'s major success, however, lay not in the creation on paper of a central government, but in the effective control of much of the countryside—*despite its occupation by a large Western army* —through the establishment of small but efficient administrative units that duplicated the existing Franco-Vietnamese administration. The French call this administrative network *hiérarchies parallèles*, i.e., a clandestine authority that annuls—or, on the contrary, reinforces—the effect of the legal authority. These, rather than the existence of guerrilla battalions, were the source of France's defeat and have also been the source of South Viet-Nam's difficulties from 1957 to the present. Since the parallel hierarchies are the true innovation of the Indochina War, it will be worthwhile to examine them more closely.

"Hierarchies Parallèles"

The establishment of parallel hierarchies can take two forms: the utilization of existing administrative structures through the infiltration of subversive individuals, or the creation of altogether new clandestine structures designed to take over full administrative responsibilities when political and military conditions are ripe. (This was thoroughly studied by the French Army and reported on in 1957.[3]) Starting in World War II, both systems have been used extensively, sometimes simultaneously with, but more often subseqent to, the infiltration of subversive individuals preceding the creation of an independent apparatus.

In Nazi-occupied France, for example, the first step involved placing anti-Vichy Resistance members in key posts of the pro-German administration. With the establishment of the CNR (Conseil National de la Résistance), in 1942, began the creation of a full-fledged nationwide parallel network of underground administrative organs. If the process of simply paralleling the existing administration does not suffice, then the underground operators will usually resort to creating new organizations whose sole purpose is to bring ever-larger segments of the population into contact with the movement and under its eventual control. As the above-cited French Army study on the subject said in evaluating the Viet-Minh's superb job of parallel organization:

> The Lien-Viet [organization of Viet-Minh subsidiary groups] included youth groups, groups for mothers, farmers, workers, "resistant" Catholics, war veterans, etc. It could just as well have included associations of flute players or bicycle racers; the important point was that no one escaped regimentation and that the [normal] territorial hierarchy was thus complemented by another which watched the former and was in turn watched by it—both of them being watched in turn from the outside and inside by the security services and the Party. The individual caught in the fine mesh of such a net has no chance whatever of preserving his independence.[4]

In the creation of its own grid of territorial administration, the D.R.V.N. proceeded with a great deal of caution. Far from disturbing existing structures (as its South Vietnamese counterpart has done—creating numerous new provinces with unfamiliar names and giving well-known cities new names, even though the old names were specifically Vietnamese and bore no association with colonialism), the Viet-Minh simply took them over from within. To this day, as far as this writer could ascertain, only two provincial boundaries in North Viet-Nam have been disturbed; the farmers go to the same district or provincial towns for their dealings with the administration as they have for eighty years. This has an undeniable psychological importance, for it leaves the bulk of the population in an administrative environment to which it has been inured—even though the system has been entirely changed from within.

Since 1945, at every level of the local administration, there has been an "Administrative Committee," which becomes more complex as the level of administration rises. At village level, it is usually composed of five members: a president, a vice-president in charge of police, a secretary in charge of all paperwork, a committee member in charge of finances, and another in charge of public works and agriculture. During the war years, when the village also had its own guerrilla unit, the vice-president (who often was a veteran of the VPA and thus had military training) would also be in charge of the village "self-defense" group. The village committee (*Uy Ban Hanh Chinh*, or UBHC-*Xà*—"*xà*" meaning "village") would be responsible to the next higher unit, entirely of Viet-Minh creation, the *lien-xà* (intervillage, or village group), whose UBHC was more sophisticated. It or the next higher unit, the *huyên* (district), would, during the war years, include an element of military command, and its committee and all those above it would be known as "Committees for Resistance and Administration" (*Uy Ban Khang Chien/ Hanh Chinh*, or UBKC/HC). Above the UBKC/HC-*Huyên* would be that of the province (*tinh*), and beyond the province would be a new grouping of several provinces entirely of Viet-Minh origin, which would be known as a zone (*khu*). In 1945–46, all Viet-Nam was split into fourteen zones, each under the command of a VPA colonel or brigadier. After the outbreak of the war, the apparatus proved too cumbersome. The *khu* were merged in March, 1948, into six interzones (*lien-khu*, followed by a Roman numeral), in whose UBKC/HC's the People's Army definitely predominated over the civilian element. Of the six *lien-khu*, I and II covered the Tonkinese mountain areas; III covered the Red River Delta; IV all of northern Central Viet-Nam; V the remainder of Central Viet-Nam, but actually the lowland provinces, which constituted the Viet-Minh bastion there; and VI covered Cochinchina. One unnumbered *lien-khu*, known simply as the "Left Bank," covers the northern part of the Red River Delta to the hill zone. Since May, 1955, and August, 1956, respectively, LK's I and II have been autonomous ethnic minority areas and are no longer referred to by their numbers.

The local administration was "demilitarized" (at least on paper) by a law of May 31, 1958, which divorced the military command zones from the UBKC/HC's; the latter again became simple "Administrative Committees," or UBHC's. Under the normal peacetime structure, each such committee, as in the Soviet model, is responsible to a locally elected People's Council, which, in turn, selects the committee members from its own numbers. Such local elections took place in North Viet-Nam in 1957–59, with predictable results. The fact that, in Hanoi itself, one of the deputy mayors, Tran Van Lai, was the town's mayor under the Japanese administration and that several People's Council members are delegates from the rump Socialist and Democratic parties still surviving in North Viet-Nam hardly modifies the over-all picture of total Communist control. As it turned out, it took the D.R.V.N. until October 27, 1962, to pass the law organizing People's Councils and Administrative Committees at all levels on a permanent basis; and very soon thereafter, on November 24, 1962, the Party newspaper *Nhan-Dan* carried a long article airing the complaints of the population about the ineffectualness of the People's Councils:

> People's Council delegates have seldom acted as local representatives to go deeply into local economic, political, and cultural problems . . . to listen to the electors' views, to know their desires. and to get a clear idea of the people's conditions of life. . . .
> . . . delegates have not set times to hold conferences with the people.
> . . . these shortcomings have somewhat loosened the ties between the government and the people and between the electorate and their representatives, thus indirectly limiting the people's right as masters of the government.

The local committees of the Communist Party—the ICP was "dissolved" in November, 1946, but was reborn as the Vietnamese Workers' Party (Viet-Nam Dang Lao-Dong, or DLD) in February, 1951—constitute yet another parallel hierarchy, which, in actual fact, controls all the others and has its own cells, committees, and assemblies from the top government ranks to the most humble village. In the view of the group of French officers who prepared the previously cited report:

> In the space of a few years, the Communist Party . . . has created a territorial organization that is both highly centralized and very flexible and which creates *unity of command* at every level from the village up. . . . Furthermore, they control the [administrative] hierarchy via the ever-present members of the Party. Thus, they are able to conduct the war as they please, without fear of the opposition or of "deviations."

Obviously, that whole elaborate structure would be of little practical use without its enforcement apparatus, but here, also, the D.R.V.N. has done its job well. Three specialized units deal very effectively with the problem: the Cong-an, the Trinh Sat, and the Dich-Van. The first is simply the civilian secret police, which operates like all other organizations of its kind. The second is the military-intelligence apparatus; an MI company is attached to each combat division, and MI groups (one sergeant and three NCO's) operate all the way down to company level. They do excellent reconnaissance work; infiltrators of the Trinh Sat precede every movement of a VPA regular unit, often by months. But it is the Dich-Van that is by far the most interesting and the least understood component of the VPA control apparatus—and by far the most dangerous.[5] The term itself stands for "Moral Intervention," a euphemism for psychological warfare but with an added "punch" that is implied in the polite phrase "armed propaganda." DV groups operate in small teams; their job is the psychological preparation of the enemy unit or territory through means ranging from friendly persuasion to murder with especially deterrent effects.

It is the Dich-Van operations which create havoc in South Viet-Nam and which, for obvious reasons, neither American helicopters nor U.S. Special Forces can cope with; the DV's make themselves felt at a specifically "Vietnamese" level of fighting upon which the foreigner simply has no effect. It will be a Dich-Van group that will capture the mayor of a recalcitrant village and cut his body to ribbons, or leave his head dangling from a bamboo pole in the middle of the village (with a note attached to it warning that anyone who takes it down will suffer the same fate); it will be a DV unit that will burst into a village meeting, call out the names of five boys who recently joined the South Vietnamese Government's youth movement, and gun them down after the reading of a "death sentence"; it was a DV operation that, on January 10, 1962, captured 100 youth-group leaders in South Viet-Nam, brainwashed them for several weeks, and then released them. Seven "incorrigibles" were held back and probably murdered. It is *that* type of operation—*the violent act for psychological rather than military reasons*—which is the source of the success of the Viet-Minh against the French-Vietnamese forces of the 1940's and 1950's and against the American-Vietnamese forces of the 1960's. This is particularly true in all combat phases where the Viet-Minh has not yet achieved its basic requirements for mobile warfare or the "general counteroffensive" (see Chapter 7).

Those are precisely the tactics the French fanatics of the Secret Army Organization in Algeria learned from the Viet-Minh: Their seemingly wanton murders and plastic bombings could not win the war, but they very nearly wrecked the cease-fire. In South Viet-Nam's guerrilla war of the 1960's, the DV's role is not to defeat a Vietnamese division, with its American advisers and with U.S. Air Force planes on call, in a Dien Bien Phu-type battle. The Dich-Van will simply go on murdering village chiefs, youth leaders, teachers, and antimalaria teams—thus isolating the Saigon government from the countryside. And in a revolutionary war, that is precisely what separates victory from defeat: the control of the rural population.

And once the system of mutual snooping and denunciation has taken hold and the little village has become a veritable empire of fear, the Dich-Van can move on, its job done. The little quiet men of the regular secret police will come in and establish their network of permanent agents. The parallel hierarchies, now solidly entrenched, can be counted upon to do the rest.

POSTWAR ORGANIZATION

The assumption of open control over 62,000 square miles of Vietnamese territory (as against South Viet-Nam's 65,000) by the D.R.V.N. brought in its wake problems that the guerrilla fighters of yesteryear did not quite know how to cope with. It is far easier to blow up a water main than to run a water-purification plant, and to sabotage the locomotive roundhouse of Hanoi than to run trains on time. Also, many of the cadres succumbed to the appurtenances of their new-found power, just as their opposite numbers in capitalist South Viet-Nam did; apparently "socialist morality" was easier to preserve in the mountain hideouts, where temptation was simply unavailable, than in the open plains. Thus, late in 1955, the Party's own organ *Nhan-Dan* openly admitted that the National Trade Service of Ho Chi Minh's native province of Nghé-An had embezzled 700 million piasters (more than $1 million at the exchange rate then prevailing), the drug-making factory of Interzone IV had embezzled 37 million piasters, and the Public Works division of Nam-Dinh had diverted 16 million to unauthorized purposes (such as building houses for its officials). A subsequent full-scale investigation of the Nam-Dinh provincial administration (reported in *Nhan-Dan* on March 22, 1956) showed that 20.4 million piasters had been misappropriated and another 578 million had been "wasted," along with 35,000 labor days and 444 tons of rice.

In addition, the D.R.V.N. simply lacked the skills necessary for proper management of the vast industrial establishments it suddenly inherited: the textile plants of Nam-Dinh, the cement plants of Hai-phong, the Hon-Gay and Dong-Trieu coal mines—not to speak of dozens of power plants and power stations, locomotive and streetcar workshops, and complicated flood-control and irrigation systems. Until the first graduating class of 633 engineers left Hanoi Poly-technical Institute in December, 1961, the 12,000 textile workers at Nam-Dinh had *no* engineers at all (the French had employed 47 engineers or supervisors), while the Hon-Gay coal-mine complex was under the supervision of *two* "technicians" where the French had used 150 engineers and supervisors to control the operations of 11,000 miners. Some of those shortages were of the D.R.V.N.'s own making: At Hon-Gay, the supervising French engineers had stayed on for two years but were never allowed to visit the coal mines. They, along with all the other Frenchmen who had accepted the difficult task of staying behind at the request of their home government or even of the regime itself, finally left, discouraged by the constant harassment and suspicion. Soviet-bloc technicians never fully filled the techno-logical gap, possibly because they were not available in sufficient numbers to be spared for a relatively low-priority area, or perhaps be-cause the Viet-Minh was reluctant to admit even to its bloc associates how much of the trained elite had moved south in 1954 and how ill-adapted to industrial production problems the guerrilla leader-ship was.

In the field of government as well, the return of peace brought its share of problems: The simplified structure that had held the move-ment together during the war period could not suffice now that cities with several hundred thousand inhabitants, such as Hanoi and Hai-phong, had to be administered. Also, the Viet-Minh leaders who had fought in isolated pockets south of the 17th parallel—men such as Pham Van Bach, Nguyên Duy Trinh, and Ung Van Khiem—de-manded their rightful share in the spoils, and the economic disloca-tion of the northern region demanded immediate control by energetic administrators. The D.R.V.N. Government no doubt had no wish to repeat the grievous errors it had committed in 1945 in that field, when, in an act of sheer demagoguery, it had abolished all taxes (hoping to survive on the customs levies of nonexistent imports) and had found itself faced with a starving population and a bankrupt administration.

Through the initial reforms carried out in September, 1955, the new Premier, Pham Van Dong, found himself flanked by two Vice-Premiers; while new separate ministries of Industry, Commerce, Public Health and Social Welfare, Public Works, and even Culture appeared on the government's table of organization. That structure was further broadened as the state took over the reins of the whole economy. In December, 1958, a Directorate for Planning was established under Nguyên Duy Trinh, along with separate ministries for Internal Trade and Foreign Trade, and one for the conservation of water resources. That executive structure remained in force until July 15, 1960.

In the legislative field, the return of peace to the D.R.V.N. had not brought about an increase in the standing of the National Assembly. Repeated promises for new elections had not been kept, in spite of the fact that total membership in the body had dropped from an initial 444 to 202 at tne ninth session, in December, 1958. In fact, the National Assembly came as close to criticism as was conceivable under the circumstances when it voted at the January, 1957, session (i.e., a few months after the abortive November, 1956, peasant rebellion, of which more will be said later) a resolution in which, among other items, it requested that "parliamentary immunities as provided under Article 40 of the Constitution of 1946 be guaranteed." Other deputies complained that there was a definite "lack of respect" among the members of the executive branch for the National Assembly, with the result that laws passed by that body in January had still not been implemented by July, in spite of the fact that the constitution provided for the promulgation of a law within ten days after its legislative approval.[6]

Finally, by December, 1958, sufficient pressure had built up for Ho Chi Minh himself to enter the picture as the conciliator among the contending factions—a role for which he seemed destined since his Paris days of the 1920's. A constitutional-reform committee, which had been perfunctorily working at a revision of the 1946 document since December, 1956, was suddenly broadened and saw its task change toward framing a totally *new* constitution. The public was invited to send suggestions to the committee, and allegedly more than 1,700 such communications were received from citizens throughout the country. In the course of the twenty-third and final session of the committee, held in Hanoi January 13–15, 1959, Ho himself broke the deadlock that appeared to have developed between the "jurists" of the committee, who favored a simple statement of guiding principles, and the "politicians," who wanted above all a propaganda document that could be employed in the impending struggle against the rival regime in South Vietnam. As always throughout his life, Ho sided with the advocates of the pragmatic approach against the "theorists." The constitutional project, which was made public on April 1, 1959, was, beyond the important structural changes it heralded, a virulent and spiteful indictment of the West, as has already been shown. But surprisingly enough, it was exactly what its name said: a *project* or a draft, subject to important changes. It is not known whether the imperfections of the document were deliberately "built in" so that later on it would be possible to make it appear that the changes that had been made were the result of public suggestions, or whether the draft was *really* meant to be discussed. The fact remains that the constitution that was finally promulgated on January 1, 1960, showed some marked differences in wording and even in structure from the 1959 draft.

THE 1960 CONSTITUTION*

As I have already said, the long Preamble (no doubt the longest ever written, since it is, in fact, a complete history of Viet-Nam since 1940, as seen through Communist eyes) is little more than a propaganda leaflet. Its transitional character is emphasized by its permeation with the "cult of personality" to an extent that probably no other Soviet-bloc nation, including Albania, would accept. Reference is made in the text to the "farsighted leadership . . . of President Ho Chi Minh," which shows both the control of the man over his Party machine and the Party's confidence in its own stability.

In Article 3, the D.R.V.N. openly acknowledges the polyethnic character of Viet-Nam, and it is the only Vietnamese regime to realize that mountain tribes of Malayo-Polynesian origin cannot be treated like Vietnamese lowland rice farmers. Thus, the country is defined as being "one nation composed of several peoples," and the mountaineers are guaranteed the right to preserve their mores, languages, and writing systems. As in the other polyethnic states of the Soviet bloc, this approach to the minorities problem has gone beyond the realm of theory and has given the D.R.V.N. a competitive advantage over all its neighbors, who still persist in a forced-assimilation policy.

The great innovation of the 1960 constitution is its Section II,

* For text, see Appendix I.

entirely devoted to the new Communist structure of the economy—and significantly placed *ahead* of the section dealing with the fundamental rights of the citizen. Its Article 9 clearly states the economic aims of the D.R.V.N. as "progressing gradually from the regime of people's democracy toward that of socialism." Although the right to private. property is still guaranteed (Article 18), the D.R.V.N. "severely forbids" its use "for the purpose of sabotaging the State Economic Plan," and reserves for itself the right to buy or "requisition" all private property in case of "absolute necessity" (Article 20).

Section III, dealing with the rights of the citizen, contains the usual references to basic freedoms, including inviolability of the home and of private correspondence (Article 28), as well as the right to complain against arbitrary or unjust decisions of the state (Article 29). Among the duties listed in that section are those of paying one's taxes (Article 41) and of serving in the armed forces (Article 42). The latter article suffered a curious change between 1959 and 1960. The 1959 version contained a phrase taken verbatim from the Soviet constitution of 1936: "Treason against the Fatherland being considered by the People the most heinous of crimes, traitors shall be severely punished." No trace of that phrase remains in the final approved version of 1960, which may represent a victory of constitutional "purists" who may have thought that penalties for treason, as for any other crime, should be subject to the provisions of the penal code and not to a constitutional provision.

Section IV concerns the powers of the National Assembly (which permanently retained its revolutionary name, dropping the term "People's Parliament"), described as "the highest organ of power in the D.R.V.N." (Article 43). Its powers are routine and largely modeled on those of the Supreme Soviet, with the bulk of the real powers going to a permanent "Committee on Current Affairs" which is a close copy of the Soviet Presidium. Except for constitutional amendments, which require a two-thirds majority of all members of the Assembly (Article 112), "all laws and all other decisions" of the Assembly are taken by a simple majority vote of one-half the total membership of the Assembly plus one vote (Article 48). Likewise, the Committee on Current Affairs operates on a simple majority basis—although thus far neither of the two bodies has been known to vote with anything less than full unanimity and standing ovations.

In the field of Presidential powers, Section V goes perhaps further than any other Communist constitution; it grants Presidential powers that have a curious resemblance to those given General de Gaulle

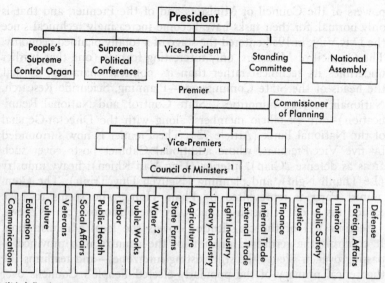

THE GOVERNMENT OF NORTH VIET-NAM, 1962-63

(1) Including the Inspector General of the Government and the Director of the National Bank

(2) Also Hydroelectric Power

under the French constitution of the Fifth Republic, of September 28, 1958. Under Article 66, the President of the D.R.V.N. "may, if he deems it necessary, participate at and preside over all the meetings of the Council of Ministers." This indeed reduces the role of the Premier to that of a "first minister."[7] Also, the post of the Vice-President was enlarged in comparison to the 1959 draft, which left him reduced to "replacing the President in some limited cases." Under the redrafted Article 68, he may "replace by proxy the President in all of his powers in each of the organs of government." Article 70 also provides for the Vice-President's assumption of Presidential powers if the President were to be compelled to take a "long rest" for health reasons, or if the post became vacant.

Article 67 introduces a completely new constitutional element in the form of a Special Political Council. It is composed of the President and his Vice-President, the Premier, the President of the Committee on Current Affairs of the National Assembly, "and other important members"; its duty consists in "examining the great problems of the state." The opinions of the Special Political Council are then transmitted for "deliberation and action" to the legislature and the executive branch. All this considerably reduces the scope of powers of the Council of Ministers and of the Premier, and that is only normal, for their tasks have become increasingly technical since the D.R.V.N. in 1958 entered the stage of a totally planned economy. The Council of Ministers' only interesting feature (one that further underlines its technical rather than its political character) is that the heads of the State Commissions—Planning, Scientific Research, Nationalities (i.e., minorities), State Control, and National Reunification)—are ex officio members, along with the Director-General of the National Bank (Article 72). The Premier is now surrounded by five Vice-Premiers, whose additional Cabinet posts cover such areas as defense (Giap), interior (Ung Van Khien), heavy industry (Lê Thanh Nghi), and planning (Nguyên Duy Trinh). The Communist Party is represented by Pham Hung, who seems to have earned his Vice-Premiership simply by the orthodoxy of his views.

Section VII of the constitution covers the local administration. It confirms the territorial division of the country into provinces—passing over in silence the still-existing interzones—and reaffirms the theoretical primacy of the popularly elected People's Councils over the executive UBHC's of their own echelon and all echelons below them (Article 85). In one field, however, the powers of the UBHC's were reduced—in comparison both to the real wartime powers they held and to the powers granted them in the draft constitution of 1959—and that was in the field of justice. Throughout the Indochina War, the president, vice-president, and secretary of the village UBHC had constituted the basic juridical organ as well, in the form of a Conciliation Committee. The 1959 draft was to extend that principle of executive interference with the judiciary even further by granting the People's Council at every echelon the power to impeach the presiding judges of the corresponding tribunal (Article 82 of the draft). No mention of such powers is made in the 1960 version of the constitution, although Article 104 states that the tribunals are "responsible" to the People's Councils.

The "Autonomous Zones," in which the majority of the ethnic minorities live, have limited self-government, which includes the administration of their own budgets and even the creation of self-defense forces. Special legislation passed by their People's Assemblies requires approval of the Committee on Current Affairs of the National Assembly (Article 95).

Another important organ in the new administration is the National Defense Council, whose functions resemble those of the National Security Council in the United States. It is headed by Ho himself, with Pham Van Dong and General Giap acting as vice-presidents; the membership includes two other senior generals of the VPA, the Minister of Public Security (i.e., police), the Minister of Heavy Industry, and two of the most experienced guerrilla leaders of yesteryear—General Chu Van Tan, the Thô tribal chieftain who corralled the fierce mountain tribesmen of northeastern Tongking for Ho, and Nguyên Duy Trinh, the tough Central Vietnamese who defended Interzone V for nine long years.

The newly created Cabinet posts further emphasize the control of the state over ever-widening sectors of the North Vietnamese economy: Thus, the Ministry of Agriculture was divided into separate departments for Agriculture and State Farms; Industry was split into Heavy and Light Industries; Interior separated into Interior (i.e., Administration) and Public Security; and the once rather rural Ministry of Water Conservancy and Forestry gave way to a more industrial Ministry for Irrigation and Hydraulic Power. New departments are likely to be created as economic activities diversify or private initiative withers away.

The judiciary of the D.R.V.N. receives a somewhat larger place in the new constitution than in the 1946 document. According to Article 97, the military tribunals are now part of the regular judiciary and presumably subject to the regular appeals procedures, and all judgeships are subject to election (Article 98); Article 100 guarantees the "independent powers" of the courts. That assertion conflicts, however, with Article 104, which stipulates that the Supreme Court is "responsible" to the National Assembly, or to its Committee on Current Affairs when the former is not in session, and "must report its activities to it." A similar responsibility of the lower courts to the People's Councils has already been mentioned.

Finally, provision was made for a new control apparatus, which seems to derive from the Communist Party "Control Commissions," the Chinese Kuomintang's "Control *Yuan*," and the Soviet "Procurator" system. Called "People's Control Organs" (Articles 105–8), they appear to have a civil and a military division and are supposed to "watch the execution of the laws" by the whole executive branch "as well as by the citizens." Presumably, they are a law unto themselves, with all the lower echelons being responsible only to the People's Supreme Control Organ which, in turn, is theoretically responsible only to the National Assembly and its Committee on Current Affairs. A law passed on July 11, 1960, on the organization of the People's Control Organs, clearly shows the all-inclusive powers of these new bodies: They "bring to justice all cases subject to inquiry, may suspend prosecution and may participate in judicial operations, and may appeal judgments of lower courts to higher tribunals." Pham Van Bach, who led the Viet-Minh guerrillas in South Viet-Nam until the Geneva cease-fire of 1954, became the first head of the People's Control Organs. He was well known for his pitiless repression of "counterrevolutionary" activities while Secretary of State for Police and Security in the Ministry of the Interior, from 1955 to 1960, and his new appointment gives a clear indication of the scope of the new organization.

The same may be said for the president of the D.R.V.N.'s new Supreme Court, Hoang Quôc Viet. He has no legal training whatever but was the leader of the Vietnamese Communist labor union since its creation on August 20, 1946. An old-line Communist who had spent five years in French jails, he took an early interest (perhaps because of his acquaintance with colonial justice) in the D.R.V.N.'s judicial system. In 1946, he wrote a now-famous circular addressed to the courts, chiding them for a too-literal application of the law; in his view, it was their duty to put "out of commission the enemies of the people, and not, by applying to the letter some obsolete text, to let them escape from just punishment of their crimes."

With the text of the new constitution on the books, all that remained was for the D.R.V.N. to apply it. This was done in the spring and summer of 1960.

THE NEW REGIME

At 7 A.M. on May 8, 1960, the sirens began to sound throughout North Viet-Nam, and the country's 5.6 million voters, many of whom had spent part of the night in front of the polling places (not so much out of patriótism as to be able to get in a full day's work at the rice fields), began to deposit their ballots in the official urns for the first time since January, 1946. By the time the polling places (there were no booths to ensure secrecy) closed, at 7 P.M., 99.85 per cent of all eligible voters had cast their ballots for members of the Vietnamese Workers' (i.e., Communist) Party and, in Hanoi, for a sprinkling of carefully screened "national bourgeois" candidates of the socialist and democratic parties of North Viet-Nam. A new electoral law had solved the age-old problem of all democracies— overrepresentation of the rural electoral districts—with a provision that gave the rural areas 1 deputy per 30,000 voters, while the cities and newly created industrial towns received 1 deputy for each 10,000.

Thus, Hanoi, with 4 per cent of the total population of the country, was allotted almost 10 per cent of the electoral seats. Finally, 458 candidates disputed a total of 404 seats. The mandates of 18 deputies from areas south of the 17th parallel were automatically renewed, making a total of 422 members in the new National Assembly.[8]

On July 7, 1960, the deputies met to elect their new officers and also the heads of new Cabinet departments and other constitutional organs created since January. It immediately became apparent that Ho Chi Minh had lost none of his effective control over the machinery and that he was, in any case, not yet ready to transfer the mantle of leadership to the shoulders of an eager young successor. The D.R.V.N.'s Vice-Presidency went to the elderly Ton Duc Thang (born in 1882). The presidency of the National Assembly went to the old Party faithful Truong Chinh, removed from the secretary generalship of the Lao-Dong (Communist Party) after the land-reform errors of 1956 but on the upswing again, probably at the behest of his friends in Peking. Pressure from the same source was presumably responsible for giving the vice-presidency of the Committee on Current Affairs to Hoang Van Hoan, who had been ambassador to Peking for a long period.

It was likewise worthy of note that Lê Duan, the up-and-coming Party bureaucrat who, as a member of the younger generation, had not been openly embroiled in the Moscow-Peking tug of war, was given no government job, although he had run for election and had won his constituency with an honorable 97 per cent of the vote (Ho Chi Minh had received 99.91 per cent). Apparently, this was but another of Ho's maneuvers to avoid trouble with the older Party members. In September, 1961, after they had all been safely ensconced in their new government positions for over a year, Ho divested himself of the party secretary generalship, which he had held since 1956, and at the Fourth Party Congress of the Lao-Dong, handed this key post to Lê Duan. This may mean that, for the time being, Lê Duan is the openly acknowledged No. Two man of the D.R.V.N., ahead of Ho's long-time associate Pham Van Dong and even Vo Nguyên Giap, the victor of Dien Bien Phu. But that was in all probability what the experts said about Truong Chinh before his discomfiture over the land-reform fiasco. It is more than likely that Ho may, in terms of health and tenure of office, become another Adenauer—in which case, he may still have ten years of effective rule ahead and not be "in the market" for a particularly strong and ambitious successor.

It is obvious that both the D.R.V.N.'s new constitution and the governmental structures upon which it rests are essentially transitional in character, just as that of the Fifth Republic is in France. An avowedly Presidential system like that of the D.R.V.N.—which, ironically, resembles very much that of its South Vietnamese rival state—occurs rarely in a Communist regime and seems to be tailor-made for Ho Chi Minh rather than destined to become a permanent signpost of constitutional development. The text's aggressive remarks against France and the United States, as well as its encomiums for the present leader, will be meaningless ten years from now, if not sooner.

Ho Chi Minh himself recognizes the temporary character of the document. Leaving the National Assembly building on December 31, 1959, after the adoption of the new text, he said to a group of cheering "Young Pioneers" who had been waiting for him: "When you grow up, you will have a Communist constitution." The one he gave the D.R.V.N. in 1960 certainly was a long step in that direction.

MINORITIES POLICIES

The relative success of the D.R.V.N.'s minorities policies, particularly in contrast to the policy of outright and total assimilation in the traditional manner practiced in Viet-Nam south of the 17th parallel, is perhaps one of the brighter aspects of the regime. The war with the French had forcefully driven home the point that Ho and his men could not survive without at least the passive cooperation of the mountaineers, who knew the country and who, unlike their Vietnamese lowland comrades, were not intimidated by the mountains and the jungle. Little wonder that several VPA divisions (notably the 312th, 316th, 320th, and the more recently formed 335th) are made up largely of mountaineers. As in the case of the land reform, the Viet-Minh did not let the war prevent it from promoting its designs for the future. A conference of 140 mountaineer delegates representing 20 ethnic groups met from August 30 to September 10, 1953, in the northern mountain areas. The conference president was Chu Van Tan, the Thô chieftain who had become a member of the Central Committee of the Lao-Dong and a VPA general. The beginnings of a mountaineer policy based on local self-government were elaborated, no doubt with the intention of reassuring the ethnic minorities who traditionally fear the expansionist designs of the Vietnamese. Implementation followed less than a year after the 1954 cease-fire.

On May 7, 1955—on the eve of the first anniversary of the fall of Dien Bien Phu—came the establishment of the "Thai-Meo Autonomous Zone," comprising almost all of North Viet-Nam west of the Red River and north of the Laotian "bulge" of Samneua, and with a population of close to 500,000, including seventeen nationality groups. In a North Vietnamese article, the "autonomous zone" was defined as being

> . . . not a separate state, apart from the D.R.V.N. [but] on the contrary an integral part of the latter and placed under the authority of the central government. However, contrary to administration in the other administrative zones, the various services of an autonomous zone are recruited from among the local cadres.[9]

In other words, there is almost no difference whatever between a lowland *khu* or UBHC and that of an autonomous zone—except that in the latter non-Vietnamese mountaineers will be in ostensible control. Thus, the UBHC elected by a "Congress of Minorities" of the Thai-Meo Zone on May 11, 1955, includes ten Thai, five Meo, two Vietnamese lowlanders, two Muong, one Man, and five representatives of smaller groups. The titular head of the zone is a Thai tribal chieftain, Lo Van Hac, and the capital of the zone is Ban Chieng Ly (Tuan Chau), a small town northwest of Son-La. In all likelihood, the new capital site, which has no historical connotations, was chosen in preference to Lai-Chau or Son-La, whose preeminence was associated with the days of the French administration. Internally, the zone is divided into the traditional sixteen *chau* (counties) of the Thai tribal federation, in addition to two counties —Thua Chua and Mu Cang Chai—that are fully Meo. But here also, a gradual integration into the normal Vietnamese administrative pattern seems to be the aim of the North Vietnamese rulers. On October 28, 1962, the D.R.V.N. National Assembly decided to change the name of the Thai-Meo Zone (which has a distinct tribal connotation) to Tay-Bac, which simply means "Northwest" in Vietnamese, and the zone was divided into three regular provinces: Lai-Chau, Son-La, and Nghia-Lô. The latter province is newly created.

A second autonomous zone, embracing all of northeastern Viet-Nam to the Red River Valley, was created on August 10, 1956, with its capital at Ho's wartime headquarters of Thai-Nguyên and its presidency going to the faithful Chu Van Tan. However, the hopeless mosaic of tribes, which had earlier given the French endless trouble, did not permit the establishment of an administrative area

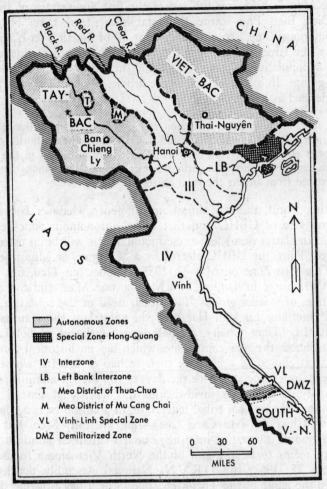

NORTH VIET-NAM'S TERRITORIAL DIVISIONS, 1963

dominated (as in the Thai-Meo Zone) by one or two major ethnic groups. The area thus was given the "neutral" name of Viet-Bac (Northern Viet-Nam); just as the French had named it Cao-Bac-Lang after the three provinces of Cao-Bang, Bac-Kan, and Lang-Son that were its major components.

A third zone presented even more serious difficulties. Carved out of the upper Red River provinces of Lao-Kay and Yen-Bay and the remote mountain area of Ha-Giang, it was known as Lao-Ha-Yen.

ts UBHC was established on March 25, 1957, but the diverse ethnic and cultural characteristics of the populations apparently made the area totally ungovernable. It was quietly abolished on March 23, 1959—"at the request of the population," I was told in Hanoi later. The two valley provinces were attached to the central administration and Ha-Giang was made a part of Viet-Bac on April 2, 1959.

At central government level, there is an advisory Committee on Nationalities (Uy Ban Dan Toc), functioning as an autonomous body subordinated to the office of the D.R.V.N. Premier. Its advice must be sought on all measures applied to the autonomous areas. The Committee was headed in 1962 by Major General Lê Quang Ba, a member of the Thô (now called "Tay") minority and former commander of the famous 316th VPA Division. The Committee operates on the guiding principles of "Union-Equality-Mutual Help" and sees to it that its charges get a fair share of the country's economic and social development. This is especially important as the North Vietnamese minorities represent, according to the 1960 census, 2.5 million people (or 14.8 per cent of the total population). (See Table 1.) That numerical strength is clearly reflected in the D.R.V.N.'s legislature, where there is a "mountaineer bloc," consisting of the 60 legislators representing the minorities and presided over by Chu Van Tan.[10] (By way of contrast, there were only three tribal representatives in the legislature elected in South Viet-Nam in 1959.)

TABLE 1

ETHNIC MINORITIES IN NORTH VIET-NAM IN 1960

Tay (formerly Thô)	503,995
Muong	415,658
Thai	385,191
Nung	313,998
Meo	219,514
Man	186,071
Chinese	174,644
Others	364,138
Total	2,563,209

There can be no doubt that this policy of limited self-government the real power lies, of course, in the hands of the majority Vietnamese operating as Party or administrative cadres in the mountain ones) has had a great impact on the mountain tribes of the South Vietnamese Highlands (PMS). A early as 1957, American social scientists in South Viet-Nam warned the Saigon government that perhaps as many as 10,000 tribesmen had gone north with the Viet-Minh in 1954 and were receiving advanced training in Hanoi. The Central Minorities School in Hanoi is a handsome campus-like college turning out teachers and political cadres for the tribes; there are also special schools for the southern Bahnar, Jaraï, and Edé (Rhadé) tribesmen living in the North. The Tay, Nung, and Meo languages and several of the southern mountain dialects have been provided with Latinized alphabets, as is shown by Communist propaganda found in the PMS. Outstanding tribesmen from the South, such as Y Ngon Niékdam of the Rhadé, were sent to the U.S.S.R. for further training and now hold seats in the D.R.V.N. legislature. Communist propaganda in the PMS tribal areas makes special mention of future "autonomous areas" that would be set up in case of a Viet-Minh victory in the guerrilla struggle. Those who today shape Vietnamese policies in both Saigon and Washington ignore the fact that because these mountain tribes have a long tradition of freedom from outside interference and high social organization within, they are easy prey for any propaganda that promises them a return to that state of affairs. It is now forgotten (if it ever was known) that the relations between the tribes and the Vietnamese rulers were about on the level of those between Viet-Nam itself and imperial China: a few gifts of tribute here and there, a meaningless affirmation of suzerainty, and noninterference by either side most of the time. The arrival of the French changed this in only a few places; some tribes did not submit to French rule until as late as 1939; others, such as the Sédang, were sufficiently organized to form a federation of tribes under a single chief, in the fashion of the American Indians. In the 1880's, a French adventurer, David de Mayréna, proclaimed himself "Marie I, King of the Sedang," in the hope of emulating the White Rajahs of Sarawak. He ruled a vast Sédang state for almost three years until the French colonial administration brought "Marie I" and the Sédang under control.

In backing a policy of local self-government for the ethnic minorities, the Communist North Vietnamese regime cannot lose in an area where the West and the indigenous governments it sponsors resolutely ignore the aspirations of the tribes in favor of a centralization that is as clumsy as it is unenforceable.

THE GREAT LEAP

When the D.R.V.N. assumed control of Viet-Nam north of the 17th parallel in 1954, it inherited an area that had been ravaged twice in less than a decade: its land plundered by the Japanese and Chinese and its communications bombed by the U.S. Air Force in 1944–45; literally plowed under by French tanks and devastated by Viet-Minh saboteurs and guerrillas from 1946 until the cease-fire. In addition, the sudden exodus of 860,000 inhabitants of the Red River Delta to South Viet-Nam created a production gap in some of North Viet-Nam's key food-producing provinces; only a Russian-financed "crash" program of importing Burmese rice (about 150,000 tons in 1955) staved off a famine that would have been about as disastrous as that with which the Viet-Minh had inaugurated its regime in 1945.

Laboring under the cadre shortages already mentioned, the regime, during a first stock-taking phase, managed only to stay above water, aided in this by a first installment of foreign aid designed mainly to keep existing services going and to repair essential communications. Although some French technicians had remained behind, they were in many cases of little help (assuming that the Viet-Minh was willing to ask for their help) since the departing Franco-Vietnamese administration had taken almost everything that was movable: dock cranes, railroad-repair equipment, and even the radium necessary for the use of the X-ray machines in the Hanoi hospitals. The French were later compelled to reimburse the D.R.V.N. for the equipment removed.

Beyond these dismal short-term prospects, the D.R.V.N.'s over-all situation was a great deal better than appeared on the surface: The exodus from the Red River Delta, though depriving it temporarily of some useful labor, solved at least in part its problem of rural overcrowding. Furthermore, it made available (in spite of pious assurances that the abandoned land would be held in escrow) close to a half-million acres of choice farm land for redistribution in an area where, as has been shown earlier, 98 per cent of the farmers *owned* the plots they farmed. Thus, it is no exaggeration to say that the mass flight of refugees—which the West encouraged—gave the Viet-Minh its best boost toward control of the North Vietnamese countryside. Although there is no doubt that hundreds of thousands of Vietnamese would have fled Communist domination in any case, the mass flight was admittedly the result of an extremely intensive, well-conducted, and, in terms of its objective, very successful American psychological warfare operation. Propaganda slogans and leaflets appealed to the devout Catholics with such themes as "Christ has gone to the South" and the "Virgin Mary has departed from the

North"; and whole bishoprics—Bui-Chu and Phat-Diem, for example—packed up lock, stock, and barrel, from the bishops to almost the last village priest and faithful.

Of the 860,000 who fled South at this time, 600,000 were Catholics. Although 65 per cent of the total Catholic population left North Viet-Nam, more than 99.5 per cent of the non-Catholics stayed put. The Tonkinese Catholics fled because they had had a long experience of persecution at the hands of their non-Catholic fellow citizens—not because of the psychological-warfare campaign. The small group of non-Catholics who left consisted mostly of dependents of soldiers in the Franco-Vietnamese forces and government officials. These figures alone should have warned the psychological-warfare planners that the operation might backfire.

Politically, the Catholic exodus helped the D.R.V.N. a great deal (which is what the French had argued), although it was finally the French who evacuated 610,000 of the refugees, with the U.S. 7th Fleet transporting the rest. Not only was land freed for redistribution by the Viet-Minh, but a vast reservoir of potential anti-Communist subversive elements was cleared from the area, and the tight northern food situation was eased at a crucial moment. The 1956 rebellion of Catholic peasants in Interzone IV (despite the fact that they had been under Viet-Minh control for ten full years!) clearly shows what this fanatically devout minority can do when it is aroused, and even in 1954, no one in the D.R.V.N. Government had any illusions as to the willingness of the Catholic minority to collaborate with a Communist regime. On the other hand, the arrival of that tightly knit community in a South Viet-Nam that is largely Taoist, spiritualist, and Buddhist created new political tensions there—the more so as the government of President Ngo Dinh Diem immediately used the Northern Catholics as its major base of political power, since he and his closest associates are Catholics themselves and originate from North or Central Viet-Nam.[11]

One-year economic plans were developed for both 1956 and 1957, aimed mainly at preparing the economic, administrative, and even statistical bases for the later longer-range plans; first of all, an intermediate three-year plan covering the years 1958 through 1960 and then the first regular five-year plan covering the years 1961–65. One of the most difficult problems of the consolidation period (1955–58) was that of land reform. As already has been pointed out, this reform in North Viet-Nam was not so much designed to establish a more equitable land-distribution pattern (since land was by and large held by its tillers) as to become a key vehicle for social change. Not even a marked increase of agricultural production could be expected from the process; in fact, it produced a decrease, at least temporarily, as the removal of some landowners left land fallow that otherwise would have been intensively used. The first step in the reform process was a "Population Classification Decree," issued on March 2, 1953, which, according to its own preamble, made it possible to "distinguish our compatriots [from each other], to separate our friends from our enemies, [and] permit the unification and direct the struggle in the sense we want."[12] It contained a set of rules so complicated as to be almost comical: For example, a piglet is equated to quarts of rice, which, added to the income in rice of the farmer, minus the salary he pays to his workers but increased by increment drawn from other sources (the whole being first expressed in quarts of rice and then in percentages of revenue over investment). These formulas established the social "rank" or "class" of the individual, with the whole population of the D.R.V.N. classified into five categories, ranging from "landlord" to "agricultural worker." The same classifications, by another ludicrous system of transfer of agricultural values to urban activities, was applied to intellectuals, artisans, professionals, etc. The Viet-Minh have made class membership an almost racial characteristic; thus, daughters of landowners who marry into a low class must first have spent one year in that new low class before being considered a part of it. Conversely, a poor farmer's daughter who "marries up" may remain married for three years before she is reclassified into the new (and less desirable) category.[13]

With the extreme narrow-mindedness that seems to be the hallmark of the Viet-Minh low-level cadre (*can-bo*), the decree was applied throughout the D.R.V.N. with utmost ferocity. Local Party officials began to "deliver" veritable quotas of landlords and rich peasants even in areas where the difference between the largest and the smallest village plots was a quarter-acre. Special "People's Agricultural Reform Tribunals" ("Toa-An Nhan-Dan Dac-Biet") began to mete out death sentences to individuals who in any case were not landlords, and who in many cases had loyally served in the war against France or had even been members of the Lao-Dong. By the summer of 1956, the Lao-Dong was for the first time confronted with a severe internal crisis: A menace to life and property from whose arbitrariness no one any longer felt safe produced a wave of disobedience and outright hatred for the Party cadres throughout the country. While it is obviously impossible to give precise figures, the best-educated guesses on the subject are that probably close to 50,000 North Vietnamese were executed in connection with the land reform and that at least twice as many were arrested and sent to forced labor camps.

On August 17, 1956, Ho Chi Minh himself openly came out in favor of putting a brake on the runaway land-reform program. In a letter addressed "To the Compatriots in the Country," he stated:

> Errors have been committed in the implementation of unity in the countryside. . . . The Party and the Government have taken up seriously the subject of those lacks and errors and have determined a plan for their correction:
>
> Those who have been wrongly classified as landlords and rich peasants will be correctly reclassified.
>
> Those members of the Party, the cadres, and the population who have been the subject of an erroneous judgment will be reestablished in their rights and prerogatives and their honorable character will be recognized. . . .

After this public acknowledgment of the problem, the other Party organs fell into line. On August 24, the authoritative *Nhan-Dan* openly admitted that loyal Party members, including UBKC chairmen, had been executed and besmirched: "Brothers from the same family no longer dare visit each other, and people do not dare to greet each other when they meet in the street." The remaining Catholics, who had been badly hit both as farmers and as Catholics, were promised the return of some of their confiscated churches and imprisoned priests.

All this came too late, however, to prevent a popular explosion on November 2, 1956—at the very time when, at the other end of the Communist bloc, Soviet tanks began to crush the Hungarians who had rebelled under precisely the same conditions. What made the Vietnamese uprising particularly humiliating for Hanoi was that it took place in the middle of the Viet-Minh bastion of Interzone IV and in Ho Chi Minh's own native province, in fact, only a few miles from his birthplace. Since, by sheer accident, Canadian members of the International Control Commission were present when the outbreak took place, its completely fortuitous and popular origin can be well substantiated: It apparently started when villagers surrounded a Commission jeep with petitions asking that they be allowed to go south of the 17th parallel. A Viet-Minh soldier or militia member tried to disperse the villagers with his rifle butt, but the enraged farmers beat him and took his rifle. Thereupon the VPA soldier found it expedient to withdraw, only to return with a squad of troops; they met a fate similar to his, and shots were exchanged. By nightfall, the movement had swept over the whole *huyên* (district), and danger mounted that the farmers, like those of the first Nghé-An Soviet of 1930, would march on the provincial capital of Vinh, just as they had marched twenty-six years earlier in protest against the colonial power. Hanoi no longer had any choice; it responded in exactly the same way as the colonial power had, sending the whole 325th Division to crush the rebels. It did so with typical VPA thoroughness; allegedly, close to 6,000 farmers were deported or executed. With headlines pre-empted by the news from Suez and Hungary, the world press had little space left for the farmers of Nghé-An. And no U.N. member—neither of the always touchy Bandung bloc so concerned about the fate of its brothers in colonial shackles, nor of the habitually anti-Communist nations— mustered sufficient courage (or marshaled sufficient facts) to present the Nghé-An case to the conscience of the world.

Ho reacted to the rebellion with eminently practical measures. The land-reform tribunals were abolished as of November 8; the unpopular Party hack Truong Chinh was removed from the secretary generalship of the Party, with Ho himself assuming it until 1961; and the Minister of Agriculture was likewise dismissed. At the same time, the regime launched a vast "Campaign for the Rectification of Errors," in which thousands of prison and concentration-camp inmates were returned to their villages. In fact, on November 22, 1956, *Nhan-Dan* printed an article titled "Our Attitude When We Return to Our Villages," which contained a sort of code of behavior for the ex-political prisoner. But the enraged prisoners had no intention of simply letting bygones be bygones. In many cases, they refused to work with the Party cadres who had sent them to prison; in many others, they dragged the cadres off to their own sessions of self-criticism and denunciation before the People's Courts. As H. C. Taussig, an otherwise not unsympathetic British eyewitness, observed later, a veritable "orgy of self-criticism" (also with quotas and statistics of "corrected errors") swept the D.R.V.N. at the end of 1956 and the beginning of 1957, with Ho himself—his own reputation surprisingly untarnished by the affair—taking to the radio and newspapers time and again to exhort his countrymen to forgiveness. But, as he himself said: "One cannot wake the dead." And there were now many dead between the regime and its people.[14] In the countryside, the Party continued to run into difficulties. On February 16, 1957, *Nhan-Dan* reported that the reinstated Lao-Dong members in Hung-Yên wanted to arrest those who had denounced them, and when prevented from doing so, they simply went "on strike"—refusing to work with Party organs. On February 19, the same paper reported that the "errors and lacunae committed during the land reform have seriously affected the basic Party units in the countryside" and once more exhorted the farmers "to forget their personal indignation and to continue to work for the union in the countryside." But the breach apparently was too wide to be bridged simply by a few good words. On April 19, 1957, the North Vietnamese press agency tersely announced that "for a definite time period, the Party shall, above all, increase its strength in the cities and industrial centers."

It was a foregone conclusion that the peasantry would eventually have to fall into line, since no one abroad supported their cause. But the problem of their *political* control remained and it apparently still dogs the Lao-Dong to this day, since, in a special resolution on the agricultural situation presented by the Central Committee of the Lao-Dong on August 20, 1961, mention is made of the need "for the reinforcement of Party leadership in the countryside . . . and to raise the level of [political] consciousness of the members of cooperatives."

The agrarian-reform law, whose gradual implementation had involved all the heartbreak of the Population Classification Decree, was in itself a fairly moderate document. Unlike its Soviet counterpart, it did not abolish private agricultural property; it provided for indemnifications for expropriated land and contained a redistribution formula with almost biblical overtones:

> One shall give much to him who needs much; one shall give little to him who lacks little; one shall give nothing to him who lacks nothing; one shall take where there is abundance and give where there is lack; one shall compensate poor lands by rich lands.[15]

Even inheritance and the right to resale are guaranteed in theory. There also is a strong emphasis on the gradual character of the implementation and the recognition of special conditions, such as in the case of the mountaineer minorities (Article 38). The reform itself was preceded, as has been shown, by the population-classification drive and a widespread process of indoctrination euphemistically known as "Mass Mobilization," which included the trials of land-

lords before the People's Agricultural Reform Tribunals. The eco
nomically absurd results of the whole process are well illustrated in
Table 2, based upon a Soviet study.[15]

TABLE 2

AVERAGE ACREAGES BEFORE AND AFTER LAND REFORM[a]

(*In Hectares*)

Social Class	Before	After
Landowner	.65	.10
Rich farmer	.21	.21
Medium farmer	.12	.17
Poor farmer	.05	.14
Laborer	.02	.15

[a] V. Zelentsov, in V*oprosy Ekonomiki* (*Problems of Economics*), September
1957, p. 62, cited in Jeanne Delattre, "L'économie vietnamienne au début de
son premier quinquennat," *Economie & Politique* [French Communist maga-
zine], June, 1961, p. 22. A hectare is equal to 2.47 acres. Thus the so-called
"landowner," even *before* the land reform, owned less than 2 acres of land.

If one is to believe the above table (much of it remained little
but theory), the "rich farmer" emerged from the reform process even
richer, in comparison to all the other classes. In fact, if he was lucky
enough to have a family of five persons over eighteen, and therefore
received more than 1 hectare of farm land, he, and possibly the
"medium farmer," were the only ones likely to approach subsistence
levels, since 1 hectare of rice land is needed per family in North
Viet-Nam to make a decent agricultural living. Furthermore, the
rich and medium farmers already possessed the necessary agricultural
implements and, above all, the very expensive draft animals required
to make the most of their land; while the other peasant categories
did not possess those essentials and were not likely to get them from
the Hanoi government. According to another Soviet source, the
whole program of prosecution of the landlords netted the D.R.V.N.
"702,000 hectares of land, 1.8 million farming implements, and
107,000 draft animals . . . which were distributed to 1.5 million
families of poor peasants and agricultural workers."[16] Simple division
shows that the poor and landless peasants would have received a
useless 0.5 hectare and 1 tool per family, and *1 buffalo for every 13
farming families!* The previously cited French Communist economist
Jeanne Delattre estimated the number of Vietnamese poor and

landless peasant families at 2.2 million, which would make the availability ratios of land, tools, and draft animals even lower than the Russian experts are willing to admit. It was obvious, then, that the D.R.V.N. land reform could lead only to starvation rations for the poor farmers and a total reversal of the letter of the land-reform law. The practice now became: "One shall give where there is abundance and take where there is lack." This confused not only the peasants but even the Party faithful who had to apply this chaotic reform, as Mlle. Delattre makes clear:

> In the fall of 1958, the Party had to proceed once more with a vast job of explanation to the cadres, the Party members, and the peasant masses. It struggled against the tendency of the medium farmers to get richer and sought to reinforce the Socialist spirit of the Party cadres and members.[17]

But it is not inconceivable that the Party was willing to accept temporary production setbacks in order to demonstrate to the North Vietnamese peasantry that the privately owned small plot was economically unviable, regardless of their traditional attachment to it. Lenin himself had given the perfect answer to the "renegade Kautsky," who had accused him of betraying the Revolution by giving each small farmer a plot of his own:

> The proletarians tell the farmers: "We shall help you realize your desires in the way of an ideal capitalism—for an equalitarian redistribution of land would be nothing but an idealization of capitalism from the viewpoint of the small holder. And then we shall prove to you the impossibility of such a system and the necessity to proceed with collective cultivation of the land."

Faced with uneconomical plots, a scarcity of draft animals, and high delivery quotas, the small and poor farmers were the first to fall by the wayside. Those who faced outright hunger provided welcome labor for the government's industrialization and irrigation projects, and the others were banded together with cooperatives launched under the innocuous name of "Work Exchange Teams." After several false starts during the earlier and disastrous land-reform "waves," the establishment of cooperatives began in earnest late in 1958. At the end of that year, there were 4,722 cooperatives; 28,775 at the end of 1959; and 41,401 at the end of 1960, including more than 85 per cent of all farming families. In March, 1963, after the cooperatives had been "rationally reorganized" (i.e., consolidated), there were only 29,824 units, but these included 87.7 per cent of all rural families. By the end of 1961, 99 per cent of the total value of agricultural production allegedly came from the cooperatives. At the same time, a move was started to transform them into "cooperatives of the higher type, i.e., fully socialistic ones," according to Jeanne Delattre, while similar drives were started among nonagricultural workers, such as fishermen and salt producers. It must be emphasized that, generally speaking, those cooperatives often do not have at their disposal improved tools, supplementary draft animals or even tractors. As a North Vietnamese specialist explained in a recent study, "contrary to what has happened in the U.S.S.R. and in the European people's democracies, the North Vietnamese cooperative movement, like those of the People's Republic of China and the Democratic Republic of Korea, begins before mechanization."[18]

Only in the pioneering system of State Farms, copied from the Russian sovkhozes, are tractors and harvesting combines used on a large scale.

In 1962, on the 55 farms in this system (33 of which were run by the VPA), a working force of 60,000 cultivated 200,000 hectares of state-owned land with the help of Soviet and Chinese motorized equipment. At least two such farms were located in the mountain tribal areas near Môc-Chau and Dien Bien Phu—an indication that sooner or later collectivization will be extended to the ethnic minority areas.[19]

The experience of the Chinese communes next door is being carefully watched in Hanoi. During my stay there in 1962, I broached the problem with experts of the State Planning Board, and it became very obvious that, for the time being at least, there was little intention of following Peking on that shaky ground. It was pointed out that the North Vietnamese policy of village-size cooperatives had been set before the Chinese began to implement their communes policy and that there existed no intention (nor the physical means) of putting such a policy into operation in the D.R.V.N. Present farm policies provide for the creation of cooperative villages grouping about 1,600 individuals, with 0.15 hectare per person, by the end of the five-year plan in 1965. The average size of the cooperatives in 1960–61 was given as 750 persons with a per capita acreage of 0.14 hectare. My questions as to the political implications of adopting (or not adopting) the communes policy were met with an evasive: "We are still too unsophisticated politically and economically to be able to judge the merits of the communes policy." That view, which is fully in line with Ho's over-all policy of local pragmatism under the guise of full Party orthodoxy, has thus far permitted Hanoi to avoid rushing head-long into a program it might later have to regret.

Even so, North Vietnamese agriculture has encountered a fair share of troubles that cannot be ascribed entirely to natural calamities. Lê Duan, the Party secretary general, in three long articles on the North Vietnamese cooperative movement published in September, 1962, in *Nhan-Dan*, warned the population that during the "period of socialist transformation . . . it may happen that production does not develop, but, instead, decreases temporarily." Lê Duan then candidly admitted that the average real income of cooperative members still included 55.5 per cent supplementary family revenue, and he clearly diverged from the Peking line in asserting that "in my opinion this situation symbolizes a farming method . . . which cannot exist in industry," and that the "subsidiary family economy is necessary not only for the co-op members, but also for the society [and] for the state-run economy, [and] is the most suitable for agricultural production."[20] It would obviously be naïve to describe this view as a return to a mixed agricultural economy. It indicates simply that when faced with the choice of either starving by the rules of Marx and Mao or eating both its rice and its principles, the North Vietnamese regime preferred the latter.

But how well or how poorly the D.R.V.N. is actually fed is statistically hard to assess with any degree of accuracy. Most Asian statistics are approximate at best—even in the non-Communist areas,[21] where their inaccuracy reflects, for the most part, poor base data. When, as in the case of Communist China or the U.S.S.R., the figures have been falsified locally by overzealous officials and centrally by over-optimistic statisticians, the result usually is total chaos until the authorities themselves find out that they have been their own worst enemy and begin a downward reappraisal of both their past achievements and future production targets. The D.R.V.N. was no exception to the rule.

When the original North Vietnamese three-year plan was launched in 1958, the 1960 production target was 7.6 million tons of paddy rice (i.e., unmilled rice, 35 per cent of which consists of inedible husks). According to Mlle. Delattre and other Communist sources, that target had been revised downward to 5.5 million tons by mid-1961; when Hanoi published the 1960 total—in January, 1962, after a year's delay—it prudently avoided absolute tonnages and cited instead an index figure, based on the previous worst year, 1957. By extension, the real tonnage produced in 1960 amounted to a startlingly low 4.1 million tons. (See Table 3.) In other words, in terms of essential rice production, the first North Vietnamese economic plan fell 3.5 million tons, or almost 50 per cent, short of its original target. After deductions for the essential reserve stocks, the seed grain

TABLE 3

RICE PRODUCTION IN NORTH VIET-NAM[a]

Year	Cultivated Area (In Hectares)	Yield (In Tons per Hectare)	Total Yield (In Tons)
1939	1,836,000	1.33	2,453,200
1944	1,833,000	1.21	2,275,000
1945	2,650,000	1.43	3,770,000
1954	1,898,100	1.37	2,600,000
1955	2,196,000	1.64	3,600,000
1956	2,280,000	1.86	4,238,000
1957	1,945,000	2.01	3,890,000
1958	2,288,450	2.04	4,576,000
1959	2,260,409	2.28	5,114,300
1960	2,354,000	3.27	4,146,700
1961	2,356,000	1.82	4,646,000
1962	2,463,000	1.95	4,738,000
1965	2,916,000	2.40	7,000,000 [b]

[a] *Note on North Vietnamese statistics:* All North Vietnamese statistics cited in this chapter come from Soviet, French Communist, or D.R.V.N. sources. As all figures are equally unreliable, no attempt has been made to reconcile the obvious discrepancies, such as in the 1960 figures above, where multiplication of the acreage figure by the excessively high ton-per-hectare figure would give a total yield of 7.7 million tons instead of the actual 4.1 million. In cases where the various sources present irreconcilable discrepancies, alternate figures are given in parentheses.

[b] Forecast as of January, 1962.

for the following year, and some small exports to Communist China's neighboring provinces,[22] this left the North Vietnamese with a dangerously low rice ration of about 10 kilograms (22 lbs.) a month. There was strong evidence from firsthand North Vietnamese sources that actual rice rations during 1961 were considerably lower in many areas. Hoarding became a major problem, and the official press pilloried whole provinces, such as rich Ha-Dong, Nam-Dinh, and Thai-Binh, which had withheld from the state purchasing agencies up to 90 per cent of their delivery quotas. The widespread floods of 1961, which also hit neighboring Cambodia and South Viet-Nam, further affected rice output. The absence of a commune system in North Viet-Nam, however, prevented the situation from getting out of hand. In 1962, most Western observers (there are British, Canadian, French, and Indian missions in Hanoi) saw no evidence that "the whole population is . . . suffering from chronic malnutrition" and that it experiences "a form of collapse from exhaustion at about 10 A.M. each day," as one writer averred.[23]

As one compares the announced crop yields per hectare with the far more modest increases planned for 1965 and the admission of such low yields as 1.8 tons per hectare in 1961, the highly overoptimistic character of the earlier figures becomes obvious; and in itself, the increasing availability of more accurate statistics has had an extremely sobering effect on the North Vietnamese economic planners. The population census of 1960 taught them that they had to reckon with an explosive yearly population increase of 3.5 per cent; thus, with about 600,000 new mouths to feed every year, rice production has to increase by at least 200,000 tons a year merely to break even. At present yield rates, that would mean that the D.R.V.N. has to put at least another 110,000 hectares to the plow every year— and not only has it failed to do so thus far, but until recently it failed even to recognize the urgency of the problem, preferring instead to attempt to increase acreage yields (in which it apparently also failed). In a frank article on the subject, a North Vietnamese stated the problem in the following terms:

> Formerly, only an increase in the yields was envisaged, the importance of clearing was underestimated. In 1961, 72,000 hectares were cleared, twice as much as from 1959 to 1960. On the new lands for growing, we are anxious to obtain increased yields. In actual fact, clearing land in our country brings a whole lot of problems in its train which must be solved simultaneously: agricultural division of the country, specialization in cultivation and animal rearing, good leadership, judicious planning, the struggle against erosion, etc.[24]

An important adjunct to rice are the secondary crops, such as corn, sweet potatoes (yams), and cassava (manioc). Although they do not constitute a popular alternative to rice, they are nonetheless important in keeping the North Vietnamese from going hungry, and the Hanoi regime emphasizes both their consumption and, above all, their growth in areas unsuitable for rice. Table 4 indicates that the regime's efforts are meeting with success.

TABLE 4

SELECTED SECONDARY CROPS IN NORTH VIET-NAM

(*In Thousand Tons*)

	1939–40	1955	1956	1957	1958	1959	1960	1961
Corn	125	23	258	187	197	228	198	279
Yams	——	——	1,062	528	540	718	557	1,217
Cassava	——	——	366	186	142	234	396	709
Peanuts	11	40	18	24	31	33	23	70
Sugar cane	109	100	168	330	361	442	403	475

In cattle breeding—also of prime importance since buffalo and oxen will remain for decades to come the major source of nonhuman agricultural energy—a series of fantastic claims in 1957–60 was supplanted by an equally drastic downward revision in the 1965 target. The statistical confusion is likewise noteworthy. (See Table 5.)

TABLE 5

LIVESTOCK PRODUCTION IN NORTH VIET-NAM

(*In Thousand Head*)

1939	1953	1956	1957	1958	1959	1960	1961	1962	1965
1,351	1,840	430	857 (2,140)	2,350	2,615	2,900[a] (2,200)	2,163	2,206	1,800[b]

[a] Three-year-plan target.
[b] Five-year-plan target.

If one assumes that the modest 1965 target figure is based on a realistic re-evaluation of the 1960 cattle potential, the latter can be estimated at equal to the 1939 figure or less—which would be clearly insufficient for a rapid expansion of agriculture, unless a vastly enlarged pool of motorized agricultural equipment were made available to the D.R.V.N. by Red China or the Soviet Union. Since in 1961 the Soviet Union made only 901,000 rubles' (less than $1 million) worth of tractors and other agricultural machines available to North Viet-Nam,[25] it is highly unlikely that a sufficient supply will be forthcoming.

In other words, the North Vietnamese agricultural economy has no doubt made important progress in certain fields and has managed to get along without the 250,000 tons of southern rice it usually imported prior to 1954 to compensate for its deficiency. However, the D.R.V.N. is far from being capable of providing its rapidly rising population with an adequate basic diet. It is, in fact, questionable whether it will be able to do so even if the 1960–65 plan is actually fulfilled, since by then the population will have risen by about 3 million souls over the 1960 base figure and will absorb much, if not all, the projected production increases. Many of the plan targets depend upon optimal conditions that will be most difficult to achieve: enlargement of the cultivated area by 20 per cent; extension of the two-crop system to all rice fields and most other crops; expansion of industrial crop acreages from 4 per cent of the total to 10 per cent (250,000 hectares); utilization of motorized agricultural equipment on about 300,000 hectares of farm land outside the already motorized State Farms, whose own acreage is expected to increase to 225,000 hectares; etc.

North Viet-Nam has made a major effort to acclimate some of the crops that were usually found only in the somewhat hotter south, notably rubber. Suitable terrain was found for the Hevea tree between the 17th and 20th parallels, and it was planned to alternate coffee bushes with the Heveas, so that the shade of the latter could protect the coffee plants. The Soviet expert V. P. Karamyichev has calculated that planting 100,000 hectares of rubber trees (yielding about as many tons of latex) would cost the enormous sum of 255 million rubles, plus about 150 million rubles for the necessary equipment, or about $450 million in all. This would make the D.R.V.N. the sole producer of natural rubber within the Communist bloc. However, there is no evidence that either the Russians or the Chinese have embarked on so ambitious a project. In any case, it would yield no appreciable dividends before 1970.

Other "industrial" crops (coffee, tea, cotton, jute, etc.) are being pushed with some energy but have thus far not been overly successful. Cotton targets, originally set at 9,000 tons for 1960, were scaled down to 7,500 tons and actually reached only 6,029 tons in 1961— which is below French production during the years of the Japanese occupation. Present North Vietnamese requirements run at about 15,000 tons annually, but the D.R.V.N. has slim hopes of reaching that level by 1965, and by then, requirements will have increased along with the population. North Viet-Nam has ample amounts of midland terrain suitable for the production of coffee, tea, and oil bearing crops (especially peanuts). Plans call for a 1965 output of 35,000 tons of coffee, 7,000 tons of tea, and 20,000 tons of peanuts. Fruits, spices, and resins can also be counted among D.R.V.N. products that have export possibilities.

One agricultural export the D.R.V.N. has understandably not boasted about is opium. Like Peking, Hanoi announced in 1956 that opium was neither used nor produced on its territory—but it apparently failed to inform the Soviet Union of its moralistic position. Thus, the Central Permanent Opium Committee in Geneva—of which the D.R.V.N. is not a member but Russia is—was informed by the latter in 1959 that it had imported 13,000 kilograms (28,600 lbs.) of opium from North Viet-Nam, and several other countries listed a total of 100 kilograms as having been imported from the D.R.V.N.[26] Control of the Lao highlands by Viet-Minh forces supporting the Pathet-Lao has given the Hanoi regime access to some of the richest opium-producing areas in the world, thus providing it with a handy source of foreign exchange and additional means for both subversion and the collection of intelligence.

In assessing North Viet-Nam's agricultural economy in the mid-1960's, it is clear that many serious difficulties have not yet been overcome. Some of the difficulties that have arisen can be directly traced to the doctrinaire application of Communist principles that were never designed for the realities of the North Vietnamese situation: low productivity, lack of agricultural tools and draft animals, and a strong dose of peasant individualism which defies proper regimentation. Ho and his associates were pragmatic enough—and the peasant rebellion of 1956 must have served as a prod—to decide late in 1961 to shift their regime's development emphasis toward a healthier balance between industry and agriculture, and, within the latter, between incentives and threats. Tax exemptions were granted for secondary crops, and tax relief was given for five years on newly planted fields, while areas switching to the two-crop system were granted three-year exemptions. But beyond this "carrot" aspect of the new production push, the "stick" was provided in the following innocent-sounding phrase in an official commentary on the agricultural program of the 1960–65 plan: "Until now, the principle of 'To each according to his labor' has not always been applied in all the cooperatives. Therefore, the struggle against equalitarianism becomes part of the order of the day."[27] In other words, far from applying the Communist theoretical principle of "From each according to his ability, to each according to his needs," Hanoi seems resigned to making eating and well-being a privilege limited to the strong and able-bodied, who are capable of fulfilling their production quotas.

But that seems to be the price the regime feels it must pay for the fulfillment of its political and ideological goals.

9

"Road to Socialism"

LENIN's definition of Communism as being "Soviet rule plus electrification" holds true, in its own way, for the underdeveloped countries that have become Communist in recent years. Both in Europe and in Asia, the peasant class has shown itself a reluctant carrier of revolution, and it is an article of faith in the Communist world that only a "politically conscious working class" can carry forward the banner of revolution. Thus, industrialization on even a modest scale is almost as necessary ideologically as economically for a backward Communist country such as North Viet-Nam.

In the D.R.V.N., the role of the peasant as the carrier of revolution—for he had effectively borne the brunt of the military struggle for more than eight years—was greatly diminished after the land-reform fiasco of 1956, and emphasis was shifted to the growth of the Party in the cities and new industrial centers among "the best sons and daughters of the working class." The political predominance of the workers, in spite of their very small numbers (it is doubtful that there were more than 150,000 industrial and mine workers in North

Viet-Nam in 1963, they are certain to increase rapidly after 1965), was further assured by giving them a greater voice at the polls and advantages in housing as well as evening classes. Little wonder, then, that the overwhelming bulk of the D.R.V.N.'s own development investments and the foreign aid it receives goes into long-range capital equipment instead of into improvements in the living standards of the population at large; while in neighboring South Viet-Nam, as will be seen in Chapter 14, the bulk of local investment and foreign aid goes into short- or medium-range projects designed for psychological impact, or simply into the day-to-day maintenance of internal security. In addition, there is one "act-of-God" factor that operates in favor of the North's industrialization: the preponderance of Viet-Nam's mineral resources, by geological accident, happens to be located north of the 17th parallel, just as, for reasons of climate, most of Viet-Nam's rubber grows in the South.

INDUSTRIALIZATION

As in the field of agriculture, North Viet-Nam's efforts in the industrial field since 1954 were headed in two directions: reconstruction and preservation of the existing industrial plant, and expansion of industrial production in all existing sectors and some new ones. But as even Communist writers—here Jeanne Delattre—observed, "in view of the lack of experience of the [Viet-Minh] planners and the absence of precise [statistical] information . . . the initial targets were set too high and had to be revised downward in most cases." It is certainly surprising that this happened, for the D.R.V.N. not only benefited from the advice of Soviet-bloc planners but also was in possession of the most realistic economic plan thus far devised for the whole Indochinese peninsula: the "Monnet Plan" of 1947.

Jean Monnet, probably best known as the father of the European Common Market, headed the French Commission of Modernization of the Economy in 1946. French plans then drawn up provided not only for the modernization of the French homeland, but also for that of the overseas possessions then under French control, including, of course, Indochina. The most interesting part of the plan was that (since it was conceived before the Marshall Plan) it did not take into account the possibilities of generous American aid, but assumed that all economic development would have to come from the resources of the colony itself, plus whatever contribution the war-shattered economy of France and perhaps some of the other colonies could make. Thus, the Monnet Plan for Indochina—drawn up by a commission of economic specialists under the leadership of Jean Bourgoin and therefore nicknamed the "Bourgoin Plan"—is a hard-headed document taking into account nearly every local asset—mineral, agricultural, and human. North Viet-Nam, with its already developed and known mineral resources, took a key place in the new scheme, and the Communist leadership of the D.R.V.N. has followed closely in the steps of Bourgoin.[1] It has fallen short of the Bourgoin targets in those areas of production where the plan had assumed that more technically qualified supervisory personnel would be available than the D.R.V.N. was capable of providing. Also, the aid provided to North Viet-Nam by its Communist brother states has not been especially more lavish than what the French had expected to contribute. And the French planners built their assumptions on a local infrastructure that had not yet suffered—as it was to, later—the extensive devastations of eight years of war. In some areas, such as steel production at Thai-Nguyên, the Bourgoin Plan ambitiously foresaw a production capacity of 400,000 tons a year within two years after completion, while the D.R.V.N., under its own revised five-year plan, expects to reach only 200,000 tons a year by 1965, seven years after construction began and about four years behind schedule.

As in the case of the agricultural statistics, it is extremely difficult to state exactly *what* the North Vietnamese industrial economy has produced, and *when*. Grandiose bulletins of achievements have been followed by quiet disclaimers, so that for each item there are several equally "authentic" figures wildly at variance with each other. (See Table 6.) That problem was brought out in the open during the Third National Congress of the Lao-Dong Party, in September, 1960, which witnessed the close of the temporary three-year economic plan and the inauguration of the first regular five-year plan of the D.R.V.N. In his presentation of the outlines of the new plan, Nguyên Duy Trinh, Minister of State for Economic Planning, bluntly stated:

> . . . in planning, we have been more or less subjective; some indices were too high, thereby bringing about a tense situation in the course of their implementation. A number of departments did not fulfil their plans, thus causing a measure of discouragement in these departments. A number of concrete policies were not formulated or amended in time; control was not very strict; cases of corruption and waste are still rather numerous.[2]

This explains the sudden reluctance of the Hanoi regime to publish hard base figures for the 1965 targets, since the latter are, in Trinh's

TABLE 6

INDUSTRIAL OUTPUT IN SELECTED SECTORS IN NORTH VIET-NAM[a]

Item	1939	1955	1956	1957	1958	1959	1960	1961	1962	1965 Planned
Coal (in thousand tons)	2,615.0	641.5	1,100.0	1,230.0 (1,085.0)	1,500.0 (1,342.0)	2,100.0	2,700.0 (2,595.0) (2,450.0)	2,804.0 (2,654.0)	n.a.	4,200.0 (5,000.0)
Cement (in thousand tons)	305.0	8.5	198.9	230.0 (165.0)	302.0	410.0 (370.0)	400.0 (380.0) (305.0)	457.0 (450.0)	n.a.	800.0 (710.0)
Phosphate (in thousand tons)	31.0 (35.0)	8.4 (6.4)	32.1	36.0 (22.5)	32.1	54.9	65.0	100.0	152.6	500.0
Steel (in thousand tons)	130.2	—	—	—	—	—	51.0	3.7	5.0	200.0
Electricity (in million KWH's)	122.5 (120.8)	53.0 (45.0)	94.0	142.3 (123.0) (121.2)	162.3	207.9 (204.3)	271.0 (254.0)	319.0 (291.0) (276.0)	391.0	700.0 (660.0)
Textiles (in million meters)	55.5	39.0 (8.5)	47.0	68.0 (65.5) (27.0)	68.5 (65.5) (34.0)	78.0 (76.5)	86.0 (83.0) (68.0)	93.2 (90.0)	93.4	134.0
Tin (in tons)	300.0	—	—	104.0	223.0	366.0	462.0	555.0	600.0	n.a.
Paper (in thousand tons)	5.7	0.8	1.9	1.2 (0.6)	1.3	2.4 (1.8)	3.3	4.1	20.0	35.5

a Sources: Delattre, op. cit.; Fall, Le Viet-Minh: La République Démocratique du Viet-Nam, 1945–1960 (Paris: Librairie Armand Colin, 1960); William Kaye, "A Bowl of Rice Divided: The Economy of North Vietnam," in P. J. Honey (ed.), North Vietnam Today: Profile of a Communist Satellite (New York: Frederick A. Praeger, 1962), pp. 105–16; P. H. M. Jones, "North Viet-Nam, Hopeful New Year," Far Eastern Economic Review (Hong Kong), March 20, 1962; and various issues of the Viet-Nam Information Bulletin. As throughout, alternate figures appear in parentheses.

own words, "for the time being" based on "the estimated degree of fulfilment of the 1960 Plan."[3] By mid-1962, the North Vietnamese economic planners were still in the process of sorting out fact from fancy in the three-year plan reports, and planning officials were still threshing out five-year plan figures with the various ministries concerned. Even so, it already seemed clear that the 7-million-ton target for rice production, originally set for 1960 and then "stretched out" to 1965, was beyond reach. A new target was set at 5.8 million tons of rice by 1965, to be supplemented by 2.5 million tons of "rice-equivalent" crops, such as yams and corn.

In terms of raw-materials potential, the D.R.V.N. occupies a choice place in Southeast Asia, because of its happy balance between fuels and metals, and their accessibility. Known coal and anthracite reserves amount to 20 billion tons, of which 12 billion are accounted for by the coastal Quang-Yên Basin, where coal can be conveyed directly from the pit heads to ocean-going ships for export, or to barges for transport to the industrial centers of the interior. Iron-ore reserves are currently estimated at 250 million tons, but recent Soviet prospecting efforts may reveal additional exploitable deposits. In addition to the present Thai-Nguyên steel-mill complex, plans are afoot for a second steel center near Yen-Bay, in the upper Red River Valley. Thai-Nguyên, like most of the other new Communist industrial centers in North Viet-Nam, has been designed with a strong emphasis on economic viability rather than on an impressive exterior. The steel center is constructed almost on top of the iron-ore deposits and will receive its fuel from the Quang-Yên coal fields by trains and river barges. On their return trip, the trains and barges will bring steel to the excellent Soviet-built machine-tool plant in Hanoi, as well as clinker, which will be used in the Haiphong cement plant.

Near the Red River, at Lao-Kay, vast apatite deposits estimated at 1 billion tons have begun to provide the wherewithal for an active fertilizer industry centered particularly around the Soviet-built superphosphate plant at Lam-Thao near Phu-Tho, which began production on June 25, 1962, with an initial production of 100,000 tons a year and is slated to reach a yearly production of 500,000 tons at the end of the 1965 plan. A smaller phosphate plant exists near Haiphong, and smaller apatite deposits are being worked in Thanh-Hoa. Of greater strategic importance are the wolfram, tin, and uranium phosphate deposits at Tinh-Tuc in the Pia-Ouac Massif near the Chinese border. Completely re-equipped with Soviet mining implements, this formerly French mining complex (which, incidentally, included the only hydroelectric power plant in colonial Indochina) allegedly has reached a production level of 3,000 tons of ore concentrate a year, which was the maximum allocated to all of Indochina under the prewar Tin Agreements. As early as 1952, French intelligence knew that the D.R.V.N. had reopened the Tinh-Tuc mines on a makeshift basis and that about 300 tons of refined tin, 90 tons of tungsten, and a small quantity of uranium phosphate were being exported yearly to Communist China. Today, small quantities of chromium are also being mined at Co-Dinh (Thanh-Hoa). It is, of course, a far cry from uranium to an atomic reactor, but the possibility that the Soviet Union might provide the D.R.V.N. with small atomic power plants or an experimental reactor cannot be discounted—if only to match that donated by the United States to South Viet-Nam and being put into operation at Dalat.

For the time being, however, the Achilles' heel of the North Vietnamese economy remains the shortage of electric power and the paucity of communications. In 1961, the nonindustrialized South produced 273 million KWH's of electricity, while North Viet-Nam produced 276 million. As a consequence, northern cities (including Hanoi) are in a state of "brown-out," and the population is exhorted not to use big bulbs and electric fans. It is not surprising, therefore, that the 1960–65 plan provides that the D.R.V.N. "must accelerate the production of means of production, mainly by developing electric power one step ahead of other departments." Both Red China and the U.S.S.R. have promised help in building a 400,000-KWH hydro-electric station at Thac-Ba on the Chay River. It does not seem to have been included in the first five-year plan, however. Present efforts seem to tend toward providing each of the industrial complexes with sufficient thermoelectric power to be self-sufficient and provide a small surplus for the surrounding area. Thus, the Viet-Tri complex has its own 16,000-KWH power plant, whose power is to be increased to 24,000 KWH's in 1963–64; it will then provide power for the initial stage of the Thai-Nguyên steel plant until the latter's own power plant can assume that task.

In the field of road and rail communications, the record of the D.R.V.N. is uneven. Emphasis seems to have been put on restoring rail communications with China via both the Yünnan railroad and Lang-Son. There also seems a deliberate policy of *not* restoring the rail net in the direction of the 17th parallel—no doubt in order to increase the communications difficulties of a potential invading force from the south. On the basis of personal observation and of talks with other firsthand observers, I would term the motor roads uniformly wretched. No road seems to have been widened beyond one-lane traffic in each direction, and in almost no case has the road itself been restored to normal standards; wide stretches of the first-class national highways are simply covered with laterite, which the heavy trucks of the various industrial projects rapidly churn into red dust. There appears to be a belated recognition among North Vietnamese planners that much of the eventual success of their ambitious industrialization plans hinges on a rapid improvement of the country's road net and power grid.

SOVIET-BLOC AID

The D.R.V.N. has unquestionably been one of the major recipients of Soviet-bloc aid. Up to 1961, in terms of strictly economic aid—obviously, no figures are available on Communist military aid to the Hanoi regime—North Viet-Nam had received more than $70 per person, which is about equal to what its southern rival received from the United States.[4] According to Lê Thanh Nghi, the D.R.V.N.'s Minister for Heavy Industry, Communist-bloc grants and loans from 1955 through 1961 totaled more than $1 billion, of which the Soviets supplied $365 million, the Eastern European countries $38 million, and Communist China $662 million. Of this sum, $280 million came from Chinese long-term loans and $47 million from Soviet long-term loans.[5] In addition, the D.R.V.N. receives sizable gifts and technical assistance from the satellite countries: city buses from Hungary, Polish meteorologists and sugar experts, East German medical personnel and a complete hospital, Mongolian cattle experts and 100,000 breed cattle, an East German ocean-fishing fleet, Czech sport and crop-dusting aircraft. The D.R.V.N.'s trade gap with Russia, though not as great as that of South Viet-Nam with the United States, is nevertheless substantial: In 1961, Soviet nonmilitary exports to North Viet-Nam amounted to about $80 million, while North Vietnamese exports to Russia were valued at about $25 million.[6]

It would be futile to recite here the entire impressive list of major industrial projects completed by the Communist bloc in North Viet-Nam; a few major examples will suffice to show the scope of the development program under way. The Thai-Nguyên *kombinat* has been mentioned. The electrochemical complex of Viet-Tri also deserves special mention because of the judicious choice of its layout and the ingenious convertibility of its facilities: a sugar-cane refinery, which, in its slack months, is slated to produce antibiotics and industrial alcohol, and whose pressed-out cane goes to the paper mill directly opposite, where it is used as the basic raw material for a yearly production of 20,000 tons of paper. The chemicals produced in the plant just beyond the paper mill are used for the paper production processes; in addition, the plant produces chlorides, sulfuric acid, and insecticides. Smaller food-processing plants are also part of the Viet-Tri complex. Not surprisingly, these *kombinats* (and at least two others, one at Haiphong and another in Thanh-Hoa) have thus far no counterpart elsewhere on the Southeast Asia mainland.

In addition to these achievements, there are two air-conditioned tea plants built by the Soviets at Phu-Tho in 1958; ten Chinese-built plants manufacturing tobacco products, matches, plywood, enameled kitchenware, plastic objects, and porcelain, completed as part of the 1957–60 plan; a Soviet canning and freezing combine at Cạt-Ba Island, capable of processing twenty tons of fish a day. The Soviet long-term loan negotiated in December, 1960, provides for the construction of forty-three industrial plants, including eight thermal-power stations of 20,000 KWH's each (one of which, at Uong-Bi in the coal fields of the Quang-Yên Basin, was nearly ready early in 1963). A Red Chinese long-term loan of $156 million was designed to double the production capacity of Thai-Nguyên and enlarge twenty-eight existing plants and installations.

While much of this industrial effort also constitutes a heavy strain on the D.R.V.N. itself—it must provide, as its "counterpart" to the foreign aid received, the local labor and its maintenance, as well as cement and coal—the results thus far achieved are nonetheless impressive, and dangerously so for the United States. One need only visit a short stretch of Road No. 6 from Hanoi to Ha-Dong, a town ten miles away. When I saw it first, in 1953, no man's land began with the last French bunker of the Hanoi perimeter; beyond that, even the rice fields were left untilled. Ha-Dong itself was a forlorn little town, surrounded by its own bunkers, and beyond it, one could hear the heavy gunfire of the French artillery strongpoints covering the outposts of the "de Lattre Line." In 1962, one spanking-new factory or school after another lined Road No. 6 from Hanoi almost up to the *city* of Ha-Dong; the big Soviet machine-tool factory and its housing blocks, the Ministry of Agricultural Hydraulics, a rubber factory, a textile plant, and the Minorities Institute were among the most conspicuous additions.

What is perhaps most important is that the Hanoi regime has thus far abstained from decking itself with useless showpieces. There exists no Stalin-Allee of pompous, useless, ugly apartment buildings as in East Berlin or on Leninskii Prospekt in Moscow; there are no foreign visitors to impress—at least, not yet—and this accounts also for the incredible shabbiness of Hanoi, which looks as if the departing French had taken with them all paintbrushes and sidewalk-repair equipment. But there has been, on the contrary, a deliberate effort to build an infrastructure that, though supplied by foreign aid, could nevertheless be maintained, if need be, by the North Vietnamese themselves. Although the D.R.V.N. could not fail to welcome this large-scale foreign aid, it appears determined not to have to depend upon it. The regime's desire to avoid a new "colonialism" (particularly by the ever-present Chinese "Big Brother") is perhaps best shown by the diminishing share foreign aid represents in the country's budget (in percentages of the total):

1955	1956	1957	1958	1959	1960	1961	1965 (est.)
65.3	(40.0)	60.8	(31.3)	(27.0)	21.0	19.9	15.0
(38.6)[a]		(36.9)			(17.7)		

[a] Figures in parentheses were provided by the D.R.V.N. in 1960. The other figures date from 1962 and show a heavier (and probably more realistic) dependence on foreign aid than had previously been admitted.

There has been much speculation over why Russia, China, and (to a lesser, but nevertheless important, extent) their satellites, are investing such comparatively large sums[7] in the economy of a rather small and exposed member of the Communist bloc. Two reasons, one political and one economic, come readily to mind: Politically, the D.R.V.N. represents a Communist wedge leading into the rest of mainland Southeast Asia—a jump-off point into not only South Viet-Nam, but Cambodia, Laos, and Thailand as well. Economically, as one Soviet technician was quoted as saying: "Up to now you are the only tropical country of the Socialist camp."[8] Although none of the D.R.V.N.'s products are essential to the Soviet bloc (it can and does buy them in Malaya and Indonesia as well), they could become an important pawn in the bloc's Cold War economic operations. Coffee, tea, rubber, or tin can be produced in sufficient quantities in North Viet-Nam to cause major regional distress. For example, the U.S.S.R. purchased $170 million worth of Malayan rubber in 1961; the loss of such sales would be deeply felt, should the D.R.V.N. step into the already jittery world natural-rubber market by 1970. Its unique location also enables the D.R.V.N. to serve

as a laboratory for the development of Communist-bloc equipment
and techniques to be used in other tropical areas.

However, the noted French political economist Tibor Mende, who
visited the D.R.V.N. in 1957, seems to have found what, more than
five years later, still seems to be the most plausible explanation of the
lavish aid the bloc is providing:

> For a certain number of reasons, I am in fact tempted to believe that
> the Communist world is in the process of making a deliberate effort
> at transforming North Viet-Nam into a show window for all of South-
> east Asia. The considerable efforts made (and particularly their secrecy)
> might well prepare the day when the doors will be opened so as to
> allow the people of the area to marvel at the progress made [by North
> Viet-Nam] on the magic carpet of Communism. . . .
>
> [The bloc countries] have had the relative luck that they can accom-
> plish this exploit in a small country with only 13 million people. With
> India or Indonesia, this would have been quite a different story and
> surely would have cost a great deal more money. . . .[9]

There can be no doubt that the sheer fact that the economic
development of North Viet-Nam can proceed without the profound
upheaval of a country-wide revolutionary war is in itself a great asset
for the Hanoi regime. Furthermore, Viet-Nam north of the 17th
parallel, while by no means a country of high living standards, has,
on the other hand, not suffered any drop in its living standards. In
recent years, there has been a leveling process, in the course of
which the most conspicuously rich North Vietnamese lost what they
had (although the bulk of them had left for the South during the
1954–55 period of grace), while the poorest at least lost their rags.
Western observers report that the regime has begun to feel secure
enough to allow its female citizens to divest themselves of the
Chinese-type uniforms in which they had been clad for some years
and to revert to the far more form-flattering Vietnamese national
costume. Although the everyday street scene still is dominated by
black, white, and faded blue, which seem to be the only colors in
which textiles are now produced, expensive and colorful older dresses
are being worn again on holidays, apparently without fear of political
reprisals.

Nevertheless, the North Vietnamese coolie or factory worker pays
for the rapid quantitative and qualitative development of his industrial economy with sacrifices whose end is not in sight. His leaders
tell him that he must provide the leadership that the politically unsophisticated peasantry cannot (or will not) provide. For the tim-

being, at least, that new class of industrial workers, coolies, and students is performing its difficult task well and apparently with little protest. But, as a Western Communist told me after he returned from North Viet-Nam, "that is what the Hungarian Government thought about *its* factory workers before they rebelled in November, 1956."

THE PARTY APPARATUS

In the last analysis, however, what gives the North Vietnamese regime its special imprint is not its industrial economy or its administrative system or its victorious army, but rather its all-encompassing Communist Party, the Dang Lao-Dong (Vietnamese Workers' Party).

Faithful to the formula of "national" Communist parties and desirous of taking the wind out of the sails of the Vietnamese nationalist opposition, the ICP took the surprising step of dissolving itself on November 11, 1945. In the last point of its communiqué of dissolution, the Party explained its gesture as designed. "to destroy all misunderstandings, domestic and foreign, which can hinder the liberation of our country."[10] In actual fact, however, the Party never ceased to exist. The final sentence of the communiqué stated that those Communists "desirous of continuing their theoretical studies will affiliate with the Indochina Association of Marxist Studies," and that newly created association became the cover organization for the Party.

How little the Party had in fact "dissolved" is best indicated by the fact that Nguyên Kien Giang's Party history, written in 1960, fails to mention the dissolution altogether but mentions, on the other hand, directives or appeals issued by the ICP Central Committee on November 25, 1945, and March 5, 1946; National Conferences of Party Cadres, held July 31, 1946, April 3, 1947, August, 1948, and January 14, 1949; and, finally, the Eleventh Congress of the ICP, held on February 11, 1951, which led, Giang asserts, to the open reconstitution on March 3, 1951, of a specifically "Vietnamese" Communist Party, the DLD.[11]

On that same day, the Viet-Minh was officially allowed to die. The National Salvation (Cu'u Quôc) Front organizations, which on May 27, 1946, had been merged in the Vietnamese United Front (Mat-tran Liên-Viet)[12] to form the parallel hierarchies of the regime, now were amalgamated through yet another "unification congress" held at the same time as the Eleventh ICP Congress, and the Viet-

Minh was superseded by the Lien-Viet. Party discipline and efficiency were considerably improved with the reappearance of an open Communist organization, but now the last genuine non-Communist nationalists who had remained in the movement faced the agonizing choice of either moving into the French-held zone and thus becoming "traitors" to their cause, or staying with the Viet-Minh and betraying their ideals. A privileged few found a third solution; they went into exile abroad. (The same dilemma existed, of course, for their opposite numbers in the South.) Although the Viet-Minh officially ceased to exist on the day the Lao-Dong was born, its name —hated, feared or admired—was to become part and parcel of the myths of the D.R.V.N. to this day. The disparaging term Viet-Công (Vietnamese Communist) is used only by South Vietnamese and American officials.

In view of subsequent changes in the Soviet bloc, the statutes of the Lao-Dong make interesting reading. Their preamble explicitly stated that "The basis of the DLD and its guiding line in all fields of its activities is the doctrine of Marx, Engels, Lenin, and Mao Tse-tung, adapted to the realities of the Vietnamese revolution." That last "mental reservation" clause and the failure to include Stalin—in 1951!—among Communism's great teachers are evidence of a sort of pragmatism that may even be called opportunism. After all, Red China and Mao were next door and helping with the war, and the Russians were on the other side of the globe and had for a long time given the Viet-Minh a cool reception. In article 2(e), however, the Party members were exhorted to study the "doctrine" of Marx, Engels, Lenin, *and* Stalin—*and* the "thoughts" of Mao Tse-tung.

A deliberate ideological scaling-down of Party aims becomes evident as one compares the statutes of the Communist Party of the Soviet Union (CPSU) and of the Chinese Communist Party (CCP) with those of the DLD. Whereas the CPSU

> . . . exercises the leadership of the working class . . . of the entire Soviet people, in the struggle for the consolidation of the dictatorship of the working class . . . for the victory of Communism . . .

and the CCP's duties

> . . . in the present stage must take the form of a new bourgeois-democratic revolution . . . under the leadership of the proletariat . . .

the DLD's struggle operated at an even lower level and was only

. . . popular and democratic, [its] mission is to eliminate the invading imperialists, to suppress the remains of feudal and semifeudal rule, and to implement the principle "to each his own piece of land" . . .

In this ranking, the Cambodian pro-Communist elements were at a still lower ideological level since the statutes of their "Khmer Revolutionary Party" did not even mention Communism and declared the purpose of the party to be simply

. . . to [unite] the whole people in the Issarak Front, to collaborate closely with the Vietnamese and Lao peoples . . . and to carry on a firm struggle so as to annihilate the French colonialists, the American interventionists and their puppet lackeys . . .

Even a cursory examination of the DLD statutes will show them to differ very little from those of the CCP, for the internal problems of the DLD are similar to those of its larger sister republic. As in most other Communist Party statutes, very little is said about the organization's *administrative* role as the *de facto* government of the country. Yet, that is precisely where the DLD's most important functions lie. In terms of ideology, it is far too weak and unsophisticated to engage in the kind of high-level theological quarrel—*querelle de clercs*—in which Mao, Liu Shao-ch'i, Ch'en Po-ta, and Lu Ting-yi like to engage with such Titoist heretics as Edvard Kardelj, or Khrushchev and Ilyichev.[13] Almost all the key members of the government are also members of the DLD Central Committee, and so on down the line at every level, with the village Party cell usually constituting the local Administrative Committee. Every factory, village, higher school, city borough, and army company has its Party cell or even cell group. The importance of the DLD administratively is thus clear: Before becoming a "parallel hierarchy" in enemy territory, the DLD is above all a parallel hierarchy on its own grounds.

But in addition to the regular Party machinery, new organizations had to be created to assume control over the various layers of the population, from children to old women, that could not readily be integrated into the DLD. In the urban areas, this problem was solved in 1957–58 by the creation of "Street and Inhabitant Protection Committees" whose avowed task it is to "make known and popularize the government's decisions dealing with city affairs . . . and to maintain order and public safety." In Hanoi alone, there are 4,600 block chiefs and deputy chiefs, plus 3,000 committee members,[14] all of whom see to it that everyone turns out for elections, for spontaneous greetings to visiting foreign Communist dignitaries, for "Hate-America-Week," or for any other collective move the regime deems useful. It may be considered a sad sign of the times that the Saigon government also started to imitate this Communist 1984-like project line-for-line in February, 1960, through the creation of "Interfamilial Groups," which are designed to "promote friendship and assistance among neighbors," but which compel every houseowner to have a "registration plate" and a list of all the inhabitants of his house. Another function of the Interfamilial Groups is to "explain the government policy to the members and acquaint the authorities with their members' problems."[15] Neither the northern nor the southern system is likely to produce free expressions of opinion.

The Lien-Viet, which had survived the Indochina War with little more than its name intact (the creation of the DLD had deprived it of its most active members), was refurbished in 1955 to meet the changed circumstances of division. It was readied for legal activities in the north and underground activities in the south, in the course of the Third Meeting of the Congress of the Lien-Viet Front, September 5–10, 1955. As had been the practice on similar occasions in the past, a member of the Presidium read a motion that was unanimously adopted by the Congress. Thereupon Ho Chi Minh entered the Congress hall and made a brief speech extolling the virtues of the new body ("The platform of the Fatherland Front of Viet-Nam is all-embracing and practical . . ."), and a few minutes later, the Mat-tran To-Quôc (Fatherland Front) was a fact.

Nothing had really changed in the internal organization of the new body despite its new name and task. Its honorary President was Ho, and its working President was Ton Duc Thang, the Black Sea mutineer who had been President of the Lien-Viet; and its twelve-man Presidium, although containing five representatives of the various major religions in Viet-Nam (including the Cao-Dai and Hoa-Hao), was staffed predominantly with such DLD stalwarts as Truong Chinh, Hoang Quoc Viet, and Chu Van Tan. The important aspect of the Fatherland Front was its program, which was resolutely directed towards reunification on terms ostensibly more moderate than the "winner-take-all" basis of the D.R.V.N. Government. In lieu of a single Vietnamese Government to be set up directly after elections, the Fatherland Front advocated in 1955 (and still does) separate legislative assemblies in both zones, which, in turn, would elect a provisional government on confederative lines; both sides would temporarily retain their separate armed forces but would be "rigidly prohibited from employing foreign instructors." A new constitution would later be drafted by the provisional government and the rights of minorities to autonomous zones would be guaranteed "wherever possible." Promising that the "economic realities" of both zones would be respected, the Front program guaranteed the landlord system of the south and the coexistence of private and state industries. On one point, the program was highly vituperative—concerning the "handful of traitors who have sold out to American imperialism." It also reiterated that "American imperialism is the chief enemy."

The Fatherland Front lost its usefulness when South Viet-Nam refused to acquiesce in the so-called reunification elections of July, 1956, which were supposedly to have resulted from the 1954 ceasefire agreements. Now being kept in reserve for a possible psychological-warfare play, the Front holds sporadic meetings. In Hanoi in March, 1958, it dutifully adopted the Lao-Dong's program without a single deviation. A second Congress of the Front took place on April 26, 1961, in the course of which it re-elected its whole Central Committee without dissent.

In the meantime, a new, more aggressive organization, the National Liberation Front of South Viet-Nam (Mat-tran Dan-toc Giai-phong Mien-Nam), was created on December 20, 1960 (one day after the fourteenth anniversary of the Viet-Minh attack against the French), in order to carry on the new policy of military-political subversion of South Viet-Nam south of the 17th parallel.

EDUCATION AND POLITICS

"For the Vietnamese Communists," says Gérard Tongas, a French ex-Communist, in a recent account of his experiences in the D.R.V.N. "the words *culture, education* and *teaching* have only one meaning, namely *indoctrination*."[16]

As in all other Communist states, in North Viet-Nam education and the arts are not ends in themselves but must also serve the regime's political aims. This does not mean that, as Tongas tends to imply, "education" in its constructive sense has disappeared altogether from the D.R.V.N., any more than the teaching of Marxism in Soviet schools has prevented the U.S.S.R. from producing able space scientists. On the contrary, a very considerable effort has been launched to spread education throughout North Viet-Nam, first through a program to eliminate illiteracy among adults and later through a revised school system for the young. The colonial school system, with its elementary, primary, and secondary schools, was replaced in 1950–51 by the single-system "Popular Schools," comprising three "cycles": a basic four-year cycle, a three-year intermediate cycle, and an advanced two-year cycle. A tenth year was added to the Popular Schools after the 1954 cease-fire. If the D.R.V.N. statistics in Table 7 may be trusted, the rise in attendance has been impressive.

TABLE 7

POPULAR-SCHOOL ATTENDANCE IN NORTH VIET-NAM[a]

	First Cycle	Second Cycle	Third Cycle
1945	182,459	7,182	2,009
1954	556,577	33,509	402
1960	1,440,000	178,000	20,000
1961	2,023,000	322,000	41,000
1962	3,156,000	(all three cycles)	
1963	3,800,000	(all three cycles)	

[a] *Sources:* Fall, *Le Viet-Minh*; *Viet-Nam Advances*, February, 1962; *Viet-Nam Information Bulletin*, No. 41/62, December 1, 1962.

Draconic measures were often used to compel adults to take literacy courses: Villagers on the way to their market town were stopped at road blocks and their literacy tested on the spot. Those who could not pass the test were compelled to take reading lessons then and there, or were barred altogether from going to the market. Viet-Minh sources claim that adult illiteracy has been wiped out among the North Vietnamese lowlanders through a massive after-hours adult education program. My personal (and unescorted as well as unannounced) inspection of several such schools in the Hanoi area confirms that such a program exists and that the problem of illiteracy is still being dealt with. Tongas's statement that "the cultural level of North Vietnam is undoubtedly one of the lowest imaginable" and that "eighty per cent of the population is illiterate,"[17] is—considering the number of North Vietnamese students working at advanced schools inside and outside the D.R.V.N.—sheer nonsense.

In terms of total figures—including the very important middle-level technical schools and the universities—the effort made by the D.R.V.N. has been noteworthy, although, as will be seen later, South

Viet-Nam's educational development has largely kept up with that of its northern rival. Again, in Table 8, the statistics provided by North Viet-Nam are confusing, and one receives conflicting figures from equally "official" sources.

TABLE 8
TOTAL SCHOOL ATTENDANCE IN NORTH VIET-NAM

	Popular Schools	Technical Schools	Universities
1954	592,095	2,928	915
1955	815,410	3,746	1,528
1957	952,485	6,500	2,305 (3,904)
1958	1,117,000 (1,283,000)	8,256	5,590
1959	1,400,000	10,054	6,200
1960	1,638,000	12,500	9,300
1961	2,386,000	31,000	15,640 (18,598)
1962	3,156,000	49,000	22,590
1963	3,800,000	64,000	20.600

The curriculums in North Viet-Nam are largely patterned on the only school system the teachers know intimately—the French—but they have been considerably lightened and, of course, Vietnamized. French is taught merely as a foreign language and not as a tool of research or higher learning. In fact, as in South Viet-Nam, English seems to be favored as the leading Western language, although a greater number of students actually study Russian and Chinese. (In 1962, I saw some French and English textbooks of a nonpolitical character available for purchase in Hanoi; the only American book for sale was a tattered paperbound copy of Dr. Spock's *Baby and Child Care.*) The translation of foreign textbooks is a major task of many educators, and many Viet-Minh sympathizers spend their days painfully translating French, British, and American textbooks into Vietnamese. In the course of this process, a whole new technical vocabulary is being created, borrowing chiefly from the Chinese, but from the Russian as well. In many cases, the North Vietnamese neologisms have nothing in common with synonymous terms being coined in the South. Thus, the division of Viet-Nam into two states is being deepened far beyond the difference of political and social systems. An increasing number of North Vietnamese now go for study to the U.S.S.R., the European satellites, and Communist China. Nearly all these students are totally ignorant of any Western language and will contribute within a short time—perhaps ten years or less—to the total alienation of North Vietnamese leadership from any intellectual ties with the West.

As would be expected, the institutions of higher learning experience certain difficulties in teaching law, political science, and what in America would be called "liberal arts." In the field of law, the absence of codification and the patchwork use of colonial law and new revolutionary law have delayed the creation of law schools. The number of defense lawyers, for example, had dwindled almost to nothing, until the re-creation of a token group became opportune when North Viet-Nam wanted to join the International Association of Jurists. Political science, as the term is understood in the West, simply does not exist; Marxism-Leninism, as a key field of teaching, on the other hand, is compulsory at all levels. In 1963, however, an Institute of Diplomatic Studies opened its doors in Hanoi as a separate school of the University of Hanoi. It specializes in training North Vietnamese diplomats, and its curriculum includes courses in comparative government and international relations.

Soon after the regime came to power, the schools were made the locus of Party youth activity. On June 6, 1946, the government ordered the dissolution of all youth movements except the Party's red-scarfed "Young Pioneers," and all schools now have their own "Pioneer" groups. There also are DLD cells if there are enough teachers and students over eighteen; the students then are treated as equals and participate actively in the cell debates. In that parallel hierarchy, the school's principal is merely another "comrade" and may be called upon by the cell's members to carry out his self-criticism in front of them, should he be guilty of an ideological error.

Another much-feared body of school government is the Hoi-dong Ky-quat (Disciplinary Council), which polices the students and school staff. It consists of the school's principal and vice-principal, two professors, and two student representatives. Each class has its own committee and is subdivided into "study cells" (To Hoc-tap), which submit reports to the Disciplinary Council on the quality and political orientation of the teachings of their professors, who then may have to justify their attitude before the Council. It is easy to imagine what all this does to both the quality of the teachers and the relations between teachers and students.

Even in the last remaining outpost of French culture north of the

17th parallel, the Lycée Albert Sarraut, which is financed by French Government funds (in exchange for which the French are allowed to maintain three teachers of French and mathematics in the school), the curriculum must conform to the set pattern. Everything else, including the physical sciences—which, in the D.R.V.N., must follow the "scientific theories of Mitchurin in biology, Filatov in medicine, and Otto Smith in cosmography"[18]—is taught according to ideological rather than pedagogical standards. The same applies to religious teaching, of course. All foreign priests and nuns were expelled in 1961. A recent Indian visitor to North Viet-Nam, K. V. Narain, described the situation in the following words:

> . . . the [D.R.V.N.] Government is trying to gradually eradicate Catholicism. Recently the Government forced the closure of the last French seminary in the country by insisting on the political indoctrination by Communist cadres of the priests under training. . . . As another step in wiping out Catholicism, the Government is also appointing pro-Communist priests. No Catholic can be taken into the Army.[19]

In 1962, there were 5 Vietnamese bishops and 320 priests left to minister to the spiritual needs of 750,000 North Vietnamese Catholics. There are, as in Red China, associations of "Progressive Catholics," "Progressive Buddhists," and other religions, and a North Vietnamese delegation participated in the World Council of Buddhists held in Cambodia in 1961.

By 1958, passive ideological obedience on the part of the schools was no longer deemed sufficient. Strong pressure was exerted upon schoolteachers and professors to "cultivate their revolutionary ideology and morality. The new Khrushchev "work-and-learn" program found an immediate echo in North Viet-Nam, and tens of thousands of students and teachers were sent to the rice fields or, worse, to the Bac-Hung-Hai canal project, where they worked for several months in water up to their waists. According to the high-brow Communist review *Hoc-Tap* (*Studies*) of December, 1958, there "they finally understood that culture, literature, and the arts come from the masses and are destined to serve the masses, because it is the latter who are the most capable of assimilating and of judging them."

But the *Gleichschaltung* of professors, students, and priests was but one facet of the massive attempt to cope with the refusal of the North Vietnamese intellectual elite to align itself completely with the official ideology.

A "Hundred Flowers"

When the Hanoi regime settled down to the humdrum life of a third-class "people's democracy," the intellectuals found themselves strapped into an ideological strait jacket. The climate of intellectual repression that had descended on South Viet-Nam had been more or less expected by the intelligentsia, but the Viet-Minh's doctrinaire narrow-mindedness was a matter of love betrayed. And while Ngo Dinh Diem and his entourage eventually resorted to such absurd measures as banning all dancing (including folk dancing) and, early in 1963, outlawed most sentimental songs as "detrimental to combat morale," they at least abstained from taking a stand on the artistic merits of free verse or abstract painting.

Neighboring China, to rouse its own intellectuals from the torpor the regime itself had induced, announced the inauguration of a more relaxed policy toward diversified intellectual and artistic endeavors, which became known as the "hundred flowers" policy. On May 25, 1956, Lu Ting-yi, chief of the Propaganda Section of the Central Committee of the Chinese Communist Party, made a speech in' Peking before a select assembly of Chinese scientists and artists on the theme of two lines of poetry attributed to Mao: "Let a hundred flowers bloom/ Let a hundred schools contend." According to Lu's comments, the new policy "permits free criticism and allows free reply to the critics."

North Viet-Nam at first tried to ignore the sudden liberalization of its gigantic neighbor, just as de-Stalinization had, by and large, been ignored as long as possible (the big picture of Stalin in Hanoi's International Bookshop remained in place until March, 1962); but the "hundred flowers" could not be ignored very long. For one thing, some of Viet-Nam's best writers had remained in the north; for another, the Hanoi intellectuals were still somewhat contaminated by the poisonous atmosphere of Paris, where many of them had studied.[20] And the return to Hanoi after 1954 of quite a few students and intellectuals who had spent ten years or more in France further intensified the problem. Thus, the blooming of the "hundred flowers" in Hanoi in the fall of 1956 produced an explosion that was far more violent than that in China, for it involved many who until then had been considered the intellectual pillars of the regime.

The liberalization movement was led by Phan-Khoi, the "grand old man" of Vietnamese letters, whose father, as governor of Hanoi, had hanged himself in shame when the city surrendered to the French in 1882, and who himself had spent nine years on the French prison island of Poulo Condore. Phan-Khoi held the editorship of two reviews: *Nhan-Van* (*Humanism*, a deliberate pun on *Nhan-Dan*, the name of the Party newspaper) and *Giai-Pham* (*Literary Pieces*). Other magazines, such as *Tram-Hoa* (*Hundred Flowers*) and *Dat-Moi* (*New Land*), were launched, and even *Van-Nghé* (*Art and Literature*), the official magazine of the Writers' Association, took up the cudgels for the new movement. A wave of criticism submerged the Party hacks and the state's propaganda machinery. As *Van-Nghé* said in an article admittedly slashed "to save space":

> . . . literature cannot avoid being superficial as long as the Party has its hands in it. . . . As far as the stereotypes are concerned which are found in all literary pieces since the August [1945] Revolution, we do not like them at all, but not at all! There is always the perfect [Party] section secretary who has all the answers, and the mass mobilization of peasants in three phases: suffering peasants, struggling peasants, and victorious peasants. . . .[21]

None of the "sacred cows" of the regime escaped criticism, and the situation became even worse after the abortive peasant rebellion of November, 1956: The Viet-Nam People's Army was accused of being anti-intellectual; the Russian experts of being overbearing and of driving around in big cars; the Party of antagonizing the peasantry and allowing corruption to flourish among its members. The Party reacted with its usual heavyhandedness—without waiting for the change of line in Peking, which came much later. The "hundred flowers" publications found themselves without newsprint and soon without printers (on strike at the behest of their union). *Nhan-Van* was forbidden to publish on December 15, 1956, after five issues—on the very day that the D.R.V.N. published a new law guaranteeing freedom of the press.

In the visual arts, the return to the approved subjects was not long in coming. As *Hoc-Tap* stated with obvious satisfaction in its October, 1958, issue, describing the yearly painting exhibition that had just taken place:

> . . . the *Nhan-Van–Giai-Pham* group had sowed doubt and discouragement among the people. . . . Poisoned by the bourgeois slogan of "art for art's sake," some [painters], instead of facing the realities of the people's work and struggle, began to study female nudes and lines and color nuances [abstract painting] without any value. . . .

On the other hand, the 1958 exhibition had purged itself fully of such aberrations, and its paintings, according to the *Hoc-Tap* art critic:

> . . . stimulated the masses to fulfill their revolutionary obligations. . . . Those paintings dealt with all the necessary subjects: the reunification struggle, the anti-American and anti-Diem struggle, the creation of work-exchange groups, etc.

The crushing of the formal intellectual opposition has not, however, eliminated the passive or potential oppositionists. Like all the other Communist countries, North Viet-Nam has its "hooligans," who, in the words of the Hanoi press, go about with "their bristling mustaches and overly long hair, engage in sterile discussions," and listen to jazz programs broadcast by Radio Saigon or the Voice of America; while others "seem to be longing for the old rot, [and] write poems expressing regret for times past."

The purging of the northern intellectuals went on for several years (it is doubtful if, in fact, it ever stopped), with some of them engaging in self-criticism—such as admitting having read the French newspaper *Le Monde*—while others simply disappeared. A group of five persons, including one woman, was put on trial for "psychological-warfare activities under the cover of the *Nhan-Van–Giai-Pham* group," and on January 19, 1960, the People's Court of Hanoi sentenced them to prison terms ranging from five to fifteen years. Phan-Khoi died a few days before he was to go on trial for deviationism. His only son, Phan Thao, editor of the Hanoi newspaper *Thong-Nhat* (*Unity*), which is the official propaganda organ of the Fatherland Front, died seven months later under unexplained circumstances.

But the end of the "hundred flowers" period (it was far shorter in North Viet-Nam than in China) did not entirely still the yearning of the North Vietnamese intelligentsia for creative freedom. One of them summed up the experience in a haunting Oriental image: "The hundred flowers died quickly, for, after all, they were made only of paper. But they nevertheless have had their spring."

Lonely Road

As the D.R.V.N. approaches the mid-1960's, it can look back upon a solid record of achievements in the military and administrative fields, and upon a not unimpressive performance in industry. But it

has squandered a vast capital of good will that the nonaligned nations of Asia extended after its victory over the French at Dien Bien
Phu and its basically reasonable attitude during the cease-fire conference at Geneva in May–July, 1954. Perhaps the best indication
of the Asians' basic sympathies is the fact that, except for Red
China, the D.R.V.N. was the only Communist regime invited to
attend the Bandung Conference; neither Outer Mongolia nor North
Korea was invited. For a while, it seemed that sweet reasonableness
was going to prevail: At Geneva, Pham Van Dong not only had
promised French Premier Mendès-France substantial guarantees for
French property but had even held out to him the possibility of having North Viet-Nam remain within the French currency zone. Some
foreign technicians, such as mining engineers or the French directors
of the Hanoi streetcar company and the Renault automobile repair
shop, were encouraged to remain, and even Western journalists
found many of the Viet-Minh leaders in Hanoi a great deal friendlier
and more relaxed than their counterparts in Saigon, whose relations
with the press have never been very cordial and who in 1955 were
facing a rebellion of religious sects, as well. But the "honeymoon"
period in the North was to be of short duration; in fact, it was over
by the time the French had evacuated their last beachhead in North
Viet-Nam, in May, 1955.

The American vice-consulate in Hanoi was virtually besieged until
its members were withdrawn at the end of 1955; on June 3, 1958,
the French and British missions were deprived of their radio communications with the outside world. France herself was placed in a
grave dilemma that is still far from solution: Her vast economic
and other interests in Viet-Nam north of the 17th parallel did not
permit her to ignore the Hanoi regime; on the other hand, her
remaining properties in the South and the presence of about 15,000
of her citizens there give the Saigon regime a near stranglehold over
French relations with any part of Viet-Nam. At first, France sent to
Hanoi as "delegate" (it maintains a full-fledged embassy in Saigon)
a man whom the Viet-Minh knew well and who, in spite of personal
wounds and grief, was still willing to "play the game": ex-Governor
Jean Sainteny. Throughout the Indochina War, Sainteny had maintained that a policy of loyal negotiation with the Viet-Minh could
have resulted in an acceptable compromise. His book *Histoire d'une
paix manquée*, published one year before Dien Bien Phu, clearly
showed that he still held this view, and the French Government
believed that, if anyone could, Sainteny would be the one who could

rebuild the burned bridges between Hanoi and Paris. When Sainteny left Hanoi in 1957 on "temporary leave"—never to return—his mission had been a total failure. All French property in North Viet-Nam had been confiscated; only the Tongking coal-mine owners received any compensation at all, and that a ridiculously inadequate 1 million tons of coal deliverable over ten years. So far, the D.R.V.N. has kept that part of its bargain. A trade agreement also was signed in 1955 and renewed every year since, covering a total of $1.8 million in both directions. In comparison, trade between France and South Viet-Nam in 1962, though much lower than in previous years, amounted to close to $40 million. On March 10, 1958, in the face of veiled threats that the French delegation in Hanoi would see its activities curtailed even further, France allowed the establishment of a D.R.V.N. "trade mission" in Paris. Hanoi answered that gesture of good will by two weeks later indicting a member of the French mission on charges of "espionage." The Frenchman, Bonfils, was expelled later, along with the last remaining French officer, who had been in charge of grave registration.

A problem that has poisoned French relations with *both* Viet-Nams is that of the repatriation of about 4,000 plantation workers of North Vietnamese origin, who had gone in the 1930's as contract laborers to the French Pacific possession of New Caledonia. In a surprising arrogation of diplomatic powers, the New Caledonia territorial government, faced with unemployment at home, negotiated a repatriation accord with the D.R.V.N. on April 30, 1958. Paris declared the agreement invalid on May 5, since New Caledonia had no more power to negotiate the repatriation of these Tonkinese than New Jersey, for example, would have to negotiate with Hungary about Hungarian refugees living within her borders. The Saigon government, however, seized upon that negotiation for a violent anti-French campaign that might perhaps have had a greater ring of sincerity if the government had informed its own public that at almost that very time anti-Communist Thailand was arranging to repatriate 70,000 Vietnamese refugees to North Viet-Nam, without giving them any real freedom of choice. In as hard-boiled a move as had been made in this field in years (and one that went totally unreported in the American press), Thailand and North Viet-Nam signed a "Red Cross" agreement in 1959, and under the indifferent eyes of "free world" observers, those Vietnamese left for Haiphong by ship in groups of about 1,500 a month. When it became clear that all the refugees could not be repatriated within the two years stipulated in the earlier agreement, a new accord was negotiated in Bangkok in November, 1962. For the North Vietnamese, those negotiations represented a considerable diplomatic victory; for while the 1959 negotiations had taken place on neutral ground in Rangoon, Burma, the new negotiations were taking place almost within the shadow of SEATO Headquarters.[22] The new agreement, extending the repatriation to 1964, will no doubt witness the full transfer of the remaining 37,000 Vietnamese (of whom a good part are practicing Catholics[23]) to the D.R.V.N. What other problems of common interest to Thailand and North Viet-Nam may have been discussed has not been reported.

In the meantime, Paris, under considerable pressure from the remaining French interests in Saigon, suspended talks on the repatriation of the Tonkinese from New Caledonia and paid for that gesture with the earlier-mentioned expulsion of all French priests, nuns, and missionaries still remaining north of the 17th parallel. By 1963, Saigon, preoccupied by somewhat weightier problems, has relaxed its anti-French campaign, and the problem of the Tonkinese in New Caledonia is in the process of being settled through the gradual repatriation of the contract workers to the Vietnamese zone of their choice—at French Government expense. Like most other French diplomatic moves concerning Viet-Nam, this one satisfies no one completely. But, under the circumstances, that in itself must be considered satisfactory.

In all other matters involving France, the D.R.V.N. has taken the orthodox Communist line. When Guinea broke away from the French Communauté in 1958, it was immediately recognized by Hanoi and—supreme insult to the culture-proud French—the D.R.V.N. provided the African republic with teachers of French after the piqued French withdrew their own personnel.[24] A high-ranking Hanoi delegation led by Ung Van Khiem, then Foreign Minister, visited all the left-leaning former French African states of Mali, Guinea, Niger, and Morocco. The delegation went also to Tunisia, where its attention did not center so much on pro-Western President Habib Bourguiba as on the Algerian nationalist regime, whose headquarters then were in Tunisia. During that spring 1961 visit, extensive contacts were made between VPA and Algerian Liberation Army officers, although rumors that General Giap himself had participated in those talks during an incognito trip to Tunisia have never been verified. The VPA provided training assistance to the Algerians, and the Algerians, in turn, provided the VPA with information on helicopter tactics (the French were using more than 600 helicopters in Algeria, of which 380 were of the H-21 type now being used by the United States in antiguerrilla operations in South Viet-Nam). In 1962, several high-level Algerian military delegations visited Hanoi and Peking, and after Algeria's independence, a special D.R.V.N. envoy, Nguyên Thanh Ha, spent several weeks in Algeria attending celebrations and making contacts.

Of the D.R.V.N.'s other non-Communist trade partners, only Britain and Japan account for substantial sums and strategically important products. A British consulate in Hanoi, though severely limited in its activities—it is accredited to the city of Hanoi rather than to the D.R.V.N. Government and is not authorized to display even a consular plaque or its national flag—is the official intermediary for D.R.V.N. trade with Hong Kong, where Hanoi also maintains a purchasing office. For prestige reasons and also in order to obtain some badly needed foreign exchange, Hanoi exported foodstuffs to Hong Kong even when its supply was grimly short. D.R.V.N. trade with Japan, after a period of coolness when Japan decided to pay war reparations to South Viet-Nam only, has reached important proportions that might well provoke concern in the United States. Trade rose from about $10 million in 1959 to more than $40 million in 1961–62 and involves such items as chemicals, machinery of all kinds, and four seagoing 5,000-ton cargo ships and one of 2,000 tons; for these, North Viet-Nam pays in raw materials, notably coal.[25] Since Japan also exports coal to South Viet-Nam under the American aid program, it is not inconceivable that North Vietnamese anthracite, after a 5,000-mile round trip and appropriate surcharges, is eventually consumed only a few hundred miles from where it was mined. But of such vagaries international economics are made in this Cold War era. Recent small coal finds in South Viet-Nam are, as will be seen, now replacing those imports.

There are no American relations whatever with the Hanoi regime, nor are there even postal relations, which goes one step further than the restrictions imposed by the two Viet-Nams upon their own citizens, who may correspond with each other on strictly censored "interzonal postcards," which are a line-for-line copy of the postcards introduced by the German military administration in France for correspondence between the Vichy-controlled zone and German-administered northern France. An American regulation of October 29, 1958, forbids foreign-chartered American vessels to dock in North Vietnamese ports.

The most significant North Vietnamese foreign relations are those between Hanoi and Moscow and Peking. Many Western pundits to the contrary, relations between the D.R.V.N. and the Soviet bloc have *not* been unfailingly friendly and close. It must be remembered that during the first four years of its existence, the D.R.V.N. was in total geographic isolation from any other member of the Communist orbit. Whatever relations with outside Communist parties there were, were maintained via the very active French Communist Party cell in Saigon.[26] As for Soviet interest in Indochina, it did not seem to go beyond the already mentioned favorable response of Stalin at Tehran and Yalta to Roosevelt's proposals for ousting the French colonial administration. In the words of Joseph Frankel, a British specialist on the problem:

> There is no evidence of any war-time liaison between Communist resistance formations in South-East Asia and the U.S.S.R.; the isolation of South-East Asia under Japanese occupation and the Soviet preoccupation with the war against Germany made such liaison unlikely.[27]

As I stated in a 1954 study: "Soviet policy towards Viet-Nam—very much as had been said about American policy—'cloaked nothing but real isolation from Indochinese events.' "[28]

What outside observers also apparently have failed to realize is that, unlike the other Far Eastern colonial powers in 1946 (Britain, the Netherlands, and the United States), France was the only one likely to become Communist-controlled. Its whole colonial empire would then have followed suit and joined the Soviet orbit along with the French homeland. As long as that chance existed, and it existed until March, 1947, the U.S.S.R. pointedly refrained from using the same propaganda tactics on France as on the other colonial powers and did not openly support Viet-Minh ambitions for independence. This explains why in 1946–47, when the Soviet press was extremely vocal with regard to the colonialism of all the other powers, it never mentioned France in derogatory terms.[29] A lengthy *Izvestia* report on the Inter-Asian Conference at New Delhi, published on May 31, 1947 (i.e., *after* the French Communist Party had lost its foothold in the French Government and after French forces had been fighting the Viet-Minh for six months), excoriated the United States, Britain, Holland, Japan, and the Chinese Nationalists, but said only the following about the Indochina **War**: The delegation from "Viet-Nam . . . told a convincing tale of how colonial powers throw off their pacifist disguises and apply armed force for the suppression of the national liberation movement." That Soviet attitude explains why the French Communist Party cell in Saigon warned the Viet-Minh, then trying to resist the French reoccupation of Saigon in September, 1945, that any "premature adventures" toward independence might "not be in line with Soviet perspectives."[30] Obviously, if Communism had succeeded in taking over France, the Viet-Minh and Ho would have been in the uncomfortable position of being taxed with "nationalist deviationism" for resisting a Communist government by force of arms! This also explains why, at home, the French Communist leaders in parliament (the Party chief, Maurice Thorez, was Vice-Premier at the time) did *not* block the first Indochina War budget and all the emergency measures connected with the prosecution of the first phase of the war.[31] There can be no doubt that a Communist-provoked government crisis in the winter of 1946–47 would have brought a military crisis in Indochina and might have caused the war to end in a compromise because of lack of supplies and manpower on the French side.

Small wonder, then, that the French conservative politicians rose in the National Assembly during a crucial appropriations debate from March 14–18, 1947, to thank their own Communist colleagues *and* the Soviet Union for leaving France to fight its war in Indochina without outside disturbance. Maurice Schumann, the leader of the Catholic middle-of-the-road Mouvement Républicain Populaire, rose in the Assembly to thank the Soviet press for its "laudable position of restraint and correctness, dictated, perhaps, by the . . . certitude that if, by ill luck, France would have to withdraw [from Indochina], her place would be taken by others." There was no doubt in anyone's mind as to who those unidentified "others" were. And France's Socialist Premier, Jean Ramadier, took the rostrum to emphasize that "in the Indochina question, we have always noted to this day the correct attitude of the Soviet Government."

It is likely that another factor restrained the U.S.S.R. from open intervention in support of Ho Chi Minh: In view of the losing fight of the Greek Communists and Stalin's deepening quarrel with Tito, there probably was little eagerness to aid yet another cause where chances of victory seemed slim. (It should also be remembered here that the Soviet Union did not establish diplomatic relations with Red China until October 2, 1949.) When the Ho Chi Minh regime made its appeal to the world for diplomatic recognition on January 14, 1950, Red China granted recognition four days later

Russia delayed until January 30, followed on the next day by North Korea. The other European satellites recognized the D.R.V.N. in the spring of 1950. Yugoslavia also recognized the D.R.V.N. but was pointedly snubbed in return by the ever-orthodox Ho. However, none of the countries that recognized the D.R.V.N. actually sent a diplomatic mission to Ho until after the cease-fire of July, 1954.

In addition to the countries of the "socialist camp," several uncommitted countries, such as India and Indonesia, have exchanged consuls general with Hanoi. In 1963, Cambodia followed suit by accepting a D.R.V.N. commercial mission in Phnom-Penh. Laos had to pay the diplomatic price of its military defeats of 1961–62 by accepting a North Vietnamese ambassador to Vientiane late in 1962. For a brief moment, the neutralist kingdom had hoped for a typically Laotian compromise: It offered to maintain recognition of South Viet-Nam by having the latter's ambassador remain in Vientiane, while the North Vietnamese diplomatic mission would reside at the royal capital of Luang-Prabang. However, South Viet-Nam refused that solution and closed its embassy, but to confuse the situation further, it retained a consulate at Paksé, a southern Lao right-wing stronghold. Laos did not reciprocate the South Vietnamese gesture and continues to maintain its own representation at the chargé level in Saigon.

However, the most momentous foreign relations problem confronting the North Vietnamese leadership in 1963 is that of the estrangement between Moscow and Peking, which has compelled the D.R.V.N. to take positions in the intrabloc ideological quarrel—a pitfall that Ho has studiously avoided until now. At the Twenty-second Congress of the CPSU, in November, 1961, the D.V.R.N.'s dilemma reached a critical point—but, as has been mentioned, Ho once more succeeded in avoiding a showdown between the pro-Peking and pro-Moscow elements within the Hanoi ruling group. The increasing bitterness of the revolutionary war in South Viet-Nam and the D.R.V.N.'s open support of the Pathet-Lao in Laos have created continuing problems. In the case of Laos, the U.S.S.R. apparently favored a negotiated settlement whose terms apparently also suited Hanoi, but almost completely "froze out" Peking's participation. Conversely, in the case of South Viet-Nam, Russia—which, particularly after the Cuban affair, seems to have lost its taste for operations far from its bases that might involve a head-on clash with the United States—appears unwilling to go as far as the North Vietnamese leadership would like. Peking, on the other hand, seems quite willing to back the D.R.V.N. fully—even beyond the point to which the present D.R.V.N. leadership is willing to go. In this unresolved divergence may lie the key to the seesawing of visits made to Hanoi throughout 1962 by high-level Soviet and Red Chinese missions, and the impassioned pleas of North Viet-Nam's Party newspaper for a reconciliation between the two major Communist powers:

> Within the socialist system, with the Soviet Union as the center, the cause of building socialism and communism has recorded great achievements . . . to defend fruitfully the world socialist system, all socialist countries must unite closely, especially the two large countries—the Soviet Union and China—because the solidarity between the Soviet Union and China is the mainstay of the solidarity within the socialist camp as a whole.[32]

On balance, it is possible to discern the following major shifts within the North Vietnamese political spectrum since 1954: The pro Peking wing was in the ascendancy until the fall of 1956, when its slavish imitation of Chinese economic methods brought about a rebellion of the peasantry. De-Stalinization never was very popular in Hanoi, but the failure of the "hundred flowers"—another Chinese import—brought a swing to a more nuanced position. Late in 1959, pro-Chinese elements began to come to the fore again, and there were some indications that late in 1960 the VPA hero, General Giap (considered a leader of the pro-Moscow wing), was temporarily out of favor.[33] Subsequent changes in the VPA General Staff, however, showed that Giap had weathered the storm: In March, 1961, Lieutenant General Song Hao replaced Brigadier General Nguyên Chi Thanh, erstwhile leader of the Lao-Dong's youth movement and then Chief of the VPA's Political Department. General Thanh, an unswerving adherent of the pro-Peking line, was shunted off to head the Ministry of Agricultural Cooperatives. Three other senior generals, known for their personal loyalty to Giap, were transferred to key jobs on the VPA General Staff. After Ho's trip to Moscow in October, 1961, the pro-Russian wing again seemed to have gained the upper hand. Much was also made of the fact that the Chinese ambassadorial post in Hanoi was vacant for more than three months in the summer of 1962, and of some sub-Cabinet changes in Hanoi in 1962 and 1963. The most remarkable example of this careful navigating between two lines was the joint statement issued by Ho Chi

Minh and Liu Shao-ch'i in May, 1963. In it, Liu emphasized faithfulness to Marxism-Leninism, while Ho just as steadfastly cautioned Peking against "dogmatism."

But the danger exists of falling into the trap of Kremlinology and trying to read too much importance into such events. The brutal truth is that for so small and exposed a country as North Viet-Nam, the number of policy choices is not infinite and that the present Hanoi leadership is painfully aware of the fearsome consequences of even a small miscalculation in a situation where it must play the brinkmanship game with as enormous an adversary as the United States. This emerged clearly in interviews given by North Vietnamese leaders to three Westerners during 1962: a London *Daily Express* correspondent in March, myself in July, and Colonel Jules Roy in December. It was obvious to all three observers that the D.R.V.N. had backed off from outright conquest of South Viet-Nam and was veering toward a negotiated solution embodying the existence of a neutral South Vietnamese state that would not be reunited with the North for a long time to come.[34]

Although such a policy may be, in the eyes of the D.R.V.N. leaders, only a smokescreen pending ultimate conquest through political means, once American troops have been removed from the scene, the fact remains that Ho Chi Minh has been a lifelong pragmatist and is today President of a truncated Vietnamese state that—if it is not the most prosperous state of Southeast Asia—at least has the merit of not being bombed to rubble. To win South Viet-Nam may be heroic and worthwhile, but not at the price of seeing all of the D.R.V.N.'s painfully rebuilt economic potential plowed under by American bombers. Enough North Vietnamese delegations have paid visits to their North Korean sister republic to know at firsthand what even obsolete B-29's could do to factories, railroads, dams, and towns —and at seventy-three, Ho may wish to leave Viet-Nam, even if only half of it, more than smoking ruins and, presumably then, in complete subjection to Communist China. In a television program on February 11, 1963, W. Averell Harriman, then Assistant Secretary of State for Far Eastern Affairs, summed up the prevailing official U.S. view of Ho's problem:

> . . . it looks as though Ho Chi Minh is trying to play both ends against the middle. He wants to get Russian support; the Viet-Minh do not wish to have the Chinese overrun them. You might say their hearts are in Moscow, but their stomachs are in China.[35]

Taking a longer view, A. Doak Barnett stated, in his excellent study on *Communist China and Asia,* that "Communist China's ambitions in Viet-Nam have been nourished . . . by China's historic traditions as well as by revolutionary zeal."[36] The same can be said for Ho Chi Minh's North Viet-Nam; its revolutionary zeal, too, has been nourished by historic traditions. And those traditions include as much independence from China as circumstances permit.

THREE

INSURGENCY IN THE SOUTH

10

The Lost Decade

WHEN Emperor Bao-Dai, confronted by Viet-Minh emissaries in his almost-deserted palace, abdicated his throne, in August, 1945, his message to the Vietnamese people had a ring of tragic foreboding in it that makes it a fitting epitaph on the failures of Vietnamese nationalism since then:

> We cannot help but feel a certain amount of melancholy at the thought of Our glorious ancestors who had struggled for 400 years to make Our country great. . . . We cannot help but have feelings of regret at the thought of the 20 years of Our reign, during which We have not been able to render any appreciable services to Our country. . . .

It is this melancholy at the thought that independence had to be bought at the price of division, these regrets at the thought that almost twenty years of rule in one form or another have not brought about closer contacts with the Vietnamese people, that often pervade the words of Vietnamese nationalists in Saigon, once the resounding formulas of "our achievements since independence" have been pronounced and organized homage to other slogans, existing leaders, and movements has been paid and can be dispensed with.

Not that the achievements of the nationalist regimes have not been real; they have been and are still notable. But they have never been of the kind that will make the average citizen tear up the pavements to make barricades and rise in defense of his government. It is one thing to have one's chest seared with napalm while leading a bayonet charge against a French position at Dien Bien Phu, and another to have peptic ulcers induced by six years of diplomatic dinners while negotiating with French officials in eighteenth-century châteaux over precisely the points the Viet-Minh sought to gain with their bayonets. But peoples and history are so made that battles are remembered but negotiations are not: Every American school child remembers Yorktown; but Benjamin Franklin is remembered for his thrift and the invention of the lightning rod, and not for his European diplomatic victories or the Treaty of Paris of 1783.

No high-level Vietnamese Government official in Saigon since 1949 has failed to vent his irritation with his sullen fellow citizens to the sympathetic foreign observer. The standard exclamation is: "*Ils ne comprennent pas tout ce que nous faisons pour eux!*" ("They just don't understand all that we're doing for them!") And that is absolutely true.

Bao-Dai obtained greater formal independence from the French in two years of hard bargaining than Ho Chi Minh had asked for in his most extreme demands of 1946. By 1954, the Saigon regime had received more international recognition, even from the newly independent countries, than the Viet-Minh jungle fighters had after eight years of bloody war; today more than thirty nations have missions of one type or another in Saigon at a time when the government is literally beleaguered in its capital, while barely a handful—perhaps four or five—of the non-Communist nations have relations with Hanoi. And while Saigon sits as a full-fledged member in every United Nations agency from which it cannot be barred by a Soviet veto, Hanoi, in an isolation that is partly self-willed, does not even provide agricultural statistics to the U.N. Economic Commission for Asia and the Far East (ECAFE). In various test votes in the United Nations on the admission of either or both Viet-Nams, South Viet-Nam has always led its northern neighbor by a sizable margin, and it garnered more votes than South Korea when the latter's admission was put to a test. These are impressive international testimonials to the regime's viability and to the validity of its claims to represent the Vietnamese people as a whole.

But proofs that carry weight in the international community have no bearing whatever on the question of the allegiance of the farming population in a country-wide revolutionary war. It is far easier for a Vietnamese Government official to travel to Washington, Paris, or Léopoldville than it is for him to stay alive in an automobile traveling from Saigon to My-Tho or Cape St. Jacques, fifty miles from his office. And that is basically where the crux of the trouble lies: Save at fleeting moments, the Saigon regime has never been able to command the loyalty, let alone the affection, of much of the Vietnamese population theoretically under its control. Indeed, the government has done things *for* the people, but only a few of them have been of the kind that are, in Bao-Dai's term, "appreciable." It takes a politician or a statesman to appreciate the importance of diplomatic recognition by eighty nations, but every illiterate peasant can test for himself whether land reform has been a reality or a sham in his district, and whether the local police and administrative officials are really civil "servants" or a gang of brutes and grafters out to make the most of their stranglehold upon a hapless population. It can be argued that, considering the evidence adduced in the previous chapters, North Viet-Nam's record in the treatment of its peasantry is hardly an improvement over that of the South; in some respects, it is even worse. Unfortunately, no one at the village level is able to make a comparison on that score, except in the areas south of the 17th parallel that were occupied by the Viet-Minh during the 1946–54 Indochina War, or have been occupied for any length of time since 1959 by Communist forces. And in those areas, the Communists— for propaganda purposes—have seen to it that their treatment of the small peasant contrasted favorably with that of the nationalist administration and, particularly, the nationalist soldiery.[1]

Thus, every non-Communist regime in Viet-Nam, whether under French or American aegis, has been faced with the terrible problem of having to reconcile its external successes and internal shortcomings —not to speak of the additional internal dilemma of political power based on a small urban middle class and civil-servant class that has to control an essentially rural society.

It is the problem of the Saigon regime's contact with the broad masses of its own population, rather than Communist subversion, that, for almost two decades, has been the major problem of the non-Communist elite of Viet-Nam, for, if such contact existed on either an institutional or an informal basis, Communist subversive efforts would, to a large extent, be unsuccessful.[2] This is the fundamental key to the complex problems of Viet-Nam's non-Communist state.

END OF AN EMPIRE

The desertion of Bao-Dai by his first nationalist government on August 7, 1945—*before* the Viet-Minh had descended from their mountain hideouts—has never received sufficient attention. Yet it is at the root of Bao-Dai's later contempt for his ministerial entourage and also of the contempt of much of the population for the later nationalist regimes. The nationalist government of Tran Trong Kim (April–August, 1945) had disintegrated because it was *afraid*; afraid of the momentous task of having to feed a starving population and having to run a wrecked economy; afraid of the fate it would meet at the hands of either the Allies or the Viet-Minh for having "collaborated" with the Japanese; afraid, finally, of the very forces of nationalist extremism and xenophobia it had unleashed and could no longer control. Tran Trong Kim's government was made up of honest and capable men (some of whom still serve with Ngo Dinh Diem), but they were not born to be heroes. And the summer of 1945, particularly in Viet-Nam, was a time for heroes.

Bao-Dai, then only thirty-two, had to deal almost alone with the crises that followed. This was still the earnest young emperor (his night club days lay in the future) who tried to do as good a job as possible under the circumstances. At the request of his father, Emperor Khai-Dinh, Bao-Dai had been educated in France in the household of Eugène Charles, who had been a French colonial official in Hué. Only once during this ten-year period beginning in 1922 had Bao-Dai returned to Viet-Nam. When he ascended the throne, he dropped the name Vinh-Thuy and assumed the dynastic name Bao-Dai, meaning, ironically, "keeper of greatness." Shy and sensitive, he tried zealously to reform Viet-Nam along modern lines, away from the sterile intrigues of a decadent court. In a love match that defied court ceremonial and endeared him to his subjects, he married a southern Catholic girl of humble origin, and in 1933, he selected as his Minister of the Interior a man who, when he was the young governor of Phan-Thiet Province, had made a name for himself for his honesty and energy. His name was Ngo Dinh Diem.

Both Bao-Dai and Empress Nam-Phuong endeavored to do their best, for time was short. On August 20, 1945, Bao-Dai sent urgent messages to President Truman, King George VI, Generalissimo

Chiang Kai-shek, and General Charles de Gaulle, requesting recognition of the independence of Viet-Nam under his rule. The plea addressed to de Gaulle, then President of the French Provisional Government, is particularly noteworthy, for it shows the deep emotion Bao-Dai must have felt at the time. And it also predicted the future with amazing accuracy:

> Even though you may be able to re-establish French administration here, it would not be obeyed any more. Each village would become a resistance nest; every former collaborator would become an enemy. . . .
>
> I beg you to understand that the only way to safeguard French interests and the spiritual influence of France in Indochina is to recognize frankly the independence of Viet-Nam and to renounce all thoughts of re-establishing French sovereignty or administration under any form whatsoever.
>
> We could easily be able to understand each other and become friends if you would cease to pretend that you want again to become our masters.[3]

Empress Nam-Phuong, a devout Catholic, addressed several messages to the Catholic hierarchy and to women's organizations, pleading for support for her country's cause. Both Bao-Dai and his empress were completely ignored abroad, just as they had been deserted at home. In both Saigon and Hanoi, red flags with a gold star in the center began to appear in the streets; and Ho's Viet-Minh units, escorted by OSS teams and followed by Chinese Nationalist troops, looked much more promising as rulers of Viet-Nam than the young couple on that archaic throne in Hué.

The only person acute enough to realize the psychological value of Bao-Dai was, of course, Ho Chi Minh himself. Far from permitting Bao-Dai to be conveniently done away with, Ho immediately made him "Supreme Adviser to the Republican Government" under the title and name of "Citizen Prince Nguyên Vinh-Thuy." While Bao-Dai's active contributions as Ho's adviser are somewhat obscure—if he actually made any—the fact that he was seen in Hanoi in company of the regime's senior members added a great deal to their prestige with both the Vietnamese and the foreigners. Particularly to such American observers as Major General Philip E. Gallagher, the ex-emperor's presence seemed to guarantee that the Viet-Minh were not Communists—as if the presence of young King Michael in Soviet-occupied Romania had in any way changed the character of the pro-Communist regime there. But in both cases, the royal figurehead served its purpose: It fooled the more gullible Western observers, and that was all that mattered at the moment. Some of the more prejudiced French sources—such as General Sabattier, who then had just returned from Yünnan—asserted that Bao-Dai was the object of "particular solicitude" on the part of OSS and already was being groomed as an alternate leader to the Viet-Minh. There is no reliable substantiation for this assertion. Nevertheless, when Bao-Dai and his family and entourage decided to flee North Viet-Nam— ostensibly they were going on a mission to Chiang Kai-shek to obtain economic and military aid for the government of Ho Chi Minh— they left Hanoi on March 18, 1946, on a C-47 aircraft of the U.S. Army Air Corps. Instead of landing in Chungking, the plane went to Hong Kong.

It was in Hong Kong that Bao-Dai first acquired his reputation as *"l'empereur des boîtes de nuit"* ("the night-club emperor"). As Professor Paul Rivet, a middle-of-the-road French legislator, said in a stormy parliamentary debate in March, 1949, "the serious people were surprised at the apparent indifference of Bao-Dai to the misfortunes that befell his country." In a somewhat less charitable vein, left-wing deputy François Mitterrand commented in another debate on January 19, 1950:

> In 1932, he ascends to the throne . . . and France pays him. . . . On March 11, 1945 . . . Bao-Dai . . . collaborates with the Japanese. Japan pays and Bao-Dai obeys. On August 25, 1945, he abdicates. . . . Ho Chi Minh appears the stronger [and] Bao-Dai hopes that, on that side, too, pay will be forthcoming.
>
> But what can such a young republic offer? . . . This does not suit Bao-Dai . . . [and he] crosses over to China. Chiang sends him back to his [Bao-Dai's] habitual moneylenders, and we find him in Hong Kong, surrounded by emissaries of the United States and of the Bank of Indochina, and by the Reverend Father Vircondelet, Procurator General of the Missions Etrangères. . . .

It is hard to determine exactly when the open break with the D.R.V.N. took place. In Hong Kong, Bao-Dai at first scrupulously stuck to the role of Ho's "Supreme Adviser." To French reporters who attempted to make him say that his abdication had been forced (with the clear implication that it was invalid and, hence, that the Ho Chi Minh regime was illegal), Bao-Dai maintained as late as July, 1947, that "my hand had not been forced—I abdicated of my own free will,"[4] and Ho Chi Minh himself stated as late as August of the same year that "many members of the [D.R.V.N.] Government and myself, friends of Counselor Vinh-Thuy, are eager to see him again. . . . The Government and the people of Viet-Nam have full confidence in the fidelity of Counselor Vinh-Thuy."[5]

There is also some obscurity as to when Bao-Dai was first thought of as an alternative to Ho Chi Minh. The idea is sometimes attributed to William C. Bullitt, wartime American Ambassador to the de Gaulle government, who met Bao-Dai late in 1947; but there is now some evidence that French General Le Bris, who commanded Central Viet-Nam in 1945–46, had been impressed with the affection and loyalty the absent ruler still commanded there and had recommended the "Bao-Dai solution" to his government as early as December, 1946.

When the French replaced the disastrous Admiral d'Argenlieu on March 5, 1947, with a civilian high commissioner, Emile Bollaert, hopes began to rise that a "new deal" could be negotiated in Indochina, and emissaries began to fly back and forth between Hanoi, Hué, Saigon, and Hong Kong—including, on several occasions, the ardent nationalist reformer Ngo Dinh Diem. Bao-Dai began to negotiate his return in earnest late in 1947, after all hopes of peaceful negotiations between the French and the Viet-Minh had collapsed, and Viet-Minh depredations and killings of anti-Communist nationalists became more widely known. The break with the D.R.V.N. appears to have become irreparable when Bao-Dai was allegedly sentenced to death and stripped of Vietnamese citizenship by a Viet-Minh drumhead court in December, 1947. A year and a half later, he was again ruling Viet-Nam.

But in one sense Bao-Dai never broke faith with the Viet-Minh: He never went back on his abdication of August 25, 1945. Viet-Nam under his later rule was never again called an "empire" but styled itself a *"quôc-gia"* ("state"); and a volume issued by the Vietnamese Provisional Central Government in 1948[6] dealing with all French-Vietnamese treaties signed since 1787 includes the French–Viet-Minh agreements of March, 1946, and the subsequent military protocols as part of the body of French-Vietnamese treaties—as if the new anti-Communist Vietnamese state were a *de facto* successor to the Ho Chi Minh regime.[7] Later on, the basic constitutional document of the Bao-Dai regime, Ordinance No. 1 of July 1, 1949, deliberately left the character of the regime in doubt until the Vietnamese people were in a position "to freely decide upon their own institutions." When they had an opportunity to do so, on October 23, 1955, they voted against Bao-Dai and for a republican regime under Ngo Dinh Diem by a reported 63,017 votes to 5.7 million.

STATE OF VIET-NAM

On the nationalist side, in the meantime, Vietnamese politics went their unhappy way. As always before, and most of the time thereafter, the nationalists split into atom-sized groups and grouplets whose names were the more resounding as they represented less and less: Thus, 1947 saw the emergence of a National Union Front, composed of the remnants of the nationalists who had followed the Chinese into Hanoi in 1945. The group's headquarters were in Nanking, China. The Front was later broadened by the inclusion of the Viet-Nam Democratic-Socialist Party, the Nationalist Youth Association, the People's League, the Cao-Dai, and, finally, some Buddhist groups. Tran Trong Kim emerged from hiding and took the leadership of the Front. In its heyday (i.e., as long as there was some hope of Chinese Nationalist support), the Front was more anti-French than Ho Chi Minh's Viet-Minh and even willing to collaborate with the latter if "by so doing it could help achieve an independent Viet-Nam."[8]

Finally, after long negotiations with Bao-Dai, led by his former regional governor in Cochinchina, Nguyên Van Sam, the National Union Front issued a manifesto on May 17, 1947, which opened the door to the return of Bao-Dai while advocating a republican structure of government—in order to attract Viet-Minh support— and full independence with loose association with the French Union; this last was a position from which Vietnamese nationalism did not depart until the French had left Viet-Nam for good. But the French were not yet ready for the type of far-reaching solution the British realistically accepted in Burma: total departure from the Commonwealth of a small country in the hope of winning the larger colonies by this demonstration of the meaning of "free association."

France's answer to the nationalists came four months later, on September 20, 1947, in a speech made by High Commissioner Bollaert at Ha-Dong in North Viet-Nam, which contained only the barest of references to an undefined future "autonomy." That broke the back of the National Union Front, whose fate was sealed one month later by Nguyên Van Sam's murder by the Viet-Minh and probably ended forever any chance of a genuine broadly based Vietnamese nationalist movement capable of competing with the Viet-Minh in patriotic appeal. Whatever proposals followed were watered down with so many compromises, mental reservations, and *double-*

entendres that they could not rival Ho's simple creed of total independence even at the price of a long and bloody war.

For this, the French had no one but themselves to blame, and most thoughtful Frenchmen recognize this. "Indecisions, contradictions, hesitations, decisions; orders and counterorders of successive governments"—this is how Professor Roger Lévy, of France's authoritative Centre d'Etudes de Politique Etrangère, in 1952 described France's policies in Viet-Nam.[9] Professor Isoart, in his 1961 study of the same problem, not only agrees with Lévy but adds that the Indochina War had simply become a French internal political football in the grand tradition of the Dreyfus case or of the question of government support for Catholic schools:

> Having inherited from our Gallic ancestors their taste for anarchy and from our Latin culture the love for drawn-out palavers, we found [in Viet-Nam] the occasion to wallow in both. Interest in the fate of France or Viet-Nam had long been lost in all this. . . .[10]

The left-wing parties, which, as has been shown, had supported the war against Ho at its beginnings, had switched to the other side once Moscow had made clear where it stood; the middle-of-the-road Socialists, though against the war, stood with the right wing because of its support on internal pork-barrel issues that were dear to the Socialists; and the remainder of the French parliament had the same outlook on Viet-Nam as it later had on Algeria and remembered the issue only long enough to complain about its increasing cost at budget time. Militarily, the war was directed by a two-headed monstrosity: Since it was, legally, not a "war" but a "police action" within territories under French responsibility (one would have to make a fine distinction between fighting in a colony such as Cochinchina and in a protectora. such as Tongking), the Ministry of Overseas France ran the war, at first, with troops it had "borrowed" from the French Ministry of Defense. Later, a special Ministry for the Associated States took over responsibilities for the three Indochinese states, and the split between the Defense and Indochina ministries continued. It led to an endless merry-go-round of shifting responsibilities; questions of a military nature were referred from Defense to Associated States and back to Defense, and the Ministry for the Associated States at one time had under its jurisdiction the bulk of France's armed forces. Although the French internal chaos did not in itself cause the military defeats and the political delays, it certainly made a concerted Viet-Nam policy completely impossible and made any achievements in the field of Vietnamese unity in alliance with France a matter of sheer accident rather than design.

On May 20, 1948, representatives of the three Vietnamese regions (*ky*) met in Saigon and entrusted a former Premier of the autonomist government in Cochinchina and former French brigadier general, Nguyên Van Xuan, with the formation of a Provisional Central Government of Viet-Nam. On May 26, Xuan presented his new Cabinet to Bao-Dai in Hong Kong. Bao-Dai had not remained inactive in the meantime. After sparring with Bollaert for more than a year in Hong Kong and at Along Bay, in Tongking, Bao-Dai had left for Europe and settled down in neutral Geneva, determined to negotiate with the French only where he could be sure of being fully independent. Bollaert had had to come all the way from Saigon to Geneva in January, 1948, to talk with him. Having received reassurances that France would interpret "generously" any agreements that would be signed, Bao-Dai had nevertheless refused to return to Viet-Nam until everything was nailed down in writing, and he had reached Hong Kong without setting foot in Viet-Nam. Only when the hard-pressed Bollaert finally was able to bring with him the necessary guarantees in writing did Bao-Dai finally consent to affix his signature to the document that was to tie his name forever to the nationalist attempt at creating a regime to compete with that of the D.R.V.N.

On June 5, 1948, a Catalina flying boat landed on the smooth waters of Along Bay, where the French cruiser *Duguay-Trouin*, with Bollaert aboard, was waiting. The document that Bao-Dai now signed in the presence of his new Premier contained, in its very first sentence, the fateful words: "France solemnly recognizes the independence of Viet-Nam." That phrase was hedged by another, stating that Viet-Nam now proclaimed "its adherence to the French Union as a state associated with France."

But the essential point had been gained. Bao-Dai had obtained from the French in two years of negotiating what Ho had not been able to obtain in two years of fighting: the word "independence." And Bao-Dai had still not "given in" to the French! The Along Bay document bears his "initialed" signature only, with the notation, "signed in His Majesty's presence" and Xuan's signature—thus leaving Bao-Dai room to maneuver should the French not fulfill the terms of the agreement. He left for Paris that same evening without returning to Hong Kong. Bao-Dai had ceased to be a neutral in the struggle between France and the Viet-Minh and had reaffirmed the right of Vietnamese nationalism to speak for itself.

On the Viet-Minh side, the news of Bao-Dai's success was received with mixed feelings. At first, it produced what the French had expected: a wave of desertions from the Viet-Minh by non-Communists who remained with them because there was no alternative. For a time, the Viet-Minh leadership was at a loss to explain the new agreements. It declared simply that Bao-Dai had been "duped" by the French imperialists. As late as February, 1949, Tran Bach Mai, the D.R.V.N.'s emissary to Thailand, declared that "we are not opposed to Bao-Dai and Xuan because they negotiate with France but because they do not represent the people."[11] While the diehard French *colons* in Cochinchina still attempted to wreck the new agreements (they did not succeed but protested loudly enough to persuade most Vietnamese that they had once more been betrayed), France herself made another bad mistake; a new French high commissioner, Léon Pignon, was appointed on October 21, 1948, to replace the liberal Bollaert. Pignon was an old Indochina hand from the Colonial Civil Service, and he brought with him a staff of old-line colonial administrators to whom the idea of a truly independent Viet-Nam meant total chaos, but who were at least competent in handling the day-to-day negotiations with the Vietnamese.

And that seemed precisely what was needed, for the negotiations *among* the Vietnamese themselves were extremely stormy, with some of the delegations to the "National Congress," which was supposed to approve the agreements between Bao-Dai and France, refusing to sit in the same room. The upshot was that the delegates from South and Central Viet-Nam met in Saigon in November, 1948; then those of North and South Viet-Nam met in Hanoi on December 5; and finally, on December 9, after the Southern delegation left for home, the Central Vietnamese met alone with their Northern colleagues. Deep in South Viet-Nam, in the meantime, the Hoa-Hao and Cao-Dai sects, which had concluded a truce, resumed their private war and ignored the Provisional Central Government. But as later in the Algerian crisis, time could not be halted: The *colon*-dominated "Assembly of the Republic of Cochinchina" discreetly changed its name to "South Viet-Nam Assembly" on December 31, 1948, and most local administrative services and the public health and postal services came under Vietnamese jurisdiction as of that date.

With the Cochinchinese hurdle out of the way, events marched on with almost lightning speed. On March 8, 1949, Bao-Dai received from French President Vincent Auriol a letter (equivalent to an American executive agreement) that contained an unequivocal sentence: "Disregarding all previous treaties . . . France solemnly reaffirms her decision not to oppose any *de jure* or *de facto* obstacle to the accession of Cochinchina to Viet-Nam. . . ."

It only remained to go through the constitutional processes of having Cochinchina hold a referendum on its fate—one shudders at the idea of what would have happened if Cochinchina had voted "No"—and having the French National Assembly ratify Cochinchina's "popular will." On March 14, the Cochinchina election project was approved by the French parliament by a 378 to 198 vote, and the elections for a new territorial assembly were held on April 10. Abstentions in the district embracing Saigon and Cholon ran 90 per cent, and the total number who voted was 1,700 out of an adult population of 3 million. On April 23, the newly elected Territorial Assembly met to cast the only vote it had been elected for and decided to accede to. Viet-Nam by a vote of 55 to 6, with 2 abstentions. The French National Assembly met on May 21, 1949, after its Easter recess, and ratified the loss of the colony of Cochinchina and its accession to Viet-Nam by a vote of 351 to 209. In a typical example of the crazy-quilt pattern of French political actions, the right-wing and middle-of-the-road conservatives voted for independence, and the traditionally anticolonial Socialists and Communists, for reasons having nothing to do whatever with the issue at hand, voted "No."

The March 9 accords between Bao-Dai and Auriol contained other points that were not very different from those the United States obtained from the Philippines in 1946: chiefly, guarantees of French bases after independence and preferential positions for French economic interests in Viet-Nam and vice versa, and for French cultural institutions. They also provided for "coordination" in the field of foreign affairs; theoretically, France had to "approve" the establishment of Vietnamese embassies abroad, but that privilege was never actually invoked (although a young senator from Massachusetts, in a speech on the Senate floor on April 6, 1953, asserted that this was the case).

Eighty-seven years after the French admirals had hoisted the tricolor over Cochinchina, and in the midst of a costly civil war, Viet-Nam had again become a unified state—thanks to the persistence of Bao-Dai rather than to the violence of the Viet-Minh or the abstentions of the wait-and-see (*attentiste*) ultranationalists. On April 24,

1949, twenty-four hours after the final vote in Cochinchina, Bao-Dai boarded an airplane for Viet-Nam.

Things went badly as soon as Bao-Dai returned: Since Cochinchina would officially become Vietnamese only after the vote of the French National Assembly in May, Bao-Dai bypassed Saigon completely and went directly to the mountain resort of Dalat, which was to become his place of work and leisure (mostly the latter) until 1954. Shy as he was, and saddled with his past role as emperor, Bao-Dai was no more capable of the "common touch" than is his mandarinal successor, Ngo Dinh Diem. As he walked off his airplane in Dalat, returning after four years of exile to his country, at long last reunified and theoretically independent, he did not, in the words of a French eyewitness, "even glance at the imperial flag raised in his honor [and] he had no word for the line of Vietnamese notables."

When Bao-Dai finally went to Saigon, on June 13, the situation was even worse: Between the Viet-Minh cadres who had received orders to make the population stay away, and the French diehards who wanted to show their distaste for the new regime, Saigon was a deserted city. As French reporter Lucien Bodard saw it: "there were many flags fluttering colorfully in the breeze; there were policemen, and there were bowing civil servants. From the people, there came not a living soul. It was a fantastic reception." To Bao-Dai, it was a jarring experience and one he probably never forgot. He never again returned to Saigon for more than a few days.

On July 1, 1949, Bao-Dai himself temporarily assumed the Premiership of his newly formed government and issued an ordinance that until the promulgation of the constitution of the Republic of Viet-Nam on October 26, 1956, remained the legal foundation of the state of Viet-Nam. Ordinance No. 1, although reiterating that "The will of the People is the source of all national activities," also stated that, "in view of present circumstances, it cannot express itself freely." The Chief of State would rule by ordinance or decree and appoint the Premier and Cabinet. A Consultative National Assembly was to be formed later under Chapter IV of the Ordinance, but even that powerless body was never appointed. A certain degree of administrative latitude was left to three regional governors, including the power to create regional assemblies based on elections. As will be seen, legislative elections for provincial assemblies were indeed held later.

Thus, a non-Communist state of Viet-Nam was born, slowly and painfully; not in a flurry of lowering French flags and rising Vietnamese flags, but in an endless shuffle of transfer agreements, protocols, and registers that excited the imagination of no one and frittered away the psychological impact of the achievement. As an attempt to set·up a regime capable of competing with the Viet-Minh for the allegiance of the Vietnamese, the "Bao-Dai solution" had failed almost from the start.

"Perfecting Independence"

The same spirit of niggardly haggling over details was to prevail during all the negotiations that followed the March, 1949, exchange of letters. In contrast to Britain, which gave total independence to Burma in 1948 in an agreement requiring 4 legal-size pages, the French conventions signed by Bao-Dai and Pignon on December 30, 1949, which were designed merely to transfer the internal authority of France to Viet-Nam, filled a 258-page, 7-by-10-inch volume. They included such matters as a·convention on the administration of the Office of Tourism (in a war-torn country) and the statute of Joint Franco-Vietnamese River Traffic Commissions (to cover the handful of ships making the Mekong run up to Phnom-Penh). For two nations with the legalistic bent of Viet-Nam and France, this was a golden opportunity to debate endlessly over phrases and paragraphs without really going anywhere—for the turn of the war made most of the conventions inapplicable or obsolete by the time they were agreed upon, and those that were agreed upon were swept away in the torrent of France's elimination from the Vietnamese scene in 1954–56.

This also applied to the system of mixed courts that was set up to try cases involving Frenchmen. A double court system (one for the natives and one for Frenchmen or "persons of assimilated status," i.e., foreign nationals, including Asians) had long been a sore point among the Vietnamese. The French argument ran that the indigenous codes offered inadequate guarantees of proper procedure and objectivity (not to speak of the somewhat inadequate comforts of indigenous jails). A joint court system was set up, which even included a Franco-Vietnamese special supreme court, installed in Paris on February 27, 1952. But the system, despite its attempts to satisfy Vietnamese sensibilities, still smacked of "concessions" and "capitulations." Although the court system did at least function—and in some measure facilitated a healthy transition—it lasted only two years and certainly was not worth the legal talent and money expended on it.

The concurrent negotiations for the independence of Cambodia and Laos—conducted in the same spirit but, mercifully, on a simpler scale—finally brought up a thorny issue that was to overshadow all others: the splitting-up of the powers as well as the property held by Indochina as a federal union. The French governor generalcy of Indochina, as has been shown in Part One, enjoyed budgetary autonomy, and like all federal states, its own resources were derived from those of its member states. Viet-Nam, in view of its predominant position on the Indochinese peninsula, had received the lion's share of the federal budget: The port of Saigon, since it served Cambodia and Laos, as well, had been vastly expanded to cover the needs of those two smaller countries; roads and railroads had received federal subsidies (with Viet-Nam again getting the major share); and, of course, the physical properties of the federation—administrative buildings, research services, communications centers, etc.—were nearly all located on Vietnamese soil, as was the Bank of Indochina, which acted as bank of issue for the three states; and the customs, which were levied at the Vietnamese ports of entry for the benefit of the three states.

All this was to be settled in a technical conference grouping delegates from the three Indochinese states and France. Governor General Albert Sarraut, the "grand old man" of Indochina, was chairman of the conference, which opened at the French Pyrenees spa of Pau on June 29, 1950. When it ended five grueling months later, on November 27, it had thoroughly soured the three Indochinese states on each other and on France. What was supposed to have been a purely technical conference on such questions as immigration, economic-development planning, navigation on the Mekong, administration of the port of Saigon, the bank of issue, and foreign-currency control had become a free-for-all in which the two smaller states accused the French of being in collusion with the Vietnamese to dominate them. For their part, the Vietnamese suspected the French of trying a new version of the divide-and-conquer technique by backing Cambodia and Laos against them.[12]

That the results would satisfy no one was a foregone conclusion, but some of the points were settled in a manner acceptable to most participants. The best that can be said for the new crop of "quadripartite" organizations and boards that emerged from the Pau Conference is that they were either dead at birth or disposed of in one last "quadripartite" conference in Paris in December, 1954, which had the merit of being brief. The Vietnamese came away from the conference table clearly the victors. Not only did they inherit the bulk of all federal property located on their territory, including full control of the port of Saigon (instead of a joint port authority), but they also were to retain 71 per cent of all customs duties collected, as against 22 per cent for Cambodia and 7 per cent for Laos. In fact, Viet-Nam went one step further: Since 1952 she has simply pocketed the customs fees she owes Cambodia and Laos rather than passing them on to their lawful recipients. By the end of 1953, Vietnamese customs debts had risen to more than $40 million. Cambodia retaliated by establishing customs control posts on June 5, 1953 (which also was a violation of the Pau agreements); Viet-Nam used these as a further pretext to arrogate for herself the funds she owed the other states. When, finally, the bank of issue was divided up among the three states in December, 1954, Viet-Nam refused to turn over a considerable share of the common funds held in bank branches in Viet-Nam, estimated at more than 3 billion piasters ($100 million). Vietnamese highhandedness in financial affairs is one of the leading items on the long list of grievances that Cambodia has formulated against the Saigon regime.

From a purely economic standpoint, an Indochinese "Common Market" covering 30 million people with a common currency and no internal customs barriers would have indeed been a desirable achievement. But France, as a retiring colonial power, was not in a position to suggest it or to impose it. And no one else, either in Indochina or outside, has had the courage to bring up the subject since French rule ended.

In the meanwhile, slowly—far too slowly in the eyes of the Vietnamese—"decolonization" ran its course. The number of French civil servants in Indochina decreased from 27,050 in 1939 to 2,574 on March 31, 1952, and kept on decreasing rapidly, until it dropped to less than 1,700 at the time of the cease-fire in 1954.[13] The year 1952 also saw the creation of a completely autonomous Vietnamese budget, with receipts of about $150 million, to which French aid added $145 million and the United States another $40.7 million. But, most important, Viet-Nam had been recognized as a sovereign state by the United States and Britain on February 7, 1950—only seven days after the U.S.S.R. had recognized the D.R.V.N. The American recognition document stated that Viet-Nam, Cambodia, and Laos were considered to be "independent states within the French Union." The United Kingdom carefully, or as Lancaster says, "with greater circumspection," recognized Viet-Nam as an "Associate State within the French Union." In less than one year, independence had taken on reality: Viet-Nam became a member of six United Nations specialized agencies (WHO, ILO, FAO, UPU, ITU, and UNESCO) and participated on its own at the San Francisco Conference to conclude a peace treaty with Japan, after which Vietnamese Premier Tran Van Huu was received in Washington by President Truman. On September 12, 1952, Viet-Nam's admission to the U.N. was championed by France in the Security Council, and ten of the eleven members of the Council voted in favor of admission. A Soviet veto blocked action and has done so ever since.

But these gains in international respectability were not followed by similar gains in internal popularity. Just as the Saigon government after 1955 was to be dominated by Central Vietnamese and Northern Catholics at a time when the burden of the freedom struggle was on the South, so the Saigon regime prior to 1954—while the burden of the war lay upon the North—was dominated by southern landowners and representatives of the feudal sects, whose interest in such matters as land reform was purely negative. Also, the *"présence française"* still made itself felt too obtrusively: For far too long the French high commissioners held onto the largest and best-situated residence in Saigon, the huge and ugly Victorian palace of the admiral-governors, while the Vietnamese Premier and Chief of State had to make do with smaller buildings (which was one reason, among others, Bao-Dai hated Saigon but rather liked Hanoi, where the French governor's residence had been handed over very early to the Vietnamese); there were still far too many French advisers in key posts; and the Vietnamese Army, after an encouraging start under Marshal de Lattre in 1951, still stagnated at about 80,000 men in 1952, while more than 200,000 Vietnamese, Cambodians, and Laotians served in the French Union Forces. However, a Vietnamese Military Academy, opened in 1949, had begun to graduate Vietnamese officers at an increasing rate; previously, all officers had been trained in French military schools. Great hopes were placed also by both the French and the Vietnamese on rapid deliveries of American aid, which began to flow into Viet-Nam after the outbreak of the Korean War had put the fighting in Indochina in a new light, transforming it from a colonial war into an anti-Communist "crusade."

A United States Military Assistance Advisory Group (MAAG) arrived in Viet-Nam in July, 1950, but the funds allocated for the fiscal year 1951–52 proved to be a disappointing $23.5 million, instead of the $146 million it was conservatively estimated that the Vietnamese Army needed. Also, the Korean War shifted priorities away from the native armies of Indochina to those of the Republic of Korea. Instead of "huge American arms deliveries to the French in Viet-Nam," by the end of fiscal year 1952 (June 30, 1952), some of the rather modest aid promised under the $23.5 million budget had been delayed as long as six months to one year.[14] Delivery deficits and shortages ranged from 52 per cent of the submachine guns so essential to small units to 100 per cent of the recoilless cannon, which by then were available in plenty to the North's VPA regulars. Shortages in signal equipment ranged from 100 per cent in the badly needed field-radio sets for small units to 40 per cent of the battalion-type sets. Naturally, this made for poor morale among the Vietnamese troops, who believed they were getting only the hand-me-downs of the French Army (which was true), and it was seized on as additional evidence by those French commanders who had little confidence in the fighting ability of an independent Vietnamese Army and who thus delayed its creation as much as they could. Nevertheless, by the spring of 1954, most of the basic military schools and service commands were in place; self-contained Vietnamese units had risen to the size of Groupes Mobiles (Regimental Combat Teams), the largest tactical unit the French regularly used for their own troops; the Vietnamese Army had its own paratroops, naval commando forces, and even the embryo of an air force, and had taken over full control of all South Viet-Nam west of Saigon and two provinces each in Central and North Viet-Nam. It still lacked an experienced staff—but when one considers the number of American advisers every ROK division required in Korea and the ever-increasing number of U.S. advisers the new Vietnamese Republican Army needs at all levels even after eight years of U.S. training, this gap, four years after the creation of the young army, was to be expected.

But relations between France and the Associated States were to receive another severe jolt: Plagued for years by the artificially high value of the French-guaranteed Indochinese piaster, which permitted fantastic smuggling schemes and other fraudulent operations at the expense of the French home treasury, the French Government, on May 11, 1953, secretly and unilaterally unpegged the piaster from its unrealistic ratio of 17 francs to 1 piaster, and reduced it to the pre-war 10-to-1 ratio. Although the devaluation did not immediately kill the goose that laid the golden eggs (for the black-market operations involved far too many well-placed Frenchmen and Vietnamese), it did reduce the strain on the French treasury. The French argued that any advance revelation of their plan would have negated the whole effect of the measure by permitting last-minute large-scale transfers of currency. In any case, that clear-cut violation of the Elysée agreements of 1949 and Pau agreements of 1950 became a handy means to push demands for the total abolition of French power. (A similar devaluation of the French franc by de Gaulle in 1959, which brought about the "economic miracle" of France in the 1960's, so angered the Vietnamese and Cambodians that they cut loose their currencies from the French franc zone.)

In France itself, the cry now was taken up not only by the Communists (who had wanted independence for Ho's Viet-Nam ever since 1947) but also by moderate elements who felt that French hesitations and contradictions were forfeiting the psychological benefits to be derived from the granting of independence. As François Mitterrand said, in a formulation that was to become famous: "We have granted Viet-Nam 'full independence' eighteen times since 1949. Isn't it about time we did it just once, but for good?"

A change of government in France in June, 1953, brought Joseph Laniel, a mild conservative, to power. One of his first acts was an unambiguous declaration, on July 3, 1953, stating that

. . . France deems it necessary to perfect the independence and sovereignty of the Associated States of Indochina in . . . transferring to them the powers she had held in the very interest of those States in view of perilous circumstances of the state of war. The French Government invites the three States to settle with it the questions each of them wishes to discuss in the economic, financial, judicial, military, and political fields.

In the case of Viet-Nam, Bao-Dai no longer felt that he could negotiate on his own with France. Since there was no elected national legislature, he appealed to all major political leaders to attend a "National Congress," to be held in Saigon on October 12, 1953. That National Congress (which this writer attended) became a monumental free-for-all in which nationalists of all hues and shades concentrated on settling long-standing scores and in outbidding each other in extreme demands on the French and on the Vietnamese Government.

Chaired by Tran Trong Kim, the ex-Premier of the short-lived

Japanese-sponsored government, the meeting heard group after group present its programs and schemes—from the old prewar nationalist parties, which wanted no part of Bao-Dai and desired a republican regime, to the religious sects' political arm, the Social Democratic Reconstruction Party, and the Can-Lao Nhan-Vi (Personalist Workers' Party), at that time a left-wing group led by Ngo Dinh Diem's younger brother Ngo Dinh Nhu. Not to be outflanked by the National Congress, Bao-Dai's own Premier, Nguyên Van Tam,[15] offered a program designed to abrogate any and all special relations between France and Viet-Nam. Whether or not the outcome of the National Congress pleased Bao-Dai (some maintain that it did, by strengthening his hand against the French), its results certainly stunned the French: On October 16, the Congress closed with a manifesto that repudiated the idea of a French union. For all prac- tical purposes, the whole laboriously constructed concept died right there, and although the actual wording was amended at the last minute to qualify the repudiation of a French union with the words "as presently constituted"—lest the French simply pull out of the fighting and leave the Saigon politicians to face the grim warriors of the Viet-Minh[16]—the intent of the manifesto nevertheless was clear.

Nguyên Van Tam resigned as Premier on December 17, after charges had been made that his mistress had invoked his backing in her illegal transactions (she was later jailed by Ngo Dinh Diem). Whether this was the cause of his resignation, Tam was, in French parliamentary slang, *"usé"*—"worn out"; his usefulness had ended. Into his place, on January 11, 1954, stepped Prince Buu-Loc, an urbane diplomat who, during World War II, had remained in France and worked for the German radio network in Paris. His government was clearly of a transitional nature; all that can be said for it is that it negotiated with the French. The negotiations began in Paris on March 8, five years to the day after Bao-Dai and President Vincent Auriol had exchanged the documents that were to start Viet-Nam on the road to independence and five days before the 308th People's Army Division stormed strongpoint "Béatrice" at Dien Bien Phu. This time, the negotiations left no doubt as to their goal: full independence without any ifs or buts. The opening speeches of the two Premiers made this apparent. While Laniel hopefully used the formula "union and association," Buu-Loc spoke only of "independ- ence and association" and he did not once pronounce the words "French union." The disaster of Dien Bien Phu sealed the fate of the French side; the treaties of "independence and association" signed on June 4, 1954 (at the same time as the cease-fire conferees in Geneva were slicing up Viet-Nam at one of several parallels), were merely a futile exercise in legalistic semantics. To this day, neither France nor Viet-Nam has bothered to submit them to legislative ratification.

After seventy years of French presence, all of Viet-Nam was free of alien domination, but at the price of division. In the Communist camp, the war had eliminated the weak and forged some bonds among men who had in common their hatred of the white invader. On the nationalist side, the battle had been waged among gentlemen in white sharkskin suits who had gone to the same schools. Actually, both sides contributed their share to the struggle for Vietnamese independence: Every Viet-Minh military victory strengthened the hands of the nationalist negotiators, and every success at the conference table strengthened Viet-Nam's international position. But the struggle at the conference table, far from uniting the nationalists, had deeply divided them. Every compromise, every article finally accepted, had been paid for by so many agonizing reversals of positions, switches of loyalties, and betrayals of old friends and temporary allies that it left indelible scars on the Vietnamese body politic.

In the end, the French were the biggest losers. The war had cost them twice as much as America had pumped into the French economy during this period, and ten times the value of all French investments in Indochina; and the same kinds of compromises and double-dealings that had undermined the Vietnamese nationalists had undermined the French as well. The French Army came out of the war a gaunt ghost of its former self, the cream of its regular officers dead or crippled, the rest of them embittered and thinking of little else but applying upon their own country the same revolutionary-warfare methods as the Viet-Minh had used upon them.

All in all, 1945–55 had been a "lost decade" for Viet-Nam.

11

Agony of a War

THE TWO months that preceded the Geneva cease-fire accord of July 21, 1954, saw the West in its customary posture of disarray—perhaps in even greater disarray than usual: The Berlin conference of foreign ministers, held at Western initiative in February, 1954, had agreed that a conference be held at Geneva in May in order to settle "outstanding issues in the Far East," such as Korea and Indochina. This gave the Soviet bloc a deadline for achieving a military decision, and with grim determination, Vo Nguyên Giap immediately set out to "deliver" it on time to his side.

It took the French somewhat longer—until the evening of March 14, the day on which the strategic hills overlooking the main positions of Dien Bien Phu fell into Viet-Minh hands—to find out that they had been maneuvered into fighting the decisive battle of the Indochina War on a ground and in a fashion not at all of their choosing. Within another fortnight—despite the expert advice of French and American antiaircraft specialists who were perfectly convinced that the French could keep the fortress's airfields open—both of Dien Bien Phu's fields were unusable, and thenceforth the fortress had to depend on airdrops for its supplies. The sheer magnitude of the preparations for parachuting 200 tons of supplies a day far outstripped French capabilities, and it soon became apparent that only American intervention could save the garrison from being annihilated. The problem was actually threefold: First, considerable amounts of large-tonnage aircraft were required to parachute the supplies; second, fighter-bombers were necessary to provide fire cover for the garrison against concentrated enemy infantry and artillery attacks; and third, heavy bombers were urgently needed to blast the Viet-Minh network of supply roads and depots leading to Dien Bien Phu. These tasks were clearly impossible for the shoestring 450-plane French Air Force in the Far East.[1]

When the French chief of staff, General Paul Ely, came to Washington on March 20, 1954, he candidly informed his American counterpart, Admiral Arthur B. Radford, and other high American officials of the likelihood of the total destruction of Dien Bien Phu and of the dangerous consequences that defeat would be liable to have for the whole Indochina War and perhaps for all Southeast Asia.[2] From official optimism, the mood switched to deep gloom. President Eisenhower, in a speech setting forth what has remained American policy in Viet-Nam for a decade, declared on April 7: "The loss of Indochina will cause the fall of Southeast Asia like a set of dominoes."

After years of inactivity on the Indochina scene, the United States began to assert itself more energetically as the pace of the war increased. Far from espousing a policy of French disengagement, the Eisenhower Administration embarked upon an effort to cajole the French to stay in the fight as long as possible, "with the obvious intention," as a *Le Monde* observer stated, on November 12, 1953, "to avoid giving France any pretext for putting an end to the conflict. As an American diplomat recently said jokingly: 'We are the last French colonialists in Indochina.'" The Eisenhower Administration was about to reap, in Indochina, the bitter fruits of its foreign-policy promises during the 1952 electoral campaign. Having branded the Democrats a "war party" and made the slogan "Peace in Korea" its major foreign-policy drawing card (along with such other phrases as "rolling back the Iron Curtain," and "unleashing Chiang Kai-shek"), it had virtually ruled out even the threat of force—much less the use of force itself. Thus, the President and Secretary of State Dulles were compelled to walk a diplomatic tightrope; Dulles continued to sell a "hard" policy to America's allies abroad, while the

President at the very same moment faced the delicate task of explaining those statements to Congress and to an anxious American public without openly contradicting Dulles.

Thus, after Dulles, on January 14, 1954, launched the concept of "massive retaliation," backed by the sending of 200 U.S. Air Force technicians to Viet-Nam to service French combat planes, the President, at his press conference of February 10, declared that he "could conceive of no greater tragedy than for the United States to become involved in an all-out war in Indochina."

What ensued is probably one of the most confused chapters of recent American diplomatic history and one that, in spite of its importance, has thus far escaped the scrutiny of American political scientists. Before it closed, it had brought a humiliating defeat in Indochina and embroiled the American leadership—the President, the Vice-President, the Secretary of State, and major Congressional leaders—in bitter squabbles. It also had created the first open rift between the United States and her major allies in Europe, a rift that was never really more than patched over until Secretary Dulles' successor, Christian A. Herter, took over the reins at the State Department.

OPERATION "GUERNICA-VULTURE"

While the President had once more assured the country that American military intervention was unlikely, the Pentagon was feverishly working out the military implications of such an intervention. Here also, sharp disagreement occurred between the American top commanders. Admiral Radford, a strong advocate of carrier-based aviation, urged American air strikes on targets around Dien Bien Phu, perhaps on a "one-shot" basis, like that first used by German and Italian aircraft to destroy the Spanish town of Guernica on April 26, 1937. A Guernica-type, single large-scale raid, which could perhaps even be carried out at night and by American aircraft bearing French insignia, was considered the operation most likely to avoid severe diplomatic repercussions. With two American carriers, the *Essex* and the *Boxer*, already operating in the Gulf of Tongking, and with American aircraft stationed in Okinawa and Clark Field in the Philippines, a Guernica-type raid had the added advantage of being feasible on a few days' notice. It was also likely to be of doubtful military value. General Matthew B. Ridgway, then Army chief of staff, had sent his own team of experts to Viet-Nam, and their report had been negative: American intervention, to be of any value at all, would have to involve ground forces, and such an operation could very well unleash the Chinese Reds, just as it had done in Korea. Ridgway thus took the forthright position that the price of a Western victory in Indochina would be "as great as, or greater than, that we paid in Korea."[3]

The conflict was resolved by the President himself in a characteristic compromise: He accepted the Radford plan of a Guernica-type raid—but only if the American position was supported by "other allies," i.e., the British and, if possible, one or two Asian nations. Eisenhower—mindful of t e adverse legislative reaction to President Truman's "police action" in Korea—also desired that intervention in Indochina be backed by Congressional approval. The resultant secret briefing Dulles gave top Congressional leaders of both parties on April 3, 1954, reportedly left them "bug-eyed"[4] and brought about an acrimonious debate on the Indochina question in the Senate on April 6, a debate that abounded with statements whose doubtful relation to the facts clearly showed how little was known about the problem even among Americans who had access to official briefings.

Thus, according to Senator John F. Kennedy, the French still "must give their consent to the sending of [Vietnamese] diplomatic missions to foreign countries." This, as has been shown, had not been the case since 1949. He then proceeded to blame much of the Indochina War on the fact that French demands upon Ho Chi Minh in 1946 had been unreasonable, and backed up his statement by citing the example of the March, 1946, agreements on French troops in North Viet-Nam, which, said the young senator and later President, "did not set any date for the [cessation of] use of French facilities in that area." As the record shows, the March 6, 1946, agreements provided for the stationing of French troops in the D.R.V.N. for a maximum of *five* years. (In July, 1946, the U.S. signed an agreement with the Philippines that provided for the continued presence of American bases in that country for ninety-nine years.) Senator Mike Mansfield provided the Senate with the statistic that the French Union Forces in Indochina numbered 591,000 troops against the Viet-Minh's 290,000. In reality (including even the poorly armed Vietnamese, Cambodian, and Laotian national armies), French forces never exceeded the 350,000 mark, and the Viet-Minh could usually count upon at least as many troops—but in a guerrilla war a 12-to-1 superiority is required for the regular force just to "break even," and more than that to win.

The Republican side was not to be outdone. Senator Everett Dirksen informed his colleagues that the Red River Delta "exported"

500,000 tons of rice to Japan and was "the rice bowl which takes care also of Burma, Thailand, Cambodia, Laos, Formosa, Indonesia, and other countries." It should be remembered that the countries cited include all the world's largest rice *exporters* along with some potential consumers—none of whom had ever bought food from North Viet-Nam, much less from the delta area, which is traditionally short of food. And while Dirksen, along with Vice-President Nixon, and Senators Knowland and Jenner, did not, in his words, "share the anxiety and concern some feel about the danger of sending American troops to Indochina, other than technicians," Senator Alexander Wiley probably summed up the feelings of the majority of his Republican colleagues when he said: "Mr. Speaker, if war comes under this Administration, it could well be the end of the Republican Party." Noninterventionist feelings ran equally high among the often-burned Democrats. Senator Edwin C. Johnson summed up the view of most of his party by saying that he was "against sending American GI's into the mud and muck of Indochina on a blood-letting spree to perpetuate colonialism and white man's exploitation in Asia."[5]

In other words, the overwhelming majority of senators of both parties were *against* American military intervention in Indochina as early as mid-April, 1954; and since President Eisenhower had made it clear in March that he would not involve America in combat operations in Indochina "unless it is a result of the constitutional process that is placed upon Congress," it was obvious that any American policy that ran against both Congressional opinion and the advice of at least part of the Joint Chiefs of Staff was pure rhetoric, if not worse. In any case, the facts do not square with the self-serving assertions in the Dulles-sponsored "brinkmanship" article in *Life* two years later:

> . . . the policy of boldness impressed the Communists. Dulles had seen to it that the Chinese and the Soviets knew that the U.S. was prepared to act decisively to prevent the fall of Southeast Asia. . . . Thus, instead of negotiating from the extreme and undisguised weakness of the French position, Mendès-France and Eden found themselves able to bargain from Dulles' strength. . .

It is certain that the Communists were at least as aware as Sir Anthony Eden of the real hollowness of the Dulles position in the matter, since Eden, even before Dulles' arrival in London on April 11 to discuss "united action," set down his own view as follows:

I cannot see what threat would be sufficiently potent to make China swallow so humiliating a rebuff without any face-saving concession in return. If I am right in this view, the joint warning to China would have no effect, and the coalition would then have to withdraw ignominiously or else embark on warlike action against China.

Eden then argued that the same threat had had little if any effect on Red China's intervention in Korea, but might give China "every excuse" to invoke its alliance with Russia and thus precipitate a world war.[6] The position the British then adopted did not exclude a warning to China at a later date, but the British felt that for the time being the best should be made of the forthcoming Geneva Conference. They maintained that position throughout the ups and downs of the conference over the next ten weeks, despite Dulles' attempts to shake it. As it turned out, it was the British position that proved to be the right one—for reasons having little to do with Indochina. Because Russia was trying to strike a bargain with Pierre Mendès-France (who had taken over the premiership on June 19 from Laniel and acted as his own Foreign Minister at Geneva) over France's membership in the European Defense Community, the Viet-Minh accepted a cease-fire on conditions a great deal less advantageous than those it could have obtained on the strength of its military successes. The fact that Mendès-France, though more liberal than his predecessors, immediately airlifted troop reinforcements into Indochina and ordered tropical inoculations for two French divisions in Germany (including, for the first time, draftees) also added to the credibility of a stiffening Western position, to which the threat of American intervention gave further weight.

RIFT AT GENEVA

But the British refusal, in Eden's words, "to endorse a bad policy for the sake of unity," gave Dulles and the Eisenhower Administration a convenient avenue of escape from the cul-de-sac of military intervention they themselves had constructed; as James Shepley was to show in the *Life* article, the whole failure of united military action was blamed on Britain.[7] In a speech in Seattle on June 10—that is, in the middle of the Geneva Conference—Dulles alleged that "some of the parties had held back," and he proceeded to compare the situation to a "rebuff" the United States received in 1931, when it tried to bring about united action against Japan in Manchuria. For months after Dulles' speech, every major American news weekly, quoting "authoritative" sources (usually unattributed statements by the Secretary of State himself), came out on one side or the other of the issue, thus adding to the confusion of conflicting assertions that will not be fully unraveled until the publication of official American documents. According to one of the best American press reports, written by Chalmers M. Roberts for *The Washington Post* of June 7, 1954, the later Eden version, as well as *Life*'s, was substantially correct. In other words, the United States *was* prepared to intervene militarily in Indochina. Dulles himself, when questioned about the accuracy of the *Life* article in a press conference on January 18, 1956, specifically confirmed that the statements attributed to him "did not require correction from the standpoint of their substance." In a debate on the Senate floor on July 9, 1954, however, two Republican senators, Homer Ferguson and Alexander Smith, solemnly denied that the subject of intervention had come up in Dulles' briefings to them; and *U.S. News & World Report*, in a headline article of August 9, quoting a highly authoritative source, asserted that "the official records show that the U.S. never was on the verge of a shooting war with Communist China over Indochina." (This did not prevent its publisher, David Lawrence, from endorsing the *Life* article two years later in a statement that the latter publication used in its advertisements.)

Yet on January 13, 1960, after Eden's memoirs had appeared, President Eisenhower contradicted both Eden and his late Secretary of State by telling a press conference that "there was never any plan developed to put into execution in Indochina" and explained Dulles' statement to the contrary by saying that Dulles had been "a very forceful man. He could very well talk about possibilities that might by then be considered as proposals, when they were not meant as that at all."

It is precisely this Janus-faced quality of presenting at times a forceful posture on the home front while being conciliatory abroad, or of being cautious at home while taking a tough stand in the councils of the world, that produces confusion about American policies in general, and on Viet-Nam in particular. The new Viet-Nam crisis that began to boil in 1961 gave a few more choice examples of that lack of a consensus based on a coolheaded estimate of the facts.

By the time the dust settled in Geneva, it was clear that "Operation Vulture"—the official designation for the Guernica-type air strike—had failed to come off not only militarily, but also politically.

Its failure had left a sour taste in the mouths of all U.S. allies involved, particularly the British, who had borne the brunt of the diplomatic battle and felt ill-rewarded when they found themselves blamed for what some Americans were comparing to another Munich or, at best, a Dunkirk. But as James Reston wrote in *The New York Times* of June 13:

> This picture, omitting any reference to Congressional or White House opposition to using force in Asia . . . is one of the most misleading oversimplifications ever uttered by an American Secretary of State, but it allocates blame and furnishes an alibi.

The last days of the Geneva Conference did not go any better than the earlier days. The Eisenhower Administration, after the failure of massive retaliation and united intervention, had found a diplomatic line of retreat in such slogans as "Peace with Honor," which the President himself translated at his June 30 press conference as "Coexistence Without Appeasement," adding that the United States would not be "a party to any agreement that makes anybody a slave." That new line seemed also to include a clear-cut dissociation of the United States from the cease-fire negotiations, reinforced by the fact that Dulles himself did not reappear at the conference and finally agreed to permit the American delegation, led by the very able Under Secretary of State Walter Bedell Smith, to remain only after Mendès-France and Eden pointed out that the United States would not escape its obligations (or save the Vietnamese from "slavery") by not participating at Geneva.[8]

Thus, during the last few days of the negotiations, it was Eden and Mendès-France, aided by a not too unreasonable Molotov and a not totally uncooperative Chou En-lai, who had to carry the ball alone. In fact, some observers felt that the absence of Dulles (who had consistently acted as if Chou were made of thin air) considerably "unbristled" the head of the Chinese delegation. The terms finally obtained by Mendès-France were well within the minimum limits set out earlier by Dulles and were definitely a diplomatic success under the circumstances.

Therefore, the American delegation's announcement that it would not sign the final declaration was not greeted as good news by the other Western allies. In Eden's eyes, "since Dulles had been at least as responsible as ourselves for calling the Geneva Conference, this did not seem to me reasonable."[9] But Molotov brought Chou En-lai around to accepting a separate declaration by the United States, on condition that the United States would also be included in the heading of the final declaration.

Thus, when his turn came to sign the final declaration, Under Secretary Smith read a declaration, according to which the United States took

> . . . note of the agreements concluded at Geneva [and] declares with regard to the aforesaid agreements that (i) it will refrain from the threat or the use of force to disturb them . . . and (ii) it would view any renewal of the aggression in violation of the aforesaid agreements with grave concern and as seriously threatening international peace and security.

The American statement went on to say that the United States was in favor of the principle of free elections under United Nations supervision and that all three Indochinese countries should be permitted to determine their own future.

If any delegation was in a more confused and ambiguous position than that of the United States, it was that of Bao-Dai's state of Viet-Nam. Bao-Dai himself managed to antagonize everybody by following the proceedings from his Château de Thorenc, near Cannes (save for a two-day trip to Evian), and the change of government from Buu-Loc to Ngo Dinh Diem, which took place on July 7, in mid-conference, did little to help matters. In Viet-Nam itself, the worsening military situation was matched, on the Vietnamese nationalist side, by a slide into total unreality; various Vietnamese politicians (none representing anything more than a few close friends and family members) were making grandiloquent statements on how they would continue to fight on "to total victory," and hatching far-reaching schemes for this end; to these, the French replied with a blunt: "What do you expect to do? Continue the war alone?" It was obvious that the Vietnamese had no good counter-argument to that point, once it had become clear that the United States was not going to fight for Viet-Nam at this juncture, and since the South Vietnamese Government had no concessions to offer (the only position that would have given it some independent bargaining power would have been a willingness to deal with the Viet-Minh, and that it was unwilling to do), it was simply ignored by all concerned in the desperate rush of meeting the July 20 deadline for achieving peace that Mendès-France had set himself. As Tran Van Do, South Viet-Nam's dedicated Foreign Minister, cabled to Ngo

Dinh Diem at the conclusion of the conference, whose declaration he also refused to sign:

> Absolutely impossible to surmount the hostility of our enemies and perfidy of false friends. Unusual procedures paralyzed the action of our delegation. ı . . . All arrangements were signed in privacy. We express our deepest sorrow on this total failure of our mission. . . .

And thus ended the first concerted international effort at saving Viet-Nam from Communism. It remained Senator Jenner's lot to perpetuate through the *Congressional Record* of August 14, 1954, a concise appraisal of what had happened at Geneva:

> The United States has been outthought, outtraded, and outgeneraled. . . .
> It does no good to say we did not physically sign the Geneva agreements. That is the old excuse of Pontius Pilate, who washed his hands to keep his conscience clear

This was perhaps true in the short run; in the long run, however, the American and South Vietnamese refusal to sign at Geneva was to have beneficial consequences for the new administration abuilding south of the 17th parallel: On the grounds of its nonsignature, South Viet-Nam refused to hold elections by July, 1956, since this would have meant handing over control of the South to Ho Chi Minh;[10] and the United States, banking upon point ii of its separate declaration at Geneva, could argue convincingly in 1962 that its military commitment in behalf of the Saigon regime was in response to North Vietnamese "renewal of the aggression in violation of the aforesaid agreements."

Another phase of the military and diplomatic struggle for Viet-Nam had drawn to an end. The struggle now began to rebuild a truncated land into a viable non-Communist Vietnamese state, around the new emerging leader, Ngo Dinh Diem.

Ngo Dinh Diem—
Man and Myth

UNTIL 1943, the French Government-General in Indochina published every year a book, always bound in red, which was in fact a "Who's Who" of actual or potential leaders in Cambodia, Laos, and Viet-Nam. It was often remarkable in its accuracy and listed, in its last three or four editions (available only to senior French colonial officials) most of the political leaders who now shape the peninsula's destinies: Princes Boun Oum, Souvanna Phouma, and Souphanouvong of Laos; Princes Norodom Sihanouk and Monireth of Cambodia, and such diverse Vietnamese leaders as Pham Van Dong and Tran Van Huu. The Ngo family was also well represented in the last editions: there was Monsignor Ngo Dinh Thuc, a Catholic bishop; and also a young intellectual who had graduated from France's famous Ecole des Chartes (an almost unique graduate school for librarians and archivists) and whose name was Ngo Dinh Nhu; another brother, Ngo Dinh Khoi, was listed as a *tong-doc*, a provincial governor in the administration of the French protectorate of Annam. Three of the Ngo brothers, however, were missing in that array of native leaders whom the French considered potentially important. One of them was Jean-Baptiste Ngo Dinh Diem.

It is, to say the least, remarkable that Ngo Dinh Diem has thus far escaped the attentions of a biographer—just as Ho Chi Minh has—with the result that, in the case of both, the information available consists either of totally uncritical eulogy or of equally partisan condemnation.[1] Most American sources stress Diem's personal integrity and unflinching patriotism; some French sources (such as Devillers) acknowledge Diem's* patriotism and devotion to his cause but also stress the doubtful value of his entourage; some others have asserted that Diem had been seen during the Japanese occupation "in a Japanese captain's uniform," and Communist sources regularly brand him a full-fledged "American puppet"—to which many Americans ruefully retort that, for a puppet, Diem is remarkably unamenable to outside advice.

There is, surprisingly enough, some mystery about Diem's exact birthplace. Official releases generally cite the imperial city of Hué, but most older sources in Viet-Nam say he was born in Dai-Phuong in Quang-Binh Province, north of the 17th parallel. All sources, however, agree that he was born on January 3, 1901, the son of Ngo Dinh Kha, a well-educated mandarin whose family had been among Viet-Nam's earliest Catholic converts, during the seventeenth century, and was said to include several members who had suffered martyrdom in defense of their religion. Ngo Dinh Kha had been Minister of Rites and Grand Chamberlain to Emperor Thanh-Thai, who reigned from 1889 to 1907, and he had conceived a deep resentment against the French when they deposed his sovereign.[2] Ngo Dinh Kha resigned his government positions, as Ho's father had done, cut himself off from all unessential contacts with the hated invaders, and began to support such Vietnamese nationalist reformers as Phan Boi Chau (1867–1940), who became Viet-Nam's Sun Yat-sen and founder of the first nationalist groups organized along modern Western lines.[3]

Ngo Dinh Kha passed on to his sons, particularly to the older Khoi and Diem, his ardent nationalism, based not on mass uprisings but on reforms through the Vietnamese elites, and also (especially to Diem) a religious fierceness bordering on fanaticism, which must be fully understood before one can understand Diem's view of his role in Viet-Nam's somber contemporary history. Marshal de Lattre de

---

* The family name of South Viet-Nam's President is Ngo, but in order to differentiate among the President and his brothers, the Western practice of using their first names is followed here.

Tassigny said of the Vietnamese Bishop of Phat-Diem, Monsignor Lê Huu Thu, that his "bishop's staff was made of the kind of wood from which truncheons are made." Ngo Dinh Diem's militancy is of that kind: His faith is made less of the kindness of the apostles than of the ruthless militancy of the Grand Inquisitor; and his view of government is made less of the constitutional strength of a President of the republic than of the petty tyranny of a tradition-bound mandarin. To a French Catholic interlocutor who wanted to emphasize Diem's bonds with French culture by stressing "our common faith," Diem was reported to have answered calmly: "You know, I consider myself rather as a Spanish Catholic," i.e., a spiritual son of a fiercely aggressive and militant faith rather than of the easygoing and tolerant approach of Gallican Catholicism.

American observers have made much of Diem's Confucianist background, in addition to his Catholicism. It remains an open question whether Diem is basically a Confucianist with a Catholic overlay, or vice versa, and one that is unimportant in evaluating his political behavior; ample justification can be found in either frame of reference for his paternalistic approach to what he considers to be proper relations between those who govern and those who are governed. Most sympathetic as well as unsympathetic sources quote Diem as giving the same answer to all queries about his policies: "I know what is best for my people." This has worried and irritated many Americans, such as William Henderson, who, in an otherwise very favorable article, says that Diem's "conversation reflects an archaic, mandarin [*sic*] temperament."[4] Another friendly American observer, Professor J. A. C. Grant, who, as an expert on constitutional law, went to VietNam in 1956 to help frame the country's constitution, stated that Diem specifically requested that the following line be added to the definition of the President's powers: "The President is vested with the leadership of the Nation." And Grant added that this supplementary line "gives the key to all that follows."[5]

A French diplomat who has had dealings with Diem before and after his rise to power likes to compare him to the late French rightwing nationalist Charles Maurras, whose absolutist views were too extreme even for the pretender to the French throne, the Count of Paris. An ample body of correspondence between Diem and Bao-Dai, dating from the years 1954 and 1955, makes clear that Diem remained genuinely attached to the Vietnamese monarchy as long as he felt that it would allow him to put his ideas of a strong executive into practice; he abandoned the monarchy only when he concluded that it had become incapable of providing Viet-Nam with the kind of strong government he believed that it needed—and that only he could provide. This resembles in more than one way Franco's relations with the pretender to the Spanish throne: Franco considers him too "weak" (or too willing to accept the idea of a parliamentary monarchy) to allow him to return to the throne. In both these cases, it is difficult to say when their loyalty to the "physical monarch" ended—if it ever existed at all—but it is certain that in both men the concept of the absolute monarchy (and not only of personal dictatorship) is very much alive. Ngo Dinh Diem has written: "A sacred respect is due to the person of the sovereign. He is the mediator between the people and heaven as he celebrates the national cult." It was perhaps out of faithfulness to the *mystique* of the monarchy as such that Diem decided in 1955 to oust its unworthy representative, Bao-Dai.

In the light of his concept of divinely anointed leadership, it should hardly be surprising that any Madison Avenue attempt to make a baby-kissing popular leader out of Diem would fail. The concept of executive power subject to popular recall simply goes against the grain of the man, and, in his own eyes, hurts his stature as a predestined leader. "Society," says Diem, "functions through personal relations among men at the top." Whether that image of history went out with Louis XIV is immaterial in the present context; that is the way Diem runs Viet-Nam. In such a *Weltanschauung*, compromise has no place and opposition of any kind must of necessity be subversive and must be suppressed with all the vigor the system is capable of. Thus, while South Viet-Nam is structurally a republic —mostly to please its American godfathers to whom that system of government is more familiar than any other—it is, in terms of the actual relations between government and governed, an absolute monarchy without a king, such as Admiral Horthy's Hungary was much of the time between the two World Wars or as Franco's Spain has been since 1939. We cannot, of course, be so naïve as to equate absolute monarchy with "bad" government. Peter the Great and Napoleon made some lasting contributions to the structure of their countries—although not in the field of civil liberties. And in all likelihood, Diem sees his own role in Viet-Nam's history from a similar angle: His key job is to consolidate truncated Viet-Nam into a viable anti-Communist state; to establish unchallenged control by the central government; and to prepare the non-Communist area for an eventual showdown with the Communist area. In other words,

Diem might consider his own position to resemble that of Emperor Gia-Long who, at the end of the eighteenth century and with the help of foreign advisers, defeated the usurpers, reunified the Vietnamese state, and gave it the codes and laws that ruled it for fifty years. In neither case was popular representation an issue, but national survival was.

If one adds to all this the fact that Diem is, in spite of his wooden outside appearance, a hot-tempered man whom even a laudatory *Time* profile, of April 4, 1955, described as capable of "explod[ing] into tantrums if interrupted"; who will, if a personal enemy is mentioned, "spit across the room and snarl 'Dirty Type!' "; who is likely to embark, at the drop of a hat, for several hours, "with transparent self-absorption, on a verbose identification of himself and his principles with the good of the nation"[6]—one has the makings of an extremely complex personality. These traits are further complicated by a deeply pious and ascetic personal life—at fifteen, Diem allegedly spent several months in a monastery to prepare himself for the priesthood, but decided, for reasons that have never been made public, against an ecclesiastical career—and by twenty-five years of self-imposed exile, first within his own country and then abroad. Those were the years of his prime, and he was deprived of making use of them by his own all-or-nothing integrity, the real or fancied intrigues of Vietnamese enemies or rivals, and the French colonial administration. Such a situation is ideal for breeding courage and a sense of mission, and also intolerance and petty hatreds. And a person who has kept his own counsel for twenty-five years is not likely to be receptive to outside advice or popular pressure.

Diem had adopted his father's rigid antagonism toward the foreign occupiers of his country (just as Ho Chi Minh had adopted a parallel hostility from his scholar father). When his father retired to his farm holdings rather than "collaborate" with the French, young Diem was left at Hué in the care of the imperial court's Premier, Nguyên Huu Bai, who, in traditional Vietnamese fashion, reared him as his son and prevailed upon him to seek an administrative career in spite of the hated French—for only service in the colonial administration would provide the independent Viet-Nam to come with cadres familiar with the intricacies of modern government.

Having completed his *lycée* studies at Hué (precisely where Ho Chi Minh, ten years his elder, had also studied), Diem entered the French-run School for Law and Administration at Hanoi. An intense debater—his habit of haranguing visitors for hours on end without letting them put in a word probably stems from this training—and an excellent student, as well, Diem succeeded brilliantly. He graduated in 1921 at the top of the twenty-man class and immediately entered the provincial administration as a district chief. In 1929, at the early age of twenty-eight, he was appointed governor of Phan-Thiet, the province and city in which Ho Chi Minh had taught school eighteen years earlier. As senior official in a rather poor and remote province that included lowland Vietnamese as well as mountaineers and remnants of the Cham minorities, Ngo Dinh Diem did a good job: He judged fairly, was known not to take bribes, and even then fought the revolutionary ideas the young firebrands of the Thanh-Nien were bringing back from Hong Kong, Canton, and Saigon. Not that Diem had thrown in his lot with the French and was against revolution as such, but he was against the kind of revolution that would not only sweep away the French but bring down the traditional leadership of the mandarins and of the monarchy along with it.

By 1932, Diem's reputation as an able and energetic administrator had filtered back to the imperial capital, where young Emperor Bao-Dai, aflame with the modern ideas he had brought back from France, wanted to reform his archaic administration. Diem was charged with a mission of inquiry by the Senior Administrative Corps, which lasted until May, 1933, when Bao-Dai appointed him over the heads of many seniors to the post of Minister of the Interior, where he could implement the reforms he had recommended. Strangely enough for a man who later on was to expect his own legislature to behave like a rubber stamp, Ngo Dinh Diem fell out with his sovereign and the French when it became apparent that the latter would not agree to endow Annam's Chamber of People's Representatives with effective legislative powers. True to his reputation for "all-or-nothing" integrity, he resigned in July after having publicly accused the emperor of being "nothing but an instrument in the hands of the French authorities," and handed back all the titles and decorations bestowed on him by Bao-Dai and the French.

Like his father before him, and like his future archenemy, Ho Chi Minh, who at that same moment also disappeared from public view for almost a decade, Ngo Dinh Diem now retired to a life of study and reading. But his role was far from cloistered and purely introspective, as his official hagiographers make it appear. Diem maintained an intense correspondence with Vietnamese nationalist leaders,

such as Phan Boi Chau or Prince Cuong-Dè, at home and in Japan,
and also with such foreign anticolonial nationalists as India's Subha
Chandra Bose and Indonesia's Sukarno, who both banked on Japan's
rising strength to help their countries toward independence. There
can be no doubt that Diem was impressed with some of their arguments, but being far more solidly anchored in his own society than
Bose and Sukarno were in theirs, he had less reason to commit himself to any one source of outside help. In his *New Yorker* profile of
Diem, Robert Shaplen says that Diem told him that he nevertheless
had "sounded out a number of the higher-ups among the newcomers
on the possibility of creating a free nation under their auspices," but
had gotten nowhere. Even after the Japanese took over the reins of
power in Viet-Nam, Diem refused to commit himself openly on their
side. Although it is apparently true that the Japanese helped him to
escape arrest by the French in July, 1944, and offered him the protection of their headquarters in Saigon until V-J Day, it is also known
that Diem refused a ministerial portfolio in the short-lived Japanese-
sponsored Tran Trong Kim Administration—thus keeping his record
free of the charge of "collaboration" with the Axis.

The collapse of Japanese power left Saigon open to the mercies of
the murderous Viet-Minh bands of Tran Van Giau. Hué, where
Bao-Dai had peacefully surrendered to the Viet-Minh, seemed the
most likely haven of peace to Diem. (An indication of the prevailing
confusion can be gleaned from the fact that Diem's younger brother
Nhu left Hué on foot for Saigon at the same time, in order to escape
probable persecution in the Viet-Minh-occupied imperial capital.)
Diem slipped out of the city and set out for Hué along the dusty
coastal road, only to be recognized and arrested by the Viet-Minh in
the little fishing port of Tuy-Hoa. Manhandled and always in danger
of being finished off by his captors at any moment—which was the
fate of his older brother, Ngo Dinh Khoi, at about that time—Diem
was dragged north and imprisoned in Ho Chi Minh's mountain
stronghold at Tuyên-Quang. But Ho, recognizing Diem's administrative gifts and the woeful ineptness of his own followers in that difficult field, summoned the mandarin to his side and offered him the
very job he had held under Bao-Dai: the Ministry of the Interior.
Diem's reply was typical of the man:

"Why did you kill my brother?" asked Diem. "It was a mistake,"
replied Ho. "The country was all confused. It could not be helped."
Angrily, Diem turned on his heel and walked out.[7]

Diem's two dominant traits—stubborn courage and, even more unshakable, family solidarity—clearly show themselves in this exchange. It was of little importance to him that the struggling republic —which, for all he knew then, was not going to be Communist-dominated, or from which the Communists could still be ousted by men of good will—needed his ability if it was to survive the forthcoming onslaught of the French colonialists. Diem did not display the generous spirit of the French nobleman who would serve the French Republic that had beheaded his father, or of the Belgian concentration-camp inmate who would build a united Europe with a West German who had once jackbooted down Brussels' main street. Diem did not object to Ho's Communism then. What counted was that Ho had allowed Diem's brother to be murdered—even though it was never proved whether that murder was indeed deliberate, or one of those "post-Liberation" killings with which Europeans from Paris to Bucharest became grimly familiar at precisely this time.

Family loyalty is a common Chinese and Vietnamese trait. In the case of Diem it extends even to relatives by marriage (such as his brother Nhu's wife, Tran Lê Xuan, who is the official hostess for the bachelor President), and its fierceness brooks no criticism, however slight. This explains why many attempts (particularly by American political experts) to wean Diem away from members of his entourage who are political liabilities have consistently failed in the past and are likely to continue to fail in the future. Thus, in 1945, having refused Ho's advances, Diem at first returned to jail but then took refuge with Canadian monks until the signing of the March 8, 1946, accords between the Viet-Minh and the French. For reasons of their own—probably in the hope of winning over able administrators—the Viet-Minh made the release of political prisoners of Diem's category an informal part of the agreements.

Returning to Hué, Diem took an active if covert part in the long-drawn-out negotiations that were to bring Bao-Dai back to power, but having achieved this, he again refused to participate in shaping the new Vietnamese state on any terms but his own. Offered the Premiership in May, 1949, Diem turned it down, alleging that the Viet-Minh might vent its displeasure upon the hundreds of thousands of Catholics residing in its zone. In reality, Diem thought the concessions made by France were not far-reaching enough for him to commit himself to their implementation. Playing again on an "all-or-nothing" basis, Diem once more withdrew his support from Bao-Dai and created in South and Central Viet-Nam a small political party with a name that in itself was a program: Phong Trao Quôc-Gia Qua Kich, or Nationalist Extremist Movement. The movement advocated resistance against both the French and the Viet-Minh (a hopeless endeavor, in 1949), but as a French political report stated:

> He aims to reorganize and increase Catholic strength in order to obtain the real unity and independence of Viet-Nam. As soon as he has gained sufficient strength, he will enter into relations with foreign powers, notably the United States, and will seek their help in the economic and diplomatic fields.
>
> Vis-à-vis France, his attitude is cordial for the time being, since the French authorities can still be useful to him. The United States [in Diem's view] should be expected to intervene only when it becomes obvious that France by herself is powerless to resolve the Indochinese conflict.[8]

That report was to prove fully prophetic six years later, but in 1948, it was ignored. The Nationalist Extremist Movement, along with several other groups created by Diem, Nhu, and Monsignor Thuc—notably a small Christian Socialist Party—quietly went into limbo when its founder, accompanied by Thuc, left Viet-Nam for the first time, in August, 1950, for a trip to renascent Japan, where his old-time ideal of nationalist resistance, Prince Cuong-Dê, was living out the last months of his life.

EXILE

The Japanese trip proved decisive for Diem's political career. Diem was snubbed by MacArthur who, with the newly launched Korean War already stirring up political as well as military problems, had no time for exiled Asian politicians. But he was well received by other Americans, among them Wesley Fishel, a young professor of political science from Michigan State College. Diem was advised to carry his case for Vietnamese independence directly to the United States, which he did during a brief visit in September and October. But he was to be disappointed again. Having been "burned" the first time it had intervened in Indochina, in 1942–45, Washington was in no mood to antagonize anyone, least of all the French. The Vietnamese nationalist leader was given a polite brush-off. His brother, Monsignor Thuc, was more successful, however, with the Catholic hierarchy. Francis Cardinal Spellman became interested in the faraway country with its small but fiercely militant Catholic community and became a strong advocate of American support for Diem over the following years. Diem and his brother traveled on to Rome and Paris, where they made contact with Vietnamese exile groups operating in France and Belgium. In 1951, with the increasing American involvement in the Indochina War, Diem saw his chances brightening. He returned to the United States in that year and established himself at Maryknoll Seminaries in Ossining, New York, and Lakewood, New Jersey. Diem promptly embarked on an energetic speaking campaign at American universities. Colleges in Michigan, Ohio, and New York invited him to address classes. Diem's theme was simple: Anti-Communism was not enough, which was the main reason the French could not hope to win the struggle; only Vietnamese nationalism could do that, and in order to be effective, Vietnamese nationalism had to be free from French control. Speaking in intense, rapid-fire French, Diem also warned his impressionable audiences as late as February, 1953 (as the mimeographed translation of his address at Cornell University shows), that France was ready to unleash a third world war for the sake of holding onto her Far Eastern domain. Ironically, another Vietnamese nationalist leader, Phan Quang Dan, who, from 1960 onward, was to be confined in Diem's prisons, was making those same points at the same time from his refuge at Harvard University, where he was completing a doctoral thesis in public health. Diem also had learned how to mend his political fences in Washington. Shepherded by Cardinal Spellman, Diem made, according to the above-cited 1955 article in *Time*, "trip after trip to Washington to harangue Congressmen and Government officials in the cause of Vietnamese independence." Congressional Asia specialists, such as Dr. Walter H. Judd, then a representative from Minnesota, Senator Mike Mansfield, and Senator John F. Kennedy, soon became his devoted advocates.

But the time was not yet ripe. Diem left the United States in May, 1953, to return to Belgium, where he took up quarters at the Benedictine monastery of Saint-André-lès-Bruges, which is also a key center of missionary activities in the Far East. His close association with Father Raymond de Jaegher, a Belgian priest who has in recent years often acted as one of his advisers, may date from that period. With the defeat of Dien Bien Phu looming early in 1954, Bao-Dai once more asked Diem to take the Premiership of Viet-Nam, but he refused the offer because it was still hedged with the restriction that over-all military command would remain in French hands while hostilities were under way (a restriction that Syngman Rhee, under similar circumstances, willingly accepted from the United States during the Korean War). Later, Diem argued, and he repeated the theme in 1963 in his interview with Shaplen, that "if we had been responsible for prosecuting the war, we would have won. The Communists were exhausted . . but the French were defeatists."

When the fall of Dien Bien Phu spelled the end of French military dominance in Viet-Nam and the final independence accords signed by Prince Buu-Loc in Paris on June 4, 1954, consecrated the political independence of the country, Diem decided that the situation now had reached the point where his conditions would be fully met both by the French and by Bao-Dai: total independence for the country and plenary powers for Ngo Dinh Diem. On June 16, 1954, Bao-Dai called upon Diem (who, in the meantime, had established headquarters in Paris) to form the new Vietnamese Government. It remains to this day a matter of speculation why Diem was pulled out of the hat at this juncture. Any of the factors widely adduced— American pressure, French pressure, or Bao-Dai's own belief that Diem would be a convenient scapegoat for a hopeless situation—may have played its part in the choice.

Yet Diem did not step into the fight unarmed. He demanded from Bao-Dai something the latter had thus far always been wise enough to refuse to his Premiers: full and complete civilian and military powers. After three days of hesitation, Bao-Dai yielded. Diem received absolute dictatorial powers on June 19. Fully realizing that he was throwing his throne away, Bao-Dai allegedly made Diem swear a solemn oath of allegiance to him, and several authoritative witnesses affirm that Diem also swore on his knees to Empress Nam-Phuong that he would do everything in his power "to preserve the throne of Viet-Nam for Crown Prince Bao-Long," son of Bao-Dai.

Ngo Dinh Diem arrived in Saigon on June 26. No cheering crowds lined the streets; there was only the constant drone of French multi-engine aircraft bringing refugees and wounded from Hanoi to Saigon and shipping ammunition and paratroop reinforcements northward to feed the last desperate battles of the Indochina War. On July 7, 1954, Ngo Dinh Diem completed his first Cabinet. The "Double Seven" (seventh day of the seventh month) anniversary of Diem's rise to power is now a holiday in South Viet-Nam.

Diem was never again to entrust his power to the incertitudes of parliamentary democracy. He retained the plenary civilian and military powers granted him by Bao-Dai until the proclamation of the Constitution of the Republic of Viet-Nam on October 26, 1956. At that date and until the expiration of his first Presidential mandate.

on April 30, 1961, his dictatorial powers were reconfirmed by virtue of Article 98 of the Constitution, which provided that "during the first legislative term, the President of the Republic may decree a temporary suspension [of virtually all civil rights] to meet the legitimate demands of public security and order and of national defense." Theoretically, that provision became inoperative at the conclusion of Diem's first term. In actual fact, little, if anything, changed, and on October 18, 1961, invoking the worsening security situation, the National Assembly proclaimed a state of urgency throughout Viet-Nam and again voted Diem plenary powers for a period of one year, to be renewed if necessary. And they were, of course, renewed.

THE TEST

Ngo Dinh Diem's finest hour came, beyond a doubt, in the spring of 1955, when his chances of remaining in office seemed almost nil. To be sure, he had succeeded in getting rid of ebullient General Nguyên Van Hinh, the Vietnamese Army's Chief of Staff, who had defied him, but it had been only after Bao-Dai personally intervened (with messages from France) in Diem's favor and after the United States threatened to cut off all but humanitarian aid to Viet-Nam. But the armed politico-religious sects were not as easy to oust; they had a measure of popular support in certain areas and, in the case of the Binh-Xuyên, they controlled the police of Saigon-Cholon and were willing to fight to retain their privileges. Here, Diem, in addition to his qualities of personal courage and stubbornness, also displayed an uncanny ability to divide his enemies by a series of intricate maneuvers. To be sure, the fact that exceedingly generous amounts of American currency were available to bribe key sect leaders was of some importance. But this in no way diminishes Diem's own talents in the affair, or those of his most intimate advisers of the time—his brothers Nhu (since 1954 Political Adviser to the President), Monsignor Thuc, Luyên (later, Ambassador to Britain and to several smaller countries), and Can (who governs Central Viet-Nam from Hué); to whom must be added Tran Trung Dung, a nephew; Mme. Nhu; and her sister's husband Nguyên Huu Chau (who fell from grace later, after his wife left him). In a succession of swift moves that left each sect chief wondering whether his sworn ally of yesterday had not sold him out for a substantial sum, Diem bought the Cao-Dai "General" Trinh Minh Thé—mastermind of the messy Saigon street bombings of 1952 so well described in Graham Greene's *The Quiet American*—for $2 million; another Cao-Dai "general," Nguyên Thanh Phuong, for $3.6 million (plus monthly payments for his troops); and a Hoa-Hao warlord Tran Van Soai for $3 million more. In all likelihood, the total amount of American dollars spent on bribes during March and April, 1955, by Diem may well have gone beyond $12 million.[9] By the time the greedy sect leaders found out that they had been outmaneuvered and began to fight back, theirs was a lost cause.

On November 11 and 12, 1960, when a rebellion by Vietnamese Army paratroops succeeded in encircling Diem and his family in the Presidential Palace, Diem skillfully parleyed with the insurgents for almost thirty-six hours in order to prevent them from overrunning the building. On November 12, Diem issued a proclamation in which he promised to dissolve his government, to form a provisional regime including the army generals, and to collaborate with the revolutionaries in broadening the regime. He ended his appeal with the words: "Be calm and have confidence in the patriotism of the President and in his unlimited love for the people."[10] On that day, when loyal troops had finally arrived around Saigon in sufficient numbers, Diem reneged on all his promises of reform and crushed the insurrection by force. Once more, his courage and cunning had prevailed and had saved his regime.

PERSONALISM

In addition to the incomparable asset of Diem's innate shrewdness, the South Vietnamese regime has an official political philosophy —Personalism. In fact, in recent speeches by such authoritative Vietnamese officials as Mme. Nhu, mention was made of a "Vietnamese Personalist Republic." Personalism as a philosophy was developed in the post-Depression 1930's, first in France by a group of young Catholics led by Emmanuel Mounier, whose work was, and still is, published in the monthly review *Esprit*. Taken up after Mounier's death by Jean-Marie Domenach, *Esprit* and the Personalist idea spread throughout Europe. Such philosophers as Martin Buber, Nikolai Berdyaev, Karl Jaspers and J. B. Coates are claimed by the Personalists as being in affinity with their ideas. It was Ngo Dinh Nhu who, during his prewar studies at the Ecole des Chartes, came into contact with Mounier and became profoundly impressed by his ideas and in turn convinced Diem that Personalism was a philosophy capable of counterbalancing the type of primitive Marxism that the Viet-Minh was trying to "sell" to the Vietnamese.

This writer will candidly admit that repeated readings of Mounier's prose[11] have not brought him closer to a clearer understanding of what exactly Personalism is in the European context, let alone in the Vietnamese context. In Viet-Nam itself, interviews with highly placed members of the regime, including Ngo Dinh Nhu himself, have brought forth various interpretations of it, some of which are at least as contradictory as Mounier himself. Perhaps the Vietnamese term for Personalism—"Nhan-Vi"—is in itself the best approach to an explanation: "Nhan" means "person," and "Vi" means "dignity." In other words, Personalism presumably emphasizes human dignity or the value of humanism in modern society, in contrast to Communism's treatment of the human being as merely a subcomponent of the "masses."

It is certain that Diem and, even more, Mme. Nhu in several speeches made in 1961–62, have expressed views on traditional forms of democracy that approach such formulations of Mounier's as the following:

> The rights that the liberal [democratic] State grants its citizens are in large part alienated by virtue of their [type of] economic and social existence. The parliamentary State is little more than an anachronism. Its wheels turn in mid-air; its speeches sow the wind and reap the whirlwind. Political democracy must be entirely reorganized on the basis of an effective economic democracy adapted to modern structures of production. . . .
>
> [Power] can be founded only upon the final destiny of man; it must respect man and promote him. . . . Popular sovereignty cannot be founded on the mere authority of numbers; [rule by] the great number (or the majority) can be as arbitrary as the [sovereign's] pleasure.[12]

Those lines, written in 1935, smack of the "corporate state" of Mussolini and Franco. With regard to religion, "Christian Personalism shall underline, in opposition to religious individualism, the collective character of the Christian faith and life, which has been too much neglected over the past two centuries." It is this collective aspect that permits South Vietnamese leaders to emphasize that the regroupment of the farming population in *agrovilles* and "strategic hamlets" is "an expression of our Personalist views." In a speech on March 11, 1962, in which she attacked the Western press (specifically, "certain American news media") for its lack of understanding of South Viet-Nam's problems, Mme. Ngo Dinh Nhu expressed the philosophy of the regime in these words:

> Our oneness will never be a disorderly collection of individuals who pull themselves in different directions for only one purpose, that of

individual self-interest. Our union, drawing its strength from unity and discipline, will track down, neutralize, and extirpate all of the society's scabby sheep, enemies of this Personalist Regime which pledges to bring forth solutions to the problems of an underdeveloped country and to ensure independence, liberty, and happiness to all.

Expressing the same doubts as Mounier in the efficacy of liberal democracy, Mme. Nhu questioned the ability of "Western democracy, with its political and philosophical ideals of which it is so proud . . . [to] succeed in drawing to it any underdeveloped and defenseless countries," and went on to say that "Personalism, which is pragmatic, [witnessed] with horror (to avoid saying nausea) . . . the progress of neutralism in the world, favored by the inability of Western Democracy to really protect all those that Communism covets."[13]

Since such a speech is certain to have been at least in large part written by Ngo Dinh Nhu, who, as Political Adviser to President Diem, is the chief theoretician of the Saigon regime, and was no doubt also approved by Diem himself, it shows a disturbing lack of understanding of, and faith in, the style of Western democracy upon whose aid the regime has to rely for its daily survival. The irony is that today European Personalism is espoused by "left-wing" Catholics who advocate socialization of industry, a "third force" policy that Americans usually term "neutralism," and a measure of East-West understanding or cooperation that would be tantamount to outright abandonment of the Western system of military alliances. It is also Mounier—not the Mounier of 1935, but the Mounier of 1950—who wrote:

> One must keep up the dissatisfaction and the drama of freedom. The end of that restlessness would also mean the end of morality and personal life. There would arise as a substitute to freedom a legalism that would prolong social pressures and childish intimidations, would eliminate moral creation, and would socialize moral criteria by classifying [people] into formal categories of "good" and "bad."[14]

Thus, the application of Personalism to Viet-Nam gives rise to much confusion, particularly in the minds of Americans (who are likely never to have heard of Mounier, much less to have read him) who like to be able to approve of Ngo Dinh Diem but find him, in the words of Lancaster, "a complex personality" endowed with "a nebulous political programme." To be sure, there is little that is objectionable in Mounier's basic idea that political freedoms without corresponding socio-economic improvements are largely meaningless. Every Western democracy which has an economically underprivileged group can vouch for that. But whereas Mounier feels that socio-economic progress can be attained *simultaneously* with political freedom (or even as a result of the latter), the Diem regime seems to feel that socio-economic development must *precede* political freedom, and that even part of the economic advances can be sacrificed on the altar of a higher "intellectual, moral, and spiritual life." In a phrase that comes directly out of Mounier's 1935 statement, Diem affirmed in his message to the Constituent Assembly of April 17, 1956, that "democracy is neither material happiness nor the supremacy of numbers . . . [but] is essentially a permanent effort to find the right political means of assuring to all citizens the right of free development. . . ."

There is truly nothing in the American political experience that would make this sort of philosophy understandable or even palatable, but by continental European standards, its development is logical in its own way. If one admits the possibility of state intervention in economic affairs through socialism, the classification of the population according to the economic interests and imperatives of the corporate state, the elitist concepts of totalitarianism and the Catholic and Confucian concepts of close family bonds and obedience to an established hierarchy, then Vietnamese Personalism must be considered a viable political concept that could be adapted to the necessities of the local political situation. *Nhan-Vi*, as expounded in Saigon, does not preclude the idea of land reform, of state industries, and of Presidential rule. In fact, it can also include, as has been shown, total disavowal of the Western system of government—and this is where it becomes dangerous. For in its attempt to become a philosophy effectively competing with Communism, not only did *Nhan-Vi* absorb far too many ex-Communists whom the regime has not digested as easily as it likes to think it did, but it also absorbed far too many of Communism's nastier modes of operation without, however, fully understanding them.

Thus, in order to compete with the Viet-Minh's anti-Westernism, South Viet-Nam also engages periodically in anti-Western (including anti-American) campaigns whose viciousness and inaccuracy of argumentation are no less expert than the Northern originals. Purges and illegal arrests have become an unpleasant feature of daily life, and not only among the known oppositionists. Of the men who came to power with Diem in 1954–55, *not one* still holds a Cabinet portfolio. Some were shunted off into faraway embassies; others followed into exile in France or the United States the very men they had helped overthrow a few months or years earlier; and a few simply retired and maintain a "wait-and-see" attitude in Saigon. Another imitation of Communist totalitarian methods is Ngo Dinh Nhu's Can-Lao Nhan-Vi Cach-Manh-Dang (Revolutionary Personalist Workers' Party), which has become the perfect *hiérarchie parallèle*, with its secret membership and five-man cells whose members know only each other, and "action groups" that can swiftly and quietly do away with bothersome oppositionists. Its cells exist not only throughout the government structure but also in the Vietnamese Army, and have a strong influence upon the advancement of civil servants as well as senior field commanders—at times, according to American military observers, at the expense of military proficiency and officers' morale; to which the Can-Lao retorts that in a guerrilla- or revolutionary-warfare situation, absolute loyalty is of greater importance than military efficiency (whose lack, in any case, can always be made up by American advisers). The fact that both the paratroop rebellion of 1960 and the aerial bombing of the Presidential Palace on February 27, 1962, were not joined by other military units seems to confirm the efficacy of the system, at least for the time being.

In his description of the Can-Lao, John C. Donnell defines the Can-Lao as a "powerful elite political party [whose] members are commonly believed to belong to other political parties also and to dominate them."[15] In other words, it does within its own system exactly what a Communist Party would do: It spies on its own friends, infiltrates its own allies, and acts as a "state within a state" in its own government's machinery. If nothing else, this would brand the South Vietnamese regime as a sort of anti-Communist "people's democracy" whose major difference with its Communist North Vietnamese twin is its attitude toward the practice of Catholicism and the ownership of rubber plantations. That, unfortunately, is not enough of a philosophical difference, unless Personalism can be made somewhat less obscure and more meaningful to the average Vietnamese citizen.

Beyond this particular theory, there exists a special cosmogony, an interpretation of world events with regard to Viet-Nam, that is peculiar to Diem's entourage, and that the regime assiduously foists on its population and on every foreigner sufficiently ignorant of the country's past to accept it. This theory holds that, basically, the whole struggle against the French and, indeed, the whole Indochina War, was fought by people who essentially were anti-French patriots and who were "betrayed" by their Communist leaders. This theme constantly recurs in official publications. Thus, a booklet called *Viet-Nam at the Crossroads of Asia*, published in 1959 by the Vietnamese Embassy in Washington, flatly asserted that there "never" was a single Chinese Red volunteer helping the Viet-Minh in its struggle against the French—although American sources (including Secretary of State Dulles) had clearly established that such advisory aid, particularly in the field of artillery, had been abundantly available. And the booklet added that, "except for a handful of Communist leaders, almost all the Viet-Minh officers and soldiers fought . . . heroically and successfully." Here again, the contradiction is obvious, but the perpetuation of that myth is being carried through to this day. In the new "Open-Arms Plan"[16] elaborated late in 1962, which is designed to induce Viet-Công soldiers to surrender, the ideological rationale that is being invoked is again that "the success of the Resistance War [against the French] was due not to the leadership of the Communists but to the work of the Nationalist members of the Resistance."

Once this assertion is accepted, only one logical step remains to be taken to endow the anti-French wartime fence-sitters or exiles with all the virtues and qualities of the guerrilla combatants who, in the service of the wrong cause, bore the brunt of the fighting. That *reductio ad absurdum* was finally foisted on the unsuspecting *New Yorker* in another article by Shaplen, which describes the reason for the outbreak of the Second Indochina War in the following Alice-in-Wonderland terms:

> In 1959, agents of the Viet Cong began trying to reëstablish in the villages. . . . Their chief talking point concerned *land that the peasants had taken over while the landlords were away fighting the long war against the French;* this land had later been reclaimed by the landlords, who, with the backing of government soldiers, were demanding payment of rentals accrued in their absence [italics added].[17]

In other words, the small farmers, no doubt in league with the French Army and colonial administration against the heroic, non-Communist, Viet-Minh and its landowning troops, were simply trying to hold onto ill-gotten land, distributed to them by Bao-Dai and his French puppet-masters. And now, the Viet-Công are presumably betraying their landlord ex-"allies" and, in a typically Communist switch, are now supporting the formerly pro-French and pro-Bao-Dai small peasants. While this peculiar type of reasoning may seem strange to the unsophisticated Western mind (it apparently was not to the sophisticated *New Yorker*) it perfectly explains what the Saigon press usually calls the "colonialist-Communist collusion." It is obvious that, in South Viet-Nam itself, such a twisted view of events can be no more useful than Personalism in communicating with the rural population.

The "Family"

One last aspect of the Ngo Dinh Diem myth is the aura of alleged corruption that surrounds some of his relatives. Since enrichment is an integral part of the appurtenances of power everywhere except in some peculiarly aberrant governments of Western Europe and North America, its existence in other parts of the world is not considered with the same distaste as in the Atlantic area. There is, however, an unwritten rule in countries that admit "corruption" as a regular practice of government that it must keep within sensible boundaries—just as in the West there is an unwritten rule about the number of sandwiches or drinks one may consume at a cocktail party. In other words, what rankles in graft-tolerating systems is either the bland denial of corruption or its monopolization by a small and unchanging group.

Much has been made in the Western press of the fact that such corruption, in the case of Diem's relatives, could not be "proved," as if their indictment or clearance by a grand jury would have solved the *psychological problem* of the popular belief that they took undue advantage of their official position. In any case, two incidents shed some indirect light on the problem: When Lê Thi Gioi, the mistress of ex-Premier Nguyên Van Tam, was put on trial for corruption in February, 1955 (i.e., at a time when the regime was far from consolidated), she "caused a sensation in court by roundly accusing . . . Mme. Ngo Dinh Nhu of indulging in similar activities on a far more extensive scale."[18] By 1957, rumors about such practices had become so widespread and precise that on August 24 both Nhu and his wife took advertisements in several Saigon newspapers to deny those charges explicitly. Needless to say, this official denial fed rather than quenched the rumors.

Similar charges have been leveled against Monsignor Ngo Dinh Thuc, who is said to have acquired large real estate and business holdings for both the Church and his family, and against another brother, Ngo Dinh Can, who ruled strategic Central Viet-Nam with a police force of his own and an ideological strictness that made

Saigon look like a haven of liberty and license (newspapers that passed government censors in Saigon were often unavailable in Hué). Only one brother, Ngo Dinh Luyên, by training a mechanical engineer, who has lived abroad since 1955 in the diplomatic service, remained largely exempt from such criticism.

Thus, both Diem and his regime were caught in a dilemma of their own making: whether to let a "loyal opposition" arise, and risk diluting the power concentrated in the hands of the ruling elite in the hope of gaining more over-all internal and external support; or to hold grimly onto every shred of power for fear that its dilution might bring down not only the regime but the Republic itself, in accordance with Alexis de Tocqueville's sardonic remark that "the most dangerous moment for a bad government comes when it tries to reform itself."

It is at this point a matter of speculation whether a divided country in Viet-Nam's precarious position can afford a greater measure of representative government than that which the Ngo Dinh Diem regime was willing to permit. There is, however, little doubt that Ngo Dinh Diem's own background of paternalistic but absolute leadership put him in a difficult position "to compete with Ho Chi Minh on Ho's own terms, as a man of the people."[19]

Diem himself rationalized his indifference to criticism and his authoritarianism as simply by-products of the situation in which his country found itself, and not as causative factors for at least a large measure of that situation. In an interview with Sol W. Sanders of *U.S. News & World Report*, he alleged that "all" underdeveloped countries were, by virtue of a "historical and general phenomenon," ruled by dictators and autocrats, whose existence—according to Diem —"corresponds to a historical need for centralization of power." And with regard to criticism in the public media, Diem declared that it cannot possibly be constructive but is designed only "to give me a complex of guilt, which I can never have."[20]

That view of his regime's place in the scheme of things and of his own role more than adequately illustrates why he was unable to adjust his regime to the increased stresses presented by the spreading insurgency.

In the face of such inflexibility, Diem's own military commanders finally resorted on November 1, 1963, to the only means of ensuring change—military revolt. Both Diem and Nhu were murdered inside an armored personnel carrier in the streets of their own capital after having been captured in a Catholic church.

13

Ngo's Republic

IT IS a recurrent theme among American writers of the extreme conservative persuasion that the Founding Fathers meant the United States to be a republic, but not necessarily a democracy. That particular definition of the republican structure of government would fit without too much difficulty the South Vietnamese regime that arose out of the shambles of the State of Viet-Nam in 1954–56. Whether or not there was ample justification for that type of regime is, at present, immaterial. But recognition of the actual character of the regime, with its advantages and defects, is important if one is not to succumb to illusions and misconceptions that make any clear-headed evaluation of the situation in South Viet-Nam impossible.

THE STRUGGLE FOR CONTROL

The transfer of power from Bao-Dai to Ngo Dinh Diem had been, with propitious American help, a rather smooth affair. It soon became obvious to Bao-Dai that he was rapidly losing whatever remote control he had over events in Saigon, and he attempted to return to

Viet-Nam on several occasions (at one time, at least, he was literally stopped on the tarmac of Orly Airport); but clearcut discouragement by the State Department prevented him from carrying out his intentions.[1] The propaganda campaign orchestrated against the admittedly discredited leader is best exemplified in a column by C. L. Sulzberger in *The New York Times* of March 14, 1955, which proclaimed that

> . . . there can be no pretense of political respectability in South Viet-Nam until the moral dead weight of Bao-Dai, so-called Emperor and Chief of State, is shed. . . . Bao-Dai rests on democracy's conscience about as comfortably as the putrefying albatross around the neck of Coleridge's Ancient Mariner.

The total collapse of the religious sects' resistance against Ngo Dinh Diem sealed Bao-Dai's doom, although it is not quite accurate to say that he fully "supported" the sects against Ngo. In fact, the telegrams exchanged between Bao-Dai and Diem during that crucial period show that Diem requested Bao-Dai's help in getting the three crack battalions of the Imperial Guard committed against the sects. Contrary to the advice given Bao-Dai by his own closest associates, he released the Guards for use by Ngo Dinh Diem, explaining his action in a curt handwritten note to a close adviser: "I do not wish it to be said later that, having to choose between his own selfish interests and the nation's survival, Bao-Dai chose his own interests." This deprived Bao-Dai of his last military leverage—and one not without importance, for it would have allowed him to fly directly from France to his mountain capital of Dalat (then held by the Guard) in defiance of any outside pressure. There was one remaining external element that could have deprived Ngo Dinh Diem of victory: the French. The latter, although in good measure responsible for Diem's rise to power, thought not only that he was slipping out of their control but that he was losing non-Communist Viet-Nam in the process; they were right on the first count, wrong on the second.

The exact nature and extent of American-French relations in those hectic days of spring 1955 in Saigon has thus far remained, on both sides, clad in official secrecy. What *seems* to have happened is that, for a short while, the "young colonels" of both nations eluded the restraints imposed by their elders, General Lawton Collins, the American Special Ambassador, and General Paul Ely, the French High Commissioner. On the American side, several officers helped Diem in psychological-warfare operations that allegedly included even inciting the Vietnamese to kill the French. On the French side, in activities that prefigured later Secret Army operations in Algeria, French officers and sergeants helped the sect warlords in their fight against loyal Vietnamese troops. On both sides, however, this was only a very small part of the picture. Both General Collins and General Ely—the latter had been stationed in Washington for several years and was known for his pro-American views—contributed much to keeping Diem in the saddle. A thoroughgoing investigation of Vietnamese charges against the French Army, made without fanfare by Ely, clearly showed that the overwhelming bulk of the French Expeditionary Corps not only had remained aloof from the situation, but had, whenever requested to do so, effectively intervened in behalf of the Vietnamese Army. When the Vietnamese Army signal center had been put out of action by enemy fire, the French Army signal center had sent specialists to repair it and, in the meantime, sent or received 373 messages in five days for the Vietnamese; the French Navy, in the period of April 25–May 13, 1955, had landed 6,000 Vietnamese troops, 500 vehicles, and 1,500 tons of equipment in Camau Peninsula (thus allowing the Vietnamese to take the rebellious sects in a "pincer") while also taking over supply runs toward the isolated Vietnamese garrisons on the islands of Poulo Condore and Phu Quoc. The report, completed on June 6, 1955, was never made public for fear of embarrassing the Vietnamese Government, and it is doubtful whether Diem, to this day, is aware of those French actions in his favor at a decisive moment. By default, the myth of a "colonialist-Communist collusion" against a struggling Viet-Nam was born.[2] It is very much alive to this day.

The next step consisted in giving an anti-Bao-Dai movement a semblance of popular underpinning. This was done on April 30, 1955, by the creation of a Revolutionary Committee, which convened a "General Assembly" of 200 delegates of 18 political parties and groups. The Committee's members had an interesting background: There were two of the expensively bought Cao-Dai "generals" in it, Phuong and Thé; two former Communist Viet-Minh political commissars; two members with Stalinist and Trotskyite connections; and two North Vietnamese ultranationalists.[3] That Committee had no difficulty in persuading the "General Assembly" to vote a platform demanding the dismissal of Bao-Dai, the formation of a new regime under Ngo Dinh Diem, and the total withdrawal of the French. But like Ho Chi Minh in 1945, Ngo Dinh Diem wanted to invest the dismissal of Bao-Dai and the demise of the monarchy with a semblance of legality. A gathering of the imperial clan was convened at Hué (under the protecting shadow of Ngo Dinh Can, Diem's brother); it obediently proclaimed Bao-Dai's dethronement on June 15, 1955, and, at the same time, proclaimed Ngo Dinh Diem the new guarantor of the nation's destiny. Bao-Dai's mother was soon thereafter deprived of her home, and the properties of the imperial family were confiscated. A last-ditch attempt to save at least the monarchical principle (as is the case in Franco Spain) by passing on the succession to Crown Prince Bao-Long[4] was also rejected. The way was now open for the proclamation of the Vietnamese Republic.

On July 7, 1955—the anniversary of the first year of Ngo Dinh Diem's leadership, the Vietnamese Government proclaimed that a nationwide referendum would be held on October 23 on the issue of monarchy vs. republic. All sources with any pretensions to objectivity agree that Bao-Dai was given very little opportunity to present his case to the voters. As Lancaster, then a senior political officer at the British Embassy in Saigon, observed: "The campaign preceding this referendum was conducted with such a cynical disregard for decency and democratic principles that even the Viet-Minh professed to be shocked."[5] It is likely that Viet-Minh shock proceeded more from a realization that Diem was using their own methods to his own advantage, and might thus turn out to be a tougher second-round opponent, than from any particular affection for the departing scion of the Nguyèn dynasty. What happened on October 23 was a foregone conclusion: The republic was swept into being by a vote of 98.2 per cent in favor and 1.1 per cent against.

There is not the slightest doubt that this plebiscite was only a shade more fraudulent than most electoral tests under a dictatorship. In nearly all electoral areas, there were thousands more "Yes" votes than voters. In the Saigon-Cholon area, for example, 605,025 votes were cast by 450,000 registered voters, and mountain or deep-swamp areas patently not even under control of the government reported as heavy voting participation as the well-controlled urban areas. *Life* magazine, in a laudatory profile of South Viet-Nam published May 13, 1957, during Diem's visit to the United States, nevertheless noted that American advisers had told Diem that a 60 per cent margin was quite sufficient and would look better, "but Diem insisted on 98 per cent." Thus, contrary to many official statements on the subject, the South Vietnamese Government must indeed be considered a revolutionary government and not one that is, in a phrase cherished by many Americans, "legally constituted." Not that this element is of any importance whatever in everyday international relations; not one out of ten governments in the United Nations today holds power from a popular source any less tainted than that of the Saigon regime. But in a propaganda war in which one side constantly brandishes the argument of legality, the fact that all its subsequent elections were just as fraudulent as that first one does constitute a psychological handicap.

The Revolutionary Committee, having done its job, was dissolved on January 15, 1956, by a series of police raids that sent most of its members into exile,[8] some to the United States, clamoring, as had their predecessors, that they had been "double-crossed." On his arrival in the United States, one of the labor leaders, Nguyên Bao Toan, attempted to tell publicly some of the hidden aspects of the Viet-Nam events of 1955–56. He was hustled out of sight and has maintained a discreet silence ever since. But the Committee had fulfilled its purpose of giving the regime a measure of the non-Communist left-wing support it needed temporarily to maintain itself in power. By 1956, the 860,000 Northern refugees had been sufficiently integrated in new villages and permanent camps to become a political force of their own, and one that was unconditionally faithful to the regime, and thus Saigon could proceed with the election of a national legislature, which took place on March 4, 1956.

The election was to choose a Constituent Assembly that would vote upon a republican constitution and would transform itself into a regular legislature upon ratification of the constitution in October. Composed of 123 members spread over 5 political parties and a few independents, it did not, needless to say, include a single candidate who could be construed to be a representative of the "loyal opposition"—let alone of the subversive (i.e., Viet-Minh) opposition. North or Central Vietnamese candidates with no popular following whatever were given newly created "refugee constituencies," which, under the leadership of their Catholic village priests, would vote to a man for the government nominee. Mme. Ngo Dinh Nhu was the recipient of such a refugee constituency. Two representatives of the old-line nationalist Dai-Viet and democratic parties attempted to run against government candidates; they were elected in spite of heavy interference but disqualified because of "electoral fraud" and replaced by government candidates in a run-off election. When one of those candidates ran in the 1959 legislative election—again in the face of heavy interference and opposition—he was elected by a Saigon constituency with the greatest plurality (35,000 votes) of *any* candidate in the election. But this candidate, Dr. Phan Quang Dan, American-trained and an OSS operative during World War II, was barred from taking his seat by armed guards and later sentenced for violations of the electoral laws.[7] Thus, the South Vietnamese legislatures elected in both 1956 and 1959, in spite of their superficial multiparty character, are as homogeneous as those elected by the Viet-Minh in 1946 and 1960, which, as will be recalled, also contain some representatives of non-Communist rump parties. In any case, the path was now cleared for the implementation of the republican structure of government.[8]

SOUTH VIET-NAM'S CONSTITUTION*

The South Vietnamese constitution was first drafted by an eleven-member Constitutional Commission composed of well-known Vietnamese lawyers and key members of the Vietnamese Government, aided by an American expert, Dr. J. A. C. Grant, and a Filipino lawyer, Juan C. Orendain. The Commission came into being by a Presidential decree of November 28, 1955. Frenchmen were carefully left out of the group, but as an official South Vietnamese publication admitted, "inevitably the strongest of Western political influences has been French."[9] In fact, all the Vietnamese lawyers on the Commission were French-trained, and the original draft of the constitution was in French.

The document is a curious mixture of various Western influences: It has a President without a Prime Minister, along American lines, but it contains specific provisions on collective bargaining, a High Council of the Judiciary, and a multicameral and extremely complicated supreme court system directly copied from the French, with the addition of the Constitutional Court, which is a compromise between the United States Supreme Court and the Judicial Committee of the Privy Council in the United Kingdom. There is an attempt at separation of powers along American lines, but there is a heavy emphasis on a strong executive beyond what would be considered proper "balance" in American terms. The National Economic Council again is a totally French institution. Articles 44 and 98 of the constitution give the President the right to proclaim a state of emergency "in one or many areas" or to rule by decree

* For text, see Appendix II. This constitution was abrogated by the military junta in November, 1963.

until 1961, which smacks heavily of the ill-famed "Article 48," which proved to be the downfall of the German Weimar Republic.

Once the Constituent Assembly had been elected, it proceeded in turn to select from its midst a fifteen-man Committee that took over the drafting of the constitution. On April 17, 1956, President Ngo Dinh Diem made known his own views on the subject in a message to the Assembly. Again in a verbatim quotation from Personalism's philosopher, Emmanuel Mounier, the President warned his legislators of the pitfalls of Western democracy, which had "brought relative freedom to a minority [while] at the same time it

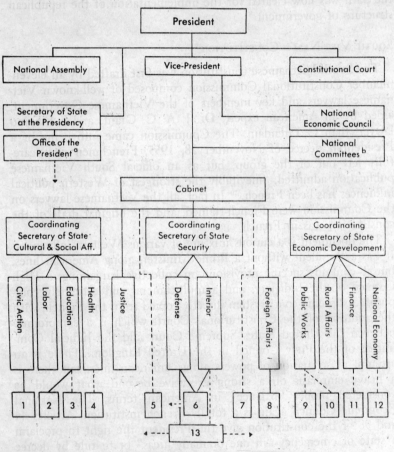

THE GOVERNMENT OF SOUTH VIET-NAM
1962-63

diminished the effectiveness of the State," but emphasized that Viet-Nam also must reject both the extremes of fascism and Communism.[10]

With five of his Cabinet ministers (who, in the meantime, had been elected to the Constituent Assembly and reappointed as members of its own Constitutional Committee) participating in the drafting, the President had little trouble in getting all his own ideas and even wording accepted.[11] When the draft came to the Assembly floor, some minor changes were also proposed by that body and the final draft returned to the President for approval on July 2. Diem kept the draft until October 15 for final perusal and then returned it once more to the Assembly for modification; the latter accepted the changes and approved the text with not one dissenting vote. On October 26, 1956, the President signed the text and it became operative. Constitution Day became the official holiday of the Republic of Viet-Nam.

On paper, the President's powers differ little from those conventionally attached to that office in a Presidential regime: elected by direct universal suffrage on a joint ticket with his Vice-President for a five-year term, he is the supreme commander of the armed forces, appoints and dismisses all senior civilian and military officials, represents the nation in foreign affairs, and ratifies international treaties after legislative approval. Mention has been made of the President's extraordinary powers in the field of security and emergencies. Article 43 gives him extraordinarily broad budgetary powers that enable him

---

THE GOVERNMENT OF SOUTH VIET-NAM, 1962–63

LEGEND: ———— Channel of subordination — — — — Channel of coordination

(a) Includes the following: Secretary General for Defense, Inspectorate General for Administrative and Financial Affairs, Planning, Budget and Foreign Aid, Civil Service, Atomic Energy, Social Action, Civil Guard (Liaison), etc.

(b) Includes the following: Money and Credit, Overseas Studies, Foreign Aid Programs, Food and Agriculture, Agrarian Reform, Education, Science and Culture, Statistics, Rural Life Study, Geodesy and Geophysics.

Special agencies: (1) Viet-Nam Press Agency, (2) Universities of Saigon and Hué, (3) Handicraft Development Center, (4) National Scientific Research Center, (5) Commercial Credit Bank, (6) Directorate General of the Civil Guard and Militia, (7) Chambers of Commerce of Saigon and Da-Nang (Tourane), (8) embassies and other diplomatic missions abroad, (9) Railroad Administration, (10) General Office for Electric Power, (11) National Bank of Viet-Nam and Currency Exchange Office, (12) Industrial Development Center, (13) Interdepartmental Commission on Strategic Hamlets: headed by the Secretary of the Interior and including the Secretaries of Defense, Education, Civic Action, Rural Affairs, and the Chief of the General Staff of the Armed Forces.

to enact his proposed budget by decree if the Assembly fails to approve it within the statutory deadline (December 31 of the preceding year). In addition to the American-type Presidential veto, the South Vietnamese President has the further weapon of being able to call referenda "with the consent of the Assembly" (Article 40). There is a three-term limit to the Presidency.

The term of the National Assembly was changed from three years (Article 51) to four by a constitutional amendment passed in June, 1962, in order to avoid holding an electoral campaign while revolutionary war was raging. After another postponement due to the Buddhist crisis, Diem held the elections on September 27, 1963, under predictably controlled conditions. Since the junta dissolved the Assembly a month later, the election result was academic.

In theory, the National Assembly's duties do not differ from those of most other legislative bodies. Resigning or deceased deputies are replaced within three months by run-off elections (Article 52). Deputies may not hold any other public office except in the field of university or secondary-school teaching.[12] They are, of course, covered by the customary immunities. They appoint four of their members to the Constitutional Court; the other four members are lawyers appointed by the President, and the Chairman is appointed by the President with the Assembly's consent (Article 86).

In spite of the guarantee provided in Article 4 that the judiciary "shall have a status which guarantees its independent character," it is in fact "neither separate nor equal."[13] Judges are, as in most states of Europe, members of a professional corps and cannot be removed from their posts. As in France, a High Council of the Judiciary constitutes a self-policing body, which is supposed to eliminate executive interference. Actually, the following situation obtains: The Secretary of State for Justice has wide powers to transfer judges to less desirable posts in outlying areas; the High Council of the Judiciary was not organized until the enactment of Law 6/61 on March 15, 1961—four and a half years after the promulgation of the constitution—and, lastly, its head is, according to Article 2 of the law, "the President of the Republic or his delegate." The Constitutional Court, which is supposed to be the ultimate guarantor of civil liberties, was finally established by Law 7/60 of December 23, 1960— likewise more than four years after the promulgation of the constitution. However, the Chief Justice was not sworn in until February 24, 1961, and the court itself came into existence later in the year.[14] There is strong evidence that the creation of both judicial bodies was a key part of the "reforms" promised by Ngo Dinh Diem after the abortive paratroop *putsch* of November 11, 1960.

The remainder of the court system is still in the process of reorganization. Whatever court procedures are now in operation are borrowed from the French system, as are the robes of the judges and the court ceremonial. The penal and civil codes are still those of the French administration, amended in many places. New codes are being prepared and may become operative in 1963. The only full-fledged law code in existence is that of Vietnamese Nationality. Although it essentially follows the European system of *ius sanguinis* (determination of nationality by filiation), it later adopted some features of the English common-law system of *ius soli* (determination of nationality by place of birth); this development was a result of the 1956 nationality decrees, which compelled all Vietnamese-born Chinese—and what is less well known, more than 500,000 Cambodians—to become Vietnamese citizens.[15]

In the field of civil rights, Chapter II of the constitution is, on the face of it, as liberal and encompassing as a European-patterned constitution written with American and Filipino help can be. It embodies the guarantees of both the French *and* the American Bills of Rights. In its own commentary on the constitution, the Vietnamese Government points with pride to the fact that, whereas both in France and the United States those basic rights are to be found either in the preamble or in amendments, in Viet-Nam those rights have been directly "built in" into the text. Thus, Article 9 provides for the citizen's "right to life, liberty and security and integrity of his person," while Article 10 provides for full protection from arbitrary arrest, and Article 11 bans torture and "inhuman or degrading punishment or treatment." Privacy of correspondence is guaranteed, along with freedom of movement and choice of dwelling place; the traditional freedoms of association and belief can be found in Articles 16 through 18, and the right to form trade unions and to strike (with the exception of public servants, mindful of the French experience in that field) is likewise guaranteed. In other words, there is very little missing in the way of constitutional guarantees—save their application.

Although the constitution, contrary to its French model, does not contain protracted discussions of economic theories, it nevertheless (in Chapter VII) provides for the creation of an Economic Council. However, its scope is far more restricted than that of its French counterpart, which has independent powers permitting it not only to give advice on economic affairs and bills related to them, but also to make studies of considerable breadth on the social impact of economic and industrial programs, some of which have become veritable classics of their kind. Here also, constitutional implementation, even on paper, was far different from inclusion in the text. Only in February, 1961, did even a draft bill on the creation of the Council pass the Vietnamese National Assembly, and only in the spring of 1962 did the Council actually see the light of day. What its usefulness in the midst of a guerrilla war can be is not readily apparent, but it at least has the merit of fleshing out the constitutional structure.

Three fairly long sections of the Vietnamese constitution (out of a total of ten) must be classified simply as "miscellaneous." Chapter VI deals entirely with a Special Court of Justice—a copy of the French Haute Cour de Justice—specifically designed to try the President, Vice-President, and the chief justices of the Court of Cassation and the Constitutional Court (Article 74). Like its French counterpart, it is essentially a political rather than a judicial court and is to be convened only when required. It is to be composed of fifteen deputies and presided over by the Chief Justice of the Court of Cassation. Should the latter be on trial himself, the Chief Justice of the Constitutional Court will preside over the proceedings (Article 75). Charges can be brought when three-fifths of the membership of the National Assembly files a motion to that effect with the Bureau of the Assembly (Article 77). Finally, Chapters IX and X are of a largely transitional character: Chapter IX provides for constitutional amendments, to be approved by three-fourths of the total number of deputies "voting in person on a roll-call vote" (Article 92). Chapter X contains the ominous Article 98, which already has been discussed.

In sum, the South Vietnamese constitution of 1956 was as good a constitutional document as could have been drawn up under the circumstances, and nothing in the text itself prevents the eventual development of reasonably representative government, with a legislature that is, if not responsive to the "enlightened popular will" (always difficult to marshal in an underdeveloped country with a high degree of illiteracy), at least conscious of its responsibilities. This writer, after having seen the Vietnamese National Assembly at work in 1957 and having spoken to some of the legislators, had expressed hopes that the legislature, government-dominated though it is, would rise to its responsibilities; some of the debates in 1956–58 showed that there was a measure of lively opposition.[16] Later writers on the subject[17] have rightly taken me to task for my unwarranted optimism; for although a measure of debate exists, the hard fact is that the government has invariably succeeded in ramming through even the most unlikely pieces of legislation, such as the "Family Law" of May 29, 1958, which, in a largely Taoist and Buddhist country, makes divorce almost impossible (each case is subject to the personal approval of a Catholic President who, presumably, would commit a mortal sin by approving it!) and makes fatherless waifs of children born in hitherto legal polygamous marriages to "secondary wives." Since Mme. Ngo Dinh Nhu, in her capacity as deputy—but who could forget that she was the "First Lady" of the country?—was the sponsor of the bill, it found few opponents. However, press reports from Saigon in April and May, 1963, show that at least 800 civil servants in the Saigon area have thus far refused to make the choice between their "first" and "secondary" wives and their various children—another indication of the difficulties of trying to legislate in the field of social mores. Nevertheless, with the country aflame and guerrillas fighting within earshot of downtown Saigon in early 1962, the Assembly found nothing better to do than to discuss a "Morality Bill" that forbade dancing, even in private homes. And knowing from where the wind was blowing, legislators competed with each other to improve the "morality" of the bill. One of them proposed the abolition of the wearing of "falsies" by the Vietnamese female population, but other legislators pointed out that the enforcement procedures would present an undue burden to the already overworked police.

When it finally became law on May 24, 1962, the "Law for the Protection of Morality" had given rise to some of the most heated controversies South Viet-Nam's National Assembly had seen since its inception. That was due not to the fact that the proposal imposed a particularly stringent type of morality upon a particularly dissolute country—for Viet-Nam's mores are, under normal circumstances, far from permissive—but to the fact that the law raised some very serious economic and moral problems that apparently had not been taken into consideration by its enthusiastic sponsors.

Thus, Article 2 forbids anyone to "provide" tobacco and alcoholic drinks to minors. However, as Deputy Pham Van Tung observed, and as anyone can see for himself in Saigon, it is usually small boys and girls who act as tobacco vendors, hawking their wares in the streets. In small restaurants, it is likewise children who often sell alcoholic drinks. In both cases, their earnings constitute an important part of the family income and one that cannot be replaced by their employment in another trade.

Likewise, it had been regarded as an extremely "respectable" sacrifice for her family if a girl took up prostitution because her family was in dire need. Deputy Truong-Hieu pointed out in the heated debate that the narrow morality of the new law clashed with the higher morality upon which the whole Sino-Vietnamese concept of the family rests, to wit, that each member of a family must do everything in his power to keep his father and mother from starving. In Viet-Nam, where, as in all underdeveloped countries, severe unemployment prevails, this is not a rhetorical question.

But it is Article 4 of the Morality Law that no doubt will provide it with a special niche in the legislative annals of the world. Its first sentence reads simply: "It is forbidden to dance anywhere at all." This is, to the best of my knowledge, the only law of that kind in existence anywhere in the world. The only similar instance I can recall occurred in Nazi-occupied Europe, where dancing was banned after Hitler's defeat at Stalingrad. Here again, economics (there were 3,000 "taxi girls" in Saigon, providing a living not only for themselves and their families, but for many seamstresses and shoemakers as well) were called into the argument, but Deputy Pham Van Tung invoked one argument that should have given pause to the abolitionists: After all, dancing was not a "degenerate" Western import; the Vietnamese had been dancing—and dancing beautifully—for two thousand years.

When Mme. Ngo Dinh Nhu, who inspired that morality crusade, was asked by American reporters in June, 1962, for the reason for that ban and its application to foreigners as well, she replied that "the Asians are not used to promiscuity between men and women, girls and boys," and that the Americans "were in Viet-Nam to help us, and not to dance." Obviously, Mme. Nhu's own education at the exclusive French Les Oiseaux convent did not encompass the reading of Chinese and Vietnamese classics that clearly discourse on the rather widespread Asian "promiscuity" with which Western dancing had very little to do. Early in 1963, a ban on sentimental songs was added to the ban on dancing, and on April 1, 1963, even the singing of "twist" songs was forbidden.

Article 5 forbids almost all types of boxing and all combat between animals, while Article 6 outlaws "spiritism and occultism" in one of the most supernatural-minded countries of the Far East. This was immediately interpreted as a Catholic-inspired stab at the highly spiritualist and occultist Hoa-Hao and Cao-Dai religious sects. A partial answer to Article 6 came on June 20, 1962, when a vast group of the faithful—500,000 of them—converged on the birthplace of the late Hoa-Hao founder in guerrilla-infested An-Giang Province to pay homage to his mother, who survived him. Article 7 provides a hilarious definition of prostitution ("a woman surprised by police with three different men at three different times," which Saigon wags immediately interpreted to mean that the law made a woman's possession of *two* lovers legal); but Article 8 imposes one of the harshest anticontraceptive penalties on record. In an interview with A. J. Fischer, a Swiss journalist writing for a great number of German-language papers, Mme. Nhu explained the severity of the sentences under this law (five years in jail for repeaters) by the "underpopulation" of the country—an allegation that is not borne out by statistics. And, as Fischer correctly points out, "even most generous American aid already does not at present suffice to resettle the majority of the farmers from the now-overpopulated areas.[18]

As foreseen, the law was rammed through the National Assembly, but it was a Pyrrhic victory. This being a question of national mores rather than of morals, even legislators from the ruling government coalition voted as their consciences dictated: On an article-by-article vote, the Law for the Protection of Morality passed by only 68 votes out of a possible total of 123.

Two more restrictive measures in the field of judicial powers and personal liberties were enacted almost at the same time without the benefit of public debate: On May 16, 1962, Diem promulgated decree-law No. 10/62 submitting to prior police authorization all meetings, gatherings, and even family reunions except in a very few cases; and on May 21, 1962, he promulgated decree-law No. 11/62, establishing three "Front-Line Military Tribunals" (one for each army corps area), which can mete out sentences up to life imprisonment without any appeal provisions whatever. Death sentences are automatically submitted for review to the President. The justice meted out by those new Front-Line Military Tribunals is even more summary than that meted out by the "Special Military Courts," whose creation in 1959 benefited at least from legislative enactment as Law 10/59.

But aside from sudden legislative tempests in a teapot such as that over the morality law or, in June, 1962, over the falsified statistics of the five-year-plan, the South Vietnamese National Assembly can do little but await the pleasure of the Chief Executive. Yet, the mere fact that the Assembly still attempts to criticize the executive branch does constitute a feeble sign of hope for the future of the country's institutions.

In terms of territorial administration, the 1956 constitution is a great deal less explicit than its Northern counterpart. In fact, nowhere is it stated what the relations between the central administration and the territorial administration should be, or what the role of the Cabinet is in relation to the President. Although Bao-Dai's regional governorships were abolished at the suggestion of the Michigan State University advisory group (known as MSUG) in 1956, "Regional Delegates" still exist as watchdogs for the central government. In fact, all American suggestions for decentralization of top control were bluntly refused or blandly disregarded—in some instances because they deviated too far from Vietnamese realities. This was the drawback to, for example, an MSUG territorial reorganization plan that provided for thirteen "areas" (instead of the traditional provinces), some with boundaries as theoretical as those of Colorado and including lowland Vietnamese-inhabited delta areas together with tribal mountaineer areas although there were no communicating roads between them. But the basically sound MSUG contention that it was impossible to run efficiently twenty-seven provinces from the Ministry of the Interior in Saigon was not only disregarded but flatly rejected. Since the creation (as always, by decree) of the provinces of Chuong Thien in the center of Camau Peninsula, on January 3, 1962, and of Quang-Tin in Central Viet-Nam, on August 1, 1962, South Viet-Nam now has forty provinces, all of which report directly to Saigon.

. . And Constitutional Realities

One is again indebted to Ambassador George F. Kennan, beyond a doubt America's greatest practitioner and student of diplomacy since Benjamin Franklin, for drawing attention to

> . . . that curious trait of the American political personality which causes it to appear reprehensible to voice anything less than unlimited optimism about the fortunes of another government one has adopted as a friend and protégé.[19]

This has been the attitude of American officialdom toward Viet-Nam from 1954 onward—an attitude that has largely been shared by the press and, to a far lesser extent, by some American scholars as well

In fact, expressions of even mixed feelings about the performance of the Saigon regime have usually been given short shrift. If the criticisms were voiced by Vietnamese nationals, they could be dismissed (if the critic could not be shown to be a Communist) as a sign of frustrated ambition[20] if not of subservience to colonialism. In the case of French observers, their very nationality has been *ipso facto* a reason to discount their words as being a reflection of, in the delightful metaphor of columnist Joseph Alsop, their "dog-in-the-manger attitude."[21] The problem has become somewhat more complicated since observers from other countries, and, later, Americans who had served in United States operations in Viet-Nam or as journalists in the area, have come forth with reports that are not one shade different from those of the earlier observers.

These criticisms have merely aroused the loyalty of the believers to a new pitch of fierceness that takes little account of development in the country itself. Thus, Leo Cherne, a very influential publicist and a leading member of the American Friends of Viet-Nam, wrote a long article in *The New York Times Magazine* of April 9, 1961, describing "President Ngo [as] emphatic in his commitment to democratic ideals"; while a Jesuit writer, Father Francis J. Corley, in a scholarly article in *Pacific Affairs* (July, 1961), asserted that the South Vietnamese Presidency "resembles the contemporary American Presidency more than the office which the Founding Father of the United States envisaged," and alleged that President Ngo Dinh Diem is "the dignified, but accountable magistrate of a free and great people." The previous pages, based entirely upon material emanating from the Saigon regime itself, should amply dispose of such optimistic views. One can similarly dispose of views that any Vietnamese regime is unworthy of our support unless it is a perfect imitation of the Anglo-American brand of parliamentarism. It is therefore worthy of note that it is an Indian political scientist who has provided us with the clearest one-sentence statement of which aspect of the Ngo Dinh Diem regime is most in need of improvement: *"What has to be discarded is not presidential leadership but the arbitrary and undemocratic exercise of executive authority."*[22] This is an aim that is certainly not subversive of the Vietnamese republic as presently constituted. Yet all efforts to attain it, whether by patriotic and thoroughly non-Communist Vietnamese or through friendly American counsel, have met with rigid refusal; or, worse, façade reforms were enacted that temporarily placated Congressional opinion in Washington but fooled no one where it counted—among the disgruntled peasants and intellectuals in Viet-Nam. This explains a cyclic process that now has become routine in Saigon: A political crisis occurs; a few surface reforms are enacted; the United States advises that those reforms be fleshed out; Saigon protests against "undue interference" or does not reply at all; Washington nevertheless asserts that "recent reforms are paying off"—and then a new crisis occurs and the whole process begins anew.

Thus, the ever-tightening controls over every kind of freedom, long before Communist guerrilla warfare gave them a semblance of justification, brought warnings from highly respected sources that could have been heeded in time. In the field of executive powers, the regular departments were shorn of many of their normal attributes in favor of a "superdepartment" called simply the Office of the Presidency, which, at one time or another, has had twenty directorates and controlled such key services as: economic planning, the Civil Guard, the National Institute of Administration, the budget and foreign aid, land reform, the Civil Service, information and youth, etc. In addition, distrust of the military leads the President not only to shuffle senior commanders around—a jocular comment, with a large element of truth in it, has been made that there are usually more Vietnamese generals in training in the United States than in troop commands in Viet-Nam—but also to interfere directly in the movement of even small units. In December, 1961, the 1st Vietnamese Paratroop Battalion sustained heavy losses in an ambush a bare twenty-five miles from Saigon simply because air support could not be cleared rapidly enough "through the Presidential coterie."[23] At one time, all passports issued to Vietnamese went directly through the President's hands, and so did a long list of other items, such as property transfers by foreigners, sales of surplus military goods, and, as has been mentioned, divorces, which are about as hard to get as Presidential pardons from a death sentence.

In the legislative field, the rubber-stamp character of the National Assembly was briefly the subject of open criticism in some of the more courageous papers of the Saigon press. In a pathetic "Letter to My Deputy," Nghiêm Xuan Thien, the publisher of what was then South Viet-Nam's largest weekly, *Thoi-Luan*, brought out in the open what many South Vietnamese were no doubt thinking:

What about your democratic election?
During the city-council and village-council elections under the "medieval and colonialist" Nguyên Van Tam Administration [under Bao-Dai, in 1953], constituents were threatened and compelled to vote;

but they were still better than your elections, because nobody brought soldiers into Saigon by the truckload "to help with the voting."

What about your Presidential regime?

You are proud of having created for Viet-Nam a regime that you think is similar to that of the United States. If those regimes are similar, then they are as related as a skyscraper is to a tin-roofed shack, in that they both are houses to live in.

In the U.S.A., Congress is a true parliament and Congressmen are legislators, i.e., free and disinterested men who are not afraid of the government, and who know their duties and dare to carry them out. Here the deputies are political functionaries who make laws like an announcer in a radio station, by reading out loud texts that have been prepared [for them] beforehand. . . .[24]

Needless to say, that was the last issue of *Thoi-Luan,* and the closing of the magazine was followed by an involved libel trial in which the publisher was sued by the various government departments that felt that they had been "insulted." He was sentenced to ten months in jail and confiscatory fines. On April 26, 1960, eighteen highly respected citizens, including several former Cabinet ministers, submitted an open letter to Ngo Dinh Diem, also warning him of the disaffection of the people:*

. . . the people do not know a better life or more freedom under the republican regime which you have created. A Constitution has been established in form only; a National Assembly exists whose deliberations always fall into line with the Government; antidemocratic elections—all those are methods and "comedies" copied from the dictatorial Communist regimes. . . .

Continuous arrests fill the jails and prisons to the rafters . . . public opinion and the press are reduced to silence. The same applies to the popular will as translated in certain open elections, in which it is insulted and trampled (as was the case, for example, during the recent elections for the Second Legislature).[25]

But it is the total erosion of the judiciary that gives the regime an all-pervading air of capricious lawlessness. Admittedly, the judges of the existing courts have, in the words of Weiner and Klein, "not been conspicuously courageous in handing down decisions unfavorable to the government,"[26] but, in addition, a large number of cases are disposed of without ever reaching a court of law. There is, for example, Ordinance No. 6 of January 11, 1956, which permits the

* For full text, see Appendix III.

arrest, imprisonment, and assignment of residence of "any person considered to be a danger to the defense of the state." Law 10 of 1959 provides for a system of drumhead military courts to judge any offense coming within the purview of "security"; in these courts, guerrilla suspects can be tried without any of the normal legal safeguards. But in addition to these summary jurisdictions, there is the arbitrary dead-of-night imprisonment in "re-education camps" by one of the many secret and semisecret police forces—the regime's own "political sects," as the grim joke goes—which crisscross the whole administrative structure with a web of conflicting jurisdictions. In 1958, four translators of French nationality disappeared one night from Saigon; although working for the French Embassy, they were not covered by diplomatic immunity. Inquiries to police authorities proved fruitless; the latter, genuinely puzzled, explained that they were not involved in the case. It turned out that the translators had been arrested by a Central Vietnamese strong-arm group run by Ngo Dinh Can that had specially "raided" Saigon for that purpose. Five years later, the four unfortunates, alleged to have been "French spies," have not yet been brought to trial. Then there was the case uncovered by a new provincial governor, upon taking over his post at Kien-Hoa (thirty-five miles from Saigon), which during the Indochina War, had been one of the most peaceful Catholic provinces. There he found 1,200 political prisoners "held in the local jail without evidence" by a local security chief who used that means to extort money from the local peasantry.[27] In Dai-Loc, Central Viet-Nam, 360 ex-Communists-turned-vigilantes one night arrested 1,000 inhabitants, beat many severely, and sent them to nine "re-education camps." Little wonder, then, that the countryside largely went Communist in 1958–60 and that even a Saigon newspaper, *Tu-Do*, finally took the desperate step of writing, on March 4, 1958: "We must have done with arbitrary arrests and imprisonment. The citizens of a free and independent country have the right to be protected in accordance with the spirit of the Constitution."

There is, however, no unanimity among observers on how all-encompassing the police-state system of South Viet-Nam really is. As this writer has pointed out earlier, the National Assembly at times still speaks its mind (at least on the minor issues it is allowed to discuss). Fishel, in *Problems of Freedom*, states that the "relaxed relationship" between the Saigon police and the citizens "suggests that accusations of authoritarianism lack solid substance."[28] That line of reasoning appears, of course, somewhat oversimplified. It would make just as much sense to deduce from the polite behavior of Moscow policemen that the secret police or the Siberian labor camps do not exist. Much, of course, can be blamed on the current insurgency—but that is when strong constitutional safeguards are especially needed in order not to add grist to the enemy's propaganda mill by lumping in too many innocents with the guilty.

With the progressive destruction of even the hope of institutional improvement from within, all opposition to the Diem regime has had to be of a revolutionary nature. The paratroop *putsch* of November 11, 1960, was the first indication of that new ugly mood, although it was conducted, as its own leaders took pains to point out, in a "gentlemanly" fashion. It was more an attempt to reform the regime (i.e., to keep Diem but compel him to shed his entourage) than to overthrow it, and many authoritative sources assert that at least some of the younger of the American military advisers to the Vietnamese Army were in sympathy with the mutineers.[29]

Having survived the *putsch*, the regime, in a first fright, announced on November 17 a "sweeping reform program." But at the same time, using once more the Revolutionary Committee gambit that had worked so well in 1955, the government established a "People's Committee" under the leadership of Truong Cong Cuu, the Vice-President of the National Assembly, and began a "purge" of known oppositionists. The Committee arrested the eighteen signers of the April 26 manifesto, and coached mobs ransacked the offices of five newspapers that had shown themselves lukewarm toward the regime; the total number of people arbitrarily thrown into jails and concentration camps in connection with the paratroop mutiny is, of course, unknown. On November 13, 1960, *The New York Times*, while musing that "much obviously now depends upon what reforms he now decides to make," nevertheless expressed its editorial happiness "that President Ngo Dinh Diem has survived this major test of his power."

When the promised reforms were finally unveiled on February 13, 1961—one week after Ngo Dinh Diem had announced that he would run for a second term as President in the April, 1961, election —they were hardly of the kind that would win the support of the villages. The bulk of the "reforms" consisted simply of promises that the various judicial and economic institutions embodied in the 1956 constitution would finally be brought to life and that—now that the villages were heavily Communist-infiltrated—provincial, municipal, and village councils would be set up again. No promise was made that they would be elective in character, as they traditionally had been in Viet-Nam before and during the colonial era and even in the midst of the Indochina War under the defunct Bao-Dai regime. When the regulation on the provincial councils was finally published almost one year later, on April 3, 1962, it showed that they were to be wholly appointive in character (their members were to be selected by Diem upon recommendation of the Ministry of the Interior) and had only consultative powers. Out of the 287 provincial councilors selected, 5 were women. In 20 provinces, there were 6 councilors each; in the other provinces, the number of councilors varied between 8 and 15. Among the councilors, the heavily conservative element dominates: 55 are businessmen, 42 are "former notables, entrepreneurs," etc., and another 48 were picked who "do not exercise any profession but have a high moral influence in their community."[30]

Thus, the long-awaited establishment of local self-government, widely considered to be essential to the success of the "strategic hamlet" program, also became a meaningless distortion. In May, 1963, however, Saigon finally yielded to American advisers who maintained that the only way to win over the village population was to give it some *real* responsibility in its own affairs—to allow it to elect its own representatives. The new "reform" took the shape of an 89-article decree that provided for elected communal councils and also for village administrative councils. The composition of the administrative councils, like that of the provincial councils, reveals clearly that the central government still intends to keep tight control over the villages: Article 51 of the decree provides that the five-man administrative council should include a "political commissioner," a "youth commissioner," and a "security commissioner," in addition to the hamlet president and the finance commissioner.[31] Of these five posts, three are politically dominated and unlikely to be permitted to go to opponents of Diem. In other words, the new "reform" will leave the villagers about as much leeway as the Communist village administration does. And the latter has at least the tactical advantage of having been in place for ten years or more.

One 1961 reform was entirely new: While a few of the myriad agencies directly subordinated to the Presidency were now put under the operating department to which they rightfully belonged, the executive departments themselves were regrouped into three "clusters," each under the control of a "Secretary of State in charge of Coordination." The job of the Coordinating Secretary is to "activate and coordinate the work of the different Departments in the same field which must submit to these [Coordinating] Secretaries their projects and action programs."[32] The executive departments in related fields were divided into three "groups": Security, Economic Development, and Cultural and Social Affairs. In a news conference, Diem asserted that this new structure had been "decided upon in answer to criticisms against red tape," but that both the Departmental Secretaries and the Coordinating Secretaries remained directly responsible to him. And thus ended that attempt at "reform." Only the departments of Justice and Foreign Affairs were left "unclustered."

It is obvious even to the nonspecialist in public administration that, far from either decentralizing or liberalizing the executive stranglehold on governmental power, the new system actually provides for an even tighter pyramid of Presidential control. Rather than increasing efficiency, the new system simply interposes an additional administrative layer on top, and one wonders what happens to the operations of departments such as Defense, Finance, or Foreign Affairs, whose responsibilities cut across the whole spectrum of governmental activity. But *The New York Times* found that a great step forward had been made; although noting that "more is needed" to win over the population to work with the government, it editorialized on June 13, 1961, that "President Ngo Dinh Diem has reorganized his Government, concentrating executive authority in three strong ministries . . . these changes promise better operating efficiency." This was a total misreading of the situation: Power, more than ever before, was concentrated in the hands of Diem alone (subject to the advice of Nhu) and the new Coordinating Secretaries were as much his creatures as was anyone else in the government. And furthermore, the *real* problem of the Diem regime did not lie in its operating efficiency—which, thanks to thousands of American experts, is probably neither worse nor better than that of most underdeveloped countries—*but in its lack of grass-roots contact with its own people*. And that cannot be obtained simply by streamlining an organization chart in an air-conditioned office.

THE NEW CRISIS CYCLE

The 1961 Presidential elections provided an open test of whether Ngo Dinh Diem had really understood the mood of his country and its deep-seated desire for genuine reforms. Indeed, the very fact that competing slates of Presidential candidates were posted was at

first hailed as "proof" of a measure of liberalization, but even a
cursory examination of the competing (it would be difficult to call
them "opposition") slates showed that they were at best what one
British journalist called an "affront to the dignity of the electorate."
Slate No. 2 was headed by Nguyên Dinh Quat, a wealthy forty-four-
year-old plantation owner and former business associate of Ngo
Dinh Nhu, whose Vice-Presidential running mate was none other
than ex-Cao-Dai "General" Nguyên Thanh Phuong, whose loyalty
to Diem, it will be recalled, had been bought rather expensively in
1955. Slate No. 3 was headed by a seventy-five-year-old practitioner
of "Oriental medicine," Ho Nhat Tan, who was too feeble even to
read his speeches, and offered as a Vice-Presidential candidate a
sixty-three-year-old chemical engineer, Nguyên Thê Truyên. Truyên
was the only truly respectable figure in that whole farce; he had a
long record of anti-French nationalism, had broken with his former
friend Ho Chi Minh when the latter began to oppress the nationalists, and had even dared to sue the French colonial government in
France's highest administrative court, alleging abuse of power.[33]
What also gave the third slate some interest was that its campaign
manager was none other than Nghiêm Xuan Thien, the former
publisher of the banned *Thoi-Luan.* Thien had at first intended to
present himself as a Presidential candidate, but as *The Washington
Post* noted on April 9, 1961, "people started 'discouraging' him
through family and friends with the reminder of his ten-month jail
sentence."

The results of the electoral contest were never in doubt. The
opposition suffered much harassment (meeting halls that had been
rented were suddenly "unavailable" or closed down by police for
"overcrowding," etc.), but it managed to get some of its case to
the public in Saigon, where foreign journalists could watch the proceedings; however, there is little evidence to show that this was the
case in the countryside. In addition, the government hedged its bets
on a possible low voting turnout by announcing loudly that the
Communist guerrillas had decided to launch a large-scale offensive to
disrupt the elections. That offensive never materialized, and there
was no increase in guerrilla fighting prior to and on election day.
The over-all participation in the April 9 election, after initial reports
of a 90 per cent turnout of the country's 7.2 million voters, was,
according to later official figures, about 75 per cent of the total, and
Diem allegedly received 88 per cent of the votes.[34]

A brief comparison of those figures with the results of the 1955 election is instructive. In 1955, Diem piled up a 5.7 million vote against Bao-Dai's 63,017. In 1961, out of a far larger total electorate, a smaller number of voters (5.4 million) went to the polls, and of those only 4.7 million voted for Ngo Dinh Diem. Thus, even according to his own accounts, Diem *lost 1 million votes* between 1955 and 1961. To this writer's knowledge, not one news analyst or columnist picked up that ominous warning. On the contrary, the reporting on the election reached new heights of blindness, if not outright stupidity. Thus, the Associated Press reported on April 10, with an apparently straight face, that "Ngo ran strongest in [the] Communist heartland to the south [of Saigon]. His lowest margin was around Saigon where his two opponents campaigned hardest. . . ." No one asked the obvious question of how Diem could possibly pile up 90 per cent majorities in outlying provinces largely under Communist control! In Saigon itself, where foreign journalists were welcome to watch the proceedings (and thus drew unwarranted conclusions as to the fairness of the election elsewhere), 36 per cent of the electorate voted for the competing slates, and Diem's support dropped from more than 600,000 votes in 1955 to 354,000 votes six years later.[35] Here again, the American press, feeling it essential to keep its reporters on the spot in Saigon, avoided antagonizing the Diem government and reported largely what suited best the official picture: *Time* concluded that the "much-abused Diem had run a reasonably honest election—and won"; while *The New York Times*, despite the objective reporting of its field staff, lent its editorial prestige to such nonsense as explaining that the heavy pro-Diem vote was due to the country's "considerable prosperity, as exemplified by the fact that the many conical hats worn by women voters today were covered with cellophane over the traditional raw straw." It commented that the election had been a "double victory," over both Diem's opponents and the Vietnamese Communists, due in the main to the "reform programs," and asserted that the over-all results had been a "crushing repudiation of Communism as well as a public tribute to the strong-willed leader."[36]

However, no matter how much the election process had fooled the American press, it did not improve the situation inside Viet-Nam or win for the regime the support of its internal or external non-Communist opposition. In Paris, the leader in exile of the Vietnamese Democratic Party, Dr. Pham Huy Co (its leader in Viet-Nam, Dr. Phan Quang Dan, had been jailed in November, 1960), called the election a "farce" and, citing the then recent examples of Syngman Rhee and Turkey's Adnan Menderes, expressed doubts that such "rigged and dishonest elections . . . can ever serve to consolidate the position of the man 'elected.'..." Inside Viet-Nam, the re-elected Administration concluded that, for the time being, there had been enough talk about reforms, although some well-publicized trials of minor officials took place on charges of abuse of power. Also, the new Kennedy Administration, before sending Vice-President Lyndon Johnson to South Viet-Nam as the first of a steady stream of high-powered American representatives, apparently decided to "link its offer of increased military aid to South Viet-Nam with stronger pressure for domestic reforms there," including faster moves on promised steps to "liberalize" the Saigon regime and rid it "of the taint of corruption."[37] But all those glittering promises sooner or later came to nought in the fact of the massive resistance the regime mobilized against any reforms that might weaken its monopoly of effective absolute power.

It was again at the prodding of a serious crisis—this time the mounting guerrilla war, compounded by floods in the Mekong Delta that affected the rice output—that the United States approached the problem of reforms for Viet-Nam. An economic-military mission under Professor Eugene Staley followed Vice-President Johnson to Viet-Nam. Surprisingly enough, that mission, though essentially of a civilian character, came forth with few recommendations that were not of a military nature, and none that involved the deep-seated political changes that other observers considered necessary. The Staley mission had hardly completed its first reports when another mission, headed by General Maxwell D. Taylor (then in retirement), in turn made its way to Saigon, late in November, 1961. Since Taylor was a military man, it was expected that his report would deal almost exclusively with the military emergency. The surprising fact was (and it was a serious shock to Saigon's ruling group) that his report was extremely hard-hitting and forthright on the subject of long-overdue political reforms, including greater freedom of speech and more effective decentralization.

The reaction in Saigon was not slow in coming. The South Vietnamese press erupted in a wave of anti-American articles whose virulence, *The New Republic* reported, "can only be matched by Peking or Havana, and on particularly bad days."[38] On November 24, *Thoi-Bao* ran an eight-column headline exclaiming: "REPUBLIC OF VIET-NAM NO GUINEA PIG FOR CAPITALIST IMPERIALISM—IS IT NOT TIME TO REVISE VIETNAMESE-AMERICAN COLLABORATION?" The accompanying article, which was taken up on November 27 by *Tu-Do* and other Saigon newspapers, contained not only accusations of "interference with the internal affairs of Viet-Nam," but also such inanities as charges that U.S. "interference" was aimed at "gaining profits under the exploitation policy of capitalist imperialism."[39] The viciousness of the attack—which the U.S. Embassy in Saigon tended to attribute to Ngo Dinh Nhu—was a jarring experience to the Kennedy Administration at a time when it was weighing whether it should risk being labeled a "war party" and commit American forces to Viet-Nam in numbers and assignments that would make combat casualties inevitable. For the first time, State Department officials let it be known that they were becoming "increasingly disenchanted" with Diem. But with dogged courage, Diem held fast. By December 6, there were hints that U.S. Ambassador Frederick E. Nolting, Jr., might be temporarily recalled "for consultations,"* which was about the strongest pressure Washington had exerted on an ally anywhere, until two months later when it deprived the right-wing Laotian Government of economic aid. In the United States, however, there was mounting pressure to go along with Diem's line that any kind of reform had to await an improvement of the military situation. The "Vietnamese lobby" clad the formula in the appealing old American maxim that "you shouldn't change horses in midstream," and Washington, instead of pursuing its overwhelming material and moral advantage, backed down. Diem called in Ambassador Nolting and told him that all further political reforms would be held in abeyance and that Ngo Dinh Nhu's powers would remain unchanged. As *Newsweek* stated tersely on December 18: "The score after the first round: Nhu 1, Nolting 0."

Then, the dreary process of plastering over the cracks created by the crisis began anew. On December 15, President Diem and President Kennedy exchanged letters in which Diem stressed that his country faced "the most serious crisis in its entire history," while President Kennedy promised that the "United States would promptly increase its aid" and stated his "full confidence in the determination of the people of South Viet-Nam." Saigon, in turn, again proceeded with some "reforms." The archaic tax system was modified somewhat to shift the tax burden to the hitherto almost unscathed business

---

* Nolting was replaced in August, 1963, by Henry Cabot Lodge. In June, 1964, as the Presidential elections neared, Lodge, a Republican, resigned, and President Johnson named General Maxwell D. Taylor to succeed him.

community, which had never lost its French-derived flair for tax evasion; and in an effort to remedy the yawning trade gap, a special tax on all imported merchandise was imposed with such suddenness that importers preferred to let their goods rot at dockside rather than pay the taxes. Finally, as was stated earlier, Ngo Dinh Diem, on January 8, 1962, created the Economic Council provided for in the 1956 constitution. This is a wholly appointive and merely consultative body, and thus represented no broadening at all of the base of popular representation. Yet, apparently clutching at any straw that could be given an optimistic hue, *The New York Times* reported this on the following day under the headline: "DIEM ACTS TO GET BROADER SUPPORT—COUNCIL IS SET) ANSWER CRITICS OF VIET-NAM REGIME."

But on January 4, 1962, both Saigon and Washington published the terms of a new socio-economic program that reflected the limited aims of the Staley report rather than the wide-sweeping and politically very astute findings of General Taylor, who, after General J. Lawton Collins' failure in 1955, thus became the second United States general to see his views on the Diem regime disregarded. The new eleven-point program promised the following:

1. Facilities will be created for the training of village officials "so as to improve the administration where it has closest contacts with the people."

2. Rural health and inoculation programs will be developed.

3. Primary schools will be created in every village.

4. Rural radio communications will be improved to enable the villagers both to listen to government broadcasts and to call for help when required.

5. New roads, particularly rural feeder-roads, will be constructed.

6. The agricultural credit system will be extended.

7. A large-scale program of insect and cattle-disease eradication will be implemented.

8. A special effort will be made to have the mountaineer minorities share in "the progress of their [lowland] compatriots."

9. Increased help will be given the flooded Mekong regions.

10. An important public-works program will be launched to reduce unemployment.

11. The industrial-development effort of the past two years will be pursued.[40]

The best that can be said for this program is that some of its points amount to locking the barn door after the horses have been stolen, while others offer the routine kind of basic aid to economic development that could be applied anywhere from Bolivia to Timbuktu, but hardly with any telling effect upon a country whose very political-administrative fabric was disintegrating under the hammer blows of revolutionary war.

Of the eleven points, only two showed any special responsiveness to Viet-Nam's own problems: the items concerned with the training of village officials and with improving the lot of the mountaineers. But as early as 1957, the cream of village officialdom had been murdered by the Communists, who had correctly identified this group as a key element in the struggle. In any event, the major problem at that level is not so much the effectiveness of the village officials in their relations with the population as the effectiveness of the central and provincial administrations in *their* relations with the village officials.

In the case of the mountaineers, the Saigon regime has much to apologize for. American scholars, including those working for the Vietnamese Government within MSUG, have warned the Vietnamese both officially and privately of the negative effects their colonization plans were having on the inhabitants of the Southern Mountain Plateau. The mountaineers were not given even the semblance of local self-government, were often illegally deprived of their ancestral lands, and until very recently were provided with fewer schools and less adequate health services than under the colonial administration. North Vietnamese Communist indoctrination programs, advanced both by infiltrators and by radio, were ignored or their importance discounted; most important, they were not opposed by more effective Southern programs.[41] More than 6,000 Rhadé and perhaps 4,000 warlike Jarai, Bahnar, and Sédang had gone north with the Viet-Minh in 1954. Many of them now reappeared south of the 17th parallel with a deceptively simple program that offered the mountaineers, downtrodden under a harsh lowland Vietnamese administration, the prospect of an "autonomous area" like the Thai-Meo and Viet-Bac zones of the D.R.V.N.[42] Since Ngo Dinh Diem, who does not envisage local self-government even for the Vietnamese lowland areas, was unamenable to real reforms in the mountain areas, any American program in the Plateau is of necessity limited to increasing the effectiveness of South Vietnamese military operations in the area and to making, as the January 4 program pledges,

a "special effort" to bring some material improvements to the mountaineers. Once more, an astute Communist psychological-political
move is matched on the Western side by an attempt to either "buy
off or kill off" the natives. In the present circumstances, this may not
be a bold enough answer.

Needless to say, Saigon accepted the new program with alacrity,
for it fully consecrated the victory of the viewpoint of Ngo Dinh
Diem and Ngo Dinh Nhu over that of Washington: All serious
attempts at political reform were to be held in abeyance until the
emergency had passed (in Malaya, for example, that took twelve
years), and all possible American military and political support would
bè given Saigon until then. The creation, on February 9, 1962, of a
full-fledged American Military Assistance Command in Viet-Nam
(USMACV), under Lieutenant General Paul D. Harkins, to take
control of the rapidly rising American military build-up, showed both
the Vietnamese and the world that the Kennedy Administration
intended to stay in the struggle for Viet-Nam and win it. But two
small psychological hurdles remained to be cleared before the commitment would be effective: Diem's internal non-Communist opposition had to be won over or at least neutralized without any
commitment on Diem's part to relax his hold on the country, and
the world press—or at least the American press—had to be reined in
from its "counterproductive" (officialese for "critical") attitude
toward Saigon.

THE STRUGGLE FOR INTERNAL UNITY

The psychological campaign to establish South Viet-Nam's new
international "image" was fought on three fronts: by American officials in Viet-Nam and the United States against both disaffected
Vietnamese citizens and critical American newspaper reporters; and
by the Vietnamese against any American criticism from any quarter.

One such major attempt at rallying the non-Communist opposition
behind Diem was a speech made by U.S. Ambassador Nolting at the
Saigon Rotary Club on February 15, 1962, in which he assured his
largely upper-class audience that the "Vietnamese Government, under
the devoted and courageous leadership of President Ngo Dinh Diem,
attempts to realize, under difficult conditions, political, social, and
economic progress for the people, with the help of the United
States." While acknowledging that "some among you found that
the advantages of a free society were not coming down to the

people," the Ambassador emphasized that the United States was giving its fullest support to the "elected and constitutional regime" and added that the key element for success would be the support of all Vietnamese of good will. "What a marvelous transformation would take place in this country," said Nolting, "if all those who criticize their government would decide to work with it and for it."[43]

The speech was well received in the Vietnamese press, and was followed up by some favorable articles in which military advisers were quoted as having fc nd "the spirit of '76" among the Vietnamese. By the beginning of March, 1962, official American opinion on Ngo Dinh Diem had made a 180-degree switch. *Time* described the process in the following terms:

> Where less than one month ago U.S. officials had privately described Diem as an unpopular dictator . . . the new line was that Diem is "very popular . . . among his people." . . . Last autumn, Nolting had personally asked Diem to fire some of his relatives, hold fair elections, and release non-Communist political prisoners. . . . Now a high [State Department] official called in newsmen and told them, unattributably, that there is no real need for reorganization of the Vietnamese Government because President Diem is "greatly respected among his people."[44]

Inside Viet-Nam, this new trend tended to take the form of a partial news blackout, which finally led the American correspondents in the country to send telegrams of protest to Secretary of State Dean Rusk and Defense Secretary McNamara. They filed lengthy dispatches, stating that American Government agencies in Viet-Nam refused to give them "much beyond the broad outlines of policy, and we cannot even be sure of that"; while Vietnamese officials branded all American journalists—including several Pulitzer Prize winners—as Communist stooges or worse, and expelled several of them. Realizing that such methods were producing exactly the opposite effect from the one desired, Ambassador Nolting finally called in the American journalists and promised better cooperation with the press, although he again cautioned them against statements that might give the South Vietnamese Government the "wrong impression."[45] Those words had hardly been spoken when two more correspondents, Homer Bigart of *The New York Times*, and François Sully of *Newsweek*, were expelled, on March 24. Only the personal intervention of Ambassador Nolting with Diem, explaining the irreparable damage that act would have upon the new "image," kept the order from actually being carried out then. Bigart was allowed to leave on his own accord, but Sully, who is a French citizen, was summarily expelled in August, 1962. James Robinson, Southeast Asia correspondent for the National Broadcasting Corporation, was expelled on October 26—the anniversary of Viet-Nam's constitution—before he had filed his first story, apparently in reprisal for earlier unflattering NBC reports about Viet-Nam filed by other reporters.

The pressure on newsmen was probably not greater in 1962 than in previous years; foreign journalists had always been expelled for one reason or another; René-Georges Inagaki, an Associated Press reporter, was expelled in October, 1960, for having openly mentioned the fact that there was a Communist guerrilla threat in South Viet-Nam; John Williams, an Australian correspondent, was ousted for having reported that the 1959 legislative elections had been rigged; and Robert Trumbull of *The New York Times* became *persona non grata* in November, 1961, after reporting that there was no factual basis to South Vietnamese allegations of Communist military installations in neighboring Cambodia. Such news policies earned South Viet-Nam the following description in the Associated Press survey on world press operations for 1960: "Viet-Nam's press printed only what it was told. It received government advisory bulletins suggesting what line to take. Foreign correspondents were watched closely. One was expelled and others were denied entry."

Although South Viet-Nam's desire to manage its own internal press is understandable—almost all Asian countries do this to some extent—relations with newsmen are particularly ill-tempered in South Viet-Nam because its leaders lack a clear understanding of how the press is handled elsewhere. Thus, when *Time* poked mild fun at Mme. Nhu for suggesting the creation of a committee of foreign correspondents that would hammer out a "general line" (preferably, according to her, headed by Joseph Alsop), she delivered a stinging reply in which she asserted—inaccurately—that "all [countries] have agencies to explain governmental policies to the press," and for the first time, she made a charge upon which she was later to expand at great length: that Western journalists in South Viet-Nam were "integrating the Communist line in our information system." The same charge was made by Dr. Tran Van Tho, South Vietnamese Director of Information, at an Asian Seminar on Press Freedom held by the U.N. Commission on Human Rights in February, 1962, at New Delhi. There he deplored the lack of understanding by the Western press, which, according to him, "takes up the slogans and destructive syllogisms of Communist psychological warfare."[46]

Matters again came to a head when Mme. Nhu, pursuing her one-woman offensive against the foreign news media, directly attacked American reporters and even previous American military-training policies in her aforementioned speech of March 11, 1962. In reply to a mild protest by the American Embassy in Saigon, she lashed out in an editorial in *The Times of Viet-Nam* of March 25 against those who "constantly and traitorously" drag South Viet-Nam's leaders in the mud:

> For years, I, like many others in this country, simply clenched my teeth and shut up when I had to listen to all the false accusations of Communist propaganda against the regime and the ideal of the Personalist Republic, all reported with glee by the U.S. press. . . .
>
> And I should continue to do this if the strange and wild behavior of the U.S. press had calmed down. But, on the contrary, it has increased to a point where it risks harming the fighting spirit of our people.
>
> The Vietnamese people do not have to be taught solidarity toward their allies . . . but they cannot allow the prestige of their leaders and of their ideals to be besmirched unjustly and foolishly by irresponsible elements.

Thus, it can be said that in two aspects of the three-cornered respectability struggle, South Viet-Nam has beaten the United States to an uneasy draw, or may—considering the extremely subdued reporting that came out of Viet-Nam during much of late 1962— even have come out ahead. But there remained the essential struggle —led mainly by the United States along the lines of Ambassador Nolting's Rotary Club speech—to win the Diem government the support of its own disaffected elites. While the internal opposition has, of course, no way of getting its reactions across to the public, *Pour le Viet-Nam*, the Paris-based organ of the Vietnamese Democratic Party, summed up the situation in March, 1962, in the following terms.

> The United States holds in its hands 90 per cent of all means of action. in South Viet-Nam . . . and exerted pressure on Diem to proceed with political reforms. The [American] failure is a matter of record.
>
> Mr. Nolting led those negotiations and lost the first and even the following rounds with a smile, in spite of the formidable means at his disposal. And it is this self-same Mr. Nolting who now asks the opposition, whose division and weakness he pointed out, to go and change the Diem regime from the inside with its bare hands.

In other words, the Ambassador of the United States kindly encourages us to do what he did not succeed in doing, or did not wish to succeed in doing.

. . . others already have attempted to work hand-in-hand with the United States in order to democratize the regime and create a legal opposition, and have disappeared without a trace. . . .

Unless the United States offers new proofs of its understanding [of the situation], it seems difficult for the opposition to offer itself the luxury of getting massacred anew.

Thus, like the French-sponsored government of Bao-Dai, the American-supported government of Ngo Dinh Diem soon ran into the problem of *attentisme*—the "wait-and-see" attitude of a large part of the elite in the face of a national crisis. Not that this elite—what there is left of it inside the country—is essential to the routine running of the government apparatus; this the Diem regime and its civil servants or the army could do well enough. But the tens of thousands of well-educated Vietnamese who are in exile in the United States, Britain, and France, or who are detained in South Vietnamese concentration camps, and who are neither pro-Communist nor pro-monarchist, could provide Saigon's stagnant mandarin bureaucracy[47] with the necessary intellectual ferment to react against the inroads of a messianic ideology—Communism—for which the nebulous pronouncements of Emmanuel Mounier's Personalism as interpreted by the Ngo family unfortunately were no match.

The victory—for it indeed was a victory, considering the heavy odds—won by the Diem regime in 1961–62 over its internal opposition, United States misgivings, and foreign press criticism, was real and impressive, and perhaps more important in the short run to the rulers in Saigon than an early victory over the Communists would have been.

But that hollow success apparently failed to impress the South Vietnamese military, who knew (apparently a great deal better than Washington) that the Diem regime stood in danger of losing all chance of winning the war, and decided to take things into their own hands. Until the insurgency problem is solved, Saigon will have to depend heavily upon the army—but, as King Jerome Bonaparte wrote his brother Napoleon from rebel-infested Westphalia: "One can do almost anything with bayonets, except sit on them."

Throughout 1963, the struggle for internal unity continued, along with the by now habitual succession of crisis cycles. On October 1, 1962, President Ngo Dinh Diem opened the autumn session of the

National Assembly by asserting that "everywhere we are taking the initiative . . . sowing insecurity in the Communists' strongholds, smashing their units one after another"; and *The New York Times* editorialized on October 6 that the "news from South Viet-Nam recently has been encouraging," and credited this improvement to such "administrative improvements" as the construction of strategic hamlets and alleged anti-Communist sentiments among the mountain tribesmen. Joseph Alsop, always closely attuned to official Saigon views, asserted in September, 1962, that the Communists had lost control of the rice crop, that the wholesale transfer of the civilian population into the strategic hamlets constituted proof that the Diem Administration had grass-roots support, and quoted General Harkins as having said that the war in Viet-Nam could be won "within one year after the [Vietnamese] army attains a fully offensive footing." The fact that rice exports were held to a virtually symbolic 15,000 tons in 1962 (as against 150,000 tons in 1961 and almost ten times as much in 1938), in order to feed the Vietnamese population, refuted the first assertion. Subsequent heavy Communist attacks took care of Alsop's other two statements. The honeymoon between the United States and Saigon, further enhanced by a vast public-relations effort on both sides,[48] lasted until the end of the year. It "crested" with President Kennedy's press-conference remark on December 12 that in Viet-Nam, "we don't see the end of the tunnel, but I must say I don't think it is darker than it was a year ago, and in some ways [it is] lighter."[49]

Then came ·the setback suffered on January 2, 1963, at Ap-Bac, near My-Tho in the Mekong Delta area, by an American-supported 2,000-man helicopter-borne and armored Vietnamese force; in the course of this, an encircled 200-man Communist force shot down 5 helicopters and killed 3 Americans. Old wounds were opened, a few new ones created. Americans were quick to blame the setback—for it was no more than that, although it stung badly after the earlier victory bulletins—on the hamstringing of the Vietnamese commanders by their civilian leadership.[50] At least one Vietnamese source openly blamed "American defective weapons and communications equipment" for the death of "many Vietnamese troops who have died unnecessarily."[51] Americans on the ground recommended direct U.S. military combat control over the Vietnamese forces, and the usual promise was given by the Vietnamese Presidency: Henceforth the Vietnamese commanders would heed the counsels of their American advisers[52]—whereupon the Vietnamese Army promptly launched an attack into extremely difficult terrain without telling its American advisers, and failed spectacularly.

Things came to a head once more on February 12, 1963, when the American Ambassador in Saigon openly invited him, in the course of a brief speech, to be more candid with the outside world about the regime's "occasional setbacks and failures." The English-language *Times of Viet-Nam* accused Secretary of State Dean Rusk of "indirectly aiding the Viet-Công Communist guerrillas" by insisting upon a modest measure of free speech in Viet-Nam.[53] The issue was quietly laid to rest again, and orders went out to the Americans in the field to apply local pressure in order to implement the assigned programs. This became known as "helicopter diplomacy"; American officers made their helicopters available only when the operation envisaged by the Vietnamese commander met their criteria.

In the civilian field, such pressures are harder to apply and demand a great deal of patience and tact. By mid-1963, at long last, the Diem regime finally considered the possibility of holding local elections for such jobs as village chiefs and youth leaders. That indeed represented a victory for the American view that grass-roots democratization was an absolute necessity in order to win the affection of the population. But it was again a half-measure typical of those that have dogged such enterprises in Viet-Nam since the days when the French tried to persuade Bao-Dai to obtain that kind of support.[54] Even Diem's *ersatz* concessions were not implemented, and the succeeding juntas of Generals Duong Van Minh and Nguyên Khanh preferred to appoint officials rather than to entrust local government to the villagers.

The first act of the new Council of Generals—officially styled the Military Revolutionary Council, or MRC—was to divest the President of any effective power (see Appendix V) in favor of a powerful Prime Minister. Diem's former Vice-President, Nguyên Ngoc Tho, became Premier of the first provisional government, which was overthrown by General Khanh on January 30, 1964. An appointed Council of Notables was to act as a quasi parliament until new institutions could be set up. In March, 1964, that body apparently proved bothersome to General Khanh, and he ordered it to "vote" itself out of existence. But new elections were promised for late 1964.

By deliberately debasing the institutions he himself had created, Diem made certain that they would disappear with him. His successors have not yet been able to rebuild a valid political structure out of the shambles he left. And thus South Viet-Nam's first republic—Diem's republic—had lasted exactly eight years and one week.

14

The Economic Base

IN REVOLUTIONARY WAR, as in any modern war, the economy of a country under attack is a prime target. This is particularly the case in guerrilla operations against an underdeveloped country, where the gradual disruption of the country's civilian economy may be as sure a path to victory—and a far less costly one—than the destruction of the country's armed forces. In the struggle that began in South Viet-Nam in 1956, the Communist insurgent forces, as will be seen in Chapter 15, followed that path with unswerving determination and marked success. The structure and orientation of the South Vietnamese economy in the 1950's and early 1960's in no small way contributed to making their task less arduous than necessary.

A Divided Economy

To make a realistic assessment of South Viet-Nam's chances of political survival it is necessary to give at least passing consideration to the country's economic and social makeup. Without American aid to Viet-Nam's military and economic machinery, the country would not survive for ten minutes—yet very little is known about the infrastructure of the machinery that is being supported at the highest per capita rate of American aid anywhere in the world.[1] And here, as in the case of South Viet-Nam's political structure, there is no lack of special pleaders and of equally fervent critics and defenders.

The State Department's December, 1961, report, A *Threat to the Peace*, lyrically asserts that "the years 1956 to 1960 produced something close to an economic miracle in South Viet-Nam." Ton That Thien, onetime chief of press relations for President Diem, averred in the April, 1961, issue of the *Malayan Economic Review* that the economy of South Viet-Nam was "poised on the threshold" of what Professor Walt W. Rostow has termed the "take-off." But one of South Viet-Nam's top economic planners, Dean Vu Quoc Thuc of the Saigon Law School, bluntly stated in *The Times of Viet-Nam Magazine* of April 1, 1962, that "1961 may be regarded, in all aspects, as having been a critical year," and "that the present economic crisis has its origin in the state of insecurity in the rural areas"; while a former American taxation adviser to the South Vietnamese Government, Professor Milton C. Taylor, in the Fall, 1961, issue of *Pacific Affairs* amply documented his assertion that "after six years of large-scale American aid, Viet-Nam is becoming a permanent mendicant."

Clearly, there is no consensus on the state of the Vietnamese economy. This is due in part to a lack of precise documentation on many key factors; as in many other underdeveloped countries, statistics are haphazard and in many cases "slanted for political ends."[2] Thus, as is the case to a lesser extent in North Viet-Nam, official sources produce different sets of figures at different times about the same items, or present them in a form that makes them hard to evaluate. It is, therefore, not too surprising that the authors of the two optimistic views cited above are not economists, and the two pessimistic viewpoints are presented by Vu Quoc Thuc and Taylor, both professional economists.

The division of Viet-Nam into two zones in 1954 left deep scars in the economic field as well as in the political field. All the country's industrial raw materials suitable for large-scale exploitation were located north of the 17th parallel, and so was most of the skilled labor. In addition, 860,000 refugees had to be absorbed by the South in a very brief time. The withdrawal of the French Army in April, 1956, at South Viet-Nam's request, also had a drastic effect on the economy. In 1954, the French Army had spent more than $500 million in Viet-Nam apart from U.S. aid, and 120,000 Vietnamese served in the French armed forces. An additional 40,000 worked in French Army arsenals and workshops throughout the country. By mid-1956, French Army expenditures had dropped almost to nothing ($1.5 million), and nearly 160,000 formerly French-employed Vietnamese were out of work, since the 150,000-man postarmistice Vietnamese Army could absorb only a small fraction of the best-skilled specialists.

South Viet-Nam was not without some valuable assets, however. First of all, it was the traditional granary of the whole Indochinese peninsula and, with Burma and Thailand, one of the world's great rice exporters. Furthermore, its whole rubber-plantation complex not only had survived the war intact but had reached production tonnages that outstripped the best prewar years. In fact, until 1954, South Viet-Nam had been short of labor and had to import plantation workers from Tongking; the refugees—although severely burdened by an unusually high proportion of children and old people, because the Viet-Minh held back many of the able-bodied men—would provide much-needed manpower to put into operation long-standing plans for the development of the Southern Mountain Plateau (PMS) and of more than 200,000 acres of rice land in the Mekong Delta and the Trans-Bassac area that had lain fallow for almost ten years because of the war.

There was also ample space for secondary food crops and for such highly valued industrial crops as jute, kenaf, tea, coffee, cane sugar, and spices. Fairly plentiful fishing, in addition to providing a balanced diet, was of sufficiently high quality for export in dried, canned, and (without proper equipment) frozen form. There existed in the Saigon area a nucleus of light industries and excellent port facilities, which could be rapidly expanded, and additional smaller industrial centers could be created in Central Viet-Nam as transportation and industrial fuels became available. In terms of the over-all economic picture, balancing long-range development possibilities with adequate subsistence levels for the population, it can hardly be said that South Viet-Nam came out second-best as a result of the Geneva Agreements of 1954.[3]

The infrastructure, however, had suffered heavily. Of a road system that Senator Mike Mansfield's Subcommittee on State Department Affairs described as having been "the most advanced in Southeast Asia,"[4] 60 per cent had been almost completely destroyed. For ex-

ample, along South Viet-Nam's major north-south communication
artery, National Highway No. 1, 134 bridges out of a prewar total
of 475 had been destroyed, and only 582 miles of railroads out of
873 miles existing before the war were in operation in 1954. In other
words, South Viet-Nam's problem—like that of its northern rival—
was not only one of economic expansion, but, more urgent, one of
reconstruction at least to prewar levels. If one adds to all this a
rapidly rising population (in 1962, more than 14.2 million, possibly
2 million more than in 1954[5]), it is obvious that, like the Red Queen
in Lewis Carroll's immortal tale, South Viet-Nam has to do all the
running she can just to stay in one place and has to run twice as fast
if she wants to get anywhere at all. This is immediately apparent in
terms of rice production and export figures.

The Rice and Rubber Mainstays

In 1937–38, all of Viet-Nam had a total population of 16.6 million
people and produced 7.74 million metric tons of rice, or 1,025 lbs.
per capita. There was an exportable surplus of perhaps 1.2 million
tons.[6] In 1960—the last year for which precise population figures are
available—all of Viet-Nam had a total population of 30.6 million
people and produced an official total of 8.7 million metric tons of
rice, or 625 lbs. per capita. More than 300,000 metric tons of rice
were available for export, but this did not represent an actual *surplus*
of food in either zone. In the south, whatever food exports there
were, were more than equaled by imports of American surplus food,
amounting to more than $20 million a year, and in the north, the
small rice exports to Communist China meant that the population
had to pull in its belts a little tighter and eat yam roots instead of
cereals.

For both zones, this means that *whereas over-all per capita food
availability in Asia since World War II has diminished by about 10
per cent, in Viet-Nam it has diminished by 48 per cent*. South Viet-
Nam, merely in order to feed its population at prewar food levels,
would require a present-day production of 6.5 million tons of paddy
(as against the 5 million tons it actually produces), and by the end of
its second five-year plan, in 1966, South Vietnamese internal rice
requirements will be at least 7.7 million metric tons at pre-World
War II consumption levels—whereas planned production by then
will be 6 million metric tons.[7] Even if the five-year plan targets are
fully met (which, in view of the impact of the guerrilla war on the

countryside, is doubtful), the average South Vietnamese will still have available only about 835 lbs. of rice per year, as against the prewar 1,025. A switch in dietary habits may, as in rice-short North Viet-Nam, be a partial palliative. Large-scale food imports (more than $23 million worth in 1961, and close to $30 million worth in 1962) will have to make up the difference. These are grim facts that clash with an official statement on rice production targets asserting that the

> . . . enormous impetus given to existing crops, and special attention given to food and industrial plants . . . will provide for an excess of 600,000 tons of rice and by-products for export by [1966], taking into account the three-percent annual increase in population.[8]

Although there is almost as much statistical uncertainty about some of the South Vietnamese statistics as there is about those of the D.R.V.N., the figures in Table 9 will provide at least an order of magnitude.

To a somewhat lesser extent than North Viet-Nam, South Viet-Nam has tried to develop supplementary crops. Some figures for 1961 production follow, with 1938 figures in parentheses to provide comparison: 24,000 tons of peanuts (20,000 tons); 26,000 tons of corn (650,000 tons); 4,251 tons of tea (15,000 tons); 4,000 tons of coffee (3,500 tons); 2,840 tons of soy beans (15,000 tons); 26,000 tons of copra (30,000 tons). Production figures for 1960 included: 57,091 tons of refined sugar (75,000 tons in 1938) and 5,460 tons of tobacco (15,000 tons in 1938). In addition, in 1961, South Viet-Nam produced 221,338 tons of sweet potatoes, 219,550 tons of yams, and 336,586 tons of fruit. With regard to fresh vegetables said to have been produced in Viet-Nam, one Vietnamese source gives a figure of 70,000 tons for 1961, while another reports that 109,586 tons were produced; the new five-year plan sets a 100,000-ton vegetable target for 1966.[9]

The above figures show clearly why South Viet-Nam is still so heavily dependent upon food imports under American aid, in spite of the fact that it is an agricultural country: for a variety of reasons (of which the growing insurgency can be invoked only for the years 1959 and later), South Viet-Nam, save for coffee, never even reached prewar levels—let alone made up for the impressive population growth, both from natural causes and from the inflow of refugees. Since the cease-fire, the value of food imports to South Viet-Nam has almost consistently exceeded the value of food exports, which

TABLE 9

RICE PRODUCTION IN SOUTH VIET-NAM[a]

Year	Cultivated Area (In Hectares)	Yield (In Tons per Hectare)	Total Yield (In Metric Tons)	Export
1938	2,464,000	2.2	5,300,000	1,200,000
1954	2,085,200	1.3	2,565,540	161,592
1955	2,243,000	1.2	2,839,324	69,624
1956	2,540,000	1.3	3,412,567	8
1957	2,719,000	1.1	3,191,567	183,872
1958	2,291,000	1.9	3,995,333	112,702
1959	2,503,000	2.0	5,311,250	245,689
1960	2,318,000	2.2	4,955,000	340,003
1961	2,028,000	2.1	4,259,000	148,700
1962	1,660,000	1.8	3,000,000	12,000
1966[b]	2,750,000	2.2	6,000,000	600,000

[a] *Note on South Vietnamese statistics:* All South Vietnamese statistics cited in this chapter come from official South Vietnamese and U.S. Government documents, unless otherwise noted. The most important such sources are: Republic of Viet-Nam, *Bilan des réalisations gouvernementales, 1954–1961* (Saigon, 1961); and the *Annual Statistical Bulletin* and the *Monthly Statistical Bulletin,* published by the U.S. Operations Mission (USOM) in Saigon over the past decade. Even those so-called official figures are subject to retroactive revisions. For example, for the cultivated acreage figures for 1958 and 1959, USOM was considerably more optimistic (2,917,000 and 3,086,000 hectares) than the South Vietnamese statisticians. And in contrast to the Vietnamese figure of 4,955,000 tons of rice produced in 1960, USOM at first reported 5.4 million tons and then revised it down to 5 million in April, 1962. Private sources vary even more sharply. Thus, the 1958 production figure given by Ton That Thien was 4.2 million tons, while the official figure was 3.9. For 1962, Roger Quilliot, in *Le Monde* (weekly air edition), January 3–9, 1963, cited a "slump" to 4.5 million tons against a supposed production of 5.4 million in 1961. Kathleen McLaughlin, in *The New York Times* of April 5, 1963, using United Nations sources, reported a "plunge" to 3 million tons. Lastly, the 1962 export figure is somewhat misleading, since it includes *imports* of 44,000 tons of rice supplied by the U.S.; the net export figure should actually show a deficit of 32,000 tons. The foregoing makes it obvious that even "Western" statistics—since they are in the postcolonial era, usually derived from local base figures—must be taken with a grain of salt.

[b] Second five-year-plan targets.

flatly contradicts the State Department's assertion in *A Threat to the Peace* that "food production rose an average of 7 percent a year and prewar levels were achieved and passed."[10] With a net population increase of more than 50 *per cent* since 1938, simply matching prewar food-production levels is obviously not enough. And the "average" rise in food production of 7 per cent at best covers the years 1956–60. While beyond a doubt South Viet-Nam's food situation is better than that of the agriculturally poorer and overpopulated north, optimism as to its future as an agricultural exporter is, for the time being, out of place.

In the field of "industrial crops," South Viet-Nam's situation shows more immediate promise: jute, ramie, and kenaf are being developed, particularly in new agricultural settlements of the northern refugees. Kenaf is usually a prized export item, but it sold rather poorly in 1961 and is subject to great price fluctuations.

Consequently, rubber remains the major cash crop of South Viet-Nam and its export mainstay for at least the foreseeable future. Here, provided that the large-scale French plantations—harassed by the kidnaping of their French supervisors, the killing of their Vietnamese subordinates, and the levying of heavy fines by the government for alleged "collusion with the enemy" when they ransom their personnel—will be able to weather the present emergency, the short-run picture is reasonably bright.

As the figures in Table 10 show, South Viet-Nam has thus far been able to sell regularly about 70,000 metric tons of rubber per year. An intensive tree-planting program in the agricultural development centers resulted in the planting of about 20,000 hectares of hevea trees up to 1962. Another 15,000 hectares were to be planted during 1962, but the program fell far short of targets because of the insurgency. This will, of necessity, affect the five-year-plan production targets. It must also be remembered that the trees require seven years to produce usable latex. Hence, the effect of the present tree-planting program will not be felt until the 1970's and will, in good part, be offset by the cutting down of overage trees. In 1960, 57 per cent of South Viet-Nam's rubber trees were over twenty-three years old, and the annual rejuvenation rate since 1946 was 1 per cent instead of the 3 per cent considered desirable. If 1960 rubber prices ($400–$500 a ton) can be maintained, South Viet-Nam can expect an export income from rubber of $70–$90 million a year in the 1970's[11]—if synthetic rubber has not by then killed the market for natural rubber. Considering South Viet-Nam's 1955–62 average yearly trade deficit of $178 million, even a fully successful rubber production program will not entirely solve the little country's economic woes.

The life-and-death importance of rubber and rice exports in the South Vietnamese economy becomes apparent when one considers

TABLE 10

RUBBER PRODUCTION IN SOUTH VIET-NAM

Year	Planted Area (In Hectares)	Output (In Metric Tons)	Export (In Metric Tons)
1938	54,000	60,000	57,000
1944	108,400	61,388	——
1954	52,996	54,917	59,472 (55,932)[a]
1955	70,156	66,337	61,770
1956	69,682	70,231	63,634
1957	69,933	69,657	75,953 (73,255)
1958	76,300	71,656	68,737
1959	100,440	75,374	66,000 (78,424)
1960	100,000	77,000	73,916 (70,118)
1961	90,000	83,755	83,403
1962	115,000[b] (80,000)[c]	85,000[b] (75,000)[c]	80,000[b] (69,634)[c]
1966[c]	200,000	120,000	100,000

[a] As throughout, alternate figures appear in parentheses.
[b] 1961 targets for 1962.
[c] Actual figures for 1962.
[d] Five-year-plan targets.

the proportion they account for in the total value of Vietnamese exports. (See Table 11.) Diversification of the economic structure is further off in the mid-1960's than it was in the colonial era or at any time between the two Indochina wars.

No aspect of Viet-Nam's industrial development can be expected to compensate for insufficient agricultural development, and the

TABLE 11

IMPORTANCE OF RICE AND RUBBER IN SOUTH VIET-NAM'S EXPORTS

(Percentages of Total Exports)

	1938	1939	1940	1956	1957	1958	1960	1961	1962
Rubber	21.4	27.4	27.4	87.1	60.9	64.0	58.6	62.5	87.6
Rice	34.8	36.0	44.1	0.0	24.8	25.5	31.4	20.3	3.6
Total	56.2	63.4	71.5	87.1	85.7	89.5	90.0	82.8	91.2

present state of insecurity is likely to affect adversely what little development has been achieved thus far. The consequences of that state of affairs on South Viet-Nam's trade balance are evident in Table 12; there has been a deficit every year since 1950. Bridging the gap between imports and exports will remain the exclusive responsibility of the United States, as it has been since 1955, when France ceased to contribute funds to the Vietnamese treasury.

TABLE 12

TRADE BALANCE OF SOUTH VIET-NAM

(*In Millions of Dollars*)

Year	Imports	Exports	Balance	(In Per Cents)
1937	34.0	83.0	+ 49.0	240.0
1950	90.2	41.9	— 48.3	47.0
1955	262.0	66.9	—195.1	27.0
1956	217.7	45.1	—172.6	21.0
1957	288.7	80.5	—208.2	28.0
1958	232.1	55.2	—166.9	24.0
1959	224.6	75.1	—149.5	33.0
1960	239.5	84.1	—155.4	36.0
1961	255.0	70.8	—184.2	28.5
1962	241.2	46.1	—195.1	19.1

The increasing pace of South Viet-Nam's commitment to a no-holds-barred counterinsurgency operation has made demands on counterpart funds even heavier, for it has brought a step-up in the importation of goods, in spite of austerity measures. Thus, there is very little in South Viet-Nam's economic picture that contradicts earlier pessimistic judgments made by Professor Taylor: that "under these circumstances, even if the exchange deficit were reduced to $100 million by the curtailment of imports, and if rice exports were doubled, a substantial exchange gap would still remain." And the *Mansfield Report* said succinctly: "There has not been any significant reduction in Vietnamese economic dependency on large aid grants from the United States, except those which coincide with congressional reductions in appropriations."

Yet, disregarding its own evidence, the official Viet-Nam weekly press bulletin of April 8, 1962, asserted that "a perusal of the figures for the past five years shows that the coverage of imports by exports becomes constantly more important."

INDUSTRIALIZATION

In the field of industrialization, South Viet-Nam faces many problems. Beyond a doubt, the most important of them is the already-mentioned paucity in raw materials; except for some small coal deposits, and such materials as limestone and glass sand, there are only traces of gold, mica, copper, and iron. More prospecting may result in some new discoveries, but such operations will have to await the return of a measure of security in the countryside. Until 1955, all southern industries were both "light" and small; there were four cigarette factories, two plants producing industrial gases (oxygen, acetylene), two soft-drink factories, two small shipyards and a naval arsenal, a distilling plant, a match factory, and two fairly large machine shops. This, plus a dozen rice mills, most of which were also located in the Saigon area, comprised the industrial picture in the country. A total of 50,000 workers out of a labor force of more than 4 million were employed in industrial jobs.

Another obstacle to Viet-Nam's industrial development was the absence of a concerted industrialization policy. Personalism also had a role in this; the government, while inviting some foreign investment, also stepped into the industrial field and became a majority "partner," owning 51 per cent of most of the newly created industries. Not to trail behind other underdeveloped countries, Viet-Nam launched, in 1957, a five-year economic plan that had an almost unique distinction in the annals of economic planning: It was kept secret. No one was ever apprised of its base figures (which Communist economic planners are likewise fond of keeping to themselves), but Saigon's secrecy went several steps further: neither targets nor exact projects were made known. Only when the first five-year period had elapsed was the public informed that such and such a project had been a part of the five-year plan and what the approximate amounts were that had been devoted to it.[12]

Roughly, the South Vietnamese first five-year plan provided for the expenditure of $500 million, of which $285.7 million was to be financed by foreign aid (mainly American and French, together with Japanese war reparations). Of the total, about $50 million was to go into industrial development, while $88 million was to be devoted to agriculture and more than $232 million to electrification and public works.[13] It is clear that industry was not considered a priority objective in the over-all scheme, and this may have been precisely what the regime wanted. As President Ngo Dinh Diem told an

American audience in New York on May 14, 1957, "we plan on a gradual industrialization program consistent with our needs and capacities. . . . We aim at producing some textiles, sugar, cement, paper, glass, and plastics; together with some other plants producing goods for daily use, this would, for the time being, be the core of our industrialization plan." In a message to the South Vietnamese National Assembly on October 3, 1960, Diem expatiated further on the subject: "The basic principle of our development remains to economize on foreign currencies by increasing exports and decreasing imports. Priority has been given in the industrialization plan to the production of consumer goods."

Although one may quarrel with the philosophical assumption behind such a program, its general target is not unreasonable, since, in 1960, for example, textiles and related items, such as yarns and raw materials, amounted to $47 million out of a total import trade of $239.5 million and a deficit of $155.4 million. Thus, elimination of imported textiles could cut South Viet-Nam's trade deficit by one-third. Self-sufficiency in such products as cement, wood, tobacco, and canned meat and fish would save another $20 million, and some effort at eliminating Western luxury foods that are not part of the Vietnamese diet would save yet another $20 million and cut the present trade gap in half.

The first five-year plan was apparently not fully implemented because of the country-wide insecurity,[14] but it did fulfill many of its modest targets: Current production has cut textile imports in half, and coal production in Nong-Son (scheduled to reach 250,000 tons in 1964) also has begun to save some foreign exchange. According to Robert Ginésy, foreign exchange savings from industrialization amounted to $37 million in 1960–61.[15] Geographically speaking, the South Vietnamese industrialization program is widely dispersed: A cement plant is being completed in Ha-Tien, at the southern tip; mining and electro-chemical industries will rise around Nong-Son–An-Hoa, in Central Viet-Nam; and Nong-Son coal will provide power for textile industries in Tourane, farther to the north. (See Table 13.) However, the Greater Saigon area received the lion's share, with a shoe factory, two textile factories, a Michelin tire plant with an initial capacity of 400,000 tires and tubes a year; a glass plant (15,000 tons per year), and a paper plant (7,000 tons per year). A total of 8,000 workers are employed in the various industrial projects thus far completed. Another 12,000 are expected to find employment in the

TABLE 13

NONG-SON COAL PRODUCTION AND SALES

(*In Tons*)

	1956	1957	1958	1959	1960	1961	1962	1964[b]
Production	2,101	12,367	20,081	19,928	27,311	25,899	56,000[a]	250,000
Sales	399	2,025	5,460	6,663	12,626	19,000	——	——

[a] 100,000 tons were planned.
[b] Second five-year-plan target.

factories to be built in the course of the second five-year plan (1962–66).

Following the example of the first five-year plan, no total figures or over-all targets have been made public, and an official handout was prepared that provided only hard-to-verify base figures. According to Ginésy, the over-all industrial investment figure thus far known seems to indicate that "for the period of 1957–65"—i.e., for the total first five-year plan, plus half of the second—about $200 million will be spent, while the French financial daily, *Les Informations Industrielles et Commerciales*, indicates that the total industrial investment figure for 1962–67 might run as high as $270 million. Among the key industrial achievements of the second five-year plan will be:

Construction of a chemical complex based on the coal and coal-generated electricity of Nong-Son, to be completed at An-Hoa in 1964. The total cost ($38 million) will be divided between Viet-Nam ($11.4 million), West Germany ($12.5 million), and France ($14.1 million). An-Hoa will produce 42,000 tons of urea, 48,000 tons of ammonium sulphate, and 8,000 tons of calcium carbide. Included in the project is a coal-burning power station that will supply 25,000 *kva* of electricity to Tourane;

Building of two paper plants in the Saigon area, which will give Viet-Nam a total yearly production of 20,000 tons of paper products;

Completion of the Ha-Tien cement plant with a French $50-million credit and construction of a small cement factory at Long Tho (near Hué) for $1.7 million, of which $0.8 million will be provided by France. In 1964, Ha-Tien will have a capacity of 250,000 tons and Long Tho of 20,000 tons;

Installation of an additional 3,000 mechanical looms (costing $46 million), which will save $5 million annually in textile imports by 1966, and of 75,000 cotton spindles;

Doubling South Viet-Nam's sugar-refining capacity to more than 100,000 tons per year by adding three smaller plants with a total capacity of 53,000 tons.[16]

In addition, other plants, such as two canning factories (one of them to provide 2 million cans of pineapple juice a year for export) and two fertilizer factories near Saigon, round out the picture of South Vietnamese industrial development during the second five-year plan. All this, as Ginésy correctly points out, whether "carried out or projected for the immediately foreseeable future, is very classic." To be sure, an American-financed and inspired Industrial Development Center (IDC) was created in November, 1957, with the purpose of serving both as an industrial promotion agency and as a development bank. But according to American experts involved in the project, "IDC withered on the vine" because of an apparent government decision to siphon off into government ownership most of those industrial projects that would have been most likely to attract foreign capital or local private investment.[17] During the first four years of its existence, IDC disbursed a total of $10 million in loans to firms and another $7 million as direct investment, and that only after an American firm of management consultants had been called in to revive the dormant organization.

Finally, the South Vietnamese themselves began to recognize what should have been evident to them for a long time: that "investments in the private sector have not reached the level necessary to maintain present living standards." In a study that was shocking in its bluntness but was nevertheless published in Saigon, one of Viet-Nam's nonsycophantic economists, Nguyên Huu Hanh, simply cited facts and figures on what needed to be done in order to win the economic battle for survival: Merely to avoid urban pauperization, 400,000–500,000 jobs would have to be created each year (there are fewer than 100,000 jobs a year opening now). Present investment, internal and foreign, amounts to about $8 million a year; about $120 million would be needed just to break even, in view of the fantastic population rise of 3 per cent per year. Direct government participation in industry is inefficient, and Viet-Nam's legislation on foreign investments—whose fifth anniversary had given rise to Nguyên Huu Hanh's article—is "ambiguous because it seeks to attract and at the same time limit such investments."[18]

But even when measured against the "forced march" industrial accomplishments of its northern rival, South Viet-Nam's development in the early 1960's does not necessarily take second place by any means, except in those fields in which the country lacks the basic raw materials in exploitable or readily accessible quantities. (See Table 14.)

TABLE 14

PRODUCTION IN SELECTED SECTORS IN NORTH AND SOUTH VIET-NAM

	1955		1961	
	South	North	South	North
Rice (in thousand tons)	2,766	3,600	4,200	4,000
Rubber (in thousand tons)	66	0	83	negl.
Coal (in thousand tons)	2	641	25	2,800
Cement (in thousand tons)	0	8	200	455
Cattle (in thousand tons)	820	430	1,940	1,800
Electricity (in million KWH's)	203	45	293	254
Textiles (in million meters)	35	8	144	68

In some cases, the real reason for the slowness of the industrialization effort was not as much the insurgency or the lack of capital, as the basic philosophy of the South Vietnamese regime, which, as will be seen in the following pages, at first did not attach very great importance to industrial development and is—all its protestations to the contrary—basically hostile to foreign investment. This may be an inevitable result of the foreign domination of the economy during the colonial era, but whatever the reason, it has, until very recently, blighted the country's economic development as a whole.

TRADE VS. AID

The one jarring element in this basically not unfavorable picture—Taylor calls it the "acid test"—is that whatever industrial development there is has in no way diminished the huge trade deficit; the deficit has, in fact, gone from bad to worse. Neither South Viet-Nam nor any other country can go on living with a trade deficit equivalent to *two-thirds of its total currency in circulation*—in 1961, $185 million out of a total of $285 million of Vietnamese currency in circulation. Foreign investment—except for the reinvestment of French capital "stuck" in Viet-Nam, which does not even benefit from rights of repatriation of legal profits—is extremely low. In 1959, French investments amounted to $22 million for the year, while the sum total of other foreign investments amounted to $4 million (including $1 million of American investments). And in 1960, foreign investments amounted to a total of $2 million in foreign currencies and another $3 million in Vietnamese currency.[19]

This is an extremely disappointing result, in spite of the Presidential Declaration on Foreign Investments of March 5, 1957, and the American-Vietnamese Investment Guaranty Agreement of November 5, 1957, which in effect ensures American investors against everything but the most normal business risks and even guarantees the repatriation of profits. Taylor ascribed this situation to a "suspicion of private businessmen [and] a fear of foreign capital" on the part of the Vietnamese Government. This is admitted by one of its defenders, Ton That Thien, who describes the economic policies of his government as "nationalistic" and involving "the freeing of the Vietnamese economy from . . . French and Chinese control." That attitude has resulted in discriminatory practices very much like those prescribed by a bill of attainder, through which the Vietnamese sought to discourage French investments without simultaneously scaring off other foreign capital. As the experience of Indonesia and Ceylon has shown, this is usually difficult to achieve.

On the Vietnamese side, American hesitancy has been severely and openly criticized by various high-ranking officials. In January, 1961, the Vietnamese Ambassador to the United States, in an address to an American business group, warned that his country could not "go very far and very long with ounces of uncertain [American] aid wrapped up in pounds of red tape," and urged his audience not to "wait in an armchair for our people to bring you keys and maps for American penetration and influence. You have enough experience and money to do it yourselves. . . ." The Ambassador's son-in-law, Ngo Dinh Nhu, stated a short while later to a French economic review that Vietnamese economic development "suffers from American slowness," and that American aid was "rigid and insufficiently adapted to the specific character of each people."[20] The inception of the "Buy American" program as of January 1, 1961, also brought sharp Vietnamese criticisms. On December 3, 1960, *The Times of Viet-Nam* asserted that the American products were 15–20 per cent higher in cost—which was indisputable—and, as in the political field, fended off American suggestions for economic and administrative reforms with a counterattack of its own:

> . . . there has been much dissatisfaction over the way this valuable aid has been dispensed to the country until now. . . .
>
> It is about time the ICA should be sounded out on the possibilities of obtaining a much-desired revision of the procedure of U.S. aid to this country.

In a gesture that should allay further South Vietnamese criticisms of private American investments, two major oil companies, Esso and Shell, joined forces in April, 1962, to construct an oil refinery costing $16 million, in which the Vietnamese Government will hold 40 per cent of the shares, and Vietnamese private investors will hold another 10 per cent. There is strong evidence that the American Government "urgently invited" the oil companies to proceed with the contract in order to show American confidence in the future of South Viet-Nam.[21] On February 18, 1963, President Ngo Dinh Diem signed a decree that guarantees foreign businesses from nationalization for twelve years and permits repatriation of profits at an annual rate of 20 per cent of the capital invested.[22] Under normal circumstances, such an incentive should produce a spurt in foreign investment, but in the case of Viet-Nam, the prevailing insecurity may deter new investments for the time being.

All this, nevertheless, does not in any way affect the hard fact that much of South Viet-Nam's trade still depends on the good will of the much-maligned ex-colonial power, France. One of the supreme ironies of the present situation is that the percentage of Viet-Nam's exports to France has *increased* since the end of colonial rule, since no other nation sees much point in purchasing the country's overpriced products. Although France's purchase of Vietnamese rubber is at least sound business (since many of the plantations are French-owned), French and franc zone purchases of Vietnamese rice (about 100,000 tons a year) are nothing but charity, since France herself produces 135,000 tons on the Camargue rice fields in southern France (for a national consumption of 85,000 tons) and uses Vietnamese rice only for economic aid to several African states. American purchases of Vietnamese goods have declined since prewar days, but on the import side, the United States and Japan have been the heavy winners. (See Table 15.) This naturally makes some French businessmen unhappy, but the fact remains that it is now American aid

TABLE 15

SHARE OF SOUTH VIETNAMESE TRADE WITH THE FRANC AREA,
THE UNITED STATES, AND JAPAN

(Percentages of Total)

	1939	1956	1960	1961	1962
Exports to:					
Franc area	32.2	67.5	42.3	38.7	42.2
United States	12.0	18.1	4.4	5.1	3.5
Japan	4.4	0.6	2.8	2.1	5.8
Imports from:					
Franc area	55.7	24.5	21.0	17.0	13.4
United States	4.2	28.0	23.5	27.0	37.4
Japan	1.7	25.6	22.0	22.8	16.6

that pays for almost all American goods imported, and—considering the minute amounts of American permanent investments in South Viet-Nam—no one can fairly accuse the United States of "economic imperialism" in the country. Should the artificial element of large-scale American aid, combined with the recently enacted "Buy American" formula, disappear tomorrow, it is doubtful whether American trade with Viet-Nam would reach even 1939 levels, since Japan now can provide almost anything the U.S. does, and at one-fourth the cost. In 1962, moreover, Taiwan appeared for the first time as a serious contender for Viet-Nam's markets and immediately took fourth place—supplying 9.4 per cent of all imports—behind France.

Another striking aspect of South Viet-Nam's economic situation is the constant rise of its gold reserve, in spite of its huge trade gap. This is due in part to the fact that American aid finances between 85 and 90 per cent of all Vietnamese imports—and that the South Vietnamese Government hoards part of the foreign-aid funds it gets, or spends foreign aid funds where it could (and should) spend its own hard currency. This delicate subject was broached in passing by the USOM *Yearly Report* for 1960, when it sought to explain why $190 million of U.S. aid had to be spent to close a trade deficit of $177 million:

In actual fact American aid financed more than $190 million in imports because Viet-Nam used part of its $55 million [of export proceeds] to meet expenses . . . abroad . . . *and to increase its foreign exchange reserves* [italics added].[23]

In September, 1960, the Vietnamese Government actually asked the United States for aid payments in dollar cash, but was turned down by the director of the U.S. aid mission to Saigon, who stated in a public address that such aid "was very hard to justify on economic grounds, as well as to the United States taxpayer." This did not prevent Saigon from building up a currency hoard of $216.4 million by December, 1960, which gave the Vietnamese piaster—in spite of a 1955–60 trade deficit of more than $1 billion—a gold and currency "cover" of 77 per cent! Taylor rightly called this "striking evidence of the misuse and superfluity of American aid."[24] And it is that kind of foreign hoarding that gives rise to many of the charges of graft and corruption within the Vietnamese Government and particularly within the President's own entourage, but that aspect still seems to be far from understood in Saigon.

Thus, when a Vietnamese opponent of the regime published a letter in *The Observer* charging that U.S. aid was in part being used to permit currency hoarding rather than for the building of "desperately needed schools and hospitals in the country," the Vietnamese Ambassador to London, Ngo Dinh Luyên (a younger brother of Diem's), replied in the same British newspaper:

> My Government has indeed built up reserves of foreign currency, rather than using them to found even more schools and hospitals. Is it not the normal policy of any country to achieve monetary independence by its own means?[25]

The fact is that by such expedients South Viet-Nam was achieving not "monetary independence" but merely the illusion of it. For even if there were no major insurgency problem, whose crushing financial burden the United States assumes almost in full, the existence of such a large unused cash hoard is a clear indication of the lack of proper balance of the South Vietnamese economy. Consequently, South Viet-Nam is in no position today or in the foreseeable future to become anything but what Taylor calls a "permanent mendicant," unless its leadership is willing to depart from its rather singular views of economic development.

Under the pressure of the guerrilla war and Washington, the regime has embarked upon some fiscal reforms on the basis of ten decrees signed by Diem on December 29, 1961, which became effective between January 1 and June 30, 1962. A heavy single tax amounting to five-sevenths of the value of an imported product is designed to reduce luxury imports; several other measures have brought about a *de facto* devaluation of the piaster from the totally unrealistic 35-to-1 exchange rate to about 60-to-1 (the 1962 free-market value of the piaster in Hong Kong being 100 to 1 U.S. dollar).[26] However, in June, 1962, a year's delay was granted to importers in paying the "5/7 Tax." This new ruling actually delays for one year all the so-called austerity measures enacted the previous January and, for the time being, leaves the financial burden of Viet-Nam's war where it had been all along—on the U.S. taxpayer.

It remains to be seen whether these economic and fiscal reforms will be of a more durable nature than the often-promised political reforms. Over the short run, however, South Viet-Nam seems to be banking on the impact of the war itself on certain economic activities to give an artificial boost to the economy, as had been the case during the earlier Indochina War, from 1946 to 1954. Saigon University Law School Dean Vu Quoc Thuc pointed out early in 1962 in an article on the country's economic prospects that the building of 12,000 strategic hamlets and the implementation of the American-Vietnamese eleven-point program of January 4, 1962, will absorb some unemployed labor; and so will the newly planned industrial projects. The presence, also, of close to 15,000 American troops and of additional thousands of American civilian personnel, with their extensive requirements for house servants and clerical labor, is likely to have a cushioning effect on inflationary pressures as long as the United States continues to funnel sufficient amounts of consumer goods into the economy. In other words, South Viet-Nam is rapidly returning to an artificial war economy. Such a situation will merely postpone the issue, not solve the problem. Yet, it has been one of the most successful gambits of the Diem regime to avoid certain unpalatable reforms until the situation itself had changed, or until the United States, faced with a critical situation, stepped in and assumed the additional burden. This was Thuc's view of the solution:

> Thus, although the people's income will increase as a direct result of military expenditures, the quantities of products supplied on the market will surely be sufficient to meet the consumers' demand.
> In conclusion, we may assume that in the year of the Tiger [February, 1962–February, 1963] the nation's economy will escape the crisis and advance toward achieving a new balance.[27]

But one year later, no "balance" of any kind had been achieved. Earlier American "polite and objective" suggestions that the burden of the war be spread more equitably than hitherto—in 1960, only

15,000 individuals out of a population of 13.8 million paid any income tax at all, and of those, 12,500 were civil servants or army officers who enjoyed special low rates[28]—were met with polite silence; the tax experts, "in spite of personal access to the highest level of the government, found their advice unwelcome."[29] And by mid-1963, the Saigon press reopened its campaign for an "early revision of American aid procedures," i.e., less strict accounting systems and more licenses for the importation of high-turnover consumer goods.[30] Chances were that, as in the political field, this new "crisis cycle" was going to be successful.

SOCIAL PROBLEMS

> However, there is mounting unrest in rural areas all over the world. What peasants increasingly crave is social justice and reform—at a minimum, the old way of life with the cruelties removed.
> This includes reform of land-tenure arrangements, reasonable rent, credit, and market facilities; and simple modern tools. . . . Finally, they crave peace and physical security.[31]

This statement, made in August, 1961, by Roger Hilsman, now Assistant Secretary of State for Far Eastern Affairs, is a clear definition of what about 90 per cent of the population wants in all the underdeveloped countries of the world. It also points out what still is wrong with much of South Viet-Nam, in spite of three land-reform programs: the Viet-Minh's, Bao-Dai's, and Ngo Dinh Diem's. Basically, as was pointed out in Part Two, North Viet-Nam had no real land-reform problem, since 98.2 per cent of all land comprised properties of 5 hectares (about 12 acres) or less. In Central Viet-Nam (now split between the two states), small holders accounted for 99 per cent of the total landholders. In South Viet-Nam proper (the former Cochinchina), of 250,000 landowners in all, 6,300 (most of them absentee landlords) owned—and still do—1,035,000 hectares of rice land, or 45 per cent of the total; while 183,000 small holders owned 345,000 hectares, or 15 per cent of the total. A situation in which 2 per cent of the landowners hold 45 per cent of the land, and 72 per cent hold 15 per cent, is an obvious field for thoroughgoing land reform.[32]

Of the three land-reform programs tried in the South, the Viet-Minh's had the unique advantage of being brutal and direct: Since most of the landlords had fled to Saigon, their holdings were there for the taking, and the Viet-Minh could reap the propaganda proceeds by issuing new ownership certificates to the former sharecroppers or the squatters. This Communist land reform also benefited from two important psychological advantages—it made no demands upon the peasants for payment; and it had been in effect in some areas from 1945 until 1955, i.e., at least three times as long as any of the competing nationalist reform measures. This is a key factor that apparently has remained unrecognized thus far.

The two nationalist land reforms ran into two major difficulties: One was that the people most likely to be hurt by the reforms were in charge of applying them; and the other was the limited and conservative outlook of the programs themselves, which usually involved a very laborious surveying and expropriation process—an invitation to delaying tactics and chicanery. The first text on land reform in South Viet-Nam was promulgated as early as May 21, 1947, by the Cochinchinese Autonomous Republic and dealt with the problem of gradually reducing land rents, which until then often amounted to 50 per cent of the harvest. With the rise to power of Bao-Dai and the consolidation of the guerrilla situation in South Viet-Nam by 1951, the problem of what to do with the Viet-Minh-encouraged squatters was tackled by Bao-Dai himself. He declared in his *Têt* (Lunar New Year) message of 1951: "Numerous humble Vietnamese, little preoccupied with politics, have gained possession of the soil. . . . The peaceful enjoyment of the fruits of their labor shall be guaranteed to them by the State. . . ." The operative phrase was "peaceful enjoyment of the *fruits*," which was interpreted to mean that they could hold onto their crops but that the title of the land remained with its rightful absentee owner, who was in no position to claim the crops anyway. In certain areas, however, the former owners arrived literally in the baggage train with the advancing French and Vietnamese soldiers and very often used the troops to force the peasants not only to surrender part of the current crops but to make back payments on past crops as well.[33] Needless to say, such practices—which still have not entirely ceased today—play into Communist hands. In North Viet-Nam, where this danger was better understood, French and Vietnamese troops were strictly forbidden to allow the return of former proprietors in front-line areas.

In July, 1952, an Agricultural Credit Service was inaugurated whose task it was to lend funds to poor farmers for the purchase of rice land from landowners, but this classic approach was neither fast nor widespread enough. As the *Manchester Guardian* of August 19, 1952, pointed out: "A little while ago, responsible members of the Bao-Dai Government announced the 'study of a plan to constitute a Study Commission for the Agrarian Reform.' If that is what is understood by agrarian reform, it will n ›t be enough."

A confidential French High Commissioner's report in the same year substantially concurred with this view, adding what seemed to be a prophetic judgment of all the subsequent land-reform measures: "From the outset, the agrarian reform of the national regime suffers from an important handicap. It wants to be equitable and pretends not to alienate any existing rights. Therefore, the national reform will be expensive and very slow."

On June 4, 1953, Bao-Dai signed the Agrarian Code—four ordinances dealing with the whole spectrum of land tenure from big industrial estates to squatters' rights.[34] Although the texts themselves constituted a great step forward, they permitted such generous safeguards for the landlords that much of the reform was rendered inoperative. For example, a tenant could no longer be summarily dismissed, but he could be removed if the landlord desired to work the property himself or have it worked by one of his adult children. All the landlord had to do to force the tenant to continue paying a usurious rent was to threaten him with the use of Article 9 of Ordinance No. 20, which covered that kind of eviction. The article was invoked even by the agents of Bao-Dai's wife and sister-in-law, when the tenants of their extensive landholdings in South Viet-Nam had the temerity to request a decrease in rent in accordance with the law.

Ngo Dinh Diem's land reform also started from the principle that "agrarian reform does not mean spoliation. It operates with justice and equality, and with respect for private property." Thus, as foreseen in the 1952 French report, it continues to be expensive and slow. Much of it is only a rehash of Bao-Dai's earlier reform, with the addition of Diem's Ordinance No. 2, of January 7, 1955, limiting land rents to 25 per cent of the crop; while Ordinance No. 7, of February 5, 1955, once more confirms squatters in their rights, just as the 1953 code had done. The only truly new measure was Ordinance No. 57, of October 22, 1956, which limits South Vietnamese landholdings to 100 hectares (247 acres), with another 30 hectares allowed if the owner farms the land himself. A new National Office of Agricultural Credit was set up to help the new landowners pay off their land in *six* years, while the government repays the former landlord at a more leisurely pace—with a 10 per cent cash payment and twelve-year government bonds. The limitations of such a reform are self-evident, and the necessity to pay for land that had often been occupied for a decade is likely to produce anger at best, and, in some cases, clashes between incensed farmers and landlords.

How badly land reform had been mismanaged in South Viet-Nam over the years became known only in its barest outlines in 1962 and is still not openly acknowledged in official circles in Washington. As John D. Montgomery points out in his solidly documented *The Politics of Foreign Aid*, "The early implementation of land reform under the Diem regime was somewhat apathetic by comparison with what the Communists had promised and in part carried out."[35] The slowness of the process appears clearly from the figures published by the South Vietnamese Government: Out of a total of 700,000 hectares of land falling within the purview of the land-reform legislation, 415,843 hectares had been expropriated as of July, 1961.[36] Of this, 232,451 hectares had been distributed to 109,438 peasants. By mid-1961, however, the Viet-Công controlled large sectors of the countryside, and further land redistribution—whose quicker implementation could have, in the words of a senior American adviser cited by Montgomery, "save[d] the day in the coming Battle for Viet-Nam"—was considerably slowed down, if not interrupted altogether. But among the *ex post facto* rationales now being sought for Viet-Nam, the explanation is often reversed: It is the guerrilla war that interrupted land reform, not the slowness of the land reform that fed the insurgency. While it is, of course, anyone's guess whether a land reform, if carried out swiftly in 1956–57, could have headed off the Second Indochina War, it remains nonetheless certain that a large floating population of landless peasants was (as it always is) an ideal breeding ground for Communist agitation. The exception to the rule would have been surprising—and Viet-Nam simply was no exception.

Many of the agricultural improvements being made now under the pressure of war could have been done much more easily and cheaply earlier. American technical and financial assistance to South Viet-Nam in that field has been extensive, and it may yet retrieve a badly compromised situation in a key sector of the struggle. France, too, has played an important role in agricultural reform by offering, on September 10, 1958, a long-term low-interest loan of $3.2 million to repurchase from French owners 246,094 hectares (another, likewise official, source says 273,844 hectares) of rice land. Although the going price for a hectare of rice land is about $200, the French owners had sold 228,858 hectares by January 31, 1961, for $13 a hectare.[37] But there is, as yet, no indication of how much, if any, of this land has been distributed to the landless.

Thus, in seven years of land-reform operations, out of a total of 1 million hectares obtained by expropriation and purchase, only about one-fourth had reached the landless farmers. The snail's pace of results deprived the program of much of the psychological impact that should have been its key aspect—since, economically speaking, the large estates were actually more efficient than the new small holdings can ever be. The slowness of agricultural reform and the even slower rate of industrial development confronts South Viet-Nam with a serious unemployment problem. In a population of more than 14 million, only 4.8 million out of 9 million potential workers are employed; of those, 3.9 million are in agriculture, and the army and the cumbersome administration absorbed another 540,000 in 1960 (this number, with additional army drafts and the expansion of security services, may well have reached more than 600,000 in 1962). This leaves about 300,000 persons (including 50,000 domestic servants)[38] for all other economic activities. Although, as Thuc hoped, the military emergency may create additional temporary jobs, a great deal more will have to be done to find jobs for the farmers driven by rural insecurity and unemployment into the urban areas, "there," says Roger Hilsman, "to form the hard core of the unemployed slum dwellers . . . [and] recruits for the city mobs that Communists and demagogues have been turning out . . . for the past fifteen years."[39] The population of Saigon-Cholon rose from 493,000 in 1943 to 1.9 million in 1955, allegedly went down to 1.4 million as of July, 1960, because refugees were being resettled, but started to rise again steeply as insecurity began to spread once more. Sooner or later, the South Vietnamese leaders will have to deal with the problem on a large scale, for even total fulfillment of the second five-year plan will make but a small dent in the ever-growing labor force. In fact, one of the genuine achievements of the regime—the rapid growth of education—will make the employment problem more explosive as time goes on.

Partition had left South Viet-Nam with more elementary and middle schools than the north, but it lost the country's only full-fledged university, which was in Hanoi. However, Saigon found itself, by virtue of the north's decision to go it alone in education or to switch to the unfamiliar ground of Chinese or Russian help, in a comparatively advantageous position: In spite of political antagonisms toward France, French patterns of education were retained until such time as adequate Vietnamese adaptations could be found; about 350 French teachers and professors were retained, and their salaries were paid by French technical aid. Also retained was a French school system, built around several excellent *lycées* maintained by the French Cultural Mission, accommodating more than 30,000 Vietnamese children. Various French Catholic missions also make contributions in that field. On the other hand, American aid has been instrumental in providing the physical wherewithal of education—classrooms, equipment, and books—for the vastly expanded school population. In addition, for six years, American aid financed the training of Vietnamese civil servants through an advisory group from Michigan State University (MSUG), which reformed the National Administration Institute along American lines and made a number of excellent studies of special problems of Vietnamese administration. Its contract was terminated when several of the American professors in the program criticized the operations of the South Vietnamese Government upon termination of their contracts —and Michigan State University refused to muzzle them. It is likely that, in spite of the relatively modest funds allocated to it, American influence in the field of education and training may well turn out to have been the best American investment in South Viet-Nam's future.

Where there had once been no full-fledged university, there are now three: the National University of Saigon, with a full range of departments; Hué University, founded in 1957, with 2,279 students in 1962 and so far largely a liberal arts curriculum, although a small medical school was opened in 1961; and the Catholic University at Dalat, founded by Ngo Dinh Diem's brother, Archbishop Thuc, in 1958. Its curriculum centers on arts and sciences; it had a student body of 463 in 1962. Many other specialized schools exist, and at Dalat, South Viet-Nam will soon have an experimental atomic reactor, whose reason for being in an underdeveloped country appears questionable, but it is perhaps considered a good morale builder. In any case, it cost South Viet-Nam very little, since it was built with U.S. aid.

Thus, in relation to the size of its population as well as in academic performance, the South Vietnamese regime is a match for its northern rival (see Table 16), but aside from the problem of how to employ those tens of thousands of college graduates without creating even more unproductive government jobs, it has a psychological problem its northern neighbor does not share: While the latter's

TABLE 16

TOTAL SCHOOL ATTENDANCE IN SOUTH VIET-NAM [a]

(*Private and Public Schools*)

	Primary Schools	Secondary Schools	Technical Schools	Universities
1954/55	400,865	22,001	2,761	2,231
1955/56	601,862	25,810	3,471	2,909
1956/57	638,104	34,474	4,416	4,201
1957/58	887,387	52,318	5,237	5,035
1958/59	1,076,523	76,346	5,540	6,712
1959/60	1,243,918	100,577	5,644	7,924
1960/61	1,365,739	103,752	6,339	10,277
1961/62	1,361,422	228,495	10,906	15,214

[a] *Sources*: Here, again, several sets of figures are available. Statistics used here are derived mostly from Republic of Viet-Nam, *Bilan des réalisations gouvernementales, 1954–1961* (Saigon, 1961). Some other figures (notably those of the *Annual Statistical Bulletin* and the *Monthly Statistical Bulletin* issued by the U.S. Operations Mission, or USOM) are often more optimistic than those provided by the Vietnamese Government. Thus, the 1960 secondary-school figure given by the USOM is 170,000, and the university figure is 11,500. The 1962 figures are drawn from the report presented by Viet-Nam to the Twenty-fifth International Conference on Education, *Situation et progrès de l'enseignement au Viet-Nam, 1961–62* (Geneva, 1962). The report explains the drop in primary-school students as being "due to a lack of security in certain remote areas." (P. 10.) The report also contradicts earlier "official" figures regarding secondary-school students, giving the number in 1960 as 199,000, in contrast to the 103,752 given by *Bilan*. This would make the increase to 228,495 in 1961 look somewhat less phenomenal.

fellowship students go only to Communist countries and seldom contract any heretical political ideas (save perhaps the wrong slant on the Khrushchev-Mao dispute, depending upon whether they study in Moscow or Peking), South Viet-Nam's 2,000 students abroad go mostly to Western countries whose code of political behavior clashes with that prevailing at home. Little wonder that recent Saigon press campaigns have been directed at the country's own "pseudo-liberals with their unrealistic Western democratic ideas."

In order to get better control over the young and, at the same time, give the regime a mass underpinning, several youth movements were created that, with their various uniforms—including ten-gallon hats, white Sam Browne belts, and U.S. carbines—smack of Mussolini's Balilla and look even more military (if not more militant) than Ho Chi Minh's red-scarved Young Pioneers. As in Europe and contrary to American practice, almost all South Vietnamese youth movements are appendages of political parties. Thus, while the once-flourishing Boy Scout movement totaled only about 2,400 adherents of both sexes in 1961, the Cong-Hoa (Republican) Youth movement had 814,000 male and 496,000 female members; and that of the National Revolutionary Movement claimed another 312,000. Another "National Revolutionary Youth" organization claimed 42,000 members; and the American-sponsored "4-T" movement (patterned on the rural 4-H clubs in the United States) numbered about 30,000 members. A few smaller groups, including a 17,000-member Buddhist youth movement and a 592-member "Police Scout" group, round out the picture. While it is doubtful that "Personalism" has made much headway among those youngsters as a political philosophy, it has nevertheless permitted the physical and psychological militarization of large numbers of young people who hitherto had managed to sit on the fence while the struggle was going on around them. Starting late in 1961, photos of Cong-Hoa girls in martial poses, holding various pieces of military ordnance, have become regular fare in the American and Vietnamese press, and Cong-Hoa groups of both sexes were assigned auxiliary military tasks early in 1962. Soon, Communist killings and kidnapings of Cong-Hoa members gave the youth movement its first martyrs.

In sum, in the economic and social fields, the Ngo Dinh Diem regime has achieved not as much as its most enthusiastic supporters would like the outside world to believe, but a great deal more than it is usually given credit for. In any case, its physical achievements easily measure up in most areas to the performance of its' northern rival. This does not mean that the regime has a "social conscience." There is perhaps no more damning statistic on that score than that on building construction in South Viet-Nam, put out by the American aid mission in Saigon: Between 1957 and 1960, South Viet-Nam built 47,000 square meters of cinemas and dance halls and 6,500 square meters of hospitals; 3,500 square meters of rice mills and 56,000 square meters of churches or pagodas; 86,000 square meters of schools but 425,000 square meters of high-rent villas and apartment buildings.[40]

That is the sort of thing—far more than weapons and infiltrators from across the 17th parallel—that makes Communist guerrillas out of peaceable peasants.

The Second Indochina War

T HE SECOND Indochina War—"Indochina" is used rather than "Viet-Nam," since the struggle once again encompasses the whole peninsula except for Cambodia—began by deliberate Communist design in South Viet-Nam early in 1957 and, abetted by American fumbling, spread to Laos in 1959.

In South Viet-Nam, after the July, 1956, deadline passed without a plebiscite on the reunification of the two Viet-Nams, the determination of Viet-Nam's non-Communist zone to become a stable and viable state was underlined by the proclamation on October 26, 1956, of a republican constitution. This fact, together with an internal leadership that was resolutely American-oriented and enjoyed fullest United States military, financial, and political support, made South Viet-Nam a prime target for the revolutionary war that was to ensue. Several easily avoidable mistakes by the Saigon leadership made the outbreak of such a war a certainty. In neighboring Laos, the mildly pro-Western regime of Souvanna Phouma, which, late in 1957, had succeeded in coming to an accommodation with the Pathet-Lao, was eliminated in July, 1958, after American aid had

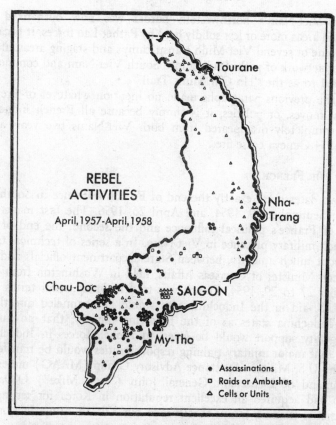

REBEL
ACTIVITIES

April, 1957-April, 1958

Tourane

Nha-
Trang

Chau-Doc

SAIGON

My-Tho

• Assassinations
□ Raids or Ambushes
△ Cells or Units

THE BEGINNING OF THE SECOND INDOCHINA WAR

been withheld. The Souvanna Phouma government was replaced by a right-wing reform regime that "was already obsessed with its American-inspired single-minded anti-Communist role"[1] and thus committed to a military showdown with the battle-toughened Pathet-Lao for which the Royal Laotian Army was far from ready. The military operations, launched at the Plaine des Jarres on May 18, 1959, ended in utter disaster for the right-wing forces two years later. The Geneva Neutralization Agreement signed on July 23, 1962—after more than a year of talks—left Laos as divided as ever, and again under the premiership of Souvanna Phouma, but with the key difference that the pro-Communist Laotian forces were twenty times larger and much better trained and equipped than in 1959. And a good part of

South Viet-Nam's northwestern border was now outflanked by
Laotian areas more or less solidly held by Pathet-Lao forces. It became
the home of several Viet-Minh transit camps and staging areas, along
with a network of paths leading into South Viet-Nam and commonly
referred to as the "Ho Chi Minh Trail."

If the previous paragraphs made no mention whatever of French
views, moves, or policies, it is simply because all French influence
had completely disappeared from both Viet-Nams two years after
the 1954 Geneva cease-fire.

EXIT THE FRENCH

Two dates mark exactly the end of French influence in Southeast
Asia: September 29, 1954, and April 26, 1956. The first marks the
end of France's political influence and the second, the end of the
French military presence in Viet-Nam. In a series of technical talks,
without much amenity, between State Department officials and the
French Minister of Overseas Affairs, held in Washington from September 27 to 29, 1954, France was told in unequivocal terms that
all U.S. aid in the Indochina area would be channeled directly to
the Indochina states as of the following January; that no further
budgetary support would be given to French forces in Indochina;
and that major military training responsibilities would be transferred
to the U.S. Military Assistance Advisory Group (MAAG) under the
command of Lieutenant General John ("Iron Mike") O'Daniel,
who had acquired an excellent reputation in Korea for setting up
divisional training camps that turned out Korean Army divisions in
almost assembly-line fashion.

The gist of those talks was further nailed down in November of
that year in the course of negotiations between Secretary of State
John Foster Dulles and French Premier Pierre Mendès-France, acting
as his own Foreign Minister. Taking place after Mendès-France had,
in the opinion of Dulles and of France's own conservatives, "sabotaged" the European Defense Community, and after the Algerian
rebellion had broken out, the meeting found Dulles unreceptive to
French arguments. And Mendès-France was sufficiently preoccupied
with new and more pressing problems in North Africa to be willing
to yield full preponderance in Vietnamese affairs to the United
States.[2]

For a short while, the façade of Franco-American "unity" was
preserved for the benefit of the outside world: The joint American-

French training program for the Vietnamese Army (Training Relations Instruction Mission, or TRIM[3]), headed by General O'Daniel,·
was placed under the over-all authority of General Paul Ely, the
French commander in chief. On the spot, however, frictions between
the Americans and the about-to-be-evicted French were bound to
occur. The Diem government, nationalistic and suspicious, was
caught in the middle. What ensued was a fairly unpleasant situation,
in the course of which the French charged an American officer with
being the author of leaflets inciting the Vietnamese against the
French; while a high-level American observer, Ambassador Angier
Biddle Duke (later on State Department Chief of Protocol), openly
accused the French of having provided the explosives and money
used in bombing raids against American offices in Saigon.[4]

Mutual antipathy built up then between American and French
military personnel as well as civilians has survived to this very day
and still occasionally poisons French-American relations in the area.[5]

With the collapse of the politico-religious sects in the summer
of 1955, a major element of Franco-Vietnamese tension disappeared,
but the very presence of French troops in Viet-Nam hurt the national
pride of the new men in the saddle in Saigon. In the ensuing negotiations, Ngo Dinh Diem remained adamant: The French would
not be allowed to maintain any military base in Viet-Nam, although
they had hoped to retain an aeronaval base near Cape St. Jacques,
and they had spent $10 million to equip it with modern facilities.
On January 19, 1956, Ngo Dinh Diem informed the French that
negotiations on the further stationing of French troops in Viet-Nam
were pointless, "as the presence of foreign troops, no matter how
friendly they may be, was incompatible with Viet-Nam's concept of
full · independence." Events later modified Diem's view on this
subject.

As far as the Geneva armistice accords were concerned, this meant
that the French Army as a signatory and guarantor of the cease-fire
provisions would disappear and that its responsibilities would have
to be assumed by a South Vietnamese successor. On April 3, 1956,
French informed Britain and the Soviet Union, as co-chairmen of
the Geneva conference, of her intent to dissolve the French High
Command in Indochina as of April 26. On April 10, almost a hundred years after the first French units had landed in Saigon, the
last parade of French troops took place in South Viet-Nam's capital:
Paratroop commandos in camouflage uniforms and amaranth berets,
Foreign Legionnaires with glistening-white kepis, and Moroccans

with fierce bearded faces crowned by tan turbans, their embroidered flags heavy with the ribbons of their unit citations and battle streamers. In the crowd, there were many Vietnamese who wore the medals they had won in the service of France, and French observers report that some of them cried as the troops marched off to their ships.[6]

With the departure of the French forces, the elimination of all remaining French influence was fairly rapid. The French broadcasting station, Radio France-Asie, had been closed down in February after an intensive press campaign accusing it of endangering Vietnamese mores with its degenerate music; the National Institute of Administration, established by the French in Dalat, was transferred to Saigon and its French staff dismissed and replaced with American professors from Michigan State University. Most other French experts were rapidly replaced, and TRIM was dissolved, with all the ground-force training remaining in American hands, while the French retained some training functions in Viet-Nam's embryonic navy and air force. The French-type rank insignia of the armed forces were burned at a symbolic bonfire and replaced with new insignia patterned upon those of Nationalist China. An American reporter described some new sartorial problems:

> United States military advisers insisted on replacing the floppy, wide-brimmed [jungle hat] popular with Southeast Asian troops with the United States . . . stiff flat-topped cap [which] with its short visor, looked "smarter." But unlike Americans, Vietnamese don't like to get suntanned and they rejected the new headgear.[7]

The Vietnamese, however, took over nearly everything else, from the complete U.S. Navy uniform to the white star on a blue field for its air force with but the smallest of red-and-yellow Vietnamese markings. As a result, Viet-Nam's neighbors accuse the United States of air-space violations for which it cannot conceivably be responsible. On May 31, 1957, the small French air and naval training mission was dismissed, and the government asked that civilian clothes be worn by the two dozen Frenchmen who had to stay on in Saigon to receive the supplies destined for the French treaty air base at Séno, in Laos.[8] What remains today of French military tradition in South Viet-Nam is the above-mentioned jungle hat (copied by the French from the Australians in 1945) and the red berets of South Viet-Nam's paratroops. All officers are now trained in Viet-Nam or the United States.

The extent to which the Diem regime wanted to rid itself of the French presence assumed at times ludicrous proportions. Thus, a Presidential decree of August 30, 1956, abolished all French first names for Vietnamese nationals, given particularly to those of the Catholic faith—including, of course, President Diem himself, whose Christian name was Jean-Baptiste. However, the name day of the President is still celebrated with great pomp.[9] In another unique demand, Viet-Nam requested the return of Vietnamese archaeological finds from French museums—a principle that, if invoked elsewhere, might strip Western museums of Egyptian, Mexican, Indian, and other art. But a new current had set in in France: a near isolationism with regard to the Far East, which made Frenchmen eager to unburden themselves of any further commitments there. In May, 1959, France returned to Viet-Nam a magnificent collection of art pieces, notably the priceless vestiges of the Oc-Eo civilization (a Greco-Roman culture that had astonishingly penetrated to this Far Eastern remove) discovered by Louis Malleret of the Ecole Française d'Extrême-Orient in 1944.[10]

De Gaulle's first Finance Minister, Antoine Pinay, a Catholic conservative with wide business interests involving Viet-Nam, was instrumental in transferring to the Saigon government whatever French holdings were left in the country. On March 24, 1960, final accords were signed that turned over all real estate still held by the French Government, including the embassy buildings and the embassy's staff housing. The French embassy then moved into the modest building of its own consulate; the latter moved into some office space a French business firm was willing to rent to it, and the French Cultural Mission had to move its files into the private homes of its staff.

In two fields, however, French influence has diminished very little: in the economic field, in which, as was shown in the previous chapter, Viet-Nam depends upon France more than ever before; and in the educational field, in which France has made a considerable effort to maintain a toehold.

The thoroughgoing noninvolvement in the political field, considering France's heavy and even heavy-handed involvement less than a decade ago, never ceases to surprise the foreign observer and is, of course, well-known to the Communists in Viet-Nam, who have repeatedly sought to gain the sympathy of the 15,000 remaining Frenchmen.[11] Their failure has led the Communists to try a different technique of persuasion—terror—and the list of French citizens murdered or kidnaped since the outbreak of the post-1954 hostilities is long and growing, and includes rubber planters as well as missionaries and teachers.

One last political problem between France and South Viet-Nam, arises from France's relations with the Hanoi regime. Although recognizing only Saigon, France nevertheless maintains a *délégation générale* in Hanoi that deals with the North Vietnamese authorities on some of the remaining problems: French properties, army deserters, war graves, etc. Its functions are little more than vestigial but the very existence of the mission (the fact that the British have a consulate general in the north is pointedly ignored)—and of a reciprocal Viet-Minh commercial mission in Paris—periodically gives rise to acrimonious remarks about French "double-dealing."

As long as the Algerian War went on—it ended on March 18, 1962—and the Vietnamese situation had not deteriorated too seriously, France's attitude remained one of studied offhandedness. To an American television correspondent who asked whether France "shared America's viewpoint" on the Vietnamese problem, Foreign Minister Couve de Murville answered on May 31, 1962: "We certainly share American preoccupations on the dangerous situation that exists there. It doubtless is full of uncertainties."

As will be shown later, France's attitude changed rapidly as it became clear that South Viet-Nam might well be engulfed in a repeat performance of the Indochina War, with the remaining French citizens and economic holdings likely to be the scapegoat for yet another Western failure.

The immediate result of France's re-entry into Vietnamese affairs was a rise in the tensions between Paris on the one hand, and Washington and Saigon on the other.

THE AMERICAN STAKE

The United States, in one way or another and often by what she failed to do as well as by what she did, has been heavily involved in Viet-Nam's fate since 1940. As has been shown in previous chapters, the occupation of North Viet-Nam by Chinese troops who brought the Vietnamese Communists with them was American-willed and American-led; the failure to bring to bear upon France in Indochina the pressures for "decolonization" that were brought to bear upon Holland in Indonesia was an American failure, just as was America's subsequent unwillingness to stand by the French militarily once the decision was made to back them in maintaining the colonial *status quo*. And, finally, responsibility for events in Viet-Nam since the 1954 cease-fire—both Ngo Dinh Diem's steadfast resistance to necessary reforms and the training of the South Vietnamese Army for a conventional war it could not conceivably have to fight—cannot be laid anywhere but at Washington's doorstep.

There is, therefore, very little point in examining in detail the execution of any specific item of American policy in Viet-Nam. It is far too easy to find fault with a particular aid program, or to find proof of inefficiency and waste in anything that involves $2 billion. In fact, it can be said that, considering the chaos that reigned after the division of the country in 1954 and the staggering problem of integrating 860,000 refugees into the South Vietnamese economic fabric, U.S. aid operations have, on the whole, been successful. After all, if South Viet-Nam should "go Communist" tomorrow, it would do so not because of a waste of dollars in a "crash" road-building program, no matter how painful that waste may be to the taxpayer.

However, South Viet-Nam may go Communist for the same reason as mainland China—because of serious errors in evaluating the exact danger that exists and the inherent weaknesses of the regime that is being supported. In the cases of both the Chiang Kai-shek and the Ngo Dinh Diem administrations, their most articulate and ardent American proponents have at the same time been the worst enemies of their own cause—for to admit their protégé's weaknesses was to criticize him. Yet, no help could be effective until his weaknesses had been admitted.

The most glaring example of this vicious circle lies precisely in the field of Communist subversion in South Viet-Nam, of which I have been a student for the past decade. Here, the postulate of Diem's most committed American followers (and they, unfortunately, included men in responsible positions) ran as follows:

1. Most Viet-Minh are not Communists, but anti-French nationalists at heart;
2. Diem, being an anti-French nationalist, will win over the Viet-Minh to his cause;
3. Therefore, the Viet-Minh will collapse in short order.
Quod erat demonstrandum.

This totally naïve belief that hard-core guerrillas could be won over by philosophical argumentation was clearly expressed in an official South Vietnamese handout given journalists in 1957:

We believe that with clear, even elementary ideas based upon facts . . we can imbue . . . first the youth and ultimately the entire population with the spirit and essential objectives of this civic humanism. We believe that this above all is the most effective antidote to Communism (which is but an accident of history), and furthermore, the most powerful incentive for the promotion of a better life. . . .

. . . *From this, we can see that the Viet-Minh authorities have disintegrated and been rendered powerless* [italics added].[12]

Thus, any continuing Viet-Minh activities in South Viet-Nam— and they were not continued simply by stragglers from 1954 but, as was admitted much too late, were gaining in strength!—were treated for years as the "dying gasps of bandit remnants." Once that myth had become official dogma, it was obviously difficult to embark upon the kind of large-scale socio-economic, political, and military anti-insurgency program that would have been necessary to nip in the bud the developing full-fledged insurgency. One is reminded of Hitler's refusal to have winter clothing distributed to German troops in Russia in the fall of 1941, because he had willed that the Russian campaign would be over before the snows had set in. And the German press continued to speak of "particularly severe autumnal storms" at a time when Germans froze by whole divisions in front of Moscow at temperatures of −40 degrees.

Thus, when I published two articles in which I expressed fear of a resurgence of Viet-Minh terrorism[13] (based upon an on-the-spot study in 1957 of the geographic "clustering" of assassinations and of the local administrative positions held by the victims), a senior adviser to the South Vietnamese Government wrote a letter to one of the publications, *The Nation*, arguing that such increasing casualty figures merely attested to the improvement in police statistics the Americans had brought about!

Until the middle of 1958, the "last remnant" theory was clung to steadfastly. Admiral Felix B. Stump, then United States commander in chief in the Pacific, testified on March 21, 1958, in Senate committee hearings, that the Vietnamese were "*still* having trouble in some areas." In testimony released in August, 1958, by the House Subcommittee on International Operations, the then U.S. Ambassador to Viet-Nam, Elbridge Durbrow, stated that "Communists and sect remnants have *regrouped* and stepped up their terrorist activities" (italics added). But Ambassador Durbrow testified later that "because of the terrorist activities in the fertile [Mekong] Delta area, the peasants, through fear or intimidation, cannot till their fields properly. . . ."

It is not without significance that the MAAG commanders, as professional senior soldiers used to the movement and training of conventional armies but unacquainted with revolutionary war, were consistently even more optimistic than any other group. To them, internal security was essentially a police problem, and for much too long a time, they saw their essential mission as training a South Vietnamese Army (ARVN) to resist a Korea-like onslaught of Viet-Minh regular forces streaming across the 17th parallel in division formation. This "Korean trauma" of American military planning in Viet-Nam was utterly disastrous, for it created a road-bound, over-motorized, hard-to-supply battle force totally incapable of besting the *real* enemy (i.e., the elusive guerrilla and not the Viet-Minh divisional regular) on his own ground.

That this was exactly the view of the earlier MAAG commanders is confirmed in an article written by Lieutenant General O'Daniel in April, 1962, in which he described the South Vietnamese Army as consisting of "eight well-organised and well-trained divisions with supporting weapons suitable for jungle warfare." Having said that at least the supporting weapons (if not the soldiers) were suitable for jungle warfare, General O'Daniel continued: "The units are *trained for fighting conventional armed forces* and find it quite a problem to bring the Communist Viet-Minh to battle . . ." (italics added).[14] What General O'Daniel did not say is that it was he who organized the Vietnamese Army on a division basis, after discarding the French organization of mobile battle groups as too weak in firepower and supply services.

His successor (General O'Daniel went into retirement and became President of the American Friends of Viet-Nam), Lieutenant General Williams, went further along O'Daniel's lines. He dissolved the 8,000-man "light divisions"—which had combined elements of the French *groupe mobile* and the full-fledged divisions wanted by MAAG and represented a compromise arrived at when TRIM was still jointly operated by American and French training elements—and replaced them by heavier "field divisions." Williams then topped off that structure by three full army corps staffs, to which a fourth army corps was added by his successor. AmericanVietnamese military training during the Williams era focused on making the South Vietnamese Army capable of withstanding a North Vietnamese invasion long enough to permit the intervention of United States forces within the framework of SEATO, or alone—in total disregard once more of the vital internal security mission that the ARVN would have to perform whether there was an invasion or not. This led to an initial refusal on the part of the United States to help the Saigon regime in equipping and training mobile police and local militia forces. This fact the always outspoken Mme. Ngo Dinh Nhu did not hesitate to bring to public attention in an official address on March 11, 1962, in which she conveniently made the United States the scapegoat for South Viet-Nam's present-day guerrilla woes:

> In 1955, the Personalist Republic of Viet-Nam was faced with the urgent necessity of building well-armed and well-trained paramilitary forces living among the people in the hamlets, villages, and districts to protect them.
> . . . But, Viet-Nam, which is poor . . . has had to face the greatest difficulties in training and equipping another paramilitary army, especially when its allies refused to recognize the need for such forces
> That is the only reason for the insecurity in the rural areas.[15]

It is obvious that only by the grossest self-delusion can one be persuaded that the United States alone is to blame for the insurgency in Viet-Nam; and one must then exclude all the mistakes made by the Ngo Dinh Diem regime itself as well as the Communists' own determination to step up their subversive operations. Yet, there is nevertheless a kernel of truth to that emotional outburst: The usefulness of paramilitary forces was indeed downgraded until the 1960's, and the training of the Vietnamese police was left largely in the hands of retired American sheriffs and police captains—as if Viet-Nam's main security problem was catching speeding motorists or controlling juvenile delinquency. Thus, no force existed that was willing to struggle for the allegiance of the local population and for the safety of the village chiefs and local officials being murdered . increasing numbers; the American and Vietnamese military refused to deal with the situation because it did not fall within the definition of "external aggression," and the local police refused to cope with it because it did not involve "crime" in the ordinary sense of the word.

The extent to which the problems of external defense were divorced from those of internal security is perhaps best illustrated in the testimony given by General Williams' deputy, Major General Samuel L. Myers, on April 17, 1959, before the Senate Foreign Relations Committee, in which he asserted that the guerrilla problems in South Viet-Nam had almost completely disappeared:

> The Viet-Minh guerrillas . . . were gradually nibbled away until they ceased to be a major menace to the [South Vietnamese] Government. In fact, estimates at the time of my departure indicated that there was a very limited number of hostile individuals under arms in the country. Two territorial regiments reinforced occasionally by one or two regular army regiments were able to cope with their depredations. . . .
>
> They [the South Vietnamese] are now able to maintain internal security and have reached the point where that responsibility could be turned over to the civilian agencies. . . . There are many Vietnamese who are even more optimistic and feel that they have the capability of counterattack.[16]

In fact, the testimony of the American military in Viet-Nam in 1959 so forcefully asserted that all was well that it completely overshadowed the far more guarded statements of American senior diplomats and aid personnel, and led Senator Mansfield's subcommittee to conclude in its February, 1960, report that it was "impressed by the apparently far greater degree of effectiveness in the administration of military, as contrasted with nonmilitary, aid programs in Viet-Nam"—effectiveness that is ascribed to "purposefulness and long-range planning lacking in civilian programs in Viet-Nam."[17]

The fact of the matter was that the American generals in South Viet-Nam had been fooled by the special character of the hostile forces they were facing, just as their French predecessors had been, and for precisely the same reasons. I still recall vividly how French senior officers explained to me in Hanoi in 1953 that French forces "controlled" the Red River Delta inside the bunker-ringed perimeter of the "de Lattre Line," although the village tax rolls at that very time showed that at least 85 per cent of the villages inside the bunker line had failed to pay taxes for more than two years.[18] A check, using the lists of village teachers showed their mounting absence in all but the urbanized areas and clearly confirmed the pattern of gradual loss of control in the administrative-political field—an area even more vital to control than is the military. The American generals evaluating South Viet-Nam's state of internal security in 1958–59 used the same standards of measurement as Generals Carpentier, Salan, and Navarre had used: Since the troops they commanded (or, in the case of the Americans, advised) were not directly challenged, these forces were considered to be "in control." Neither of the two military machines was technically or psychologically geared to evaluate the far subtler challenges presented by revolutionary war.

In the meantime, however, the *Mansfield Report* confidently concluded:

> . . . on the basis of the assurances of the head of the military aid mission in Viet-Nam . . . at least the U.S. Military Aid [*sic*] Advisory Group (MAAG) can be phased out of Viet-Nam in the foreseeable future.

This was published at a time when local officials in Viet-Nam were being killed at a rate of more than *ten a day*.[19] But even a year earlier, murders of minor officials had reached the ominous rate of more than a hundred a month and should have set alarm bells ringing all over Washington. Moreover, officials concerned with the problem were now caught in the iron logic of their own argument: They could not assert that everything was fine in Viet-Nam and, at the same time, ask for higher appropriations and more military and security experts to combat the rising guerrilla threat.

During the latter part of the tenure of Lieutenant General Williams as MAAG commander in Viet-Nam—he retired in September, 1960—a serious difference of opinion on the success of the training program existed between MAAG and other Western experts on the spot. Even the American military attachés (some of whom had had combat experience in Burma) feared that the "big war" approach would lead the South Vietnamese Army to a military dead end. The British concurred. Colonel H. C. B. Cook, who had been British Military Attaché in Saigon from 1959 to 1961, wrote an unusually blunt article in the spring of 1962, in which he openly voiced many of the complaints that had only been whispered about until then:

> . . . [the Vietnamese Army's] main difficulty is that it has to find many good officers for civil Government posts. Nearly all the provincial governors are soldiers. . . .
> Another difficulty has arisen from the fact that until two years ago its American advisers trained it to fight a purely conventional war. Vietnamese officers were heard to talk about the "American-type of war we train for and the Indo-China war we will have to fight." . . .
> Unfortunately the Pentagon has in the past been reluctant to accept any assistance in the military sphere.[20]

Another British colonel very well described the optimistic atmosphere which must have then prevailed:

> There was little or no realism in the sense of appreciating facts and conditions as they really were or were going to be. . . . The cause was fundamental, consisting of an academic bureaucratic outlook based on little realistic practice and formed in an environment utterly different to that we experienced in war. In the case of the Staff this environment was the cool of an office or the comfort of the road, scarcely ever the rubber jungle with its sweat, thorns and claustrophobic oppressiveness. All seemed good in a good world. There was no inducement to look below the surface or to change prior appreciations.

What makes the above passage especially shocking is that it does *not* deal with American operations in Viet-Nam—but with Britain's defeat in Malaya at the hands of the Japanese in 1941! In other words, and this perhaps is the major cause for discouragement about the war in Viet-Nam in 1963, there is very little evidence that the West has learned anything at all in more than two decades.

With regard to combat operations in the jungle, the British officer had this to say about his unit's performance:

> Unit organization was not amended to meet conditions entirely different to those it was designed for . . . under European conditions infantry battalions were organized on the basis of high automatic firepower. Our manpower remained unaltered when jungle war negatived the effectiveness of automatics and required high manpower.

At this writing, American doctrine in Viet-Nam still is predicated upon the use of high firepower (which has resulted in the delivery of ultramodern Lockheed "Armalite" automatic rifles to Viet-Nam) and against the commitment of extensive manpower to constant offensive patrolling, although extensive training of Vietnamese and American troops for jungle war is now under way. As the same British officer wrote, "jungle war is a war of highly-trained specialists where the actual man and minor infantry tactics are dominant."[21]

In September, 1960, when Lieutenant General Lionel C. McGarr became the commander of MAAG Viet-Nam upon the retirement of General Williams, he inherited a situation that already was beyond salvaging with the MAAG force at his disposal. However, McGarr did succeed in persuading Diem to allow American advisers to accompany Vietnamese units at battalion level (hitherto they had been limited to regimental headquarters and higher) and put back into operation the old French commando-training school in Nha-Trang, which McGarr's predecessors had used as a spit-and-polish NCO academy.[22] Yet, after seven years of training for a linear war likely never to come, it was hard to get the Vietnamese to accept radical changes in outlook and even harder to have those changes accepted in Washington by the very people who had praised the achievements of McGarr's predecessors. Thus, as the security situation in Viet-Nam deteriorated to a new low late in 1961, McGarr was made the scapegoat and was shipped back to the United States in March, 1962, for "health reasons." MAAG Viet-Nam was superseded on February 9, 1962, by a U.S. Military Assistance Command Viet-Nam (USMACV) under four-star General Paul D. Harkins, whose command was extended in May to include also the American troops stationed in Thailand.

Since the very size of the guerrilla operations had demolished the "last remnant" theory of the situation in Viet-Nam, it now became imperative to find another rationale to explain the huge guerrilla build-up, virtually before the eyes of the Saigon regime and its American advisers, without having to admit that the former was unpopular and that the latter may have erred in their optimistic judgments. The theory of a large-scale "invasion" of South Viet-Nam by North Vietnamese infiltrators came just in time to save face for everyone concerned.

Not that such infiltrations do not take place. They do indeed, as the following pages will show, and by mid-1963, may have involved 12,000 men. Certainly at least a part of the guerrilla depredations can be blamed on "invaders," as the State Department's White Book of December, 1961, shows. But that does not explain the extent or the persistence of the insurgency—still estimated in 1963 at about 25,000 armed men although the South Vietnamese forces claimed to have killed 30,000 guerrillas in both 1961 and 1962—any more than does Mme. Nhu's explanation, which blames it all on the United States. The hard fact is that Washington, under Eisenhower and to a considerable extent under Kennedy, as well, has shied away from looking the problem squarely in the face and now must pay the price of this shyness with a direct American military commitment whose extent in size and length of time is unforeseeable at present. Various highly placed government officials have cited the example of the successful Malayan antiguerrilla campaign in order to prepare the American public for a military commitment over a five-to-seven-year span. The time span of seven years, currently cited for the Malayan insurrection, is highly inaccurate: The state of emergency was proclaimed on June 18, 1948, and lifted on July 31,

1960—more than twelve years later. Actually, fighting in Malaya had gone on since late in 1946.

Even terrorism against Americans in Viet-Nam—depicted in most newspapers as a recent development—has been an integral part of the situation almost since the beginning. In June, 1955, grenades were thrown at the U.S. Information Service headquarters, the house of an aid official, and an American car near the Ambassador's home. In October, 1957, thirteen American servicemen were hurt when a bomb exploded in a potted palm in front of their quarters, and another bomb once again wrecked the USIS office and library. In June, 1958, Americans found "U.S. Go Home" signs and threatening leaflets in their mailboxes. On July 8, 1959, a MAAG major and a sergeant were murdered in their billets in the ARVN's Bien-Hoa training camp when Viet-Minh guerrillas made a raid in a deliberate attempt to discredit Diem. For on the previous day, July 7—which, as the anniversary of Diem's rise to power in 1954, is celebrated as a holiday—the Vietnamese President had made a speech in which he stressed the "country-wide return to peace and security" his rule had brought about; the spectacular murder of the two Americans eloquently dispatched that boast. In November, 1960, an American public-safety adviser was killed not far from the seaside resort of Cape St. Jacques, with the result that the United States Embassy imposed a curfew on out-of-town driving on its personnel. In 1961, attacks against Americans included the throwing of a hand grenade at the car of the newly appointed Ambassador, Frederick E. Nolting; the planting of a time bomb in a MAAG jeep; the kidnaping of an American sergeant on the outskirts of Saigon on Christmas Day and the killing of another NCO in an ambush three days earlier. From that time on, Americans killed, maimed, and kidnaped simply became combat casualties. The granting of Combat Infantryman's Badges to American soldiers in Viet-Nam starting in April, 1963, merely made official something the American servicemen in Viet-Nam had known for more than a year: they were at war in Viet-Nam and deeply committed to the outcome of the battle.

The Eisenhower Administration left office apparently without ever having understood the extent to which America was committed to Viet-Nam's survival. It is to the credit of the succeeding administration that it addressed itself to the problem with a sense of urgency. An interagency "Viet-Nam Task Force" was set up, military aid was accelerated, and a never-ending stream of inspection missions of all kinds[23] began to invade Saigon.

Vice-President Lyndon B. Johnson, accompanied by his wife, one of President Kennedy's sisters, and a top-level staff, visited Viet-Nam in May, 1961. The result of the visit was a joint American-Vietnamese announcement in which Viet-Nam (faithful to the "crisis cycle" theory developed in Chapter 13) promised reforms and America promised more aid.[24] Another upshot of the Johnson mission was the dispatching of the mission headed by Professor Eugene Staley, whose recommendations included the increase of the ARVN to 170,000 men and the stepping-up of its antiguerrilla training; doubling of the effectives of the Bao-An (Civil Guard) from 60,000 to 120,000 men; equipping the Dan-Vê (Village Militia) with modern small arms and radio communications; construction of strategic hamlets and villages, and increase of the *agrovilles* from 22 to 100 in one year.[25]

Again, as always before, the symptoms rather than the illness were being treated, and this for the simple reason that the people back in Washington who were in charge of drawing policy conclusions from the reports were precisely those who had devised the earlier policies whose failure has not yet been admitted. And the far more probing recommendations of the Taylor mission were by and large sidetracked, according to Brigadier General S. L. A. ("Slam") Marshall, the noted military writer, who asserted in March, 1962, that "no more than about one-fourth of the program recommended by Gen. Maxwell D. Taylor . . . was bought by the administration."[26]

In the meantime, however, the crisis cycle had once more gone one full turn. On April 6, General Harkins announced that Diem had agreed to two key elements for ultimate victory: the immediate implementation of an ambitious "pacification plan," involving ten Mekong Delta provinces and thus known as the "Delta Plan"; and immediate cessation of Presidential interference in military operations. One month later, newcomer Harkins in turn had learned his lesson: Nothing at all had been done, and on May 10, Secretary of Defense Robert S. McNamara had to exert his own powers of persuasion to exact yet another promise that the earlier promises would be implemented.[27] None of them was.

And thus, degree by degree, the United States slid into the Second Indochina War. It took Washington until March 10, 1962, to admit that American pilots were flying combat missions in Viet-Nam, and it was left to *Time* to state on May 11, 1962, that the decision to hold South Viet-Nam "at all costs" had been made in *October, 1961*—i.e., *after* General Taylor had returned from Viet-Nam. Finally, in February, 1963, Americans were authorized to "shoot first." But all this still lacks a grand design. It is still a Korea-type improvisation, with American troops being committed piecemeal as "advisers" along the principle of the Wehrmacht's sending of German detachments with the somewhat wobbly Italian, Romanian, and Hungarian divisions in Russia. Those detachments were aptly known as *"korsettstangen"* ("corset stays"), for without them, those non-German units usually broke and ran—but the system also consumed a great many advisers. This will do in the short run—*but it is not a concerted policy*, and it rests on the assumption that all will be well in South Viet-Nam on the day that the last Viet-Minh infiltrator has been killed and the last Vietnamese farmer is safely behind the fences of a "strategic hamlet."

As the Second Indochina War settled down to what could be called "cruising speed," with bloody skirmishes and engagements being fought with varying degrees of luck by either side, Saigon and Washington again began to engage in a new phase of wishful thinking that resembled that of the French generals of 1953 and that of the MAAG generals of 1959. In opening a new session of the South Vietnamese National Assembly on October 1, 1962, President Diem announced to his obedient legislators, as well as to the world, that "Government forces had taken the initiative against Communist guerrillas . . . sowing insecurity in the Communists' reputedly impregnable strongholds."[28] But during the following six months, the war went badly for the South Vietnamese forces: Raids against "Resistance Zone D," north of Saigon, failed to locate the enemy and did not achieve permanent occupation of the area; and "Operation Waves of Love," which was in part designed to flush out the enemy redoubt of Camau Peninsula, also fell short of significant results.[29]

Yet, the commander in chief in the Pacific, Admiral Harry D. Felt, declared in Washington on January 30, 1963, that the "South Vietnamese should achieve victory in three years," and he went on to define victory "as the situation wherein the South Vietnamese controlled 90 percent of the rural population." He added that the Saigon regime "now controls about 51 percent of the rural population, the Viet Cong about 8 percent, and the remainder were still uncommitted."[30] One must marvel at the ability to define the loyalty of villagers in percentages (in a country where no census has taken place in thirty years), but this creates an illusion of victory, since in American business or electoral terms, 51 per cent of the stock or the vote constitutes a "controlling interest." Unfortunately, it must be feared that the results of a struggle for the allegiance of the peasantry of an underdeveloped country cannot be as easily calculated.

On the civilian side as well, the problem was being further "refined"—i.e., oversimplified until one aspect of it became manageable —and thus, a new "image" of the whole Vietnamese problem was being created. High-level planners now conceded that Ngo Dinh Diem was perhaps no knight in shining armor, but they asserted that, basically, he was being criticized only in the cities by the unimportant (and impotent) bourgeoisie and intelligentsia, while the peasantry on the whole was not interested in politics but in security and a measure of physical well-being.[31] This they were now receiving in the strategic hamlets, which, by the end of 1962, were to contain close to 10 million Vietnamese. It is perhaps the tendency to equate residence inside a strategic hamlet with "control," and "control" with loyalty toward Saigon that led *The New York Times* of April 4, 1963, to report that unnamed

> . . . United States policy planners believe that the Communist guerrilla attack has been blunted and that there is room now for political and social efforts to convey a greater sense of progress to both the restive urban and rural populations of the wartorn nation.

The most that can be said for this estimate is that, in view of developments in other similar insurgencies and of the military situation inside Viet-Nam, it is somewhat premature. And, above all, it indicates the continuing refusal to face the vital ideological aspect of the insurgency problem. Specialists have repeatedly warned that illiteracy is not necessarily an indication of total naïveté; as Peter Paret and John W. Shy eloquently wrote, "unlike machinegun-bolts, ideologies are not readily interchangeable."[32] Neither, one might add, is it possible to trade ideologies for better village sewage or notebooks for schoolchildren.

Although the absence of a grand design beyond the mechanics of stopping the Viet-Minh seems not to trouble the American public, which is more immediately concerned with the fate of the American soldiers involved in the struggle, this lack seems to be apparent to Europeans, such as the West Germans, whose own fate resembles that of Viet-Nam. Some of the best reporting on the Viet-Nam crisis is the work of German-speaking journalists, whose articles unfortunately receive little attention in the United States. One such eyewitness, writing for the conservative *Die Welt* of Hamburg, states his views in the following terms:

> I have now been in Saigon for a week. I have met dozens of people, from Cabinet ministers to taxi drivers; from businessmen to hotel porters; and from officers to housewives and diplomats. I have asked each and every one of them what they were struggling for and what they thought could be done to wrest away the initiative from the Communists. They gave me uncounted numbers of tactical proposals: to further reinforce the army or to improve the weapons and pay of the village militia; to liberalize the administration and to commit American combat units directly.
>
> But no one had [any concept of] a political aim. And no one ever mentioned a desire to see the country reunified.[33]

It is this political and spiritual void—which the South Vietnamese Government seeks to fill with its slogans of Personalism—that is perhaps the major weakness of the Western position today, just as it was when the French sought to prop up the Bao-Dai government a decade earlier. Similarly, the Americans now fighting the Viet-Minh apparently have acquired the kind of grudging respect for their enemy that the French also acquired ten years ago. "They have the same spirit," said Lieutenant Colonel Frank B. Clay, son of the general who was a symbol of American determination in Berlin, "as the Crusaders and Saracen soldiers who established the medieval empires—all fired up for a cause."

Thus, the real stake America has in Viet-Nam is not whether or not it can defeat 25,000 guerrillas with helicopters, napalm, weed-killing chemicals, or other special gadgets. The key problem is not even whether victory will be won by carrying the war to Hanoi or by bloody and tedious infighting below the 17th parallel. In fact, the real stake did not even have any relation to the question as to whether one must "Win with Diem," "Swim with Diem," or "Sink with Diem"—or whether he had to be replaced by a military junta. The real stake is purely and simply whether or not the United States and, for that matter, the West as a whole, is still capable of instilling enough confidence in the humble people who have put their trust in us to make them stand up and fight for our common cause, and they will do this only because they are finally convinced that the defeat of our adversaries does not mean an unconditional return the bondage of a morally and politically bankrupt leadership.

The events that led to the anti-Buddhist repressions of mid-1963 are a case in point. Anti-Buddhist discrimination had existed from the beginning of the Diem regime, although it may not have been as serious as it was later portrayed. Actually, what most enraged the non-Catholic majority of the population was the outright favoritism in every field shown the doubly alien Catholic minority—alien because of its Western spiritual allegiance and because of its largely North Vietnamese refugee origin. A regime more flexible than Ngo's could easily have handled what was essentially a problem of "communalism."

But the Buddha's 2,506th anniversary, on May 8, 1963, was the spark that set off the tinderbox of accumulated political and social frustrations under which South Viet-Nam had been laboring for almost a decade. Probably fearing that the overlapping of the Buddhist holiday and of the ninth anniversary of the defeat at Dien Bien Phu might lead to antigovernment demonstrations, heavy-handed officials at Hué broke up a Buddhist meeting with 37-mm. cannon, killing one woman and seven children. Instead of condemning the outrage, the regime closed ranks around its perpetrators, and Mme. Nhu made a series of ill-timed remarks about "barbecuing" Buddhists and "clapping hands" when several Buddhist monks of both sexes chose self-immolation as a means of protest.

Throughout the crisis, Ngo Dinh Diem and his entourage acted true to type: As in 1955 with the sects and in 1960 with the paratroops, they engaged in dilatory negotiations while carefully preparing a brutal and total counterblow. During the night of August 20–21, 1963, the most important pagodas throughout South Viet-Nam were surrounded and Buddhist leaders captured; the interiors of the pagodas were looted and smashed. Those acts of gratuitous savagery reduced to a shambles whatever rationale remained for American policies in Viet-Nam. The "Nolting mission" of conciliating the Saigon rulers at any price, for the sake of winning the guerrilla war, had utterly failed. It remained for incoming Ambassador Henry Cabot Lodge, and after him, General Maxwell D. Taylor, to construct from the shambles a new rationale of the kind that would make the average South Vietnamese willing to endure the horrors of yet another decade of revolutionary war.

This may, under the circumstances, be a most difficult task.

16

Insurgency: Myths and Facts

I~N~ the United States, "insurgency," as a different and far more difficult art than "guerrilla warfare," was discovered after the American setbacks in Cuba and Laos in April, 1961. Those events brought in their wake a spate of hasty books and studies, most of them based on insufficient field data or unwarranted comparisons— in short, the phenomenon of overcompensation began to operate. From total ignorance of the problem at the level where it should have been dealt with, the new concern with this subject spread to embrace even agencies of the government whose functions normally were utterly removed from the shadow land of Revolutionary War: Even the Chaplains Corps developed a counterinsurgency program. *The New York Times*' outspoken Military Editor, Hanson W. Baldwin, explained that

> these operations . . . have become almost a fetish with the President
> . . . and, of course, all the military schools are reflecting this White
> House interest. The result is . . . a stress upon the obvious, and—if it

continues—a perhaps dangerous overemphasis upon one, but only one, type of warfare.[1]

One might add also that this overemphasis applies not only to the military aspects of revolutionary war (a term that seems to be officially eschewed,[2] no doubt because of its political implications), but also to the few successful military counterinsurgency operations rather than to the large number of such operations lost precisely because they were fought on almost wholly military terms. A further semantic confusion exists between the terms "guerrilla warfare" and "jungle warfare." This explains why some "neo-realists" in the United States advocate the use of Japanese troops in Southeast Asia because of their good jungle-fighting record—completely forgetting that the Japanese counterguerrilla record was perhaps one of the worst known because of the Imperial Army's unerring ability to antagonize the civilian population of occupied areas by its arrogance and cruelty. Revolutionary warfare can be fought from the jungles of Asia to the pavements of Paris; jungle warfare is geographically more limited and thus easier to comprehend.

PATTERNS OF REVOLUTIONARY WAR

Although I have disposed of those facile and fallacious comparisons in greater detail elsewhere,[3] I shall briefly repeat some of the facts here. In the Pacific from 1942 to 1944, save in New Guinea and Luzon, operations dealt with small islands that left the enemy almost no space to maneuver in depth once an initial beachhead had been secured. Usually deprived of his supply lines by American sea and air power, and enjoying no popular support whatsoever (this was, of course, also the case among the Papuans of New Guinea and the Filipinos), the enemy was soon starved into submission or cornered against a mountain chain or beach—with no rescue forces behind him. And it must be emphasized that the Japanese fought, as long as it was tactically and logistically possible, like any other modern army, with airplanes, tanks, and artillery; they resorted to small-unit and sniper tactics only when no other course was left for them. The tactics they employed then—and one must admire them for having been able to make the switch so effectively—were those of jungle warfare but not of guerrilla warfare, and even less of revolutionary warfare.

In Burma—and the same can be said for New Guinea—there was ample room for maneuver on both sides, and in Burma both sides had native partisans. The Japanese had the lowland Burmese on their side until late 1943, and the hill tribes remained loyal to the Allies throughout the war. The hill tribes proved to be the far better fighting investment—another lesson that was forgotten until late in the day in South Viet-Nam. The "Chindits" of Britain's General Orde Wingate and the American "Marauders" of General Frank Merrill wreaked havoc behind Japanese lines, greatly helped by the fact that the Japanese had succeeded in making themselves more detested by the native population than the white colonizers ever had been. Even so the cost in human lives and health was appalling: Merrill's Marauders were, for all practical purposes, wiped out in six months of jungle fighting—about par for the course in cases of whites committed to jungle combat.[4] As for the New Guinea campaign, the agony of the U.S. Army 32d Division in the "Hell of Buna" is well remembered. Thus, contrary to the confident talk of "American experience in jungle war," it was in fact neither very extensive nor of the kind that gives much cause for rejoicing. And it is twenty years old.

The British experience in Malaya comes one shade closer to the *physical* environment of the fighting in Viet-Nam, but is totally different in the sociological, political, and ethnic factors so crucial to winning such a battle. First and above all, Malaya has no common border with another Communist country. That single factor is so vitally important as to affect radically all other elements in the equation. Second, Malaya is split right down the middle between the Malayan and Chinese components of its population, which is not the case in Viet-Nam, where the ethnic Vietnamese represent about 85 per cent of the country's inhabitants. Third, in Malaya, the terrorists came from the Chinese population only—and within that segment, only the 423,000 "squatters" who had nothing to lose but their illicitly acquired rice fields could really be counted upon to give more than halfhearted support to the Communist terrorists (CT's in British parlance).[5] This, coupled with a series of tactical mistakes by the CT leadership, caused the Malayan emergency to evolve in ways that were highly unfavorable to the CT's. In search of a new remedy to the spreading South Vietnamese insurgency after the failure of the *agroville* program,[6] the South Vietnamese Government, particularly at the insistence of Ngo Dinh Nhu in his capacity as Political Adviser, decided on April 17, 1962, to transfer the Malayan experience to Viet-Nam lock, stock, and barrel—including the British officers who had devised part of the "New Villages" system.

(Unsurveyed)

● Incidents involving killings

Long-An

Kien-Hoa

Camau

INSURGENCY SPREADS
April, 1959-April, 1960

A base is being established in the Camau area, and the rich Mekong Delta is being cut off from Saigon through widespread terrorism in Kien-Hoa and Long-An provinces.

One year earlier, when the first glib comparisons were made between the Malayan and the Vietnamese emergencies, warnings were sounded against what seemed a tendency in official quarters to overlook or de-emphasize the vast differences between the two situations:

A more fundamental difference is that Malaya (especially for the Chinese) did not offer an agrarian theater of hostilities. The Chinese in Malaya were primarily employed on rubber plantations and in the tin mines. The "squatters" who had turned to agriculture to supplement their income and who proved the most available collaborators for the Communists did not have a way of life that held them by sentiment and mystique to a particular place. Thus when the British introduced the New Villages program under which the squatters were brought together in new communities which could be isolated from the terrorists, there was some complaining but not the extreme reaction of people who were having their basic way of life altered. . . .

By contrast, the Vietnamese peasant is closely tied to the land and has deeply resented the effort to move him to more secure concentrations. . . .[7]

The prime reason that the comparison between the Malayan and Vietnamese situations is fallacious lies right here: The squatters could not provide the CT's with the demographic "water" that Mao's guerrilla "fish" needs to survive; no sizable outside support (except for a very few weapons and medical supplies from Thailand) ever succeeded in reaching the CT"s; and popular grievances were not sufficient to make a Chinese guerrilla look like a "liberator" to a Malayan peasant. But *even so*, the 8,000 CT's of the Malayan emergency tied up 80,000 Britons, Australians, New Zealanders, Fijians, Dayak headhunters, and Nepalese Gurkhas for twelve years—not to speak of 180,000 Malayan special police, constables, and village-militia members. And the fight is still not over. In 1963, a hard-core remnant of perhaps 470 CT's still held out in the jungle thickets of the Yala-Betong salient on the Thai-Malayan border. In fact, fighting flared up on the Thai side of the border early in 1963.

In addition, politically the CT's represented Chinese domination to all ethnic Malays, and Communist terror to all wealthy Chinese. The alternative leadership of Malays that was being developed by the Malays and British together was on all counts more palatable to the great majority of the population, and unrigged elections soon proved its genuine popularity. In Viet-Nam, Ho Chi Minh's regime does constitute an alternate "Vietnamese" solution (i.e., one not dominated by an alien ethnic group), and North Vietnamese promises of permitting the further existence of a separate "bourgeois" but neutralist southern state are made precisely in order to split away from Diem those middle-class elements that may still cling to him as an alternative to a social revolution.

Thus, any comparison between British victories in Malaya and the situation in Viet-Nam in the 1960's is nothing but a dangerous self-delusion, or, worse, a deliberate oversimplification of the whole problem.

Another example of a Western success in Southeast Asia is less often cited because of its explosive political implications, and that is the victorious American-Filipino struggle against the Huks from 1947 to 1952. A veteran of that struggle, Brigadier General Edward G. Lansdale, has stated unequivocally that "purely military tactics failed completely to stop the Huks" because the latter

> . . . had analyzed the people's grievances and made the righting of these wrongs into their slogans. And the change came when Ramón Magsaysay became Defense Minister. He was from the people, loved and trusted them. He and the army set about making the constitution a living document for the people. As they did so, they and the people emerged on the same side of the fight. The Huks lost support and had to go on the defensive.[8]

This is a masterful plea for the essential *political changes* that are indispensable to the winning of a revolutionary war—and that the Ngo Dinh Diem regime has resisted unceasingly. The truth of General Lansdale's assertion is further verified by the fact that the corrupt and inefficient García Administration, which followed the Magsaysay era, saw a resurgence of Huk guerrilla attacks. Concentrating, as in Viet-Nam, on village officials and landowners, those renewed attacks proved sufficiently troublesome to García's successor, Diosdado Macapagal, for him to order mop-up operations in Central Luzon in April, 1962.

In sum, South Viet-Nam combines the worst features of all the other theaters in which the West has had to fight Communism thus far. And in addition, the enemy that is faced there is one who has not only read all the classics of guerrilla warfare, but also added a few chapters of his own.

Although it is important to define what the insurgency in South Viet-Nam is not, it is equally important to define what it is. It is first and foremost a *war*, with the classic objective of all wars: to break the enemy's will to resist.

Whether the Viet-Minh can attain this aim at the polls, as it hoped to do in the aborted reunification referendum, or must resort to outright invasion or the subversion of the south's administrative structures, is largely immaterial to the men of Hanoi. It is certain that if they could get South Viet-Nam by gentle persuasion, they would gladly do so. This not being the case, North Viet-Nam resorts to the tactics that are best suited to attain its central objective of destroying the enemy's will to resist: It does *not* attack the ARVN in showdown battles—a practice it gave up after its disastrous experience in the Red River plains in 1951[9]—but concentrates instead upon destroying the administrative and economic fabric that every government requires to stay in business. From the first, the Viet-Minh knew that this was a *political war fought for political objectives*, and its troops, unlike the South Vietnamese or the Americans, are specifically geared toward that task. It was the VPA's commander in chief, Vo Nguyên Giap, who stated in his *People's War, People's Army*:

> The People's Army is the instrument of the Party and of the revolutionary State for the accomplishment, in armed form, of the tasks of the revolution. Profound awareness of the aims of the Party, boundless loyalty to the cause of the nation and the working class, and a spirit of unreserved sacrifice are fundamental questions for the army, and questions of principle. Therefore, the political work in its ranks is of the first importance. *It is the soul of the army.*[10]

We have nothing on our side to counter that kind of theory of war. A U.S. Marine or Special Forces officer can perhaps fly a helicopter better than anyone else or even outwrestle a Communist guerrilla in judo or karate; he may be able to live in the jungle by trapping animals and, through grueling training may outtrot a native while carrying a heavy pack (though this is doubtful)—but he simply cannot indoctrinate a South Vietnamese peasant or intellectual with an ideology that is worth fighting for. This "our" Vietnamese must do for us, or rather, for themselves—and, to all accounts, they are not doing it. They simply have no valid philosophy to sell.[11]

How little this whole process appears to be understood even in the highest circles is nowhere better evidenced than in an address made on June 28, 1961, by Walt W. Rostow (then the President's Special Assistant for National Security Affairs and now Chairman of the State Department's Policy Planning Council) to the graduating class of the U.S. Army Special Warfare School at Fort Bragg. The speech contained the following revealing passage:

> . . . It is important that the world become clear in mind, for example, that the operation run from Hanoi against [South] Viet-Nam is as certain a form of aggression as the violation of the 38th parallel by the North Korean armies in June, 1950.
>
> In my conversations with representatives of foreign governments, I am sometimes lectured that this or that government within the free

world is not popular; they tell me that guerrilla warfare cannot be won unless the peoples are dissatisfied. These are, at best, half-truths. The truth is that guerrilla warfare, mounted from external bases—with rights of sanctuary—is a terrible burden to carry for any government in a society making its way toward modernization. For instance, it takes somewhere between ten and twenty soldiers to control one guerrilla in an organized operation. Moreover, the guerrilla force has this advantage: Its task is merely to destroy, while the government must build and protect what it is building. A guerrilla war mounted from outside a transitional nation is a crude act of international vandalism. There will be no peace in the world if the international community accepts the outcome of a guerrilla war, mounted from outside a nation, as tantamount to a free election.[1]

Were it not for the highly specialized audience to which the speech was made and the attendant publicity given to it as a statement of national policy, one might dismiss it as merely another one of those commencement addresses that most speakers prefer history to forget. But it illustrates the muddled thinking of high Administration officials:

The first assertion—that North Vietnamese infiltration into South Viet-Nam is the direct equivalent of the North Korean invasion of the ROK—omits the embarrassing fact that anti-Diem guerrillas were active long before infiltrated North Vietnamese elements joined the fray. The second assertion—that popular support of a government is of secondary importance in winning a guerrilla war—flies straight in the face of all the evidence so painfully amassed on the guerrilla battlefields of three continents over the past three decades. For civilian support is *the* essential element of a successful guerrilla operation, and a national guerrilla-warfare policy that downgrades that element[13] most certainly warrants rethinking if victory is ever to be achieved.

The third assertion—that the guerrilla merely destroys while the government always builds—is likewise unsupported by the facts of the mid-twentieth century. It arises from a semantic confusion between "partisan," "guerrilla," and "revolutionary-warfare fighter." The first two are designed to operate *in support* of a regular force engaged in open warfare; the third, as has been explained in Chapter 8, seeks primarily to *establish a rival regime* via the system of *hiérarchies parallèles*. Indeed, a guerrilla force *must* eventually build up a working administrative structure, maintain or provide schooling and a modicum of economic life (i.e., "construct" rather than simply destroy) within its area of operation, if it wants to survive and succeed in the long run. This was the case of the anti-Nazi underground movements in Europe, of the Chinese Communists in Yenan, of the Algerian Liberation Front, and, of course, of the Viet-Minh and Viet-Công. Any guerrilla movement that remains in a sterile destructive phase either is only a commando force or degenerates into pure banditry.

Finally, Professor Rostow's assertion that outside support of a guerrilla movement is a "crude act of international vandalism" can be wholeheartedly concurred with—but it seems anachronistic when addressed to the Special Forces graduates at Fort Bragg, whose ob is to fight, and train others to fight, in the shadowy marginal areas of the Cold War. True, a bit of self-righteous anger is always good for the soul, but after the successful overthrow of the pro-Red Arbenz government in Guatemala in 1954 by "outside helpers" and the less successful attempt of April, 1961, to rid the Cubans of Castro, discreet silence on the subject would not have been out of place. For let us remember that the debasement of international law and comity has reached such a stage in the 1960's that UN members could for years openly provide bases for a rebel movement— as was the case of Tunisia and Morocco in the Algerian war—without having to fear the wrath of the attacked. And it seems probable that the time is not far off when, contrary to earlier practice, the sanctity of the outside harasser will become a principle solidly anchored in international mores. Whether it be Egypt's *fedayeen* infiltrators in Israel, Moroccan infiltrators based in Mali for the purpose of subverting Mauritania, Congo-based Angolans attacking the Portuguese, South Vietnamese arming and training Cambodian rebels, or, finally, North Vietnamese sending infiltrators into South Viet-Nam—the principle is always the same. If the United States adopted Professor Rostow's view that a guerrilla movement supported from outside cannot bring about a political change acceptable to the international community, then this country would have to embark upon a policy of nonrecognition of about a dozen states with which she now maintains full diplomatic relations—Laos and Algeria are but two examples.

Thus, I believe that the whole problem of the meaning of "war" in the new context will have to be re-examined sooner or later, to take into account the facts that parallel hierarchies, revolutionary warfare, and active sanctuaries are here to stay and that our present response of concentrating on the external military symptoms of the problem simply has no bearing on the preponderant politico-socio-economic components.

While this essential truth apparently has thus far failed to make headway in high-level councils, operational analysts have begun to realize the built-in limitations of the military approach, and, for that matter, of all severely coercive methods without corresponding improvements not only economic, but also political. In one of the best, yet most concise, studies on the subject of the relative priorities in revolutionary war, James Eliot Cross, a member of the Institute of Defense Analyses, described the traditional position:

> . . . the [local] government's official policy line is usually that reforms will be considered and granted only after the insurgents have been defeated and peace restored. The authorities then concentrate on the police and military operations which they hope will smother the disaffection and try to postpone political action until later.
>
> It has been demonstrated again and again in unconventional wars that this government policy is the highroad to disaster. The government locks itself into the stand-pat position of fighting to defend all the inequities which gave the rebellion its first impetus.[14]

Specific examples of such a situation abound; and the British, whose military methods were identical in Palestine, Cyprus, Kenya, and Malaya, lost hands down against the Israelis and the Cypriot Greeks of EOKA, but won in Kenya and Malaya. Yet, in Palestine and Cyprus, the British had the benefit of precisely the same socioethnic and military advantages as in Malaya! Part of the population was pro-British (the Arabs in one case, the Cypriot Turks in the other) for a variety of reasons, just as the Malays were in Malaya—and in all four cases, the British had overwhelming control of the supply routes. In all four cases, population regroupment, curfews, surprise searches and raids, etc., were widely used, and the ratio of counterinsurgent forces to insurgents was sufficient to ensure victory. Without going into the details of what in itself should be the subject of a book, it can be concluded that it was not the British who "won" in Kenya and Malaya, but the Mau Mau and CT's who "lost" by their failure to win popular support for their causes and by allowing themselves to be drawn into a purely military contest with forces that were clearly superior.

The French also have encountered the problem of revolutionary war three times in less than a quarter-century: once as active practitioners (in Nazi-occupied France) and twice in repressive operations (in Indochina and Algeria). In Indochina, only too few of them recognized the fact that the Viet-Minh enjoyed exactly the same advantages with regard to the French as the French had enjoyed with regard to the Wehrmacht. By the time that recognition dawned and corrective measures were attempted, the situation had deteriorated beyond salvaging.

In Algeria, the lessons learned from the Communist enemy were applied in their whole horror, from psychological "intoxication" to the limited but methodical use of torture. And the lessons brought results: As described in grim detail in Jean Lartéguy's novel *The Centurions*, the city of Algiers was cleared of bomb-throwing Moslem terrorists in 1957–58 by General Massu's famous 10th Parachute Division, and by 1960, all battalion-size units of the Algerian National Liberation Army (ALN) had been destroyed. In a relentless series of highly mobile operations with *"commandos de chasse"* ("hunting commandos"), the ALN's field units were slowly cut down to squads and platoons, while at the same time, dozens of specialized officers—many of them "graduates" of Communist indoctrination in Viet-Minh prison camps—proceeded to break up the OPA (Organisation Politico-Administrative), which was the parallel hierarchy of the Algerian nationalist movement. By the time the cease-fire was signed at Evian on March 18, 1962, the ALN inside Algeria had been reduced, even according to French left-wing sources, to a remnant force of fewer than 10,000 full-time fighters (French Army sources said that fewer than 4,000 remained) out of a total of close to 60,000 in 1959.[15]

The French had no Dien Bien Phu in Algeria, but the war simply became *politically* "unwinnable" because of the two active sanctuaries—Tunisia and Morocco—and the pressure of world opinion. Thus, here again, the nonmilitary components of revolutionary warfare finally accomplished what the revolutionary force could not win on the battlefield alone. In other words, even the Mao Tse-tung–imbued French colonels of the new school[16] had failed to read the fine print of their favorite author and had concentrated on repression instead of offering the Algerian Moslems a valid political alternative to the appeals of the National Liberation Front (FLN). After the coup of May 13, 1958, they hoped that "integration," i.e., the complete equalization of rights between Moslems and Europeans, could have an overwhelming appeal—and the fanatics of the Secret Army Organization (OAS) probably believe this even today. De Gaulle and the rest of the world knew this was inadequate; it might have

worked thirty years earlier—Ferhat Abbas, the first Premier of the
Algerian Provisional Government in Exile, said so himself—but in
1958, "integration" no longer was a match for "independence." To
win the military battle but to lose the political struggle may increasingly be the unsatisfactory conclusion of a revolutionary war, for,
as Paret and Shy said in a passage cited earlier, "unlike machinegun-
bolts, ideologies are not readily interchangeable."

Yet the OAS colonels attempted once more to apply the politico-
military aspects of revolutionary war in the futile terrorism in western
Algeria during the spring of 1962. Once more, they eloquently proved
their own and Mao's theories by being able to reduce the modern European cities of Algiers and Oran to rubble-strewn Gomorrahs—as long
as the presence of a million of their countrymen provided them with
a human sea in which to disappear and hide. But as their terrorism
drove the French civilian population into mass flight to the motherland, the OAS dug its own grave. Its only attempt at creating a
"maquis" in the countryside, in the Ouarsenis hills, failed miserably
precisely because in the heavily Moslem-inhabited rural areas, the
OAS was totally without the civilian support it needed to survive.

Unfortunately, scant attention seems to have been paid to the
over-all French experience in the revolutionary warfare field, in spite
of an informal staff paper recommending study of French work in
that area, published in April, 1961, with the endorsement of the
then Chief of the U.S. Army's Research and Development Branch,
Lieutenant General Arthur G. Trudeau.[17] The prevailing attitude
seems to be that there is little to be learned from people who "lost"
wars (if this were so, one might well wonder why German scientists
and military specialists were so much in demand after V-E Day, all
the way from Moscow to White Sands, New Mexico), with the result
that only a few generalizations from the French experience seem to
have found their way into American specialized literature. How
remote the notion of political purpose or political use of insurgency
seems to be from official thinking is best illustrated by the fact that
all officially approved glossaries on the subject limit their definition
to the acts themselves without ever giving an indication of their
ultimate purpose.[18] And they assiduously avoid the term "revolutionary war," which is precisely the one that was initially used in its new
sense by Mao Tse-tung as early as 1936, and was adopted by the
French when they encountered the phenomenon in Indochina.

In one particularly important French work on the subject, Colonel

Gabriel Bonnet defined revolutionary warfare by a quasi-mathematical formula:

$$RW = G + P$$

That is, revolutionary warfare is the result of the application of guerrilla-warfare methods and psychological-political operations for the purpose of establishing a competing ideological system or political structure.[19] And this is basically where the Communists, in spite of their professed materialism, apparently have understood the rules of the game a great deal better than the United States, which professes to defend spiritual values: The Communists have correctly identified as the central objective of a revolutionary war—and, in fact, its only worthwhile prize—the *human beings* who make up the nation under attack. On our side, the securing of communication lines, the control of crops and industrial installations, and the protection of one particular power group seem to be the overriding considerations. The population at large becomes an object that is manipulated, transferred, searched and seized, shoved out of the way when it impedes military operations, and, finally, strafed and napalm-bombed until the mounds of innocent dead overshadow the negligible damage inflicted on the battle-hardened guerrillas operating in its midst.

Official South Vietnamese casualty figures bear evidence of this. For three years in a row, "enemy" casualties were estimated at more than 30,000 killed, while the number of Viet-Công combatants remains stationary at about 25,000–30,000. On the other hand, the number of weapons captured amounts to less than one weapon for every three or four casualties, and, in reality, the figure is even lower, since during the first eleven months of 1962, the South Vietnamese captured only 4,100 weapons while losing 4,700.[20] Since it is hardly credible that the guerrillas always succeed in retrieving the weapons of their dead comrades, there exists a very strong feeling (confirmed by impartial ground observers) that many of the "Viet-Công killed in action" are innocent bystanders. As James Eliot Cross says: "The speed of even the slowest fixed-wing aircraft is so great that the pilot has little chance of positively identifying an enemy who is not wearing a distinctive uniform, unless the latter obligingly waves a rifle or shoots at him."[21] This obvious fact of revolutionary war has not deterred the Diem government from requesting various types of "high-performance aircraft" from the U.S. That request, though now being held in abeyance, has received some encouragement from Air

Force quarters that would like to see a broadening of their role in counterinsurgency operations.[22]

How the tactical aircraft now in Viet-Nam are used can be discerned from the official reports of the South Vietnamese Air Force. In a not untypical operation in January, 1964, the VNAF destroyed 500 VC structures (i.e., houses), 219 tons of unmilled rice, 3 "training centers," 395 acres of crops, and 155 cattle.[23] The rationale behind attacks on such targets seems to be that these "villages had to be destroyed, for the strength of the [South Vietnamese] government had to be impressed upon them [the population]. They had to be shown that the Viet-Công could not live up to its promise to protect them."[24] During the "Big Minh" era, the South Vietnamese press, unmuzzled as almost never before, openly criticized the indiscriminate use of napalm:

> Cases have been reported of wanton bombing or shelling of entire villages. . . . The merciless destruction of unharvested ricefields under a column of armored personnel carriers, or the scorched earth of napalm bombing are examples of types of [peasant] grievance.[25]

Although it is encouraging that Secretary McNamara in March, 1964, cautioned U.S. pilots in Viet-Nam against the overuse of area-destruction weapons, past excesses may well have created more Viet-Công adherents than the Viet-Công's own propaganda. It apparently has been forgotten that these aircraft are not operating on foreign enemy targets, but upon a population whose allegiance Saigon *must* regain if it wishes to win this war.

Indiscriminate use of force, particularly with weapons that readily permit wide-ranging destruction of the only possessions of any worth the peasant has—his house and his rice crop—may backfire dangerously.[26] The same principle applies, of course, to the operations of the insurgents themselves; overreliance on terror on their part will surely drive the population into the arms of the government forces.

All this, and a great deal more, make up the intricate patterns of revolutionary war that are being woven in South Viet-Nam in the 1960's. They do not lend themselves to easy definitions and even less to patent-medicine solutions. But few human endeavors do.

THE ENEMY

The enemy the United States has to face in the Second Indochina War differs somewhat from that the French faced from 1946 until 1954. During the earlier war, a distinct division between the tasks assigned to the Viet-Minh regulars and to the guerrillas emerged only when the former came into their own in 1950, and for almost two years thereafter there must have been discussion as to whether the Viet-Minh regulars should be used for limited offensives or should be held in reserve for the Tong Tan-cong—the "general counter-offensive" that was to break the back of the French Union Forces. In fact, Giap used his main battle force for both tasks, and with great success.

In the 1959–63 phase of the Second Indochina War, the Viet-Minh regular divisions have been carefully kept north of the 17th parallel, both for political reasons and on sound military grounds: In view of the excellent equipment made available to the South Vietnamese in quantities far greater than the French had ever received, the commitment of several Viet-Minh divisions would certainly have been premature. However, at least two full division staffs seem to have been infiltrated for the purpose of coordinating the operations of the Liberation Front forces. The basic organization of the earlier Viet-Minh forces has been maintained: At the bottom, there are *du-kich* (militia) units raised in each village; above the *du-kich*, there are *dia-phuong-quan* (regional troops); and at the top of the ladder are the *chu-lac* (main force) regulars.[27]

The *du-kich* constitutes the hapless cannon fodder. Its task is to lay local ambushes, to sabotage roads and dikes, and to provide supplies and intelligence to the other two categories. It operates at squad and platoon level; here and there, several hamlets may temporarily form a company. But in any case, the *du-kich* usually "melts" back to its villages once its tasks have been accomplished.

The regionals are better trained, better armed, and more mobile than the *du-kich*. Although still capable of "melting" back into its original villages, since it is usually raised in the province in which it operates, the regional battalion can be counted upon to provide an effective screen for a *chu-luc* unit in its area. It also engages in a firefight or, on its own, may attack a small convoy. The regional unit is also prepared to yield some of its elite combatants to a nearby *chu-luc* unit if the need for replacements arises.

The *chu-luc*, both as a unit and as an individual, is part of an educational, political, and military elite. He can always read and write and often has completed six or eight years of school, often was trained in North Viet-Nam, is a Communist Party member or aspires to become one, and is competent at handling a multitude of weapons and at carrying out the variegated and intricate tactics involved in irregular warfare. And, above all, he is proud of doing the job he is doing; the captured diaries of North Vietnamese soldiers, published in the State Department's *White Book*, bear eloquent witness to that. Like all soldiers, the regulars gripe about poor food and accommodations; in fact, they break regulations by keeping diaries at all—but those diaries also show how extremely well briefed they are for their mission:

> Our [mountaineer] allies have great admiration for us. But precisely for this reason we must not show any vanity which could lead our allies to think that the [lowland] Vietnamese do not have any modesty.

> See to it that our troops use only our own dry food supply and do not touch the property of the population. Beware of relationships with women. . . . Political cadres must reaffirm this before departure. . . .

> Think of the problem of unity between the army and the population, between the political cadres and the army. . . .

> Having been away for several years from the territory of Inter-Zone 5 "Quang-Nam" [South Central Viet-Nam], my heart is both happy and sad. What shall I do now to be a worthy son of Inter-Zone 5? . . .

> For the third time [the Viet-Minh had fought in North Viet-Nam against the French, then in Laos prior to going to South Viet-Nam] my life turned to war again. For the liberation of our compatriots in the South, a situation of boiling oil and burning fire is necessary! . . . Now my life is full of hardship. . . . But in my heart I keep loyal to the Party and to the people. I am proud and happy.[28]

In North Viet-Nam, divisions are numbered with three-digit figures beginning with 304 and ending, so far, with 351, a "heavy division" (artillery and combat engineers). The regular infiltrated forces are usually renumbered in order to maintain the pretense that they are separate entities under the control of the National Liberation Front of South Viet-Nam. Those battalions seem to be numbered from 502 upward, with the component companies being numbered in three digits beginning with the number 2: 209, 227, etc.

Some battalions are known by a particularly significant name drawn from Vietnamese history ("Ly Thuong Khiet" in Vinh-Long Province; "Tay Son" near Qui-Nhon) or drawn from an area ("Dong-Nai," "Phu-Loi," a notorious South Vietnamese concentration camp, etc. As of mid-1963, only a few regular regiments, or elements thereof, have been identified in South Viet-Nam; significantly, most of them are Mountain Regiments, made up of Jarai, Rhadé (Edé), and

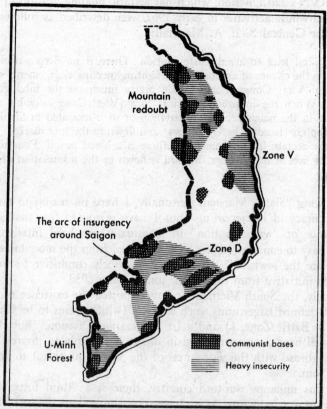

Mountain
redoubt

Zone V

The arc of insurgency
around Saigon

Zone D

U-Minh
Forest

Communist bases

Heavy insecurity

REVOLUTIONARY WARFARE IN SOUTH VIET-NAM
1962-63

Hré mountaineers who had gone north in 1954. There are elements of Regiment 120 in the Binh-Dinh–Quang-Ngai area. That regiment is commanded by Colonel Y-Bloc, a Hré mountaineer. Then there is Regiment 126, reinforced by a special 600-man battalion, infiltrated into South Viet-Nam in May, 1961, and likewise operating in the mountains west of Quang-Ngai; and lastly, there is the famous 803d Infantry Regiment, which had been the scourge of the French back in 1952–54 on the Southern Mountain Plateau, where it is now operating again. In 1954, it had hounded to death a French motorized battle group of more than 3,000 men,[29] and it is likely to have lost little of its combativeness. It operates on its old hunting grounds in the northern Central Plateau area and is more than a match for the ARVN's 22d Division, which has a static holding mission in the area and whose activities in early 1962 were described as follows by Brigadier General S. L. A. Marshall:

> The 22nd tries to avoid waste motion. There is no deep patrolling just on the chance of ambushing, or fighting meeting engagements with roving [Viet] Congs. Forces guide pretty much on the intelligence data. When the information points to a [Viet] Cong assembly any-where in the neighborhood, a battalion or so is mounted in Shawnee helicopters (handled by U.S. crews) and flown to the spot marked "X" on the acetate [map]. Sometimes there is a blood payoff. Four times out of five, at least, either the bird is flown or the information proves wrong.[30]

Knowing "Slam" Marshall personally, I have no reason to doubt the accuracy of his reporting—but I have reason to fear that such avoidance of "waste motion" in an area where hard intelligence is not easy to come by (it has to be obtained from the mountaineers, who hate the lowland Vietnamese!) is scarcely conducive to wrest-ing the initiative from the tough, jungle-going 803d.

Finally, the South Vietnamese have reported the existence of cer-tain ill-defined larger units, such as CK-I (which seems to be Chien-Khu, or Battle Zone, I) and a 1st "Liberation Division." But these may well have been mentioned in dispatches simply to impress the public abroad with the seriousness of the Viet-Minh threat to South Viet-Nam.

In this unhappy war-torn country, there is a "third force," the Hoa-Hao sect remnants. As we have seen, the bulk of the sect forces were destroyed by the ARVN in 1955, and there was one reason for this success: The rural population, long oppressed by the sect war-lords, at first received the government forces with open arms, until it learned (these cases were well substantiated even in the South Vietnamese press) that the returning government forces and admin-istrators treated them with no more kindness. A temporary truce ensued between the Hoa-Hao and the Viet-Minh guerrillas, and the Hoa-Hao began slowly to reinfiltrate their old strongholds: Battalion Lê-Loi operated in the Phong-Dinh area; Bay-Dom in west-ern Chau-Doc; 117 in Long-Xuyên; and 104 in An-Giang.

Late in 1961, the Viet-Minh felt strong enough in South Viet-Nam to shed their temporary alliances with the "reactionary" sect leaders, and in typical Communist fashion, the Viet-Minh regulars attacked the sect units, which soon found themselves squeezed between the Viet-Minh and the ARVN. In May, 1962, Hoa-Hao Battalion 104, under the command of "General" Truong Kim Cu, was caught in a simultaneous drive by the ARVN and Viet-Minh Battalion 510, and was totally destroyed. Truong Kim Cu and a few members of his staff and family managed to escape into Cambodia. This "polarization," in which many of the non-Communist, anti-Diem elements are driven into the arms of the Viet-Minh, is probably unavoidable under the circumstances. It is, however, a far from satisfactory solution.

In terms of its political-administrative apparatus, the South Vietnamese insurgency operated until December, 1960, as simply an extension of the then-existing Communist underground apparatus. Then, following its customary practice of staging important events on anniversaries of earlier auspicious events, the Viet-Minh proclaimed a National Liberation Front of South Viet-Nam (Mat-tran Dan-toc Giai-phong Mien-Nam) on December 20, 1960, the day after the fourteenth anniversary of the 1946 uprising against the French. According to the State Department's *White Book*, the "overall direction of the Viet Cong movement is the responsibility of the Lao Dong Party," whose special Committee for Supervision of the South includes Lê Duc Tho, a Politburo member; Pham Hung (a Vice-Premier who prior to 1954 was a top guerrilla leader in Cochinchina); and VPA Brigadier General Nguyên Van Vinh, an alternate member of the Lao-Dong's Central Committee.

Inside South Viet-Nam, the Viet-Minh seems to have maintained its old administrative structure of Interzones (*lien-khu*) V and VI, the former covering Central Viet-Nam south of the 17th parallel, and the latter covering the Nam-Bô (the southern part, i.e., South Viet-Nam proper, or Cochinchina). Each *lien-khu* has, as before, its executive committee of about ten members; in turn, each zone is subdivided into four "interprovinces" (*lien-tinh*), which cover four or more provinces of the South Vietnamese territory and the Special Zone of the national capital. From the provincial to the hamlet level, the standard parallel hierarchies exist.[31]

On the military side, the two zone commanders are equals and apparently get their orders directly from Hanoi. In 1960–62, they were Brigadier General Nguyên Don for Interzone V and a "civilian" guerrilla leader, Nguyên Huu Xuyên, for the Nam-Bô. On May 27, 1962, all the bombing aircraft of the South Vietnamese Air Force then available (about 45 planes) were concentrated for a saturation raid on Nguyên Don's jungle headquarters in the Mang Xim redoubt on the Kontum–Quang-Ngai boundary; 100 tons of bombs were dropped on groups of huts in the jungle. On May 29, General Nguyên Khanh, chief of staff of the ARVN, announced that the raid had been a "total success." American observers, however, somewhat dampened the official optimism; they estimated that perhaps 50 enemy personnel had been killed in the raid. Nguyên Don was not among them.

At lower levels of command, provincial commanders control all military units in their area, although certain "independent battalions" and highly specialized roving units, such as the sampan-borne 634th Battalion, are at the direct disposal of their zone commanders.

The wholly artificial character of the National Liberation Front, at least during the first year of its operation, is perhaps best shown by the fact that until April 13, 1962, it had not disclosed the names of its alleged leaders, in spite of the fact that its program (see Appendix IV) had been made public almost at the inception of the Front. Even so, the leaders thus far known are hardly of the caliber to constitute a "shadow government" ready to take over from the Saigon regime at the first sign of disintegration: the Chairman of the Front is Nguyên Huu Tho, a Saigon lawyer who had participated in the last-ditch negotiations with France in the spring of 1947, which failed to end the Indochina War. In 1949, it was Tho who organized the anti-French and anti-Bao-Dai demonstrations in Saigon. Returning to legality in 1954, he became a member of the clandestine "Peace Protection Movement" in Saigon, which advocated reunification elections in 1956. When the existence of the movement was discovered by the authorities, Tho fled to Hanoi. He returned to South Viet-Nam late in 1961 but is said to have returned again north of the 17th parallel.[32] The Secretary General of the Central Committee of the National Liberation Front is "Professor" Nguyên Van Hieu, a leader of Viet-Nam's minuscule Radical Socialist Party. A journalist rather than a teacher, Hieu joined the anti-French resistance in 1950 and became head of the "Overt and Covert Propaganda" section of the Viet-Minh's Nam-Bô information committee. He is well known among newspapermen in Saigon and is said to have created an extensive Viet-Minh cell among them.

The other members of the committee include a carefully selected cross section of South Vietnamese society: Phung Van Cung, M.D., Chairman of the South Vietnamese "Peace Committee," in hiding since October, 1960; Huynh Tan Phat, Secretary General of a defunct "Democratic Party," in hiding since 1958; Superior Bonze Son-Vuong, a Buddhist monk of the 500,000-strong Cambodian minority living in westernmost South Viet-Nam; and Ibih Aléo, a former noncommissioned officer of the French Union Forces and a member of the Edé (Rhadé) mountain tribe. Still, both the Viet-Minh and the Liberation Front are fully conscious of the fact that the latter could not be considered a representative group, and in making public a list of only thirty names of Committee members, the Front asserted that the remaining seats on the fifty-two-member Committee would be reserved for "collectivities, political parties, or important persons which will join the Front later."

In order to promote the concept that the Front and the Lao-Dong Party were separate entities, Hanoi informed the world on January 20, 1962, that a "conference of representatives of Marxists-Leninists in South Viet-Nam" had taken place on December 19, 1961, in the course of which it was decided to set up the Viet-Nam People's Revolutionary Party (Dang Nhan-Dan Cach Mang), which officially came into existence on January 1, 1962.

In its manifesto, the new party declared itself to be "the party of the working class and laboring people of South Viet-Nam . . . a party wholeheartedly devoted to serving the fatherland, serving the people,"[33] but, like the National Liberation Front itself, the Revolutionary Party failed to announce the names of any of its founding members. According to two circulars emanating from the Lao-Dong authorities and infiltrated into South Viet-Nam, members of the Lao-Dong were notified as early as December 7, 1961 (twelve days before the founding meeting) that the new party was created merely out of tactical necessity but would remain under the over-all control of the Lao-Dong.[34]

There are two explanations for the creation of a "separate" South Vietnamese Communist Party. According to the Saigon authorities, it is a sign of weakness, an indication that the Viet-Minh wants to win over many oppositionists who were holding back from joining the movement as long as it was overtly Communist-dominated. Another interpretation, widely held by French observers, is that the situation follows very closely the 1946–51 pattern: As long as the situation was precarious, the Communists played down their own presence within the Viet-Minh movement; but as soon as they felt strong enough to go it alone, they discarded the camouflage, created the Lao-Dong in 1951 and henceforth sailed under their own flag.

In all likelihood, the establishment of a "separate" Communist organization for South Viet-Nam follows the same pattern as the dissolution of the old ICP in the 1940's to give the Laotian and Khmer Communist movements a semblance of national autonomy, and provides for a "legal struggle" organization in the event of the rise to power in South Viet-Nam of a regime willing to attempt peaceful coexistence with Hanoi. The appointment, in 1963, of separate Liberation Front delegations of a pseudo-diplomatic nature to such countries as Cuba and Algeria lends further weight to the theory that Hanoi wishes to invest a possible nonaligned South Vietnamese regime of the future with the appurtenances of a separate sovereign state.

A last rationale for the autonomous rise of a resistance movement in South Viet-Nam, advanced notably by the French writer Philippe Devillers, is that "the insurrection existed before the Communists decided to take part, and that they were simply forced to join in" by Diem's oppressive measures.[35] Devillers, however, advances no evidence to the effect that the movement was not taken in hand by Hanoi *later*, precisely because it had a popular character, and thus was useful. This, of course, is too often confused with direct operational everyday control, which, in a guerrilla war, is obvious nonsense.

In the fields of political-administrative, economic, and military subversion, the operations of the insurgents have gone through several phases. During the first phase, lasting roughly from the 1954 cease-fire until mid-1957, the Viet-Minh devoted itself mainly to adapting its underground structure to the changed conditions; for from mid-1955 until perhaps late 1958, the police forces of the South Vietnamese Government were in far better control of the countryside than the French had been. Also, the division at the 17th parallel, with the attendant repatriation of the armed forces of both sides to their respective zones, had produced one unexpected bonus for the Communists: Close to 100,000 South Vietnamese of Communist obedience left the southern area for North Viet-Nam, thus providing the latter with native southerners aplenty who were given extensive training for later operations in their home areas; among them were close to 10,000 mountaineers from the Central Plateau area. At the same time, the repatriates going north included the dependents of the hard-core fighters who were ordered to go underground in the south, as well as the raw recruits with whose training and protection the southerners had been burdened until then.

Thus, ironically, the population exchange of 1954 benefited North Viet-Nam at least as much as the Saigon regime: The latter received many of the Catholic refugees who still constitute its most loyal backing, but the north received land that was cleared for agricultural reforms and a large and excellent reservoir of infiltrators. At the same time, the population exchange enabled the hard-core regulars who stayed behind in the south to engage in mobile warfare, without having to worry about reprisals against their relatives, who, during the earlier Indochina War, were often the first victims of their operations.

In mid-1957 the first deliberate offensive of the insurgents began. Their target was simple and well-chosen: the village official. In a country in which 80 per cent or more of the population lives in 17,000 hamlets spread over 8,000 villages, the village chief or secretary, and the "notables" who make up the village council, are the key links between the central government and the people. Once this link is broken by terror, "feedback" ceases and the central authorities gradually become isolated from the country at large. Orders given from above no longer are enforced at the village level, and the government begins to, in a beautiful French word-image, *"légiférer dans le vide"* ("to legislate in the great void"). It still has an extensive bureaucracy, a ubiquitous police, and a powerful army, but it no longer may control much outside of the key cities and (during the day) the major roads. One is reminded here of Dean Acheson's observation, during a press conference of January 20, 1950, on the causes of the loss of the Chinese mainland:

> What has happened is . . . that the patience of the Chinese people in their misery ended. They did not bother to overthrow this [Nationalist] government. There was simply nothing to overthrow. They simply ignored it throughout the country.

The same could have been said of the Bao-Dai government in 1955 or the right-wing Laotian regime in 1962. The Ngo Dinh Diem regime in Saigon had traveled a long way along that road by the time the world outside awakened to the grim facts of the situation. Professor Robert Scigliano, who spent several years in Viet-Nam as an administration adviser, asserts that late in 1961 "the Communists had in fact extended their influence, in varying degrees, to about 80 per cent of the Vietnamese countryside."[36] In both the Chinese and the Vietnamese cases, Communist terror had helped matters a great deal.

Losses of South Vietnamese village officials were extremely heavy before anyone in a position to know was willing to admit how desperate the situation really had become. According to President Kennedy's earlier cited May, 1961, message, 4,000 low-level officials were killed between May, 1960, and May, 1961. Other partial figures published earlier show that perhaps 2,500 had been killed in 1959–60 and perhaps half that many the year before and more than 700 in 1957. Since the killings continued throughout 1961–63 as well (in some cases, the very Dan-Vê guards who are supposed to protect the village officials hand them over to the Viet-Công[37]), perhaps as many as 13,000 small officials have been killed in South Viet-Nam. That figure alone clearly differentiates the Vietnamese from the Malayan insurgency—where village leader killings never reached dangerous proportions—and will, in any case, produce some sort of social revolution in South Viet-Nam's village administration. The new village leadership, if only because of the deterrent effect of the earlier wave of murders, is likely to be more responsive to the needs of the village population upon whose loyalty it depends for its survival.

Another favorite human target in the Second Indochina War is schoolteachers, which is comprehensible in a war where the allegiance of the people is the chief prize of victory. Schoolteachers form young minds and educate them to love their country and its system of government; to close such schools or to cow the teachers into spreading antigovernment propaganda can be a more important victory than to defeat an army division—particularly in countries where 50 per cent or more of the population is of school age. Thus, in 1959 the Viet-Minh launched an energetic campaign against schoolteachers, notably in the provinces of Long-An, Dinh-Tuong, and Kien-Hoa. At one time in Long-An, teachers were killed or kidnaped as fast as village officials. The result was that by late 1960, more than 30,000 schoolchildren were deprived of schooling, and, according to findings of a field survey of the World Confederation of Organizations of the Teaching Profession carried out in South Viet-Nam in the spring of 1962, almost 80,000 schoolchildren had been deprived of schools because of terrorist action, and 636 schools were closed. Approximately 250 teachers had been kidnaped and another 30 allegedly killed.[38] South Vietnamese Government figures are considerably grimmer: The South Vietnamese United Nations observer, Mme. Tran Van Chuong (mother of Mme. Ngo Dinh

Nhu, wife of the South Vietnamese Ambassador to Washington, and aunt of ex-Emperor Bao-Dai), informed UNESCO on June 4, 1962, that more than 1,200 teachers had been kidnaped. In that same month, after a plot against the regime had been discovered in Saigon schools, along with a clandestine "Students for Liberation" organization, several South Vietnamese newspapers suggested that schools in the threatened areas should be closed altogether.

Another valuable human target of the insurgents is social workers and medical personnel, because their activities create good will for the government and also because the rebel units are short of trained medical personnel and adequate drugs. Thus, the very promising malaria-eradication program was stopped late in 1961 because of the casualties among its personnel (22 killed and 60 kidnaped in less than one year) and the losses of equipment (an average of 6 spray cans a day between January and November, 1961).[39] Medical doctors, Vietnamese as well as foreign, have often been captured to tend heavy Viet-Minh casualties; this is usually the reason for raids on plantation hospitals, village first-aid kits, and leprosaria, but such raids also spread fear of the guerrillas and point up the inability of the government to defend its servants.

Here again, the warnings had been clear and early: "Today the menace is heavier than ever," wrote the Saigon newspaper *Thoi-Luan* on December 15, 1957, "with the terrorists no longer limiting themselves to the notables in charge of security. Everything suits them, village chiefs, chairmen of liaison committees, simple village guards, even former notables. . . ." Two days later, *Tu-Do*, another Saigon newspaper, warned the government that "the security question in the provinces must be given top priority." By the spring of 1958, insecurity had become sufficiently widespread for many farmers to desert their villages—a fact that, as we have seen, was reported to Congress by the then U.S. Ambassador in Saigon—and for President Diem to plead in his May Day message that "those who once lived on farms . . . resume their former occupation in order to boost the nation's farm production."[40] By 1959, the situation had grown worse rather than better, and on April 28, *Tu-Do* warned that "the Viet-Công intend to make us relive the troubled days of 1945; terrorism spreads anew."

Insurgent operations are also directed against foreigners, for political and economic reasons. Americans, both civilians and military, are captured in combat or killed or injured in grenade-throwing incidents for the express purpose of showing that even the foreign "advisers" can be effectively challenged. Clemency measures for foreigner prisoners are always timed for maximum psychological impact: Two U.S. Special Forces sergeants were released on May Day, 1962, and another military prisoner was released on Christmas Day. All three had signed statements favorable to the Communist cause.[41] Missionaries, both American and French, also have been killed, but on a selective basis, that is, where the Viet-Công suspected them of having given Saigon or the U.S. advisers information of military value.[42] Another example of Communist psychological pressure is the unilateral truces proclaimed by the Viet-Công during such traditional holidays as the Lunar New Year in February, 1962, or the Buddhist New Year in April. They were fully observed, thus giving both the sorely tried population and the ARVN a welcome breathing spell reminiscent of the off-and-on bombardment policy of the Red Chinese at Quemoy and Matsu.

The killing or kidnaping of Frenchmen operating in key economic sectors has materially affected the rubber economy of the country, as has been discussed earlier. Other nationals, such as Filipino surveyors or Japanese engineers, also have been killed. One Australian expert for the Colombo Plan, kidnaped by the rebels, was traded by them for a typewriter. Contrary to its operations during the 1946–54 hostilities, when the Viet-Minh did not hesitate to resort to scorched-earth tactics, the People's Southern Liberation Front seems to aim at paralyzing rather than destroying the South Vietnamese economy. After all, Hevea trees need seven years to produce tappable rubber, and as long as the Liberation Front has any hope of winning the struggle, it has no reason to resort to irreparable destruction. The damage to the plantations has been serious, and is due largely to the fact that the Saigon regime has disarmed them. During the First Indochina War, the plantations had, as in Malaya, raised their own defense units and fortified all their vital installations, while continuing to produce. Loc-Ninh plantation was once cut off for forty-five days by Viet-Minh units and held out, with the women of the plantation firing the guns along with the men. In 1954, however, Saigon forbade any Frenchman in the country to keep weapons but, on the other hand, failed to provide the plantations with adequate government security forces. It is likely that the plantations will, by and large, be able to survive the emergency once more; the only difference this time will be that they are "buying" peace on a local scale by staying out of the fight, whereas before they contributed to the over-all defense of the area.

Charcoal is the chief urban fuel in Viet-Nam. Fresh wood is not dry enough in that climate, and only Europeans or rich Vietnamese can afford bottled gas. By destroying or capturing hundreds of kilns in Camau Peninsula and intercepting charcoal convoys, the Viet-Minh created acute fuel shortages (and price rises) in Saigon late in 1961. On February 27, 1962, the government appealed to the population to switch to Nong-Son coal instead of trying to buy charcoal, whose black-market price began to soar. Heavily armed river warships began to escort the charcoal-boat convoys, but any shipment to Saigon risks serious casualties.

Similarly, communications throughout the country are severely menaced. With a competence that denotes central direction, the insurgents hacked to pieces the country's single north-south railroad leading from Saigon to the 17th parallel, which shortly before, on August 7, 1959, had reopened for through traffic after an interruption of fourteen years. In the first six months of 1962 alone, the Viet-Minh blew up or derailed sixteen trains, machine-gunned thirteen others and sabotaged the railroad at about thirty places, including an important arch of the Quang-Ngai bridge, thereby cutting off through traffic (including the very Nong-Son coal with which the Saigonese are supposed to cook) into northern Central Viet-Nam. In one powerful ambush at Song-Phan on June 5, two troop trains with supplies, escorted by an armored train, were completely destroyed after the armored train had prudently abandoned its charges. Another armored train coming from the opposite direction, from the town of Phan-Thiet, was ambushed in turn at a bridge that was blown up as the train began to cross. All night trains were discontinued as of April 7, 1962, and prices were increased in May, to pay for the heavy expenses of replacing destroyed equipment.

The road net suffers from a similar fate, although great efforts are made to keep the roads open during the daytime. Thanks to large amounts of available engineering equipment and numerous advisers, no major road remains out of commission for a long time.

As in the earlier Indochina War, all this places great strain on air transportation. The national airline, Air Viet-Nam, started "grasshopper flights" in five-seater planes connecting Saigon with outlying provincial towns often only a few miles apart but inaccessible overland because of the unsafe roads.[43] Although air transportation and the extensive use of transport helicopters for the armed forces can up to a point take the place of overland communications, it cannot reduce the psychological impact of the "siege syndrome" in many

areas. Thus, the provincial capital city of Quang-Ngai is now separated from the rest of the province by thirty-five miles of moats and
hedges—a system that is being adopted in other areas as well—and
one town, Bô-Tuc, a bare fifty miles north of Saigon, is one of many
that is being supplied entirely by air.[44] As the French found out during their Indochina War, keeping the major roads open during the
daytime cost on the average three casualties per kilometer per month,
but they believed the price had to be paid if any control at all was
to be maintained over the countryside.

One particularly important facet of all Viet-Công operations is
the attention paid to giving "convincing explanations" (i.e., propaganda) to various elements of the population. There are very few
blanket appeals in the Viet-Công arsenal. On the contrary, all
propaganda is channeled through local organizations most likely to
be able to gain the ear of their particular target. The effectiveness
of the Dich-Van has been discussed previously, but at least three
other propaganda organizations work on specialized targets: the
Binh-Van, which specializes in inducing ARVN soldiers to defect
or to switch sides; the Dan-Van, which operates solely among the
peasants; and the Tri-Van, which seeks to create support for the
Liberation Front among the intellectuals. Tri-Van groups are particularly active in the Saigon area and also have sunk roots into the
schools and even the Buddhist community. On March 25, 1963, the
Saigon Military Court tried a whole Tri-Van network led by a woman
pharmacist, Pham Thi Yen; the group included three senior Buddhist
bonzes and a professor at the highly respected Lycée Petrus-Ky.[45]
A similar network, involving many of the senior officials of South
Viet-Nam's geographical-survey service, had been arrested earlier, and
large networks also were reported in several provincial headquarters,
notably in the Mekong Delta.

Communist military tactics have continued thus far to keep pace
with the changes in technology on the American and South Vietnamese side. An American combat officer in Viet-Nam is reported
to have observed: "These boys never quit in their self-appraisal and
self-criticism. That aspect of them is pretty impressive."[46] The
arrival of American helicopters in force—more than 200 were said
to be operating in Viet-Nam by mid-1963—for a while diminished
Communist daytime attack capabilities. However, they soon adapted
to the changed conditions, which no longer permitted them to lay

siege to a fortified village or post; instead, they learned to batter its defenses to pieces in one hammer blow early enough in the night to be able to crush its resistance before daybreak and to remove booty and prisoners to safe hiding places before the helicopters could begin to operate. As the French found out in Algeria (an experience that should be studied a great deal more than it is), helicopters turned out to be very vulnerable once the adversary learned how to direct his machine-gun fire against a moving aerial target. The insurgents soon set up "helicopter traps" in which a fight was deliberately started for the purpose of drawing the planes to an area where several heavy machine guns lay in wait. Operations in the Quang-Ngai, Camau, and Plaine des Joncs areas in January, April, and May, 1963, in which numerous American helicopters were hit very accurately, may be the forerunner of such a situation. Also, the possession of an increasing number of field radios by the Communists soon enabled them to set up farly effective air-raid-warning nets.

Military planning, on the Communist side—apart from over-all direction by the Vietnamese People's Army—seems to be well directed by the two regional staffs in Interzones V and VI. Communist operations denote the existence of region-wide objectives. For example, after the establishment of almost invulnerable bases in the far western tip of South Viet-Nam in 1957–59, the Communists in 1960–61 began to cut Saigon off from its hinterland. By late 1961, the "arc of insurgency" around Saigon was almost complete, with all roads leading from Saigon subjected to constant harassment and sometimes outright attack. Government attempts to break through the arc with American help, by establishing its own belt of strategic hamlets to the north of Saigon, began in April, 1962. By 1963, it became obvious that establishing strategic hamlets in heavily infiltrated areas was an invitation to disaster, and that the clearing and holding of the area must precede the establishment of the hamlets, and not vice versa.

In Central Viet-Nam, 1957–59 saw the methodical infiltration of tribal cadres and of lowland Vietnamese who had been trained to speak the mountain languages, and who even filed their teeth to sharp points so that they would resemble the mountaineers. This was followed by the establishment of a network of relay bases, some of which crossed the most inaccessible parts of southern Laotian territory while others directly crossed the 17th parallel;[47] this complex of relay bases and jungle paths is known as the Ho Chi Minh Trail. Although some of the camps were captured by the ARVN during months of bitter fighting in 1962, many others still exist, and the Viet-Công had, by and large, succeeded in maintaining its positions on the PMS. Although about 150,000 mountain tribesmen out of a total of about 700,000 sought refuge in government-controlled areas during 1962—more often because of air raids rather than out of affection for the lowland Vietnamese[48]—the Communists still retained their strong position in the hills. In December, 1962, American-trained tribals, who had been carefully selected for their loyalty to Saigon, suddenly attacked their American advisers and the Vietnamese garrison of Plei-Mrong; on April 14, 1963, Viet-Công forces launched a coordinated large-scale attack on twelve strategic hamlets and the provincial capital of Quang-Ngai, 250 miles northeast of Saigon; while on April 27, a jungle garrison was overrun north of Kontum. American sources found comfort in the fact that in the case of the Quang-Ngai attack, some of the villagers informed the pursuing ARVN forces about the Viet-Công's path of retreat. Nevertheless, the VC remains firmly established in its wartime stronghold of Interzone V, and it has the capability of almost interdicting rail and road travel along the key coastal communication artery connecting South with Central Viet-Nam. The deteriorating situation in neighboring Laos, which abuts on Central Viet-Nam and where the neutralist government of Prince Souvanna Phouma never succeeded in making its authority felt in the hinterland, also had a negative influence on ARVN and American operations in the PMS.

In the Mekong Delta lowlands and the Camau Peninsula, fighting, during 1962, made little headway, in spite of the open rice fields that should, theoretically, facilitate aerial surveillance, which is plentifully available. By late 1962, 10,000 Vietnamese troops with American advisers, helicopters, amphibious carriers, and armored launches, had thrown what was expected to be an airtight blockade around the Camau swamp redoubts of U-Minh Forest. But some astute observers, notably *The New York Times*' David Halberstam, noted that in the lowlands, "the war is not going so well as might be expected, nor in fact is it going so well as 10 months ago."[49] That became apparent late in April, 1963, when, in a series of lightning strikes, the VC forces annihilated a string of government positions, captured hundreds of modern weapons, including recoilless artillery, and then loaded the mutilated bodies of some of the defenders, as well as their weeping widows and children, on a barge as a sign of defiance, leaving them to be picked up downriver by ARVN troops.[50]

Camau had once more, in Halberstam's words, become "like traveling in North Viet-Nam."

In the use of small-unit tactics, the Communist forces have added a few new "twists" to their earlier considerable body of knowledge in that field. Attacks are planned according to a "Five-Point Field Order" known as "One Slow Action, Four Fast Ones." This is explained as follows:

SLOW and meticulous attack preparations and rehearsals;
FAST closing in with the enemy and attack;
FAST and determined destruction of enemy resistance;
FAST mopping-up of the battle area (arms, prisoners, own casualties);
FAST withdrawal to base areas.

These five points are generally well respected, especially now that American helicopters can provide support at dawn. This explains why Communist attacks in South Viet-Nam are often broken off seemingly with no reason and at a point where, with little extra effort, the objective would have been fully attained. But perhaps the extra half-hour devoted to attainment of the objective would have exposed the unit to strafing on the way back to its hideouts; the Viet-Minh frowns on this sort of "adventurism."

Mine ambushes are also a specialty of the Vietnamese Communists. In eight years of fighting, the French lost almost 500 armored vehicles (tanks, armored cars, and amphibians), of which 84 per cent blew up on mines. Another 8.7 per cent were destroyed in direct human-wave attacks, and the remainder more conventionally disposed of by antitank weapons. A survey of present operations shows that the Communists continue to place heavy emphasis on mining roads, bridges, rail beds, and even open rice fields where they are likely to constitute obligatory points of passage.

Most recently, the new strategic hamlets have become a prime target, not only because they harbor much desirable booty (rice, aid kits, a small radio transceiver, and weapons), but because the destruction of a strategic hamlet constitutes a psychological setback for the scheme's British-American authors and thus shakes the faith of the South Vietnamese in the existence of a panacea against the insurgency. Though looking impressive with their moats and varying thicknesses of wooden palisades, they are easy prey every time the Viet-Minh attacks them with an incendiary device. Another and more peaceful way of penetrating into a strategic hamlet came to light recently when insurgents halted a passenger bus, removed the legitimate riders, and then simply rode the vehicle into the village they wished to raid.

Much has also been said about the Viet-Minh's intention to set up a permanent "liberated area" south of the 17th parallel in order to install a "South Vietnamese Liberation Government" there that would emerge from the present "Liberation Committee." While such an idea is not entirely inconceivable, the military realities of the situation—the relative accessibility of South Viet-Nam's terrain, in comparison to Laos, for example, or North Viet-Nam—make this highly unlikely unless the situation of the present South Viet-Nam regime deteriorates radically. In any case, such a "Liberation Government" could always be set up in the jungles to the north of the 17th parallel if North Viet-Nam decides that such a government is politically desirable. After all, the fact that the Algerian nationalist regime never succeeded in setting foot on Algerian soil while hostilities were in progress did not prevent it from gaining victory. Retrospectively, it may perhaps even be asserted that the clamor in February and March, 1962, about such a "Liberation Government" came mostly from Saigon, where it suited the authorities to impress the United States with the overwhelming magnitude of the Communist threat the Ngo Dinh Diem regime faced.

In sum, in this war in which the peasantry of South Viet-Nam is the primary target, the Communists were given a three-year head-start—from 1957 until 1960—before it was even admitted that a real threat existed, and almost two more years elapsed before any organized attempt was made to distinguish between routine military countermeasures and a proper combination of constructive socio-economic endeavors and military tactics adapted to the war that was being fought.

But the situation in South Viet-Nam will remain parlous and indecisive as long as officials in Washington or Saigon continue to believe that popular support in a revolutionary war is a minor factor in the eventual achievement of victory.

COUNTERINSURGENCY

To win a revolutionary war is no easy task at best, even when, as in Malaya, the authorities were willing to recognize very early that they were in fact faced with such a war. In the case of South Viet-Nam, it already has been shown that, after establishing in 1957 as official dogma that the Communist guerrilla threat had disappeared, it was awkward for both the Vietnamese Army and MAAG to engage in large-scale antiguerrilla operations. During that period, such antiguerrilla measures as there were, were limited to the "Communist Activities Denunciation Campaign" (*to-cong*) in which, in a perfect replica of measures in Communist North Viet-Nam, anyone and everyone could denounce as a "Communist" anyone he or she did not like. The only effect of that kind of counterinsurgency was that it clogged the security apparatus with thousands of trumped-up cases that had to be investigated and also sent thousands of innocent people into concentration camps, where *real* Communist fellow-internees took them in hand and made Communist sympathizers out of them. The arbitrariness of the South Vietnamese security apparatus, though unknown to the public in the United States, is openly admitted and discussed in South Viet-Nam. On December 26, 1962, Nguyên Van Luong, the Vietnamese Secretary of Justice (the equivalent of the U.S. Attorney General), replying in open session to questions put to him by South Vietnamese legislators, stated candidly that

> . . . in the present state of [government] organization, the security services, in spite of the fact that they have a judicial character in that they are the auxiliaries of the prosecutor, are not under the jurisdiction of the Justice [Department]. For that reason, it is difficult to ensure that controls are carried out under conditions assuring that investigations are conducted in accordance with the law.[51]

On the American side, active concern with the problem began only late in 1960. It resulted in the inception of an eighteen-month "Counterinsurgency Plan," upon which the Staley Mission built its own recommendations in 1961. All that can be said of both the Counterinsurgency Plan and the Staley Mission recommendations is that neither gave much evidence of being alert to the realities of the South Vietnamese situation.

General Maxwell Taylor's report, presented late in 1961, brought an increased appreciation of the comprehensiveness of revolutionary warfare. As has been noted earlier, however, not many of the key sociopolitical recommendations of his plan seem to have been "bought" in Washington, and even fewer in Saigon. The joint American-Vietnamese eleven-point declaration of January, 1962, clearly is the result of a compromise in which the Vietnamese (or their defenders within the Administration) watered down whatever "bite" there was in the Taylor report to little but a few minor technical measures.

Yet, in one of the many cautiously optimistic phrases that henceforth became the hallmark of official announcements on South Viet-Nam, the January 2 accords gave Washington the following grounds for hope:

> 1. The will shown by the Vietnamese government to maintain its independence and to insure a more efficient use of its own resources and of American aid;
> 2. The hope that the next six months would see a vigorous counter-offensive not only in the military field, but also in the socio-economic fields;
> 3. The good will shown by the Ngo Dinh Diem administration to implement the reforms desired by the United States in favor of democratization, so as to put an end to corruption, nepotism and waste.[52]

By July, 1962, it was obvious that none of the three points had satisfactorily materialized; but even before then, several other measures had been taken either jointly by the Vietnamese and American authorities in Viet-Nam, or by the Vietnamese at American behest. The putting into the field of "Ranger" companies—called Biet Dong Quân (literally, Detached Action Forces)—which were ferried into action by American-manned helicopters, gave the ARVN a new offensive edge. On the American side, advisers were attached to each of the provincial governors in March, 1962, fulfilling the role the French "Fifth Bureau" and "Pacification Advisers" had played in the earlier Indochina War. This direct and lower-level action was further reinforced by a group called MATA, for "Military Advisory Training Assistance." The "Matadors," as they are unofficially referred to, emphasize "civic action" as their major job and train the Civil Guard and Dan-Vè (village militia) to become more effective in counterguerrilla operations. Another of their tasks, according to Warren Rogers, Jr., is to "try to win greater support from isolated villagers for the efforts by the South Vietnamese government forces."[53]

If any alien soldier, equipped, as Rogers reports, with a four-week course in Vietnamese history and customs and a 750-word vocabulary, can win over the ever-suspicious South Vietnamese villagers, this will have to be reckoned as a major sociological breakthrough. The MATA program is too new, however, for any definitive judgment on its success.

One countertactic with which American and South Vietnamese planners have flirted is the possibility of "re-exporting" the guerrilla war to North Viet-Nam. In 1961, a special unit for operations above the parallel was set up, known as the "First Observation Group." Initially composed of 350 men, it is being increased to about 800 men. The unit is all Vietnamese, but it has a strong American advisory detachment; it was originally organized in three companies, each comprising three fifteen-man combat teams and a twenty-four-man headquarters and support team. One such unit was captured near Ninh-Binh (180 miles north of the 17th parallel) in July, 1961, when its aircraft developed engine trouble.

In general terms, it is difficult to proceed with "antiguerrilla-guerrilla" operations as long as one's home area is infiltrated by guerrillas, for the chances of betrayal are enormous and those of success rather slim. Also, the all-encompassing Communist police-state system makes early detection of the infiltrators likely. But that does not mean that the effort should not be made.

It is not generally known that for several years the French ran effective guerrilla operations behind Viet-Minh lines; but, in 1954, when the curtain rang down after Geneva, the guerrilla units, composed of mountain tribesmen who could not abandon their families to Communist reprisals, stayed put and fought to the bitter end along with the French sergeants and officers who could not fight their way back alone across enemy territory. The Viet-Minh later announced that several thousand such guerrillas were killed after 1954. In France, the government remains closemouthed about the fate and operations of the GCMA (Groupements de Commandos Mixtes Aéroportés, or Composite Airborne Commando Groups).[54] Yet recent reports from North Viet-Nam indicate that "bandits" still operate in some of the highland regions.

However, although the possibility of counterinfiltration cannot be ruled out, its value as a deterrent to North Vietnamese infiltration in South Viet-Nam is dubious. And the frightful cost of the operation in terms of human lives—not to speak of the diplomatic complications when such infiltrations are accompanied by airplanes, which may be shot down—must be clearly understood before it is undertaken on a sizable scale.

But the heart and soul of counterinsurgency in South Viet-Nam seems to have gone into the scheme to establish strategic hamlets and villages. It is a measure of the importance the Diem government placed on the program that Ngo Dinh Nhu personally supervised it.

Basically, the plan implies the recognition that civilian support is one of the essential factors of the enemy's strength and that, consequently, he must be deprived of it. Besides this aspect of "denial," there is also the hope that the strategic hamlet, by providing the inhabitants with better social services (infirmaries, schools, etc.) and by putting the villagers within the reach of government administrators and propagandists, may eventually convince them that the cause of the insurgents not only is "wrong" (a moral notion that is difficult to convey), but is also losing (a notion that is easier to prove and far more important).

The strategic-hamlets idea is neither new nor revolutionary. To cut off civilian support from resistance forces is an objective occupation commanders the world over have attempted to achieve at one time or another. Usually, however, controls were necessary for brief periods only, and could be handled by such methods as curfews or the issuance of passes and other means of restricting civilian travel. The British, however, resorted on several occasions to the full control of large civilian populations in order to cut off hostile elements from their civilian support: At the turn of the century, the Boer civilians were either assigned to their own towns or "concentrated"—this gave rise to the term "concentration camp"—in areas where contact with Boer forces was impossible. A similar method was employed during the Mau-Mau emergency in Kenya (1950–57) with some degree of success[55] and, simultaneously, in Malaya.

In Indochina, the British Malayan experience was followed with great attention, for it seemed to promise a good solution to the problem the French faced. It was the then commander of the northern theater, the late General François Gonzalès de Linarès, who, in 1952, launched the idea of what he called "protected villages," and implementation began later that year. I visited two of these villages—Khoi-Lac in Quang-Yen Province and Don-Quan in Ha-Dong Province—early in 1953. They resembled their British prototypes line for line, as do their South Vietnamese successors today: attractive market areas, well-built houses, electricity, and, in the case of Don-Quan, not only earth-and-wood fortifications but standard French concrete bunkers.

The major difference between the British and the French strategic villages was—the enemy. In Malaya, the CT's, fighting at 8,000 against 300,000, were simply never strong enough to take on the New Villages; in Indochina, with 500,000 Viet-Minh against 380,000 French Union troops, the problem was reversed, and the Viet-Minh also possessed the mortars and recoilless cannon necessary to breach even sophisticated defensive positions. Also, the New Villages in Malaya not only regrouped and concentrated the population, but in most cases *completely removed* it from the CT's zone of influence; since the squatters represented less than 6 per cent of the population and made almost no contribution to the economic life of the country, this was feasible. In the case of the French experience in North Viet-Nam, which eventually failed, or the present American experiment in South Viet-Nam, the number of people to be resettled is staggering. About 3 million were moved within the Red River Delta, the magnitude of the program in South Viet-Nam will make it the most mammoth example of "social engineering" in the non-Communist world. On October 1, 1962, seven months after the program had been inaugurated, President Ngo Dinh Diem announced to his National Assembly that

> . . . at the present time, the population living in safety and revolution*
> inside the strategic hamlets already built (3,074) or about to be com-
> pleted (2,679), numbers 7,267,517 souls. A completion figure of 600
> strategic hamlets per month has been set. Thus, by the end of 1962,
> 9,253,000 persons, or two-thirds of the population, will live [in strategic
> hamlets].[56]

That target, apparently, has not been met. On April 11, 1963, almost a year after the program's official launching, it was reported that 5,917 (instead of 7,500) hamlets had been built, housing 8,150,187 inhabitants out of a total population given as 13,813,066.[57] The ultimate goal is to build at least 12,000 hamlets by the end of 1963, which will house all the rural inhabitants of the country, and simultaneously to equip the urban areas with "strategic boroughs," which will give Saigon the aspect of a vast stockade.

Again, the differences in the Malayan situation come to mind: In a food-deficit area, such as Malaya, "starving out the enemy was a practical possibility," an American noted recently, after having observed the Vietnamese experiments.[58] Further, with only 423,000 people involved, the British could manage to feed them out of field kitchens, if need be, in order to diminish the chances of food smuggling. With 10 million people, in a food-surplus area, it will be a

---

* The official view of the Ngo Dinh Diem government, and particularly of Ngo Dinh Nhu, is that the strategic hamlets will become the cradle of a "Personalist Revolution." That is the "revolution" the President of South Viet-Nam refers to here.

great deal more arduous to reap the military benefits of the population regroupment process. And there are indications that the social, economic, and political amenities with which the strategic villages will be furnished (good schools, clinics, waterworks, unfettered elections of village officials) take second place to the government's urgent drive to insulate the Viet-Công from its civilian support environment.[59]

Hasty or inadequate planning has also hampered the success of the program in some cases. For example, the pilot strategic village of Bên-Tuong, with which the whole program was inaugurated in March, 1962, under the code name of "Sunrise" (*"Binh-Minh,"* in Vietnamese), was so far away from the nearest market town, Bên-Cat, that the farmers had to pay the prohibitive sum of $2.85 per person for a motor pedicab ride into town.[60] Bên-Tuong turned out to be a mistake in other ways as well: Too deep in Communist-held territory, it was overrun in 1963 along with many other ill-planned hamlets, and by the end of 1963, a major reappraisal of the program was under way.

After individual fortified hamlets had been in operation for several months, a comprehensive attempt was made to solve the insecurity problem of a whole district or even the better part of a whole province in a concerted operation. A British Advisory Mission under R. K. G. Thompson, an ex-brigadier who had been Secretary for Defence for guerrilla-racked Malaya, was instrumental in working out the basic plans for what was to become "Operation Sunrise." MAAG provided aid and coordination; the U.S. aid mission to Viet-Nam appointed a special Rural Rehabilitation Committee (which is now becoming the dominant channel for U.S. aid operations in the country) and supplied an initial sum of $300,000 for distribution to the resettled families—at the rate of $21 per family for all property lost and destroyed in the course of the transfer. The U.S. Information Service printed a special pamphlet, entitled *Toward the Good Life,* and the ARVN's 5th Division furnished the troops and trucks to proceed with the population transfer.

The province of Binh-Duong, directly north of Saigon and lying athwart National Highway No. 1, was chosen as the test site for "Operation Sunrise." The southernmost district of the province, Cu-Chi, had been at least partly cleared in an arduous seven-month campaign beginning in August, 1961; but the Bên-Cat district, surrounded by a vast network of rubber plantations and wild forests, had become a redoubt for two active and well-trained Communist

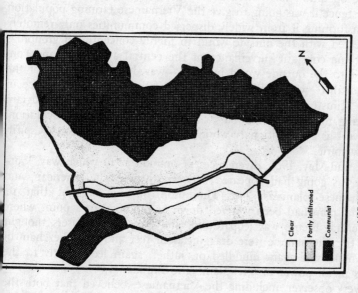

CU-CHI AFTER CLEARING OPERATIONS
August 2, 1961-March 20, 1962
Official South Vietnamese View

30 mi. to Cambodia

Road No. 1

20 mi. to Saigon

MILES
0 1 2 3

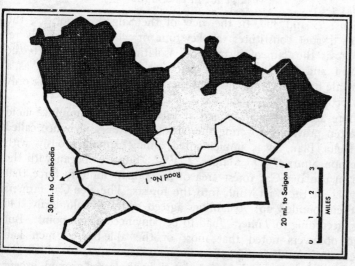

INSECURITY IN CU-CHI DISTRICT
April-August, 1961
Official South Vietnamese View

N

Clear
Partly infiltrated
Communist

battalions, 55 and 300. In the view of the Saigon authorities, the Bên-Cat district constitutes the keystone of what is commonly referred to as the "arc of insurgency" isolating Saigon on both the southwest and the northeast; therefore it not only qualified as a worthwhile first target but also had the advantage of containing only 38,000 people.

A more ambitious plan, aimed at breaking the Communist hold on the ten provinces covering the Mekong Delta, and hence called the "Delta Plan," was implemented almost simultaneously with "Operation Sunrise." On March 22, 1962, "Sunrise" began with the arrival in the Bên-Cat forest area of a 600-man military force that simply swept the Viet-Minh into the forests. The Bên-Cat farmers were then rounded up: 70 families agreed to move voluntarily; 140 others, according to *Time*,[61] "had to be convinced at gunpoint." But foreign observers noted that most of the able-bodied men had escaped the round-up. The Bên-Tuong village area, to which the farmers were being moved, consisted mainly of cleared ground, except for a concrete infirmary and administration building, around which the farmers had to construct their own thatch houses, and moats and walls for defense. In the meantime, the farmers' former hamlets were leveled in accordance with "a relentless scorched-earth program."[62]

The operation was hailed as a vast success, and the new pattern of existence it was going to give the Vietnamese farming population —transforming it from widely dispersed communities only remotely connected with the outside world to highly concentrated groupings under the constant surveillance of the central authorities and connected to the outside world by radio—was described as part of the "Personalist" way of life, which all Vietnamese are to embrace in time. Minister of the Interior Bui Van Luong explained the program as being totally "revolutionary": "The way is a way of revolution; the work is a revolutionary work; the spirit is a revolutionary spirit, a new spirit."[63]

By mid-May, 1962, divergences of opinion as to which way "Sunrise" was going had appeared between the British, American, and Vietnamese planners. The Thompson mission thought that its original plan had been watered down or modified to a point where its central theme was jeopardized, and American advisers thought that the Vietnamese were dragging their feet and that the chain of command was again muddled or, rather, again led directly to the locus of all power in Viet-Nam—the Presidency.[64]

Every observer, including the Vietnamese, believed that both the

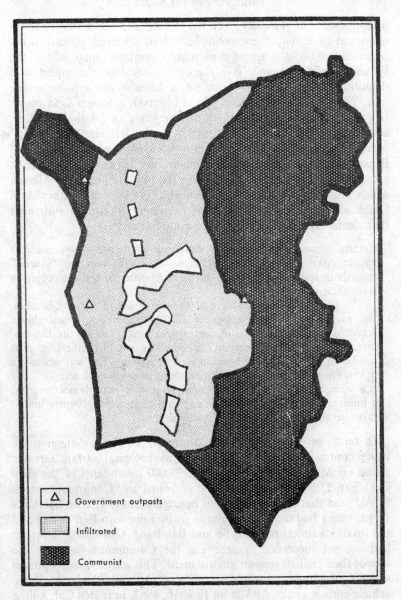

INSECURITY RETURNS
August 15, 1965
United States View

△ Government outposts

░ Infiltrated

▓ Communist

insignificant sum of money given the farmers and the drastic methods employed to regroup them would be bitterly resented, at least in the beginning. Also, the egress and ingress controls upon which the system hinges necessarily give the strategic village the aspect of a detention area rather than that of a harmonious socio-economic unit. *The Wall Street Journal*'s local observer, a former OSS operative who was wholly sympathetic to the cause of South Viet-Nam, nevertheless felt that a visit to such a hamlet left one with the impression of having "blundered into some sort of prison camp." Reporters from Europe made comparisons between the strategic villages and a similar relocation system used by the French in Algeria, which involved 2 million Moslems. Such articles led the Information Office of the South Vietnamese Government to issue a statement that clearly showed the authorities' exasperation:

> Certain journalists—particularly American journalists—have made it appear, either through wickedness or naïveté, that Operation "Sunrise" consists in applying totalitarian methods in order to compel people to leave their villages.
> . . . It is easily conceivable that the uprooting of peasant families, and particularly the destruction of abandoned villages, is not always accepted with joy, in spite of the explanations given by the Government. Nevertheless, Operation "Sunrise" is not a pacification plan similar to that which has been applied in Algeria. The war which we fight against Communism is the opposite of a colonial war . . . but is a salvaging operation, not affecting the principles of democracy, and a humanitarian action which the government of a free country undertakes because it is afflicted by Communism.

In terms of statistical accomplishments, *Tu-Do*, a Saigon newspaper controlled by the government psychological-warfare services, stated on May 13, 1962, that of the 38,000 inhabitants of the Bên-Cat district, 60 per cent must be reckoned as "Communist-intoxicated," and that after six weeks of operations, only 2,769 inhabitants (7 per cent) had moved voluntarily or by force into Bên-Tuong and the smaller hamlets of Dong-So and Ban-Bang. Obviously, "Sunrise" had not yet succeeded in depriving the Communist forces in the area of their civilian support environment. This was eloquently proved when Communist guerrillas in full daylight ambushed an eleven-vehicle convoy of the ARVN on June 16, 1962, near Bên-Cat, killing twenty-six Vietnamese soldiers, several civilian public-works technicians and a contractor, and two American officers. The ambush was carried out to perfection, thanks to the fact that the civilian population—thoroughly intimidated or willingly cooperating—failed to notify the local ARVN posts of the impending attack, and also did its share in sabotaging the roads leading to the ambush area so reinforcements did not reach the convoy until afternoon. By that time, following his "One Slow Action, Four Fast Ones" principle, the enemy had filtered back into the forest with the convoy's equipment. One year later, the situation had not altered. Some strategic villages withstood VC attacks—in fact, reportedly better than many a better-armed regular ARVN unit—while others were overwhelmed, or even betrayed. Among the casualties was Bên-Tuong, the pilot project, which was overrun by the VC on August 20, 1963.

In sum, the strategic-village concept, though sound in principle, will have to undergo many changes, both in physical design and, above all, in human approach, before it can be considered a truly effective counterinsurgency weapon that can be indiscriminately applied wherever revolutionary wars occur. Considering the physical and psychological magnitude of the problem, it would be unfair to expect immediate and wide-ranging dividends. In any case, the stakes are high—very high—for on it (and on very little else) rides the reputation of the United States and the South Vietnamese regime it supports.[65] One year after the program had started, *The New York Times* observed that there still reigned in Viet-Nam

> . . . a subtle feeling that the population has not yet really committed itself to the hamlet idea.
> Nothing is more important at present than the hamlet program. . . . Americans frankly acknowledge that they have few alternatives if it fails to cure present ills.[66]

If that is a correct interpretation of the situation, one hopes that the exploration of other alternatives has not been discarded altogether.

In the area of offensive military operations, very few innovations seem thus far to have been introduced—chiefly, the lavish use of helicopters as airborne trucks. Watchtowers, long—and, in the view of this writer, rightly—derided as a symbol of the French Maginot Line spirit, are back in favor with the Vietnamese, although their American advisers maintain that they give their occupants a "false sense of security" and encourage the Vietnamese to wait passively until the enemy strikes.[67]

But the classic hunt-and-kill operation, with thousands of troops sealing off an area that is then mopped up as thoroughly as possible, still constitutes the tactical mainstay of the Vietnamese-American forces; and the expressions of frustration from American senior officers remind me very much of similar expressions of frustration couched by French senior officers in almost the same words.

"This is a grubby, dirty method of fighting," said an American paratroop colonel whose Vietnamese regiment had just spent twelve fruitless days chasing an elusive guerrilla band. "If we could corner all the Viet-Cong operating on the highland on open ground we could lay them flat in twenty-five minutes. But it takes weeks to find even fifty of them."[68]

"We should be able to chase these guys down," another colonel remarked, "push them against the wall, and make them fight on our terms. Then we've got them cold."[69]

In other words, what those officers are looking for in a revolutionary war is precisely what their French predecessors had looked for— the old-fashioned "set-piece battle," where the enemy will come out from his corner with regulation gloves and fight according to the rules of the Marquess of Queensberry. In the First Indochina War, the enemy did the French that kind of favor only twice: First, when Giap tried out his regulars on Marshal de Lattre in 1951 and lost all taste for such affairs, and the second time, at Dien Bien Phu, when, after eight frustrating years of searching out the enemy, the French finally baited the trap with the top 5 per cent of their battle force and found the bait swallowed by an enemy who had learned a great deal. The "heliborne" aspect of the war has merely added a new dimension of speed to our side of the war but has not essentially modified its ground rules: In order to succeed in his operations, the enemy must plan more carefully; must prepare for covered withdrawal routes and a measure of antiaircraft protection or, at least, "deterrence"; and must expect more persistent search operations after a successful attack. And the enemy does all that, and thus far rather successfully.

It should have been obvious from the start that jungle-covered terrain (49 per cent of Viet-Nam's area) or deep bush or swamp (another 30 per cent) would make aerial surveillance unrewarding and that other means of intervention are not limited to the "eight-to-five" hours of heliborne operations (helicopters are almost useless at night and are too vulnerable to be left overnight in the operations area). The technical limitations of the heliborne search operation are best evidenced in cases where heliborne troops were committed to tracking down specific Communist units whose approximate distance from the contact area was easily within a given marching radius—such as the units that captured American Special Forces sergeants in Central Viet-Nam or those that took American medical missionaries near Ban Me Thuot. In both cases, search forces in large numbers were committed within a short time after the incident, i.e., when the guerrillas, burdened by prisoners, had covered only a few miles. In both cases, and in most other subsequent similar instances, aerial searches proved fruitless.

Thus, it is clear that there still is no panacea in the field of counterguerrilla operations when one has to commit 5,000 men for three days, with all the paraphernalia of a D-Day landing, to come up with a dead count of 9 out of perhaps 500 enemy troops under attack;[70] or at the now famous Battle of Ap-Bac (known to the Vietnamese as the Battle of My-Tho), where the VC broke through the South Vietnamese encirclement in broad daylight, just as they had done ten years earlier against the French.[71] Another broad-gauged pincer operation undertaken in the northern PMS area by the elements of 3 ARVN divisions and ARVN Marines in early May, 1963, also failed to produce sizable results, although it allegedly proved that hostile airdrops were taking place on South Vietnamese territory.[72]

As the year 1963 ended, it had become obvious that the confident predictions made by the senior U.S. military commanders in the area and by the Secretary of Defense had failed to materialize. On March 5, 1963, General Harkins had asserted that there prevailed in South Viet-Nam "a firm belief that victory was in sight."[73] By August, as the Buddhist crisis had affected Vietnamese combat morale and the VC had shifted its operations deep into the Mekong Delta (the most vulnerable part of South Viet-Nam), a briefing officer in Saigon was quoted by Pulitzer Prize-winning reporter Marguerite Higgins as asserting that

> . . . there has been no evidence of any increase in the number of Viet-Công units in the delta even though we expected there would be because our strategy is to sweep them steadily southward and finally corner them.[74]

If this quote is true, that officer was saying that the current strategy was aimed at sweeping guerrilla units from the sparsely populated highlands, where food is not readily available, into the delta area, which is Viet-Nam's granary, holds 65 per cent of its population, and is closest to the country's most sensitive targets. That would be military idiocy. In all likelihood, the guerrilla shift to the delta simply could not be prevented, and Miss Higgins had apparently swallowed a cover story.

Nevertheless, despite their concentration of attacks in the Mekong Delta area, the VC's strength in Central Viet-Nam showed no appreciable drop. In the old Interzone V provinces from Quang-Tin to Binh-Dinh, "the Reds force[d] the people to hold anti-government, pro-neutralist mass meetings even in daytime and close to National Highway No. 1" and kept sentencing landlords before "People's Courts" in February, 1964.[75] A "secret" agreement concluded in early April, 1964, between General Khanh and Laotian right-wing General Phoumi, allegedly to allow Vietnamese forces to pursue VC units into Laos, is hardly likely to be of immediate value in view of the notoriously doubtful military prowess of the Phoumi forces.

Official American optimism was maintained despite the tensions patently gathering about Diem and his government. On the very day that Diem and Nhu were murdered, the U.S. Army's authorized paper *The Stars & Stripes* quoted General Harkins, in inch-high headlines, as asserting that "Viet Victory [Was] Near" and that "victory in the sense that it would apply to this kind of war" was just months away. His deputy, Major General Charles J. Timmes, averred in the same article that the South Vietnamese forces—at that very moment seething with multiple conspiracies and about to mutiny—were essentially unmoved by the crisis that was besetting their country: "Sure," Timmes said, "they worry about political and religious disputes but, just like the American soldier, they're loyal to their government."[76] That issue of *The Stars & Stripes*, printed in Tokyo, arrived in Saigon at almost the very hour when those "loyal" Vietnamese soldiers murdered their President and while their generals were sharing among themselves the spoils of political power. There can be little doubt that the American senior commanders in Viet-Nam, like their French predecessors, totally underestimated the complexity of the war and managed to convey their overoptimism to their own military and civilian superiors at home.

An old issue of an American news magazine eloquently shows how such oversimplified views can reach even sophisticated news channels. Describing Viet-Nam at an earlier stage, it outlined the Saigon leader's task as follows:

> He needs time to organize an effective government, train an army and militia that can restore order in the villages, win over the doubting fence-sitters among the intelligentsia. Besides a military shield, he also

needs a display of winning strength and patient understanding by his Western allies.

. . . the military problem is the No. 1 problem, and . . . Western men and arms must lick it. Given sufficient U.S. equipment, they think they can crush [the Viet-Minh] within three years.

All the ingredients of present planning in Viet-Nam are there: the village militia, the display of Western strength, the necessity to commit large American funds and Western manpower, the primacy of military over politico-economic measures, etc. And as Secretary McNamara said in his key speech on Vietnamese policy, on March 26, 1964, the "long twilight struggle" may not be finished "in the first 1,000 days" of the Johnson Administration (i.e., three years). The disturbing fact is that the paragraphs quoted above were printed in *Time* magazine on *May 29, 1950,* and that the optimistic predictions they contained were made by French generals. The title of the article was "Indochina—The New Frontier."

Thus, as the Second Indochina War grinds on, it appears as devoid of easy solutions and as full of pitfalls as the earlier one. This must be ascribed to the fact that most of the presently developed counter-measures are essentially conventional guerrilla (rather than revolutionary-warfare) tactics, with the word "counter" added as a prefix: counterguerrilla, countersubversion, counterterrorism, counterinfiltration, etc. In addition to these, several old standbys are used: sealing off the insurgent area from external sanctuaries—no matter how much of a strain in manpower or in linear defenses this may be— and regroupment of the civilian support environment. Successful completion of such a first phase is then to be followed by the traditional methods of pacification by means of *quadrillage* or *tache d'huile* (which, as we have seen, had failed the French in the First Indochina War).

But all these techniques can merely supplement, but not replace, the need for political action. In South Viet-Nam, such action, parallel to the "All-Out Force and All-Out Friendship" motto applied during the Hukbalahap emergency in the Philippines, was finally launched on April 17, 1963. Christened the "Movement to Regroup Misled Members of the Resistance" ("Phong Trao Chieu Tap Khang Chien Lam Duong"), it is usually referred to in English as the "Open-Arms Plan" and shortened in Vietnamese to "Chieu Hoi." It promises complete amnesty and a safe return home to the guerrilla fighters.[77] Ngo Trong Hieu, Secretary for Civic Action and President of the Chieu Hoi Committee, denied on April 22 that there were any limitations to the surrender appeal, as had been reported "by a foreign press agency" (*The New York Times*).[78] The hard fact is that the original plan did state that "we must destroy, i.e., kill, all persons in this category [hard-core Communists]." According to official figures, a total of 12,067 VC returned to the government side in the twelve-month period ending February 18, 1964. To judge from the few weapons they brought along with them (an average of 1 or 2 per 100 returnees), they could hardly have been hard-core VC, but were probably peasants caught in the wake of clearing operations. Over-all, of the 23,500 presumed VC officially counted as killed in 1963, "thirty-seven per cent . . . or 7,500 were attributed to the fixed-wing tactical air strikes of the Vietnamese Air Force."[79] As James Eliot Cross stated, in a passage cited earlier, it is extremely difficult to distinguish between combatants and peasants in aerial bombardment. This is likely to hold true in Viet-Nam, as elsewhere.

In any case, pardon for the transgressors does not obviate the necessity to improve the physical and, above all, the moral and political lot of the Vietnamese peasantry. Its overwhelming share in the suffering of this murderous war entitles it to a voice in the decision-making that has thus far been withheld from it. Until that type of reform is effectively implemented by the South Vietnamese Government, the United States will have to carry virtually single-handed the physical burden of the counterinsurgency—and the moral responsibility for the way it is being prosecuted.

17

The Two Viet-Nams
in Perspective

As one surveys Viet-Nam's somber history over the past 2,000 years, one cannot escape the feeling that it seems destined to a course like that of a Greek drama: dynastic rivalries, deep clan hatreds, rank betrayals, as well as fortitude in adversity, shining heroism, and deep love of country—all appear at regular intervals and sometimes simultaneously.

Neither the division that occurred in 1954, nor the South Vietnamese revolutionary war that followed it, need have come about if forces beyond Viet-Nam itself had not intervened, or failed to intervene, in shaping the country's destiny. But now the deed is done, and the two Viet-Nams have lived as separate entities for more than a decade.

This in itself is tragic enough, but events since the 1954 cease-fire have contributed to exacerbate on both sides an already unsatisfactory situation. In the North, Ho Chi Minh's regime utterly failed to take advantage of the golden opportunity it had won at Geneva to make of the D.R.V.N. a state that, albeit Communist, would

385

have left itself with some windows on the non-Communist world. It could have become, if not a Yugoslavia or a Guinea, at least a Poland. There were Frenchmen, Britons, and other Europeans who were willing to "play the game"—had the D.R.V.N. been willing to play at all. And with a long border on non-Communist Laos and good ports on the open sea, with a disciplined 350,000-man army solidly behind its leaders and proud in the knowledge that it had defeated the forces of colonialism with relatively little outside support, North Viet-Nam had the basic strength to chart its own "road to Socialism," if that was what its leaders wanted.

Instead, it chose not only full orthodoxy, it chose also to surround itself with a wall of aggressive suspicion. Little Laos had been subjected to an increasing number of "border incidents" even before the outbreak of hostilities between the Pathet-Lao and the Vientiane regime. And even as early as the 1955 Bandung Conference, the Lao Government asked Red China's Chou En-lai to make his weight felt in Hanoi in order to stop Viet-Minh interference in Lao affairs. In relations with states outside the Sino-Soviet bloc, the D.R.V.N. stands, along with Albania, on the lowest rung of the ladder. And Albania is, moreover, a member of the U.N. Despite repeated promises of cultural exchanges, no North Vietnamese student has thus far been allowed to pursue his studies outside the Sino-Soviet bloc—although to have to switch from French to Russian or Chinese as a language of advanced research may mean the loss of two to three years of time. Even though accords exist with France in the cultural field, one French cultural institution in Hanoi after another has been compelled to close its doors. French professors, such as Dr. Pierre Huard, former Dean of Hanoi Medical School and a personal friend of senior Viet-Minh leaders for three decades, finally left Hanoi in despair. Three French teachers in Hanoi maintain a last Western cultural foothold, but the personal restrictions imposed on Western foreigners in Hanoi rob them of any influence whatever.

Perhaps there is no more explicit indicator of conditions in North Viet-Nam than the fact that the hundred-odd deserters from the French armed forces who went over to the enemy in the early 1950's, and subsequently married and settled down in Hanoi, sought repatriation to France (it was granted in November, 1962) in the full knowledge that prosecution before a military court and prison sentences awaited them there.

While suspicion of the West may have some emotional justification, it is difficult to understand why relations between the D.R.V.N.

and noncommitted Asian nations are little closer than those with Western countries. Eastern European satellites seek Western tourists in the hope both of earning foreign exchange and of convincing the naïve; no such activity takes place in North Viet-Nam. Visas are handed out very parsimoniously and, by all accounts, the only "tourists" thus far seen in North Viet-Nam (which has, as I know, from personal experience, far more beautiful tourist sites than the south) were a few Poles late in 1961. By cutting itself off from the Asian neutrals, North Viet-Nam has committed a diplomatic blunder of the first magnitude, whose full price it may well have to pay should the matter of covert aggression against South Viet-Nam ever come up before an international forum. The International Control Commission report on the war in South Viet-Nam, presented in June, 1962, by India and Canada (Poland dissented) to the British and Russian co-chairmen of the 1954 Geneva cease-fire accords, may well be a straw in the wind on that score.

Thus, having thrown away leverage against its Sino-Soviet backers by turning its back on the outside world, North Viet-Nam must seek to preserve its identity within the Communist bloc by a dangerous game of playing off the demands of both its mighty sponsors while extracting aid from each. In this, the North Vietnamese leadership— notably Ho Chi Minh himself—has displayed uncommon skill. How delicate this tightrope walk can be is revealed best in small things: In December, 1963, Hanoi was host for the soccer tournament of the "Armies of the Socialist Countries," which included both the U.S.S.R. *and* Albania. And fate would have it that the final elimination match pitted the Soviet team against the Albanians. Radio Hanoi stated that the event took place—but in its English-language broadcasts, it sedulously avoided mentioning who won the match. On the openly ideological plane, the ninth session of the Lao-Dong's Central Committee, in December, 1963, also toed Ho's adopted line in its final communiqué, which cautioned Party members

> . . . to oppose revisionism and right-wing opportunism [i.e., the Soviet Union's position], which constitute the main danger, and at the same time oppose dogmatism and sectarianism [i.e., Red China's position], and to contribute to enhancing cohesion and unity within the Socialist camp. . . .[1]

However, a good part of the D.R.V.N.'s success in maneuvering between the Chinese and the Soviet roads to socialism may be due to Ho's personal prestige as an "Old Bolshevik" and may well not be

transferable to whoever succeeds him. If the Lao coalition government manages to survive, it will have been due in good part to the
fact that North Viet-Nam found it in its interest to play the Russian
card rather than Peking's, for the time being. In that case, modera-
tion on the South Vietnamese situation may also be possible, for
the north, despite all its disciplined hordes of toilers and its battle-
wise People's Army, is still a fragile edifice that could be reduced to
rubble in a single "conventional" fire raid by the American aircraft
right now on Okinawa, Taiwan, the Philippines, and in Thailand
and South Viet-Nam.

The world, as seen from Hanoi, must be full of menace; and while
reunification may be worth a limited war engaging less than a division
of regulars and mostly booty weapons, it is not worth the risk that
North Viet-Nam may be wiped off the map. If the Vietnamese Communists have displayed one consistent quality in their thirty-year
struggle for power, it is their sense of cold realism. By 1964, it must
have become clear in Hanoi that the United States means to stay in
South Viet-Nam as long as necessary, and that the American build-
up (or, as seen from North Viet-Nam, "American interference") in
South Viet-Nam will increase rather than diminish while Communist
guerrilla pressure continues. As in Korea after the Inchon thrust, the
men in Hanoi must be beginning to realize that the overthrow of
the Saigon regime by revolutionary warfare is unlikely. In fact, if the
successors to the Ngo Dinh Diem Administration gain wider Western
support, this would render the chances of Communist victory only
more remote.

Thus, having failed in its first bid for victory, North Viet-Nam,
just like North Korea and Red China in late 1951, may be ready to
talk terms—not because it thinks it can impose a pro-Communist
regime upon Saigon, but simply because the price of victory may be
too high. In that sense, the American commitment to Saigon already
has paid dividends. However, a swing of the political pendulum inside
the Hanoi leadership toward Peking (which some experts predict
in the wake of the ministerial changes that took place in the
D.R.V.N. in the spring of 1963), may well produce an escalation of
the South Vietnamese struggle into a Korea-type war. The guarantee
Khrushchev offered the D.R.V.N. against any attack by "Messrs.
Imperialists,"[2] might well widen the dimensions of the conflict.

It is probably harder to obtain a balanced picture of South Viet-

Nam than of North Viet-Nam today—and not, as some of the southern regime's ardent exponents aver, because the Communists have succeeded in "integrating their propaganda into Western information channels." The really basic problem of Diem's South Viet-Nam was that in its efforts to stem the Communist threat, it had gradually come to adopt methods in every field of endeavor which tended to blur the differences between its brand of totalitarianism and that of the Communist north: rigid controls in every field of communication; indefinite detention without trials; concentration camps; drumhead courts; an impotent legislature; and, finally, direct interference in every individual's private life—all this smacked of the futuristic totalitarian state George Orwell described in his unforgettable 1984. Very little has changed under Diem's successors.

Nor is a "New Class" of rulers missing in South Viet-Nam even now; it is, as in the Communist countries, a bureaucratic elite that owes everything to the top leadership and very little to the people it is supposed to serve. Under Diem, the Presidency was the fount of all honors, and of all material privileges, as well. Under the government of General Nguyên Khanh, which seized power on January 30, 1964, the Presidency has been reduced to a purely ceremonial job, and effective power resides with Khanh himself. But unlike the pattern in other nondemocratic systems in underdeveloped areas, in South Viet-Nam the armed forces, which were about to lose the last shreds of their autonomy under the Diem regime, have, as in Pakistan, Burma, and, to some extent, Indonesia, become an alternate source of national leadership. Through a shrewd system of frequent transfers and of mutually counterbalancing authorities with equal access to the ear of the political leadership, Khanh has kept the armed forces as dependent on his personal impulse as the bureaucracy is. Powerful paramilitary formations, increasingly better-armed Civil Guards possessing their own artillery and armor, and local militia forces have been put under tight military control. Key units are now under direct command of the Premier. After all, the only serious (and ultimately successful) attempts at disposing of the political leadership *have* come from the armed forces.

The major differences between south and north are, at first glance, very few: the unquestionably higher southern consumption standards, the existence of private ownership, and the unfettered freedom to practice Catholicism.[3] But here again, a look beneath the surface may disclose facts that might disturb this somewhat oversimplified view. In the case of agricultural ownership, the Ngo Dinh Diem regime advocated private ownership and implemented, albeit slowly, reform programs that to a limited extent broadened the base of agricultural small holdings. However, with rural indebtedness and usury still widespread, theoretical title to the land is a hollow gift indeed. In addition, emergency measures prompted by the guerrilla war have meant that farmers have been summarily removed from their land, and many are compelled to carry out public works (rebuilding destroyed roads and dikes, building *agrovilles* and strategic hamlets), with little or no compensation, under conditions of duress like those of the *corvée* of early colonial days. In the field of industrial development, the Personalist philosophy did not look kindly upon private enterprise in which the state did not have an important share; and a constant stream of petty rules and regulations discouraged foreign investment—in spite of many official inducements —even before the guerrilla emergency.

South Viet-Nam today seems to resemble a diseased body previously weakened from other illnesses; it has become incapable of spontaneously producing the antitoxins necessary to combat the onslaught of new bacilli. In other words, there simply is not yet enough of a difference between the two regimes, in their relations between themselves and their citizens—and the north has the more efficient politicomilitary apparatus—to make the citizens of the south rally to its defense. That is why there can be no genuine comparison between the Berlin Wall and the 17th parallel: In Berlin, the barrier separates a total dictatorship from a true working democracy; in Viet-Nam, it separates two systems practicing virtually the same rituals, but invoking different deities.

In the field of foreign relations, however, South Viet-Nam has been far more successful than its northern counterpart. Its leaders understood early in the struggle that foreign support (particularly American support) would be a decisive element in their eventual survival, just as it had been in the cases of South Korea, Taiwan, and Thailand; and they have made a determined effort to line up allies willing to back them unconditionally. But while both sides have several such allies, South Viet-Nam also has succeeded in gaining acceptance from countries of the Afro-Asian bloc to an extent the dour North Vietnamese rulers have thus far been unable to match. South Viet-Nam is represented in every international organization to which it can lawfully be admitted. North Viet-Nam is not a member even of the international organizations, such as the Universal Postal Union, in which such abject dependencies as the Spanish and Portuguese colonies have their own seats.

While North Viet-Nam does not even broadcast meteorological reports that would facilitate aerial and sea navigation in the Tongking Gulf, South Viet-Nam is represented at every conceivable international gathering, no matter how abstruse: In the space of a few weeks in the spring of 1962 (and this was not an exceptionally busy period), South Vietnamese delegations attended a conference on "Education for Women in Rural Areas," another on the "Conservation of Nature and Natural Resources," a third on "Asian Education," one on "International Limited-Access Highways," a gathering of the World Veterans' Federation, and an "International Meeting on the Sciences of the Sea," while, no doubt because of an error in geography, the South Vietnamese chargé d'affaires in Jakarta was appointed on February 5, 1962, to go to Ethiopia as his country's delegate to the Fourth African Economic Conference. South Viet-Nam, though not a member of the U.N., has bought U.N. bonds to finance operations in the Congo; is on the board of UNESCO; and has also made a cash contribution to the World Campaign Against Hunger.

All this has given South Viet-Nam an international standing of no mean consequence, and the highly personable Mme. Ngo Dinh Nhu must be accorded a large share of the credit for this achievement; there is no better illustration of her ability in personal diplomacy than the reception given her in April, 1962, in Mexico, one of the few American states that still maintain diplomatic relations with Castro, and in the United States in the fall of 1963.

And even though South Viet-Nam may perhaps not receive all the journalistic praise its leadership *thinks* it deserves, it receives nevertheless more praise and less incisive criticism than its performance usually merits. As a day-to-day survey of the non-Communist press shows, very few newspapers are in a position to obtain more than wire-agency news about Viet-Nam, or to comment on it editorially. Even the "liberal press"—*The Washington Post* or the independent *New York Times*—for years reined its editorial temper before finally asking, as *The Times* did in an explosive editorial, whether it was still possible to "Win With Diem." In fact, thanks to an extremely lavish public-relations campaign and an efficient volunteer propaganda organization in the United States, Saigon had very little trouble getting its message before the public.

All this made the vociferous campaign the Ngo Dinh Diem Administration waged against its foreign critics (particularly those who reached the American public) somewhat superfluous, and the "You're-either-for-us-or-you're-a-Communist" theme[4] may well boomerang as it brings back to mind the unhappy era of the great China debates of the late 1940's.

To this tangled situation must be added what the United States viewed as the new irritant of French reinvolvement in Asia. Even before her recognition of the Peking government, on January 31, 1964, France had made clear her intention to regain in the Indochina peninsula a voice commensurate with her stakes in the area. In addition to 17,000 French nationals and an immovable investment of $500 million still remaining there, France also felt a "moral responsibility" for the Cambodians, Laotians, and South Vietnamese whose independence she had underwritten in Geneva in 1954—while the United States had not.

On August 29, 1963, the French Government issued a statement expressing understanding for

> . . . the role [the Vietnamese people] could play in Asia's present situation, for their own progress and to the benefit of international understanding, as soon as they could deploy their activity in independence vis-à-vis the outside, in peace and unity at home, and in concord with their neighbors. . . . any national effort undertaken by Viet-Nam with that aim will find France ready, within the means at its disposal, to enter into cordial cooperation with that country.

In Washington, the phrases "independence vis-à-vis the outside" and "unity at home"—though ostensibly addressed to *both* Viet-Nams—were received as a deliberate slap against American policies in South Viet-Nam and viewed as part of de Gaulle's "hate-America" campaign. President John F. Kennedy took advantage of a special Labor Day interview to reply directly to the French President:

> . . . he doesn't have any forces there or any program of technical assistance, so while these expressions are welcome, the burden is carried, as it usually is, by the United States. . . . we are glad to get counsel, but we would like to get a little more assistance.

Aside from the fact that the President had obviously not been informed of the existence of a large French educational-aid program

(340 teachers in 1962) and extensive French commitments in such activities as land reform, the irritation with what was considered French "interference" was further heightened by France's support for an international conference to guarantee the neutralization of Cambodia, which Prince Norodom Sihanouk had repeatedly demanded. From that moment onward, both the United States and her French ally took their gloves off in the Far East. Joseph Alsop, in several syndicated columns published in September, 1963, adduced precise allegations—unconfirmed by any other source—to the effect that French diplomats were acting as go-betweens in negotiations between Ngo Dinh Nhu and Ho Chi Minh.[5] Paris replied that this charge was "beneath denial." Mme. Nhu later said that her husband had had contacts not with Hanoi, but directly with leaders of the National Liberation Front of South Viet-Nam.[6]

The level of American-French discord rose a notch further when the French at first conspicuously failed to recognize the "Big Minh" junta for almost three weeks and then proposed as new French ambassador to Saigon the French ambassador to Cuba. (Saigon refused to accept him.) And the last straw came when France recognized Communist China, and accompanied that recognition with statements whose gist seemed to be that Paris had written off as lost the cause of a non-neutralized South Viet-Nam. The French press, represented for the first time since the end of the Indochina War by top-notch reporters (all of whom had been expelled by Diem), such as Max Clos, Georges Chaffard, and Jean Lartéguy, fully agreed with that view: "The Americans," said Clos, "are caught in the treadmill [and] must send to Viet-Nam more dollars, more guns, and more men. Like the French ten years before them, they are quagmired [*enlisés*] in the Indochina War."

In Saigon, such statements were branded as yet another example of "colonialist-Communist collusion," and South Vietnamese officers known for their French sympathies were purged as being likely to harbor neutralist feelings. The overthrow of the "Big Minh" junta by General Khanh was resented in Paris as an anti-French move engineered with American help.[7] But inasmuch as France, unlike Britain and Australia, was unwilling to participate in the conflict on America's side even in token form, her leverage on the Vietnamese scene—unless it became as hopelessly stalemated as the Korean War and required an intermediary for negotiation—was almost nil. Although at the end of the SEATO conference, in Manila, in April of 1964, all the powers—except France—pledged "to remain prepared if necessary to take further concrete steps within their respective capabilities in fulfillment of their obligations under the treaty," the problem of Viet-Nam, both North and South, had become almost totally the burden and responsibility of the United States.

Thus we come to the last panel of the Vietnamese triptych—the United States. Whatever America's mistakes in Viet-Nam may have been, it must be said that they were the faults of her virtues. It would be well to remember here Kennan's previously cited observation about

> . . . that curious trait of the American political personality which causes it to appear reprehensible to voice anything less than unlimited optimism about the fortunes of another government one has adopted as a friend and protégé.

Once the adoptions have been made, the missions sent by the United States to investigate conditions in such countries usually return "breathing sweetness and light, confidence and reassurance, about the situation," with the result that a radical deterioration of that situation usually evokes deep shock and righteous indignation. Kennan then speaks of the American

> . . . tendency to view any war in which we might be involved not as a means of achieving limited objectives in the way of changes in a given *status quo* but as a struggle to the death between total virtue and total evil. . . From this there flowed, of course, the congenital reluctance of American statesmen and military leaders to entertain the suggestion that there could be considerations of a political nature that could conceivably take precedence over those of military efficiency and advantage.
> . . . Finally, there was a disposition on the part of the President and his advisers . . . to assume that something had occurred [which transformed] various statesmen from the hard, ruthless, and realistic figures they were into humane, enlightened people . . . guided by a new-found devotion to the principles of democratic self-government and a liberal world order.[8]

The fact that Kennan's statements refer to America's policies toward Russia in 1917 and China in 1945 merely underlines how deep-rooted that streak of idealism and blind good will seems to be in American diplomatic behavior, for every one of those statements fits as a description of the relations between Saigon and Washington from 1954 through 1964. Even in such organizations as SEATO, the United States, until late in 1959, defended tooth and claw against all her other major Western allies her viewpoint that guerrilla activities in South Viet-Nam fell into the "last remnant" category rather than representing a dangerous resurgence of large-scale revolutionary war.

There also seems a repeated determination to neglect the political factors of the insurgency and concentrate on its relatively simpler military factors; the former would of necessity involve a reshaping of the Saigon regime, whereas the latter can be handled by the Pentagon alone and, on the surface at least, may involve little more than additional American troops and arms. This, then, also encourages the "crusade" aspect of the situation: No quarter has to be given, no other consideration entertained but the total extermination of the guerrilla threat. This is the transposition of the "unconditional surrender" concept to revolutionary war, although experience in Kenya, Cyprus, Malaya, Algeria, and the Philippines has shown that "reconversion" of the guerrilla threat through amnesties and other forms of forgiveness can do much to reduce its insurrectional aspects.

Finally, the view that South Viet-Nam's leadership is neither hard nor ruthless, nor realistic enough to know when it has reached the limits of its resistance against American pressure, deprives Washington of any control over a situation in which it is making its potentially most far-reaching commitment since NATO. American reluctance to make its influence felt upon the behavior of a "total protégé," while understandable to a political philosopher like Kennan, is incomprehensible not only to the Communist bloc but also to those of America's friends and allies who hold to the more conventional view of international relations expressed in the old American proverb: "He who pays the orchestra has a right to call the tune."

The successive military juntas that replaced the defunct Diem regime had at least the merit of fully recognizing their own military and political weaknesses; this led to an intimate and harmonious relationship between American and Vietnamese leaders. But with General Khanh, the process of overglorification of the protégé described by Kennan began once more, even though the chances appeared slim for long-term survival of Khanh and his Military Revolutionary Council as a working government. Hence, it was unavoidable that successive purges of military commanders and civilian ministers should be attributed in part to American influence and even desires. *The Washington Post* of April 8, 1964, stated that "American authorities are known to have been encouraging Khanh to secure his position [through purges of potential rivals] because they fear another coup would cause irreparable harm to the anti-communist cause in South Viet-Nam."

A policy of ignoring all aspects of the Vietnamese situation except the insurgency is simply not feasible today—nor was it yesterday, for that matter. Kennan, and with him many anti-Communist Eastern Europeans, hold the United States responsible for the loss of their homelands to Soviet influence, because the United States refused to entertain any thoughts about Soviet postwar motivations and aims as long as the struggle against the common enemy was in progress. And as Kennan points out, it is *while* the danger is great, while the outcome of the struggle is uncertain, that the hard-and-fast commitments must be exacted upon which not only the war, but the peace as well, will be won. This is a hard law of politics, one that the United States has, on the whole, obeyed successfully in her relations with her European allies. American pressure upon Britain, France, and Israel in the Suez affair is an extreme example, but there are many others, of which pressure on France not to build her own atomic striking force was one of the more recent and obvious. And, closer to Viet-Nam, the American role in Laos shows how effective, for ill or for good, pressure can be in the case of countries that are economically or militarily as vulnerable as those in the Southeast Asia area.

Yet until recently, Washington shied away from that approach. In his report on Viet-Nam, made to the Senate Foreign Relations Committee in February, 1963, Senator Mansfield distinguished between "popularly responsible" (freely elected) government and "responsive" government, that is, a regime that may perhaps be authoritarian but keeps the needs of its people in mind. And Senator Mansfield, who earlier expressed wholehearted admiration for the Diem regime, explicitly stated that, "after 7 years of the Republic, South Viet-Nam . . . appears more removed from, rather than closer to" both responsibility as well as responsiveness.[9] Since that was so—and this writer fully shares the Senator's view—then Saigon should have been made aware that there were other approaches to the Vietnamese problem besides the issuance of a blank check on American economic and military aid to the Ngo Dinh Diem Administration. The failure of the post-Diem governments to reach the people is made plain by an official report released on April 1, 1964, which admitted that only 34 per cent of Viet-Nam's villages were government-controlled; 24 per cent were "neutral"; and 42 per cent were outright Viet-Công. And MAAG Viet-Nam's own weekly, *The Observer*, stated on January 24, 1964, that "some 4 to 5 million people support the NLF [National Liberation Front] in varying degrees."

Thus, what hurt the war effort in South Viet-Nam was *not* that the Diem regime was removed but that it was not removed early enough. If the bulk of the peasantry were effectively behind the anti-Communist cause, South Viet-Nam could, up to a point, even afford a somewhat ineffective central administration. But without effective grass-roots support, even the most efficient central regime is only a shell.

Furthermore, despite the Cassandra cries of the pro-Diem diehards today, success in Viet-Nam was nowhere in the cards even *before* the Buddhist crisis—a fact that has to be clearly established lest it fall victim to the new mythology that the deterioration of the situation came about through the "artificially created" Buddhist clashes with Diem and their "exaggerated" reporting in the United States press.[10] The hard fact is that the highest weekly incident rate of the insurgency (1,034) prior to Diem's death was reached in February of 1963, while the first Buddhist clash did not occur until May 8.

To lay to rest once and for all the myth that the whole Buddhist crisis was a "plot" and that Diem never persecuted the Buddhists,[11] here is an eyewitness account by the Australian journalist Denis Warner:

> In *July, 1961*, I went from Saigon to Vinh Binh Province to watch six army and newly trained Civil Guard battalions with artillery and naval support launch a major drive. . . . But the Viet Cong slipped away [as] the artillery blazed fruitlessly into the line of advance. No one saw anything wrong in this. . . .
>
> The following month, after the army had retired, leaving thousands of unhappy peasants behind it, *Buddhist bonzes* petitioned the province chief in Tra Vinh *against the shelling of hamlets and pagodas and to demand the release of their imprisoned fellows.* Some months later their leader, Superior Bonze Son Vong, appeared on the lists of the central committee of the Viet-Cong's National Liberation Front [italics added].[12]

Warner's book, otherwise quite complimentary to Diem and finished long before the 1963 crisis, made this point merely as a matter of reportorial accuracy. In my own doctoral thesis, written in 1953

(i.e., before Diem had returned to Viet-Nam and while the Confucianist Bao-Dai was chief of state and a Buddhist was Prime Minister), I mentioned the fact that Catholic North Vietnamese villages,
using the weapons the French had supplied, had gone on "crusade
raids" against neighboring Buddhist villages. As I have shown in a
preceding chapter, many Vietnamese leaders have displayed religious
intolerance in the past, and Diem was simply no exception.

In addition, the strategic-hamlet program was already in serious
difficulty before the Buddhist outbreaks, but it was not until 1964
that it was finally admitted that the Diem regime had grossly over-
extended the program by using the hamlets as spearheads—rather than
as the end product—of pacification, and that hastily fortified and
poorly defended hamlets were only an invitation to disaster. Over-
exposed hamlets and outposts were evacuated under General Khanh's
rule. The remaining hamlets (rebaptized "New Life Hamlets" afte
Diem's fall) were consolidated and their worst compulsory features
made less harsh.

Finally, after years of official optimism over political and military
progress in South Viet-Nam, Secretary McNamara's gloomy reports
to Congress in January and February, 1964, indicated a departure
from the earlier confidence, and the outlines of the beginning of a
"Viet-Nam debate" began to emerge. Senators Bartlett, Gruening,
Morse, Mansfield, Fulbright, and others began to speak out on the
problem (generally in opposition to the Administration's position).
The respected Harris public-opinion poll brought forth the surprising
information that Viet-Nam had apparently become a matter of
widespread concern, similar to that generated by Korea in 1952. Of
the persons polled, 35 per cent were in favor of South Viet-Nam's
neutralization, 28 per cent were opposed, and the remainder were not
sure; only 26 per cent favored extending the war into North Viet-
Nam if need be, as against 45 per cent opposed. It is not unlikely that
the Korean War, with its inconclusive march into North Korea and
the ensuing bloody stalemate on the original dividing line, left deeper
psychological scars than had been thought.

This makes the finding of a proper political and ideological rationale for South Viet-Nam even more imperative than before. The
empty slogans of "Personalism" have shown their bankruptcy in the
Vietnamese context. Buddhism is a force in the negative sense only:
it will react if directly threatened, but thus far, it tends to become
diffuse again when the pressure lessens. In the absence of a genuine
South Vietnamese rationale, it will be difficult to avoid the psycho-

logical pitfalls the French fell victim to when they tried to prop up the Bao-Dai government—the pro-Western Vietnamese leader is always backed by "foreigners" while the guerrilla (even if his ultimate backers are in Peking or Moscow) is always a native son fighting in an underdog position.

It must be clearly realized in Washington that—regardless of the objective facts of the matter—the United States is held responsible both inside Viet-Nam and abroad for the performance of the Saigon regime. Therefore, unconditional support of that regime in a costly war should have been based on a hardheaded evaluation of what this meant in terms of American world-wide responsibilities, rather than on misplaced sentimentality. With a commendable sense of realism, the Saigon leadership understood this long ago, and its virulent criticisms[13] of certain American policies and of the American press simply mean: "We do not like you or your policies, but we need your help in order to survive and we know that it is to your advantage to see us survive. So, let us have your aid and stop meddling in our affairs." This, by the way, is not a unique reaction on the part of recipients of American aid. Tito's Yugoslavia and Franco's Spain fit that description equally well—but so far, at least, neither of those two regimes has required the services of American troops to keep it in power.

In South Viet-Nam, the net result of that absence of a clear policy in the matter was that the United States was finally placed in the legally uncomfortable position of having to "suggest" the removal of the Diem regime by military *coup d'état* while simultaneously condemning such coups in Honduras and the Dominican Republic. There is absolutely nothing immoral in tying continued support of a given regime to that regime's fulfillment of criteria imposed by the donor.[14] Until something better comes along, national interest will have to remain a major guide of foreign policy. Any other motive risks becoming mired in emotional considerations unlikely to serve anyone's interests.

WHAT NEXT IN VIET-NAM?

The question then remains as to what is likely to develop out of the present conflict—on both sides of the 17th parallel. The present situation permits of several alternatives:

1. Reunification except on Communist terms is out of the ques-

tion as a short-run prospect. Under the present circumstances, it would spell the doom of the southern regime. The stepped-up guerrilla war and increasing American commitment have further contributed to make the estrangement durable. By April, 1964, U.S. casualties had reached 1,000 (including 211 dead), and the rate for the first third of the year was double that for the same period in 1963; American expenditures were running to $700 million annually—the same level as U.S. expenditures at the end of the Indochina War, in 1953–54. The magnitude of the U.S. involvement *precisely to prevent reunification on Communist terms* makes it unlikely that any choice remains to the Vietnamese on both sides of the parallel except to learn to live as separate entities.

2. Economically, the two Viet-Nams are Siamese twins, mutually complementary, i.e., one has the food and the other the minerals. In the past, North Viet-Nam has made several overtures in the economic field, but South Viet-Nam has turned them down by making counterproposals in the political field (e.g., free travel between the zones) that it knew would be unacceptable. Both areas would do well to heed the example of the two Germanies, who keep their economic relations divorced from their political relations. In the economic field, South Viet-Nam may well have the greater leverage and could make offers—if and when the guerrilla threat is at least stabilized—to establish some sort of economic relations on condition that a stop is put to North Vietnamese subversion.

3. Neutralization of South Viet-Nam along the lines of Laos or Cambodia has been repeatedly proposed, and has, of course, met stiff resistance from the Ngo Dinh Diem regime and its successors. The most cogent point that can be made against neutralization is that not even General de Gaulle, its most authoritative Western exponent, has yet come forth with a workable proposal on how to match the neutralization of the south with that of the north. Unilateral neutralization of South Viet-Nam without far-reaching North Vietnamese concessions would indeed be a "sell-out" from which any non-Communist government in Saigon would rightfully recoil. Bilateral neutralization, on the other hand, would run into exactly the same enforcement troubles as the 1954 or 1962 Geneva cease-fires: The Indian-Canadian-Polish Control Commission, which supervises them, has proved incapable of preventing either side (or their foreign friends and allies) from shipping in any kind of war materials and any number of instructors it wants. However, it would be well to remember that the 1954 Geneva cease-fire accord on Viet-Nam does

not refer to neutralization. But Article 19 of the agreement provides that the two Viet-Nams "do not adhere to any military alliance and are not used for the resumption of hostilities or to further an aggressive policy." On February 12, 1964, North Viet-Nam announced that it would like to see the South Vietnamese conflict settled "on the basis of the 1954 Geneva agreements"—a considerable retreat from immediate reunification or unilateral neutralization, and a position that could well provide an approach to a mutually acceptable solution.

4. A subvariant of the above that might be considered further is the creation of a "neutral belt" comprising Burma, Laos, Cambodia, and South Viet-Nam, and guaranteed by the major powers involved. This has been proposed several times by Prince Norodom Sihanouk of Cambodia, but to date, it has met with about as much resistance as unilateral neutralization. Since in the cases of both Laos and Cambodia, neutrality has thus far meant the presence of Western military-training missions without a Communist *quid pro quo*, it seems possible that South Vietnamese neutrality within a larger bloc and with the presence of an American MAAG at 1954 level (685 men) may not be unviable. And American advisers, whose retention would be part of the bargain, would be a deterrent to a sudden resurgence of subversive warfare.

There are those who view such a settlement as "unrealistic" since it removes the "protection" offered by the presence of a large corps of American military advisers. I have discussed the fallacy of that approach elsewhere,[15] but it might bear repeating here: The presence of a relatively large group of American advisers did not prevent the Laos debacle in 1962, and the sight of heavily armed Americans being stymied in South Viet-Nam by lightly armed peasants does perhaps more harm to American prestige than if the Americans were not there at all. The battles fought in the Mekong Delta and the Camau Peninsula during the spring of 1964 are typical of that kind of situation. American strength in the Far East rests ultimately on what it *might* do to North Viet-Nam and Red China—and for that American air and sea power in the area is more than adequate to enforce a cease-fire.

5. The element of danger inherent in *any* type of neutralization is, of course, the *coup de Prague*—the overthrow of the non-Communist regime by bloodless political sleight of hand. That danger is, admittedly, real. But it could just as easily happen tomorrow morning, with 17,000 Americans going about the Vietnamese countryside.

After all, the ARVN has been involved in revolts against the civilian regime, and (as the Algerian War and the First Indochina War showed) it is impossible to fight a revolutionary war without "politicizing" the forces on both sides. While the plotters of November, 1963, and January 30, 1964, were stanchly anti-Communist, the possibility remains that somewhere in this ever-increasing South Vietnamese military machine there is another officer—a South Vietnamese Kong-Lê—who one day may step forward and claim for himself the power other contenders have failed to grasp. And that obscure officer may be anti-American.

6. Much has been said lately, particularly by conservative Republicans, such as Senator Barry Goldwater and former Vice-President Richard Nixon, to the effect that an invasion of North Viet-Nam would be an appropriate response to the problem of insurgency in the south. This could be carried out in three different ways: the infiltration of guerrilla teams; aerial bombardment; or the landing of ground forces. The first alternative has been repeatedly attempted over the past years and has met with dismal failure for reasons that have been indicated in an earlier chapter. Present losses are estimated to run at 85 per cent of the total personnel engaged in such operations. Aerial bombardment, even with conventionally armed bombers, would of course succeed in wiping out all North Viet-Nam's conventional industrial and military targets, but it would probably have little immediate effect on its armed forces. After all, they successfully fought the French for eight years from hidden guerrilla bases and without making use of electric-power plants and railroads. As is, the South Vietnamese Air Force has a difficult time finding suitable targets for militarily effective air strikes even within South Viet-Nam. Lest it be forgotten, the United States Air Force was unable successfully to interdict Communist supply operations in Korea despite the fact that all conventional targets had been effectively destroyed.

The alternative of a massive landing force in North Viet-Nam would amount to "conventionalizing" the whole war, inasmuch as Hanoi would most certainly respond to such an action by committing its regular combat divisions, which have thus far been idle.

Such a course of action would then necessarily entail the commitment of equally large-size American and South Vietnamese units, and this would in all likelihood broaden the war to Korean proportions, with all the military and political consequences this would involve. Further, an operation of that scale against North Viet-Nam would not necessarily mean that the 100,000 guerrillas that are now wreaking havoc in South Viet-Nam would lose much of their combativeness. In other words, that course of action—for all its appealing simplicity—may merely enlarge the area of conflict and vastly increase the casualties on both sides without, however, much improving the situation of South Viet-Nam proper. In addition, its most fearsome consequences might well be the reappearance of Chinese "People's Volunteers" and the facilitation of a Sino-Soviet reconciliation.

7. The "straight zigzag line" that North Viet-Nam has been pursuing under Ho Chi Minh leaves ample room for negotiating a settlement based not on the present position of weakness but on a position of strength created out of a sober-minded appraisal of Communist weaknesses and Western strength in the Far East as a whole.

This alternative is often conveniently confused with "neutralization" followed by a Communist takeover. In actual fact, the U.S. position in the area is sufficiently strong to give pause for reflection to any would-be aggressor (nothing, of course, could prevent a *coup de Prague*, as mentioned in alternative 5). The Seventh Fleet has since 1949 managed to thwart Communist designs for Quemoy and Taiwan, and the encounters between American destroyers and North Vietnamese PT-boats in August, 1964, in the Gulf of Tonkin appear to show that it could well perform similarly in the case of a settlement between the two Viet-Nams.

Further, both internal and external divisions plague North Viet-Nam. There are reputedly differences between Hanoi and the National Liberation Front, the latter apparently being somewhat more amenable to a compromise settlement. Hanoi also can count on only limited support from the Red Chinese. Without the bolstering of Soviet support and supplies, the Chinese have little equipment to donate to the North Vietnamese. Communist China's air force, deprived for several years of Soviet spare parts and new aircraft, is in all likelihood less prepared to engage the United States in 1964 over Viet-Nam than it was in 1950 over Korea.

It would by no means be as easy for Red China to supply, say twenty "People's Volunteers" divisions across the chaotic geography of Yünnan as it was to supply a similar force in Korea from the excellent Manchurian communications network backed up by nearby Soviet supply points.

In addition to the incertitude as to the effectiveness of Chinese aid, there is the 2,000-year-old distrust in Viet-Nam of everything Chinese. The North Vietnamese, in particular, having lived through one Chinese occupation in 1945–46, do not look with particular fondness upon the prospect of another Chinese invasion merely for the sake of proving to Washington and Saigon that they are not "paper tigers" and that Mao's policy of liberation wars is better than Khrushchev's policy of peaceful coexistence.

In short, Hanoi cannot really afford a total victory in South Viet-Nam if the price is total destruction of its own industrial and political base. It is such considerations that might eventually lead Hanoi to settle for far less than it has intended; and to stick to the bargain, once it is made.

The United States has yet another card to play. It is largely up to the United States whether to push North Viet-Nam into the arms of the Chinese, or to allow it to retain or even enhance its present "straight zigzag line." If trade were normalized between the two Viet-Nams—so that food and rubber produced in the south could travel to the north, and minerals and manufactured goods produced in the north were sent to the south—Hanoi might then be less dependent on China and in a better position to follow a course of national self-determination within the Communist bloc. Only Washington can make this possible.

Considering the state of Sino-Soviet relations, it might just be worth Moscow's while not to oppose American attempts at stabilizing the situation in Viet-Nam.

All this should not be construed to mean that Hanoi can simply be bullied into submission and into abandoning the National Liberation Front. The non-Communist regime in Saigon will have to come up with policies and men willing to fulfill popular aspirations,[16] or all attempts at the military salvation of South Viet-Nam will remain doomed to failure. As of mid-1964, that regime still seems to be concerned with the "streamlining" of administrative procedures, regardless of the fact that further concentration of governmental powers could hardly be construed as an increase in popular responsiveness.

8. In light of the character the Diem regime displayed—autocratic, arrogant, dogmatic, unwilling to take advice[17] and fiercely resisting any suggestion for real reform—its successors now must prove to their fellow-citizens that more has taken place in Saigon than a mere change of faces. *For the character of the enemy and of the war has not changed:* Popular support remains as essential an ingredient of victory as it was yesterday, no matter what the technologists of counterinsurgency may say. But peace, it must be clearly realized, can be found only in Hanoi. To refuse to face the fact that Hanoi will have to be talked to, sooner or later no matter what the military outcome of the insurgency, is as unrealistic as to have wished to "end" the Korean War by a unilateral proclamation of a cease-fire,

Appendixes

Notes

Bibliography

Index

Appendix I

TEXT OF THE NORTH VIETNAMESE CONSTITUTION OF 1960

Preamble

Viet-Nam is a single entity from Lang-Son to Camau.

The Vietnamese people, throughout their thousands of years of history, have been an industrious working people who have struggled unremittingly and heroically to build their country and to defend the independence of their Fatherland.

Throughout more than eighty years of French colonial rule and five years of occupation by the Japanese fascists, the Vietnamese people consistently united and struggled against domination by the foreign aggressors in order to liberate their country.

Note: The texts of these Appendixes, with the exception of Appendix IV, are official translations. The text of Appendix IV is an unofficial translation from the French. In all cases, spelling and punctuation have been altered where necessary for stylistic consistency.

From 1930 onward, under the leadership of the Indochinese Communist Party—now the Viet-Nam Lao-Dong Party—the Vietnamese revolution advanced into a new stage. The persistent struggle, full of hardship and heroic sacrifice, of our people against imperialist and feudal domination won great success: the August Revolution was victorious; the Democratic Republic of Viet-Nam was founded; and, on September 2, 1945, President Ho Chi Minh proclaimed Viet-Nam's independence to the people and the world. For the first time in their history, the Vietnamese people had founded an independent and democratic Viet-Nam.

On January 6, 1946, the entire Vietnamese people, from north to south, enthusiastically took part in the first general elections to the National Assembly. The National Assembly adopted the first Constitution, which clearly recorded the great successes of our people and highlighted the determination of the entire nation to safeguard the independence and unity of the Fatherland and to defend the freedom and democratic rights of the people.

However, the French imperialists, assisted by the U.S. imperialists, again provoked an aggressive war in an attempt to seize our country and once more enslave our people. Under the leadership of the Vietnamese working-class party and the government of the Democratic Republic of Viet-Nam, our entire people, united as one, rose to fight the aggressors and save their country. At the same time, our people carried out land-rent reduction and land reform with the aim of overthrowing the landlord class and restoring the land to those who till it. The long, hard, and extremely heroic war of resistance of the Vietnamese people, which enjoyed the sympathy and support of the socialist countries, of the oppressed peoples, and of friends of peace throughout the world, won glorious victory. With the Dien Bien Phu victory, the Vietnamese people defeated the French imperialists and the U.S. interventionists. The 1954 Geneva Agreements were concluded; peace was restored in Indochina on the basis of recognition of the independence, sovereignty, unity, and territorial integrity of our country.

This major success of the Vietnamese people was also a common success of the liberation movement of the oppressed peoples, of the world front of peace, and of the socialist camp.

Since the restoration of peace in completely liberated North Viet-Nam, our people have carried through the national people's democratic revolution. But the South is still under the rule of the imperialists and feudalists; our country is still temporarily divided into two zones.

The Vietnamese revolution has moved into a new position. Our people must endeavor to consolidate the North, taking it toward socialism, and to carry on the struggle for peaceful reunification of the country and completion of the tasks of the national people's democratic revolution throughout the country.

In the last few years, our people in the North have achieved many big successes in economic rehabilitation and cultural development. At present, socialist transformation and construction are being successfully carried out.

Meanwhile, in the South, the U.S. imperialists and their henchmen have been savagely repressing the patriotic movement of our people. They have been strengthening military forces and carrying out their scheme of turning the southern part of our country into a colony and military base for their war preparations. They have resorted to all possible means to sabotage the Geneva Agreements and undermine the cause of Viet-Nam's reunification. But our southern compatriots have constantly struggled heroically and refused to submit to them. The people throughout the country, united as one, are holding aloft the banner of peace, national unity, independence, and democracy, resolved to march forward and win final victory. The cause of the peaceful reunification of the Fatherland will certainly be victorious.

In the new stage of the revolution, our National Assembly must amend the 1946 Constitution in order to adapt it to the new situation and tasks.

The new Constitution clearly records the great revolutionary gains in the recent past and clearly indicates the goal of struggle of our people in the new stage.

Our state is a people's democratic state based on the alliance between the workers and peasants and led by the working class. The new Constitution defines the political, economic, and social system of our country, the relations of equality and mutual assistance among the various nationalities in our country, and provides for the taking of the North toward socialism, the constant improvement of the material and cultural life of the people, and the building of a stable and strong North Viet-Nam as a basis for the struggle for the peaceful reunification of the country.

The new Constitution defines the responsibilities and powers of the state organs and the rights and duties of citizens with a view to developing the great creative potentialities of our people in national construction and in the reunification and defense of the Fatherland.

The new Constitution is a genuinely democratic Constitution. It is a force inspiring the people throughout our country to march forward enthusiastically and win new successes. Our people are resolved to develop further their patriotism, their tradition of solidarity, their determination to struggle, and their ardor in work. Our people are resolved to strengthen further solidarity and unity of mind with the brother countries in the socialist camp headed by the great Soviet Union and to strengthen solidarity with the peoples of Asia and Africa and peace-loving people all over the world.

Under the clear-sighted leadership of the Viet-Nam Lao-Dong Party, the government of the Democratic Republic of Viet-Nam, and President

Ho Chi Minh, our entire people, broadly united within the National United Front, will surely win glorious success in the building of socialism in North Viet-Nam and the struggle for national reunification. Our people will surely be successful in building a peaceful, unified, independent, democratic, prosperous, and strong Viet-Nam, making a worthy contribution to the safeguarding of peace in Southeast Asia and the world.

CHAPTER I. THE DEMOCRATIC REPUBLIC OF VIET-NAM

Article 1. The territory of Viet-Nam is a single, indivisible whole from north to south.

Article 2. The Democratic Republic of Viet-Nam, established and consolidated as a result of victories won by the Vietnamese people in the glorious August Revolution and the heroic Resistance, is a people's democratic state.

Article 3. The Democratic Republic of Viet-Nam is a single multinational state.

All the nationalities living on Vietnamese territory are equal in rights and duties. The state has the duty to maintain and develop the solidarity between the various nationalities. All acts of discrimination against, or oppression of, any nationality, all actions which undermine the unity of the nationalities are strictly prohibited.

All nationalities have the right to preserve or reform their own customs and habits, to use their spoken and written languages, and to develop their own national culture.

Autonomous zones may be established in areas where people of national minorities live in compact communities. Such autonomous zones are inalienable parts of the Democratic Republic of Viet-Nam.

The state strives to help the national minorities to make rapid progress and to keep pace with the general economic and cultural advance.

Article 4. All power in the Democratic Republic of Viet-Nam belongs to the people. The people exercise power through the National Assembly and the People's Councils, at all levels elected by the people and responsible to the people.

The National Assembly, the People's Councils at all levels, and the other organs of state practice democratic centralism.

Article 5. Election of deputies to the National Assembly and the People's Councils at all levels proceeds on the principle of universal, equal, direct, and secret suffrage.

Deputies to the National Assembly and People's Councils at all levels may be recalled by their constituent before their term of office expires if they show themselves to be unworthy of the confidence of the people.

Article 6. All organs of state must rely on the people, maintain close contact with them, heed their opinions, and accept their supervision.

All personnel of organs of state must be loyal to the people's democratic system, observe the Constitution and the law, and wholeheartedly serve the people.

Article 7. The state strictly prohibits and punishes all acts of treason, opposition to the people's democratic system, or opposition to the reunification of the Fatherland.

Article 8. The armed forces of the Democratic Republic of Viet-Nam belong to the people; their duty is to safeguard the gains of the revolution and defend the independence, sovereignty, territorial integrity, and security of the Fatherland, and the freedom, happiness, and peaceful labor of the people.

CHAPTER II. ECONOMIC AND SOCIAL SYSTEM

Article 9. The Democratic Republic of Viet-Nam is advancing step by step from people's democracy to socialism by developing and transforming the national economy along socialist lines, transforming its backward economy into a socialist economy with modern industry and agriculture and an advanced science and technology.

The fundamental aim of the economic policy of the Democratic Republic of Viet-Nam is continuously to develop the productive forces with the aim of raising the material and cultural standards of the people.

Article 10. The state leads all economic activities according to a unified plan.

The state relies on the organs of state, trade-union organizations, cooperatives, and other organizations of the working people to elaborate and carry out its economic plans.

Article 11. In the Democratic Republic of Viet-Nam, during the present period of transition to socialism, the main forms of ownership of means of production are: state ownership, that is, ownership by the whole people; cooperative ownership, that is, collective ownership by the working masses; ownership by individual working people; and ownership by the national capitalists.

Article 12. The state sector of the economy, which is a form of ownership by the whole people, plays the leading role in the national economy. The state ensures priority for its development.

All mineral resources and waters and all forests, undeveloped land, and other resources defined by law as belonging to the state are the property of the whole people.

Article 13. The cooperative sector of the economy is a form of collective ownership by the working masses.

The state especially encourages, guides, and helps the development of the cooperative sector of the economy.

Article 14. The state by law protects the right of peasants to own land and other means of production.

The state actively guides and helps the peasants to improve farming methods and increase production and encourages them to organize producers', supply-and-marketing, and credit cooperatives, in accordance with the principle of voluntariness.

Article 15. The state by law protects the right of handicraftsmen and other individual working people to own means of production.

The state actively guides and helps handicraftsmen and other individual working people to improve their enterprises and encourages them to organize producers' and supply-and-marketing cooperatives, in accordance with the principle of voluntariness.

Article 16. The state by law protects the right of national capitalists to own means of production and other capital.

The state actively guides the national capitalists in carrying out activities beneficial to national welfare and the people's livelihood, contributing to the development of the national economy in accordance with the economic plan of the state. The state encourages and guides the national capitalists in following the path of socialist transformation through the form of joint state-private enterprises and other forms of transformation.

Article 17. The state strictly prohibits the use of private property to disrupt the economic life of society or to undermine the economic plan of the state.

Article 18. The state protects the right of citizens to possess lawfully earned incomes, savings, houses, and other private means of life.

Article 19. The state by law protects the right of citizens to inherit private property.

Article 20. Only when such action is necessary in the public interest does the state repurchase, requisition, or nationalize, with appropriate compensation, means of production in city or countryside, within the limits and in the conditions defined by law.

Article 21. Labor is the basis on which the people develop the national economy and raise their material and cultural standards.

Labor is a duty and a matter of honor for every citizen.

The state encourages the creativeness and the enthusiasm in labor of workers by hand and brain.

CHAPTER III. FUNDAMENTAL RIGHTS AND DUTIES OF CITIZENS

Article 22. Citizens of the Democratic Republic of Viet-Nam are equal before the law.

Article 23. Citizens of the Democratic Republic of Viet-Nam who have reached the age of eighteen have the right to vote, and those who have reached the age of twenty-one have the right to stand for election, whatever their nationality, race, sex, social origin, religion, belief, property status, education, occupation, or length of residence, except insane persons and persons deprived by a court or by law of the right to vote and stand for election.

Citizens serving in the army have the right to vote and stand for election.

Article 24. Women in the Democratic Republic of Viet-Nam enjoy equal rights with men in all spheres of political, economic, cultural, social, and domestic life.

For equal work, women enjoy equal pay with men. The state ensures that women workers and office employees have fully paid periods of leave before and after childbirth.

The state protects the mother and child and ensures the development of maternity hospitals, crèches, and kindergartens.

The state protects marriage and the family.

Article 25. Citizens of the Democratic Republic of Viet-Nam enjoy freedom of speech, freedom of the press, freedom of assembly, freedom of association, and freedom of demonstration. The state guarantees all necessary material conditions for citizens to enjoy these freedoms.

Article 26. Citizens of the Democratic Republic of Viet-Nam enjoy freedom of religious belief; they may practice or not practice a religion.

Article 27. Freedom of the person of citizens of the Democratic Republic of Viet-Nam is guaranteed. No citizen may be arrested except by decision of a people's court or with the sanction of a People's Organ of Control.

Article 28. The law guarantees the inviolability of the homes of the citizens of the Democratic Republic of Viet-Nam and inviolability of mail.

Citizens of the Democratic Republic of Viet-Nam enjoy freedom of residence and movement.

Article 29. Citizens of the Democratic Republic of Viet-Nam have the right to complain of and denounce to any organ of state any servant of the state for transgression of law. These complaints and denunciations must be investigated and dealt with rapidly. People suffering loss owing to infringement by servants of the state of their rights as citizens are entitled to compensation.

Article 30. Citizens of the Democratic Republic of Viet-Nam have the right to work. To guarantee to citizens enjoyment of this right, the state, by planned development of the national economy, gradually creates more employment and better working conditions and wages.

Article 31. Working people have the right to rest. To guarantee to working people enjoyment of this right, the state prescribes working hours and holidays for workers and office employees and gradually expands material facilities to enable working people to rest and build up their health.

Article 32. Working people have the right to material assistance in old age and in case of illness or disability. To guarantee to working people enjoyment of this right, the state gradually expands social insurance, social assistance, and public health service.

Article 33. Citizens of the Democratic Republic of Viet-Nam have the right to education. To guarantee the citizens enjoyment of this right, the state enforces step by step the system of compulsory education, gradually extends the various types of schools and other cultural institutions, extends the various forms of supplementary cultural, technical, and professional education in public services and factories and in other organizations in town and countryside.

Article 34. Citizens of the Democratic Republic of Viet-Nam enjoy freedom to engage in scientific research, literary and artistic creation, and other cultural pursuits. The state encourages and assists creative work in science, literature, art and other cultural pursuits.

Article 35. The state pays special attention to the moral, intellectual, and physical education of youth.

Article 36. The state protects the proper rights and interests of Vietnamese resident abroad.

Article 37. The Democratic Republic of Viet-Nam grants the right of asylum to any foreign national persecuted for demanding freedom, for supporting a just cause, for taking part in the peace movement, or for engaging in scientific activity.

Article 38. The state forbids any person to use democratic freedoms to the detriment of the interests of the state and of the people.

Article 39. Citizens of the Democratic Republic of Viet-Nam must abide by the Constitution and the law, uphold discipline at work, keep public order, and respect social ethics.

Article 40. The public property of the Democratic Republic of Viet-Nam is sacred and inviolable. It is the duty of every citizen to respect and protect public property.

Article 41. Citizens of the Democratic Republic of Viet-Nam have the duty to pay taxes according to law.

Article 42. To defend the Fatherland is the most sacred and noble duty of citizens of the Democratic Republic of Viet-Nam.

It is the duty of citizens to perform military service in order to defend the Fatherland.

CHAPTER IV. THE NATIONAL ASSEMBLY

Article 43. The National Assembly is the highest organ of state authority in the Democratic Republic of Viet-Nam.

Article 44. The National Assembly is the only legislative authority of the Democratic Republic of Viet-Nam.

Article 45. The term of office of the National Assembly is four years.

A new National Assembly must be elected two months before the term of office of the sitting National Assembly expires.

The electoral procedure and the number of Deputies are prescribed by law.

In the event of war or other exceptional circumstances, the National Assembly may decide to prolong its term of office and take necessary measures to ensure its activities and those of Deputies.

Article 46. The National Assembly meets twice a year, convened by its Standing Committee. The Standing Committee of the National Assembly may convene extraordinary sessions of the National Assembly according to its decisions, or at the request of the Council of Ministers or of a minimum of one-third of the total number of Deputies.

The Standing Committee of the National Assembly must convene the new National Assembly not later than two months after the elections.

Article 47. When the National Assembly meets, it elects a Presidium to conduct its sittings.

Article 48. Laws and other decisions of the National Assembly require a simple majority vote of all Deputies to the National Assembly, except for the case specified in Article 112 of the Constitution.

Article 49. Laws must be promulgated not later than fifteen days after their adoption by the National Assembly.

Article 50. The National Assembly exercises the following functions:

1. to enact and amend the Constitution;

2. to enact laws;

3. to supervise the enforcement of the Constitution;

4. to elect the President and Vice-President of the Democratic Republic of Viet-Nam;

5. to choose the Prime Minister of the government upon the recommendation of the President of the Democratic Republic of Viet-Nam and the Vice-Premiers and the other component members of the Council of Ministers upon the recommendation of the Prime Minister;

6. to choose the Vice-President and the other component members of the National Defense Council upon the recommendation of the President of the Democratic Republic of Viet-Nam;

7. to elect the President of the Supreme People's Court;

8. to elect the Procurator General of the Supreme People's Organ of Control;

9. to remove the President and Vice-President of the Democratic Republic of Viet-Nam, the Prime Minister, the Vice-Premiers and the other component members of the National Defense Council, the President of the Supreme People's Court, and the Procurator General of the Supreme People's Organ of Control;

10. to decide upon national economic plans;

11. to examine and approve the state budget and the financial report;

12. to fix taxes;

13. to decide the establishment and abolition of ministries and of organs having a status equal to that of a ministry;

14. to ratify the boundaries of provinces, autonomous regions, and municipalities directly under the central authority;

15. to decide on general amnesties;

16. to decide on questions of war and peace; and

17. to exercise other necessary functions as defined by the National Assembly.

Article 51. The Standing Committee of the National Assembly is a permanent executive body of the National Assembly and is elected by it. The Standing Committee is composed of: the Chairman; the Vice-Chairmen; the Secretary General; and other members.

Article 52. The Standing Committee of the National Assembly is responsible to the National Assembly and reports to it.

The National Assembly has power to remove any member of the Standing Committee.

Article 53. The Standing Committee of the National Assembly exercises the following functions:

1. to proclaim and conduct the election of Deputies to the National Assembly;

2. to convene the National Assembly;

3. to interpret the laws;

4. to enact decrees;

5. to decide on referenda;

6. to supervise the work of the Council of Ministers, the Supreme People's Court, and the Supreme People's Organ of Control;

7. to revise or annul decisions, orders, and directives of the Council of Ministers which contravene the Constitution, laws, and decrees; to revise or annul inappropriate decisions issued by the People's Councils of provinces, autonomous regions, and municipalities directly under the central authority; and to dissolve the above-mentioned People's Councils if they do serious harm to the people's interests;

8. to decide on the appointment or removal of the Vice-Premiers and the other component members of the Council of Ministers when the National Assembly is not in session;

9. to appoint or remove the vice-presidents and judges of the Supreme People's Court;

10. to appoint or remove the deputy procurators general and procurators of the Supreme People's Organ of Control;

11. to decide on the appointment or removal of plenipotentiary diplomatic representatives of the Democratic Republic of Viet-Nam to foreign states;

12. to decide on the ratification or abrogation of treaties concluded with foreign states, except when the Standing Committee considers it necessary to refer such ratification or abrogation to the National Assembly for decision;

13. to decide on military, diplomatic, and other grades and ranks;

14. to decide on the granting of pardons;

15. to institute and decide on the award of state orders, medals, and titles of honor;

16. to decide, when the National Assembly is not in session, on the proclamation of a state of war in the event of armed attack on the country;

17. to decide on general or partial mobilization;

18. to decide on the enforcement of martial law throughout the country or in certain areas.

Apart from these functions, the National Assembly may, when necessary, invest the Standing Committee with other functions.

Article 54. The decisions of the Standing Committee of the National Assembly must be approved by a simple majority vote of its members.

Article 55. The Standing Committee of the National Assembly exercises its functions until a new Standing Committee is elected by the succeeding National Assembly.

Article 56. The National Assembly elects a Commission for examination of the qualifications of Deputies to the National Assembly. The National Assembly will base itself on the reports of this Commission in deciding on the recognition of the qualifications of Deputies.

Article 57. The National Assembly establishes a Law-drafting Committee, a Planning Board and Budget Commission, and other committees which the National Assembly deems necessary to assist the National Assembly and its Standing Committee.

Article 58. The National Assembly or its Standing Committee, when the National Assembly is not in session, may, if necessary, appoint commissions of inquiry to investigate specific questions.

All organs of state, people's organizations, and citizens concerned are required to supply all information necessary to these commissions when they conduct investigations.

Article 59. Deputies to the National Assembly have the right to address questions to the Council of Ministers and to organs under the authority of the Council of Ministers.

The organs to which questions are put are obliged to answer within a period of five days. In the event of investigations having to be carried out, the answer must be given within one month.

Article 60. No Deputy to the National Assembly may be arrested or tried without the consent of the National Assembly or, when the National Assembly is not in session, of its Standing Committee.

CHAPTER V. THE PRESIDENT OF THE DEMOCRATIC REPUBLIC OF VIET-NAM

Article 61. The President of the Democratic Republic of Viet-Nam is the representative of the Democratic Republic of Viet-Nam in internal affairs as well as in foreign relations.

Article 62. The President of the Democratic Republic of Viet-Nam is elected by the National Assembly of the Democratic Republic of Viet-Nam. Any citizen of the Democratic Republic of Viet-Nam who has reached the age of thirty-five is eligible to stand for election as President of the Democratic Republic of Viet-Nam.

The term of office of the President of the Democratic Republic of Viet-Nam corresponds to that of the National Assembly.

Article 63. The President of the Democratic Republic of Viet-Nam, in pursuance of decisions of the National Assembly or its Standing Committee, promulgates laws and decrees; appoints or removes the Prime Minister, the Vice-Premiers, and the other component members of the Council of Ministers; appoints or removes the Vice-President and the other component members of the National Defense Council; promulgates general amnesties and grants pardons; confers orders, medals, and titles of honor of the state; proclaims a state of war; orders general or partial mobilization; and proclaims martial law.

Article 64. The President of the Democratic Republic of Viet-Nam receives plenipotentiary representatives of foreign states; and, in pursuance of decisions of the National Assembly or its Standing Committee, ratifies treaties concluded with foreign states, appoints or recalls plenipotentiary representatives of the Democratic Republic of Viet-Nam to foreign states.

Article 65. The President of the Democratic Republic of Viet-Nam is the Supreme Commander of the armed forces of the country and is President of the National Defense Council.

Article 66. The President of the Democratic Republic of Viet-Nam has power, when necessary, to attend and preside over the meetings of the Council of Ministers.

Article 67. The President of the Democratic Republic of Viet-Nam, when necessary, convenes and presides over the Special Political Conference.

The Special Political Conference is composed of the President and Vice-President of the Democratic Republic of Viet-Nam, the Chairman of the Standing Committee of the National Assembly, the Prime Minister, and other persons concerned.

The Special Political Conference examines major problems of the country. The President of the Democratic Republic of Viet-Nam submits the view of this conference to the National Assembly, the Standing Committee of the National Assembly, the Council of Ministers, or other bodies concerned for their consideration and decision.

Article 68. The Vice-President of the Democratic Republic of Viet-Nam assists the President in his duties. The Vice-President may exercise such part of the functions of the President as the President may entrust to him.

The provisions governing the election and term of office of the President apply also to the election and term of office of the Vice-President.

Article 69. The President and Vice-President of the Democratic Republic of Viet-Nam exercise their functions until the new President and Vice-President take office.

Article 70. Should the President of the Democratic Republic of Viet-Nam be incapacitated for a prolonged period by reason of ill health, the functions of President shall be exercised by the Vice-President.

Should the office of President of the Democratic Republic of Viet-Nam fall vacant, the Vice-President shall fulfill the functions of President until the election of a new President.

CHAPTER VI. THE COUNCIL OF MINISTERS

Article 71. The Council of Ministers is the executive organ of the highest organ of state authority; it is the highest administrative organ of the Democratic Republic of Viet-Nam.

The Council of Ministers is responsible to the National Assembly and reports to it or, when the National Assembly is not in session, to the Standing Committee of the National Assembly.

Article 72. The Council of Ministers is composed of: the Prime Minister; the Vice-Premiers; the Ministers; the Heads of State Commissions; and the Director-General of the National Bank.

The organization of the Council of Ministers is determined by law.

Article 73. Basing itself on the Constitution, laws, and decrees, the Council of Ministers formulates administrative measures, issues decisions and orders, and verifies their execution.

Article 74. The Council of Ministers exercises the following functions:

1. to submit draft laws, draft decrees, and other drafts to the National Assembly and the Standing Committee of the National Assembly;

2. to centralize the leadership of the ministries and organs of state under the authority of the Council of Ministers;

3. to centralize the leadership of the administrative committees at all levels;

4. to revise or annul inappropriate decisions of the ministries, and organs of state under the authority of the Council of Ministers; to revise or annul inappropriate decisions of administrative organs at all levels;

5. to suspend the execution of inappropriate decisions of the People's

Councils of provinces, autonomous zones, and municipalities directly under the central authority and recommend to the Standing Committee of the National Assembly revision or annulment of these decisions;

6. to put into effect the national economic plans and the provisions of the state budget;

7. to control home and foreign trade;

8. to direct cultural and social work;

9. to safeguard the interests of the state, to maintain public order, and to protect the rights and interests of citizens;

10. to lead the building of the armed forces of the state;

11. to direct the conduct of external relations;

12. to administer affairs concerning the nationalities;

13. to ratify territorial boundaries of administrative areas below the provincial level;

14. to carry out the order of mobilization, martial law, and all other necessary measures to defend the country;

15. to appoint and remove personnel of organs of state, according to provisions of law.

Besides these functions, the National Assembly or its Standing Committee may invest the Council of Ministers with other functions.

Article 75. The Prime Minister presides over the meetings of the Council of Ministers and leads its work. The Vice-Premiers assist the Prime Minister in his work and may replace him in the event of his absence.

Article 76. The Ministers and Heads of organs of state under the authority of the Council of Ministers lead the work of their respective departments under the unified leadership of the Council of Ministers.

Within the jurisdiction of their respective departments, in accordance with and in pursuance of laws and decrees, decisions, orders, and directives of the Council of Ministers, they may issue orders and directives and supervise their execution.

Article 77. In the discharge of their functions, members of the Council of Ministers bear responsibility before the law for such acts as contravene the Constitution and the law and do harm to the state or the people.

CHAPTER VII. THE LOCAL PEOPLE'S COUNCILS AND THE LOCAL ADMINISTRATIVE COMMITTEES AT ALL LEVELS

Article 78. The administrative division of the Democratic Republic of Viet-Nam is as follows:

The country is divided into provinces, autonomous zones, and municipalities directly under the central authority.

Provinces are divided into districts, cities, and towns.

Districts are divided into villages and townlets.

Administrative units in autonomous zones will be determined by law.

Article 79. People's Councils and administrative committees are established in all the above mentioned administrative units.

Cities may be divided into wards with a ward People's Council and administrative committee, according to decision of the Council of Ministers.

Article 80. Local People's Councils at all levels are the organs of state authority in their respective areas.

People's Councils at all levels are elected by the local people and are responsible to them.

Article 81. The term of office of the People's Councils of provinces, autonomous zones, and municipalities directly under the central authority is three years.

The term of office of the People's Councils of districts, cities, towns, villages, townlets, and wards is two years.

The term of office of the People's Councils at all levels in autonomous zones is fixed by law.

The electoral procedure and the number of representatives to People's Councils at all levels are determined by law.

Article 82. The People's Councils ensure observance and execution of state laws in their respective areas; draw up plans for local economic and cultural development and public works; examine and approve local budgets and financial reports; maintain public order and security in their areas; protect public property, protect the rights of citizens, and safeguard the equal rights of the nationalities.

Article 83. The local People's Councils issue decisions for execution in their areas on the basis of state law and of decisions taken at higher levels.

Article 84. The People's Councils elect administrative committees and have power to recall members of administrative committees.

The People's Councils elect and have power to recall the presidents of the People's Courts at corresponding levels.

Article 85. The People's Councils have power to revise or annul inappropriate decisions issued by administrative committees at corresponding levels, as well as inappropriate decisions issued by People's Councils and administrative committees at the next lower level.

Article 86. The People's Councils at all levels have power to dissolve People's Councils at the next lower level when the latter do serious harm to the people's interests. Such a decision must be ratified by the People's Council at the next higher level prior to its application. A decision of dissolution issued by the People's Councils of provinces, autonomous zones, and municipalities directly under the central authority is subject to endorsement by the Standing Committee of the National Assembly prior to its application.

Article 87. The administrative committees at all levels are the executive organs of the local People's Councils at corresponding levels and are the administrative organs of state in their respective areas.

Article 88. The administrative committee is composed of President, one or several Vice-Presidents, a secretary, and a number of committee members.

The term of office of an administrative committee is the same as that of the People's Council which elected it.

On the expiration of the term of office of the People's Council or in the event of its dissolution, the administrative committee continues to exercise the above functions until a new People's Council has elected a new administrative committee.

The organization of administrative committees at all levels is determined by law.

Article 89. The administrative committees at all levels direct the administrative work in their respective areas, carry out the decisions issued by People's Councils at corresponding levels and the decisions and orders issued by organs of state at higher levels.

The administrative committees at all levels, within the limits of the authority prescribed by law, issue decisions and orders and verify their execution.

Article 90. The administrative committees at all levels direct the wc of their subordinate departments and the work of administrative committees at lower levels.

The administrative committees at all levels have power to revise or annul inappropriate decisions of their subordinate departments and of administrative committees at lower levels.

The administrative committees at all levels have power to suspend the carrying out of inappropriate decisions of People's Councils at the next lower level, and to propose to People's Councils at corresponding levels the revision or annulment of such decisions.

Article 91. The administrative committees at all levels are responsible to the People's Councils at corresponding levels and to the administrative organs of state at the next higher level, and shall report to these bodies.

The administrative committees at all levels are placed under the leadership of the administrative committees at the next higher level, and under the unified leadership of the Council of Ministers.

The People's Councils and Administrative Committees in Autonomous Zones

Article 92. The organization of the People's Councils and administrative committees in autonomous zones are based on the basic principles governing the organization of the People's Councils and administrative committees at all levels, as defined above.

Article 93. In the autonomous zones where a number of nationalities live together, they are entitled to appropriate representation on the People's Councils.

Article 94. The People's Councils and the administrative committees in autonomous zones work out plans for economic and cultural development suited to the local conditions, administer their local finances, and organize their local self-defense and public security force within the limits of autonomy prescribed by law.

Article 95. The People's Councils in autonomous zones may, within the limits of autonomy, and basing themselves on the political, economic, and cultural characteristics of the nationalities in their respective areas, draw up statutes governing the exercise of autonomy and regulations concerning particular problems to be put into effect in their areas, after endorsement by the Standing Committee of the National Assembly.

Article 96. The higher organs of state must ensure that the People's Councils and administrative committees in the autonomous zones exercise their right to autonomy and assist the minority peoples in the full promotion of their political, economic, and cultural development.

CHAPTER VIII. THE PEOPLE'S COURTS AND THE PEOPLE'S ORGANS OF CONTROL

The People's Courts

Article 97. The Supreme People's Court of the Democratic Republic of Viet-Nam, the local People's Courts, and the military courts are judicial organs of the Democratic Republic of Viet-Nam.

Special courts may be set up by the National Assembly in certain cases.

Article 98. The system of elected judges according to the procedure prescribed by law applies to the People's Courts.

The term of office of the President of the Supreme People's Court is five years.

The organization of the People's Courts is determined by law.

Article 99. Judicial proceedings in the People's Courts must be carried out with the participation of people's assessors according to law. In administering justice, people's assessors enjoy the same powers as judges.

Article 100. In administering justice, the People's Courts are independent and subject only to law.

Article 101. Cases in the People's Courts are heard in public unless otherwise provided for by law.

The right to defense is guaranteed the accused.

Article 102. The People's Courts ensure that all citizens of the Democratic Republic of Viet-Nam belonging to national minorities may use their own spoken and written languages in court proceedings.

Article 103. The Supreme People's Court is the highest judicial organ of the Democratic Republic of Viet-Nam.

The Supreme People's Court supervises the judicial work of local People's Courts, military courts, and special courts.

Article 104. The Supreme People's Court is responsible to the National Assembly and reports to it or, when the National Assembly is not in session, to its Standing Committee. The local People's Courts are responsible to the local People's Councils at corresponding levels and report to them.

The People's Organs of Control

Article 105. The Supreme People's Organ of Control of the Democratic Republic of Viet-Nam controls the observance of the law by all departments of the Council of Ministers, all local organs of state, persons working in organs of state, and all citizens.

Local organs of the People's Organ of Control and military organs of control exercise control authority within the limits prescribed by law.

Article 106. The term of office of the Procurator General of the Supreme People's Organ of Control is five years.

The organization of the People's Organs of Control is determined by law.

Article 107. The People's Organs of Control at all levels work only under the leadership of their higher control organs and the unified leadership of the Supreme People's Organ of Control.

Article 108. The Supreme People's Organ of Control is responsible to the National Assembly and reports to it or, when the National Assembly is not in session, to its Standing Committee.

CHAPTER IX. NATIONAL FLAG, NATIONAL EMBLEM, CAPITAL

Article 109. The national flag of the Democratic Republic of Viet-Nam is a red flag with a five-pointed gold star in the middle.

Article 110. The national emblem of the Democratic Republic of Viet-Nam is round in shape, has a red ground with ears of rice framing a five-pointed gold star in the middle and with a cogwheel and the words "Democratic Republic of Viet-Nam" at the base.

Article 111. The capital of the Democratic Republic of Viet-Nam is Hanoi.

CHAPTER X. AMENDMENT OF THE CONSTITUTION

Article 112. Only the National Assembly has power to revise the Constitution. Amendments to the Constitution require a two-thirds majority vote of all Deputies to the National Assembly.

Appendix II

TEXT OF THE SOUTH VIETNAMESE
CONSTITUTION OF 1956

PREAMBLE

Confident in the glorious and eternal destiny of the Vietnamese state and nation, a destiny which is guaranteed by the victorious struggles of our ancestors and the indomitable will of our people;

Confident in the perpetuity of our civilization which rests on spiritualist foundations and the propagation of which is the duty of all citizens;

Confident in the transcendent value of the human person whose free, harmonious, and complete development on the individual as well as on the communal plan must be the object of all state activity;

Conscious that the Constitution must satisfy the aspirations of the entire nation from the point of Camau to the gate of Nam-quan, these aspirations being:

the consolidation of national independence and the struggle against all forms of domination and imperialism;

the safeguard of the liberty for each individual and for the nation; the erection, in the respect for the human person, for the benefit of all classes of the population of a political, economic, social, and cultural democratic regime;

Conscious that liberty, which is the ability to obey reason and moral precepts, can only be preserved if collective security is assured and the legitimate rights of men respected;

Conscious that our nation, being located at the crossroads of international lines of communication and migrations, our people is ready to receive all currents of progress with a view to perfecting before the Almighty and before humanity its mission which is the edification of a humanistic civilization for the safeguard and the development of man in his entirety;

We, members of the National Constituent Assembly,

After deliberation, adopt the Constitution, the purpose of which is as follows:

CHAPTER I. BASIC PROVISIONS

Article 1. Viet-Nam is an independent, unified, territorially indivisible republic.

Article 2. Sovereignty resides in the whole people.

Article 3. The nation vests the executive functions in a President, elected by the people, and the legislative functions in a National Assembly, also elected by the people. The separation of powers between the executive and the legislative agencies must be clear. The activities of the executive and legislative agencies must be brought into harmony.

The President is vested with the leadership of the nation.

Article 4. The executive, the legislative, and the judiciary have as their responsibility the defense of freedom, democracy, the republican form of government, and public order.

The judiciary shall have a status which guarantees its independent character.

Article 5. All citizens, without distinction of sex, are born equal in dignity, rights, and duties, and must act toward each other in a spirit of fraternity and solidarity.

The state recognizes and guarantees the fundamental rights of the human person in his individual capacity and in his capacity as member of the community.

The state shall endeavor to establish for all equal opportunities and the necessary conditions for the enjoyment of their rights and the performance of their duties.

The state shall aid the economic development, cultural creation, scientific and technical expansion, and progress.

Article 6. Every citizen has duties toward the Fatherland, the community, and fellow-citizens in the pursuit of the harmonious and complete development of his personality and that of others.

Article 7. All activities having as their object the direct or indirect propagation or establishment of Communism in whatever form shall be contrary to the principles embodied in the present Constitution.

Article 8. The Republic of Viet-Nam shall adhere to the principles of international law which are not contrary to the exercise of national sovereignty and the realization of the equality of nations.

The republic shall endeavor to contribute to the maintenance of world peace and security as well as to strengthen the bonds of friendship which unite it with other peoples on a basis of freedom and equality.

CHAPTER II. RIGHTS AND DUTIES OF THE CITIZEN

Article 9. Every citizen has the right to life, liberty, and security and integrity of his person.

Article 10. No one may be illegally arrested, detained, or exiled.

Except in cases of *flagrante delicto*, no arrest may be carried out without a mandate of the competent authorities and which does not conform with the conditions and procedures prescribed by law.

In accordance with the procedures prescribed by law, the accused in cases of crimes or misdemeanor shall have the right to choose their defense or request that one be designated for them.

Article 11. No person may be tortured or subjected to brutal, inhuman, or degrading punishment or treatment.

Article 12. The private life, family, home, dignity, and reputation of every citizen shall be respected.

The privacy of correspondence may not be violated except on order of the courts or in cases necessitated by the protection of public security or the preservation of public order.

Everybody shall be entitled to the protection of the law against illegal interference.

Article 13. All citizens have the right to circulate and likewise reside freely on the national territory, except in those cases prohibited by law for reasons of public health or public security.

All citizens have the right to go abroad, except in the cases of restrictions by law for security, national defense, economic, financial reasons, or in the public interest.

Article 14. Everyone has the right and the duty to work. Pay shall be equal for equal work.

Everyone who works shall be entitled to an equitable remuneration guaranteeing to him and to his family an existence consistent with his human dignity.

Article 15. Every citizen has the right to freedom of thought and, within the limits set by law, of meeting and association.

Article 16. Every citizen has the right to freedom of expression. This right may not be used for false accusations, slander, outrages against public morals, incitations to internal disturbances, or for the overthrow of the republican form of government.

Every citizen has the right to liberty of press in order to establish a truthful and constructive opinion which the state must defend against all effort to distort the truth.

Article 17. Every citizen has the right to freedom of belief, religious practice and teaching, provided that the exercise of these rights shall not be contrary to morality.

Article 18. In accordance with the procedures and conditions prescribed by law, every citizen has the right to vote and to take part in the direction of public affairs, either directly or through his representatives.

Article 19. Every citizen has the right to hold public office, according to his abilities and on a basis of equality.

Article 20. The state recognizes and guarantees the right of private property.

The law shall fix the procedures of acquisition and enjoyment of the right of property so that everyone may become a proprietor and in order to assure to the human person a worthy and free life and at the same time to construct a prosperous society.

In the circumstances prescribed by law and on the condition of compensation, the state may expropriate private property in the public interest.

Article 21. The state shall facilitate the use of savings in acquiring dwelling, agricultural land, and shares in business corporations.

Article 22. Every citizen has the right to set up economic associations, provided the aim of such associations is not to establish illegal monopoly in order to engage in speculation and manipulation of the economy.

The state shall encourage and facilitate associations for the purpose of mutual aid, the intent of which is not speculation.

The state does not recognize business monopoly except in cases determined by law for reasons of national defense, security, or public utility.

Article 23. The right to free trade-unions and the right to strike are recognized and shall be exercised in conformity with the procedures and conditions prescribed by law.

Public officials have no right to strike.

The right to strike is not recognized in regard for the personnel and the workers in those activities related to national defense, public security, or the needs indispensable to the life of the community.

A law shall determine the branches of activities mentioned hereabove and guarantee to the personnel and workers of these branches a special status with the purpose of protecting the rights of the personnel and workers in those branches.

Article 24. Within the limits of its capacity and economic progress, the state shall take effective measures of assistance in cases of unemployment, old age, illness, natural disaster, or other misfortunes.

Article 25. The state recognizes the family as the foundation of society.

The state shall encourage and facilitate the formation of families and the fulfillment of the mission of the family, especially in regard to maternity and infant care.

The state shall encourage the cohesion of the family.

Article 26. The state shall endeavor to give every citizen a compulsory and free basic education.

Every citizen has the right to pursue his studies.

Those who are capable but lack private means shall be helped in the pursuit of their studies.

The state shall recognize the right of parents to choose the schools for their children and of associations as well as individuals to open schools in accordance with conditions fixed by law.

The state can recognize private institutions of university or technical education which satisfy the legal requirements. The diplomas granted by these institutions can be recognized by the state.

Article 27. Every citizen has the right to participate in cultural and scientific activities and to enjoy the benefits of the fine arts and of technical progress. Authors shall enjoy legal protection for their spiritual and material rights relating to scientific inventions, literary or artistic production.

Article 28. The rights of each citizen shall be exercised in conformity with the procedures and conditions prescribed by law.

The rights of each citizen shall be subjected only to those legal restrictions fixed by law in order to ensure respect for the rights of other citizens and satisfaction of the legitimate requirements of general security, morality, public order, national defense.

Whoever abuses the rights recognized by the Constitution with the object of jeopardizing the republican form of government, the democratic regime, national freedom, independence, and unity shall be deprived of his rights.

Article 29. Every citizen has the duty of respecting and defending the Constitution and the law.

Every citizen has the duty of defending the Fatherland, the republican form of government, freedom, and democracy.

Every citizen must fulfill his military obligations in conformity with the procedure and in the limits prescribed by law.

Everyone has the duty of contributing to public expenditure in proportion to his means.

CHAPTER III. THE PRESIDENT OF THE REPUBLIC

Article 30. The President of the Republic shall be elected by universal and direct suffrage with secret ballot in an election in which all electors throughout the country may participate.

A law shall determine the procedures of the election of the President of the Republic.

The Vice-President of the Republic shall be elected simultaneously with the President of the Republic and on the same ticket.

Article 31. Those citizens shall have the right to be a candidate for President or Vice-President of the Republic who shall have fulfilled all of the following conditions:

1. to have been born on Vietnamese territory and possess Vietnamese nationality without interruption since birth or to have recovered Vietnamese nationality prior to the date of the promulgation of the Constitution;

2. to have had residence on the national territory with or without interruption for a period of at least fifteen years;

3. to be forty years of age;

4. To enjoy the rights of citizenship; the office of President or Vice-President of the Republic shall be incompatible with any other paid or unpaid activity in the private domain.

Article 32. The President and the Vice-President of the Republic shall be elected for five years.

They shall be eligible for re-election for two terms.

Article 33. The terms of the President and of the Vice-President of the Republic shall expire exactly at noon, on the last day of the sixtieth month beginning from the day they effectively take office, and the terms of the new President and Vice-President shall begin at the same moment.

The functions of the President and of the Vice-President of the Republic may come to an end before the normal term, in the following circumstances:

1. death.

2. incapacity, because of serious and prolonged illness, to exercise the powers and fulfill the duties of the office; this incapacity must be ascertained by the National Assembly with a majority of four-fifths of the total number of Deputies, after medical examination and cross examination;

3. resignation duty tendered to the National Assembly;

4. deposition by the Special Court of Justice, under Article 81.

Article 34. The election of a new President and of a new Vice-President of the Republic shall take place on a Sunday, three weeks before the expiration of the terms of the President and Vice-President of the Republic in office.

In case of cessation of function before the expiration of the Presidential term, the Vice-President of the Republic shall exercise the functions of President until the end of the term.

Under the circumstances mentioned in the preceding paragraph, in the case in which there shall be no Vice-President of the Republic or in which the Vice-President of the Republic for some reason cannot fulfill the Presidential function, the President of the National Assembly shall temporarily exercise the function of President of the Republic in order to expedite current affairs and to organize the election of a new President and a new Vice-President of the Republic within a maximum period of two months. In this case, the first Vice-President of the Assembly shall assume the acting Presidency of the National Assembly.

Article 35. The President of the Republic shall conclude and, after approval by the National Assembly, ratify international treaties and conventions.

The President of the Republic shall appoint ambassadors, accredit foreign diplomatic representatives, and represent the nation in its relations with foreign countries.

Article 36. With the agreement of one-half of the members of the National Assembly, the President of the Republic shall declare war and conclude treaties of peace.

Article 37. The President of the Republic shall appoint and dismiss all military and civil servants in conformance with existing laws, except in cases where the Constitution shall prescribe special procedures.

The President of the Republic shall be the Supreme Commander of the armed forces.

The President of the Republic shall bestow all decorations.

The President of the Republic shall exert the right of pardon, of mitigation, communication, cancellation of penalty.

Article 38. In case of war or internal disturbances, the term of office of the Deputies such as defined in the Constitution shall be automatically extended at the expiration of their normal terms of office.

In case an electoral district shall be placed in a state of emergency, of alert or of siege, the President of the Republic may extend the term of office of the Deputies of that district.

However, general or partial elections must be organized at the latest within six months of the end of the special circumstances referred to in the two previous paragraphs.

Article 39. The President of the Republic shall communicate with the National Assembly by means of messages.

The President of the Republic may attend the sessions of the National Assembly and speak before it.

Each year, at the beginning of the second regular session of the National Assembly and whenever he deems it necessary, the President of the Republic shall inform the National Assembly on the state of the nation and on the domestic and foreign policies of the government.

Article 40. The President of the Republic may, with the consent of the Assembly, organize a referendum. The results of the referendum must be respected by the President of the Republic and the National Assembly.

Article 41. Between two sessions of the National Assembly, the President of the Republic may, for reason of emergency, sign orders in council.

The orders in council shall be transmitted immediately after their signature to the Bureau of the Assembly. If the National Assembly does not reject these orders in council during its next regular session, they shall become laws.

Article 42. In cases of emergency, war, internal disturbances, or financial or economic crises, the National Assembly may vote a law conferring on the President the power to sign orders in council for a definite time and within definite limits with a view to enforcing the policy defined by the National Assembly in the law by which it delegates power to the President.

The orders in council must be communicated to the Bureau of the National Assembly immediately after their signature. Thirty days after the expiration of the time limit defined in the law delegating the power, these orders in council shall become laws proper if the National Assembly does not reject them.

Article 43. In case the budget should not have been voted upon within the period defined in Article 60, the President of the Republic may sign budgetary orders in council for the financial period following. In each quarter, the President of the Republic may expend one-fourth of the budget until the time when the National Assembly shall have taken a final vote on the law concerning the budget.

In the budgetary law, the National Assembly must solve the problems resulting from the rejection or alteration of the provisions of the budgetary orders in council.

Article 44. The President of the Republic may sign a decree proclaiming a state of emergency, alert, or siege in one or many areas; this decree may temporarily suspend the application of one or many laws in these areas.

Article 45. Upon assuming office, the President of the Republic shall take the following oath: "I solemnly swear:

to fulfill the obligations of President of the Republic to the best of my ability,

to respect and defend the Constitution,

to serve the Fatherland faithfully and to devote myself entirely to the public interest."

Article 46. The President of the Republic shall be assisted by a Vice-President of the Republic, Secretaries of State, and Undersecretaries of State. The two last mentioned shall be appointed by the President of the Republic and shall be responsible to him.

Article 47. Secretaries of State and Undersecretaries of State can confer with the President and the Vice-President of the National Assembly and the Chairmen of the committees of the National Assembly in order to give explanations on problems relative to legislation.

CHAPTER IV. THE NATIONAL ASSEMBLY

Section 1. The Deputies

Article 48. The electoral law shall fix the number of Deputies to the National Assembly and the electoral constituencies.

Article 49. The Deputies shall be elected by universal and direct suffrage with secret ballot, according to procedures and conditions fixed by the electoral law.

Article 50. Those citizens may be candidates for the National Assembly who:

1. possess Vietnamese nationality without interruption since birth, or have obtained Vietnamese nationality at least five years prior thereto, or recovered Vietnamese nationality at least three years prior thereto exclusive of those who have recovered Vietnamese nationality before the date of the promulgation of the Constitution;

2. enjoy their rights of citizenship;

3. are fully twenty-five years of age before election day;

4. fulfill all the other conditions laid down in the electoral law.

However, in special cases where persons have recovered or acquired Vietnamese nationality and have rendered exceptional service to the Fatherland, the President may by decree reduce the five- and three-year requirements cited above.

Article 51. The term of office of the Deputies shall be three years. The Deputies may be re-elected.

The election of a new National Assembly shall take place one month prior to the expiration of the term of the existing legislature.

Article 52. When a Deputy resigns, dies, or terminates his mandate for any reason whatsoever, the election of a replacement shall take place within three months. There shall be no election for a replacement if the vacancy occurs less than six months prior to the end of the original term of office.

Article 53. The mandate of a Deputy is incompatible with any other remunerated public function or with any other elected office. Civil servants who are elected shall take leave of absence; military personnel elected shall be demobilized.

The mandate of a Deputy is incompatible with the office of a Secretary or Undersecretary of State.

However, Deputies may be charged with special missions lasting not more than twelve months each nor exceeding *in toto* one-half of the life of the legislature. While discharging such special assignments, Deputies shall not have the right to debate or vote in the National Assembly or its committees.

Deputies may serve as teachers in universities and higher technical schools.

In no case may Deputies participate in competitive bidding sponsored by government organs or enter into contracts with them.

Article 54. No Deputy may be pursued, arrested, incarcerated, or sentenced because of anything he may have said or any vote he may have cast in the Assembly or any of its committees.

Except in cases of high treason, injury to the security of the state, or *flagrante delicto*, no Deputy may be pursued, arrested, incarcerated, or sentenced during the whole period of National Assembly sessions, including the time for repairing to the Assembly and returning from it.

Section 2. The Powers of the National Assembly

Article 55. The National Assembly votes the laws. It approves international treaties and convocations.

Section 3. Legislative Procedures

Article 56. Deputies may introduce proposals for laws in the National Assembly; the President of the Republic may submit bills of law to the National Assembly for its examination.

Article 57. Bills of law and proposals for laws which are approved by the Assembly shall be transmitted to the President within a period of seven full days. The President must promulgate such laws within a period of thirty full days from the date of receipt. In a case declared by the Assembly to be urgent, the period for promulgation shall be reduced to seven full days.

Article 58. During the period allowed for promulgation, the President may transmit to the Assembly an explanatory message calling upon that body to reconsider one or several provisions of a law which it has approved.

With a second reading of the bill, the Assembly, if it rejects the modifications proposed by the President's message, will enact the law by a roll call vote of three-fourths of its membership.

Article 59. If, during the period provided in Article 57, the President of the Republic neither promulgates nor returns to the National Assembly for reconsideration a text which it had earlier approved, that text shall become law.

Article 60. Budget proposals must be sent to the Bureau of the Assembly before the thirtieth of September. The budget shall be voted before December 31.

Article 61. Deputies have the right to initiate expenditures, but at the same time, they shall propose corresponding new receipts.

Section 4. Functioning of the National Assembly

Article 62. The National Assembly shall meet in regular and special sessions.

Article 63. Each year there shall be two regular sessions—one beginning on the first Monday of April and one beginning on the first Monday of October. Neither regular session shall last longer than three months.

Article 64. The National Assembly shall be convened in special session if the President of the Republic or more than one-half of the membership of the Assembly so demand. When convened by the President, the agenda of the special session is to be fixed by him.

When convened on the demand of the Deputies, the agenda is to be fixed by the Bureau of the Assembly.

The duration of each special session may not exceed thirty days.

Article 65. The National Assembly shall meet in public. However, it may meet in closed session if a majority of over one-half of the members present or the President of the Republic so demand.

Verbatim accounts of the discussions and documents produced in the Assembly except for the accounts of closed sessions shall be published in the Official Journal.

Article 66. To control the regularity of the elections of its members, the National Assembly shall set up a Control Committee with the responsibility to report on this matter.

The National Assembly has the full power of decision.

Article 67. The National Assembly will elect a Bureau composed of a President, 2 Vice-Presidents, 1 Secretary General, 3 Assistant Secretaries General, and the necessary staff.

The Assembly shall designate various committees.

Article 68. The National Assembly shall prescribe its own internal regulations, especially with regard to:

the internal organization of the Assembly and its Bureau;

the Assembly's rules of procedures and the powers of the Bureau;

discipline within the Assembly and disciplinary sanctions;

the composition and functions of committees.

Article 69. A bill of law or proposal for law approved by the National Assembly shall be valid only if the majority vote received is not inferior to one-third the total number of Deputies.

CHAPTER V. THE JUDGES

Article 70. To discharge the duties set forth in Article 4, the judicial system shall be organized in accordance with the principles of the equality ot all persons before the law and of the independence of the magistrates on the bench.

Article 71. Judges shall make decisions according to their own consciences, with respect for the law and the interest of the nation.

Article 72. Under the supervision of the Department of Justice, the public prosecutors shall supervise the application of the law, the respect for morals, and public order.

Article 73. There shall be established a High Council of the Judiciary with the mission of supervising the application of the statute of the public prosecutors.

The organization, functions, and powers of the High Council of the Judiciary shall be determined by law.

CHAPTER VI. THE SPECIAL COURT OF JUSTICE

Article 74. The Special Court of Justice shall be a court competent to judge the President and Vice-President of the Republic, the President of the High Court of Appeals, and the President of the Constitutional Court in cases where charges of treason or high crimes are brought against them.

Article 75. The Special Court of Justice shall include the following: President of the High Court of Appeals—President; fifteen Deputies elected by the National Assembly for each legislature—Counselors.

When the President of the High Court of Appeals is the accused, the President of the Constitutional Court shall sit as President of the Special Court of Justice.

Article 76. The Commission of Inquiry of the Special Court of Justice shall include five Deputies elected by the National Assembly for each legislature.

Article 77. Charges shall be brought in accordance with the following conditions:

a) a motion containing the reasons for the charges shall be signed by three-fifths of the membership of the Assembly and presented to the Bureau of the Assembly fifteen days before debate begins;

b) that motion shall be approved by two-thirds of the membership of the Assembly;

c) Deputies sitting on the Special Court of Justice or on the Commission of Inquiry shall not have the right to present a motion of charges or to vote on that motion.

Article 78. The functions of the accused shall be suspended from the date of passage of the motion of accusation by the National Assembly until the decision of the Special Court of Justice is rendered. During that period, the procedures set forth in Article 34, paragraphs 2 and 3, shall obtain.

Article 79. The Commission of Inquiry has the right to summon wit-

nialism; from terror to terror, from sacrifice to sacrifice—in short, from promise to promise, until finally hope ended in bitter disillusion.

Thus, when you were on the point of returning to the country, the people as a whole entertained the hope that it would find again under your guidance the peace that is necessary to give meaning to existence, to reconstruct the destroyed homes, put to the plow again the abandoned lands. The people hoped no longer to be compelled to pay homage to one regime in the morning and to another at night, not to be the prey of the cruelties and oppression of one faction; no longer to be treated as coolies; no longer to be at the mercy of the monopolies; no longer to have to endure the depredations of corrupt and despotic civil servants. In one word, the people hoped to live in security at last, under a regime which would give them a little bit of justice and liberty. The whole people thought that you would be the man of the situation and that you would implement its hopes.

That is the way it was when you returned. The Geneva Accords of 1954 put an end to combat and to the devastations of war. The French Expeditionary Corps was progressively withdrawn, and total independence of South Viet-Nam had become a reality. Furthermore, the country had benefited from moral encouragement and a substantial increase of foreign aid from the free world. With so many favorable political factors, in addition to the blessed geographic conditions of a fertile and rich soil yielding agricultural, forestry, and fishing surpluses, South Viet-Nam should have been able to begin a definitive victory in the historical competition with the North, so as to carry out the will of the people and to lead the country on the way to hope, liberty, and happiness. Today, six years later, having benefited from so many undeniable advantages, what has the government been able to do? Where has it led South Viet-Nam? What parts of the popular aspirations have been implemented?

Let us try to draw an objective balance of the situation, without flattery or false accusations, strictly following a constructive line which you yourself have so often indicated, in the hope that the government shall modify its policies so as to extricate itself from a situation that is extremely dangerous to the very existence of the nation.

POLICIES

In spite of the fact that the bastard regime created and protected by colonialism has been overthrown and that many of the feudal organizations of factions and parties which oppress the population were destroyed, the people do not know a better life or more freedom under the republican regime which you have created. A constitution has been established in form only; a National Assembly exists whose deliberations always fall into line with the government; antidemocratic elections—all those are methods and "comedies" copied from the dictatorial Communist regimes, which obviously cannot serve as terms of comparison with North Viet-Nam.

Continuous arrests fill the jails and prisons to the rafters, as at this precise moment; public opinion and the press are reduced to silence. The same applies to the popular will as translated in certain open elections, in which it is insulted and trampled (as was the case, for example, during the recent elections for the Second Legislature). All these have provoked the discouragement and resentment of the people.

Political parties and religious sects have been eliminated. "Groups" or "movements" have replaced them. But this substitution has only brought about new oppressions against the population without protecting it for that matter against Communist enterprises. Here is one example: the fiefs of religious sects, which hitherto were deadly for the Communists, now not only provide no security whatever but have become favored highways for Viet-Minh guerrillas, as is, by the way, the case of the rest of the country.

This is proof that the religious sects, though futile, nevertheless constitute effective anti-Communist elements. Their elimination has opened the way to the Viet-Công and unintentionally has prepared the way for the enemy, whereas a more realistic and more flexible policy could have amalgamated them all with a view to reinforcing the anti-Communist front.

Today the people want freedom. You should, Mr. President, liberalize the regime, promote democracy, guarantee minimum civil rights, recognize the opposition so as to permit the citizens to express themselves without fear, thus removing grievances and resentments, opposition to which now constitutes for the people their sole reason for existence. When this occurs, the people of South Viet-Nam, in comparing their position with that of the North, will appreciate the value of true liberty and of authentic democracy. It is only at that time that the people will make all the necessary efforts and sacrifices to defend that liberty and democracy.

ADMINISTRATION

The size of the territory has shrunk, but the number of civil servants has increased, and still the work doesn't get done. This is because the government, like the Communists, lets the political parties control the population, separate the elite from the lower echelons, and sow distrust between those individuals who are "affiliated with the movement" and those who are "outside the group." Effective power, no longer in the hands of those who are usually responsible, is concentrated in fact in the hands of an irresponsible member of the "family," from whom emanates all orders; this slows down the administrative machinery, paralyzes all initiative, discourages good will. At the same time, not a month goes by without the press being full of stories about graft impossible to hide; this become's an endless parade of illegal transactions involving millions of piastres.

The administrative machinery, already slowed down, is about to become completely. paralyzed. It is in urgent need of reorganization. Competent people should be put back in the proper jobs; discipline must be re-established from the top to the bottom of the hierarchy; authority must go hand in hand with responsibility; efficiency, initiative, honesty, and the economy should be the criteria for promotion; professional qualifications should be respected. Favoritism based on family or party connections should be banished; the selling of influence, corruption, and abuse of power must be punished.

Thus, everything still can be saved, human dignity can be re-established; faith in an honest and just government can be restored.

ARMY

The French Expeditionary Corps has left the country, and a republican army has been constituted, thanks to American aid, which has equipped it with modern matériel. Nevertheless, even in a group of the proud elite of the youth such as the Vietnamese Army—where the sense of honoi should be cultivated, whose blood and arms should be devoted to the defense of the country, where there should be no place for clannishness and factions—the spirit of the "national revolutionary movement" or of the "personalist body" divides the men of one and the same unit, sows distrust between friends of the same rank, and uses as a criterion for promotion fidelity toward the party in blind submission to its leaders. This creates extremely dangerous situations, such as the recent incident of Tay-Ninh.*

The purpose of the army, pillar of the defense of the country, is to stop foreign invasions and to eliminate rebel movements. It is at the service of the country only and should not lend itself to the exploitation of any faction or party. Its total reorganization is necessary. Clannishness and party obedience should be eliminated; its moral base strengthened; a noble tradition of national pride created; and fighting spirit, professional conscience, and bravery should become criteria for promotion. The troops should be encouraged to respect their officers, and the officers should be encouraged to love their men. Distrust, jealousy, rancor among colleagues of the same rank should be eliminated.

Then in case of danger, the nation will have at its disposal a valiant army animated by a single spirit and a single aspiration: to defend our most precious possession—our country, Viet-Nam.

* *Author's note:* This refers to the destruction of a complete Vietnamese Army Battalion in February, 1961, when Communist forces slipped into their camp through treachery and captured several hundred weapons.

ECONOMIC AND SOCIAL AFFAIRS

A rich and fertile country enjoying food surpluses; a budget which does not have to face military expenditures;* important war reparations; substantial profits from Treasury bonds; a colossal foreign-aid program; a developing market capable of receiving foreign capital investments—those are the many favorable conditions which could make Viet-Nam a productive and prosperous nation. However, at the present time many people are out of work, have no roof over their heads, and no money. Rice is abundant but does not sell; shop windows are well-stocked but the goods do not move. Sources of revenue are in the hands of speculators who use the [government] party and group to mask monopolies operating for certain private interests. At the same time, thousands of persons are mobilized for exhausting work, compelled to leave their own jobs, homes, and families, to participate in the construction of magnificent but useless "agrovilles" which weary them and provoke their disaffection, thus aggravating popular resentment and creating an ideal terrain for enemy propaganda.

The economy is the very foundation of society, and public opinion ensures the survival of the regime. The government must destroy all the obstacles standing in the way of economic development; must abolish all forms of monopoly and speculation; must create a favorable environment for investments coming from foreign friends as well as from our own citizens; must encourage commercial enterprises, develop industry, and create jobs to reduce unemployment. At the same time, it should put an end to all forms of human exploitation in the work camps of the agrovilles.

Then only the economy will flourish again; the citizen will find again a peaceful life and will enjoy his condition; society will be reconstructed in an atmosphere of freedom and democracy.

Mr. President, this is perhaps the first time that you have heard such severe and disagreeable criticism—so contrary to your own desires. Nevertheless, sir, these words are strictly the truth, a truth that is bitter and hard, that you have never been able to know because, whether this is intended or not, a void has been created around you, and by the very fact of your high position, no one permits you to perceive the critical point at which truth shall burst forth in irresistible waves of hatred on the part of a people subjected for a long time to terrible suffering and a people who shall rise to break the bonds which hold it down. It shall sweep away the ignominy and all the injustices which surround and oppress it.

* *Author's note:* The military expenditures of the Vietnamese budget are paid out of U.S. economic and military aid.

As we do not wish, in all sincerity, that our Fatherland should have to live through these perilous days, we—without taking into consideration the consequences which our attitude may bring upon us—are ringing today the alarm bell in view of the imminent danger which threatens the government.

Until now, we have kept silent and preferred to let the Executive act as it wished. But now time is of the essence; we feel that it is our duty—and in the case of a nation in turmoil even the most humble people have their share of responsibility—to speak the truth, to awaken public opinion, to alert the people, and to unify the opposition so as to point the way. We beseech the government to urgently modify its policies so as to remedy the situation, to defend the republican regime, and to safeguard the existence of the nation. We hold firm hope that the Vietnamese people shall know a brilliant future in which it will enjoy peace and prosperity in freedom and progress.

Yours respectfully,

1. TRAN VAN VAN, *Diploma of Higher Commercial Studies, former Minister of Economy and Planning*
2. PHAN KHAC SUU, *Agricultural Engineer, former Minister of Agriculture, former Minister of Labor*
3. TRAN VAN HUONG, *Professor of Secondary Education, former Prefect of Saigon-Cholon*
4. NGUYEN LUU VIEN, *M.D., former Professor at the Medical School, former High Commissioner of Refugees*
5. HUYNH KIM HUU, *M.D., former Minister of Public Health*
6. PHAN HUY QUAT, *M.D., former Minister of National Education, former Minister of Defense*
7. TRAN VAN LY, *former Governor of Central Viet-Nam*
8. NGUYEN TIEN HY, *M.D.*
9. TRAN VAN DO, *M.D., former Minister of Foreign Affairs, Chairman of Vietnamese Delegation to the 1954 Geneva Conference*
10. LE NGOC CHAN, *Attorney at Law, former Secretary of State for National Defense*
11. LE QUANG LUAT, *Attorney at Law, former Government Delegate for North Viet-Nam, former Minister of Information and Propaganda*
12. LUONG TRONG TUONG, *Public Works Engineer, former Secretary of State for National Economy*
13. NGUYEN TANG NGUYEN, *M.D., former Minister of Labor and Youth*
14. PHAM HUU CHUONG, *M.D., former Minister of Public Health and Social Action*
15. TRAN VAN TUYEN, *Attorney at Law, former Secretary of State for Information and Propaganda*

16. TA CHUONG PHUNG, *former Provincial Governor for Binh-Dinh*
17. TRAN LE CHAT, *Laureate of the Triannual Mandarin Competition of 1903*
18. HO VAN VUI, *Reverend, former Parish Priest of Saigon, at present Parish Priest of Tha-La, Province of Tay-Ninh*

April 26, 1960

Appendix IV

PROGRAM OF THE NATIONAL LIBERATION FRONT
OF SOUTH VIET-NAM

[On December 20, 1960, the day of its founding, the National Liberation Front of South Viet-Nam issued a manifesto and published its ten-point program, the text of which follows:]

I. *Overthrow the camouflaged colonial regime of the American imperialists and the dictatorial power of Ngo Dinh Diem, servant of the Americans, and institute a government of national democratic union.*

The present South Vietnamese regime is a camouflaged colonial regime dominated by the Yankees, and the South Vietnamese Government is a servile government, implementing faithfully all the policies of the American imperialists. Therefore, this regime must be overthrown and a government of national and democratic union put in its place composed of representatives of all social classes, of all nationalities, of the various political parties, of all religions; patriotic, eminent citizens must take over for the people the control of economic, political, social, and cultural interests and thus bring about independence, democracy, well-being, peace, neutrality, and efforts toward the peaceful unification of the country.

II. *Institute a largely liberal and democratic regime.*

1. Abolish the present constitution of the dictatorial powers of Ngo Dinh Diem, servant of the Americans. Elect a new National Assembly through universal suffrage.

2. Implement essential democratic liberties: freedom of opinion, of press, of assembly, of movement, of trade-unionism; freedom of religion without any discrimination; and the right of all patriotic organizations of whatever political tendency to carry on normal activities.

3. Proclaim a general amnesty for all political prisoners and the dissolution of concentration camps of all sorts; abolish fascist law 10-59 and all the other antidemocratic laws; authorize the return to the country of all persons persecuted by the American-Diem regime who are now refugees abroad.

4. Interdict all illegal arrests and detentions; prohibit torture; and punish all the Diem bullies who have not repented and who have committed crimes against the people.

III. *Establish an independent and sovereign economy, and improve the living conditions of the people.*

1. Suppress the monopolies imposed by the American imperialists and their servants; establish an independent and sovereign economy and finances in accordance with the national interests; confiscate to the profit of the nation the properties of the American imperialists and their servants.

2. Support the national bourgeoisie in the reconstruction and development of crafts and industry; provide active protection for national products through the suppression of production taxes and the limitation or prohibition of imports that the national economy is capable of producing; reduce customs fees on raw materials and machines.

3. Revitalize agriculture; modernize production, fishing, and cattle raising; help the farmers in putting to the plow unused land and in developing production; protect the crops and guarantee their disposal.

4. Encourage and reinforce economic relations between the city and country, the plain and the mountain regions; develop commercial exchanges with foreign countries, regardless of their political regime, on the basis of equality and mutual interests.

5. Institute a just and rational system of taxation; eliminate harassing penalties.

6. Implement the labor code: prohibition of discharges, of penalties, of ill-treatment of wage earners; improvement of the living conditions of workers and civil servants; imposition of wage scales and protective measures for young apprentices.

7. Organize social welfare: find work for jobless persons; assume the

support and protection of orphans, old people, invalids; come to the help of the victims of the Americans and Diemists; organize help for areas hit by bad crops, fires, or natural calamities.

8. Come to the help of displaced persons desiring to return to their native areas and to those who wish to remain permanently in the South; improve their working and living conditions.

9. Prohibit expulsions, spoliation, and compulsory concentration of the population; guarantee job security for the urban and rural working populations.

IV. *Reduce land rent; implement agrarian reform with the aim of providing land to the tillers.*

1. Reduce land rent; guarantee to the farmers the right to till the soil; guarantee the property right of accession to fallow lands to those who have cultivated them; guarantee property rights to those farmers who have already received land.

2. Dissolve "prosperity zones," and put an end to recruitment for the camps that are called "agricultural development centers." Allow those compatriots who already have been forced into "prosperity zones" and "agricultural development centers" to return freely to their own lands.

3. Confiscate the land owned by American imperialists and their servants, and distribute it to poor peasants without any land or with insufficient land; redistribute the communal lands on a just and rational basis.

4. By negotiation and on the basis of fair prices, repurchase for distribution to landless peasants or peasants with insufficient land those surplus lands that the owners of large estates will be made to relinquish if their domain exceeds a certain limit, to be determined in accordance with regional particularities. The farmers who benefit from such land distribution will not be compelled to make any payment or to submit to any other conditions.

V. *Develop a national and democratic culture and education.*

1. Combat all forms of culture and education enslaved to Yankee fashions; develop a culture and education that is national, progressive, and at the service of the Fatherland and people.

2. Liquidate illiteracy; increase the number of schools in the fields of general education as well as in those of technical and professional education, in advanced study as well as in other fields; adopt Vietnamese as the vernacular language; reduce the expenses of education and exempt from payment students who are without means; resume the examination system.

3. Promote science and technology and the national letters and arts; encourage and support the intellectuals and artists so as to permit them to develop their talents in the service of national reconstruction.

4. Watch over public health; develop sports and physical education.

VI. *Create a national army devoted to the defense of the Fatherland and the people.*

1. Establish a national army devoted to the defense of the Fatherland and the people; abolish the system of American military advisers.

2. Abolish the draft system; improve the living conditions of the simple soldiers and guarantee their political rights; put an end to ill-treatment of the military; pay particular attention to the dependents of soldiers without means.

3. Reward officers and soldiers having participated in the struggle against the domination by the Americans and their servants; adopt a policy of clemency toward the former collaborators of the Americans and Diemists guilty of crimes against the people but who have finally repented and are ready to serve the people.

4. Abolish all foreign military bases established on the territory of Viet-Nam.

VII. *Guarantee equality between the various minorities and between the two sexes; protect the legitimate interests of foreign citizens established in Viet-Nam and of Vietnamese citizens residing abroad.*

1. Implement the right to autonomy of the national minorities:

Found autonomous zones in the areas with a minority population, those zones to be an integral part of the Vietnamese nation.

Guarantee equality between the various nationalities: each nationality has the right to use and develop its language and writing system, to maintain or to modify freely its mores and customs; abolish the policy of the Americans and Diemists of racial discrimination and forced assimilation.

Create conditions permitting the national minorities to reach the general level of progress of the population: development of their economy and culture; formation of cadres of minority nationalities.

2. Establish equality between the two sexes; women shall have equal rights with men from all viewpoints (political, economic, cultural, social, etc.).

3. Protect the legitimate interests of foreign citizens established in Viet-Nam.

4. Defend and take care of the interests of Vietnamese citizens residing abroad.

VIII. *Promote a foreign policy of peace and neutrality.*

1. Cancel all unequal treaties that infringe upon the sovereignty of the people and that were concluded with other countries by the servants of the Americans.

2. Establish diplomatic relations with all countries, regardless of their political regime, in accordance with the principles of peaceful coexistence adopted at the Bandung Conference.

3. Develop close solidarity with peace-loving nations and neutral countries; develop free relations with the nations of Southeast Asia, in particular with Cambodia and Laos.

4. Stay out of any military bloc; refuse any military alliance with another country.

5. Accept economic aid from any country willing to help us without attaching any conditions to such help.

IX. *Re-establish normal relations between the two zones, and prepare for the peaceful reunification of the country.*

The peaceful reunification of the country constitutes the dearest desire of all our compatriots throughout the country. The National Liberation Front of South Viet-Nam advocates the peaceful reunification by stages on the basis of negotiations and through the seeking of ways and means in conformity with the interests of the Vietnamese nation.

While awaiting this reunification, the governments of the two zones will, on the basis of negotiations, promise to banish all separatist and war-mongering propaganda and not to use force to settle differences between the zones. Commercial and cultural exchanges between the two zones will be implemented; the inhabitants of the two zones will be free to move about throughout the country as their family and business interests indicate. The freedom of postal exchanges will be guaranteed.

X. *Struggle against all aggressive war; actively defend universal peace.*

1. Struggle against all aggressive war and against all forms of imperialist domination; support the national emancipation movements of the various peoples.

2. Banish all war-mongering propaganda; demand general disarmament and the prohibition of nuclear weapons; and advocate the utilization of atomic energy for peaceful purposes.

3. Support all movements of struggle for peace, democracy, and social progress throughout the world; contribute actively to the defense of peace in Southeast Asia and in the world.

Appendix V

PROCLAMATIONS BY SOUTH VIETNAMESE
COUNCIL OF GENERALS

[Issued on November 1, 1963.]

Military Order No. 1 of the Council of Generals:

Martial law is now proclaimed throughout the territory. As of November 1, 1963, the Vietnamese Republican Armed Forces assume the responsibility of protecting public security throughout the territory. The people are forbidden:

1. To leave their houses from 2000 to 0700 hours in the morning.
2. To hold meetings harmful to public security and order.
3. To engage in violations of public security and order, such as printing, circulating, and keeping documents, newspapers, and leaflets aimed at destroying the national security and order. All printing material and tables must be censored.
4. All organizations and individuals having weapons must immediately hand weapons and ammunition, including sharp weapons, over to the nearest military authorities.

Those who violate the above articles will be prosecuted before the military court in accordance with emergency procedures.

MAJ. GEN. DUONG VAN MINH
Chairman of the Council of Generals

Soldiers in the army, security service, civil defense force, and people's forces:

During the last nine years countless numbers of us have sacrificed our blood and flesh to defend the country against the Communists. Innumerable soldiers have fallen on the battlefield in order to score glorious victories for the Fatherland. Meanwhile, the Ngo Dinh Diem Government, abusing power, has thought only of personal ambition and slighted the Fatherland's interests.

The people's lawful rights were trampled upon, thus creating great injustices in society. It maintained an incompetent system of cadres. If our sacrifices and victories won the people's confidence and love, the rottenness and corruption of the Ngo Dinh Diem clique destroyed the confidence of the people and of friendly nations in the free world.

Thus, let us ask whether all our merits achieved up to the present time had any chance of bringing about any result or security to the country at a time when the people are fed up with the family-rule regime, which places money and power above all.

Never has our soldiers' honor been damaged as it is now. Ngo Dinh Diem has utilized the army's name to carry out dark acts for personal aggrandizement and to consolidate his position. Countless genuine national elements have been arrested. It has abused the army's name to infringe on freedom of religion, arrested priests, and aroused immeasurable disgust and indignation among the people. . . .

Dear comrades in arms, will the tradition allow us to sit idly by and let the despots lead the nation to annihilation? Will it allow us to make sacrifices and bow our heads in obedience to a regime whose rottenness, injustice, and dictatorship are being condemned by all the people, and the whole world?

No. We will never allow ourselves to remain silent. As you know, we have carried out a revolution to save the country and to rebuild a powerful army not controlled by incompetent cadres or an unjust rule.

We have no political ambitions; we act not for fame or benefit but to save our beloved Fatherland, which 'is in danger. Our acts have an urgent nature, because unless we act, we ourselves will be sacrificed, one by one and uselessly.

The army has swung into action. The task of you all is to unite. Obey discipline and clearsightedly see the dangerous situation caused by the Communists and the Ngo Dinh Diem clique.

We officers call on you to continue the anti-Communist work that you have been valiantly carrying out on all battlefields and to unite and be single-minded in order to save our beloved Fatherland.

The revolution will certainly be successful. The army will certainly be victorious in building a sound country. You will be correctly and efficiently commanded. The people have confidence in you. We officers place all our expectations in you.

Salute of certain victory,

LIEUT. GEN. DUONG VAN MINH, LIEUT. GEN. TRAN VAN DON, LIEUT. GEN. NGUYÊN NGOC LE, LIEUT. GEN. TRAN VAN MINH, BRIG. GEN. LE VAN NGHIEM, BRIG. GEN. NGUYÊN GIAC NGO, BRIG. GEN. MAI RUU XUAN, BRIG. GEN. TRAN TU OAI, BRIG. GEN. LE VAN KIM, BRIG. GEN. NGUYÊN VAN LA, BRIG. GEN. PHAM XUAN CHIEU, BRIG. GEN. TRAN THIEN KHIEM, BRIG. GEN. TON THAT DINH, BRIG. GEN. TRAN NGOC TAM, COL. DO BUU, COL. NGUYÊN PHUONG, LIEUT. COL. NGUYÊN VAN THIEN, LIEUT. COL. LE YEN THANG, COL. DUONG NGOC LAM, LIEUT. COL. PHUNG VAN TUONG, LIEUT. COL. DO NGOC NHUAN, and MAJ. NGUYÊN NGOC THIEN

Appendix VI

DECISION OF THE REVOLUTIONARY COUNCIL

According to the Provisional Constitutional Charter No. 1, dated November 4, 1963, and considering that the Executive Committee of the Military Revolutionary Council, set up on November 1, 1963, has proved ineffective in the face of the tense situation at home and abroad, the Military Revolutionary Council, following a vote, has decided as follows:

Article 1. To put an end to the duties of the Executive Committee of the Military Revolutionary Council set up on November 1, 1963;

Article 2. To appoint Major General Nguyên Khanh to take over the office of Chairman of the Military Revolutionary Council;

Article 3. This decision is effective as of January 30, 1964.

MAJ. GEN. NGUYÊN KHANH, COMMANDER OF IST ARMY CORPS; MAJ. GEN. TRAN THIEN KHIEM, COMMANDER OF IIID ARMY CORPS; MAJ. GEN. DO CAO TRI, COMMANDER OF IID ARMY CORPS; BRIG. GEN. NGUYÊN HUU CO, COMMANDER OF IVTH ARMY CORPS; ETC. . . .

Appendix VII

PROCLAMATION BY GENERAL NGUYÊN KHANH ON THE COUP D'ÉTAT OF JANUARY 30, 1964

On November 1, the main cause prompting the Republican Army to rise up and overthrow the dictatorial, rotten, and incompetent regime of Ngo Dinh Diem was to strive to carry out a comprehensive revolution in order to build a truly democratic regime, to increase effective measures against Communism, and to ensure a free and happy life for every citizen.

But for three months following the coup, the political, economic, and social situation, especially in the rural areas; has not brought any promise for the future of the country and has not compensated for the daily sacrifices of soldiers. Therefore, the aspirations of the compatriots and soldiers are not satisfied. The governmental organization has proved incompetent and counterrevolutionary. A number of persons desiring to promote their individual interests do not hesitate to ally themselves with the colonialists and have a tendency to advocate neutrality, thereby paving the way for the Communists to enslave our country.

The armed forces have decided to rise up and continue to carry out the national revolution to satisfy the aspirations of all the people. They are determined to sweep away the Communists and the Vietnamese traitors who advocate neutrality. The army is determined to join the compatriots to re-establish security and order so as to bring all people a plentiful and happy life. The army is determined to join the compatriots in building the future of the Fatherland on the basis of freedom and democracy. The army insistently calls on the compatriots to unite in order to achieve the final victory quickly.

Notes

Chapter 1. THE PHYSICAL SETTING

1. Joseph Buttinger, *The Smaller Dragon* (New York: Frederick A. Praeger, 1958), p. 75.

2. Archaeological discoveries made in 1960 at Thiêu-Dong (Thanh-Hoa, Central Viet-Nam), where Vietnamese Bronze Age artifacts were found *under* layers of Chinese Han artifacts, tend to be "a refutation of the thesis that the Bronze [Age] objects of Dong-Son were the fruits of the civilization of the Posterior Hans introduced into Viet-Nam during their domination of this country." (Nguyên Van Nghia and Pham Van Kinh, "Archeological Finds in Thiêu-Dong," *Viet-Nam Advances* [Hanoi], October, 1961, pp. 18–21.)

3. In a speech made on March 1, 1962, Prince Sihanouk, the Chief of State of Cambodia, declared: "Suppose that we could retake Cochinchina [South Viet-Nam] or even that someone offered it to us. It is hardly necessary to show you that coexistence between 5 million Khmer and 12 million Vietnamese would not be without danger. We would be only a minority and would soon be dominated by this alien mass in which the Khmer nation would disappear." (*Agence Khmère de Presse* [AKP]. Phnom-Penh, March 2, 1962, p. 4.)

Chapter 2. A GLIMPSE OF THE PAST

1. In his very complete (and thus far the only one) English-language history of Viet-Nam prior to 1900, Buttinger, *op. cit.*, pp. 69–70, to judge from his

references and bibliography, apparently did not have at his disposal Maurice Durand's *Miroir complet de l'Histoire du Viêt* (Hanoi: Ecole Française d'Extrême-Orient, 1952), an extremely interesting translation of diplomatic correspondence between Viet-Nam and China during the years 258–112 B.C.

In one diplomatic exchange between a Han empress and "old Trieu Da," a Chinese general who had made himself king and later emperor of Viet-Nam, the empress expressed her regret at being compelled to shed much valorous blood on both sides merely because Da had made himself an emperor, too. The latter answered that he had been compelled to do so by virtue of the fact that his two viceroys had made themselves "kings." The matter was settled by a typically Oriental compromise: The Vietnamese king would style himself "emperor" within his own country but would use the title of "king" in relations with other countries. Thus bloodshed was avoided.

This incident perhaps explains later confusions by authors who alternately describe the rulers of Viet-Nam as kings or emperors.

2. From *dôn* (fort) and *diên* (rice field). The process was also used by the Chinese themselves during their push southward, and the Vietnamese system was an adaptation of the earlier Chinese model.

3. A. Dauphin-Meunier, *Histoire du Cambodge* (Paris: Presses Universitaires de France, 1961), pp. 71–104 *passim*. Buttinger fails to give any more weight to the problem of Vietnamese colonialism in Cambodia, which to this day poisons the relations between the two countries, than to state that Viet-Nam "had shown its vitality by steadily growing at the expense of Cambodia." (*Op. cit.*, p. 270.) Buttinger errs when he asserts that the Cambodian rulers resided in Phnom-Penh "all the time" save between 1796 and 1802. (*Ibid.*, p. 305.) Oudong was the royal capital; Phnom-Penh became Cambodia's capital on June 3, 1864, with the enthronement of King Norodom.

4. Paul Isoart, *Le Phénomène National Vietnamien* (Paris: Librairie générale de droit et de jurisprudence, 1961), p. 25.

5. Pham Huy Thong, *L'esprit public vietnamien hier et aujourd'hui* (Paris: Union Culturelle des Vietnamiens en France, 1949), p. 10.

6. Donald Lancaster, *The Emancipation of French Indo-China* (London and New York: Oxford University Press, 1961), p. 31n.

7. *Op. cit.*, p. 333.

8. Isoart, *op. cit.*, p. 94. Fifty-two French priests were executed between 1815 and 1856. According to the American publication *Catholic Digest* of February, 1962, "in the persecutions of the last century, tiny Viet-Nam had 100,000 martyrs, far above any single nation's quota since the early Roman persecutions." (P. 17.)

9. Lê Thanh Khoi, *Viet-Nam* (Paris: Les Editions de Minuit, 1955), p. 365.

10. *Op. cit.*, p. 349.

Chapter 3. COLONIAL INTERLUDE

1. Another reason for fallacious criticism is the practice of judging a country's colonial performance by the manner in which it occupied a colony. America's over-all performance in the Philippines, which was good, began nevertheless with the bloodiest colonial war (in proportion to population) ever fought by a white power in Asia; it cost the lives of 300,000 Filipinos. (Leon Wolff, *Little Brown Brother* [Garden City, N.Y.: Doubleday & Company, 1961].) In fact, the heavy .45-caliber bullet was especially designed for the Moro war because of its stopping power. High Moro losses were also due to the fact that this was the first time that automatic guns (the Gatlings) were used in Asia.

2. K. M. Panikkar, *Asia and Western Dominance* (New York: The John Day Company, 1950), p. 221.

3. *Op. cit.*, p. 227.

4. John T. Cady, *The Roots of French Imperialism in Eastern Asia* (Ithaca, N.Y.: Cornell University Press, 1954).

5. Henri Brunschwig, *Mythes et réalités de l'impérialisme colonial français, 1870–1914* (Paris: Armand Colin, 1960), p. 16. The anti-English bent of French colonialism is very little understood in the United States. Claude Farrère, the first French writer to give an incisive portrait of French colonial society in Saigon around 1910, in his *Les Civilisés*, builds the climax of his story on a suicide attack of French torpedo boats against a British fleet off Cape St. Jacques!

6. See table in Brunschwig, *op. cit.*, p. 99.

7. Strachey, a member of the Labour Party and former British Secretary of War, shows in his *The End of Empire* (New York: Random House, 1960) that Britain's trade picture has never been more favorable than it has been since she lost nine-tenths of her empire; and Myrdal conclusively shows (as the newly independent countries are finding out the hard way) that the relative trade position of the underdeveloped countries tends to worsen rather than to improve as they are cut loose from the protected markets of the colonial powers.

8. In comparison, in 1961, American foreign trade amounted to $20 billion out of a total gross national product of $550 billion, or about 3.5 per cent.

9. "Economic Development in South Viet-Nam, 1954–60," *The Malayan Economic Review*, April, 1961, pp. 55–80. D. G. E. Hall, in his monumental *History of South-East Asia* (London: Macmillan & Co., 1955), p. 657, makes the point that between 1911 and 1920, only 19.6 per cent of all Indochinese exports went to France, while the latter accounted for less than 30 per cent of Indochina's imports during the same period.

10. *Op. cit.*, p. 101.

11. Isoart, *op. cit.*, p. 187.

12. Any American who professes to be shocked by this inequality should remember that to this day the United States Government pays its American and foreign employees on vastly different wage scales even though they may hold exactly the same jobs. The only sizable group to protest against this so far is the local employees in the Panama Canal Zone.

13. An American reader who is shocked by the unrepresentativeness of those colonial legislatures will do well to remember that the legislatures of the eleven Southern states of the U.S. are singularly devoid of representatives of the Negro segments of their populations.

14. Nguyên Thê Truyên v. The French Protectorate of Annam, in *Recueil des arrêts du Conseil d'Etat* (Paris: Imprimerie Nationale, 1936), session of May 19, 1936, p. 568. Nguyên Thê Truyên, a Vietnamese nationalist of long standing, ran unsuccessfully as a South Vietnamese Vice-Presidential aspirant on a ticket opposing President Ngo Dinh Diem in 1961.

15. *Op. cit.*, p. 200. The population figure cited for Indochina is probably slightly exaggerated.

16. J. Lun, "The Popular Movement in Indochina," *Communist International* (Moscow), XIV, No. 3 (1937), 910–11.

17. Nguyên Kien Giang, *Les grandes dates du parti de la classe ouvrière du Viet Nam* (Hanoi: Foreign Languages Publishing House, 1960), pp. 32–34 *passim*.

18. One nationalist rebellion (involving a Tonkinese rifle battalion at Yên-Bay) and one Communist-led peasant rebellion (involving 6,000 farmers in

Nghé-An) had taken place in 1930, but neither developed more than local importance.

19. Notably Lê Thanh Khoi, *op. cit.*; and Jean Chesneaux, whose interesting *Contribution à l'histoire de la nation vietnamienne* (Paris: Editions sociales, 1955) uncritically espouses every cliché of the Party line.

Chapter 4. WHITE MAN'S END

1. Telegram cited in General [Georges] Catroux, *Deux actes du drame indochinois* (Paris: Librairie Plon, 1959), p. 55. Italics in original text.

2. Cordell Hull, *Memoirs* (New York: The Macmillan Company, 1948), I, 906.

3. The foregoing is based on interviews with senior officers involved and on correspondence in the files of the French Army Historical Services, Paris. On March 27, 1962, the Department of State released the 1941 volume of Far Eastern diplomatic papers, which cites a meeting on July 31, 1941, between Admiral Leahy, then U.S. Ambassador to the Vichy regime, and Marshal Pétain and Admiral Darlan (then Pétain's heir presumptive). Darlan expressed to Leahy his deep disappointment at the United States' refusal to send its Manila squadron to Saigon to prevent further Japanese encroachments and added: "As usual, the Americans will be late."

4. The Burma Road had been opened only the year before, and under Japanese pressure, Britain closed her supply lines to Chiang Kai-shek on June 27, 1940.

5. In his extensive chronology, Buttinger merely notes that a "clash" between the French and Japanese brought about nationalist and Communist uprisings which the French quelled with "bombardments, mass executions, and mass deportations." (*Op. cit.*, pp. 439–40.) Not to be outdone in biased historiography, Ellen J. Hammer, in her *Struggle for Indochina* (Stanford, Cal.: Stanford University Press, 1954), states that French resistance to the Japanese "was mainly notable for its brevity." (P. 117.)

6. Catroux, *op. cit.*, pp. 55–56.

7. *Op. cit.*, p. 92.

8. Bernard B. Fall, "La politique américaine au Viet-Nam," *Politique Etrangère*, No. 3 (July, 1955), pp. 299–322. See also Lancaster, *op. cit.*, p. 92.

9. General Jean Marchand, *L'Indochine en guerre* (Paris: Les Presses Modernes, 1954), p. 59.

10. The main primary sources concerning wartime Japanese policy are the documents and proceedings of the International Military Tribunal for the Far East (IMTFE), which sat in judgment over Japanese war criminals from May 3, 1946, until November 12, 1948. Other important sources are: Togo Shigenori, *The Cause of Japan* (New York: Simon and Schuster, 1956), and Charles A. Beard, *President Roosevelt and the Coming of the War, 1941* (New Haven: Yale University Press, 1948), and Hull's *Memoirs*.

11. Shigenori, *op. cit.*, p. 85.

12. *Ibid.*, p. 217.

13. Admiral Jean Decoux, *A la barre de l'Indochine* (Paris: Librairie Plon, (1949), p. 164.

14. In 1940, there were 525,000 children in 7,164 schools in Viet-Nam. In 1944, the number had risen to 960,000, attending 13,384 schools. In 1955, the first peacetime year after the Indochina War, 1,077,000 children attended 8,905 schools in both Viet-Nams.

15. Nguyên Kien Giang, *op. cit.*, pp. 41–47 *passim*. One platoon of Indochinese guards rebelled at Do Luong, in Central Viet-Nam, on January 13, 1941.

16. Admiral William D. Leahy, *I Was There* (New York: McGraw-Hill, 1950), p. 44.

17. George F. Kennan, *Russia and the West under Lenin and Stalin* (Boston: Little, Brown, 1961), p. 5.

18. Hull, *op. cit.*, II, 1595. At least one French authority on the history of Indochina, Georges Taboulet, expressed to this writer the interesting theory that Roosevelt's particular hatred for the French in Indochina stemmed from his maternal grandfather, Warren Delano (Delaneau), who had lost a great deal of money in 1867 in prematurely selling two parcels of real estate at the entrance of the "Chinese Arroyo" into the Saigon River. Today, the area is still one of the choice spots in Saigon and is owned by a French industrial concern. The French consulate is also located there. There is no evidence that Roosevelt was ever informed of his grandfather's interests in the area, but Taboulet's information provides additional evidence of the United States' century-old interest in Viet-Nam.

19. Elliott Roosevelt, *As He Saw It* (New York: Duell, Sloane and Pearce, 1945), p. 115.

20. General Joseph W. Stilwell, *The Stilwell Papers* (New York: William Sloane, 1948), p. 246.

21. *Foreign Relations of the United States, Diplomatic Papers: The Conferences at Cairo and Tehran 1943* (U.S. Department of State [Washington, D.C., 1961]), pp. 485 and 509 and *passim*. It is most improbable that Roosevelt meant his remark jocularly, especially in view of his statement at the Yalta Conference, on February 4, 1945, when he "told the [Joint Chiefs of Staff] that he favored anything that was against the Japanese so long as the United States was not aligned with the French." (Charles F. Romanus and Riley K. Sunderland, *Time Runs Out in CBI* ["U.S. Army in World War II: The China-Burma-India Theater," published by the Office of the Chief of Military History] [Washington, D.C.: Government Printing Office, 1956], chap. viii.)

22. Henry A. Wallace, *Toward World Peace* (New York: Reynal and Hitchcock, 1949), p. 97. Wallace, then Vice-President, personally carried the offer to Chiang. He has fully confirmed his earlier statements in correspondence with this writer.

23. Samuel I. Rosenman (ed.), *The Public Papers and Addresses of FDR* (New York: Harper & Brothers, 1950), XIII, 562. This discussion took place on the return from Yalta, during a press conference aboard the *Quincy*, February 23, 1945. In the 1941 diplomatic papers, published in March, 1962, mention is made of a heated exchange of correspondence between the then French representative in Washington, Henri Hoppenot, and the State Department, in which the former objected to the Chinese occupation of Tongking, on the historical grounds that the Vietnamese and Chinese were "hereditary enemies." A. A. Berle, then Assistant Secretary of State, commented in a memorandum that the President should resolve the problem "whether we are in the Far East to re-establish the Western colonial empires" or whether the Asian peoples should be left to liberate themselves "if they were able to do so." He also objected to Hoppenot's accurate reference to the traditional enmity between Vietnamese and Chinese in a memorandum to Under Secretary of State Edward Stettinius, who, in a memorandum of November 8, 1943, agreed that Hoppenot's views "appeared ill-founded." On the following day, Roosevelt adopted Berle and Stettinius's viewpoint and decided that Indochina would be considered as "essentially a military problem," i.e., one that would be handled

by the China Command and not be subject to political discussion with Free French leaders. See Chapter 5 for the consequences of that decision.

24. James K. Eyre, *The Roosevelt-MacArthur Conflict* (Chambersburg, Pa.: Craft Press, 1950), p. 156.

25. There are several good sources on the resistance aspects of the struggle: Lancaster, *op. cit.*; G. Sabattier, *Le destin de l'Indochine* (Paris: Plon, 1952); and Romanus and Sunderland, *op. cit.* A very valuable source of primary documents as well as of Free French views are the memoirs of General de Gaulle, *Mémoires de guerre* (Paris: Librairie Plon, 1954–59), 3 vols.

26. General Claire L. Chennault, *Way of a Fighter* (New York: G. P. Putnam's Sons, 1949), p. 342. According to some sources, Chennault's dismissal on August 7, 1945, as 14th Air Force commander was due to his intervention in behalf of the French. In correspondence with this writer, General Wedemeyer affirmed that the tenor of his orders with regard to Indochina was still a restricted matter.

27. General Albert C. Wedemeyer, *Wedemeyer Reports!* (New York: Henry Holt, 1958), pp. 340 and 343.

28. Leahy, *op. cit.*, p. 338.

29. De Gaulle, *op. cit.*, III, 167.

30. Sabattier, *op. cit.*, p. 455. On p. 466, he gives the number of officers killed as 250.

31. De Gaulle, *op. cit.*, III, 163.

32. Isoart, *op. cit.*, p. 323. The full French text is in Philippe Devillers, *Histoire du Viet-Nam de 1940 à 1952* (Paris: Editions du Seuil, 1952), p. 125.

Chapter 5. "Doc-Lap!"

1. *Op. cit.*, p. 108.

2. Nguyên Kien Giang, *op. cit.*, p. 42. Note that the citation comes from a North Vietnamese Communist source.

3. Truong Chinh, *The August Revolution*, in *Primer for Revolt*, ed. and with an Introduction and Notes by Bernard B. Fall (New York: Frederick A. Praeger, 1963), p. 14.

4. In a doctoral thesis completed in August, 1962, for Pennsylvania State University, a young Chinese scholar pieced together many parts of the puzzle of Chungking's Viet-Nam policies of 1945. The Chinese Central Government had sent to Viet-Nam an advisory group attached to Lu Han's headquarters. One of its members, Chu Ch'i (now in Peking), later wrote a book on his group's operations that sheds much light on those little-known but important events: *Yueh-nan shou-hsiang jih-chi* (*Diary of Accepting the [Japanese] Surrender*) (Shanghai: Commercial Press Co., 1946). Cf. King Chen, *China and the Democratic Republic of Viet-Nam* (1945–1954), pp. 74–83 *passim*.

5. Pierre Celérier, *Menaces sur le Viet-Nam* (Saigon: I.D.E.O., 1950), p. 48.

6. Bernard B. Fall, *Le Viet-Minh*, 1945–1960 (Paris: Armand Colin, 1960), pp. 45–47 *passim*.

7. As has already been mentioned, the Trotskyite leader Ta Thu Thau, a personal friend of Ho Chi Minh, was murdered by the Viet-Minh while returning from a meeting with Ho in Hanoi.

8. Isoart, *op. cit.*, p. 331.

9. Unpublished report in the Library of Congress.

10. In his own memoirs on those events, General Lionel-Max Chassin, former commander of the French Far Eastern Air Force, states that, contrary to Wedemeyer's orders, supply drops and even fighter support for the retreating French

continued to be provided by Chennault's 14th Air Force until at least April 26, 1945. (*Aviation Indochine* [Paris: Amiot-Dumont, 1953], pp. 33–41.)

11. Jean Sainteny, *Histoire d'une paix manquée*, (Paris: Amiot-Dumont, 1953), pp. 91–124 *passim*. All telegrams cited are based upon Sainteny. See also Pierre Maurice Dessinges, "Intrigues Internationales en Indochine," *Le Monde*, April 14, 1947.

12. For example, in the first briefing handed by the Department of State to President Harry S. Truman, on April 13, 1945—less than twenty-four hours after he had been sworn in—it was said that "in certain cases, notably in connection with Indochina, [the French] showed unreasonable suspicions of American aims and motives." Harry S. Truman, *Memoirs* (New York: Doubleday & Company, 1956), I, 15.

13. George K. Tanham, *Communist Revolutionary Warfare: The Vietminh in Indochina* (New York: Frederick A. Praeger, 1961), p. 4. A Rand Corporation Research Study.

14. *Ibid.*, p. 67. Until 1950, the Viet-Minh openly maintained a purchasing office for U.S. equipment and medical supplies in Bangkok (in "anti-Communist" Thailand) within one block of the local U.S. Information Service. It closed after the outbreak of the Korean War and shifted its operations to Rangoon.

15. General Pierre Boyer de Latour, *De l'Indochine à l'Algérie: Le martyre de l'armée française* (Paris: Les Presses du Mail, 1962), p. 47.

16. Lancaster, *op. cit.*, p. 143.

17. *Traités, Conventions, Accords passés entre le Viet-Nam et la France (1787–1946)* (Gouvernement Central Provisoire du Viet-Nam [Hanoi: Imprimerie d'Extrême-Orient, 1948]), pp. 41–47 *passim*.

18. *Le Monde*, September 24, 1946 *et seq.*

19. Bernard B. Fall, *Street Without Joy: Insurgency in Indochina, 1946–1963* (3d rev. ed.; Harrisburg, Pa.: The Stackpole Co., 1963), p. 27.

20. This version of the facts is based on reports by such firsthand observers as Paul Mus, *Viet-Nam. Sociologie d'une guerre* (Paris: Editions du Seuil, 1952), and Devillers, *op. cit.*, and on perusal of French Army telegrams of the time. Tanham gives the following truncated version:

On November 23, 1946, after a series of incidents in Haiphong, the French ordered the Vietnamese, under threat of reprisals, to evacuate their section of the city within two hours. Compliance with such an order was clearly impossible, and the French, true to the letter of their ultimatum, bombarded and wiped out the Vietnamese sections of Haiphong that same day. (*Op. cit.*, p. 6.)

One simple point could be added to explode this myth: Had the French really bombarded the city of Haiphong (300,000 inhabitants!), there would have been a great many more than 6,000 dead. Yet even the Communists accept this figure as correct.

21. Giang, *op. cit.*, p. 59. In a recent West German study by Wolfgang Appel, *Südostasien im Brennpunkt der Weltpolitik* (Würzburg: Marienburg Verlag, [1960], the author asserts that the "French troops had received their marching orders on December 19, 1946, signed by the leader of the French Communist Party, Maurice Thorez, then deputy Prime Minister" (p. 123). There is no documentary support for that assertion

Chapter 6. THE RISE OF HO CHI MINH

1. In all, only three non-Communist Westerners have thus far attempted to chronicle Ho's life in any depth, two of them using firsthand research. In

France, Jean Lacouture, in *Cinq hommes contre la France* (Paris: Editions du Seuil, 1961), interviewed many French politicians and officials who had dealt with Ho. I attempted a biography of Ho in my *Le Viet-Minh, 1945–1960*, and was fortunate enough to be able to interview Ho Chi Minh and several of his close associates in Hanoi in July, 1962. Much of what follows in this chapter is based on notes, printed material, and tape-recorded interviews collected during my 1962 stay in North Viet-Nam. Ho himself refused at first to talk about his own past ("I'm an old man and like to hold onto my little secrets. Wait until I'm dead"), but later allowed his associates to fill in many of the gaps. In some cases, they provided me with verifiable printed references of the facts cited.

The only English-language biographical essay on Ho is an unpublished master's thesis by R. L. Spencer (George Washington University, 1957), based entirely on older American and Communist sources. Pham Van Dong, Ho's long-time associate, published in 1961 in Hanoi a small brochure entitled *Le Président Ho Chi Minh*, which clears up several mysteries in Ho's biography, but adds still more inaccuracies.

2. Unpublished ms. in the archives of the Service Historique de l'Armée. Paris.

3. Pham Van Dong, *op. cit.*, states those are the correct names. Since his study is backed by the Historical Commission of the Vietnamese Communist Party, it must be considered an authorized statement.

4. Lacouture, *op. cit.*, p. 14.

5. Ernst Degner, "Das schlaflose Herz," *Freie Welt* (East Berlin), No. 45, (November 9, 1961), p. 14.

6. Cf. Jean-Pierre Demariaux, *Les secrets des îles Poulo-Condore* (Paris: Peyronnet, 1956). The author gives a detailed description of most of the important prisoners, particularly Ho's associates. Nowhere is the imprisonment of Ho's father mentioned.

7. Pham Van Dong, *op. cit.*, p. 35. Quôc-Hoc was then classified as an "academy" in the traditional Vietnamese sense and only later was classified as a regular *lycée*. It still exists today at Hue.

8. *Ibid.*, p. 40.

9. Lacouture, *op. cit.*, p. 19.

10. André Marty later became a senior French Communist leader and the Soviet Navy named a battleship after him. He was purged from the Party by its Stalinist wing, in 1951, and died without having been reinstated.

11. Ruth Fischer, *Von Lenin zu Mao* (Düsseldorf: Eugen Diederichs Verlag, 1956), p. 178. The official *History of the Communist Party of the U.S.S.R.*, 1960 ed., confirms that Lenin's last public appearance was at the 1922 Comintern Congress.

12. *Nhan-Dan* (*The People*) (Hanoi), May 12, 1961.

13. Robert Shaplen, "The Enigma of Ho Chi Minh," *The Reporter*, January 27, 1955, pp. 11–19.

14. Truyên later broke with Ho and, in 1961, unsuccessfully ran against Ngo Dinh Diem in the Presidential election in South Viet-Nam. Other Soviet-trained Vietnamese with their Russian cover names are: Duong Bach Mai (Blokof), Ha Huy Tap (Siniskin), Lê Hong Phong (Livinov), Nguyên Van Phong (Polya), Nguyên Khanh Toan (Minime).

15. Pham Van Dong, *op. cit.*, p. 47.

16. Lê became the second secretary general of the Indochinese Communist Party in 1935, but was captured by the French in June, 1939, and executed in

late 1940. The first secretary general, Tran Phu, was captured by the French in March, 1931, and died in jail on September 3 of that year. Ho held the secretary generalship only between 1956 and 1960, but he is "President" of the Party.

17. Franz Faber, *Rot leuchtet der Song-Cai* ([East] Berlin: Kongress-Verlag, 1955), p. 169.

18. See, for example, S. R. Mohan Das, *Ho Chi Minh–Nationalist or Soviet Agent?* (Bombay: Democratic Research Service, 1952), p. 3.

19. Gene Z. Hanrahan, *The Communist Struggle in Malaya* (New York: Institute of Pacific Relations, 1954), p. 12.

20. Lacouture, *op. cit.*, p. 32.

21. Pham Van Dong, *op. cit.*, p. 57.

22. Lacouture errs in asserting that "Ho, after making a first regroupment [of the Vietnamese Communists] in March, 1930 . . . ratified in October, 1930, the creation of the Indochinese Communist Party." (*Op. cit.*)

23. This is also why Pham states (on. p. 57) that "our Party was born on February 3, 1930."

24. Tran Huy Lieu, *Les Soviets du Nghé-Tinh* (Hanoi: Editions en Langues Etrangères, 1960), p. 55. In a conversation with me, Tran Huy Lieu affirmed that the Communists refrained from intervening in the Yen-Bay mutiny—unlike their later involvement in the Nghé-An rebellion—only because they were not yet strong enough.

25. The French captured every secretary general of the ICP, one by one, until Truong Chinh took that post, and in November, 1939, most of the members of the ICP Central Committee had been captured by the Sûreté.

26. King Chen, *op. cit.*, p. 41. General Chiang now lives in comfortable retirement in Hong Kong and is active in the Moral Rearmament movement.

27. Ho Chi Minh, *Prison Diary*, trans. Aileen Palmer (Hanoi: Foreign Languages Publishing House, 1962).

28. Appel, *op. cit.*, p. 119.

29. Letter dated October 14, 1954, from Colonel Helliwell to the author. In view of later correspondence with other OSS members, Helliwell's statements on arms deliveries seem to have been limited to the activities of the OSS intelligence unit.

30. Shaplen, *op. cit.* Shaplen, who during World War II was in China, interviewed several OSS officers who had been parachuted to Ho's units in 1945.

31. As Paul Mus (*op. cit.*) observed, the Viet-Minh (whose insigne was a five-pointed yellow star on a red field) had persuaded the Vietnamese population that the American fighters and bombers (whose insigne is a five-pointed white star) flying overhead in North Viet-Nam were part of their own mighty air force, and thereby greatly increased Viet-Minh prestige.

32. Bernard B. Fall, "North Viet-Nam's Constitution and Government," *Pacific Affairs*, September, 1960, pp. 282–90.

33. Ho Chi Minh, "Problèmes de l'Asie," *Temps Nouveaux* (Moscow), No. 47 (November 22, 1961), pp. 4–6.

34. *The Washington Post*, January 30, 1963. See also *Newsweek*, February 11, 1963.

Chapter 7. THE ROAD TO DIEN BIEN PHU

1. *News from Viet-Nam* (weekly bulletin of the Vietnamese Embassy in the United States) (Washington, D.C.), November 2, 1959.

2. For the best English-language account of *l'affaire Revers*, see Lancaster, *op. cit.*, pp. 407–10. Revers was cashiered in June, 1950.

3. The Thai Highlands cover about 17,500 square miles of northwestern Tongking. The name is often spelled *T'ai* in French documents to avoid confusion with neighboring Thailand (Siam).

4. Commandant Y. G., French Marine Paratroops, (Unpublished ms., Paris, 1961), pp. 2–21 *passim*.

5. *Street Without Joy*, p. 30. It should be remembered that at precisely the same time (October 24, 1950), Red Chinese "volunteers" made their appearance at the North Korean border and inflicted upon the U.S. forces there their most costly defeat since Corregidor. The equipment abandoned intact by those American forces armed several Viet-Minh divisions one year later and can be found to this day in Laos and South Viet-Nam.

6. Most writers lump together in one single sum (1) the funds allocated by the U.S. to France under NATO and the Mutual Security Program, (2) the funds *voted* by Congress for Indochina, and (3) the funds *actually expended by the time of the cease-fire*. The first amounted to $4 billion; the second to about $1.4 billion, and the third, according to several competent authorities in Washington, to $954 million (France spent $11 billion on the Indochina War). In reality, there was a thoroughgoing cleavage between NATO arms deliveries and weapons used in Indochina. General Chassin has written that, until 1950, the United States insisted that American-produced propellers be removed from British aircraft sent to Indochina, which would give the lie to charges of American support of French colonialism. (*Op. cit.*, p. 67.) A similar American attitude was observed in Algeria. The fact that *commercially* purchased American equipment was used by *both* sides in *both* wars had nothing to do with American policies.

7. Mao Tse-tung, *Strategic Problems of China's Revolutionary War* (Peking: Foreign Languages Publishing House, 1954), pp. 36–38 *passim*.

8. Tanham, *op. cit.*, p. 15.

9. For example, a Pentagon spokesman announced on March 22, 1962, that the guerrilla-war situation in South Viet-Nam "would show radical improvements within three months" (cf. *Journal d'Extrême-Orient* [Saigon], March 24, 1962), although it must have been obvious to the spokesman or to his responsible superiors that the kind of war that was being fought in South Viet-Nam was not of the type that would radically improve in ninety days. However, since American troops were committed, American public opinion had to be persuaded that such a commitment would yield quick results. Yet the propaganda on the Communist side constantly emphasizes the indecisiveness and protracted character of the struggle. To a people who have fought the Chinese for a thousand years and the French for eight, "radical improvements" after five years of fighting, or even a prolonged stalemate, are perfectly acceptable.

10. Vo Nguyên Giap, *People's War, People's Army* (Hanoi: Foreign Languages Publishing House, 1961), p. 47. A facsimile edition has been published in the United States (New York: Frederick A. Praeger, 1962).

11. For an interesting, though at times too uncritical, biography of de Lattre, see Sir Guy Salisbury-Jones, *So Full a Glory* (New York: Frederick A. Praeger, 1955).

12. Tanham, *op. cit.*, p. 15.

13. Wilfred Burchett, *Mekong Upstream* ([East] Berlin: Seven Seas Book Corporation, 1960), p. 289. Thus, from the Communist viewpoint, the VPA

regulars operating in Laos or Cambodia had the status of "volunteers" along the same lines as the "Chinese People's Volunteers" in Korea.

14. Henri Navarre, *Agonie de l'Indochine* (Paris: Plon, 1956).

15. *Le Monde*, March 13, 1954. In a parliamentary debate on March 9, 1954, French Foreign Minister Bidault also did not deny a charge that large-scale American aid had been made dependent upon a pledge he gave the U.S. Ambassador to France, on September 29, 1953, that France would cease all negotiations with Red China and the Viet-Minh. This prompted a French non-Communist newspaper to comment that "the Indochina War had become France's number one dollar-earning export." And that was the absolute truth.

16 Dwight D. Eisenhower, *Mandate for Change, 1953–1956* (Doubleday & Company, 1963), p. 338.

17. Nguyên Van Hinh, dismissed by President Ngo Dinh Diem for insubordination in the autumn of 1954, has served since in Algeria in a fighter-bomber command and later as chief of a French Air Force testing center. He became French Deputy Chief of Staff for Reorganization in 1963.

18. A French paratroop raid on Lang-Son in July, 1953, in which the French reoccupied the town, was ignored; so was the destruction of Regiment 95 on the Annam coast between July 28 and August 4, and the severe mauling given the 320th Division at Phu-Nho-Quan in September. At no time did Giap commit the error of throwing good troops after bad ones; thus, he preserved the hard core of his battle force for the main effort.

19. Navarre, *op. cit.*, p. 191.

Chapter 8. GARRISON STATE

1. *Cu'u Quôc* (*National Salvation*, the Viet-Minh's daily newspaper) (Hanoi), November 1, 1946.

2. Thus, Tanham avers that it was only "by the early 1950's [that] the Viets had won a tight hold on the military apparatus and were pursuing Communist ends in addition to their nationalist objectives" and "as late as 1952 . . . they were still cautious about preaching pure Communism outside their own organization." (*Op. cit.*, pp. 34 and 54.) The foregoing chapters should have made it amply clear that the Viet-Minh controlled the whole D.R.V.N. apparatus long before the 1950's. It is also normal Communist tactics to preach "pure Communism" only inside a Communist organization. After all, the Communists consider themselves an elite movement with a mass following, and not a "mass party" *per se*.

3. Jean Hogard, "Guerre révolutionnaire et pacification," *Revue Militaire d'Information* (cited henceforth as *RMI*), No. 280 (February, 1957). See also the superb special issue of *RMI* devoted to revolutionary warfare, No. 281 (March–April, 1957), which is still one of the best over-all studies of the problem. A very poor unofficial English translation of this issue was prepared by the Pentagon in 1960. The best recent study of the problem, embodying the Algerian experience, can be found in Roger Trinquier, *Modern Warfare* (Frederick A. Praeger, 1963).

4. *RMI*, No. 281, p. 30.

5. Tanham, who had French secret documents at his disposal, said only the following about the DV's: "Certain Viet-Minh adherents (known as *Dich-Van*) even attached themselves to French units. . . ." (*Op. cit.*, p. 24.) The problem of parallel hierarchies is not even mentioned.

6. *Thoi Moi* (Hanoi), September 19, 1957.

7. Cf. E. Drexel Godfrey, Jr., *The Government of France* (New York: Thomas Y. Crowell, 1961), p. 44: ". . . the premier's role has developed largely in the province of coordinating the activities of the government ministries."

8. Cf. Fall, "North Viet-Nam's Constitution and Government." Some contemporary Hanoi sources put the total number of constituencies at 362, while others, in July, 1960, showed that 422 deputies were seated in the National Assembly, including 18 from South Viet-Nam. This would have meant a total of 404 constituencies in North Viet-Nam.

9. *Le Viet-Nam en marche* (Hanoi), June, 1958.

10. I was given the figure of 60 in 1962 at the Uy Ban Dan Toc in Hanoi, but the official newspaper *Nhan-Dan*, in its edition of March 3, 1960, cited a figure of 55 mountaineer representatives prior to the 1960 elections. Since 9 additional seats were allocated on March 22, 1960, it is possible that part of them went to minority representatives.

11. Contrary to what might be expected, South Viet-Nam is not a "Christian" (or a "Catholic") country in the same sense as, for example, the Philippines, which is 78 per cent Catholic. Although government ceremonies commonly employ Catholic practices such as masses and blessings upon army and youth units, South Viet-Nam is at the very most 10 per cent Catholic, while the Hoa-Hao and Cao-Dai religious sects count about 5 million adherents. The Buddhist demonstrations in the spring and summer of 1963 were ample proof of the strength of anti-Christian feelings in Viet-Nam.

12. Decree No. 239/B. TLP of March 2, 1953. Translation in Bernard B. Fall, *The Viet-Minh Regime* (New York: Institute of Pacific Relations, 1956), pp. 172–78.

13. *Ibid.*, Article 12 (a) and (b).

14. "Land Reform Abuses," *South China Morning Post* (Hong Kong), November 28, 1956. See also Georges Chaffard, "Le gouvernement nord-vietnamien doit affronter à son tour le mécontentement populaire," *Le Monde* (Paris), December 5, 1956.

15. Article 26, Section III.

16. V. P. Karamiychev, in *Zemledeliye* (Moscow), October, 1957; and in *Ekonomika Sel'kogo Khozyaistva* (Moscow) V (1957). Cf. Fall, *Le Viet-Minh*, p. 282.

17. Jeanne Delattre, "L'économie vietnamienne au début de son premier quinquennat," *Economie & Politique*, June, 1961, p. 23.

18. Vo Nhan Tri, "Une importante résolution concernant notre politique agraire," *Le Viet-Nam en marche*, January, 1962, p. 4. See also his very thorough "La politique agraire du Nord-Vietnam," *Tiers-Monde* (Paris), July–August, 1960, pp. 352–72.

19. According to the *Viet-Nam Information Bulletin* (cited henceforth as VNI) (Rangoon), No. 37/62 (November 3, 1962), 74.5 per cent of all farmers in the Viet-Bac Autonomous Zone are cooperativized, and 15 State Farms have recently been set up in Viet-Bac.

20. *Nhan-Dan*, September 11–13, 1962, cited in VNI, No. 31/62 (September 22, 1962). *Nhan-Dan* of November 27, 1962, carried the text of a long cable addressed by Premier Pham Van Dong to various local authorities, drawing their attention to the fact that the use of "rice to make alcohol, noodles, and cakes is spreading daily to many localities," and would create severe food-supply difficulties.

21. As will be seen in Chapter 14, dealing with the South Vietnamese economy, American figures on South Vietnamese rice production had to be

revised downward when it became obvious that the earlier figures had been grossly exaggerated.

22. When questioned about food exports, North Vietnamese officials stated in 1962 that straight exports had been stopped as of 1960. Foodstuffs could only be part of barter deals, i.e., in which other foodstuffs would be received in trade.

23. P. J. Honey, "Daily Life in North Viet-Nam," *The Times of Viet-Nam* (weekly) (cited henceforth as *TVN*) (Saigon), July 16, 1962.

24. VNI, No. 41/62 (December 1, 1962).

25. *Vneshnyaya Torgovlya Soyuza S.S.R.* (Moscow: Vneshtorgizdat, 1962), cited in *The YUVA Newsletter* (published by the Central Asian Research Centre, London), II, No. 1 (January, 1963).

26. Jacques Armand-Prevost, *Opium—Monnaie Forte* (Paris: La Table Ronde, 1962), p. 82.

27. Vo Nhan Tri, "Une importante résolution . . . ," p. iv.

Chapter 9. ROAD TO SOCIALISM

1. The report was published as: *Premier Rapport de la Sous-Commission de Modernisation de l'Indochine* (République Française, Présidence du Conseil, Commissariat Général du Plan de Modernisation et d'Equipement [Paris, 1948]). North Vietnamese economic planners explained to me in 1962 that part of their erstwhile errors were due to deliberately falsified economic data left behind by the French in 1954. While this possibility cannot be entirely excluded, it nevertheless sounds like a convenient *ex post facto* alibi for planning errors such as most Communist economists have made at one time or another elsewhere in the Soviet bloc.

2. *Third National Congress of the Viet-Nam Workers' Party* (Hanoi: Foreign Languages Publishing House, 1961), II, 31. Those problems apparently proved harder to solve than expected. Thus, the Soviet-built Hanoi machine-tool plant was reported on December 4, 1962, to be "encountering difficulties in fulfilling the 1962 plan." The problem, as elsewhere in the Communist bloc, was sub-standard output.

3. *Ibid.*

4. According to Agency for International Development figures, South Viet-Nam had received through June 30, 1961, a total of $1.44 billion in grant aid and $95 million in loans. Of this, however, only $160 million was allocated to specific economic aid projects.

5. Speech by Lê Thanh Nghi at the opening of the Viet-Tri complex on March 18, 1962. A highly qualified West German expert confirms this pre-ponderant role of the Red Chinese in the field of economic aid to the D.R.V.N. According to Professor Klaus Mehnert, in his *Peking und Moskau* (Stuttgart: Deutsche Verlags-Anstalt, 1962), p. 508, through 1959, Chinese aid represented 64.4 per cent of all aid received; the U.S.S.R.'s 27.8 per cent, and the satellites (including Mongolia, presumably) provided the remaining 7.7 per cent.

6. *The YUVA Newsletter*, pp. iv–vi.

7. East Germany, for example, claims to have provided Hanoi with 60 million rubles' worth of equipment, including twenty fishing cutters, a hospital, a printing plant, a telephone communications center, and a glass factory. Cf. *Deutsche Aussenpolitik* (East Berlin), special issue "Südostasien zwischen Gestern und Morgen," 1962, pp. 208–9.

8. Vu Can, "Spring in Red Soil Phu Quy," *Viet-Nam Advances* (Hanoi), August, 1962, p. 5.

9 Tibor Mende, "Les deux Vietnam," *Esprit*, June, 1957, pp. 945–46. Ironically, Mende's favorable views about North Viet-Nam's economy were translated into English by the Vietnamese lobby in the United States and distributed with a cover letter pleading for increased American aid to Viet-Nam to match Communist aid to Hanoi.

10. Cited in full in I. Milton Sacks, "Marxism in Viet-Nam," in Frank N. Trager (ed.), *Marxism in Southeast Asia* (Stanford: Stanford University Press, 1959), p. 158.

11. Giang, *op. cit.*, pp. 53–68 *passim*.

12. Sacks, *op. cit.*, p. 160. Giang, *op. cit.*, p. 57, gives the date as May 29.

13. A perfect example of the theological quarrel pushed *ad absurdum* is Kardelj's recent book *Vermeidbarkeit oder Unvermeidbarkeit der Krieges* (Hamburg: Rohwolt, 1961). Here, in the dullest imaginable Party jargon, Yugoslavia's Vice-President and Foreign Minister makes a point-by-point comparison of the Red Chinese theses with the Yugoslav—which had, in the interim, become Khrushchevian.

14. Radio Hanoi, July 24, 1958.

15. *Viet-Nam Press* (Saigon) (weekly English-language ed.), February 7, March 6, and May 15, 1960. The sign on each house looks as follows:

$$\frac{I \quad 5}{378}$$

meaning that the house whose street number is 378 belongs to Section I and Interfamilial Group 5. There are supposed to be 650 sections and 10,687 groups in the Saigon area. The system was reinforced in 1961 by the creation of urban self-defense groups and "strategic boroughs" similar to the rural "strategic hamlets."

16. Gérard Tongas, "Indoctrination Replaces Education," in P. J. Honey (ed.), *North Vietnam Today: Profile of a Communist Satellite* (New York: Frederick A. Praeger, 1962), p. 93.

17. *Ibid.*

18. VNI, December 24, 1953. See also Gérard Tongas, *J'ai vécu dans l'enfer communiste du Nord Viet-Nam et j'ai choisi la liberté* (Paris: Débresse, 1960), a book as indigestible as its title but which gives some firsthand insights into the D.R.V.N. school system, in which Tongas taught French.

19. *The Hindu Weekly Review*, February 6–13, 1961.

20. To date, South Viet-Nam has failed to produce a single writer of any stature whatever, while Vietnamese exiles in France (including a former South Vietnamese ambassador) win French literary prizes almost every year. This in itself is a fitting comment on the influence of authoritarian government on literary output.

21. *Van-Nghé (Art and Literature)*, No. 162 (March 7, 1957).

22. *Bangkok World*, November 20, 1962.

23. I had occasion to visit several of the refugee camps in Northeast Thailand in 1959, and to talk to refugees, their priests, and the head of the South Vietnamese Information Office in Ubon-Rajtani. The priests affirmed to me that the refugees had never been given freedom of choice in privacy, but had to make their choice *en masse*, in the midst of their pro-Communist compatriots and the Viet-Minh underground camp cadre. Saigon has made no move beyond one perfunctory diplomatic protest to save them from their fate.

24. *Le Monde* (weekly airmail ed.), January 17, 1962.

25. *Industriekurier* (Düsseldorf, West Germany), March 27, 1962.

26. Paul Mus gives details of a meeting in October, 1945, between General

Leclerc and French Communists in Saigon, who told him: "There are no French and Vietnamese Communists. There is *one* Communist Party, and here we [happen to be] in Indochina." (*Op. cit.*, p. 342.)

27. "Soviet Policy in South-East Asia," in Max Beloff, *Soviet Policy in the Far East, 1944–1951* (published for the Royal Institute of International Affairs by Oxford University Press, 1953), p. 208.

28. Bernard B. Fall, "As Seen from Moscow," in "The Political Development of Viet Nam: V-J Day to Geneva" (unpublished doctoral dissertation, Syracuse University, 1954), pp. 950–51.

29. See, for example, Y. Viktorov's editorial in *Pravda*, September 28, 1946. For the 1946–50 period, there were more articles published on every other Asian colonial area than Viet-Nam. Cf. Fall, "The Political Development of Viet-Nam . . . ," pp. 952–53.

30. Cited in Harold Isaacs, *No Peace in Asia* (New York: The Macmillan Company, 1947), p. 173. For the whole development of French Communist policies concerning Indochina, see Bernard B. Fall, "Tribulations of a Party Line: The French Communists and Indochina," *Foreign Affairs*, April, 1955, pp. 499–510.

31. Oliver E. Clubb, Jr., in his *The United States and the Sino-Soviet Bloc in Southeast Asia* (Washington: The Brookings Institution, 1962), cites Ellen J. Hammer as his authority for the assertion that Thorez signed in March, 1947, "the order for military action against the Republic of Viet-Nam." (P. 14.) I could find no evidence for that assertion, the more so as military action had begun in December, 1946, and not in March, 1947.

32. An editorial, "Imbue with the Common Political Program of the International Communist Movement—Strengthen Solidarity and Unity of Mind to Struggle Against U.S.-Led Warmongering Imperialists," in *Nhan-Dan*, December 5, 1962.

33. Honey (ed.), *North Vietnam Today* . . . , pp. 56–57 *passim*. Honey states that Giap was not heard from in October–December, 1959, and May–August, 1960.

34. *Daily Express* (London), March 28, 1962; *The Saturday Evening Post*, November 24, 1962; *L'Express*, January 10, 1963.

35. *Red China and the U.S.S.R.* (Department of State [Washington, D.C., 1963]), pp. 27–28.

36. A. Doak Barnett, *Communist China and Asia* (New York: Vintage Books, 1961), p. 304.

Chapter 10. THE LOST DECADE

1. In his very first, and never published, report on South Viet-Nam, Wolf Ladejinsky—until 1962 President Diem's chief agricultural adviser—was extremely critical of the overbearing attitude of Vietnamese officialdom and soldiery. There was no evidence that his recommendations were acted upon, and in 1962 he resigned from his post.

2. For example, the Philippines have done very little to abolish many of the social and economic inequalities of their society. But on an informal basis, such popular Presidents as Magsaysay and Macapagal have been able to command a nationwide rural following that has stemmed the inroads of Communist subversion.

3. *Viet-Nam Tan-Bao* (*Official Journal of Viet-Nam*) (Hué), August 20, 1945.

4. *L'Union Française* (Saigon), July 3, 1947.

5. *Bulletin d'Information* (Délégation de la D.R.V. en France [Paris]), August, 1947.

6. *Traités, Conventions, Accords* . . . .

7. Cf. the doctoral thesis of Marie-Thérèse Blanchet, *Naissance de l'Etat Associé du Viet-Nam* (Paris: Genin, 1954). Mlle. Blanchet was a member of the legal staff of the French Army High Command in Indochina.

8. *Political Alignments of Vietnamese Nationalists* (Department of State, OIR Study No. 3708 [prepared by Milton Sacks]), October 1, 1949 (declassified February 14, 1950), p. 107.

9. Roger Lévy, *Regards sur l'Asie* (Paris: Librairie Armand Colin, 1952), p. 117.

10. Isoart, *op. cit.*, p. 381.

11. *Liberty* (Bangkok), February 2, 1949.

12. *Conférence Inter-Etats* (Government of France, La Documentation Française, Notes et Etudes Documentaires, No. 1447 [Paris, March 9, 1951]). Cf. also *Conventions Inter-Etats* (Ministère des Relations avec les Etats Associés [Saigon: I.D.E.O., 1951]).

13. Senator Mike Mansfield stated in a Senate Subcommittee report on U.S. operations in Viet-Nam:

> . . . less than a decade ago, there were in all of Indochina . . . not more than 100 official Americans of all kinds. The increase of American personnel to 1,500 in Viet-Nam alone . . . has coincided with a great decrease in the numbers of official French personnel, particularly in Viet-Nam.
>
> In consequence, the U.S. Government now has the largest single block of employees, as compared with other foreign nations, in Viet-Nam . . . More than 80 per cent of this community is concentrated in the Saigon area [italics added].

(*United States Aid Program in Viet-Nam* [Subcommittee on State Department Affairs of the United States Senate Committee on Foreign Relations (Washington, D.C.: U.S. Government Printing Office, February 26, 1960)]; cited henceforth as the *Mansfield Report*.)

And this was, of course, before the guerrilla war necessitated the stationing of U.S. troops in the country.

14. Cf. Chapter 7, n. 6. See also the chapter "Armed Forces of Viet-Nam," in Fall, *The Political Development of Viet-Nam* . . . ," pp. 500–47.

15. Nguyên Van Tam was born in the South, of humble origins. By hard work, he acquired a law degree and then went into the colonial administrative service, becoming a district officer. In 1945, he was tortured by the Japanese, and his youngest sons were murdered by the Viet-Minh. When the French returned, he was the first Vietnamese to become a provincial governor and was assigned to one of the most difficult provinces, Tan-An, which included the ill-famed Plaine des Joncs. He personally hunted Viet-Minh with a carbine and earned for himself the nickname of "the Tiger of Tan-An." As Minister of the Interior for Bao-Dai in 1952, he broke the back of the Viet-Minh underground inside Saigon by torture and other means (there was not one bombing in Saigon from 1952 to the cease-fire). His youngest son, Nguyên Van Hinh, as stated before, was chief of staff of the Vietnamese Army until 1954. One of his daughters is married to a physician who was the chief of the People's Army medical services. Exiled by Ngo Dinh Diem, Tam lives in France.

16. Lancaster, *op. cit.*, pp. 282–83 *passim*. He also notes that it was Ngo Dinh Nhu, then leading a "Movement for National Union and Peace," who in December, 1953, declared that the French were ready to "betray the Vietnamese."

Chapter 11. Agony of a War

1. In a theater of similar size during World War II, the U.S. 10th and 14th Air Force and the British Southeast Asia Command operated a total of about 7,000 aircraft. Further, in 1954, the French did not have a single B-29 bomber that could have delivered eight tons of bombs as far away as the Chinese border, but had to make do with World War II-vintage AD's or F4U Corsairs which had a small bomb-carrying capacity and only enough fuel to stay over Dien Bien Phu for ten minutes. Also, the slowness of these planes did not permit them to intervene rapidly in case of a Communist attack; it took them about ninety minutes to reach the fortress in an emergency. A jet fighter of the then routine F-86 type could have flown the same distance in thirty-five minutes.

2. Cf. "The Asia-First Admiral," by my late colleague Edgar Kemler, in *The Nation*, July 17, 1954.

3. General Matthew B. Ridgway and H. H. Martin, *Soldier: Memoirs of Matthew B. Ridgway* (New York: Harper & Brothers, 1956), pp. 274–78.

4. Fletcher Knebel, "We Nearly Went to War Three Times Last Year," *Look*, February 8, 1955. See also James Shepley's "How Dulles Averted War," in *Life*, January 16, 1956. Knebel's article, though in retrospect far more factual, never received the publicity of Shepley's article, which benefited from Dulles' personal views and brought "brinkmanship" into the vocabulary of American politics.

5. All citations from *Congressional Record*, April 6 to 19, 1954, pp. 4402–4977 *passim*.

6. Sir Anthony Eden, *Full Circle* (London: A. S. Cassell & Co., Publishers, 1961), pp. 93–94 *passim*.

7. For an Administration viewpoint of these events, see Robert J. Donovan's chapter "Dilemma Over Indo-China" in his *Eisenhower: The Inside Story* (New York: Harper & Brothers, 1956), pp. 259–68.

8. For an excellent French study, based on interviews with most non-American participants, see Jean Lacouture and Philippe Devillers, *Genève 1954: Fin d'une guerre* (Paris: Editions du Seuil, 1961), which is beyond a doubt one of the finest pieces of diplomatic history recently written anywhere.

9. Eden, *op. cit.*, p. 142.

10. Russell H. Fifield, *The Diplomacy of Southeast Asia: 1945–1958* (New York: Harper & Brothers, 1958), pp. 301–4.

Chapter 12. Ngo Dinh Diem—Man and Myth

1. The wife of an American official in Saigon once attempted to write a biography of Ngo Dinh Diem. It was said that the manuscript, although extremely sympathetic, did not entirely meet with the approval of Ngo Dinh Diem and his brothers and thus was not published in order to avoid embarrassment.

2. Thanh-Thai was replaced by Duy-Tan, his son, who also resisted French encroachments (see p. 34) and was deposed in 1917. He was replaced by Khai-Dinh, the son of Thanh-Thai's predecessor, Dong-Khanh, who had put up very little resistance to the French. Khai-Dinh's son, Vinh-Thuy, later ascended to the throne under the name of "Bao-Dai" ("Keeper of Greatness"). The fact that Bao-Dai was the descendant of emperors who had been weak in their resistance to the French also may account for Diem's contempt for him.

3. It is a little-known fact that Sun Yat-sen directed his Chinese reform movement largely from Hanoi in 1907–9. A few years later, Phan Boi Chau in turn was granted asylum in China and operated from Canton.

4. William Henderson, "South Viet-Nam Finds Itself," *Foreign Affairs*, January, 1957..

5. J. A. C. Grant, "The Viet-Nam Constitution of 1956," *American Political Science Review*, June, 1958, p. 445.

6. Robert Shaplen, "A Reporter in Viet-Nam: Diem," *The New Yorker*, September 22, 1962.

7. *Time*, August 4, 1961.

8. *Partis Nationalistes Vietnamiens, Année 1948* (French Army, Commandement en Chef en Indochine [Saigon (1949), mimeog.]), p. 69.

9. Cf., among other sources, *Life*, May 13, 1957; *Paris-Match*, May 14, 1955; and Joseph Alsop in the *New York Herald Tribune*, March 31, 1955.

10. *Journal d'Extrême-Orient*, November 12, 1960.

11. Emmanuel Mounier, *Le Personnalisme* (Paris: Presses Universitaires de France, 1961). There are two sources in English on Vietnamese Personalism. One is the excellent contribution by John C. Donnell, "Personalism in Viet-Nam," in Wesley R. Fishel (ed.), *Problems of Freedom: South Viet-Nam Since Independence* (New York: The Free Press of Glencoe, 1961), pp. 26–67. (Except for Donnell's chapter, the balance of this book is an uninterrupted paean of praise for the Diem regime.) The other is the hopelessly unreadable *Asia: Challenge at Dawn—Personalism versus Marxism*, by M. K. Haldar (New Delhi: Siddharta Publications, 1961), which is little more than a compendium of President Ngo Dinh Diem's speeches, direct but unattributed excerpts from other books, and citations from the Greek classics.

12. Mounier, *op. cit.*, pp. 127–28. One American expert who spent eighteen months in Saigon trying to reform South Viet-Nam's taxation system defined Personalism as a "confused mélange of papal encyclicals and kindergarten economics . . . [combined with] a suspicion of private businessmen, a fear of foreign capital, and an attitude that little can be accomplished in Viet-Nam without direct government ownership and control." Cf. Milton C. Taylor, "South Viet-Nam: Lavish Aid, Limited Progress," *Pacific Affairs*, Fall, 1961, p. 252.

13. From the English text published in *The Times of Viet-Nam Magazine* (weekly) (henceforth cited as *TVN Magazine*), March 18, 1962. Mme. Nhu's invocation of "independence, liberty, and happiness" must have been a Freudian slip because those three words, *in precisely that order*, are the official motto of the North Vietnamese Communist regime!

14. Mounier, *op. cit.*, p. 95.

15. *Op. cit.*, pp. 48–49.

16. The plan, first worked out by the State Secretariat for Civic Affairs in Saigon in December, 1962, is designed to bring about the voluntary surrender of Communist fighters through a combination of psychological appeals and threats backed up by force. It superficially resembles a British surrender plan applied in Malaya.

17. Robert Shaplen, "A Reporter in Viet-Nam: The Delta, the Plateau, and the Mountains," *The New Yorker*, August 11, 1962.

18. Lancaster, *op. cit.*, p. 381, n. 10. Mme. Lê Thi Gioi received a five-year jail sentence.

19. Wells C. Klein and Marjorie Weiner, "Viet-Nam," in George McT. Kahin (ed.), *Governments and Politics of Southeast Asia* (Ithaca, N.Y.: Cornell University Press, 1959), p. 362.

20. "How to Beat the Reds in Southeast Asia," *U.S. News & World Report*, February 18, 1963.

Chapter 13. Ngo's Republic

1. *Manchester Guardian,* April 30, 1955, and other sources.

2. Ellen J. Hammer, "The Struggle for Indochina Continues," special issue of *Pacific Spectator,* IX, No. 3 (Summer, 1955).

3. *Le Monde,* May 4, 1955; Lancaster, *op. cit.,* pp. 391–92.

4. Prince Bao-Long is a curious personage who seems deliberately to have rejected every one of his father's most objectionable traits. After graduating from the French Army's military academy, he volunteered for service with a crack paratroop regiment in Algeria, where he distinguished himself for bravery on many occasions. More recently, he reportedly received thirty days' disciplinary punishment for "Secret Army" activities.

5. Lancaster, *op. cit.,* p. 398.

6. *Le Monde,* January 17, 1956.

7. For an account by a participant who tried to run on the government slate without endorsement by Mme. Nhu, see Mme. Nguyên Tuyêt Mai, "Electioneering: Vietnamese Style," *Asian Survey,* November, 1962.

8. For an incisive study of South Vietnamese electoral processes, see Robert G. Scigliano, "The Electoral Process in South Viet-Nam: Politics in an Underdeveloped State," *Midwest Journal of Political Science,* IV, No. 2 (May, 1960), 138–61. Dr. Scigliano spent two years in Viet-Nam as an adviser under the Michigan State University program, and, like Dr. Milton C. Taylor, returned to the United States thoroughly discouraged.

9. *The Constitution of the Republic of Viet-Nam* (Republic of Viet-Nam, State Secretariat for Information [Saigon, 1956]), p. 19.

10. *Ibid.,* p. 4.

11. Grant, *op. cit.*

12. Here again the French experience was considered. In France, there are numerous *député-maires,* legislators who are at the same time mayors of sizable cities and thus unable to devote their full attention to two equally demanding jobs. On the other hand, and again as in France, university professors are mostly civil servants, but their duties are not considered to conflict with their legislative obligations.

13. Klein and Weiner, *op. cit.,* p. 356.

14. *Viet-Nam Press* (weekly English-language air ed.), February 26, 1961.

15. *Bilan des réalisations gouvernementales* (Republic of Viet-Nam, State Secrétariat for Information [Saigon, 1961]), pp. 151–60. For the impact of the forced naturalization of the Chinese, see Bernard B. Fall, "Viet-Nam's Chinese Problem," *Far Eastern Survey,* May, 1958.

16. Bernard B. Fall, "South Viet-Nam's Internal Problems," *Pacific Affairs,* September, 1958, p. 253.

17. Klein and Weiner, *op. cit.,* p. 357 n.; and K. R. Bombwall, "Presidential Leadership in the Republic of Viet-Nam," *International Studies* (New Delhi), October, 1961, p. 155.

18. *Tages-Anzeiger* (Zurich), May 4, 1962, p. 10.

19. Kennan, *op. cit.,* p. 26.

20. Ellen J. Hammer, "Progress Report on Southern Viet-Nam," *Pacific Affairs,* September, 1957, pp. 283–94.

21. When this writer, in an article entitled "Will South Viet-Nam Be Next?", *The Nation,* May 31, 1958, first sounded the alarm about Communist infiltration in South Viet-Nam, he immediately became the target of a concentrated smear campaign.

22. Bombwall, *op. cit.*, p. 158. (Italics added.)

23. *Newsweek*, December 18, 1961, p. 36. According to complaints voiced by American military advisers and even Vietnamese officers, that situation had not noticeably improved two years later.

24. *Thoi-Luan*, No. 440 (March 15, 1958). A letter sent by Nghiêm Xuan Thien on April 30, 1958, to Alfred Friendly, managing editor of *The Washington Post*, in which Thien exposed Viet-Nam's problems as he saw them, was never printed because, according to Friendly, "it might look like we're knocking Viet-Nam too much."

25. See Appendix III for the full text. Most of the signers have served jail terms since. Dr. Phan Huy Quat again called upon Diem to liberalize his regime in an open letter addressed to U.S. Ambassador Frederick E. Nolting in March, 1962. (*Newsweek*, March 26, 1962.) He received no answer.

26. Klein and Weiner, *op. cit.*, p. 356.

27. *Time*, April 21, 1961. Colonel Albert Pham Ngoc Thao, the governor of Kien-Hoa, had been head of the Viet-Minh's intelligence apparatus in Cochin-china from 1946 to 1954 and had later switched to Ngo Dinh Nhu's Can-Lao.

28. Fishel, *op. cit.*, p. 25.

29. Stanley Karnow, "Diem Defeats His Own Best Troops," *The Reporter*, January 19, 1961, and Pierre and Renée Grosset, "Les ennuis du Président Diem," *Le Figaro*, November 21, 1960. These authors fully concur on the fact that the mutineers asked the chief of MAAG Viet-Nam, Lieutenant General McGarr, and U.S. Ambassador Durbrow to arrange for a meeting between them and Diem or his authorized representative. Both refused, but *I VN*, inspired by Ngo Dinh Nhu, later accused "false Western friends" of having supported the *putsch*.

30. *Journal d'Extrême-Orient*, April 3, 1962.

31. Decree 45/NV of May 3, 1963. It is noteworthy that such an important measure was adopted by decree rather than law, while less important measures, such as those regulating dancing or polygamy, were subject to legislative debate.

32. *Viet-Nam Press* (weekly English-language ed.), February 19, 1961. It must be remembered that Viet-Nam had abolished the title of "Minister" and adopted the American-style "Secretary" and also retained the French term "of State"—Secrétaire d'Etat. Thus, every department head is a "Secretary of State"—with the department's name following the title.

33. See Chapter 3, n. 14.

34. *Time*, April 21, 1961.

35. In fact, since there were officially 732,000 voters in Saigon in 1961, Diem received less than 50 per cent of the total vote in the city.

36. *The New York Times* (henceforth cited as *NYT*), April 10, 1961.

37. United Press International (henceforth cited as UPI), in *The Washington Post*, May 8, 1961.

38. Z., "The War in Viet-Nam: We Are Not Told the Truth," *The New Republic*, March 12, 1962.

39. *NYT*, November 27, 1961; *Times of India* (New Delhi), November 29, 1961.

40. *Agence France-Presse*, January 4, 1962.

41. See, among others, the excellent reports by Gerald Hickey for the Michigan State University Group, 1957–58; and Frederick Wickert, "The Tribesmen," in Richard W. Lindholm (ed.), *Viet-Nam: The First Five Years* (East Lansing, Mich.: Michigan State University Press, 1959).

42. Robert Trumbull, "Laos-Based Reds Use Tribes in South Viet-Nam as Guerrillas," *NYT*, June 5, 1961; Peter Smark, " 'Battle of Minds' in Vietnamese

Mountains," *Bangkok World,* December 7, 1961. Yet, after almost two years of American-inspired reforms in the relations between the mountain tribes and the lowland Vietnamese administration, an on-the-spot American observer noted in March, 1963, that "worst of all, the Vietnamese have savagely bombed and shelled villages" of tribesmen, which made "thousands of *montagnards* turn to the Communist Viet Cong." (Jerry A. Rose, "I'm Hit! I'm Hit! I'm Hit!," *The Saturday Evening Post,* March 23, 1963.)

43. *Agence France-Presse,* February 16, 1962. Since no English text was available, the quotations have been retranslated from the French and may differ slightly from the original.

44. *Time,* March 5, 1962.

45. *The Stars & Stripes* (Pacific ed.), March 21 and 29, 1962; *NYT,* March 24, 1962.

46. *Journal d'Extrême-Orient,* February 22, 1962. Ironically, a Japanese delegate, Yuji Isobe, Assistant Managing Editor of the huge *Tokyo Shimbun,* accused American reporters at the same meeting of being extremely biased in favor of the government in their dispatches from South Viet-Nam and Laos. (*Bangkok World,* February 28, 1962.)

47. See the excellent articles by Roy Jumper: "Mandarin Bureaucracy and Politics in South Viet-Nam," *Pacific Affairs,* March, 1957; and "Problems of Public Administration in South Viet-Nam," *Far Eastern Survey,* December, 1957.

48. See, for example, an extremely flattering profile of Mme. Ngo Dinh Nhu ("Joan of Arc or Dragon Lady?") by Milton Orshefsky in *Life,* October 26, 1962; or Robert Shaplen's articles in *The New Yorker.*

49. Warren Unna, "One Year Later, Money and Men Bring Light to Viet-Nam," *The Washington Post,* December 17, 1962.

50. Neil Sheehan, of UPI, "Vietnamese Ignored U.S. Battle Orders," *The Washington Post,* January 7, 1963.

51. Ton That Thien, Chief of President Diem's Press Office (on leave), in a letter to *NYT,* February 20, 1963.

52. Beverley Deepe, "Saigon Telling Officers to Heed U.S. Advisers," *The Washington Post,* January 20, 1963.

53. Warren Unna, "Nolting Urges Viet-Nam Give More Candid News," *The Washington Post,* February 13, 1963; David Halberstam, "U.S.–Viet-Nam Tie Is in Tense Stage," *NYT,* February 15, 1963.

54. For an examination of earlier failures to produce effective local legislatures in non-Communist Viet-Nam, see Bernard B. Fall, "Representative Government in the State of Viet-Nam," *Far Eastern Survey,* XXIII (August, 1954).

Chapter 14. THE ECONOMIC BASE

1. According to Taylor, Viet-Nam's 1960 per capita share of U.S. aid was $13.7, as against Taiwan's $12.5, Korea's $8.6, Pakistan's $3.9, India's $1.9, and Thailand's $1.2. Before Laos was neutralized, it topped the list at $17.0, but the total Laos program ran to about $400 million, as against South Viet-Nam's $2.4 billion through 1962–63. (*Op. cit.,* p. 244.)

2. Taylor, *op. cit.,* p. 248.

3. For an explanation of the possibilities of the South Vietnamese economy, see the report by Professor Carter Goodrich for the United Nations, *Les perspectives du développement économique au Viet-Nam* (U.N. Restricted Document, TAA/173/101/04 [New York, 1956]). The report also exists in English. See also Taylor, *op cit.,* and Buu Hoan, "The Consequences of the Geneva Peace for the Vietnamese Economy," *Far Eastern Economic Review,* December 11, 18, and 25.

4. *Mansfield Report*, p. 25.

5. A South Vietnamese census planned in 1960 was called off because of the prevailing insecurity. However, an "estimate" by the National Institute of Statistics gave a figure of 13,789,300 in mid-1960.

6. Isoart cites a total 1937 export figure for the port of Saigon of 1,548,000 tons. (*Op. cit.*, p. 177.) That figure in all likelihood also includes about 300,000 tons of Cambodian rice; hence, the 1.2 million-ton estimate is given here.

7. Viet-Nam Press (South Vietnamese Government press agency), "Big Boost for Food and Industrial Crops," *TVN*, April 3, 1962.

8. *Ibid.*

9. "Productions du Viet-Nam," *Asie Nouvelle* (Paris), March, 1962. Other sources used are cited in the note to Table 9.

10. *A Threat to the Peace: North Viet-Nam's Effort to Conquer South Viet-Nam* (Department of State [Washington, D.C., 1961]), p. 6.

11. *Agence France-Presse*, March 9, 1962. For a detailed article on the difficulties experienced by the rubber plantations, see Jean-Pierre Lefèvre, "Subversion communiste dans les plantations du Sud-Viet-Nam," *Le Figaro*, March 12, 1963.

12. Robert Ginésy, "L'industrialization au Viet-Nam au lancement du second plan quinquennal," supplement to the *Journal d'Extrême-Orient*, February 27, 1962: ". . . the first plan never constituted a document to be publicly distributed. It has no formal existence."

13. *Ibid.* Since Ginésy's text had passed official censorship, it can be considered to represent facts and figures not far from Vietnamese Government estimates.

14. *Agence France-Presse*, April 13, 1962, and Vu Quoc-Thuc, "Viet-Nam's Economic Prospects for 1962," *TVN Magazine*, April 1, 1962.

15. Ginésy, *op. cit.*

16. *Les Informations Industrielles et Commerciales* (Paris), April 13, 1962; *Handelsblatt* (Duesseldorf), April 6, 1962; and *European Chemical News* (London), March 23, 1962.

17. Taylor, *op. cit.*, pp. 251–52. "IDC has not become . . . the leading organization for promoting industrial progress in Viet-Nam, nor has it evolved a program for assisting a broad range of industrial enterprises." (M. N. Trued, "South Viet-Nam's Industrial Development Center," *Pacific Affairs*, September, 1960.)

18. Nguyên Huu Hanh, "Après cinq années de 'Privilèges d'investissement,'" *Journal d'Extrême-Orient*, June 23, 1962.

19. *Viet-Nam Press* (weekly English-language air ed.), January 29, 1961.

20. *La Vie Française*, May 15, 1958.

21. *Le Monde*, April 7, 1962.

22. *The Washington Post*, February 20, 1963.

23. *Op. cit.* This changed somewhat in 1962, when South Viet-Nam covered about 25 per cent of its total imports with its own dollars.

24. Taylor, *op. cit.*

25. *The Observer* (London), April 8 and 22, 1962.

26. *L'Asie Nouvelle*, April 12, 1962; *La Vie Française*, April 20, 1962. See also: "Viet-Nam's Economic Growth Said Not Keeping Pace with U.S.-Backed Military Buildup," Associated Press (henceforth cited as AP) dispatch in *Bangkok World*, May 1, 1962.

27. Thuc, *op. cit.* In an article in the same publication on May 13, 1962, significantly entitled "Remarks on Foreign Aid—Matter of Major Concern," Thuc followed the Saigon government's new counterattack line on American aid and American critics who, said Thuc, listen too much to individuals who "usually are sources of pertinent criticism in the light of Western democracy." Thuc then

went on to warn his American readers that while South Viet-Nam will continue to accept "conditions required by the need of common defence, we still have the right to refuse other political conditions," i.e., American suggestions for political reform. Finally, Thuc asserted that making the Vietnamese peasant aware of the usefulness of American aid to him "constitutes a different problem which falls within the cognizance of the agencies which the American government has set up to defend and explain its policy throughout the world." Apparently, the recipient government also shrugs off this job.

28. John D. Montgomery, *The Politics of Foreign Aid: American Experience in Southeast Asia* (New York: Frederick A. Praeger, 1962), p. 114.

29. *Ibid.*, p. 118.

30. *Dan Moi* (*The New People*) (Saigon), March 26, 1963.

31. Roger Hilsman, "Internal War: The New Communist Tactic," in Lieutenant Colonel T. N. Greene (ed.), *The Guerrilla—And How to Fight Him* (New York: Frederick A. Praeger, 1962), p. 31.

32. For further information on South Viet-Nam's land reforms after 1955, see David Wurfel, "Agrarian Reform in the Republic of Viet-Nam," *Far Eastern Survey*, June, 1957; Price Gittinger, "Rent Reduction and Tenure Security in Free Viet-Nam," *Journal of Farm Economics*, May, 1957; and "Vietnamese Land Transfer Program," *Land Economics*, May, 1957. For the earlier nationalist reforms, see Fall, "Early Postwar Reforms," in "The Political Development of Viet-Nam . . . ," pp. 602–50.

33. Cf. Robert Shaplen's rationale, cited earlier (p. 251), that the "landlords [who had been away] fighting the long war against the French" were asking for those payments which—according to Shaplen and the official Saigon view—then precipitated the outbreak of fighting in 1959.

34. Fall, "Early Postwar Reforms," p. 632.

35. *Op cit.*, p. 122.

36. *Bilan des réalisations gouvernementales*, p. 370.

37. *Viet-Nam Press* (weekly English-language air ed.), February 26, 1961.

38. USOM, *op. cit.*, p. 9. However, a U.N. International Labor Office study published on April 20, 1962, comes up with the startling figure of 1 million urban workers, *not* including the government or armed forces, and 4.17 million Vietnamese employed in agriculture. (*Viet-Nam Presse* [weekly French ed.], April 22, 1962.)

39. Hilsman, *op. cit.*, p. 32.

40. *Annual Statistical Bulletin* (USOM), No. 4, p. 105. Later monthly figures show no change in trends, but the massive construction of strategic hamlets is likely to affect the situation.

Chapter 15. THE SECOND INDOCHINA WAR

1. Stuart Simmonds, "Independence and Political Rivalry in Laos 1945–61," in Saul Rose (ed.), *Politics in Southern Asia* (London: Macmillan & Co., 1963), p. 183.

2. Department of State *Press Release No. 662*, November 20, 1954.

3. The meaningless name of "Training Relations Instruction Mission" was adopted only because it abbreviated to the meaningful TRIM, reflecting the fact that the Vietnamese Army was to be pared down from 250,000 to 150,000 men.

4. *NYT*, August 18, 1955.

5. When questioned by members of the Senate Foreign Relations Committee in 1959 about difficulties in Viet-Nam, the then MAAG commander, Lieutenant General Samuel ("Hanging Sam") Williams attributed them to die-hard "French

colonialists"; while his predecessor, Lieutenant General O'Daniel, in an article published in Viet-Nam in April, 1962, said of the Vietnamese oppositionists in France that they "are Frenchmen at heart."

6. [Major] Paul Grauwin, *Seulement Médécin* (Paris: France-Empire, 1955.)
7. John G. Norris, *The Washington Post*, August 20, 1961. The ARVN adopted the stiff flat-topped cap somewhat later, but also kept the French-type bush hat. How far this nonsense went is best illustrated by the fact that a Special Forces colonel was reproved by a public-relations-conscious higher echelon when his photograph appeared in *Life*, March 16, 1962, while he was wearing the French bush hat.
8. Rising road insecurity and further administrative harassment finally made the French switch to alternate facilities at the Cambodian port of Sihanoukville.
9. *Journal d'Extrême-Orient*, June 25, 1962.
10. Pham Dinh Khiem, *Extrême-Asie* (Saigon), May 19, 1962.
11. "Guerrillas Ask Support of French in Viet-Nam," AP dispatch in *Bangkok World*, April 5, 1962.
12. *The Fight Against Communist Subversive Activities* (Republic of Viet-Nam, Department of Information [January, 1957]).
13. Fall, "Will South Viet-Nam Be Next?" and "South Viet-Nam's Internal Problems."
14. Lieutenant General John W. O'Daniel, "A Finger in the Dike Is Not Enough," *TVN Magazine*, April 29, 1962.
15. *Ibid.*, March 18, 1962.
16. *Situation in Viet-Nam* (U.S. Senate Committee on Foreign Relations [July 30–31, 1959]), p. 171. Statement read into the record by Senator Mike Mansfield.
17. *Mansfield Report*, p. 8.
18. Fall, *The Political Development of Viet-Nam* . . . , pp. 462–99.
19. The number of deaths was given as "four thousand civil officers in the last twelve months in Viet-Nam alone" by President Kennedy in his special message to a joint session of Congress on May 25, 1961.
20. Colonel H. C. B. Cook, "Shaky Dike Against a Red Flood," reprinted from *Daily Telegraph* (London), in *Bangkok World*, March 15, 1962.
21. Anon., "Lessons from Malaya," (British "Secret" document No. 850 8/42 W.O.P. 11382 [London, (1942)]; unclassified by U.S. Department of the Army Bulletin 18, 1953). All citations from pp. 6–7.
22. Simon Poore, "General McGarr's Jungle Tigers of Viet-Nam," *Saga*, October, 1961.
23. The *Mansfield Report* notes that in 1958–59, "official courtesies" were extended on 1,905 occasions, or about three times a day. Since then, the situation has grown worse.
24. *Washington Post*, May 14, 1961.
25. Anon., "Le Sud-Est Asiatique en Danger," *Revue de Défense Nationale*, Paris, May, 1962, p. 785, n.
26. [Brigadier General] S. L. A. Marshall, " 'Pedee' Harkins' New Problem," *Bangkok World*, March 8, 1962.
27. Homer Bigart, *NYT*, April 7, 1962 and May 11, 1962. In the latter article, Bigart referred to "United States impatience and . . . vexation" over the slowness of the implementation of the Delta Plan and over continuing "political interference with the military chain of command." A year later, the situation had not improved and the Delta Plan had been quietly shelved.

28. David Halberstam, "Diem Asserts Guerrillas Are on Defensive," *NYT*, October 2, 1962.
29. Peter Kalischer, CBS "Report on Asia," February 9, 1963. Of the 275,000 inhabitants of An-Xuyen Province, which occupies a good part of Camau Peninsula, about 75 per cent were then estimated to be Communist-controlled." The share of the Viet-Công "take" from tax revenues derived from the sale of charcoal was estimated at better than 40 per cent.
30. U.S. Department of the Army Release No. 16, January 30, 1963.
31. See, for example, the panel discussion between Under Secretary of State W. Averell Harriman, Senator Claiborne Pell, and Richard Dudman over WAMU, Washington, D.C., March 8, 1963. Harriman: "Diem is being criticized in the cities, but the battle i. fought in the villages. And what they want is security. . . . Our surveys show that this is what they want. . . . President Diem is a determined fighter; he is deeply interested in democratizing his regime."
32. Peter Paret and John W. Shy, *Guerrillas in the 1960's* (New York: Frederick A. Praeger, 1962), p. 50.
33. Peter Grubbe, "Verfluchte Paradiese," *Die Welt* (Hamburg), May 22, 1962.

Chapter 16. INSURGENCY: MYTHS AND FACTS

1. *New York Times Book Review*, November 11, 1962.
2. It cannot be found in the U.S. Air Force Counterinsurgency Course Manual or in the Department of Defense pamphlet *Alert*, No. 6 (November 16, 1962), both of which contain glossaries of counterinsurgency terms.
3. *Street Without Joy* (3d rev. ed.), pp. 15–17 *passim*.
4. Charlton Ogburn, *The Marauders* (New York: Harper & Brothers, 1959); and *Merrill's Marauders* (Historical Division, U.S. War Department [Washington, D.C., 1945]).
5. For two excellent analyses of the Malayan insurgency, see Lucian W. Pye, *Guerrilla Communism in Malaya* (Princeton, N.J.: Princeton University Press, 1956), and Gene Z. Hanrahan, *The Communist Struggle in Malaya*.
6. Joseph J. Zasloff states that the farmer was "compelled to abandon a traditional pattern of life . . . build a new home . . . till a fallow plot which he had not chosen, but was required to buy." ("Rural Resettlement in South Viet-Nam: The Agroville Program," *Pacific Affairs*, Winter, 1962–63, p. 338.) The author had been Smith-Mundt professor at the University of Saigon.
7. Editorial "Commitment in Saigon," *The New Republic*, May 22, 1961.
8. *Newsweek*, February 12, 1962. For a full-scale analysis of the victory over the Huk, see Colonel Napoleon O. Valeriano and Lieutenant Colonel Charles T. R. Bohannan, *Counterguerrilla Operations: The Philippine Experience* (New York: Frederick A. Praeger, 1962).
9. Dien Bien Phu was a "target of opportunity"—created by French stupidity —that Giap simply could not forgo, but on his own he never undertook a "human-wave" offensive again.
10. Giap, *op. cit.*, p. 55.
11. Homer Bigart, "Saigon Is Losing Propaganda War," *NYT*, January 18, 1962; Malcolm Browne of the AP wrote: "Government propaganda uses too many big words (such as 'personalism' and 'infra-structure') and involves too many complicated ideas." ("Viet Cong Propaganda More Forceful, Viet Nam Steps Up War for Minds," *The Stars & Stripes* [Pacific ed.], January 26, 1962.)
12. W. W. Rostow, "Guerrilla Warfare in Underdeveloped Areas," *Marine*

Corps Gazette, January, 1962, pp. 48–49 (special "Guerrilla Warfare" issue). Reprinted in Greene (ed.), *op. cit.*, pp. 59–60.

13. In fact, the Fort Bragg training manual, April 1961 edition, lists Civilian Support as the first of the "Nine Principles of Guerrilla Operations." The other eight are: Outside Assistance, Favorable Terrain, Effective Leadership, The Will to Resist (The Cause), Unity of Effort, Propaganda, Intelligence, and Discipline.

14. James Eliot Cross, *Conflict in the Shadows: The Nature and Politics of Guerrilla War* (New York: Doubleday & Company, 1963), p. 98.

15. Albert-Paul Lentin, "L'Histoire de la Révolution Algérienne," *France-Observateur*, March, 1962.

16. Cf. Trinquier, *op. cit.*

17. *Army, Navy, Air Force Journal*, April 8, 1961.

18. Cf. publications cited in n. 2.

19. [Colonel] Gabriel Bonnet, *Les Guerres insurrectionnelles et révolutionnaires* (Paris: Plon, 1958), p. 60.

20. NYT (Western ed.), February 28, 1963. See confirmation of this pattern in other sources: TVN, January 10, 1964, states that for 1,888 Viet-Công killed or captured in 1963, only 399 weapons were captured; while the crack 7th Division, in operations from June, 1961, to January, 1963, caused the enemy 10,329 casualties (of which 6,849 were killed) and captured 3,791 weapons. TVN, January 7, 1963, reported that Gia-Dinh Province claimed 844 VC casualties for 1962, but only 50 individual weapons captured. In the case of ARVN losses, casualties and lost weapons match fairly closely.

21. Cross, *op. cit.*, p. 77. See also Jerry A. Rose, "The Elusive Viet Cong," *The New Republic*, May 4, 1963.

22. NYT (Western ed.), February 23, 1963.

23. *The Observer* (weekly newspaper of the U.S. Military Advisory Command, Viet-Nam), February 1, 1964.

24. Rose, "I'm Hit! . . ."

25. "To Rally the Peasants," *The Saigon Post*, January 10, 1964.

26. Stewart Alsop asserts in his preface to Cross, *op. cit.*, that the "conviction of ultimate victory" is an important condition for an effective guerrilla movement. Wars such as the uprising of Spartacus, the American-Indian wars, and the French Revolution show the effectiveness of rage born out of despair as a motive for resistance.

27. Cf. David Halberstam, "VC Trains Three Guerrilla Units," NYT, May 5, 1963. The structure has not changed for the past fifteen years, however.

28. *White Book*, II, 42–67 *passim*.

29. Cf. *Street Without Joy*, chap. ix, "End of a Task Force," pp. 182–246.

30. S. L. A. Marshall, "The Hardening Process," *Bangkok World*, May 28, 1962. All Communist units mentioned here or shown on maps have been mentioned in the press. None of the material cited comes from official sources.

31. *White Book*, p. 19; "Viet Cong Has Shadow Regime," UPI, April 21, 1962; "Red Government Believed Planned for South Viet-Nam," Reuters, January 18, 1962.

32. *Thoi-Bao* (Saigon), April 21, 1962; "V-N Liberation Leaders' Names," *Bangkok World*, April 15, 1962.

33. VNI, January 27, 1962, pp. 11–12.

34. Circulars No. 510 and 511/AQ of December 7, 1961, cited in *Journal d'Extrême-Orient*, June 8, 1962.

35. Philippe Devillers, "The Struggle for the Unification of Vietnam," in Honey (ed.), *North Vietnam Today* . . . , p. 42. Stanley Millet also makes the

point that "the conditions of insurrection in South Viet-Nam make [outside] military and political direction seem very unlikely." ("Can Viet-Nam Be Neutralized?," *War/Peace Report* [New York], April, 1964, p. 3.)

36. Robert Scigliano, "Viet-Nam: A Country at War," *Asian Survey*, January, 1963.

37. Report of a Vietnamese Army court-martial involving three such cases and one of sales of grenades and ammunition by soldiers to the VC. *Journal d'Extrême-Orient*, February 12, 1963.

38. AP, May 28, 1962.

39. Robert Trumbull, "Malaria Teams Beset in Viet-Nam," *NYT*, November 7, 1961.

40. Fall, "South Viet-Nam's Internal Problems."

41. The release on May Day, 1962, of Special Forces Sergeants Francis Quinn and George E. Groom was an incredible example of mismanagement of public relations. They had been released by the Communists only a few miles from the place where they had been captured (and after South Vietnamese troops and American helicopters had scoured the area unsuccessfully for three weeks) and permitted to walk back on their own. The South Vietnamese convinced the local American command that the men had been freed by South Vietnamese troops, and President Kennedy immediately sent Ngo Dinh Diem a warm telegram of thanks, which was made public almost simultaneously with the correct account that a Communist act of clemency, rather than South Vietnamese prowess, had resulted in the liberation of the men. (Homer Bigart, in *NYT*, May 3 to 7, 1962. See also "GI Claims Reds Made Him Sign," in *The Washington Post*, December 27, 1962.)

42. The Rev. Elwood Jacobsen, killed on March 3, 1963, knew mountain tribal languages and was probably suspected of having taught them to Special Forces soldiers operating in the PMS. The French Rev. Father Bonnet, killed in 1962, apparently had also been accused by the Viet-Công of having given information to the ARVN.

43. AP, "Saigon Takes 'Siege' in Stride," *The Stars & Stripes* (Pacific ed.), February 7, 1962.

44. *Thoi-Bao*, March 9, 1962.

45. *Dan Moi* (*New People*), March 27, 1963.

46. NYT, October 12, 1962.

47. *White Paper*, II, 22–23 *passim*.

48. Rose, "I'm Hit! . . ."

49. *NYT* (Western ed.), March 11, 1963.

50. *Chicago Tribune*, April 25, 1963; *NYT*, May 5, 1963.

51. *Thoi-Bao*, December 27, 1962.

52. *Agence France-Presse* (Washington), January 10, 1962. As one American press-agency reporter explained to me in the Indochina area, in May, 1962, " 'cautious optimism' is the official American watchword here, whether it's Secretary of Defense McNamara or a simple lieutenant colonel from the Pentagon who comes out here for a look-around. So we just ask them about the 'degree of cautious optimism' to which they would be willing to admit, in order to get some idea of which way things are going."

53. Warren Rogers, Jr., "New U.S. Army Group at Work in Viet-Nam," *Bangkok World*, April 18, 1962.

54. Cf. *Street Without Joy*. Even ten years later, virtually nothing has been said about the GCMA. The French Historical Service in Paris, which is the repository of all French Army files, has absolutely no material on the GCMA

except the general orders establishing and dissolving them. During my research there, I was told that everything else had been removed by the French central intelligence services.

55. Cf. the excellent *Historical Survey of the Origins and Growth of Mau Mau,* written by F. D. Corfield for the British Colonial Office (London: Her Majesty's Stationery Office, 1960).

56. *Bulletin du Viet-Nam* (Embassy of Viet-Nam in Paris), No. 226 (October-November, 1962). For authoritative statements on the over-all aims of the strategic-hamlets program, see the speeches of Bui Van Luong, Minister of the Interior of South Viet-Nam, and Ngo Dinh Nhu, *Journal d'Extrême-Orient,* July 25, 1962.

57. *Saigon Moi (New Saigon),* April 17, 1963.

58. Richard Dudman, "Political Reaction a Problem in the Use of 'Dirty' Tactics to Fight Viet Cong Guerrillas," *St. Louis Post-Dispatch,* February 6, 1963.

59. *Ibid.* See also Zasloff, *op. cit.*

60. *Tu-Do* (Saigon), May 13, 1962.

61. *Time,* April 6, 1962.

62. "Tactic in Viet-Nam," *NYT* (international ed.), April 2, 1962.

63. *TVN Magazine,* May 27, 1962.

64. Homer Bigart, "U.S. Prods Saigon on Resettlement," *NYT,* May 9, 1962. See also "The War in Viet-Nam," *The Economist,* May 19, 1962: "there is no indication that ["Operation Sunrise"] has achieved any definite and permanent result." The "Delta Plan" was never implemented at all.

65. Malcolm Browne, "Viet-Nam's Hamlets Go Strategic," *TVN Magazine,* May 6, 1962.

66. *NYT,* May 5, 1963. However, R. K. G. Thompson, "father" of the New Villages in Malaya and one of the chief authors of the strategic-hamlets plan in South Viet-Nam, expressed his fullest confidence in its early success to President Kennedy on a visit to Washington in April, 1963. (*Newsweek,* April 15, 1963.)

67. *The Stars & Stripes* (Pacific ed.), May 10, 1962.

68. *Newsweek,* January 1, 1962.

69. *Ibid.,* April 23, 1962.

70. *TVN,* December 31, 1962.

71. Rose, "The Elusive Viet-Cong." See also Department of Defense News Release No. 16-63, January 5, 1963.

72. *NYT,* May 7, 1963. From personal experience, I am astonished that the Communists did not bury the parachutes or tear up the highly prized material for other purposes. Other details of the story strain credulity.

73. *The Washington Post,* March 6, 1963.

74. Marguerite Higgins, in the *New York Herald Tribune,* August 28, 1963.

75. "Viet Cong Step Up Subversion in Central VN," *The Saigon Post,* February 24, 1964.

76. *The Stars & Stripes* (Pacific ed.), November 1, 1963.

77. *NYT,* April 18, 1963. See article by Halberstam and also editorial.

78. *Ngon Luan* (Saigon), April 22, 1963.

79. *The Observer* (Viet-Nam), March 21, 1964. Under the "Open-Arms" surrender program, up to December, 1963, 642 VC in Tay-Ninh Province brought 16 weapons; 452 VC in Kien-Phong brought 10 weapons; 484 VC in Kien-Hoa brought 3 rifles, and 710 VC in Binh-Duong brought 18 weapons. These are typical results.

Chapter 17. The Two Viet-Nams in Perspective

1. *Nhan-Dan*, January 21, 1964.
2. NYT, February 28, 1963.
3. In an extremely well-documented cover article, the authoritative *Informations Catholiques Internationales*, No. 188 (March 15, 1963), reports warnings from the Vietnamese clergy about unfavorable reaction against a too-blatant "Christianization" of what is basically a Confucianist and Buddhist country; and cites the example of certain Vietnamese bishops who refuse military escorts and others who refuse to raise specifically Catholic militia forces, and cites those two significant phrases: "A Catholic may be in politics . . . but there is no political system that represents Catholicism as such," and "It is not obedience that is a virtue, but freedom." (Pp. 17–26.) In view of the Buddhist demonstrations that followed two months later, that warning should have been given careful consideration.
4. An extreme but not untypical example of that "tarbrush" technique is an article written by Suzanne Labin, a French Socialist with extreme right-wing leanings, in the May, 1962, issue of the U.S. Army's most respected publication, the *Military Review* of the U.S. Army Command and General Staff College.

Entitled "Killing Our Ally" and subtitled "A Disclosure of Communist Methods Used to Discredit and Undermine the Government of South Vietnam," the article flatly accuses anyone who does not support Ngo Dinh Diem (who, in that kind of treatment, is equated with South Viet-Nam) of being a participant in "an immense campaign . . . launched by the Communists and their dupes to discredit the government of Ngo Dinh Diem so that its support would be unbearable for all the democratic governments of the West." She then adduces patently erroneous "facts" (the guerrillas' weapons are "ultrasilent, ultrarapid, ultralight . . . latest products of Czechoslovakia's armament factories," and the guerrilla fighters are "unknown" in the villages and trained "for years" in such places as Peking or Prague "to earn a regular pay," etc.) or half-truths (South Viet-Nam's agricultural production doubled from 1954 to 1960; but she forgets to say that 1954 was one of the worst recent years and far below prewar production) to ram home the point that to criticize the Diem regime "flatters the taste of some commentators for dissenting and their appetite for reforming. And to satisfy that appetite, they do not hesitate to eat and sell Communist dishes."

This, of course, is the old syllogism that (1) all that the Communists do is bad; (2) the Communists have Mother's Day; (3) therefore, Mother's Day is a Communist plot.
5. For a more complete appraisal of that phase, cf. Fall, "What de Gaulle Actually Said About Vietnam," *The Reporter*, October 24, 1963.
6. *Candide*, February 13, 1964.
7. Jean Lartéguy, "Les généraux vietnamiens sentaient trop la France," *ibid.*
8. Kennan, *op. cit.*, pp. 26 and 384.
9. *Viet-Nam and Southeast Asia* (88th Cong., 1st sess., U.S. Senate [Washington, D.C.: U.S. Government Printing Office, 1963]), p. 8.
10. Thomas J. Dodd, *Saigon Summary* (reprint from *Congressional Record*, January 14, 1964).
11. Cf. Clare Boothe Luce's "The Lady *Is* for Burning," *The National Review*, November 5, 1963; Senator Dodd's pamphlet; Marguerite Higgins, in *America*, January 4, 1964.

12. Denis Warner, *The Last Confucian* (New York: The Macmillan Company, 1963), pp. 128–29.

13. The title of a leading article in Saigon's weekly *Nhan-Quyên* (*Human Rights*), No. 17 (April 13, 1962), was: "Is American policy in Laos knavery mixed with naïveté?" See also Mme. Ngo Dinh Nhu's speeches referred to earlier, and her press interview in West Berlin on May 14, 1962.

14. Two equally interesting cases of limited support for otherwise inimical regimes come to mind: Britain's temporary alliance with Israel against Egypt in 1956, which ran counter to Britain's usually pro-Arab policies; and West Germany's considering giving the hated East German regime a ten-year $687-million loan for purchases of machinery and food in the West, as of 1963. West Germany argues that such a grant may delay the integration of the East German economic structure into that of the Soviet bloc, and may also permit it to extract firm commitments on Berlin. The fact that East Germany would even consider asking for such a huge loan after the Berlin Wall episode—and that West Germany gives that proposal active consideration—shows a degree of political maturity thus far lacking in dealing with Viet-Nam.

15. "Our Options in Viet-Nam," *The Reporter*, March 12, 1964. Walter Lippmann made the same point in his yearly televised interview on April 8, 1964.

16. It is not without significance that French Foreign Minister Couve de Murville warned his colleagues at the SEATO conference on April 14, 1964, that "the absence in Saigon of a government benefiting from popular support is the essential problem of South Viet-Nam." (*Le Monde*, April 15, 1964.) The over-all reception to Couve de Murville's remarks was negative.

17. Tanham concludes in his RAND Corporation study based on findings of July, 1961, that "Diem has been unable to win popular support either on a nationalist basis or with personal loyalty as a motivating force. Until his government has the active and continuing support of the Vietnamese masses and the troops, all the economic and military aid in the world, though it may delay it, will not halt the Communist advance." (*Op. cit.*, p. 157.)

One year later, Oliver E. Clubb, Jr., wrote that "the outlook . . . would likely be for increasing rather than decreasing strains in the United States–Diem relationship as the struggle in Viet-Nam continues." (*Op. cit.*, p. 125.) These judgments were fully confirmed by later events.

18. Eisenhower, chap. vii, "Korea: The End of Bloodshed," *op. cit.*, pp 171–91.

19. Max Clos, "Le Viet-Nam après Diem," *Le Figaro*, December 24, 1963.

20. Hannah Arendt, *On Revolution* (New York: Viking, 1963), p. 49.

21. *Ibid*, p. 219.

Bibliography

It has become symptomatic of the Old Heidelberg influence on American scholarship in recent years that nonfiction books contain ever-longer bibliographies and more and more voluminous footnotes. Often more scholarship and research seems to have gone into the bibliography and other paraphernalia than into the text itself. Having devoted more than a decade to research on Indochina, I can assure the reader that I have used all the sources dealing with my subject that can be found in other standard works and specialized bibliographies. In addition, I have engaged in a considerable amount of field research, including personal interviews with many of the key personages involved in the Vietnamese drama.

Thus, to burden the present book with a mere duplication of the bibliographies of earlier writers or of my own earlier writings, would add little to constructive scholarship. The books of Miss Hammer or Messrs. Buttinger and Fifield, in addition to my own works on North Viet-Nam and th≥ Indochina War, contain ample bibliographies; and various newspaper indexes and guides to periodical literature will help the aspiring specialist or graduate student find his way through the enormous stream of articles that have recently appeared on the subject.

The books and articles listed here are being mentioned because they were either omitted in the bibliographies mentioned above or have appeared since their publication.

I. THE COMMON GROUND

Bone, Robert C. *Contemporary Southeast Asia*. New York: Random House, 1962.

Durand, Maurice. *Texte et Commentaire du Miroir Complet de l'Histoire du Viêt*. Hanoi: Imprimerie Minsang, 1950.

Isoart, Paul. *Le Phénomène National Vietnamien: de l'indépendance unitaire à l'indépendance fractionnée*. Paris: Librairie générale de droit et de jurisprudence, 1961.

Lancaster, Donald. *The Emancipation of French Indochina*. London and New York: Oxford University Press, 1961.

Lê Thanh Khoi. *Histoire de l'Asie du Sud-Est*. Paris: Presses Universitaires de France, 1959.

Legrand, J. *L'Indochine à l'heure japonaise*. Paris: published by the author, 1963.

Masson, André. *Histoire du Vietnam*. Paris: Presses Universitaires de France, 1960.

Savani, A. M. *Visage et images du Sud Viet-Nam*. Saigon: Imprimerie Française d'Outre-Mer, 1955.

Tran Minh Tiet. *Histoire des persécutions au Viet-Nam*. Paris: Nouvelles éditions latines, 1961.

Tran Van Chuong. *Essai sur l'esprit du droit sino-annamite*. Paris: Librairie générale de droit et de jurisprudence, 1922.

Vu Quôc Thong. *La décentralisation administrative au Viet-Nam*. Hanoi: Presses Universitaires du Viet-Nam [1952].

II. REVOLUTION IN THE NORTH

Appel, Wolfgang. *Südostasien im Brennpunkt der Weltpolitik*. Würzburg: Marienburg Verlag [1960].

Cole, Allan B. (ed.). *Conflict in Indo-China and International Repercussions: A Documentary History, 1945–1955*. Ithaca, N.Y.: Cornell University Press, 1956.

Brimmell, J. H. *Communism in South East Asia*. London and New York: Oxford University Press, 1959.

Burchett, Wilfred. *North of the 17th Parallel*. 2nd rev. ed. Hanoi: published by the author, 1957.

Fall, Bernard B. *Le Viet-Minh, 1945–1960*. Paris: Armand Colin, 1960.

———. *Street Without Joy: Insurgency in Indochina, 1946–1963*. 3d rev. ed. Harrisburg, Pa.: The Stackpole Co., 1963.

————. "Master of the Red Jab," *The Saturday Evening Post,* November 24, 1962.

Ho Chi Minh. *Oeuvres choisies.* Vol. I. Hanoi: Foreign Language Publishing House, 1960.

Honey, P. J. (ed.). *North Vietnam Today: Profile of a Communist Satellite.* New York: Frederick A. Praeger, 1962.

Hunebelle, Danielle. "North Vietnam: Communism's most disquieting experiment," *Réalités* (English ed.), May, 1963.

"L'expérience [nord-] vietnamienne," special issue of *La nouvelle critique,* March, 1962.

Mehnert, Klaus. *Peking und Moskau.* Stuttgart: Deutsche Verlags-Anstalt, 1962.

Shchedrov, I. M. *Yushnii vietnam sevodna (South Viet-Nam Today).* Moscow: Izdatel'stvo vostochnoy literaturi, 1962.

"Südostasien zwichen Gestern und Morgen," special issue of *Deutsche Aussenpolitik.* East Berlin: Rütten & Löning, 1962.

Trager, Frank N. (ed.). *Marxism in Southeast Asia.* Stanford, Cal.: Stanford University Press, 1959.

Truong Chinh. *Primer for Revolt.* New York: Frederick A. Praeger, 1963.

"Viet-Nam," special issue of *Les Temps Modernes,* August-September, 1953.

III. INSURGENCY IN THE SOUTH

A Threat to the Peace: North Viet-Nam's Effort to Conquer South Viet-Nam. 2 vols. (Department of State [Washington, D.C., 1961].)

Bilan des réalisations gouvernementales, 1954–1961. (Republic of Viet-Nam, State Secretariat for Information [Saigon, 1961].)

Clubb, Oliver E., Jr. *The United States and the Sino-Soviet Bloc in Southeast Asia.* Washington, D.C.: The Brookings Institution, 1962.

Cross, James Eliot. *Conflict in the Shadows: The Nature and Politics of Guerrilla War.* New York: Doubleday & Company, 1963.

Devillers, Philippe, and Lacouture, Jean. *La fin d'une guerre.* Paris: Editions du Seuil, 1960.

Dudman, Richard. "Asia's Frontiers of Freedom. U.S. Policy: Pluses, Minuses and Questions," *St. Louis Post-Dispatch,* February 3, 4, 5, 1963.

Halberstam, David. "Coup in Saigon: A Detailed Account," *The New York Times,* November 6, 1963.

Jordan, Amos A., Jr. *Foreign Aid and the Defense of Southeast Asia.* New York: Frederick A. Praeger, 1962.

La politique agressive des Viet Minh communistes et la guerre subversive communiste au Sud-Viet-Nam. (Government of the Republic of Viet-Nam [Saigon, July, 1962].)

Lartéguy, Jean. *Le mal jaune.* Paris: Presses de la cité, 1962.

Lindholm, Richard W. *Viet-Nam: The First Five Years*. East Lansing, Mich.: Michigan State University Press, 1959.

Millet, Stanley. "Terror in Vietnam: An American's Ordeal at the Hands of Our 'Friends,'" *Harper's Magazine*, September, 1962.

Montgomery, John D. *The Politics of Foreign Aid: American Experience in Southeast Asia.* New York: Frederick A. Praeger, 1962.

Nguyên Kien. *Le Sud-Vietnam depuis Dien Bien Phu*. Paris: Maspéro, 1963.

Nguyên Thai. *Is South Viet-Nam Viable?* Manila: Carmelo & Bauerman, 1962.

Nguyên Tuyet Mai. "Electioneering: Vietnamese Style," *Asian Survey*, November, 1962.

Rigg, Robert B. "Catalog of Viet Cong Violence," *Military Review*, December, 1962.

Rose, Jerry A. "I'm Hit! I'm Hit! I'm Hit!," *The Saturday Evening Post*, March 23, 1962.

Scigliano, Robert. *South Vietnam: Nation Under Stress*. Boston: Houghton Mifflin Co., 1964.

Tanham, George K. *Communist Revolutionary Warfare: The Viet-Minh in Indochina*. New York: Frederick A. Praeger, 1961.

Trinquier, Roger. *Modern Warfare: A French View of Insurgency*. New York: Frederick A. Praeger, 1964.

Warner, Denis. *The Last Confucian*. New York: The Macmillan Company, 1963.

Index